booksonline

Read this book online today:

With SAP PRESS BooksOnline we offer you online access to knowledge from the leading SAP experts. Whether you use it as a beneficial supplement or as an alternative to the printed book, with SAP PRESS BooksOnline you can:

- Access your book anywhere, at any time. All you need is an Internet connection.
- Perform full text searches on your book and on the entire SAP PRESS library.
- Build your own personalized SAP library.

The SAP PRESS customer advantage:

Register this book today at *www.sap-press.com* and obtain exclusive free trial access to its online version. If you like it (and we think you will), you can choose to purchase permanent, unrestricted access to the online edition at a very special price!

Here's how to get started:

1. Visit *www.sap-press.com*.
2. Click on the link for SAP PRESS BooksOnline and login (or create an account).
3. Enter your free trial license key, shown below in the corner of the page.
4. Try out your online book with full, unrestricted access for a limited time!

Your personal free trial **license key** for this online book is:

ihgr-amxn-qwvz-t9uj

Controlling with SAP®—Practical Guide

 PRESS

SAP PRESS is a joint initiative of SAP and Galileo Press. The know-how offered by SAP specialists combined with the expertise of the Galileo Press publishing house offers the reader expert books in the field. SAP PRESS features first-hand information and expert advice, and provides useful skills for professional decision-making.

SAP PRESS offers a variety of books on technical and business related topics for the SAP user. For further information, please visit our website: *www.sap-press.com*.

John Jordan
Product Cost Controlling
2009, 572 pp.
978-1-59229-167-0

Marco Sisfontes-Monge
Controlling-Profitability Analysis (CO-PA) with SAP
2008, 407 pp.
978-1-59229-137-3

John Jordan
100 Things You Should Know About Controlling with SAP
2011, 289 pp.
978-1-59229-341-4

John Jordan
Production Variance Analysis in SAP Controlling
2011, 292 pp.
978-1-59229-381-0

Janet Salmon

Controlling with SAP® — Practical Guide

Bonn • Boston

Galileo Press is named after the Italian physicist, mathematician and philosopher Galileo Galilei (1564–1642). He is known as one of the founders of modern science and an advocate of our contemporary, heliocentric worldview. His words *Eppur si muove* (And yet it moves) have become legendary. The Galileo Press logo depicts Jupiter orbited by the four Galilean moons, which were discovered by Galileo in 1610.

Editor Meg Dunkerley
Copyeditor Ruth Saavedra
Cover Design Graham Geary
Photo Credit iStockphoto.com/pxel66/aldomurillo/Tolimir
Layout Design Vera Brauner
Production Graham Geary
Typesetting Publishers' Design and Production Services, Inc.
Printed and bound in Canada

ISBN 978-1-59229-392-6

© 2012 by Galileo Press Inc., Boston (MA)
1st edition 2012

Library of Congress Cataloging-in-Publication Data
Salmon, Janet.
Controlling with SAP : practical guide / Janet Salmon. — 1st ed.
   p. cm. — (SAP press)
Includes index.
ISBN-13: 978-1-59229-392-6
ISBN-10: 1-59229-392-1
1. SAP ERP—Handbooks, manuals, etc. 2. Corporations—Accounting—Handbooks, manuals, etc. 3. Controllership—Handbooks, manuals, etc. I. Title.
HF5686.C7S266 2012
657.0285'53—dc23
               2011023377

All rights reserved. Neither this publication nor any part of it may be copied or reproduced in any form or by any means or translated into another language, without the prior consent of Galileo Press GmbH, Rheinwerkallee 4, 53227 Bonn, Germany.

Galileo Press makes no warranties or representations with respect to the content hereof and specifically disclaims any implied warranties of merchantability or fitness for any particular purpose. Galileo Press assumes no responsibility for any errors that may appear in this publication.

"Galileo Press" and the Galileo Press logo are registered trademarks of Galileo Press GmbH, Bonn, Germany. SAP PRESS is an imprint of Galileo Press.

All of the screenshots and graphics reproduced in this book are subject to copyright © SAP AG, Dietmar-Hopp-Allee 16, 69190 Walldorf, Germany.

SAP, the SAP-Logo, mySAP, mySAP.com, mySAP Business Suite, SAP NetWeaver, SAP R/3, SAP R/2, SAP B2B, SAPtronic, SAPscript, SAP BW, SAP CRM, SAP Early Watch, SAP ArchiveLink, SAP GUI, SAP Business Workflow, SAP Business Engineer, SAP Business Navigator, SAP Business Framework, SAP Business Information Warehouse, SAP inter-enterprise solutions, SAP APO, AcceleratedSAP, InterSAP, SAPoffice, SAPfind, SAPfile, SAPtime, SAPmail, SAPaccess, SAP-EDI, R/3 Retail, Accelerated HR, Accelerated HiTech, Accelerated Consumer Products, ABAP, ABAP/4, ALE/WEB, Alloy, BAPI, Business Framework, BW Explorer, Duet, Enjoy-SAP, mySAP.com e-business platform, mySAP Enterprise Portals, RIVA, SAPPHIRE, TeamSAP, Webflow and SAP PRESS are registered or unregistered trademarks of SAP AG, Walldorf, Germany.

All other products mentioned in this book are registered or unregistered trademarks of their respective companies.

Contents at a Glance

1	Introduction	25
2	Reporting	51
3	Master Data Owned by Controlling	89
4	Master Data Where Controlling Is a Stakeholder	143
5	Planning and Budgeting	201
6	Actual Postings	257
7	Period Close	325
8	Reporting in SAP NetWeaver BW and SAP BusinessObjects	387
9	Master Data in a Multisystem/Shared Service Environment	427
10	Planning in SAP NetWeaver BW or SAP SEM	457
11	Allocations Using SAP Cost and Profitability Management	497
12	Period Close Using SAP Financial Closing Cockpit	527

Dear Reader,

If you use Controlling in SAP ERP Financials, this book is a must-have resource for your daily work. You'll learn how to perform transactions with fewer steps and less effort, and you'll discover how to troubleshoot minor problems and system issues. In addition to the core areas of Controlling, you'll also find coverage of more advanced topics, such as SAP NetWeaver BW, SAP BusinessObjects, and the Financials Closing Cockpit. There are also several appendices dedicated to quick-reference materials, such as transaction lists and menu paths. It is everything you need to know about Controlling, organized in a way that is intuitive and easy to reference.

Janet Salmon is a dream of an author, and I'd work with her again in a heartbeat. She is knowledgeable, conscientious, and a first-class communicator. Janet has gone above and beyond what was expected of her, and I have every confidence that she has provided you with the best book on this topic.

We appreciate your business, and welcome your feedback. Your comments and suggestions are the most useful tools to help us improve our books for you, the reader. We encourage you to visit our website at *www.sap-press.com* and share your feedback about this work.

Thank you for purchasing a book from SAP PRESS!

Meg Dunkerley
Editor, SAP PRESS

Galileo Press
Boston, MA

meg.dunkerley@galileo-press.com
www.sap-press.com

Contents

Preface 15

1 Introduction 25

1.1 Basic Controlling Functions 28
    1.1.1 Goals of Controlling 29
    1.1.2 Cost Accounting in the United States 31
    1.1.3 Standard Costs and Actual Costs 32
    1.1.4 Investment and Project Controlling 32
    1.1.5 Lean Accounting 33
1.2 Essential Record Keeping Functions 33
    1.2.1 Record Keeping by Cost Center 35
    1.2.2 Record Keeping by Order 38
    1.2.3 Record Keeping by Project 39
1.3 Managing Close and Valuation Processes 40
    1.3.1 Valuation of Goods Movements 40
    1.3.2 Work in Process 41
    1.3.3 Scrap 41
    1.3.4 Work in Process for Projects 42
1.4 Preparing Budgets and Planning 43
    1.4.1 Driver-Based Cost Planning 43
    1.4.2 Driver-Based Cost Planning Between Cost Centers 45
    1.4.3 Budgeting 46
1.5 Process Analysis and Internal Controls 47
    1.5.1 Master Data Controls 47
    1.5.2 Workflow 48
    1.5.3 Process Controls 48
1.6 Summary 49

2 Reporting 51

2.1 Cost Center Line Items 52
    2.1.1 Classic Cost Center Line Item Report 52
    2.1.2 Simplified Cost Center Line Item Report 59
    2.1.3 Totals Records for Cost Centers 61

2.2		Order Line Items	62
	2.2.1	Classic Order Line Items	63
	2.2.2	Simplified Order Line Items	65
2.3		Product Costs: Itemization	65
	2.3.1	Classic Reports for Product Cost Reporting	67
	2.3.2	Simplified Reports for Product Cost Reporting	70
2.4		Product Costs: Cost Objects	72
	2.4.1	Product Cost by Order	72
	2.4.2	Product Cost by Period	74
	2.4.3	Product Costs by Sales Order	76
2.5		Material Ledger	77
2.6		Profitability Analysis Reports	80
2.7		Summary	87

3 Master Data Owned by Controlling ... 89

3.1		How to Set Up Cost Centers	90
	3.1.1	Responsibility for a Cost Center	92
	3.1.2	Embedding the Cost Center Design in SAP ERP	93
	3.1.3	Ensuring that Cost Center Expenses Are Handled Correctly	95
	3.1.4	Cost Center Hierarchies	97
	3.1.5	Enterprise Organization	102
	3.1.6	Reporting of Cost Center Master Data	103
3.2		Internal Orders	105
	3.2.1	Internal Orders and Cost Centers	108
	3.2.2	Settlement Rules for Internal Orders	108
	3.2.3	Statistical Internal Orders	110
	3.2.4	Order Groups	111
	3.2.5	Reporting Order Master Data	112
3.3		Statistical Key Figures	114
	3.3.1	Statistical Key Figure Groups	117
3.4		Activity Types	117
	3.4.1	Direct and Indirect Activity Allocations	120
	3.4.2	Settings for Activity Price Calculation	121
	3.4.3	Activity Type Groups	122
	3.4.4	Reporting Activity Type Master Data	122
3.5		Secondary Cost Elements	123

		3.5.1	Cost Element Groups	127
		3.5.2	Reporting on Cost Element Master Data	128
	3.6		Product Cost Collectors	130
	3.7		Cost Object Hierarchies	132
	3.8		Maintenance Issues	134
		3.8.1	Time-Dependent Fields	135
		3.8.2	Status Management	136
	3.9		Change Requests for a SOX-Compliant Master Data Process	137
	3.10		Summary	141

4 Master Data Where Controlling Is a Stakeholder ... 143

	4.1		Material Masters	144
		4.1.1	Basic View	146
		4.1.2	Accounting View	147
		4.1.3	Costing Views	151
		4.1.4	MRP View	154
		4.1.5	Sales View	154
		4.1.6	Batches	155
	4.2		Customer Masters	156
	4.3		Bills of Material	158
		4.3.1	Quantity Definition	161
		4.3.2	Co-Products and By-Products	161
		4.3.3	Recursive BOMs	164
		4.3.4	Configurable BOMs	165
	4.4		Routings	168
		4.4.1	Types of Routing	168
		4.4.2	Operation Values	170
		4.4.3	Operation-Level Costing	172
	4.5		Work Centers and Resources	173
	4.6		Procurement Alternatives and Mixed Costing	175
		4.6.1	Internal Processing	176
		4.6.2	External Procurement	177
		4.6.3	Plant to Plant Transfer	177
		4.6.4	Subcontracting	178
		4.6.5	Mixing Ratios	178
	4.7		Projects	179
		4.7.1	Work Breakdown Structure Elements	180
		4.7.2	Networks and Network Activities	181

4.8	Investment Programs		183
	4.8.1	Appropriation Requests	185
4.9	Primary Cost Elements and P&L Accounts		186
	4.9.1	Chart of Accounts	187
	4.9.2	Controlling and the Financial Accounts	189
4.10	Setting Prices for Product Costing		191
	4.10.1	Setting Standard Costs for Raw Materials	192
	4.10.2	Balance Sheet Valuation	195
	4.10.3	Calculating Actual Costs	196
	4.10.4	Cross-Company Costing	196
4.11	Summary		198

5 Planning and Budgeting — 201

5.1	Complete Sales Plan in a Manufacturing Environment		203
	5.1.1	Sales and Operations Planning	205
	5.1.2	Cost Center Planning	211
	5.1.3	Calculate Standard Costs for Products to Be Manufactured	230
	5.1.4	Profitability Planning	245
5.2	Planning and Budgeting For Investment Programs		246
	5.2.1	Investment Program	247
	5.2.2	Overall Plan	247
	5.2.3	Cost Element Planning	248
	5.2.4	Budgeting	251
	5.2.5	Displaying and Changing a Budget	254
5.3	Summary		256

6 Actual Postings — 257

6.1	Integrated Process Flows: Buy, Make, and Sell		257
	6.1.1	Procure to Pay	258
	6.1.2	Plan to Manufacture	267
	6.1.3	Order to Cash	281
6.2	Distribution of Usage Variances		289
	6.2.1	Capturing Physical Inventory Documents	290
	6.2.2	Distribution of Usage Variances	292
	6.2.3	Distribution of Activities	293
6.3	Integrated Process Flows: Other Logistics Scenarios		295

		6.3.1	Product Cost by Order	295
		6.3.2	Product Cost by Period	300
		6.3.3	Product Cost by Sales Order	302
		6.3.4	Project Controlling	307
	6.4	Corrections or Adjustment Postings		313
		6.4.1	Reposting Line Items	314
		6.4.2	Correcting an Activity Allocation	317
		6.4.3	Reposting Values	318
	6.5	Cross-Company Postings		319
	6.6	Summary		324

7 Period Close 325

	7.1	Allocations		326
		7.1.1	Steps Prior to the Start of the Period Close	328
		7.1.2	Depreciation of Fixed Assets	328
		7.1.3	Allocations Between Cost Centers	330
		7.1.4	Allocations to Profitability Analysis	343
		7.1.5	Target Costs and Variances on Cost Centers	347
	7.2	Calculations and Settlement		352
		7.2.1	Overhead Calculation	355
		7.2.2	Work in Process	357
		7.2.3	Target Costs and Variances in Production	361
		7.2.4	Settlement	367
		7.2.5	Product Cost by Sales Order	369
	7.3	Multilevel Actual Costing in Material Ledger		371
		7.3.1	Types of Costing Run	372
		7.3.2	Periodic Costing Run	372
		7.3.3	Alternative Valuation Run	378
	7.4	CO-PA Processes		384
		7.4.1	Revaluation	384
		7.4.2	Top-Down Distribution	385
	7.5	Summary		386

8 Reporting in SAP NetWeaver BW and SAP BusinessObjects ... 387

	8.1	Reporting on Large Data Volumes in SAP ERP	388
		8.1.1 Using Extracts to Accelerate Cost Center and Internal Order Reports	388

		8.1.2	Using Summarization Levels to Accelerate CO-PA Reports	392
		8.1.3	Using Summarization in Product Cost Reports	393
	8.2	How to Decide Whether You Need SAP NetWeaver BW for Reporting		395
		8.2.1	Performance Concerns	395
		8.2.2	Multidimensionality	401
		8.2.3	Navigation Attributes	404
		8.2.4	Inclusion of Non-SAP Data	408
		8.2.5	Building Queries	409
	8.3	Cost Center Reporting in SAP NetWeaver BW		413
	8.4	Reporting with SAP BusinessObjects Tools		418
		8.4.1	Crystal Reports for Controlling	418
		8.4.2	Dashboards for Controlling	422
		8.4.3	SAP BusinessObjects Explorer for CO-PA Reporting	423
	8.5	Summary		426

9 Master Data in a Multisystem/Shared Service Environment ... 427

	9.1	Change Requests in SAP ERP		430
	9.2	New Solutions for Handling Master Data in a Multisystem Environment		436
		9.2.1	Data Modeling in SAP Master Data Governance for Financials	437
		9.2.2	Editions in SAP Master Data Governance for Financials	438
	9.3	Governance Requirements for Master Data		443
		9.3.1	Creating a Change Request	443
		9.3.2	Finding Change Requests	448
		9.3.3	Workflow Steps for a Change Request	449
	9.4	Creating Change Requests in a Shared Service Center		451
	9.5	Summary		456

10 Planning in SAP NetWeaver BW or SAP SEM ... 457

	10.1	New Options for Planning		459
		10.1.1	Structure of Planning Applications in SAP ERP	459
		10.1.2	Structure of Planning Applications in SAP NetWeaver BW	462

		10.1.3	Multidimensional Database Layer in SAP NetWeaver BW	464
		10.1.4	Data Entry and Planning Functions	469
	10.2	Options in SAP ERP from SAP Enhancement Package 6 for SAP ERP 6.0		472
		10.2.1	Role Project Planner and Cost Estimator	473
		10.2.2	Overall Planning	474
		10.2.3	Cost Element Planning	476
	10.3	Express Planning as a Framework for the Planning Process		479
		10.3.1	Creating a Planning Round	480
		10.3.2	How Cost Center Managers Submit Their Data	487
		10.3.3	Monitoring, Reviewing, and Approving the Planning Process	491
		10.3.4	Embedding Overall and Cost Element Planning in Express Planning	493
	10.4	Summary		495

11 Allocations Using SAP Cost and Profitability Management 497

	11.1	New Tools for Performing Allocations in SAP ERP		500
		11.1.1	Template Allocations in SAP ERP	501
	11.2	New Tools for Performing Allocations in SAP BusinessObjects PCM		510
		11.2.1	Mapping the Costing Model in SAP BusinessObjects PCM with SAP ERP	512
		11.2.2	Dimensions of the Costing Model	513
		11.2.3	Assignments in the Costing Model	518
		11.2.4	Loading Data to the Model	521
	11.3	Customer Value Analysis Using SAP BusinessObjects PCM		523
	11.4	Summary		525

12 Period Close Using SAP Financial Closing Cockpit 527

	12.1	New Options for Accelerating the Period Close		528
		12.1.1	Orchestrating Your Closing Tasks	530
		12.1.2	Executing Your Close Tasks	533
		12.1.3	Automating Closing Transactions	536
		12.1.4	Creating Program Variants for Your Close Tasks	539

		12.1.5	Scheduling Tasks	541
		12.1.6	Using Workflows In the Close	546
		12.1.7	Handling Costing Runs in Your Close	551
		12.1.8	Handling Organizational Units in the Closing Cockpit	552
		12.1.9	Closing Cockpit and SAP Financial Closing Cockpit	557
	12.2	Closing Tasks in Multiple Systems		559
	12.3	Summary		564
	12.4	Post-Script		564

The Author	565
Index	567

In this chapter, I'll discuss my own roots in the Controlling component of SAP ERP Financials (CO), how I came to write this book, and what I am trying to achieve as I introduce the individual chapters.

Preface

When I joined SAP back in 1992, the documentation available in English was minimal, and what there was came in blue binders. It was to be my job to translate some of these binders into English. The short form was a series of cardboard quick reference guides, which listed the transaction codes needed to perform the tasks and the tables required to configure the system in each module. I spent my early weeks in Germany in the training center working my way through RK, RM, and RF courses (in those days we were still on SAP R/2). Each week I would add another German binder and quick reference guide to my pile. In theory, I was learning lots, but I was frustrated because I couldn't see the big picture and couldn't relate what I found in my heap of English accounting books with what I was learning about SAP. It was soon clear that translating CO was going to require more than a good dictionary.

The breakthrough came when a colleague suggested I read Wolfgang Kilger's cost accounting bible, *Flexible Plankostenrechnung und Deckungsbeitragsrechnung*. Given my level of business German at that time, I sometimes wonder how much I actually took in. In retrospect, it hardly matters. Kilger's book told me how the pieces fit together and how my ever growing list of transactions related to the business world. It allowed me to ask the right questions of the consultants who would spend time in our office testing the new software. When SAP R/3 came along, I stopped translating and started writing documentation.

For most English speakers the breakthrough came with the publication of *Product Costing Made Easy* in 1998. This book walked users through every posting performed in Product Costing, giving the T-accounts for each step in the process. I still meet controllers and consultants who go misty eyed at the mention of this book and confess to a terror of losing their copy. This book was the ultimate reference, and

Preface

I still pull it out when I'm testing new functions and trying to remember how they should work.

In 2009 I made a presentation at SAP Financials in Prague that was based on the postings described in *Product Costing Made Easy* to a full house. It showed me that 10 years on, people were still struggling to relate the business processes in Sales, Production, and Purchasing with the T-accounts in Financials and the various cost objects used to provide information to management. There were still people searching for the big picture as I had been back in 1992. The germ of this book was contained in that presentation.

However, things have moved on in the last 10 years, not least in the fact that SAP R/3 has become SAP ERP. I'll give you the same menu paths and transaction codes that I would have given 10 years ago. I loved the menus when we moved from transaction codes in R/2 to menus in R/3, but the sheer number of transactions means the menus are now becoming as unwieldy as my quick reference guides for R/2. So I'll also show you how to use roles to present those transactions in a more user-friendly manner.

I'll show you where to find the reports you'll need in SAP ERP, but I'll also tell you where SAP NetWeaver Business Warehouse (SAP NetWeaver® BW) fits into the picture. I'll introduce the new reporting options available with SAP BusinessObjects. I'll show you how to plan in SAP ERP, but I'll also show you how to use the newer planning options. I'll tell you how to set up your master data in SAP ERP but also how to use a change request to document why you need to make changes to your master data at all and introduce the newer solutions for managing master data in a multisystem or shared service environment. I'll talk about allocations in SAP ERP but also about when to consider SAP BusinessObjects Profitability and Cost Management. I'll walk you through the period close activities, but I'll also show you how to use SAP's Financial Closing cockpit to provide a framework for the close.

In 2010 I took over the role of chief product owner for management accounting and now manage new developments that are taking place in CO. This book will explain the basics for a reader new to CO, but it will also look at the enhancements that affect CO in all releases up to SAP enhancement package 5 for SAP ERP 6.0, so it should provide information relevant for more experienced controllers and consultants. Things are not changing as fast as they did in the 1990s, but there are still changes that affect CO as International Financial Reporting Standards (IFRS) become more prevalent or corporate controlling attempts to take a group view that would have been pure fantasy back in the early 1990s.

However, this book is not a configuration guide. I spent the mid-1990s writing implementation guides, so it didn't seem fair to write about configuring cost components and costing variants now, when there are others better qualified than me to do so. I'll generally assume that you have a configured system before you, though I might show you things that were not available or that your implementation didn't know about when it was carried out. When this happens, I'll try to include enough information to enable you to find what you need in the SAP documentation.

This book is also not a white paper, though I've written plenty of them too. I wanted to fill the space between the high-level white paper and the detailed implementation guide, since for me this is where the most interesting questions lie. If you understand how the pieces fit together, then you should be able to ask the right questions, whether these are general questions such as where to plan or report or specific questions about the handling of an individual business process from a controlling perspective.

Over the last several years, I have had the pleasure of working with controllers at many customer sites, and these conversations are reflected in the pages of this book. I may not be a controller, but I am in constant discussions with controllers working with SAP ERP. I hear where they are struggling, whether in conversations with user groups, answering a customer message asking for help on a specific issue, or when we are developing new functions in collaboration with some of our key customers. It is these conversations that make this a practical guide.

As for the examples in this book, I've tried to take my screenshots from the standard demo system, IDES, wherever possible so that anybody with access to that demo landscape can follow the examples for themselves. This may mean the examples I show are not specific to your industry, though I do try to mention industry variants when I consider them relevant. The screenshots were, with a handful of exceptions, made using a system on SAP enhancement package 5, though when I talk about the new functions I was often using a quality system, since at the time of writing not all new functions were reflected in the standard demo landscape. Some of the examples are a little simplistic, since I wanted them to be easy to understand, unlike some of the real-life examples I see at customer sites. If there are issues surrounding more complex examples, such as performance or locking, I've tried to mention them, though clearly I can't know every detail concerning your organization's particular implementation.

A Practical Guide to Controlling with SAP

Let's briefly look at what is covered in each of the chapters. I've tried to make it easy for a new controller with basic accounting experience to start at the beginning and work from front to back. Experienced controllers may prefer to use the index to find the key features that interest them or use the downloadable appendix on new business functions to find out about areas they have not yet explored.

Introduction

In **Chapter 1** we'll explain basic concepts such as cost elements, fixed and variable costs, standard costs, and actual costs as they apply to CO. We'll introduce the roots of CO, explaining where there are differences with respect to typical cost accounting practices in the United States and where there is common ground. We'll introduce record keeping by cost center, order, and project and introduce the main tasks to be performed at period close. We'll also look at planning and budgeting as a key element of CO and introduce the internal controls necessary for the business processes involved in CO.

Reporting

In **Chapter 2** we'll introduce cost center line items, order line items, and line items in Profitability Analysis in terms of the information they offer but also as an introduction to the way controllers work with such data. We'll look at the key functions in SAP List Viewer so you'll learn how to use existing layouts and create new layouts for your particular purposes. We'll also look at your reporting options for Product Cost Controlling and the various tree reports that allow you to view the structure of bills of material, both for standard costs and actual costs. Finally we'll introduce the data flows to Profitability Analysis and explain the record types available for reporting.

Master Data Owned by Controlling

In **Chapter 3** we'll look at the master data for which the controlling department is responsible, showing how to create cost centers, internal orders and settlement rules, statistical key figures, activity types, secondary cost elements, product cost collectors, and cost object hierarchies. We'll look at how to group this master data to ease selection for reporting and allocations and how to handle time-dependent master data. We'll look at statuses on internal orders and discuss how to create change requests to initiate a master data change.

Master Data Where Controlling Is a Stakeholder

In **Chapter 4** we'll look at the master data for which the controlling department is one of several stakeholders, showing the relevant fields in the material master, customer master, bill of material (BOM), routing, and work center. We'll look at different types of bills of material, including BOMs for joint production, BOMs for configurable materials, and recursive BOMs, and different types of routings, including master recipes and rate routings. We'll also look at production alternatives and how to mix them for Product Costing. We'll then look at the master data for projects and investment programs and discuss the fields that matter to the controlling department. We'll explain the link between the operational chart of accounts and the primary cost elements used in CO. Finally we'll look at the price information in the material master and purchasing info records for the raw materials, since this key information has to be in place before we start planning in Chapter 5 or performing goods movements in Chapter 6.

Planning and Budgeting

In **Chapter 5** we'll look at a complete planning cycle, starting with the sales plan in Profitability Analysis, transferring the results to sales and operational planning in Logistics, bringing a scheduled activity from the production plan back to the cost center plan, and then planning cost center expenses for both operational and supporting cost centers and taking account of activity-dependent and activity-independent costs. We'll then calculate the activity price for those cost centers and look at how to generate a primary cost component split for that activity price before looking at how to create a costing run to calculate the standard costs for all the materials we plan to manufacture. We'll then mark and release the cost estimates to transfer the results to the material master and use valuation to pull the results of the cost estimate into Profitability Analysis. We'll also look at investment planning, starting with an investment program and planning values for the projects assigned to that program, preparing budgets for these projects, and learning how to initiate a change request to change or transfer a budget.

Actual Postings

In **Chapter 6** we'll walk through the typical steps in a procure-to-pay, plan-to-manufacture, and order-to-cash process to show you what a controller typically monitors in each step and where variances can potentially occur. We'll then look at how to handle differences identified during a physical inventory and assign them to the work orders or product cost collectors processed during the time between inventory counts. Next we'll look at how to handle co-products, perform an order split or rework, work with product cost collectors, use configurable materials and sales order stock, and work with work breakdown structure (WBS) elements as account assignments. We'll discuss how to make correction postings, and we'll end the chapter by looking at a cross-company stock transfer from both a legal and group perspective.

Period Close

In **Chapter 7** we'll look at the main tasks taking place at period close, including allocations both between cost centers and to Profitability Analysis and, explain the differences between real-time direct activity allocations and the typical period close allocations. We'll look at the different forms of allocation, including assessment cycles, distribution cycles, reposting cycles, and indirect activity allocation cycles. We'll then look at target costs and variances on cost centers and how to calculate an activity price based on actual costs. Having completed the close steps in Cost Center Accounting, we'll look at the close activities in Cost Object Controlling, including calculating work in process, variances, and settlement. If you're using the Material Ledger, we'll also look at the periodic costing run and the alternative valuation run as a means of calculating actual product costs once the period is complete. Finally we'll look at the revaluation and top-down distribution tasks in Profitability Analysis.

Reporting in SAP NetWeaver® BW and SAP BusinessObjects

In **Chapter 8** we'll look at how to analyze large volumes of data in SAP ERP, explaining the use of extracts and variation in Report Writer and summarization levels in Profitability Analysis and Cost Object Controlling. We'll look at some of the criteria that might affect a decision to move to SAP NetWeaver Business Warehouse (BW), including performance issues, multidimensionality, and a need to mix data from multiple systems. This chapter won't have the depth of a book dedicated to reporting in SAP NetWeaver BW, but it will show you how to find the delivered DataSources, InfoProviders, and queries for CO and bring data from an existing operating concern into SAP NetWeaver BW. We'll explore examples of querying data in Cost Center Reporting, using physical, virtual, and transient InfoProviders, and wrap up with an introduction to Crystal Reports, Xcelsius Dashboards, and the brand new High-Performance Analytic Appliance (SAP HANA™).

Master Data in a Multisystem/Shared Service Environment

In **Chapter 9** we'll return to the internal service request we introduced in Chapter 3 and look at the configuration required to prepare the form, workflow, and notification to document the requested change and the proper execution. We'll then introduce a solution for master data maintenance in a multisystem environment, available from enhancement package 4. We'll look at the data model, editions, change requests, and distribution services delivered with SAP Master Data Governance for Financials. Finally we'll look at master data maintenance in the context of a shared service scenario delivered with the SAP shared service framework.

Planning in SAP NetWeaver BW or SAP SEM

In **Chapter 10** we'll return to the planning layouts we looked at in Chapter 5 and discuss how they are used to structure the data available for planning in SAP ERP before moving on to discuss your options for planning in SAP NetWeaver BW or SAP Strategic Enterprise Management (SAP SEM®), where we'll look at examples of investment planning and product cost planning using SAP NetWeaver BW. We'll then introduce new solutions in enhancement package 6 that combine the flexibility of an input-enabled query in SAP NetWeaver BW with the ability to write the planned data directly to the SAP ERP tables, where there is no business requirement for full data modeling. Finally we'll introduce Express Planning as a way of managing the collaboration between the controller and cost center managers during cost center planning.

Allocations Using SAP Cost and Profitability Management

In **Chapter 11** we'll look at more sophisticated ways of allocating overhead, using both template allocation if most of your allocations can be made using drivers in SAP ERP or a new solution, SAP Cost and Profitability Management, that allows you to load the relevant data into a dedicated environment and perform allocations and what-if simulations with the goal of understanding the cost to serve a customer segment or the true profitability of an individual customer.

Period Close Using SAP Financial Closing Cockpit

In **Chapter 12** we'll pick up where we left off in Chapter 7 and look at ways to document which steps are performed as part of your period close, automate the close steps by using executable programs and workflows, handle errors occurring during the period close, and handle a close process that crosses multiple systems.

> **Appendices**
>
> The appendices for this book are available for you to download at *www.sap-press.com*.
>
> In **Appendix A** we'll look at how to use SAP NetWeaver Business Client or SAP NetWeaver Enterprise Portal to display transactions, reports, and web applications, so your administrator will be able to make your system look like the examples shown in the book.
>
> In **Appendix B** we'll look at how to configure a report launchpad to make it easier for your users to find the reports relevant to their roles, so your administrator can re-create some of the screens shown in Chapter 2.
>
> In **Appendix C** we'll discuss how to activate the enterprise extensions and business functions needed for the newer functions described in this book.

Acknowledgments

This book wouldn't have been possible without the help and support of many colleagues. Hendrik Ahlgrimm, Michael Alexander, Dirk Degrell, Mario Franz, Johannes Gierse, Markus Königstein, Hartmut Körner, Ralf Ille, Stefan-Claudius Müller, Stephan Rehmann, Thomas Pike, Alfred Schaller, Sadaf Shakil, Stefan Tex, Marco Valentin, and Klaus Weiss answered many of the questions that came up during the writing process and corrected the manuscript. To them I extend my sincerest thanks.

I'd also like to thank Dondogmaa Lkhamdondog for her help and support when I needed changes to the SAP ERP demo systems, Thomas Schultze for his support when working with the SAP Business Objects demo systems and Birgit Starmanns for preparing the original T-Account presentation, shown at SAP Financials in Las Vegas. In the course of writing this book I was helping train our China team, and their questions inevitably flowed into the text. In this context, I'd like to thank Alex Hu, Emily Li, Bill Liu, Alex Ouyang, Zhiqiang Wu, and Ivan Zhang from the Shanghai office.

I'd also like to thank Meg Dunkerley and the SAP PRESS team for their help in guiding me through my first book.

And finally, the biggest thank you to my family: husband, Nick, and children, Martin and Lucy. I am particularly grateful to Nick for his help in keeping me cycling while the book was in progress.

This chapter discusses the roots of Controlling with SAP ERP Financials and introduces the basic Controlling functions. You'll learn what might be different from other systems you have encountered and where there is common ground.

1   Introduction

People taking their first class on Controlling with SAP ERP Financials (which we'll refer to as CO moving forward) are often daunted by the sheer range of functions, since CO is actually several costing systems rolled into one, covering Responsibility Accounting, Planning, Activity-Based Costing, Product Cost Accounting, and Profitability Management, whereas most other systems handle each of these areas separately. A quick glance at the SAP menu (see Figure 1.1) shows you a series of folders that you may not instantly be able to map to your current approach to cost accounting.

Let's start with the top menu point: COST ELEMENT ACCOUNTING. This can sound like an alien concept if you're used to seeing cost centers and orders simply as an account assignment in the general ledger, with postings made to an account and a "center." You may only be familiar with the term *account* and never have encountered the term *cost element* at all. The cost element provides the link to the General Ledger accounts, so typical cost elements are wages and salaries (for recording the costs associated with your workforce), materials and services (for recording the costs associated with the goods you buy and sell), depreciation (for recording the costs associated with your assets), utility costs, and so on. It's really just a word, so if it helps to carry on thinking of a cost element as an account, by all means do, at least for *primary cost elements*. Cost elements are also used to store the results of any allocation, so you'll also use several additional cost elements to define how costs flow through your organization. These cost elements are known as *secondary cost elements,* and we'll look at how to define the two types in Chapters 3 and 4. When defining your cost elements, it's also important to understand how the costs behave. Energy costs are *variable,* rising as the output of the cost center rises, but rent costs are *fixed*, remaining constant irrespective of how much work the cost center performs.

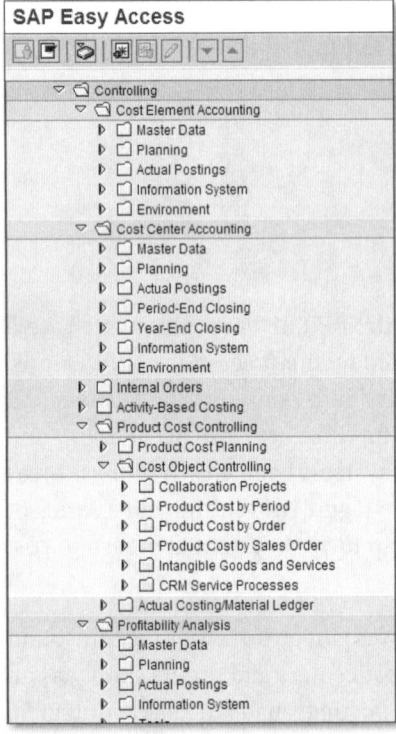

Figure 1.1 Controlling in the SAP Easy Access Menu

If the cost element answers the question of the *type* of costs incurred, the question of *why* such costs were incurred is answered in the next folders: COST CENTER ACCOUNTING and to a lesser extent INTERNAL ORDERS. Every posting in the SAP General Ledger recorded under an account with a sister cost element (the primary cost element) also requires you to enter the following:

- The *cost center* for which the costs were incurred (in the example of wages and salaries, for which department the employees were working)
- The *order or project* for which the costs were incurred (in the example of goods and services, which project required the purchase to be made).

Within this type of posting there is an idea of *responsibility accounting*, in other words of making the cost center manager responsible for the costs incurred for his cost center and the project manager responsible for the costs incurred for his project. For small projects, you may not even need a project in SAP ERP but will find that an internal order is adequate for your needs. The word *accounting* is related to *accountability*. It's the controller's task to ensure the accountability of the relevant managers for their spending on each cost center, order, or project.

With Cost Center Accounting and internal orders we are essentially looking at cost or expense accounting, If we now look at how to capture sales *revenue*, we move into the realm of Profitability Analysis (often shortened to CO-PA) (the bottom folder in Figure 1.1). If you're new to SAP, you need to understand that Profitability Analysis is essentially a data warehouse in SAP ERP where you can capture the costs and revenue associated with each customer and product and analyze your profitability by region, sales organization, business area, company code, and so on. Profitability Analysis is a very powerful tool but may provide a degree of granularity that differs from what you're used to if you currently capture costs and revenue mainly in your general ledger. It offers two alternative taxonomies for viewing the relevant values: by cost element (account-based) and by value field (costing-based). While most people can imagine costs and revenue accounts, the value fields represent a different view that can be more or less detailed than the account view, depending on business requirements.

If you now look more closely at the menus for COST CENTER ACCOUNTING, INTERNAL ORDERS, and PROFITABILITY ANALYSIS, you'll see that each of them contains a folder called PLANNING. The idea of planning and setting standards is central to CO, and we'll talk later about how to plan and why a plan is necessary in SAP ERP. This is especially important because it's usually the controller who drives the creation of the plan, establishing the framework and collaborating with all the involved parties until agreement is reached.

If you're performing any kind of manufacturing, then the process of turning the materials you buy into products you can sell is covered in Product Cost Controlling. Again, if you're used to managing work orders in a separate system, the idea that every work order in SAP ERP is a cost object in CO may be new. In the course of this book we'll discuss the different levels of detail you can use to capture the information on work orders. We'll compare the classic approach to standard costing with newer approaches, including *lean accounting*, which rejects the work order as the sole focus of cost accounting.

Finally, there is a folder for Activity-Based Costing, allowing you to capture costs for business processes such as quality control or product configuration that cannot be described in routings and master recipes. We'll return to this in more detail in Chapter 11.

Figure 1.2 may help you visualize the value flows through CO, with the cost centers and internal orders capturing expenses from the SAP General Ledger at the top; the business process as an optional account assignment for Activity-Based Costing below; the production orders, sales orders, and projects that are used to handle the organization's operations in the middle; and the multidimensional cube that is Profitability Analysis at the bottom. The boxes on the left represent the inputs to CO from the other components, and the boxes on the right represent the way costs flow from Cost Center Accounting to production orders, sales orders, and projects and via order settlement to Profitability Analysis.

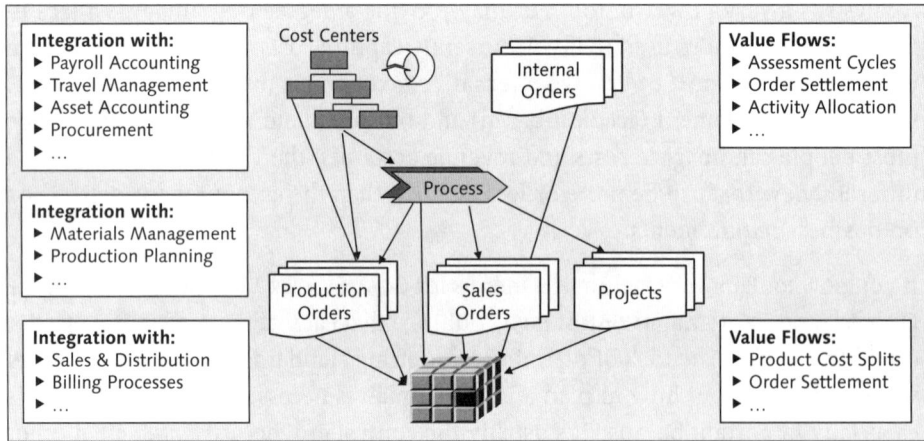

Figure 1.2 Value Flows in Controlling

1.1 Basic Controlling Functions

To understand how CO started out, we need to look at the work of Hans-Georg Plaut, an automotive engineer who became involved in management accounting in the late 1940s. His legacy is the system of *Grenzplankostenrechnung* (GPK), variously translated into English as "marginal planned cost accounting" or "flexible analysis cost planning and accounting," which has been the mainstay of German cost accounting for over 60 years. This approach shaped what we now know as CO when he and his consultants worked with the SAP developers to build the RK components in SAP R/2 and the early CO components in SAP R/3. This being said, you certainly don't need to have studied cost accounting (aka controlling) in Germany to understand controlling in SAP, but it's worth taking a few minutes to look at the basic principles of cost accounting before we look at the software in detail.

1.1.1 Goals of Controlling

In this section, we'll take Hans-Georg Plaut's ideas about cost accounting as a starting point. The goal of controlling is to provide meaningful insight and analysis of accounting information for the benefit of internal users, such as controllers, cost center managers, project managers, plant managers, and so on. It's the controller's job to put a structure in place that provides meaningful cost information to the various managers. This is achieved as follows:

- **Building clearly defined cost center structures**
  Each *cost center* represents the cost of resources employed, where a resource could be a machine, a building, or people working in a department. Each cost center should be homogenous in purpose. Generally, a single cost center is the responsibility of one manager. This is important in the sense that the cost center is not an anonymous pool of costs, but an entity for which one person is responsible. Accounting is effectively being used to drive accountability, with each manager being held responsible for the cost of the resources his cost center uses and what that cost center provides, whether it's the provision of goods and services or the support of other cost centers. It's the controller's job to ensure that a workable structure is in place that supports both the reporting needs of each cost center manager and the business needs of corporate reporting.

- **Separating fixed and proportional costs**
  Costs behave differently depending on their type. So costs such as rent and insurance generally remain the same (*fixed*), while costs such as energy (*proportional*) rise if the production line runs for longer or the department has to handle more orders. The goal is to understand how costs behave under changing output levels and to explore capacity limitations and the utilization of available capacity. This is important because it's the reason why CO is separated from Financial Accounting. The rent payments or the energy payments are recorded in the financial accounts, but the explanation of what drives changes to the level of payments is in CO. The notion of fixed and variable costs is an area of endless debate among cost accountants who have to balance the practicality of their approach against

absolute accuracy. In recent years, there has been a trend toward unraveling and simplifying some of these assignments to make it easier for cost center managers and project managers to understand their costs and take effective action.

- **Establishing clearly defined activities and drivers**
  The aim is to define at least one representative output measure, such as machine hours, for each cost center and to ensure a linear relationship between the product and the output measure (for example, machine hours) and between the output measure and the cost pool (costs incurred by the production cost center to provide machine hours). This approach focuses on outputs or drivers, whether it's the quantity of goods to be sold or produced in a given period or the quantity of work to be performed by a cost center, as a way of determining whether resources are being used efficiently. This approach applies to both the actual outputs and to planning, which is output-driven in the SAP approach. It's the controller's job to work with the cost center managers in this area. Some cost centers are easy: It's quite clear that a production line provides work in the form of machine hours. Whether an energy cost center is merely an expense that should be allocated to the operational cost centers or carries an output in the form of kilowatt hours of energy used will be a subject for discussion, and you'll find that there are no hard and fast rules governing how to determine the output of a cost center.

- **Using analytical cost planning**
  The goal is to prepare a plan for each cost center that reflects realistic expectations for budget setting and operational performance. This plan is based on the output of the cost center (i.e., the machine hours required to perform the work) as a realistic expectation that is modeled during planning. The cost center output is, in turn, driven by the demand from production and sales for output (goods to be sold). This planning approach involves more work but provides greater insight than the "last year plus X%" approach that prevails in some organizations. It's the controller's job to coordinate and manage this plan in a collaborative effort, involving the sales managers, cost center managers, and so on, since the plan is not just about gathering the numbers but is also about reaching agreement about realistic goals for the next planning period.

- **Setting standards**
  The aim is to set stable standards for the period that allow users to understand the variances, and it's the controller's job to ensure that such a standard is in place. Standard setting is an important part of the cost accounting approach,

providing a standard for the provision of a given level of activity by a cost center or a standard for the production of a given lot size of a product. In both cases, variances with respect to this standard are analyzed at period close to explain the source of the variance (price change, quantity change, and so on). Variance analysis is initially the controller's task, but for high variances or scrap this typically involves discussions with the relevant plant managers to understand the underlying cause of the variance and where it indicates problems on the shop floor. Variance analysis should be treated not as an academic exercise, but as a need to ask "Why?" Was the standard wrong or do we need to make some changes to reduce rework or scrap?

▶ **Correctly allocating internal service costs**
The goal is to reflect the true supply-and-demand conditions for usage of each resource. This applies not only to production cost centers, but potentially to all cost centers for which output measures can reasonably be established, so you'll find cost centers for IT services, human resources, finance, and so on being modeled as service providers alongside more obviously measurable cost centers. It's the controller's job to set up a model that supports the proper allocation of all internal services.

1.1.2 Cost Accounting in the United States

While the notion of standard cost accounting and variance analysis is well established in the United States, there are some fundamental differences between Germany and the United States.

▶ U.S. organizations typically have fewer cost centers than their German counterparts, making it sometimes difficult to establish a single output for each cost center.

▶ U.S. organizations often separate the accounts into fixed and variable accounts, rather than separating the idea of the account from the idea of the cost element. In CO, costs are categorized in terms of how they respond to the changing output of the cost center and to the changing production output. Indeed, it's often clearer to use the word *proportional* rather than *variable* to represent the way this relationship works. To understand this, think of how the energy costs for the cost center will rise if the number of machine hours produced in the period rises and how the number of machine hours needed in the period will rise if more units are produced.

- U.S. organizations often plan using software that is not integrated with their cost accounting system, rather than seeing planning as an integral part of controlling and the basis for all variance analysis.

1.1.3 Standard Costs and Actual Costs

The central importance of planning and standard-setting brings us to one of the first myths about CO, namely that it's only possible to work with *standard costs*. When we discuss the material master in Chapter 4, we'll cover how setting a standard price for the manufacture of a unit of the product is an option and that it makes sense to apply a standard price to goods movements, where finished goods are received to stock and issued to sales before all actual costs (invoices, time recording, etc.) have been recorded. However, since Release 4.6C, it has been possible to use the Material Ledger to calculate true actual costs at period close that take account of all price variances and production variances. We'll look at this in detail in Chapters 6 and 7. The wording on some of the screens only adds to the confusion, since many of the delivered reports use the term *actual costs* simply to mean the actual quantity multiplied by a standard price, whereas the *true* actual costs are only calculated at period close when the periodic costing run is executed. We'll look at this whole process when we consider the period close in Chapter 7.

1.1.4 Investment and Project Controlling

Alongside production controlling, sales controlling, and so on, we'll also explore investment controlling. You'll find the functions for Investment Management in a separate part of the menu (see Figure 1.3), but there is so much overlap in the assignment of costs to internal orders and projects that no book on CO can afford to leave out the subject of Investment Management. If you're completely new to the subject, think of the investment program simply as a reporting layer structuring the investment portfolio and providing budgeting functions over and above a simple plan/actual comparison at the project or order level. The area is of interest for the controller whenever there is significant expense involved in bringing a new product to market or building a new production line that is not captured if you only look at sales or production controlling.

If you compare the CO menu and the Investment Management menu, you'll notice that the INTERNAL ORDERS folder for INVESTMENT MANAGEMENT contains exactly the same entries as the INTERNAL ORDERS folder for CONTROLLING. The difference is in the definition of investment programs to which the investment orders and projects are assigned and the use of appropriation requests to initiate an investment proposal.

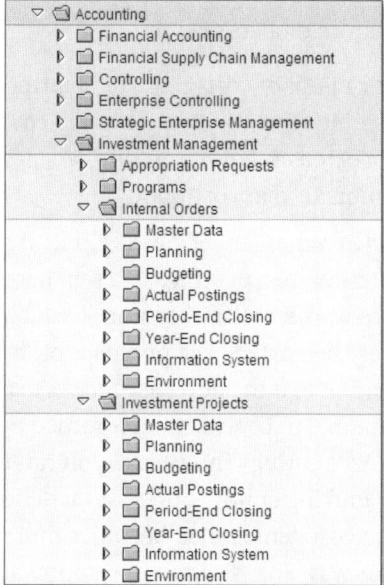

Figure 1.3 Investment Management in the SAP Easy Access Menu

1.1.5 Lean Accounting

One function you won't find in the SAP Easy Access Menu, but you'll find discussed throughout the book is the idea of lean accounting. The practice of lean accounting can provide a useful guide to many implementation questions, encouraging the use of clean master data, simple reporting structures, and data that everyone (not just the controller) can understand and act upon.

Now that we've introduced the main elements, let's look at CO as a bookkeeping function and how expenses move from the SAP General Ledger into CO.

1.2 Essential Record Keeping Functions

Apart from the general ideas underpinning controlling, it's also important to understand that CO is not stand-alone software taking feeds from financial and operational logistics systems. It's embedded in SAP ERP and is essentially the glue that links operational logistics to finance. What a financial accountant sees as essential bookkeeping, the controller sees as a dialog between purchasing and finance or between production and finance.

To understand what we mean, think about the nature of a cost center.

- In a stand-alone system, a cost center describes a pool of costs that are incurred by a department, a group of workers, or a machine. The assignment to the cost center may be made in the general ledger as an extension of the account assignment, or it may involve mapping certain accounts to that cost pool.

- In SAP ERP, the cost center is part of the SAP General Ledger posting, but it's also part of the Logistics transaction that initiates the cost posting. So a purchase request is created and approved with reference to the cost center under which the costs for the purchased goods will ultimately be posted. The purchase order and invoice from the supplier carry the information that the purchase relates to a specific cost center. So the purchase costs are captured in Logistics and recorded in both the SAP General Ledger and Cost Center Accounting. This means you can't design your cost center structure without also looking at how purchases will be initiated with reference to the cost center. The cost center thus becomes more than just an account assignment, affecting the way you design your approval processes, so that the cost center manager can authorize all purchases carried out with reference to the cost center.

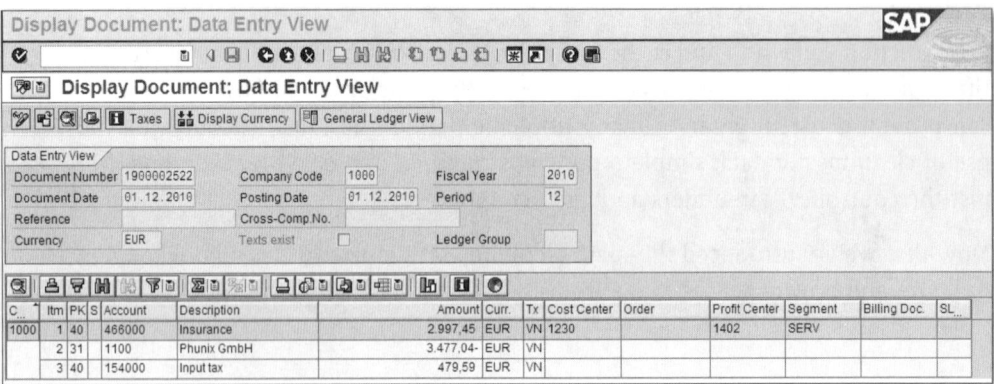

Figure 1.4 Expense Posting to a Cost Center

Figure 1.4 shows a posting for insurance expenses to a cost center. This posting will be passed from the SAP General Ledger into Cost Center Accounting under the cost element associated with the profit and loss (P&L) account for the insurance expenses. You'll also notice that the expenses have also been assigned to the profit center and segment in the cost center master. What you need to remember is that in a fully integrated SAP ERP implementation the majority of postings coming into CO originate not in the General Ledger, but in purchasing, production, human resources, and so on and that the account assignment is automatically populated based on the cost center in the relevant application (the purchase order in purchasing, the organizational unit for payroll, and so on).

The same basic principle applies to orders and projects.

- A stand-alone system can also capture order or project costs as an extension of the general ledger posting and even support basic time recording.
- What makes CO unique is the way the order is embedded in Logistics and in Time Recording in human resources. A cost allocation takes place automatically when an order confirmation is recorded in Logistics to record that an operation has been completed, a quantity of product finished, or even a quantity scrapped. The same thing happens when an employee records his working time with reference to the order or project in human resources. This cost assignment utilizes the planned activity rate for the machine or labor hours confirmed to the production order or the hourly rate for the employee charging time to a project to make an immediate charge to the order or project. This may be corrected at period close, when the actual costs for the period are known.
- This tight integration has its challenges in the sense that you have to make sure that the master data in production and the organizational units in human resources tie in with the cost center master data. On the other hand, the basis for many of the allocations is being collected not in finance but where the activity is carried out on the shop floor or an employee's time sheet. Bills of material (BOMs), routings, master recipes, maintenance plans, and so on provide the basis for cost calculations requiring only basic monitoring work from the controlling department. By comparison, most organizations' attempts to capture activity drivers in Activity-Based Costing systems have been quite difficult, with frequent reliance on spreadsheets and slightly unreliable data integration.

1.2.1 Record Keeping by Cost Center

As we discussed, the cost center represents the cost of resources employed, where a resource might be a machine, a building, or people working in a department. This helps you answer simple questions, such as the amount of travel expenses incurred by a given department or the level of rent and maintenance costs for a building, but also the level of efficiency of a production line or an oven.

It's best to design cost centers so a single manager is responsible for each. This may simply be a management view for reporting purposes, but it's also relevant in operational processes, since the cost center manager approves purchase requests, travel expenses, and working time.

Cost Center Expenses

Let's look first at the types of costs that might be assigned to a cost center. We already mentioned that purchase costs are assigned to the cost center via the purchase order. Travel expenses are captured in a similar way, with all travel requests containing the assignment to the employee's cost center. When the travel expense is paid out, it's automatically assigned to the employee's cost center.

Cost centers can also represent production resources, including machines and equipment. In production, the machine is represented as a work center or resource, and in Plant Maintenance, the machine is represented as equipment. Generally, the machine is also a fixed asset, the costs of which have to be depreciated according to whichever generally accepted accounting principle (GAAP) applies in the relevant company code. The amount of depreciation according to each accounting principle is calculated in fixed asset accounting and transferred to the cost center during the depreciation run that takes place once a month.

Payroll is another significant cost input. The costs of employing staff and workers are captured in SAP ERP Human Capital Management and paid out based on the organizational unit to which the employee is assigned. In SAP ERP, the organizational unit is linked with a cost center, and all payroll expenses are transferred to the general ledger with the correct cost center assignment.

Cost centers can also receive costs from other cost centers. This might be in the form of general expenses (i.e., rent and insurance that are captured centrally and then allocated) or work performed by other cost centers (i.e., maintenance work, quality checks, or the cost of hiring or training new workers).

Cost Center Outputs

In CO, cost centers represent both where the costs were incurred in the organization and what was done with these costs. For a machine this may seem obvious. The production cost center receives depreciation expenses, payroll costs, energy costs, maintenance costs, and so on and provides machine hours. Assuming you have established routings or master recipes to describe the production steps, confirmations in Logistics record how many hours of machine time are required for each order. Even if you don't have detailed routings yet, there are ways to capture machine time, which we'll discuss in Chapter 6.

For a maintenance department, the same principle applies. The cost center receives payroll costs, operating supplies, and so on and provides maintenance hours. Assuming you have established maintenance plans, the costs of each maintenance task are assigned to the maintenance order when you make a confirmation.

For a sales department, the question of output may be more difficult. The Plaut approach advocates having an output measure for all cost centers, so you may find an activity such as sales hours being captured, but how can this be charged? What typically happens in these circumstances is that some form of allocation takes place. Either the expenses incurred by the sales department or the sum of the sales hours worked in the period are allocated to the customers served. We'll discuss the various forms of allocation in more detail when we look at the master data for activity types in Chapter 3, how to perform allocations in Chapter 7, and new options for allocations in Chapter 11.

For other departments, it may be possible to establish time recording in human resources, where time worked is charged to orders or projects. These might be research departments, development departments, consulting departments, and so on.

Handling Inventory

One source of confusion if you're moving from a U.S. legacy system is that the cost center output is always machine time, labor time, setup time, and so on (in other words, work provided), but not inventory (in other words, material produced). This is important in a manufacturing scenario, because although the costs of operating supplies might be assigned to a cost center, the inventory of raw materials and semifinished and finished products don't flow through the cost center, but are recorded on production orders, sales orders, projects, and so on. We'll look at this process in more detail in Chapter 6.

1.2.2 Record Keeping by Order

We've already met production orders for manufacturing a product and maintenance orders for repairing an asset, but there are many more types of orders in SAP ERP, from investment orders for capital expenses to service orders for performing external maintenance work and internal orders that represent activities outside of SAP ERP. There are also internal orders that the controlling department creates as cost collectors where more detail is required than is possible on a single cost center (such as for each vehicle assigned to a car pool).

Order Expenses

Regarding expense postings, all these orders behave the same way. You can assign purchasing costs, travel costs, and payroll costs to an order instead of a cost center by adjusting the account assignment. The underlying business question is simply why the purchase is necessary.

- Will the purchase provide equipment, such as a laptop or cell phone, for an employee assigned to the cost center or operating supplies, such as oil or grease, that are needed for the work of the cost center? If this is the case, the costs should be assigned to the cost center.
- Will the purchase provide goods or services that are specific to the order, such as buying consulting services to deliver on a project or order, buying materials for a building that is under construction, whose costs will later be capitalized as assets under construction, or buying materials for a special project? If this is the case, the costs should be assigned to an order.

For production orders and maintenance orders, it's also common to issue goods from stock to the order, whether as raw materials for use in a production order or as service parts for use in a maintenance or service order.

Other Postings to an Order

In addition to general overhead costs, you'll also find orders used in a *time and materials* approach, where the time part can be as significant as the materials. The SAP approach records time from external contractors as a primary cost via the purchase order, but time worked by people in the same organization is captured using the Time Recording functionality in SAP ERP HCM or Direct Activity Allocation in CO. In both cases, the employee enters working time in the form of the number of hours worked for the order, and a standard rate for one unit of this time is applied to the order. This takes us back to the output measure for each cost center. The activities of the employees would be represented on the cost center as research tasks, development tasks, maintenance tasks, and so on. When the employee charges his development time to the order or project, his cost center is credited and the order debited for his work.

Order Settlement

Once costs have been accumulated on an order, they are *settled*, or charged to another object. There are as many settlement options as there are types of orders. Maintenance orders and quality orders generally settle their costs back to the "parent" cost center. Production orders generally settle their production variances to Profitability Analysis. Investment orders generally settle their costs to assets under construction or fixed assets. Internal orders that represent a detailing of the cost center's activities, such as attending trade fairs, may settle either to the parent cost center (here the marketing cost center) or to the regions and customer groups attending the trade fairs. You'll also find mixed assignments, where some of the construction costs are assigned to a fixed asset and others to a cost center. We'll look at settlement in more detail in Chapters 3 and 7.

1.2.3 Record Keeping by Project

Sometimes an order does not provide adequate detail for the activity to be undertaken. A complex research project or construction project may need to be broken down into separate phases and activities for transparency. It can also be that parts of the project are being handled by different parts of the organization and in extreme cases by different companies in the organization. This breakdown of the project activities is known as a work breakdown structure, with each element represented as a *work breakdown structure element* (WBS element).

In complex engineering environments, you may find the work breakdown structure being used in conjunction with networks. In this case, the WBS elements represent the organizational view of the project, while the networks represent the logistics view providing scheduling tools for handling different work dependencies. WBS elements, networks, and network activities are all cost objects and can carry costs just like an internal order. WBS elements can also carry budgets since it's common in these scenarios to set an upper limit on spending in a given time frame.

With commercial projects, alongside the expense postings and time and materials postings, it's common to also capture revenue, since the customer is invoiced when certain milestones are reached. The billing process differs from the billing process for a make-to-stock product in that the delivery of the finished product is not the trigger. Instead, billing has to be triggered either based on an invoice plan or based on the resources spent on the project. In this situation, it's usual for the project costs to be settled to the sales order item.

While cost collection by cost center, order, or project essentially takes place in real time whenever a goods movement is posted and controlling is largely in a *monitoring* role, the controller is in the front seat at period close when the time comes to handle the close and the valuation of work in process and assets under construction, which we'll cover in the next section.

1.3 Managing Close and Valuation Processes

We've looked so far at many of the transactions that result in costs being assigned to cost centers and orders. One of the things that make CO confusing if you're coming from a stand-alone costing system is that some of the transactions, such as goods movements, asset acquisitions, invoice receipts, and so on, result in postings in the SAP General Ledger in *real-time*, whereas other postings take place at *period close*, such as allocations and order settlement. This is perhaps the most difficult part of the SAP approach to controlling. Inventory movements are valued immediately at standard costs but may be adjusted to account for variances later. Work in process, on the other hand, is moved to the balance sheet at period close and then reversed when the order is complete.

1.3.1 Valuation of Goods Movements

SAP recommends that you value finished and semifinished products at standard costs. This is because the delivery of these goods to stock and removal for sale can take place before all cost information relating to the production order has been posted. The standard cost thus represents the best guess for valuation purposes, even though, as we said earlier, the inventory value can be adjusted later if you use the Material Ledger. This approach also takes away the danger of inconsistencies during settlement, where goods are only revalued if there are still goods in stock.

1.3.2 Work in Process

In most U.S. systems, the movement of raw materials to the shop floor and on completion from the shop floor to finished goods inventory is treated as a reclassification of the balance sheet from raw materials inventory to *work in process* (WIP) and from there to finished goods inventory.

In CO, while the issue of the raw materials to the shop floor and the delivery of the finished product to the stores are *immediately* visible in the balance sheet, work in process is only calculated once per period. So the raw materials issued to the production order are treated as an expense on the profit and loss (P&L) statement during the period. Any work performed to convert the raw materials into a product is also expensed to the production order.

If the order is not complete at period close, the difference between the actual costs on the order and the value of any deliveries of the finished goods to stock is captured as work in process. On settlement the value of the work in process is moved to the balance sheet. If work continues in the next period, the value of the work in process increases. The difference from the previous period is moved to the balance sheet using settlement. Finally, when the order is complete, the value of the work in process is reversed and the balance sheet value is zero.

1.3.3 Scrap

In most U.S. systems, *scrap* is treated as a balance sheet item. In CO, the value of scrap is calculated during variance calculation. In the SAP approach, a distinction is made between normal and abnormal spoilage. Normal spoilage arises under efficient operation conditions and is an inherent result of the production process. The costs of normal spoilage are viewed as part of the costs of good units manufactured and included in the standard costs as *planned scrap*. Abnormal spoilage is not expected to arise under efficient operation conditions, and most abnormal spoilage is regarded as avoidable and controllable. The costs of abnormal spoilage are written off as losses of the accounting period in which the detection of the spoiled units occurs. In the SAP approach, abnormal spoilage is treated as a *scrap variance*.

1.3.4 Work in Process for Projects

In large-scale projects, the costs and revenues may not be representative of the actual stage of completion. At the beginning of the project high costs may be incurred to procure the correct components and begin work. On the revenue side, the billing schedule to the customer may not correspond with the amount of work completed or the costs incurred.

In this case, *results analysis* is used to smooth the pattern of the postings. There are two main approaches:

- **Percentage of completion (POC)**
  The POC method involves looking at the costs incurred compared to the planned costs to determine the percentage of completion. The revenue to be recognized in the period is then calculated based on the percentage of completion. Generally the actual revenue is lower than the revenue calculated according to the POC method, and a posting is prepared for revenues in excess of billings.

- **Revenue-based results analysis**
  The revenue-based results analysis method involves comparing the revenues to the planned revenues and planned costs to calculate the cost of goods sold that relate to these revenues. Normally the actual costs are higher than the calculated cost of goods sold because expenses have been incurred that have yet to be billed for, so work in process is calculated for the difference. Occasionally the actual costs are lower than the calculated costs, because time recording and invoices from contractors are missing, so reserves for missing costs are calculated for the difference.

Normally your implementation team defines which methods of results analysis are active in your system, but it's the controller's job to execute the valuation tasks at period close. We'll come back to results analysis when we look at period close activities in Chapter 7.

If period close has the controller in the hot seat for several days each month, the other area where the controller is active is the area of preparing budgets and planning, as described in the next section.

1.4 Preparing Budgets and Planning

As we noted earlier, Analytical Cost Planning is a key element of a good costing system and an area where the integration between the different plans in SAP ERP makes the approach feasible. People are often confused by this in the English-speaking world since the terms *planning* and *budgeting* tend to be used synonymously. In SAP systems, the *cost plan* refers to the exercise of valuating a sales plan or preparing a plan for individual cost centers or orders. A plan is just a plan—a set of assumptions about future business performance. A *budget* is something else. A budget may be derived from a plan, but it refers to the fixed budget to complete the order or project. The budget is checked whenever postings are made that will affect costs, whether these are expense postings in the general ledger or purchase orders that will result in costs in the future.

1.4.1 Driver-Based Cost Planning

The driver-based planning approach is considered a best practice in the manufacturing industry, where the sales plan or the production plan defines the expected output. Companies in the service industries also use driver-based planning, but instead of a physical quantity of goods to make and sell, a bank, for instance, might plan the clerical hours required to handle the loan applications it hopes to process in a given region or the clerical hours required to issue the new credit cards it hopes to issue in the next planning period.

The objective of planning is to provide a more accurate picture of expected future business performance by planning and monitoring the key operational activities that drive these results. This sounds easy enough but can mean completely rethinking the way you approach planning. With the SAP approach, you start the planning process not with the monetary values for the period, such as dollars per line of business, but with the sales quantities and production quantities. You then use these to calculate how much work you'll need to put in to meet your targets. Ultimately, the amount of work required takes you to the capacity per resource, whether this is a cost center supplying machine time or a call center providing clerical hours. You then plan your expenses against these drivers to calculate the resources you'll consume on each cost center to execute your plan.

We'll walk through the whole process in Chapter 5, but to get an idea of the scope of the plan, consider the following steps:

1. Create sales plan. This is where you can enter the quantities of product to sell to each customer and check the planned revenue (sales managers).
2. Create production plan. You can transfer the sales quantities to production and adjust them if necessary (production planners).
3. Transfer production requirements to cost center plan. You can use the production quantities to calculate the number of production activities required to complete the necessary work and transfer these quantities to the cost center plan as the *scheduled activity* (administrator).
4. Match cost center capacities against scheduled activity from production. You can check the capacities for each cost center and activity against scheduled activity to provide a reality check regarding the amount of activity requested by production (controllers).
5. Plan activity-dependent costs per cost center and activity type. This is probably the most fundamental difference between the way many organizations plan monetary values per cost center and the way the SAP approach distinguishes between costs such as rent and insurance that are fixed and costs such as energy that vary with the amount of activity provided in each period. The two are planned in separate *planning layouts* (cost center managers).
6. Calculate standard rate for activity types. For a cost center with a single output, or one activity type, this activity price calculation divides the expenses by the activity type to provide a rate per hour. If the cost center provides more than one activity, then activity price calculation first splits the expenses to the activity types using either equivalence number. The result is a rate per hour for each of the activities (controllers).
7. Calculate standard costs for products to be manufactured. From here, you can calculate standard costs for all the finished products in the original sales plan. This uses the bill of material to determine the material usage and the routing to determine the number of machine hours and so on needed. The activity rate per hour is then applied to these machine hours (controllers).
8. Transfer standard costs to sales plan to determine planned profitability. Finally you can use the valuation function in the sales plan to pull the standard costs for the materials into the sales plan to determine profitability (controllers).

1.4.2 Driver-Based Cost Planning Between Cost Centers

While the above approach to sales planning is widely used in the United States, the business of planning activities between cost centers is not very common outside of the German-speaking world. Most organizations plan expenses by cost center and then compare the actual costs with the planned costs for the period and analyze the variance. However, such an approach has its limitations in that it doesn't take into account whether the cost center did more or less work in the period.

In CO, if you have captured an output quantity for the cost center, the planned costs will be adjusted to reflect the actual output for the period. The adjusted costs are known as *target costs*. While production cost centers usually have a planned output in terms of the number of machine hours, labor hours, and so on, service cost centers often don't. The SAP approach is to plan activities for most cost centers. It involves planning:

- **What the cost center output is**
  The activity types to be performed and the quantities of that activity (output) to be provided.

- **What the cost center will spend to perform this activity**
  SAP differentiates here between activity-dependent costs and activity-independent costs.

- **How the output of this cost center is to be used**
  How much of each activity will flow to other cost centers and orders in the course of the planning period.

This is a much more detailed form of cost center planning than many organizations currently perform, but it provides a very powerful way of establishing the targets for the cost center and measuring whether these targets have been achieved. This form of planning also presupposes that the activity flow is *reconciled*—supply reflects demand—and that the flow of activities will be valued with a price, that is calculated by dividing the planned costs by either the planned activity or (more rarely) the planned capacity for the cost center. In theory this reconciliation is technical in nature, but the controller provides the human element, negotiating with both the supplying and the requesting cost center to determine whether the plan is reasonable. We'll walk through this process in detail in Chapter 5.

1 | Introduction

1.4.3 Budgeting

It's also common to perform very detailed cost planning for projects prior to approval, and it's the controller's job to coordinate the planning process with the individual project managers and ensure that their demands are reconciled with the goals set by corporate controlling. This may start with a rough plan, called the *overall plan*, which provides rough values per WBS element and year. The work breakdown structure is hierarchical. Values can be entered for the top WBS elements and distributed down to lower WBS elements or entered for lower WBS elements and aggregated up to the higher-level WBS elements. The process thus involves both *top-down* and *bottom-up planning*. Figure 1.5 illustrates the flow in both directions, with the budget for Europe being distributed down to the individual projects on the left and the order and project plans for the United States being rolled up to the corporate level on the right.

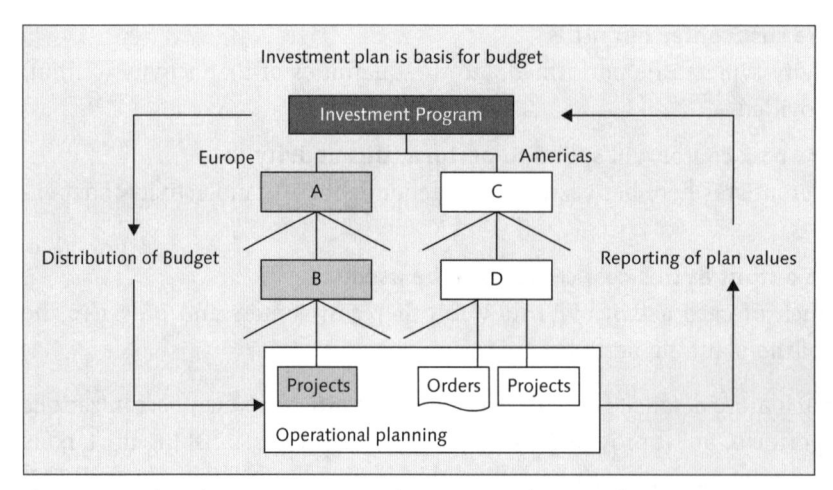

Figure 1.5 Value Flow in Top-Down and Bottom Up Planning of Investments

This plan is often created more than a year before execution is expected to begin in order to provide supporting information for the investment decision. This may be supplemented by detailed cost element planning where sufficient information exists to support this type of planning.

Once the plan is approved, it's often copied to the *budget*. This represents a binding plan that is used to determine how resources can be spent on the project. There are two types of budgeting:

- Passive budgeting involves the use of reports to monitor spending and commitments and to alert managers to potential budget overruns.
- Active budgeting or *active availability control* is used to set a ceiling on spending. If the ceiling is reached, you won't be allowed to create another purchase order or post costs to the project. This may take the form of a warning message or an error message that effectively blocks spending.

Since the budget is so critical, processes exist in controlling to document the level of the original budget and to allow you to assign additional budget to the project (a *supplement*), return unused budget (a *return*), and request a budget transfer from another project. These processes are handled as separate transactions and can involve the use of a workflow to handle the necessary approvals.

Now that you understand budgets and planning, let's move on to process analysis and internal controls.

1.5 Process Analysis and Internal Controls

The material we've covered up to this point could have been written at any point since SAP R/3 Release 4.6C. What changed at the turn of the century was the massive failure in financial reporting, governance practices, and risk prevention that created a need for sustainable improvement in these areas, leading to the Sarbanes-Oxley Act (SOX) in the United States and similar mandates and regulations in other countries. In terms of financial compliance, Section 302 of SOX states that CEOs and CFOs must personally sign off on their company's financial statements. Section 404 mandates that well-defined and documented processes and controls must be in place for all aspects of company operations that affect financial reports.

A whole industry has risen around the concerns of governance, risk, and compliance, and this guide cannot cover all the internal and external risks facing organizations. What is important in this context is to understand where you need to look at your controlling processes to achieve compliance.

1.5.1 Master Data Controls

The obvious place to start is the area of master data controls. The master data underlies all business processes, and poor master data quality can lead to significant risks. There needs to be a clear process in place to govern who can create or change any object to which costs can be assigned. This includes the creation of cost elements, cost centers, orders, projects, and so on. We'll return to this in Chapters 3 and 4. We'll also look at a new solution, SAP Master Data Governance in Financials, in Chapter 9.

1.5.2 Workflow

Once the master data is correctly in place, it makes sense to review all workflows and approval procedures to understand who is authorized to approve purchases, travel expenses, time recording, and anything else that can result in costs. Normally this sort of procedure applies mainly to incidental expenses, such as the purchase of a new laptop for a cost center, while the purchase of goods for use in production is not handled via a single workflow item. Here it's important to ensure that system controls are in place to check the three-way match required for logistics invoice verification (purchase order, goods receipt, and invoice receipt) and how price variances are handled in Purchasing.

For budget approval, SAP has its own transactions for releasing budgets and documenting the issue of budget supplements, budget returns, budget transfers, and so on. We'll look at these in Chapter 5.

1.5.3 Process Controls

Because of the huge impact of the standard costs in determining how goods movements are valued, it's important to properly document the planning process, including how activity rates are calculated and checked, how standard costs are calculated and checked, and who can mark and release the standard cost estimate and thus trigger a balance sheet adjustment for the inventory of that material currently in stock.

Similarly, if you have commercial projects or investment projects, it's important to understand how planning for these projects is performed, who signs off on the plan, and which planning values are used in results analysis to calculate work in process or put a value on assets under construction, so that your projects are correctly represented in the balance sheet at period close.

It's also important to review every step of the period close, to understand who signs off on each step, and what checks are performed. This is especially important in the area of order settlement, where expenses are capitalized as work in process, assets under construction, and so on. If you're using the Material Ledger, it's also important to document carefully which checks are performed after each stage of the costing run to ensure that the values are correct, how manual changes are performed and documented, and who can create the inventory adjustment postings to take account of the newly calculated actual costs.

1.6 Summary

In this chapter we introduced the roots of the SAP approach to controlling and explained how it differs in certain respects from common practices in the United States and other countries. We looked at recommendations for cost center design, a subject we'll return to along with what output measures to use and how to create internal orders in Chapter 3. We looked at how cost centers, orders, and projects provide the link between operational processes, such as purchasing and production and the general ledger, a subject we'll return to in Chapter 4. We introduced some of the actual postings that result in costs being applied to a cost center and order, which we'll return to in Chapter 6, and some of the period-end close processes, which we'll return to in Chapter 7. We also looked at the underlying assumptions behind planning and budgeting, a subject we'll return to in Chapter 5. Finally we looked at the type of process controls that may be needed when working with CO. Our next step will be to look a little closer at the software to understand the reports available to support you in these tasks.

In this chapter we'll discuss the basic reports that every organization needs to run its core business, including coverage of general Controlling, Product Cost Controlling, and Profitability Analysis reports.

2   Reporting

Almost all SAP documentation and training materials cover reporting in the final chapter as something of an afterthought, once the main topics surrounding the business processes and underlying master data have been explained. However, if you're a controller, the need to analyze business performance each month is at the heart of your job, the very reason for doing controlling in the first place, so it makes sense to start by looking at some of the standard reports that controllers use every day. This way, you'll get a sense of what information is available in each area of the Controlling component of SAP ERP Financials (CO) and what you can expect from the chapters to follow.

The other reason to start with reporting is that we'll have covered the basic functions, such as changing the column structure or downloading the report contents to a spreadsheet, when we walk through how to post expenses to a cost center or production order later.

This chapter will look at your reporting options in SAP ERP. If your organization is already using a data warehouse for reporting, you'll find a discussion of when to use SAP NetWeaver Business Warehouse (SAP NetWeaver BW) in Chapter 8. However, even controllers whose organizations have implemented SAP NetWeaver BW still tend to use the line item reports in SAP ERP for detailed cost tracking and analysis.

> **Note**
>
> Wherever possible in this book, we'll use the new-look user interfaces that are available from SAP enhancement package 5 for SAP ERP 6.0. For readers not yet using this version of the software, we'll also provide the menu path and transaction, to make sure you can follow the instructions, whichever version of SAP ERP you're running. You'll find information about how to install the SAP NetWeaver Business Client in SAP Note 1029940 and on how to implement the new user interfaces in Appendix A, which you can download at *www.sap-press.com*.

2.1 Cost Center Line Items

Let's start our journey in Cost Center Accounting. The cost center line item report that helps you monitor expense postings to a cost center and allocations from the cost center is one of the most widely used transactions in SAP ERP Financials. If you know how to use it properly, you'll already be well on the way to being an expert in CO with SAP ERP Financials.

2.1.1 Classic Cost Center Line Item Report

In the SAP EASY MENU, all transactions and reports are grouped into folders for the main application areas, such as COST CENTER ACCOUNTING, INTERNAL ORDERS, PRODUCT COST CONTROLLING, PROFITABILITY ANALYSIS, and so on. These *application areas* are delivered as *roles* in SAP enhancement package 5 for SAP ERP 6.0. When you log on, you'll see all the roles assigned to your user as folders along the top of the screen. Since we're going to be looking at most of the CO functions, the user used for the screenshots has all the roles delivered for CO throughout the chapter. In a real-world example, a user would have fewer folders. Since COST CENTER ACCOUNTING is selected, this folder is highlighted, as shown in Figure 2.1.

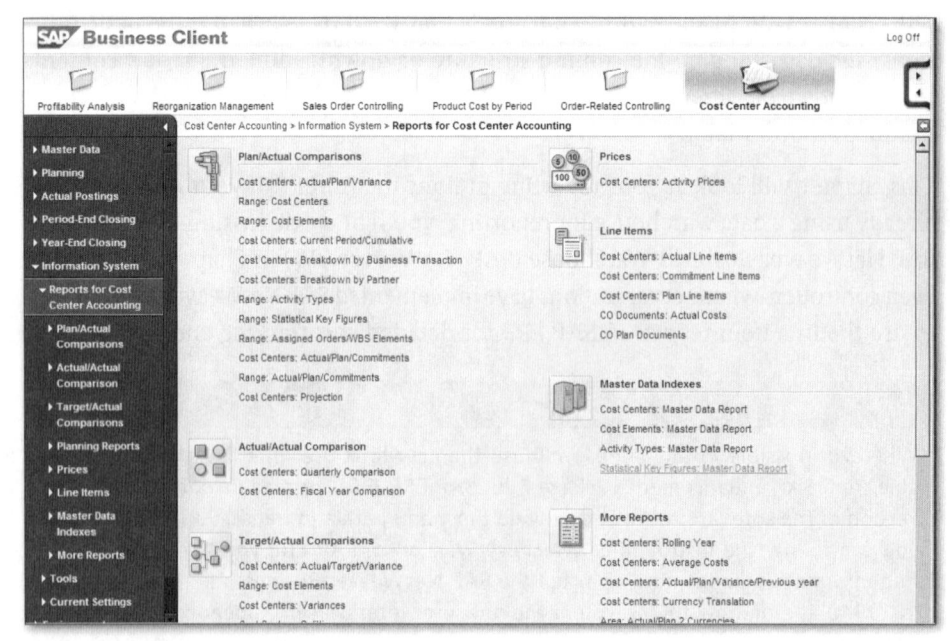

Figure 2.1 Classic Reports for Cost Center Reporting

Along the left side of the screen is a navigation panel that allows you to access the next level of folders, such as the planning functions, actual postings, period-end close functions, and so on. This grouping corresponds to the fourth-level navigation in the SAP EASY MENU, which you access by following the menu path FINANCIALS • CONTROLLING • COST CENTER ACCOUNTING • MASTER DATA, PLANNING, ACTUAL POSTINGS, and so on. To access the reports, select INFORMATION SYSTEM in the navigation panel and then REPORTS FOR COST CENTER ACCOUNTING.

This corresponds to the menu path FINANCIALS • CONTROLLING • COST CENTER ACCOUNTING • INFORMATION SYSTEM • REPORTS FOR COST CENTER ACCOUNTING in earlier versions of the software. In the LINE ITEMS folder, select the link COST CENTERS: ACTUAL LINE ITEMS. The *actual line items* document every posting taking place to CO (such as the expense posting we looked at in Chapter 1) and in CO (such as the allocations we'll look at in Chapter 7).

The selection screen for the cost center line item report now appears in the canvas area of the screen (see Figure 2.2). Experienced controllers will recognize this as Transaction KSB1. From this point onward, all functions will be the same as in the classic transaction. The new user interface simply changes the way the transaction is accessed, replacing a menu or transaction call with a role-based approach.

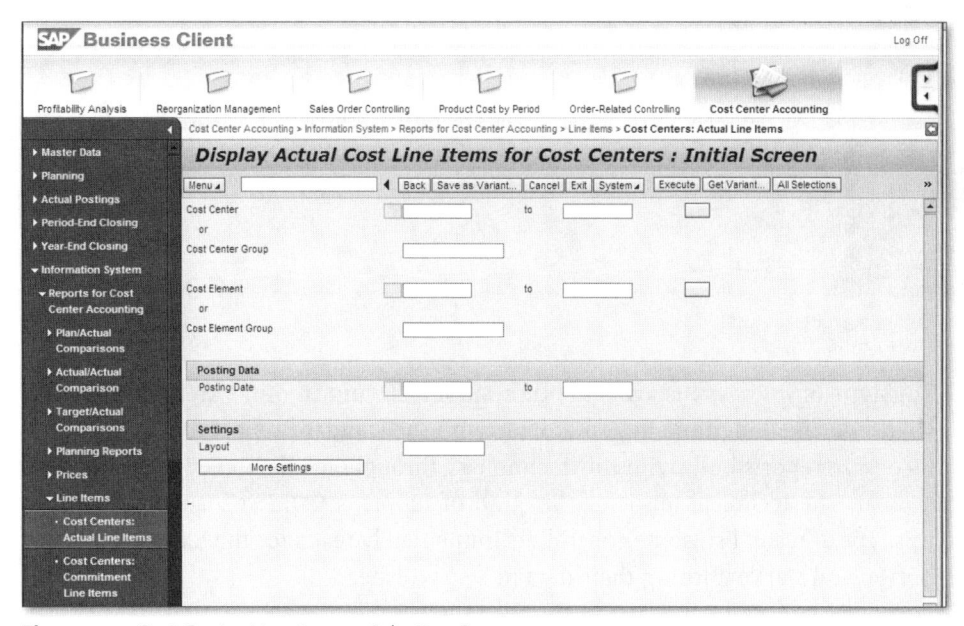

Figure 2.2 Cost Center Line Items – Selection Screen

To remove the navigation panel to have more space to work with the figures in the report, use the small toggle icon in the top-right corner of the navigation panel.

To select the relevant line items for analysis, enter cost center 1230 (Power), cost element 466000 (Insurance Expenses), and posting dates between 01.01.2010 and 31.12.2010 in the selection screen, and then click on the EXECUTE button. The result is a list of all postings for insurance expenses to the cost center in 2010, as shown in Figure 2.3. This is the CO view of the expense posting we used as our example in Chapter 1.

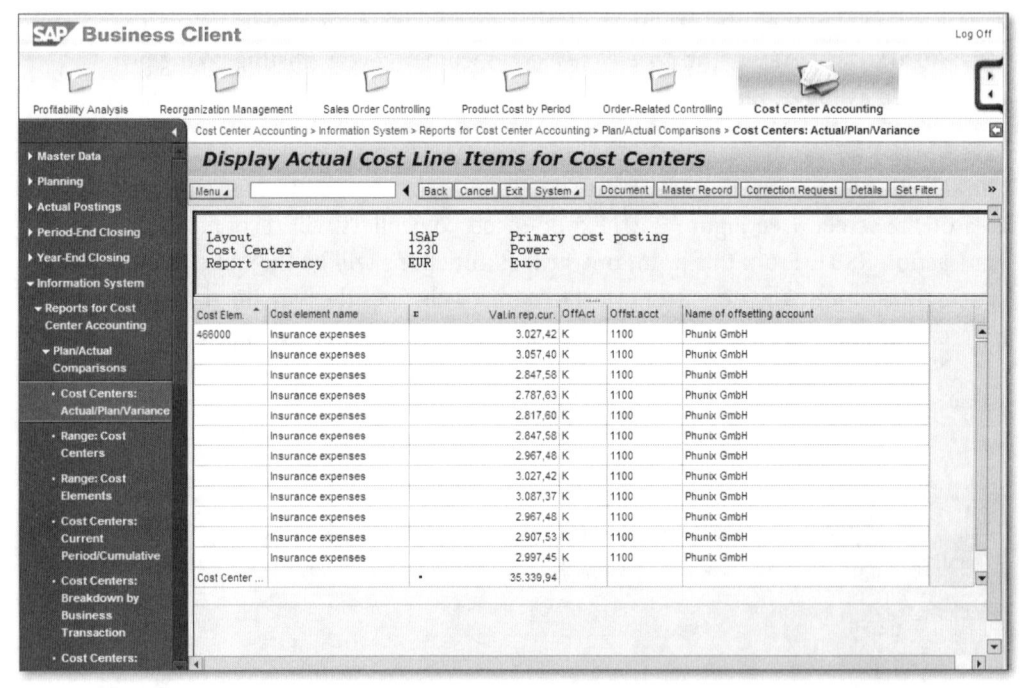

Figure 2.3 Result List

This type of *list report* is available throughout CO and in other areas of SAP ERP, so it's worth taking time to get familiar with the standard report functions. You'll recognize reports built with this technology throughout the book by the standard toolbar. The technical term for this kind of report is *SAP List Viewer*. To explore this type of result list, some controllers immediately reach for the EXPORT TO EXCEL button and start exploring their data in a spreadsheet.

You should know, however, that SAP List Viewer has its own spreadsheet-like functions. You can sort columns, include totals and subtotals, and so on in any list. To remove unnecessary columns, position the cursor on the column, right-click, and select HIDE.

Generally speaking, you are more likely to add fields to such reports than remove them, since the line item includes far more fields than can reasonably be displayed on a single screen. The group of fields displayed in SAP List Viewer at any point is called the *layout*. SAP delivers several layouts for use with cost centers. You can change these using the CHANGE LAYOUT dialog which you can reach by clicking on the CHOOSE LAYOUT button, as shown in Figure 2.4.

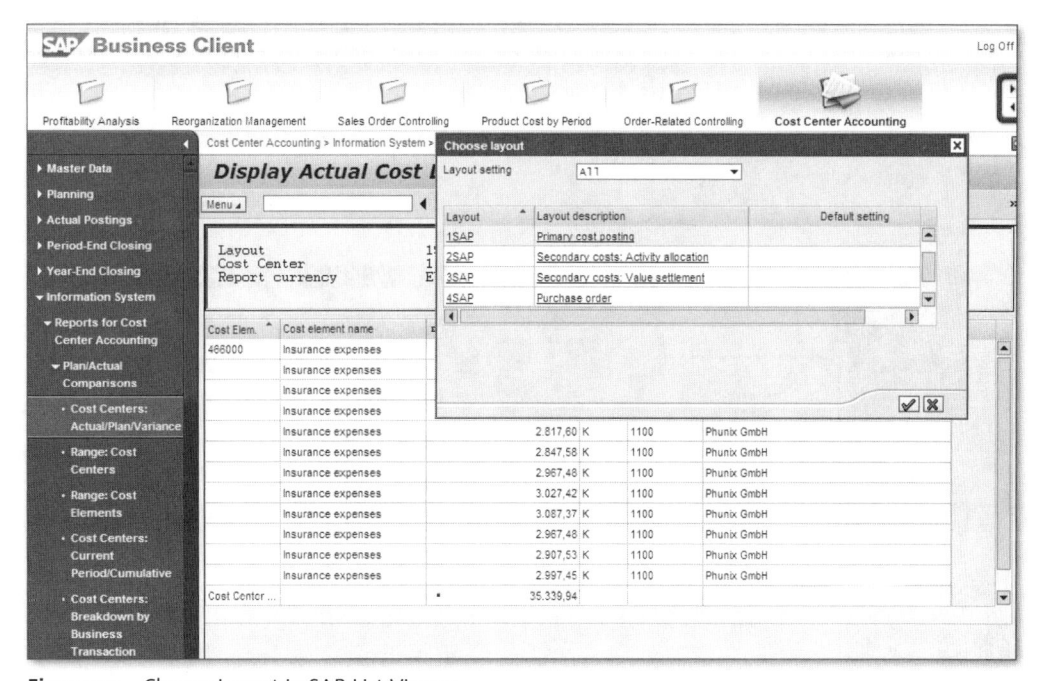

Figure 2.4 Change Layout in SAP List Viewer

The cost center line item includes layouts for:

▶ PRIMARY COST POSTING
  Use this layout to analyze expense postings from the general ledger.

▶ SECONDARY COSTS: ACTIVITY ALLOCATION
  Use this layout to analyze direct activity allocations charged from another cost center (see Chapter 6).

- **SECONDARY COSTS: VALUE SETTLEMENT**
  Use this layout to analyze order values that have been settled to the cost center (see Chapter 7).

- **PURCHASE ORDER**
  Use this layout to analyze purchase orders whose account assignment is the cost center (see Chapter 6).

- **MATERIAL MOVEMENT**
  Use this layout to analyze goods movements charged to the cost center (see Chapter 6).

While these layouts will get you started, you'll almost certainly want to create more layouts to organize the data in the list the way you want to see it. To change a layout or to create a new one, click on the CHANGE LAYOUT button, which takes you to the CHANGE LAYOUT dialog shown in Figure 2.5.

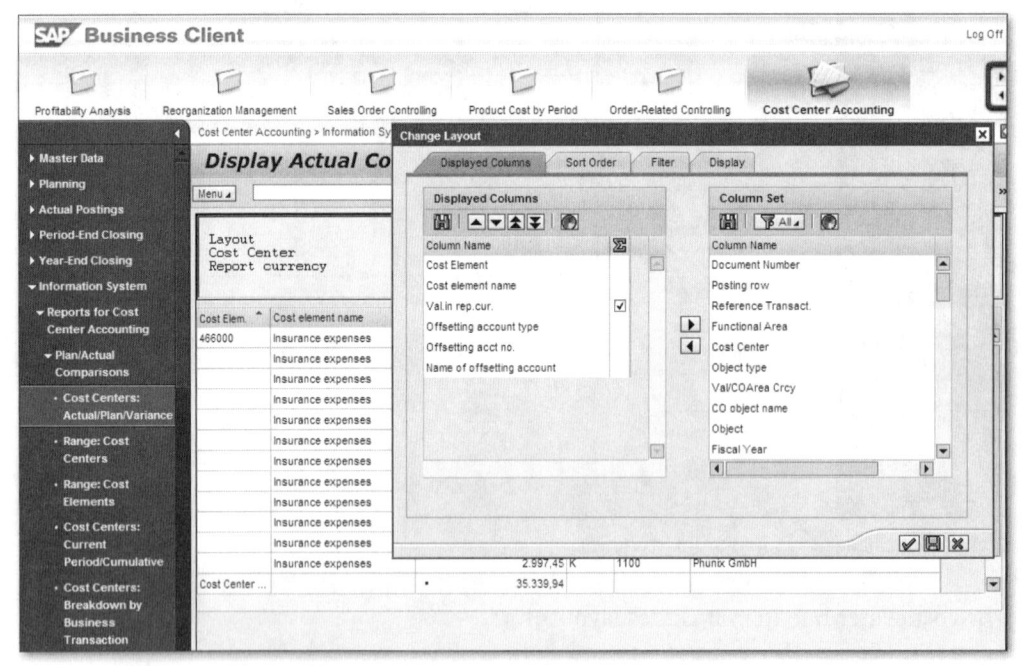

Figure 2.5 Adding Fields Using SAP ABAP List Viewer

To add fields, move them to the left by marking the relevant field in the right-hand column (COLUMN SET) and selecting the left-facing arrow button in the center. To hide columns, move them to the right by marking the relevant fields in the left-hand column (DISPLAYED COLUMNS) and selecting the right-facing arrow button in the center. If the result is a layout that you want to use regularly, it's worth saving the layout under a meaningful name by clicking on the SAVE button. The new layout is assigned to your user, so nobody else will see your layout. To help you explore the potential of this list, let's consider the data available in the line item report.

Primary Cost Postings

The layout shown in Figures 2.4 and 2.5 is for primary cost postings. It explains expense postings that originated in the General Ledger and shows the cost element in CO that mirrors the profit and loss account in the General Ledger and the offsetting reconciliation account for the vendor in Accounts Payable. We'll look at cost elements and accounts in more detail in Chapters 3 and 4. The layout also includes details of the offsetting account type — the insurance company whose services have been purchased. So the layout includes account type K for vendors and document type KR for vendor invoice in our example.

If you want to reconcile your cost center documents against the data in the General Ledger, you can extend this layout to include the following fields, all of which are defaulted from the cost center master record:

- COMPANY CODE
  If you're looking at cross-company postings, you may want to know in which company code each posting was made.
- BUSINESS AREA
  This is the main way of segmenting your business activities in the general ledger.
- FUNCTIONAL AREA
  This is used to segment activities for Cost of Goods Sold (COGS) reporting and in Public Sector Accounting.
- SEGMENT
  This is used for Segment Reporting according to International Financial Reporting Standards (IFRS). The segment is derived from the profit center in the cost center.

One field you won't find in the layout is the controlling area. Every posting in CO takes place in a controlling area. Depending on your configuration, the controlling area may cover one or more company codes. In recent years there has been a trend in global organizations toward a global controlling area. Whatever your settings, the golden rule is that all postings in CO and all reporting activities take place in a single controlling area. The only way to show data in multiple controlling areas is to report in SAP NetWeaver BW.

Secondary Postings or Allocations

If we assume that the cost center allocates the insurance expenses to several other cost centers, you might want to explain these postings by creating a new layout to show the *partners* participating in the allocation. This layout still includes the cost element and the cost center as the sender of the allocation, but you can extend it to include the following fields for the *sender*:

- OBJECT TYPE
  The type of object against which the posting was made. In our example the cost center is CTR. For the order line item that we'll look at later, the object type is ORD, and so on.
- OBJECT
  The object against which the posting was made. In our example this is cost center number 1230.
- DR/CR INDICATOR
  Whether the posting was a debit (D) or a credit (C).

To explain the other side of the *partner relationship*, include the fields:

- PARTNER TYPE
  The type of object to which you made the allocation. This might be CTR if you are using assessment cycles or distribution cycles or ORD (order) if you are charging a department's costs to an order using time recording.
- PARTNER OBJECT
  The key of the other cost center or the order that received the allocation.
- PARTNER OBJECT NAME
  The name of the other cost center or the order that received the allocation.
- BUSINESS TRANSACTION
  This enables us to distinguish between different types of allocations for auditing purposes. We'll see examples of the different codes for the business transactions

when we look at the various forms of allocations that take place at period close in Chapter 7.

Multiple Currencies

If you work with several currencies, it's is also a good idea to create a separate version of your chosen layouts for each of the relevant currencies and another layout that shows relevant combinations.

- CO AREA CURRENCY
  This is usually the group reporting currency and is set for the controlling area.
- OBJECT CURRENCY
  This is the currency of the object (in our case, the cost center) and is set in the cost center master record. For example, a cost center based in the United States would have U.S. dollars as the object currency.
- TRANSACTION CURRENCY
  This is the local currency in which the transaction was performed. For example, if the U.S. cost center purchases goods in Canada, the Canadian supplier would invoice in Canadian dollars (transaction currency).
- REPORT CURRENCY
  This is set centrally for reporting purposes.

Most of the other fields are fairly technical and tend to be used for troubleshooting or when extracting data to another system, such as SAP NetWeaver Business Warehouse (SAP NetWeaver BW).

2.1.2 Simplified Cost Center Line Item Report

In SAP enhancement package 3 for SAP ERP 6.0, SAP modernized the user interface for the cost center line item report, so that the whole user interface is on the Web. In this example, we include the new cost center reports under ANALYTICS. Other reports labeled LIST in Figure 2.6 behave exactly the same way as the cost center line item report. There are also reports labeled ANALYSIS and CRYSTAL REPORT. We'll come back to these reports when we look at alternative reporting options using SAP NetWeaver Business Warehouse (for the analysis reports) and SAP BusinessObjects (for Crystal Reports) in Chapter 8.

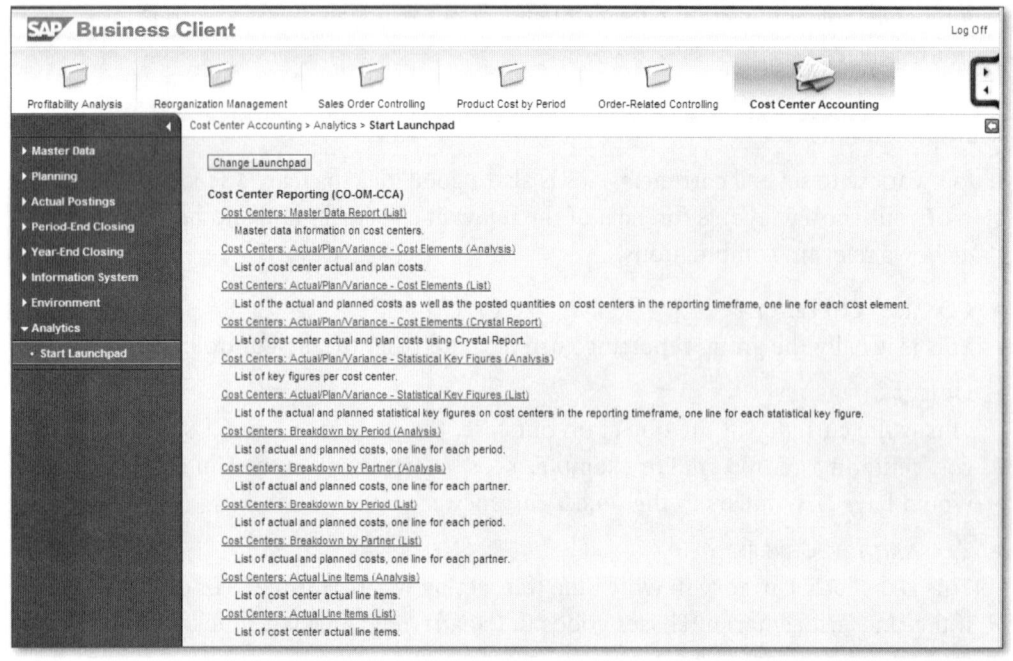

Figure 2.6 Simplified Reports for Cost Center Reporting

Clicking on COST CENTERS: ACTUAL LINE ITEM (LIST) takes you to the new report. Enter the same search criteria as before. Figure 2.7 shows the resulting layout. Without getting too technical, notice that the screen rendering of an application built specifically for the Web looks "cleaner" than a transaction that was built in pre-Web days and has simply been called via the role. However, the costs displayed are identical, since both reports read the same underlying data from SAP ERP. This report looks slightly different, in that the selection screen can be toggled on and off using the SEARCH CRITERIA button, rather than being left behind once the report is executed. To export this list to a spreadsheet, click on the EXPORT button above the result list. The basic principles for list reporting that we just discussed are the same. To create layouts and change the fields displayed, click on the SETTINGS button. Beware, however, that this time the hidden columns are on the left and the displayed columns on the right (see Figure 2.7).

Cost Center Line Items | 2.1

> **Simplified Reporting and the SAP Easy Menu**
>
> Although the first enhancements for Simplified Reporting were introduced in SAP enhancement package 3 for SAP ERP 6.0, activating the business function FIN_REP_SIMPL_1 does not activate new transaction codes or bring these reports into your SAP Easy Menu. The way to work with the list reports delivered for Simplified Reporting is to make them part of a report launchpad that is included in the user's role. To find out how to configure a report launchpad like the one shown in Figure 2.6, refer to Appendix B (found at *www.sap-press.com*).

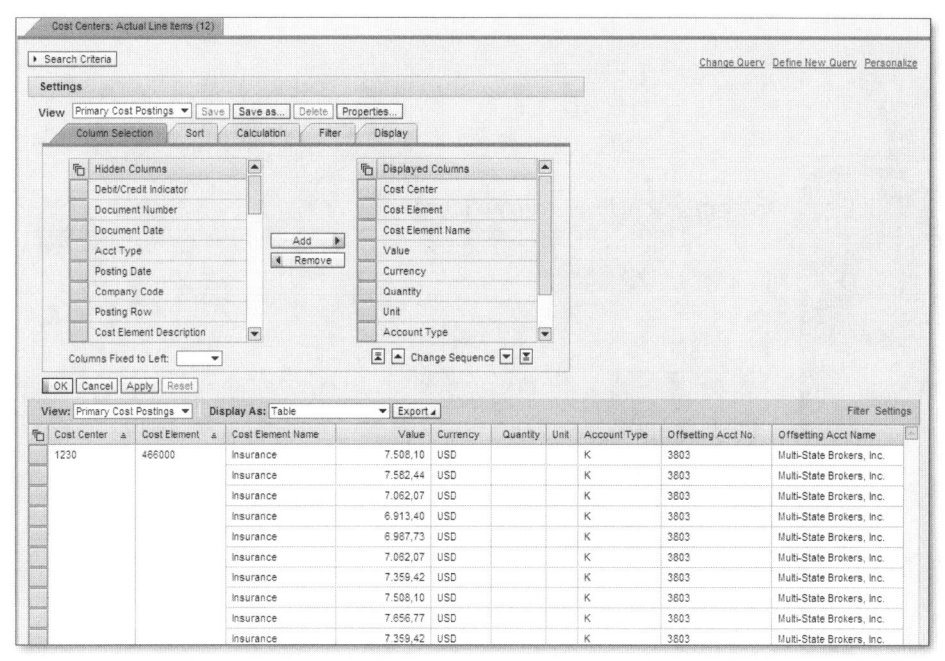

Figure 2.7 Simplified Cost Center Line Item Report

2.1.3 Totals Records for Cost Centers

The line item is by far the most commonly used data record for reporting. However, selecting such a huge record during allocations and settlement can be unwieldy, so every line item has its sister *totals record* that stores a subset of the data available in the line item. Most of the other reports in Cost Center Accounting, including the plan/actual comparison, target/actual comparison, and so on (see Figure 2.1) read the totals records rather than the line items for performance reasons. Generally, you can display the line items from these reports by selecting the line you're interested in and double-clicking. The selection parameters (cost center, cost element, time frame, and so on) are passed to the line item report using the *Report to Report Interface*. As an example, select PLAN/ACTUAL COMPARISON REPORT (in Figure 2.1) and enter the cost center 1230 and the periods January to December 2010 in the selection list. The result is a formatted report (see Figure 2.8) designed to show the cost center manager the state of spending on his cost center in that time frame. To display the line item, double-click on the line for insurance expenses, and select COST CENTER: ACTUAL LINE ITEMS from the pop-up. This passes the parameters from your selection, and you then see the line item report we used as our initial example.

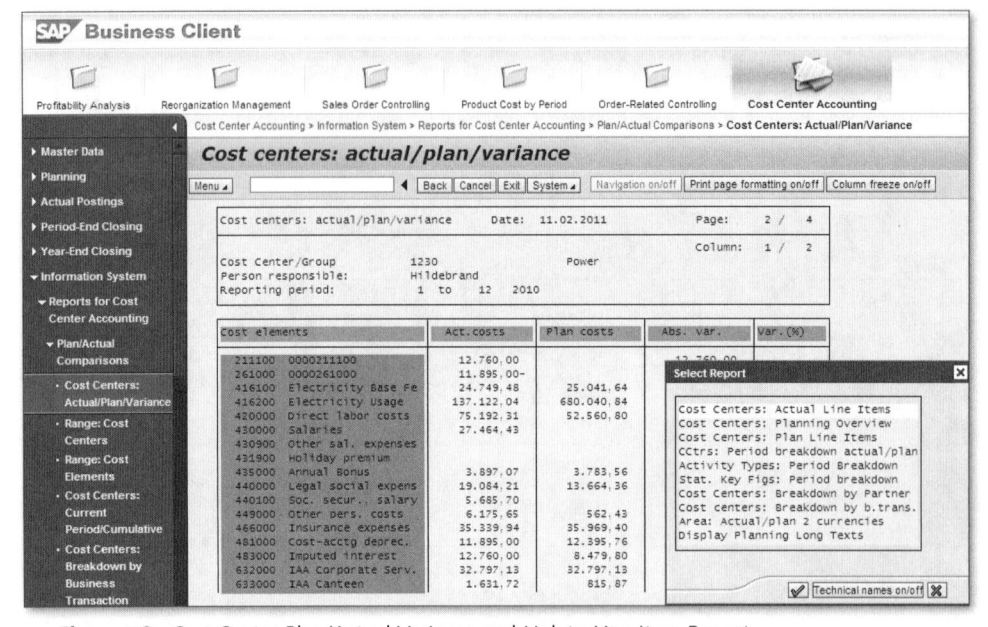

Figure 2.8 Cost Center Plan/Actual Variance and Link to Line Item Report

It's unlikely that you'll work with cost centers alone, so let's now look at the reports for internal orders.

2.2 Order Line Items

Let's continue our journey by looking at internal orders. Orders have many uses in SAP ERP, either detailing the activities on a cost center or representing activities going on completely separate from the cost center, such as capital investments. Others are purely statistical and are entered as an additional account assignment alongside the real cost center or order. There are also many orders that don't originate in CO but are created in Logistics (production orders, process orders, maintenance orders, QM orders, networks, and so on). The costs for these orders can be analyzed using the same report, which probably explains why the order line item report is one of the most widely used transactions in SAP ERP Financials.

2.2.1 Classic Order Line Items

Order line item reports follow the same basic principles as cost center line item reports. To access the order reports, select the role INTERNAL ORDERS at the top of the INFORMATION SYSTEM screen in the navigation panel and then select REPORTS FOR INTERNAL ORDERS, as shown in Figure 2.9. This corresponds to the menu path FINANCIALS • CONTROLLING • INTERNAL ORDERS • INFORMATION SYSTEM • REPORTS FOR INTERNAL ORDERS in earlier versions of the software.

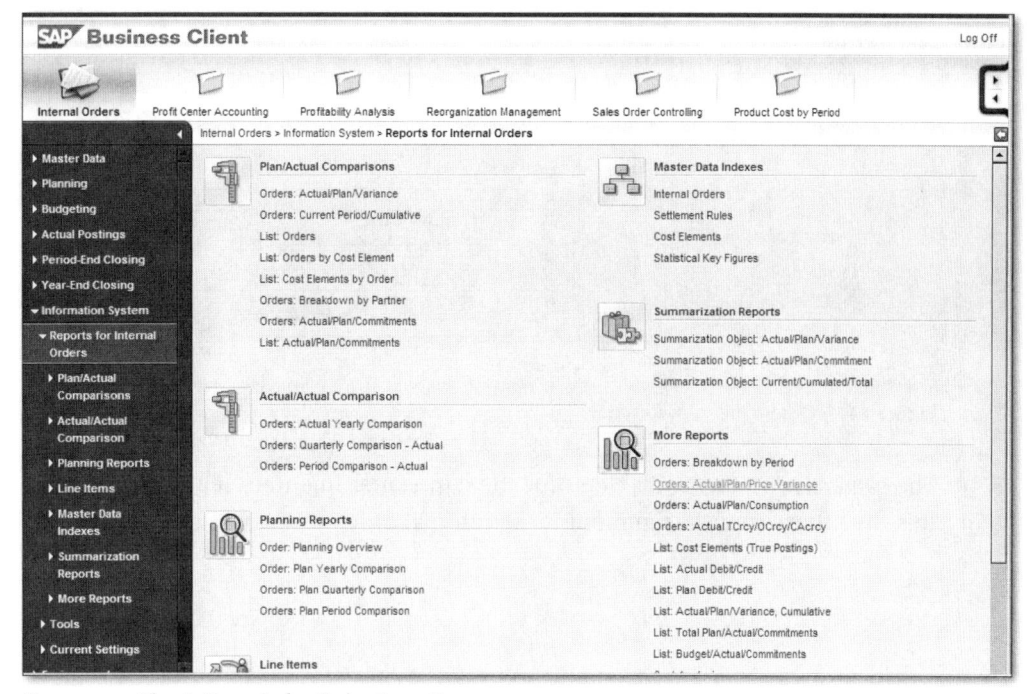

Figure 2.9 Classic Reports for Order Reporting

2 | Reporting

Now select the LINE ITEMS folder and then ORDERS: ACTUAL LINE ITEMS. Experienced controllers will recognize this as Transaction KOB1.

To select the relevant line items for analysis, enter order 400199, leave the cost element group blank, and enter posting dates between 01.12.2010 and 31.12.2010 in the selection screen. Then click on the EXECUTE button. The result is a list of all postings for order 400199 in December 2010, as shown in Figure 2.10.

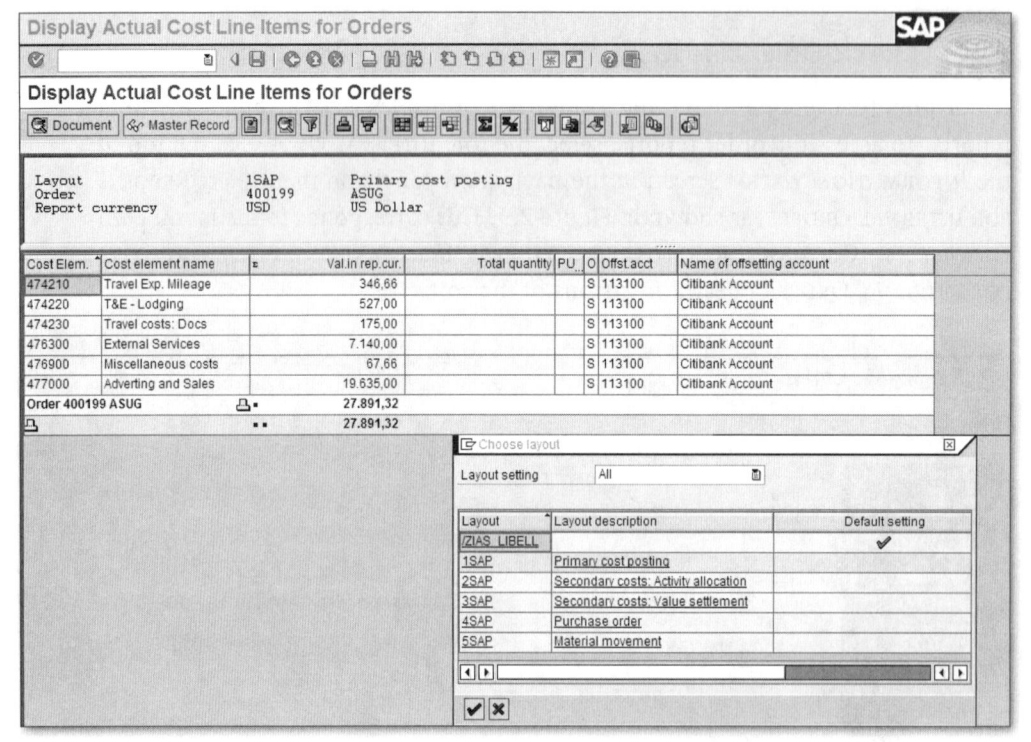

Cost Elem.	Cost element name	Val.in rep.cur.	Total quantity	PU	O	Offst.acct	Name of offsetting account
474210	Travel Exp. Mileage	346,66			S	113100	Citibank Account
474220	T&E - Lodging	527,00			S	113100	Citibank Account
474230	Travel costs: Docs	175,00			S	113100	Citibank Account
476300	External Services	7.140,00			S	113100	Citibank Account
476900	Miscellaneous costs	67,66			S	113100	Citibank Account
477000	Adverting and Sales	19.635,00			S	113100	Citibank Account
Order 400199 ASUG		27.891,32					
		27.891,32					

Choose layout — Layout setting: All

Layout	Layout description	Default setting
/ZIAS_LIBELL		✓
1SAP	Primary cost posting	
2SAP	Secondary costs: Activity allocation	
3SAP	Secondary costs: Value settlement	
4SAP	Purchase order	
5SAP	Material movement	

Figure 2.10 Order Line Item Results

The same layouts are available as for the cost center line item report, except that this time the account assignment is the internal order.

2.2.2 Simplified Order Line Items

Just as we saw with the cost centers, SAP modernized the user interface for reporting on internal orders in SAP enhancement package 3 of SAP ERP 6.0. Figure 2.11 shows the simplified reports for internal orders. All reports labeled LIST behave just like the line item reports we've been looking at.

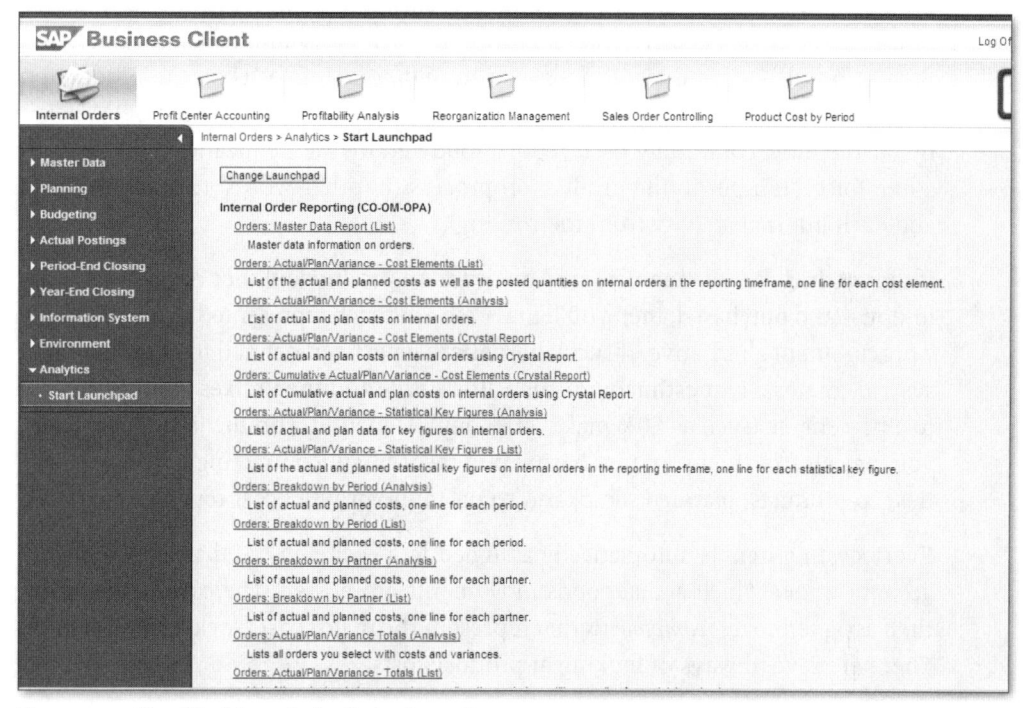

Figure 2.11 Simplified Reports for Order Reporting

While cost centers and internal orders are the simplest account assignments, if you work for a manufacturing company you'll also want to understand how to report on product costs, which we cover in the next section.

2.3 Product Costs: Itemization

The concept of cost center line items and order line items is easy for most accountants to grasp because of the affinity between a line item and a document in the general ledger. When we come to product costing, the data structures change as the document takes something of a back seat and the focus moves to multilevel production structures, a familiar view for engineers but a new world for some accountants. The standard costs for each manufactured product are calculated using a product cost estimate. The first step in costing is to read the bill of material (BOM) in Logistics to determine the materials to be used. The BOM is a multilevel structure that describes which raw materials are used to make a quantity of semifinished product and which semifinished products are used to make a quantity of finished product. The costs of converting the raw materials into semifinished products and then into finished products is described in *routings*. This focus on the production master data is also apparent in the reports, with the multilevel costed BOM being by far the most commonly used report, followed by the itemization that displays a line for each input to the production process (in other words, for each material and each internal activity from the routing).

If the product can be manufactured on different production lines or manufactured in-house and purchased, then you'll find each approach represented in the reports as a procurement alternative. If such alternatives have been defined for a product, the system creates a cost estimate for each alternative and then mixes them according to a percentage (such as 60% make, 40% buy). Depending on the implementation, you may also see items for purchasing info records, subcontracting, external activities, co-products, planned scrap, and so on in the product cost reports.

Every costing item is automatically assigned to a cost element that represents the account under which actual goods movements are posted. The cost elements are then assigned to *cost components* that represent the major cost blocks in production. There are several ways of looking at product costs:

- **Cost of goods manufactured**
  This sees the product costs as material costs, internal activities, external activities, overhead, and so on. There can be up to 40 cost components, and the assignment is based on the cost elements under which the actual postings are captured in the system.
- **Primary cost component split**
  This split looks at what is behind the internal activity. In other words, to provide an internal activity, a cost center uses energy, wages, depreciation, and so on.
- **Partner cost component split**
  This split looks at the value added by each plant, company code, or business area involved in the manufacturing process.

2.3.1 Classic Reports for Product Cost Reporting

To access the reports needed for Product Cost Planning, select the PRODUCT COST PLANNING folder shown in Figure 2.12, select INFORMATION SYSTEM in the navigation panel and then REPORTS FOR PRODUCT COST PLANNING. In earlier versions of the software, follow the menu path CONTROLLING • PRODUCT COST CONTROLLING • PRODUCT COST PLANNING • INFORMATION SYSTEM • REPORTS FOR PRODUCT COST PLANNING.

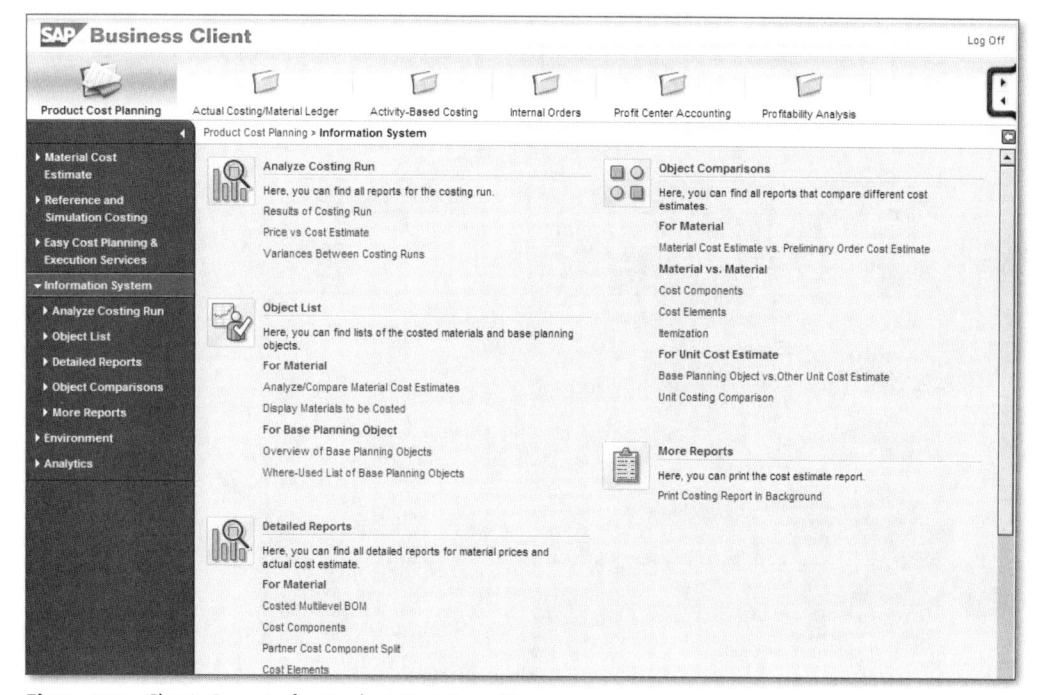

Figure 2.12 Classic Reports for Product Cost Reporting

Let's start with the DETAILED REPORTS folder and select COSTED MULTILEVEL BOM. Enter the following and execute the report:

▶ **Material number and plant**
This identifies the product you're interested in.

▶ **Costing variant**
This provides the link to the configuration settings, telling you the purpose of the cost estimate (setting standard costs, determining the accuracy of current standard

costs, balance sheet valuation for annual close), how the bill of material and routing should be selected, and what prices will be used in this calculation.

- **Costing version**

  Normally this is 1 unless you're using mixed costing (where multiple cost estimates are weighted) or group costing (where the same BOM and routing are costed first using the local prices and again using the group costs).

- **Costing lot size**

  The reference quantity for the cost estimate against which all variable costs will be adjusted.

Figure 2.13 shows the bill of material together with the cost per item.

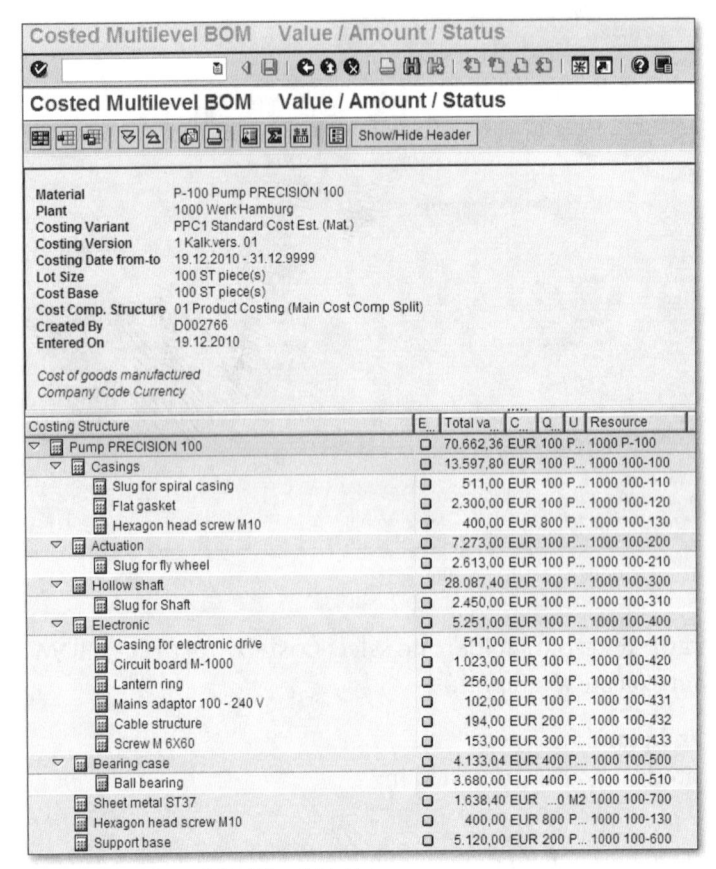

Costing Structure	E.	Total va.	C	Q	U	Resource
▽ 🏭 Pump PRECISION 100	☐	70.662,36 EUR	100	P...		1000 P-100
▽ 🏭 Casings	☐	13.597,80 EUR	100	P...		1000 100-100
🏭 Slug for spiral casing	☐	511,00 EUR	100	P...		1000 100-110
🏭 Flat gasket	☐	2.300,00 EUR	100	P...		1000 100-120
🏭 Hexagon head screw M10	☐	400,00 EUR	800	P...		1000 100-130
▽ 🏭 Actuation	☐	7.273,00 EUR	100	P...		1000 100-200
🏭 Slug for fly wheel	☐	2.613,00 EUR	100	P...		1000 100-210
▽ 🏭 Hollow shaft	☐	28.087,40 EUR	100	P...		1000 100-300
🏭 Slug for Shaft	☐	2.450,00 EUR	100	P...		1000 100-310
▽ 🏭 Electronic	☐	5.251,00 EUR	100	P...		1000 100-400
🏭 Casing for electronic drive	☐	511,00 EUR	100	P...		1000 100-410
🏭 Circuit board M-1000	☐	1.023,00 EUR	100	P...		1000 100-420
🏭 Lantern ring	☐	256,00 EUR	100	P...		1000 100-430
🏭 Mains adaptor 100 - 240 V	☐	102,00 EUR	100	P...		1000 100-431
🏭 Cable structure	☐	194,00 EUR	200	P...		1000 100-432
🏭 Screw M 6X60	☐	153,00 EUR	300	P...		1000 100-433
▽ 🏭 Bearing case	☐	4.133,04 EUR	400	P...		1000 100-500
🏭 Ball bearing	☐	3.680,00 EUR	400	P...		1000 100-510
🏭 Sheet metal ST37	☐	1.638,40 EUR	...0	M2		1000 100-700
🏭 Hexagon head screw M10	☐	400,00 EUR	800	P...		1000 100-130
🏭 Support base	☐	5.120,00 EUR	200	P...		1000 100-600

Figure 2.13 Costed Multilevel BOM

Notice that some of the icons in this report are familiar from the cost center line item report. This is because this report also uses SAP List Viewer, but it uses a tree structure to represent the quantity structure in production, with each level in the tree representing an assembly with its own bill of material.

To display the costs per operation in the routing, select the ITEMIZATION report in the DETAILED REPORTS folder. Because of the sheer number of ways of looking at data for a cost estimate (by item category, by operation, by cost element, by cost component, and so on), SAP delivers many layouts. To view the operations in the routing, select the OPERATIONS layout before executing the report.

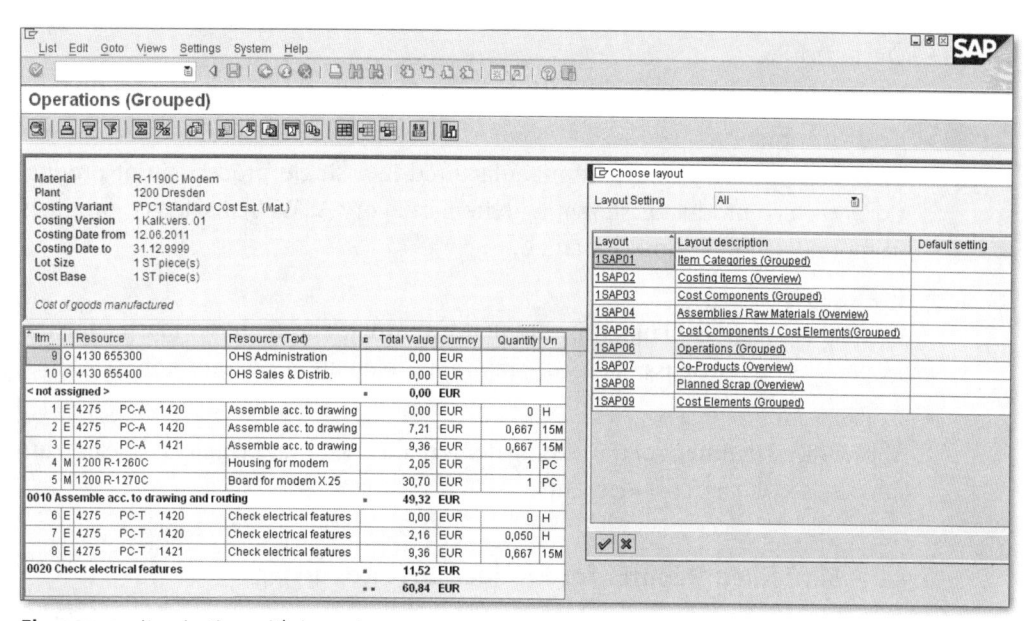

Figure 2.14 Itemization with Layouts

Figure 2.14 shows the items by operation, together with the delivered layouts. These include:

- ITEM CATEGORIES
  Groups the items of the cost estimate by the internal categories Material, Internal Activity, Overhead, and so on.
- COSTING ITEMS
  Lists the items of the cost estimate by their technical ID.

- COST COMPONENTS
  Shows the assignment of each costing item to one of up to 40 cost components.

- ASSEMBLIES/RAW MATERIALS
  Shows the raw materials (materials without BOMs, i.e., purchased materials) and assemblies (materials with own BOMS, i.e., manufactured materials) used in the final product.

- COST COMPONENTS/COST ELEMENTS
  Used to check the assignment of the items to cost elements and from there to cost components.

- OPERATIONS
  Shows the assignment of the costing items to the operations in the routing.

- CO-PRODUCTS
  Where multiple products are manufactured in a single process (joint production), each co-product is shown with item category A. We'll discuss co-products in more detail in Chapters 4 and 6.

- PLANNED SCRAP
  Normal spoilage is planned in the BOM, routing, and material master for the assembly. We'll discuss planned scrap in more detail in Chapter 4.

- COST ELEMENTS
  Shows the assignment of the costing items to the accounts/primary cost elements and the secondary cost elements.

2.3.2 Simplified Reports for Product Cost Reporting

In SAP enhancement package 3 for SAP ERP 6.0, the main reports for Product Cost Planning were reworked. Figure 2.15 shows the details. The new reports include some that display the results of Product Costing (in other words, the standard costs for each product) and some that display the costs for a production order (including work in process and variances). In the next section we'll look at the various options for monitoring your product costs and the role of the production order in each case. At the time of writing, there probably aren't enough new reports for Product Cost Planning to cover all your reporting needs, but you may still find some examples in this list that will allow you to modernize the look and feel of your product cost reports. Another key element of reporting in this area is the analysis of the costing run that acts as a framework during the process of calculating the standard costs. We'll look at these reports in more detail when we work through the process of creating a costing run and performing the relevant steps as part of the annual operating plan in Chapter 5.

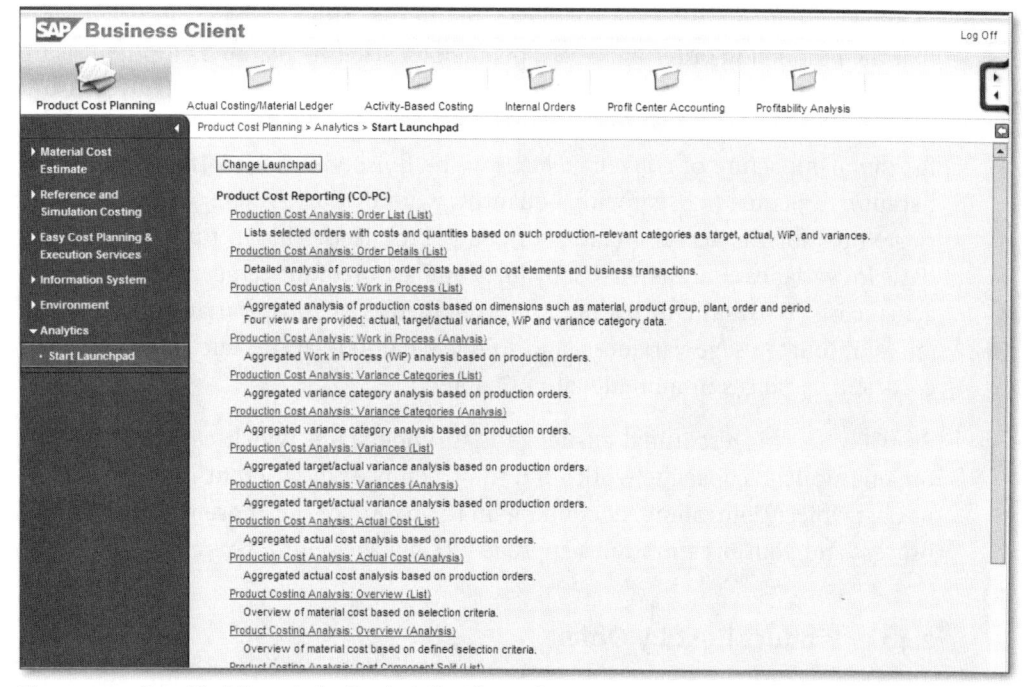

Figure 2.15 Simplified Reports for Product Cost Reporting

The product cost reports we've looked at so far help us analyze the *standard costs* for the product and support us mainly during the planning process (see Chapter 5). We'll now look at the reports available during the manufacturing process to explain how the costs are captured for production orders and similar objects. These are later compared against the standard costs during variance analysis.

2.4 Product Costs: Cost Objects

Product Cost Planning almost never exists in isolation but exists as a preparation for Cost Object Controlling, where the costs of executing the individual work orders are monitored. While the reporting for Product Cost Planning introduced many new concepts, the reporting for Cost Object Controlling is similar to the reports for the internal order. The data structures for the line items and totals records are identical. The main difference between an internal order and a *production order* is that the production order includes a planned lot size (the planned output measure for the order; see Chapter 1). So while an internal order for a research project simply collects the costs associated with the research, a production order collects costs for the manufacture of a given *quantity* of the finished product. This is important because all planned costs for this quantity will be adjusted later to calculate the *target costs* for the actual quantity of goods produced. This in turn provides the basis for variance analysis — a line by line comparison of the target costs against the actual costs, where the differences are explained as quantity variances, price variances, resource usage variances, and so on. We'll look at the calculation of target costs and variances in more detail in Chapter 7.

Probably the biggest initial challenge is to understand which cost objects your organization has chosen to work with, since a number of different approaches exist in Cost Object Controlling, depending on the nature of the chosen manufacturing process and your organization's approach to management accounting.

2.4.1 Product Cost by Order

The product cost by order approach is used when the individual production order or process order is the focus for cost management and the production costs for each individual lot are regularly monitored. The idea of the work order as the key element is an approach that has been around since the 1930s. The business goal is to monitor how each order gradually accumulates costs as goods are issued to the shop floor, operations confirmed, scrap reported, and so on. This approach makes sense where setup costs are significant and full cost traceability for each order is a business requirement and is widely used. But practitioners of lean accounting argue that focusing on the work order in isolation encourages a "push" approach that potentially results in excessive inventory for which there is not necessarily a demand. Cost collection by order is also necessary in the case of *joint production*, in other words, where multiple products are produced in the same manufacturing process and the order costs have to be split to the co-products. The PRODUCT COST BY ORDER menu offers a number of reports for tracking the costs of *production campaigns*, where a series of production orders are manufactured in sequence because of the high costs of initial setup and cleanup on completion. This is particularly common in the chemical and pharmaceutical industries.

In controlling terms, this approach is characterized by the delivery of the finished product to stock, the calculation of variances on completion of the order, and the calculation of work in process if the production or process order happens to be open at the time of the period close. We'll look at this process in detail in Chapter 7.

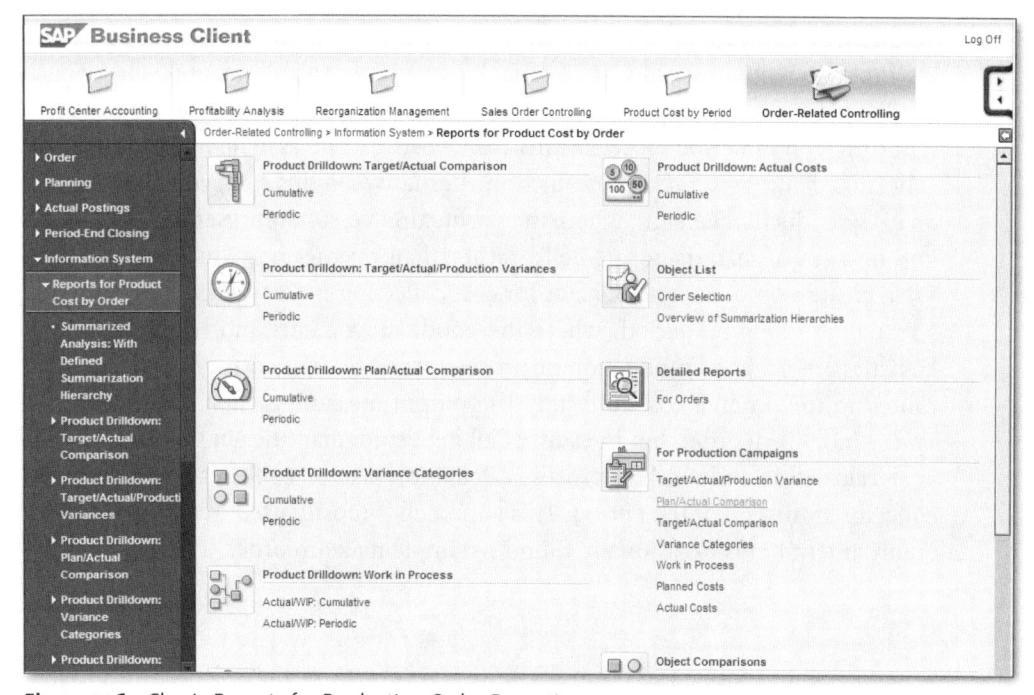

Figure 2.16 Classic Reports for Production Order Reporting

Figure 2.16 shows all reports for product cost by order. You can find this by following the menu path FINANCIALS • CONTROLLING • PRODUCT COST CONTROLLING • COST OBJECT CONTROLLING • PRODUCT COST BY ORDER • INFORMATION SYSTEM • REPORTS FOR PRODUCT COST BY ORDER. Because of the number of production orders being processed at any given time, the detailed reports we looked at for the internal orders are supplemented by various mass reports that select, for example, all materials in a given plant or for a given product group. We'll look at these reports when we look at mass reporting in Chapter 8. It's also common to move such orders to a data warehouse for reporting on account of the huge data volumes. Some organizations choose the PRODUCT COST BY PERIOD option simply because they believe this is the only way they'll be able to handle the data volumes in question.

2.4.2 Product Cost by Period

At some sites, the volume of production orders is so high that it's nearly impossible for CO to monitor the costs successfully. This can be the case in the food industry, where the production orders can be very short lived (less than a day). It can also be the case with continuous, repetitive production with minimal setup that there is simply no requirement for individual lot-oriented controlling, and storing each production order as a separate order in CO represents an unnecessary burden for reporting and at period close. In this case, costs can be assigned to product cost collectors that represent each production alternative. In this case, you might report on each production version, where the production version represents a production line or a set of manufacturing cells, rather than on the individual work orders. We'll create a product cost collector for cost collection in Chapter 3. These provide a lean controlling by period, where the goods movements and confirmations in Logistics are made by production or process order, but the costs are automatically routed to the product cost collector. The output measure is then not the lot size on the individual order, but the sum of all delivered quantities in the period. Variance calculation and work in process calculation take place for each product cost collector at the end of the period. This approach is mostly used in a make-to-stock environment but is occasionally found in simple make-to-order scenarios.

> **Lean Accounting Tip**
>
> Lean accounting encourages organizations to move away from the collection of costs by work order and toward a value stream-based view of the organization. The product cost collector fits nicely into this concept, capturing the costs for each production version by period. If the value stream involves multiple products, then such costs can be rolled up to the value stream level in reporting, where the value stream is typically represented by a product group or material group.

The main difference between the product cost by period approach and product cost by order is that the status of the production order plays no role in the period close. At the end of every period the confirmations to the product cost collector are analyzed to determine which operation quantities are work in process (in other words, have been started but not completed), which operation quantities are complete and can be analyzed for variances, and for which operations scrap has been confirmed. Figure 2.17 shows the standard reports for product cost by period. You can find this by following the menu path FINANCIALS • CONTROLLING • PRODUCT COST CONTROLLING • COST OBJECT CONTROLLING • PRODUCT COST BY PERIOD • INFORMATION SYSTEM • REPORTS FOR PRODUCT COST BY PERIOD. While most of the reports are similar to those for product cost by order, you'll also notice line items for a cost object. The cost object hierarchy is used to create a cost object for which the cost of internal activities can be captured when there is no routing or the routing does not capture all manufacturing activities. These costs can then be distributed to the assigned product cost collectors or production orders at period close. Alternatively, the costs on the production orders or product cost collectors can be summarized to the cost objects and then settled. We'll look at how to create cost object hierarchies in Chapter 3.

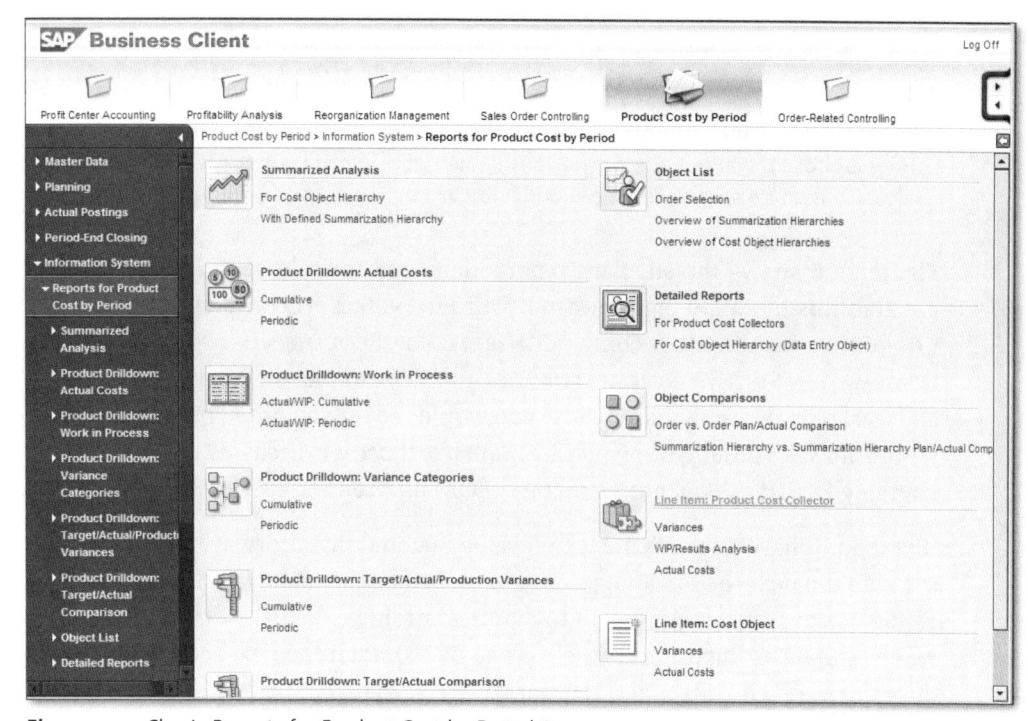

Figure 2.17 Classic Reports for Product Cost by Period Reporting

2.4.3 Product Costs by Sales Order

The product cost by order and product cost by period approaches are mainly used in a make-to-stock environment. In this case, sales controlling takes place in Profitability Analysis, where the sales orders and associated invoices are captured. Product cost by sales order is used when the manufacturing process is linked to the sales order, generally because a customer-specific configuration has taken place in the order, as might happen in the automotive, steel, or high-tech industries. In this case, there can be no standard costs for the product since the product is unique to that sales order. Generally a cost estimate is created for each such item in the sales order, and this cost estimate may be used to price the sales order. To ensure that the finished product cannot be taken from stock and shipped to a different customer, delivery from the production line is made to *sales order stock*, and the delivery to the customer can only be made from this stock. Because there are no standard costs, the sales order cost estimate is also used to value goods movements to and from sales order stock.

> **Lean Accounting Tip**
>
> Lean accounting encourages the use of make-to-order, where the sales order initiates, or "pulls," the manufacturing process in its wake. This is the opposite of the classic work order approach, where work orders "push" their goods into inventory in the hope that sales will then be able to sell the product in stock.

Figure 2.18 shows the standard reports delivered for sales order reporting. You can find this by following the menu path FINANCIALS • CONTROLLING • PRODUCT COST CONTROLLING • COST OBJECT CONTROLLING • PRODUCT COST BY SALES ORDER • INFORMATION SYSTEM • REPORTS FOR PRODUCT COST BY SALES ORDER. The line items and total records are similar to those you would see for any order, but you also have reports for sales order costing that are more like those we discussed for Product Cost Planning in that the quantity structure (BOM and routing) is very prominent.

If you don't have a requirement to revalue material inventory at actual costs, you can skip the next section and go straight to Profitability Analysis. If you work in a country with a legal requirement to report according to actual costs, or an industry where actual costing prevails (such as chemicals), then the next section will introduce the Material Ledger as a tool for collecting actual costs.

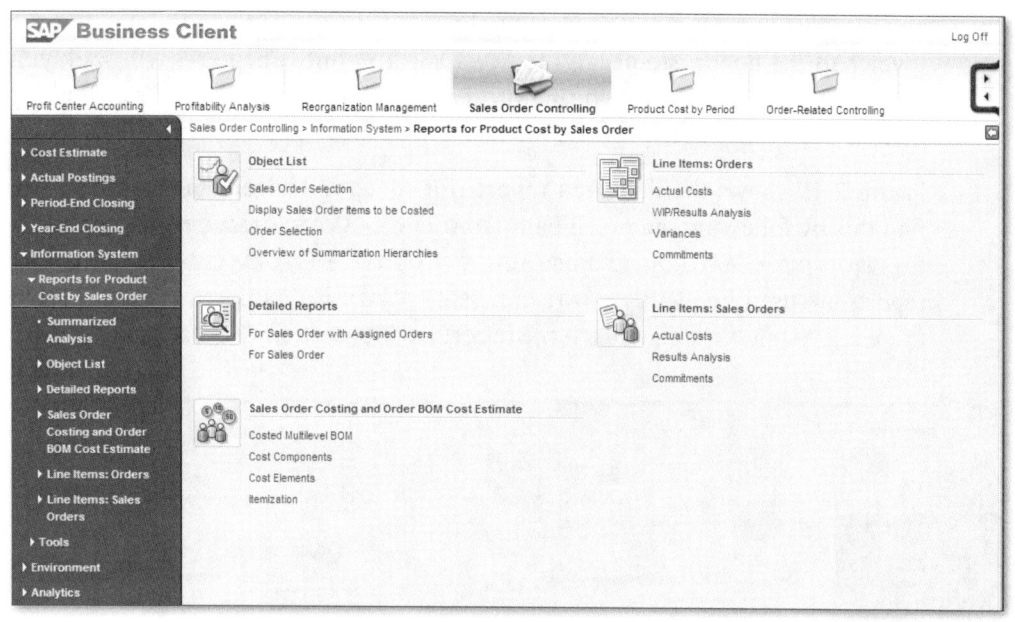

Figure 2.18 Classic Reports for Sales Order Reporting

2.5 Material Ledger

Not all sites use the Material Ledger. Your organization may use it if you have a legal requirement to value inventory at actual costs (common in Asia and South America), if you have highly volatile raw material prices or unstable production structures that make standard costing with detailed variance analysis impractical, or if you use it to provide a second inventory valuation approach for legal reporting.

From a reporting point of view, the Material Ledger differs from cost center and order reporting in that the reports display the *inputs and outputs* in each procurement, production, and sales process. The Material Ledger has its own documents for every goods movement, every business transaction that affects material prices (invoices, order settlement, etc.), and its own calculations at period close. So if you call up a report for a raw material, you'll see the goods receipt and invoice from the supplier in the RECEIPTS line and the goods issue to production in the CONSUMPTION line, along with details of any stock currently in inventory. If you call up the same report for a finished material, you'll see the goods receipt from raw material inventory in the RECEIPTS line and the goods issue to sales and the invoice to the final customer in the CONSUMPTION line. Chapter 6 will walk you through a complete manufacturing process from procurement to sales, showing you the Material Ledger postings for each goods movement.

Figure 2.19 shows the delivered reports for Material Ledger reporting. You can find this by following the menu path FINANCIALS • CONTROLLING • PRODUCT COST CONTROLLING • MATERIAL LEDGER/ACTUAL COSTING • INFORMATION SYSTEM. Two reports are used frequently: MATERIAL PRICE ANALYSIS (Transaction CKM3N) and the VALUATED MATERIAL QUANTITY STRUCTURE (Transaction CKMLQS).

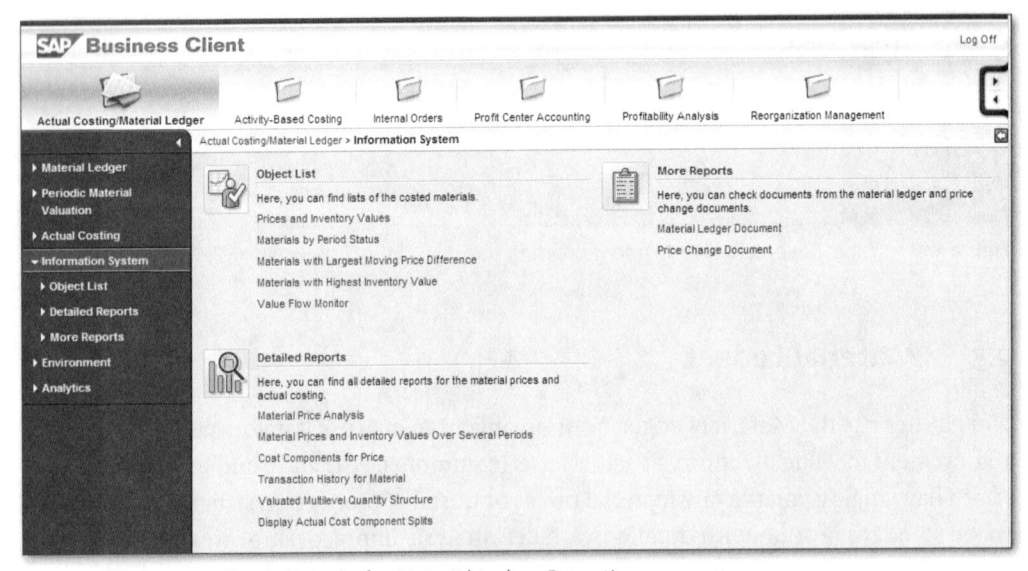

Figure 2.19 Classic Reports for Material Ledger Reporting

Figure 2.20 shows the material ledger postings for a raw material that has been purchased from an external supplier and then issued to an internal production process for conversion into a finished product. Technically this is a list viewer tree report like the one we saw for the multilevel costed BOM in Product Cost Planning.

Figure 2.21 shows the quantity structure for a finished product (PCG-FERT-01) that has required three semifinished products, PCG-SEMI-01, PCG-CO-PRODUCT-01, and PCG-SEMI-SV-01, in its manufacture. PCG-SEMI-01 was procured from another plant in the UK (so the values are in British pounds), while PCG-SEMI-SV-01 was manufactured in the same plant. Manufacturing activities were performed to convert the raw materials into PCG-SEMI-SV-01 and the three semifinished products into PCG-FERT-01. This report first became available in Release 4.7 of SAP R/3 (see the downloadable Appendix C at *www.sap-press.com*).

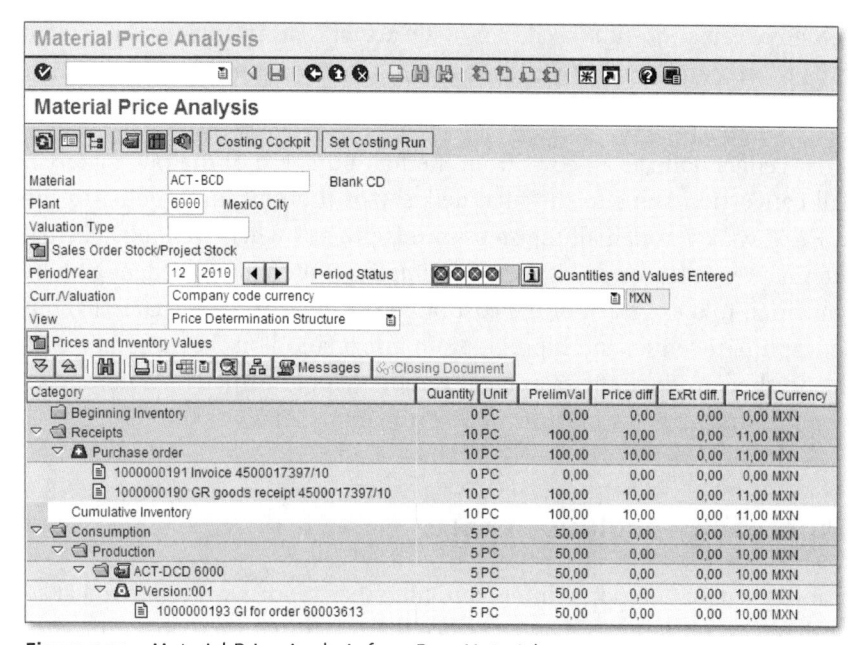

Figure 2.20 Material Price Analysis for a Raw Material

Figure 2.21 Valuated Quantity Structure

In addition to these two detailed reports for the material and the quantity structure, much reporting in the Material Ledger is performed in the context of the period close (see Chapter 7), where each step in the periodic costing run (used to calculate the weighted average costs per material at the end of each period) and each step in the alternative valuation run (used to provide actual costs in a wider time frame or according to a second accounting approach) has its own supporting report that allows you to check the values calculated in that step.

The Material Ledger collects all costs from the first purchase of the raw material, through all conversion steps to the final delivery of the finished product to the customer. We'll walk through all the steps in this process when we look at actual postings in Chapter 6. However, as the name implies, the Material Ledger gathers costs by material. It keeps track of the cost of goods sold for these materials, but it does not capture revenue, and it provides no information on the customer who bought the finished product, the sales organization that performed the sale, and so on. For such information, we must move to Profitability Analysis (or CO-PA).

2.6 Profitability Analysis Reports

The Profitability Analysis reports differ from the other reports we've looked at so far in that there are no standard layouts, since the structure of the operating concern is determined during implementation. The only commonality in Profitability Analysis reports is that certain standard events write data into the Profitability Analysis application. For reporting, these are distinguished by the *record type*. The following transactions transfer data to Profitability Analysis:

- Incoming sales orders (record type A)
- Direct postings from Financial Accounting (record type B)
- Order and project settlement (record type C)
- Cost center allocations (record type D)
- Single transaction costing (record type E) — industry-specific, so you might not use it
- Billing documents from Sales and Distribution (record type F)
- Customer agreements (record type G) — used in some industries

- Statistical key figures (record type H)
- Transfer of sales orders from projects (record type I) — used for commercial projects that are linked with sales orders for billing

If the above list sounds fairly technical, consider instead the different levels of detail captured for the main record types in Profitability Analysis.

- Let's start with an *incoming sales order* (record type A). We'll see in Chapter 6 that an incoming sales order includes the name of the customer, the product or products purchased, the sales organization making the sale, the distribution channel, the division, the sales office, the sales group, and so on. This is the lowest level of granularity available in Profitability Analysis.
- Usually the same characteristics are captured when the customer is *billed* for his purchase (record type F). Again, this is extremely detailed information.
- A *direct posting* from Financial Accounting (record type B) may be made at this level of detail if the person making the posting has all the listed information. However, as we'll see in Chapter 6, it may be possible to know only the affected material at the time of the posting, but not the customer who will ultimately purchase the finished product. In this case the record includes the product as a characteristic, but not the customer.
- *Production variances* (carried in the settlement document — record type C) always apply to the product produced, but only to the customer if it's a make-to-order scenario and the production process is triggered by the sales order.
- *Cost allocations* (record type C) offer the most options. In Chapter 7 we'll learn how to set up assessment cycles that can be very granular, breaking all expenses down to individual customers or products. We'll also see that it's possible to do an allocation to a much higher-level characteristic, such as a region or a country. This might be the case for marketing expenses, where it's clear that a trade fair took place in the northwestern region of the United States but unclear which customers participated.

The Profitability Analysis (CO-PA) reports also distinguish between actual and planned data. Actual data is captured during the sales transactions, while planned data is captured as part of the sales and profit planning process. We'll look at that in more detail in Chapter 5.

> **Note**
>
> The implementation team determines all other fields when they configure your system. Since the focus is on sales reporting, most organizations have the dimensions product, customer and sales region, and other dimensions that can be derived from these entities (product group, customer group, division, sales office, and so on). You'll find details of the recommended size of the operating concern (generally, the maximum number of characteristics is 50 and the maximum number of value fields is 120, but this can be extended) in SAP Note 1029391.

There are two types of fact tables, depending on whether you use account-based CO-PA or costing-based CO-PA or both. You'll find a full description of the difference between the two approaches in SAP Note 69384.

- Account-based CO-PA records data to a cost element that represents the account used to post the data originally. This makes it much easier to reconcile the cost elements and the accounts by company code, business area, and so on. But you should be aware that low-level characteristics such as customers and products are not captured in the General Ledger, so they won't be available for reconciliation.

- Costing-based CO-PA assigns all postings to *value fields* that capture the individual elements of a contribution margin (sales, cost of goods sold, general overhead, and so on). This approach provides the ability to break down account-level information into further detail, such as fixed and variable costs for the same cost element, and separate the components of the standard cost into different value fields.

In costing-based CO-PA, the value fields are determined during implementation, so some teams break out the price conditions for the sales deductions into many separate value fields, while others lump them into one field. Most implementations distinguish between fixed and variable costs for their product cost estimate, but some implementations keep a lot of detail from their cost components, while others lump the cost components together. The same variability applies to allocations, order settlement, and the settlement of production variances and to the transfer of cost components from the Material Ledger.

If the underlying tables are different at every site, so are the reports, since you can only report on the data captured in the underlying tables. Figure 2.22 shows the classic reports for Profitability Analysis. You can access this by following the menu path FINANCIALS • CONTROLLING • PROFITABILITY ANALYSIS • INFORMATION SYSTEM. Note the DEFINE REPORT folder, which did not exist in the other application areas. Creating reports is part of the implementation effort for Profitability Analysis, since Transaction KE30 (Execute Report) only shows data if you've properly configured your operating concern and built the appropriate reports first.

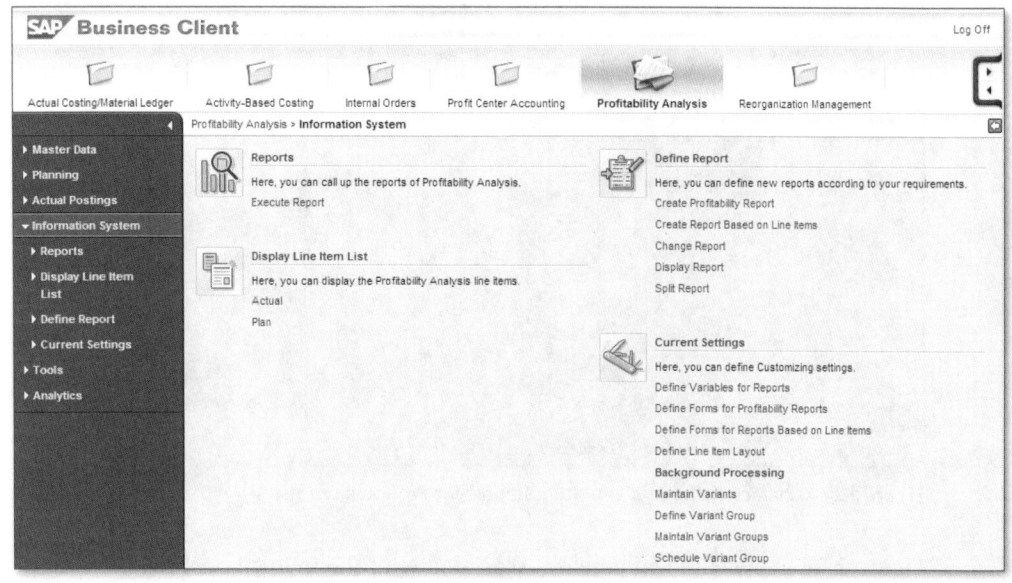

Figure 2.22 Classic Reports for Profitability Reporting

Figure 2.23 shows the document created in Profitability Analysis when an invoice or billing document was created in Sales and Distribution. The customer Industrias Pacificas, with customer number 6666, purchased the goods Demo CD with material number ACT-DCD in the sales organization. Customer group, product group, and various organizational units have also been read from the invoice document or derived using logic set up when configuring CO-PA. In addition to the line item reports, every organization builds its own reports that select the data for drill-down reporting, whether they do this in Transaction KE30 or in SAP NetWeaver BW. Regardless of the reporting tool, you'll use the entries you see in Figure 2.23 either to provide an initial selection, such as all postings in a particular company code, or to allow drill-down. The drill-down potential of CO-PA is almost unlimited, with organizations slicing and dicing their data by customer, by product, by distribution channel, and so on to try to understand where and with whom they are making or losing money.

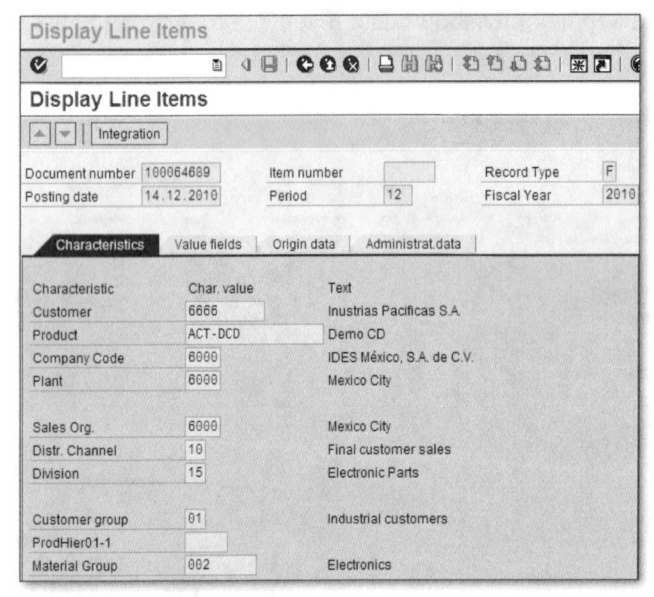

Figure 2.23 Characteristics in a Line Item Report for Profitability Analysis

Figure 2.24 shows the value fields associated with the invoice posting. We see the invoiced quantity (5 pieces), the sales revenue (150 Mexican pesos), the cost of goods sold (100 Mexican pesos), and the breakdown of the product costs into the components material input, fixed labor costs, variable labor costs, fixed machine costs, variable machine costs, and material overhead. In SAP NetWeaver BW terms, these are the "facts" that are displayed in all reports. In the bottom of the screen are buttons for switching between currencies and for switching between the legal view and the profit center view (dimensions in SAP NetWeaver BW terms). We'll look at the options for legal and group valuation in more detail in Chapter 6.

While the line items are useful for checking the integrity of the data in Profitability Analysis, it's more common to view the data in a drill-down report or to move the entire operating concern to SAP NetWeaver BW for analysis. In SAP enhancement package 4 for SAP ERP 6.0, SAP defined new reports for Profitability Analysis as shown in Figure 2.25. Notice that there are no list reports here, but that all reports are labeled ANALYSIS. This is consistent with trends in profitability reporting generally, where the operating concern is often transferred to SAP NetWeaver BW to make querying multidimensional structures such as product/customer combinations faster. We'll return to this in Chapter 8.

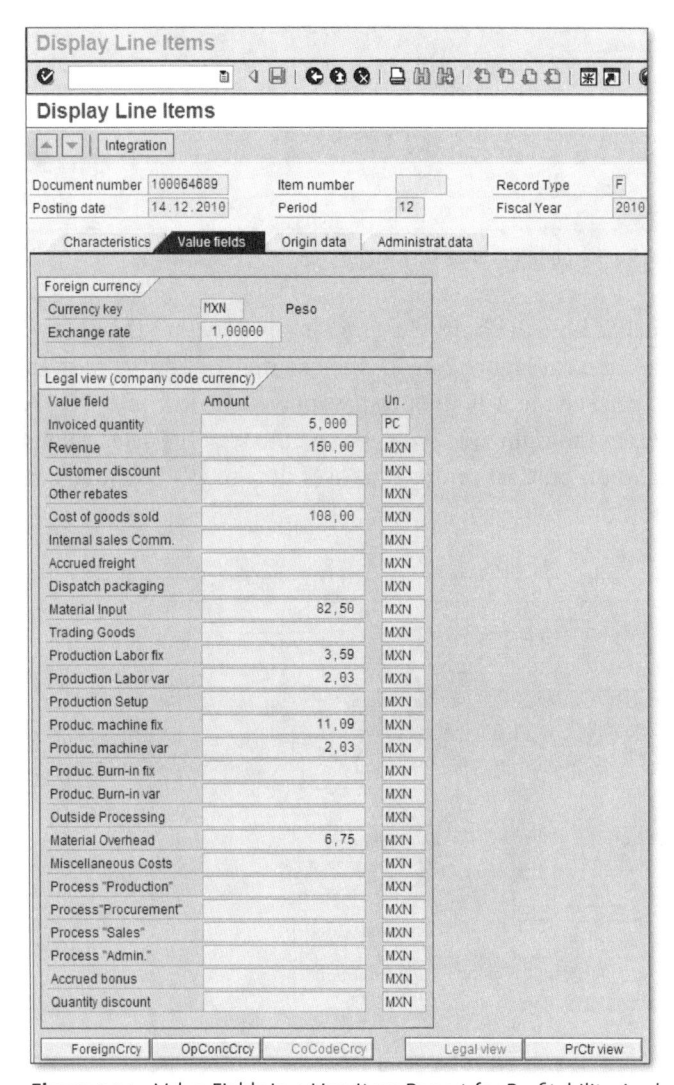

Figure 2.24 Value Fields in a Line Item Report for Profitability Analysis

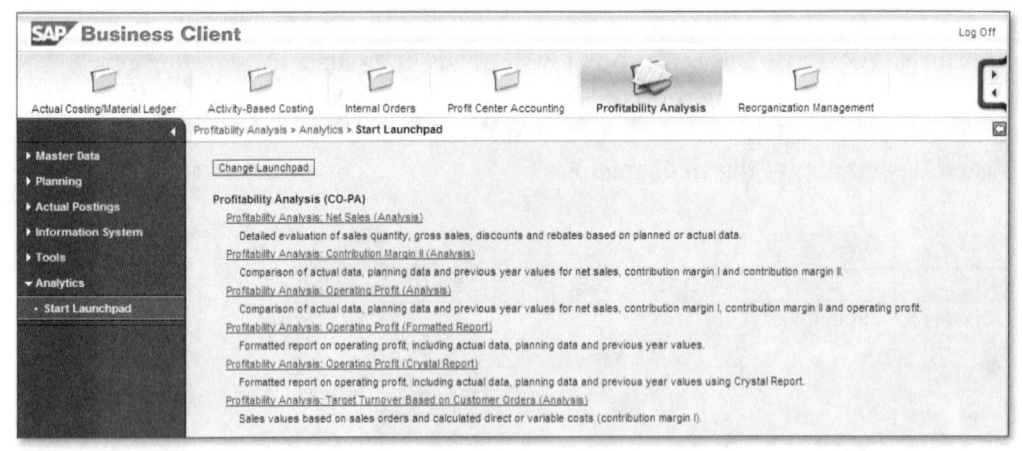

Figure 2.25 Simplified Reports for Simplified Profitability Reporting

If you're struggling to visualize how the individual line items flow into the operating concern in CO-PA, take a look at Figure 2.26 as one example of how values can flow. On the left side, you can see the way the production values flow into CO-PA via the material and plant. On the right side, you can see the way the sales values flow into CO-PA via the sales order. Cost center expenses flow to CO-PA either via the product or via an allocation.

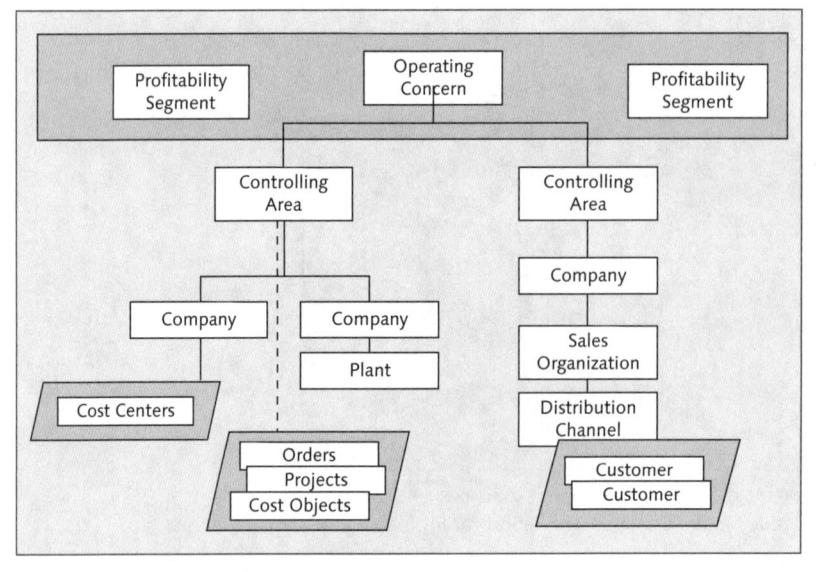

Figure 2.26 Organizational Structures in CO-PA

2.7 Summary

In this chapter, you learned about the basic list reports for Cost Center Accounting, internal orders, and Cost Object Controlling and some tree reports for Product Cost Planning and Material Ledger/actual costing, and we explained how an operating concern is defined for Profitability Analysis.

As we work through the chapters that follow, we'll refer to any reports that support the process, so you'll find the master data reports in Chapter 3 and the line items for planning in Chapter 5. All reports shown in Chapters 1 to 7 are based on reporting capabilities inherent in the SAP ERP system and don't require an additional data warehouse.

We'll return to the subject of reporting in Chapter 8 to look at SAP NetWeaver Business Warehouse and the case for moving data to a dedicated data warehouse. There we'll also discuss some of the newer options made possible using the SAP BusinessObjects tools and specifically how to use a generic function in SAP List Viewer to call Crystal Reports.

But first we'll look at the master data that needs to be in place before you can run any of these reports.

The master data defines the resources in your organization, the output measures for these resources, and other measures needed for allocations. We'll look at how to group your master data to ease selection and discover some new account assignments.

3   Master Data Owned by Controlling

In Chapter 1 you learned about the process controls needed for master data management following the passage of the Sarbanes-Oxley Act. In this context, it makes sense to distinguish between master data where the controlling department is the main stakeholder (such as cost centers and activity types) and master data where the controlling department is one of several stakeholders, as is the case for the material master record or a customer master record. In this chapter we'll discuss the master data where the controlling department is in the lead, namely cost centers, cost center hierarchies (standard and alternative), internal orders, order groups, statistical key figures, activity types, secondary cost elements, product cost collectors, and cost object hierarchies. So we'll look not only at the master data, but also at the issues you need to consider during maintenance (i.e., time-dependent fields and status management). We'll also review the concept of change requests for providing a SOX-compliant master data process.

After reviewing the principles in Chapter 1, we need to set up proper master data in the form of a cost center structure that represents the resources in the organization, such as a department, group of people, machine, or building. Wherever possible, we'll define output measures for these cost centers in the form of *activity types* that represent work time, machine time, and so on. In some cases, this will not be practical. There can also be cost centers that are simply used for general cost collection, such as paying the bills for rent or power, and whose costs are then charged to the operational cost centers via a simple resource driver, such as square footage of floor space or number of employees at each operational cost center. Such resource drivers are defined as *statistical key figures*.

For reporting, the cost centers are grouped into hierarchies, allowing you to select a whole hierarchy or simply a group of related cost centers. This can simply aid selection, allowing you to report on the costs for all production cost centers or all sales cost centers or plan on these cost centers. The groups are also the basis for setting up allocation structures, where a cost center may charge its costs to all production cost centers or all sales cost centers, or you may choose the cost groups that will take part in such an allocation.

We'll also look at some of the other *account assignments* that we covered briefly in Chapter 2, namely, the internal order, the product cost collector, and the cost object hierarchy, and we'll learn how to create cost elements in the Controlling component of SAP ERP Financials (which we'll refer to as CO throughout the rest of this chapter) to document the different sorts of allocation being performed.

3.1 How to Set Up Cost Centers

For most organizations, Cost Center Accounting is the first phase of an SAP ERP implementation along with setting up the General Ledger. If establishing the chart of accounts is the first challenge of Financial Accounting, then establishing the proper cost center structure is the first challenge of CO, since the cost center represents the first contact between operational processes such as purchasing and reporting on such processes in finance. If you're unsure what constitutes a cost center, you need to understand that in SAP ERP a cost center represents a *stable, manageable* unit, such as a department or business unit, while orders and projects exist only for the *duration* of their execution.

> **Master Data and Customizing**
>
> Setting up master data and reporting structures can either be considered part of the initial implementation effort or an ongoing task. To ensure consistency, some organizations maintain their master data in the same client as their configuration settings and then transfer them to their productive systems. Others see maintenance of such master data as an ongoing part of running their business and make changes directly in the productive system. Make sure you know which approach your organization has chosen before making critical master data changes.

To set up your cost centers, use the role Cost Center Accounting and select the Cost Center folder, as shown in Figure 3.1. Alternatively, you can go to Accounting • Controlling • Cost Center Accounting • Master Data • Cost Center • Create or use Transaction KS01.

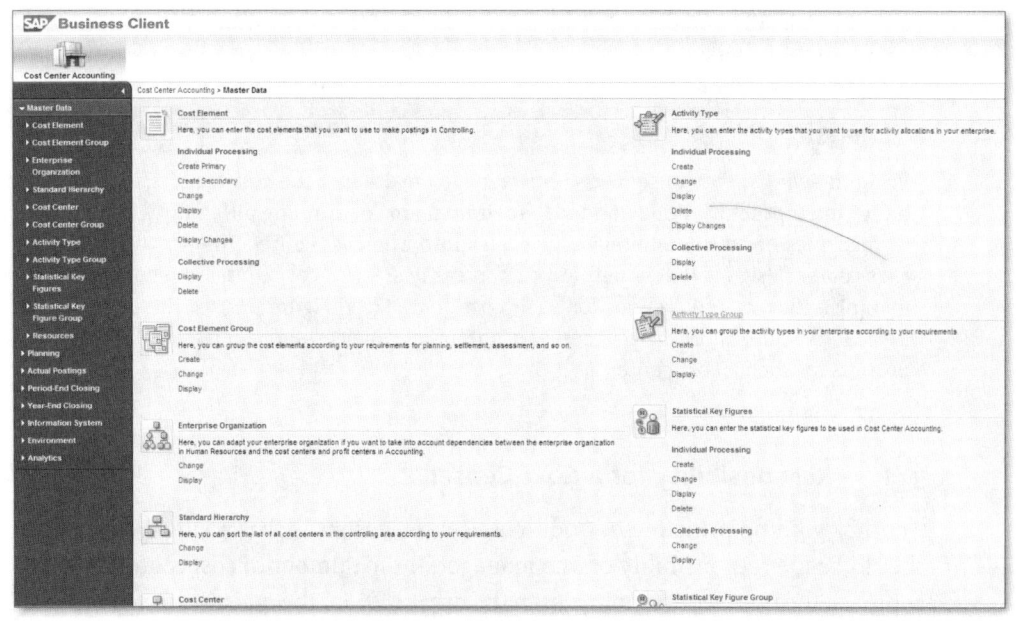

Figure 3.1 Master Data for Cost Center Accounting

The cost center represents the resources employed by the organization. A resource could be a machine, building, or people working in a department. Sometimes it's easier just to look at the departments you have (i.e., research, sales, or corporate services). At other times, it may be better to represent the production department as a whole production line or split it to cover each of a group of machines on a factory floor. When establishing your cost center design, it can also be helpful to distinguish between *operational* cost centers and *supporting* cost centers.

- The *operational* cost centers are those that provide work to production, maintenance, and so on. We'll link these cost centers with *work centers* in Chapter 4 and use them to charge work to a production order or to a project in Chapter 6.

- The *supporting* cost centers provide general services such as energy or telecommunications. We'll explore the various ways of allocating costs from the supporting cost centers to the operational cost centers in Chapter 7. At this stage it's important to decide whether the cost center will be used to capture *expenses* (such as rent or telephone costs) that will later be split to the operational cost centers using an *assessment cycle* or whether there is a *quantity* in play, such as the kilowatt hours supplied by an energy cost center. In this case, you'll be able to use an *indirect activity allocation cycle* to assign the kilowatt hours to your operational cost centers.

> **Tip**
>
> When drawing up the design, it's important to ensure that the cost centers are homogenous in purpose. It's not a good idea to lump teams performing different types of work or machines of hugely different efficiencies into one cost center. The first test of your cost center design will be whether you can easily select a cost center category, such as administration or production, for each cost center (see Figure 3.2). If the category is unclear, the purpose of the cost center is potentially unclear, and you'll struggle to define outputs for such a cost center.

3.1.1 Responsibility for a Cost Center

Another guiding principle of good cost center design is that a single cost center should be the responsibility of one manager. If the number of cost centers starts to approach the number of employees in the organization, the question of who "owns" each cost center can be a good way of pruning the list of potential cost centers and ensuring that each cost center has an owner. Figure 3.2 shows the master data for a corporate services cost center. As you can see, there are two fields to hold the name of the manager:

- The PERSON RESPONSIBLE field has been in the cost center master from the very beginning and allowed organizations to document the name of the cost center manager at a time when the manager was likely to receive paper reports on the performance of his cost center prepared by the controlling department. The ADDRESS and COMMUNICATION tabs date from the same era and are rapidly becoming redundant, because organizations employ new mechanisms to notify their managers about the spending on their cost centers online.

- The USER RESPONSIBLE field was added in SAP ERP 6.0 and illustrates how cost center management has evolved. With more recent developments such as Manager Self-Service (a Web application for managers, available with SAP ERP 6.0), it's now commonly assumed that the cost center manager is an SAP user, accessing his reports and entering his own planning data online. The USER RESPONSIBLE field is used in Manager Self-Service to prefill the selection screens in various reports, to ensure that managers see data for only their cost centers (a process known as *personalization*), and in Express Planning to determine which cost centers managers will be invited to plan, a process we'll discuss in more detail in Chapter 10.

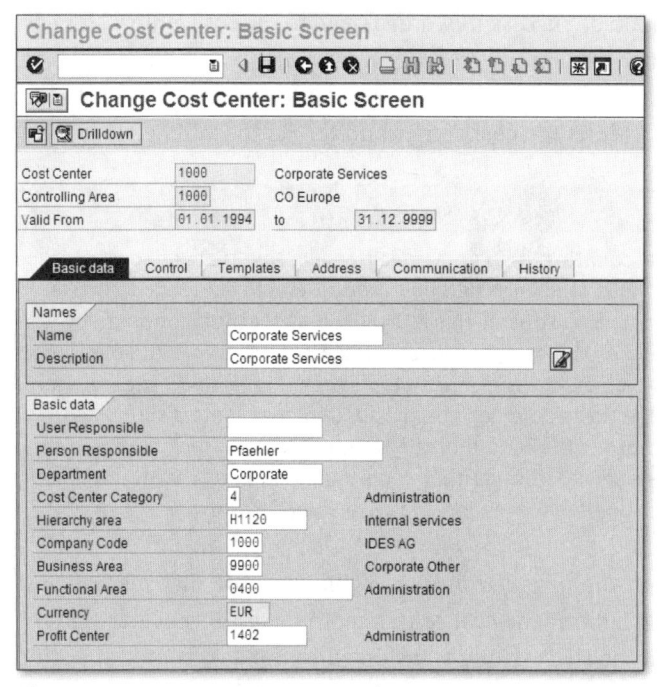

Figure 3.2 Cost Center Master Record

> **Extending the Cost Center Master Data**
>
> One of the most commonly asked questions about the cost center master data is whether it's possible to add extra fields. This is usually a matter of having additional attributes available for reporting. If you find yourself involved in this kind of discussion, talk with your IT department about the possibility of activating user exit COOMKS01 (cost center: customer-specific additional fields in the master record). This allows you to extend the structure of the cost center master record and include whatever attributes you feel would help with your reporting.

3.1.2 Embedding the Cost Center Design in SAP ERP

The cost center design can't be undertaken in isolation. Since all employees who perform the work of the cost center are also assigned to an organizational unit in human resources, you'll need to ensure that your cost center design harmonizes with your organizational structure. Entering the name of the relevant cost center in the master data of the relevant organizational unit ensures that the costs for payroll, benefits, travel, and so on can be successfully transferred to the cost center. This cost center is also credited when the employee posts work time to an order or project using a time sheet. In Chapter 6 we'll show how an employee posts his work time to a project and how this credits the cost center and debits the WBS element.

> **Lean Accounting Tip**
>
> If you're considering lean accounting, it's a good idea to make sure that your cost center design meshes with your value stream design and that all employee-related costs are being assigned to the correct value stream. This is usually easy for shop floor employees who operate or maintain one or more machines but can be tricky for employees on supporting cost centers. If you can't assign such employees to one value stream, then use an allocation to split the costs between the production cost centers supported by these employees. Sometimes it's the nature of the business to have such cost centers. IT departments and shared service centers that serve many parts of the business are examples of cost centers that will never assign neatly to value streams.

Likewise, the machines on the production line are likely to be managed as *fixed assets* in Asset Accounting. Linking the cost centers with the assets ensures that the depreciation expenses can be successfully transferred to the cost center at period close. This cost center assignment also determines the profit center and the segment to which the asset is assigned. From SAP enhancement package 5 for SAP ERP 6.0, the link between fixed assets and the cost center has been extended to include the profit center and the segment in the asset master record. This is done to ensure that the profit center for the asset is not derived on-the-fly during the relevant cost center-related postings but is permanently available in the asset master record, allowing asset reporting by segment and profit center. To see the new fields in the asset master record, check whether your organization has activated the business function FIN_GL_REORG_1. Note also that the link between the cost center and the fixed asset is *time-dependent*, because the assignments can change over time and a new data slice will be created for each assignment. You can refer to Section 3.9 for more information on this concept.

The same linkage to the cost center is made for equipment in Plant Maintenance in SAP ERP. This ensures that the costs of equipment are correctly captured on the cost center. This assignment is used to display the assigned assets and equipment in Manager Self-Service.

If the machines perform work during production, they'll normally be defined as *work centers* in production or *resources* in the process industries. Linking the cost centers with the work centers ensures that the costs performed at the work center can be charged to the production orders correctly during order confirmation. We'll return to this assignment in Chapter 4.

3.1.3 Ensuring that Cost Center Expenses Are Handled Correctly

Figure 3.2 shows the assignment of the cost center to organizational entities, such as the company code, business area, functional area, and profit center. These are important since they determine how expenses assigned to this cost center are treated in the general ledger and related ledgers.

Company Code

If the controlling area (the main organizational unit for CO) contains multiple company codes (which is usually the case), you need to assign each cost center to a company code. This determines the object currency of the cost center (euros, in our example). This may be different from the controlling area currency, which is usually the group currency.

The company code assignment is important not just for capturing expenses, but also for allocations. If a cost center allocates costs to another cost center and the partner cost center is in a different company code, two things may happen:

- If you use the classic General Ledger (available in all releases prior to SAP ERP 5.0), this cross-company allocation is stored in a reconciliation ledger. At period close these values are moved to the other company code, via Transaction KALC or the menu path ACCOUNTING • CONTROLLING • COST ELEMENT ACCOUNTING • ACTUAL POSTINGS • RECONCILIATION WITH FI.

- If you use the SAP ERP General Ledger (also known as the new General Ledger), this cross-company allocation results in a transfer to the cost center in the other company code being made immediately. The configuration settings are described in the implementation guide under scenario FIN_CCA (Cost Center Update) and the entries Real-Time Integration of Controlling with Financial Accounting.

Business Area

The *business area* represents one way of segmenting your business within the general ledger. So any posting to the Corporate Services cost center is automatically assigned to business area 9900 (see Figure 3.2) in the general ledger, and any allocation also updates the business area.

If you use the SAP ERP General Ledger, it's worth checking whether scenario FIN_GSBER (business area) is active, since this determines whether the business area and the partner business area are updated in the General Ledger during an allocation. If you've activated Real-Time Integration of Controlling with Financial Accounting, allocations between different business areas will also be updated in real-time.

Functional Area

The most common use of the functional area is in the context of Cost of Sales Accounting, which is a legal requirement in many countries, but the field is used differently in Public Sector Accounting. The functional area is then used to classify expenses by economic purpose, so any posting to the Corporate Services cost center is automatically assigned to functional area 0400 (Administration).

- If you use the classic General Ledger, Cost of Sales Accounting is handled in the Special Ledger, and a substitution rule is used to derive the correct functional area from the CO postings and update it to the Special Ledger (sometimes called the Cost of Sales (COS) ledger).
- If you use the SAP ERP General Ledger, you can capture this assignment immediately, provided scenario FIN_UKV (Cost of Sales Accounting) is active. This means you can obtain financial statements according to Cost of Sales Accounting by using the standard balance sheet report and drilling down by functional area.

Profit Center

The *profit center* represents another way of segmenting your business. In principle, it supersedes the business area, but in many organizations the two continue to be used in parallel. The profit center began as a management way of viewing revenue and costs but was subsequently extended to include payables and liabilities. From SAP ERP 5.0 on, the profit center was linked with the *segment* to support the legal requirements for Segment Reporting according to IFRS 8 (International Financial Reporting Standards) or IAS 14 (International Accounting Standards).

- If you use the classic General Ledger, the assignment to the profit center results in expense postings to the cost center being assigned to the Profit Center Ledger (technically this is ledger 8A).
- If you use the SAP ERP General Ledger, the assignment to the profit center results in expense postings to the cost center updating both the profit center and the segment, provided you have activated scenarios FIN_PCA (Profit Center Accounting) and FIN_SEGM (Segmentation).

> **Note**
> When assigning the profit center, you should also consider the use of splitting in the SAP ERP General Ledger. When goods are purchased for the cost center, the expense items are automatically posted to cost center 1000 and profit center 1402. However, the vendor payable item and the tax item are normally stored at the company code level. Splitting allows the system to use rules to automatically assign the vendor item and the tax item to the correct profit center (usually the profit center assigned to the cost center).

3.1.4 Cost Center Hierarchies

All cost centers are assigned to a hierarchy area, as shown in Figure 3.2. The hierarchy area is a node in the *standard cost center hierarchy*. This assignment ensures that it's possible to report across all cost centers in a single controlling area, since the top node of the standard cost center hierarchy is linked to the controlling area and all cost centers are assigned to one of the nodes in this hierarchy. Generally, organizations use both the standard cost center hierarchy and alternative cost center hierarchies to aggregate their cost centers for reporting.

Standard Cost Center Hierarchies

All cost centers have to be assigned to a node of the standard cost center hierarchy (the HIERARCHY AREA field in the cost center master). To check the structure of your cost center hierarchy, you can take the following steps:

1. Use the role COST CENTER ACCOUNTING.
2. Select STANDARD HIERARCHY, as shown in Figure 3.1, or go to ACCOUNTING • CONTROLLING • COST CENTER ACCOUNTING • MASTER DATA • STANDARD HIERARCHY • CHANGE (Transaction OKEON). You cannot create a new hierarchy but can only change the existing one. This is because the root node of the cost center hierarchy is already assigned to the controlling area in Customizing.

What makes the standard cost center hierarchy special is that it's *complete:* It shows every cost center in a given controlling area. Just to make sure you haven't created cyclical relationships when defining your hierarchy nodes, select EXTRAS • AMBIGUITY CHECK to make sure your tree is correctly defined.

Some organizations use the standard cost center hierarchy as their only reporting structure and ensure that the nodes are detailed to the extent required for corporate reporting. Other organizations treat the standard cost center hierarchy as something of a formality, with only a few nodes, and then create alternative cost center hierarchies for different reporting purposes. The assignment to the alternative cost center hierarchy is made not in the cost center master, but in a separate transaction.

Figure 3.3 shows a sample cost center hierarchy from the IDES demo system.

> **Note**
>
> Since Release 4.6C, you can maintain the nodes that make up the tree structure and the cost centers in a single transaction. In earlier releases, the maintenance transaction is identical to the user interface for the alternative cost center hierarchy we'll show next. If you have an extremely large standard cost center hierarchy, SAP recommends that you continue to use the old transaction (Transaction OKEO) for hierarchy maintenance. You'll find more information and links to other notes associated with system performance for the hierarchies in SAP Note 402088.

Alongside reporting, the other use of the cost center hierarchy is as a basis for allocations. The nodes of the hierarchy can be the sender or, more commonly, the receiver of an allocation. As you can see in Figure 3.4, there's an assessment cycle, in which the costs for cost center MFC_1040 are to be allocated to all cost centers in group MFC_A_4000. You can view assessment cycles like this one by following the menu path ACCOUNTING • CONTROLLING • COST CENTER ACCOUNTING • PERIOD-END CLOSING • SINGLE FUNCTIONS • ALLOCATIONS • ASSESSMENT and then EXTRAS • CYCLE • CHANGE or by using Transaction KSU2. We'll return to allocation cycles in Chapter 7. For now it's sufficient to know that cost center groups can be both the sender and the receiver of an allocation. In the real world, the receivers of an allocation are almost always cost center groups—all production cost centers, all maintenance cost centers, all sales cost centers, and so on. With the senders, it depends how different the cost centers themselves are. Sometimes you'll want to handle each sender cost center in a separate segment of an assessment cycle (as we'll see in the examples in Chapter 7), whereas if the cost centers are very similar, you can put them into a group and handle them in a single segment.

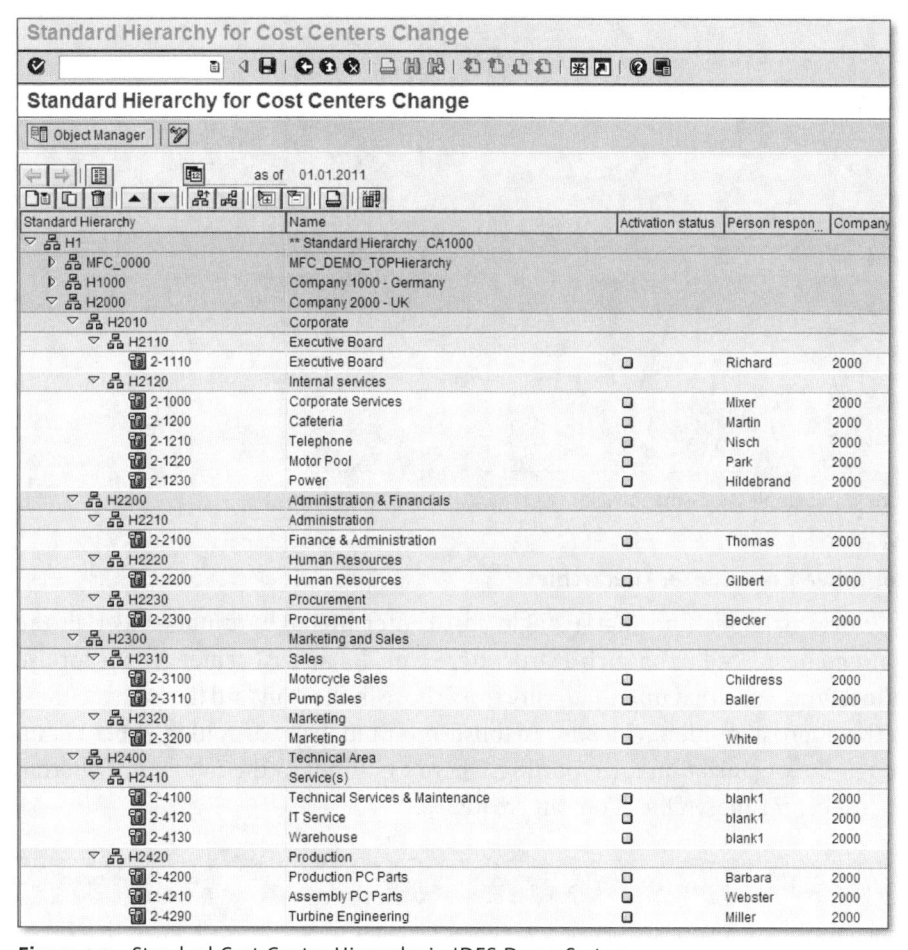

Standard Hierarchy	Name	Activation status	Person respon...	Company
H1	** Standard Hierarchy CA1000			
MFC_0000	MFC_DEMO_TOPHierarchy			
H1000	Company 1000 - Germany			
H2000	Company 2000 - UK			
H2010	Corporate			
H2110	Executive Board			
2-1110	Executive Board	☐	Richard	2000
H2120	Internal services			
2-1000	Corporate Services	☐	Mixer	2000
2-1200	Cafeteria	☐	Martin	2000
2-1210	Telephone	☐	Nisch	2000
2-1220	Motor Pool	☐	Park	2000
2-1230	Power	☐	Hildebrand	2000
H2200	Administration & Financials			
H2210	Administration			
2-2100	Finance & Administration	☐	Thomas	2000
H2220	Human Resources			
2-2200	Human Resources	☐	Gilbert	2000
H2230	Procurement			
2-2300	Procurement	☐	Becker	2000
H2300	Marketing and Sales			
H2310	Sales			
2-3100	Motorcycle Sales	☐	Childress	2000
2-3110	Pump Sales	☐	Baller	2000
H2320	Marketing			
2-3200	Marketing	☐	White	2000
H2400	Technical Area			
H2410	Service(s)			
2-4100	Technical Services & Maintenance	☐	blank1	2000
2-4120	IT Service	☐	blank1	2000
2-4130	Warehouse	☐	blank1	2000
H2420	Production			
2-4200	Production PC Parts	☐	Barbara	2000
2-4210	Assembly PC Parts	☐	Webster	2000
2-4290	Turbine Engineering	☐	Miller	2000

Figure 3.3 Standard Cost Center Hierarchy in IDES Demo System

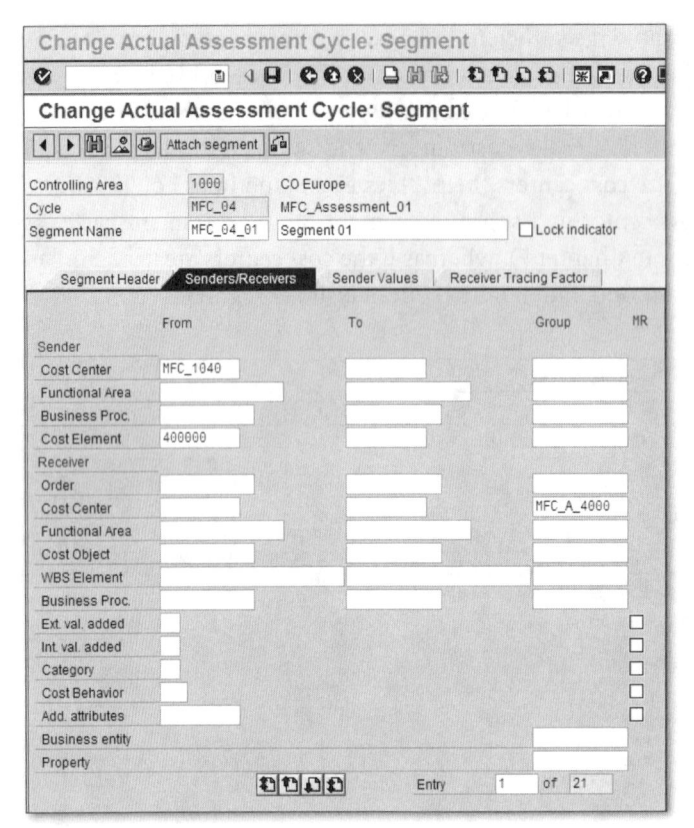

Figure 3.4 Sample Assessment Cycle

Alternative Cost Center Hierarchies

Many organizations find that a single cost center hierarchy cannot meet all the requirements placed upon such a structure. Some define cost center groups for use in allocation cycles that differ radically from those in the standard hierarchy. Others use the alternative hierarchies to establish multiple ways of rolling expenses up through the organization for reporting. There's no limit to the number of alternative cost center hierarchies you can create.

> **Lean Accounting Tip**
>
> One obvious use for an alternative cost center hierarchy is to construct nodes that represent the main value streams in your organization. This allows you to report along these lines and along the more traditional reporting lines of your departmental structure.

To create an alternative cost center hierarchy, use the role COST CENTER ACCOUNTING and select COST CENTER GROUPS, as shown in Figure 3.1. You can also use Transaction KSH1 or go to ACCOUNTING • CONTROLLING • COST CENTER ACCOUNTING • MASTER DATA • COST CENTER GROUP • CREATE.

Alternative cost center hierarchies are built as *groups*, and the tool bar used to maintain cost center groups within an alternative cost center hierarchy is the same for order groups, cost element groups, activity type groups, statistical key figure groups, and so on.

During group maintenance, you build up the tree structure by entering nodes with texts either on the same level as the root node or on the lower level, until you have built up a tree structure that meets your requirements. You can use nodes in an alternative hierarchy as receivers of an allocation in exactly the same way as we saw in Figure 3.4.

> **Tip**
>
> You then assign the cost centers to these nodes. If you have labeled your cost centers with meaningful codes (such as 1XXX for internal services, 2XXX for administration, 3XXX for production, and so on), it will save time if you enter intervals or ranges, such as 3000-3999.
>
> Assuming you follow the naming convention that any cost center beginning with a 3 is assigned to production, then all new cost centers will automatically be assigned to the production node. Figure 3.5 shows a sample hierarchy.

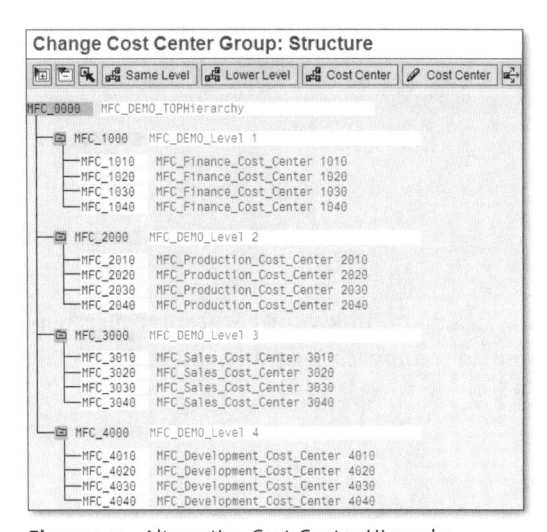

Figure 3.5 Alternative Cost Center Hierarchy

You can also include a suffix in the cost center hierarchy to represent the year in which it's valid or the purpose of the reorganization. Some organizations create copies of their hierarchies each year and then adjust them to take account of changing operational requirements. To copy a cost center hierarchy with a suffix, use Transaction KSH1, go to COST CENTER • COPY, and enter a four-digit suffix, as shown in Figure 3.6.

Once you have copied your hierarchy and started to change it, it makes sense to run the ambiguity check we saw in the standard cost center hierarchy. If you're building an alternative cost center hierarchy that aims to provide a complete view of all the cost centers in a controlling area, you should make sure you have included every cost center in the controlling area, by selecting EXTRAS • CHECK AND HELP FUNCTIONS • CHECK COMPLETENESS. Once you have pruned your structure, you can also remove groups that are now empty by selecting EXTRAS • CHECK AND HELP FUNCTIONS • DELETE UNUSED GROUPS.

While you're building your hierarchies, it also makes sense to consider how you'll use the groups within your hierarchies for reporting. With this in mind, refer to Chapter 8, Section 8.1 for information on how to create extracts for each cost center group to speed up the response time of reports that use large cost center groups.

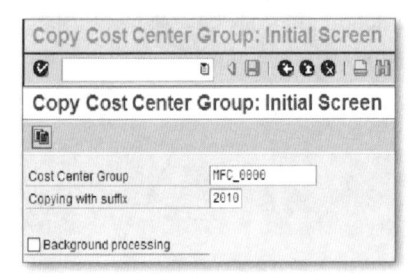

Figure 3.6 Copy Function with Suffix

3.1.5 Enterprise Organization

You'll also find an entry in the SAP Easy Menu to link your cost center hierarchy with the organizational hierarchy in human resources. Generally, this is not widely used and can be ignored.

3.1.6 Reporting of Cost Center Master Data

When the cost center structure is complete, you can check the consistency of your cost centers with the help of the cost center master data report. The traditional report is Transaction KS13. You'll find this in the MASTER DATA INDEXES folder shown in Chapter 2, Figure 2.1. You can also use the simplified report Cost Centers: Master Data Report (List), shown in Figure 3.7.

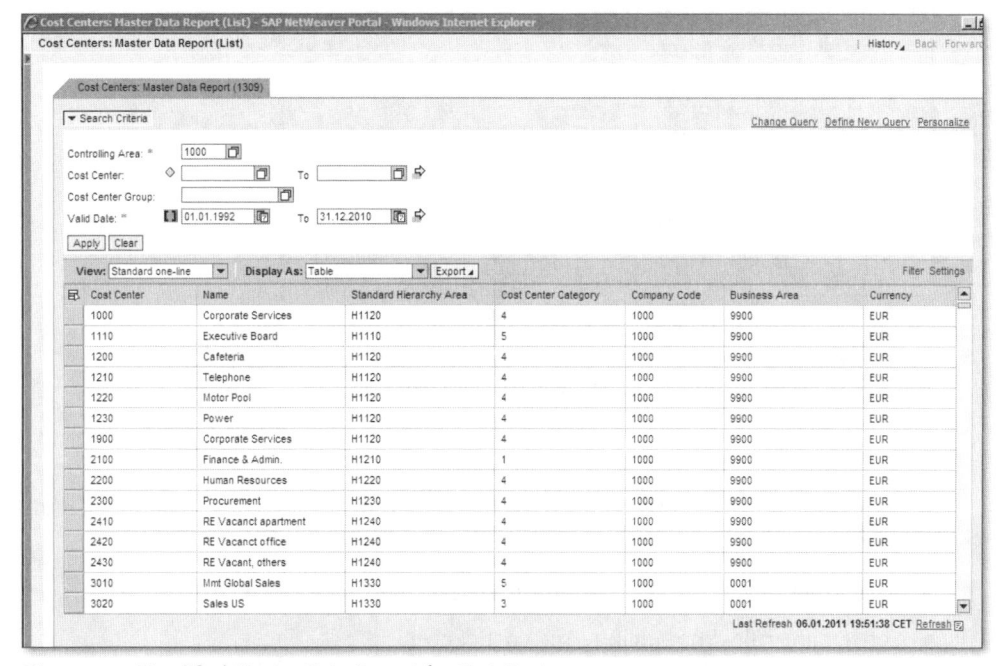

Figure 3.7 Simplified Master Data Report for Cost Centers

We've discussed how intertwined the cost centers are with other master data in SAP ERP. This means that before executing any kind of change, it's worth taking a look at the *where-used lists*. You can find these in the cost center master record under EXTRAS • WHERE USED LISTS. Figure 3.8 shows the fixed assets that are linked with cost center 1000, which is just one of the delivered where-used lists.

Where-used lists are also available to display the following:

- Activity types assigned to the cost center (e.g., machine hours)
- Splitting structure to display how the costs from a single cost center are split to multiple activity types

3 | Master Data Owned by Controlling

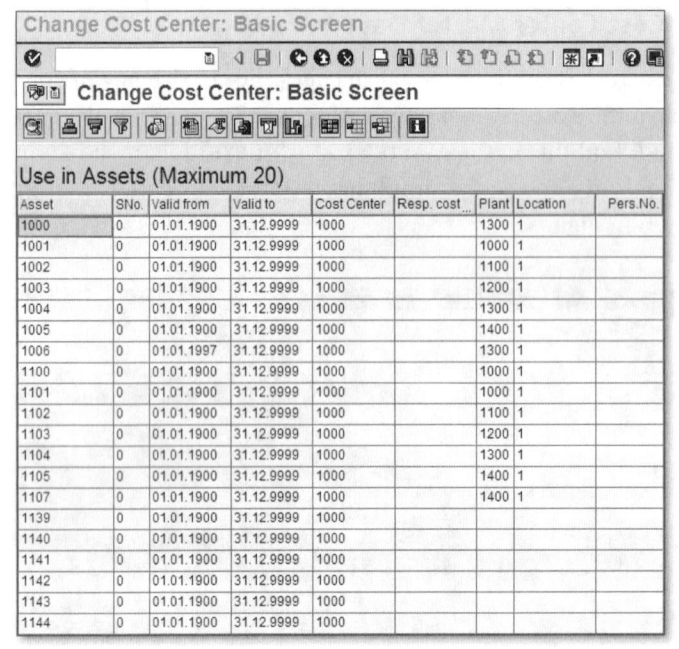

Change Cost Center: Basic Screen

Use in Assets (Maximum 20)

Asset	SNo.	Valid from	Valid to	Cost Center	Resp. cost	Plant	Location	Pers.No.
1000	0	01.01.1900	31.12.9999	1000		1300	1	
1001	0	01.01.1900	31.12.9999	1000		1000	1	
1002	0	01.01.1900	31.12.9999	1000		1100	1	
1003	0	01.01.1900	31.12.9999	1000		1200	1	
1004	0	01.01.1900	31.12.9999	1000		1300	1	
1005	0	01.01.1900	31.12.9999	1000		1400	1	
1006	0	01.01.1997	31.12.9999	1000		1300	1	
1100	0	01.01.1900	31.12.9999	1000		1000	1	
1101	0	01.01.1900	31.12.9999	1000		1000	1	
1102	0	01.01.1900	31.12.9999	1000		1100	1	
1103	0	01.01.1900	31.12.9999	1000		1200	1	
1104	0	01.01.1900	31.12.9999	1000		1300	1	
1105	0	01.01.1900	31.12.9999	1000		1400	1	
1107	0	01.01.1900	31.12.9999	1000		1400	1	
1139	0	01.01.1900	31.12.9999	1000				
1140	0	01.01.1900	31.12.9999	1000				
1141	0	01.01.1900	31.12.9999	1000				
1142	0	01.01.1900	31.12.9999	1000				
1143	0	01.01.1900	31.12.9999	1000				
1144	0	01.01.1900	31.12.9999	1000				

Figure 3.8 Where-Used List for Cost Center 1000 Showing Assigned Assets

- Activity types used in time recording in human resources (CATS)
- Assessment cycles, distribution cycles, and reposting cycles that include the cost center
- Assessment cycles to Profitability Analysis that include the cost center
- Settlement rules that include the cost center
- Internal orders where the cost center is defined as the responsible cost center
- Work breakdown structure elements for Project Management where the cost center is defined as the responsible cost center

> **Using Where-Used Lists**
>
> Where-used lists are the controller's primary checklist for master data management. Before any change is made to the cost center master data, controlling checks what other areas will be affected by the change. The most common use case is a reorganization where two cost centers are merged or one is split. Before implementing any such change, controlling checks which assets are currently assigned to the cost center and notifies the accountant that these assets need to be moved to another cost center before locking the cost center.

> On a smaller scale, if an employee changes a cost center, he checks which assets and equipment (such as his mobile phone and laptop) he is taking with him and ensures that such equipment is transferred to the new cost center. In the run up to the period close, these lists are used to check that the allocation cycles relating to each cost center are up to date.

The cost center is the backbone of any CO implementation and meshes tightly with the organizational structure of the company in terms of the assigned employees and assets. Wherever you need to capture costs for items that exist for a shorter time frame, you should look at internal orders as a way to capture costs.

3.2 Internal Orders

Some organizations manage to assign all their costs to cost centers, but most need an alternative account assignment in the form of internal orders (or sometimes projects). This is typically the case if there is to be some capital expenditure to replace a production line or overhead expense, such as research and development that needs to be captured in more detail than simply the R&D cost center. Depending on the design, an internal order can either provide more detail on the postings to an individual cost center, such as a single vehicle belonging to the cost center Car Pool or a trade fair belonging to the cost center Marketing, or can be considered a separate entity, such as a research order or an investment order for which individual departments work. You can distinguish orders by assigning them to a special order type. This determines how expenses assigned to the order are settled and what fields are displayed in the user interface.

To create an internal order, use the role INTERNAL ORDERS, select the MASTER DATA folder, and then select ORDER MANAGER as shown in Figure 3.9. You can also use Transaction KO04 or go to ACCOUNTING • CONTROLLING • INTERNAL ORDERS • MASTER DATA • ORDERS • ORDER MANAGER.

The Order Manager is an early example of a work list allowing you to select and store a list of orders that you work on regularly. The work list appears on the left side of the screen, and selecting an item in the list takes you to the master data for that object on the right side of the screen (see Figure 3.10). Note the REFERENCE ORDER field in this list. If you have to create a lot of similar orders where most of the master data will be similar and only a few fields change, then it's worth working with references or setting up a dedicated order type to serve as a reference or model order.

3 Master Data Owned by Controlling

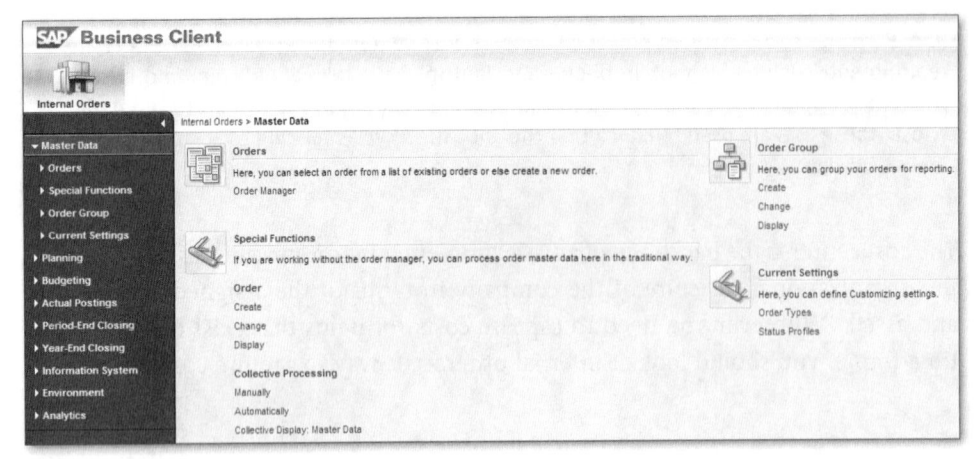

Figure 3.9 Internal Order Master Data

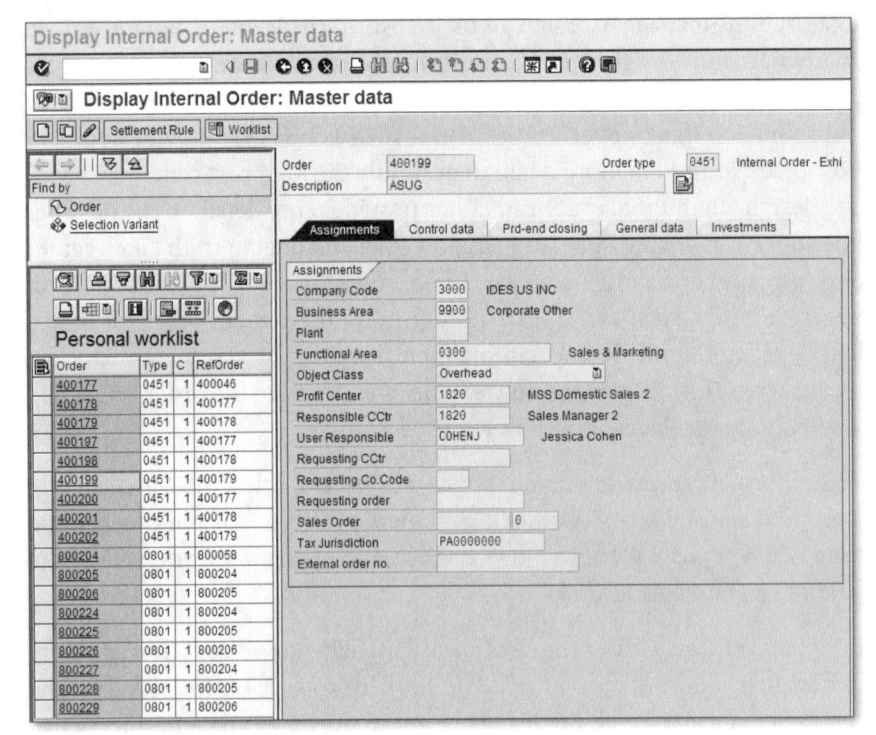

Figure 3.10 Internal Order with Work List

Since the number of internal orders in an organization can be huge, many organizations use *selection variants* to ease the selection of orders for reporting and settlement. The selection variant is used to select all orders with entries in particular fields, such as all internal orders of order type 0100 that have the status Released. Figure 3.11 shows the fields available to create a selection variant. We'll cover other options for selecting orders as work lists when we look at optimizing close activities in Chapter 12.

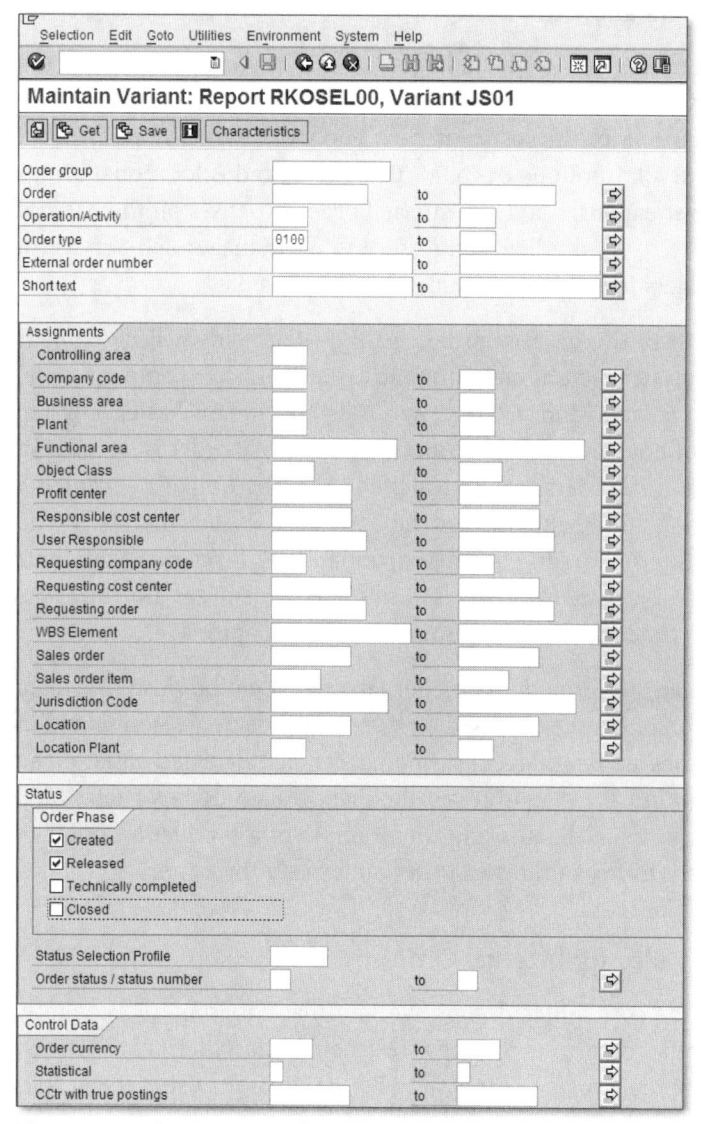

Figure 3.11 Selection Variant for Internal Orders

3 | Master Data Owned by Controlling

> **Selection Variants**
>
> Once you understand how selection variants work, you can use them for all the master data in CO. You'll find an option to use selection variants in all the master data reports.

3.2.1 Internal Orders and Cost Centers

You can connect internal orders with their parent cost centers by entering the cost center in the RESPONSIBLE CCTR field. This link was evaluated in the where-used lists that we discussed for the cost centers. If you work with SAP NetWeaver Business Warehouse (BW), InfoCube 0COOM_C02 (Costs and Allocations) brings together the cost center expenses and the internal order expenses on the basis of this combination. It's also used when you're setting up Manager Self-Service to derive the internal orders for which the manager is responsible.

As you look at the rest of the internal order, many of the fields will be familiar from the cost center master record, including the assignment to a company code, business area, functional area, and profit center. This assignment has exactly the same effect in terms of how an expense posting to an internal order is updated in the General Ledger. Internal orders are also assigned to a plant (unlike cost centers). There are also additional fields, maintained on the GENERAL DATA tab, that show who requested the order. Internal orders that are part of a larger investment initiative can also be assigned to investment programs using the fields in the INVESTMENTS tab. We'll look at investment programs in more detail in Chapter 4.

Certain standard tasks are performed for an internal order at period close. The main tasks are the calculation of overhead, based on a costing sheet that's configured in the IMG and, sometimes, an overhead key. Interest can be calculated based on an interest profile. You'll find these settings on the PERIOD-END CLOSING tab. We'll look at these options in more detail using the example of a production order in Chapter 7, but the options for an internal order are exactly the same.

3.2.2 Settlement Rules for Internal Orders

When we looked at the cost center design, we saw that cost centers frequently charge their costs to other cost centers using assessment cycles. Internal orders, on the other hand, charge their costs to other account assignments using the entries

3.2 Internal Orders

in a *settlement rule*. Figure 3.12 shows a very simple settlement rule, where all the costs for an internal order for attending ASUG events are charged back to the parent cost center, 1820. The user interface for the settlement rule is highly dynamic depending on the approaches allowed and potential receivers as defined in the *settlement profile*, so you may find that your settlement rules look slightly different, showing fewer fields or a different number of potential distribution rules. Depending on your configuration, each order type can have a different settlement profile. When we look at production orders in Chapter 6, we'll see settlement rules that look similar to this one but assign costs to materials and profitability segments, and when we look at settlement rules for sales orders, we'll see settlement rules that assign costs to profitability segments.

Figure 3.12 includes several empty lines, allowing you to create more than one DISTRIBUTION RULE in a single settlement rule. This can allow you to create a first distribution rule where 80% of the investment costs for an order are assigned to a fixed asset and a second distribution rule where 20% of the investment costs are assigned to a cost center. To make sure all costs on your internal order are cleared during settlement, ensure that the sum of the percentages for the distribution rules is 100%.

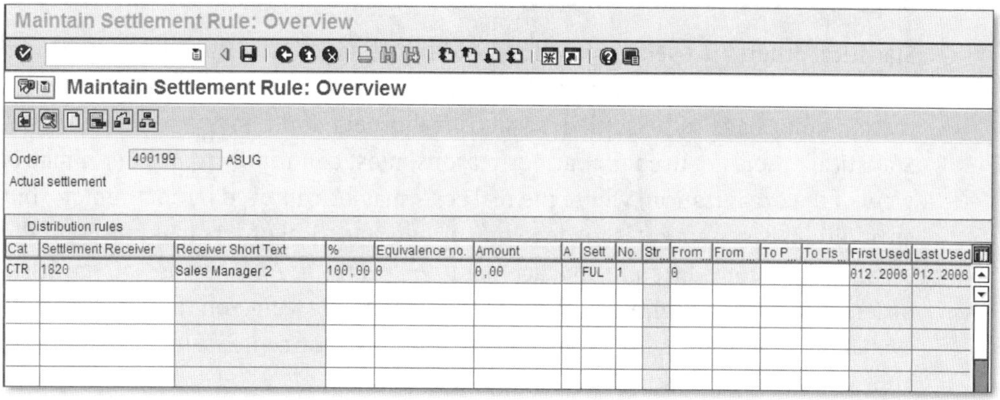

Figure 3.12 Settlement Rule for an Internal Order

You can also see that there is a validity period for each distribution rule. This allows you to settle to an asset under construction until order completion and then create a new distribution rule with a new validity period that settles all costs to the final

109

fixed asset on order completion. You do this by creating a first distribution rule that was valid until the date when the asset was taken into productive use. You then define a second distribution rule valid from the same date where the settlement receiver would be the relevant asset.

Also note the HIERARCHY icon. If the order is assigned to a project or other order it can be useful to visualize where your order is in the settlement hierarchy to understand how the costs will flow from one order to another or from an order to a project.

> **Generating Settlement Rules Automatically**
>
> If you are worried about errors in your settlement rules, it's also possible to configure the system to generate settlement rules automatically (in this case there's an entry in the STRATEGY column). This is essential if orders are generated for objects in other systems, such as CRM service orders that are initiated in SAP Customer Relationship Management (CRM) and cProjects that are initiated in SAP Product Lifecycle Management (PLM). For internal orders, you might consider automatically generating a settlement rule to the requesting cost center or the responsible cost center based on the fields in the order.

3.2.3 Statistical Internal Orders

Statistical orders are used to provide an additional statistical posting when expenses are posted to a cost center or real internal order. These costs are purely statistical and don't have to be settled, so statistical orders don't have a settlement rule. Statistical orders get used for various reasons, most commonly to provide a matrix view of the organization, where the real costs may be captured by cost centers, but an additional assignment is made to one or two statistical orders that represent the organization from different management perspectives. Another use of statistical orders is to act as a shadow of the real cost center, allowing you to perform active availability control for the order representing the cost center. Full details of this approach are provided in SAP Note 68366.

Figure 3.13 shows an example of a statistical internal order. In this example, various marketing campaigns are defined as statistical orders, and the actual costs are posted to cost center 1000 (ACTUAL POSTED CCTR field).

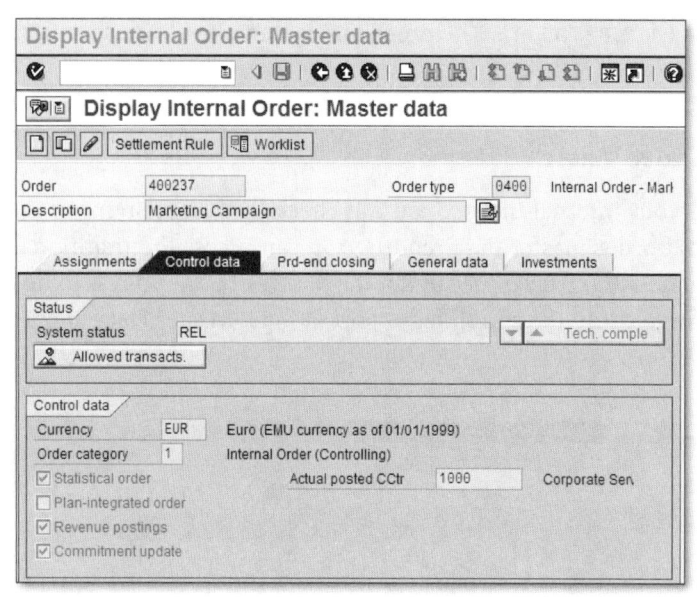

Figure 3.13 Statistical Internal Order

3.2.4 Order Groups

Since organizations typically have many orders, it also makes sense to consider how you are going to select them later:

- *Order groups* are used for reporting and for selecting orders during an allocation (the same procedure applies as we saw for cost centers). When we look at allocations in Chapter 7, we'll see many examples of order groups being used to group orders as potential receivers of an allocation. We'll also see them during cost center and order planning in Chapter 5, where they're used to select the orders for which planned costs can be entered. They're typically used for long-living orders that tend to be treated as one unit.

- *Selection variants* can be easier to use for selecting internal orders for settlement, rather than manually assigning orders to an order group since the selection variants offer more dynamic selection.

To create an order group, use the role INTERNAL ORDERS and select the MASTER DATA folder and then ORDER GROUP • CREATE as shown in Figure 3.9. You can also use Transaction KOH1 or go to ACCOUNTING • CONTROLLING • INTERNAL ORDERS •

MASTER DATA • ORDER GROUP • CREATE. The procedure is then the same as for cost center groups.

3.2.5 Reporting Order Master Data

When you've created your internal orders, you can check their consistency with the help of the internal order master data reports. You can access the traditional report by using Transaction KOK5 (available under the MASTER DATA INDEXES folder in Reporting). Alternatively, use the simplified report Orders: Master Data Report (List), shown in Figure 3.14.

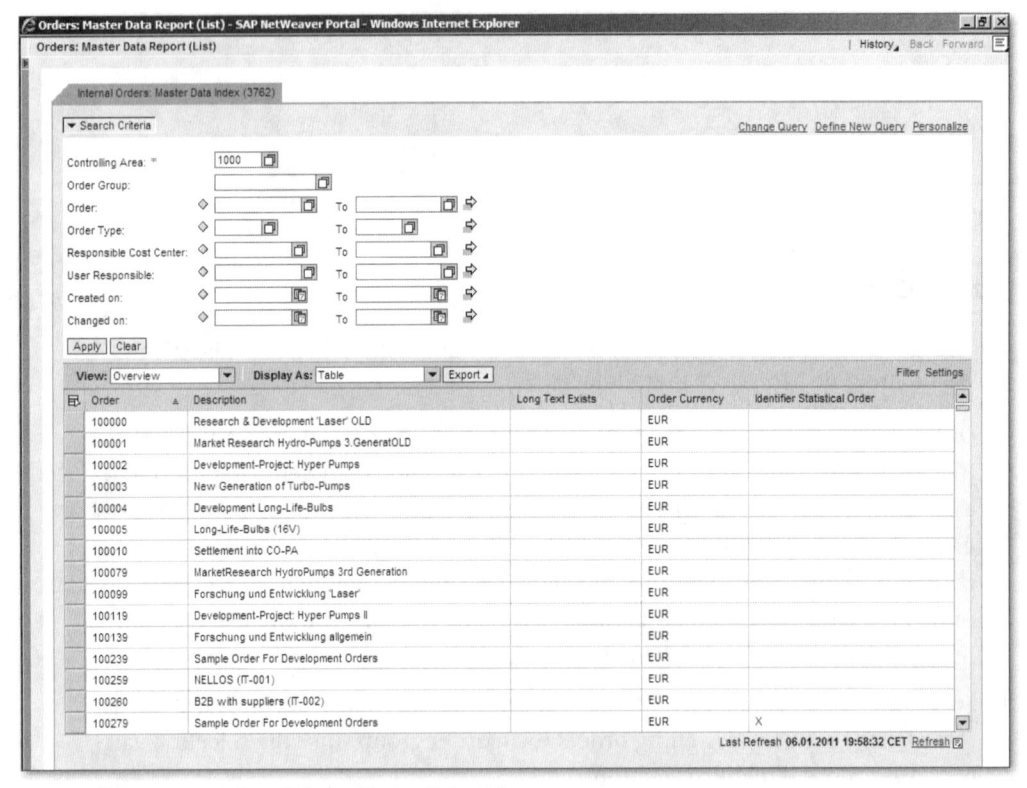

Figure 3.14 Internal Order Master Data List

In addition, you can display a list of the settlement rules by using Transaction KOSR_LIST. This is also available under the MASTER DATA INDEXES folder in Reporting and is especially useful in the run up to the period close, when you want to make sure the correct settlement parameters have been maintained for all internal orders. The list in Figure 3.15 shows how all the internal orders for marketing events settle their costs back to the parent cost center.

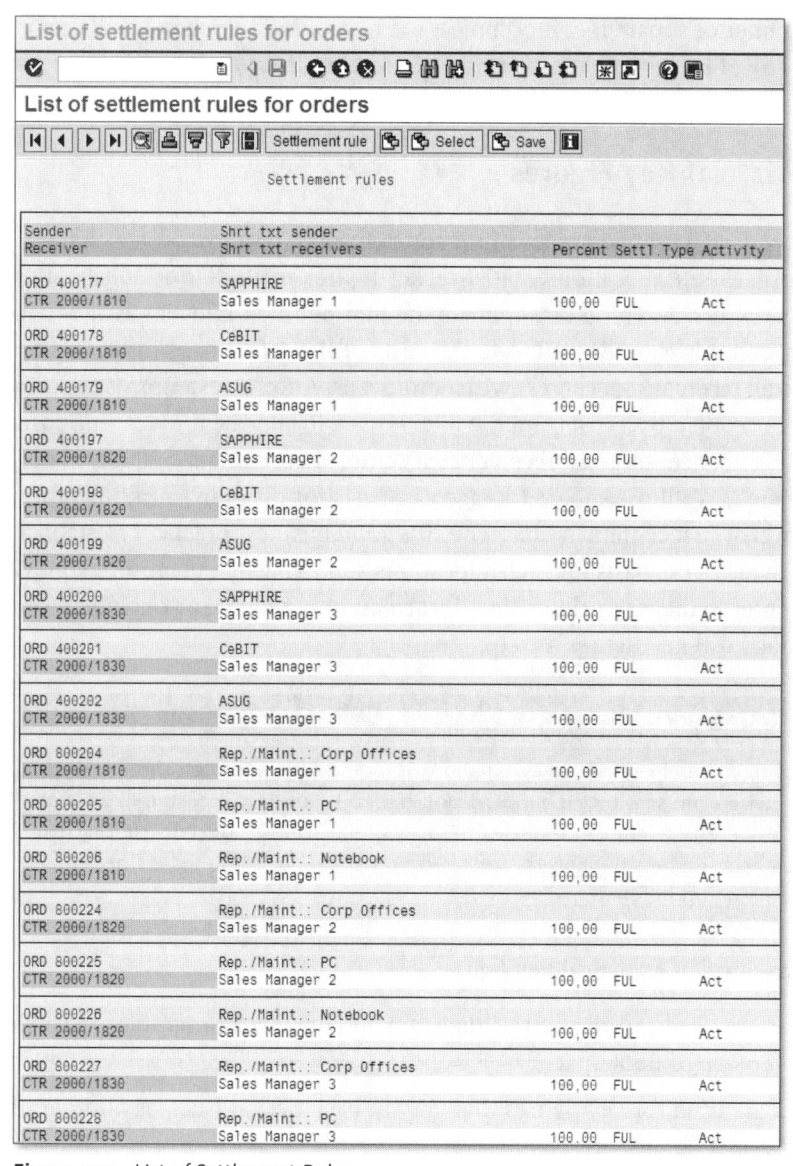

Sender / Receiver	Shrt txt sender / Shrt txt receivers	Percent	Settl.Type	Activity
ORD 400177 / CTR 2000/1810	SAPPHIRE / Sales Manager 1	100,00	FUL	Act
ORD 400178 / CTR 2000/1810	CeBIT / Sales Manager 1	100,00	FUL	Act
ORD 400179 / CTR 2000/1810	ASUG / Sales Manager 1	100,00	FUL	Act
ORD 400197 / CTR 2000/1820	SAPPHIRE / Sales Manager 2	100,00	FUL	Act
ORD 400198 / CTR 2000/1820	CeBIT / Sales Manager 2	100,00	FUL	Act
ORD 400199 / CTR 2000/1820	ASUG / Sales Manager 2	100,00	FUL	Act
ORD 400200 / CTR 2000/1830	SAPPHIRE / Sales Manager 3	100,00	FUL	Act
ORD 400201 / CTR 2000/1830	CeBIT / Sales Manager 3	100,00	FUL	Act
ORD 400202 / CTR 2000/1830	ASUG / Sales Manager 3	100,00	FUL	Act
ORD 800204 / CTR 2000/1810	Rep./Maint.: Corp Offices / Sales Manager 1	100,00	FUL	Act
ORD 800205 / CTR 2000/1810	Rep./Maint.: PC / Sales Manager 1	100,00	FUL	Act
ORD 800206 / CTR 2000/1810	Rep./Maint.: Notebook / Sales Manager 1	100,00	FUL	Act
ORD 800224 / CTR 2000/1820	Rep./Maint.: Corp Offices / Sales Manager 2	100,00	FUL	Act
ORD 800225 / CTR 2000/1820	Rep./Maint.: PC / Sales Manager 2	100,00	FUL	Act
ORD 800226 / CTR 2000/1820	Rep./Maint.: Notebook / Sales Manager 2	100,00	FUL	Act
ORD 800227 / CTR 2000/1830	Rep./Maint.: Corp Offices / Sales Manager 3	100,00	FUL	Act
ORD 800228 / CTR 2000/1830	Rep./Maint.: PC / Sales Manager 3	100,00	FUL	Act

Figure 3.15 List of Settlement Rules

Cost centers and internal orders are both account assignments; in other words, you can charge costs to these objects. For a controlling implementation, it's rarely enough to draw up a list of cost centers and a list of internal orders. You also need a way of defining the nature of the cost center—the number of employees that work there, the number of square feet it occupies, the number of telephones it has, and so on. This type of information is captured as a *statistical key figure*.

3.3 Statistical Key Figures

The cost center design is not complete until you define the resource drivers that you need to perform simple allocations. Statistical key figures are used to establish ratios between cost centers. A typical key figure is the number of employees assigned to a cost center, and this is used to allocate the costs of the cafeteria from the sender cost center to all receiver cost centers with employees. Another example is the area in square feet occupied by a cost center, which is used to allocate the cleaning costs from the sender cost center to all receiver cost centers in accordance with the footage to be cleaned. We'll use square footage as a basis for assigning administration costs to a group of cost centers in Chapter 7. It's good business practice to establish *measurable* drivers as the basis for such allocations and to make it the responsibility of the cost center manager to check such information regularly so controlling can update the statistical key figures as required.

> **Lean Accounting Tip**
>
> Lean accounting generally strives to avoid allocations and to assign costs directly to the value stream wherever possible. If an allocation has to be used, a measure like square footage is considered preferable, because it's easily understood by the cost center manager, easy to check, and encourages the cost center manager to try to reduce his square footage by clearing up his "patch."

There are two types of statistical key figure:

- *Fixed values* are used for key figures that remain constant in each period (such as square footage of floor space).
- *Total values* are used for key figures that vary in each period (such as number of telephone units).

3.3 | Statistical Key Figures

> **Note**
>
> There is sometimes confusion between the use of statistical key figures and the use of activity types, since they both act as "resource drivers" and have a unit of measure (such as pieces). Statistical key figures can only be used to establish ratios or equivalences for allocations. If you want to charge work time to a project or operation time to a production order, you need to define activity types, which we'll discuss in the next section.

If you need to use data for your allocations that is already being captured somewhere in Logistics, it's possible to link statistical key figures with key figures in the Logistics Information System. This saves you from having to manually enter, for example, the number of telephone units used each month.

You'll find the master data for the statistical key figures in the STATISTICAL KEY FIGURES folder in Figure 3.1. You can also use Transaction KK01 or go to ACCOUNTING • CONTROLLING • COST CENTER ACCOUNTING • MASTER DATA • STATISTICAL KEY FIGURE • CREATE. Figure 3.16 shows a statistical key figure for the square footage of office space occupied by each cost center.

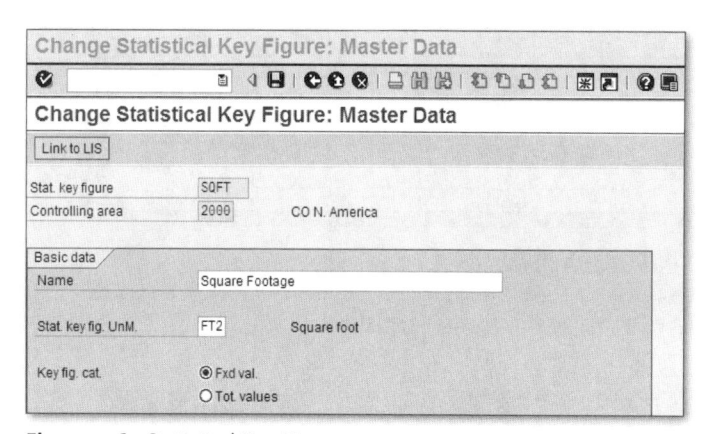

Figure 3.16 Statistical Key Figure

To link this statistical key figure with a cost center, you can take the following steps:

1. Go to ACCOUNTING • CONTROLLING • COST CENTER ACCOUNTING • ACTUAL POSTINGS • STATISTICAL KEY FIGURE • ENTER or use Transaction KB31N. This takes you to the screen shown in Figure 3.17.

115

2. Enter cost center 1000.

3. Enter the statistical key figure (SQFT) and the relevant square footage for the cost center (100 square feet in our example).

4. Save your entries.

If you set up your assessment cycles to read the statistical key figures by cost center, this can be the starting point for the allocation, as we'll see in Chapter 7.

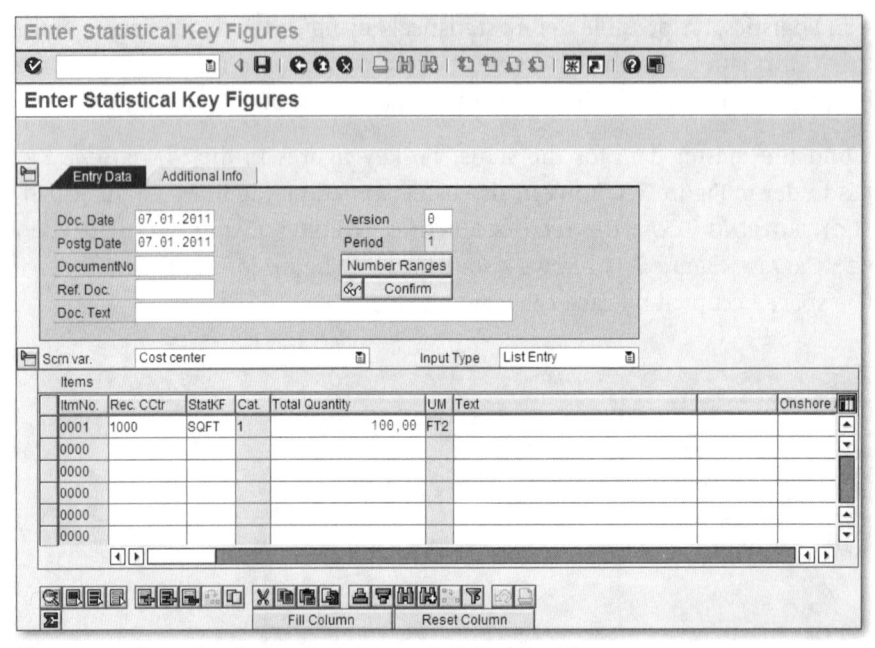

Figure 3.17 Recording Square Footage as a Statistical Key Figure

> **Fixed Values and Total Values**
>
> When you record a statistical key figure, make sure you know whether it's a fixed value or a totals value (see Figure 3.16). If the square footage is a *fixed value*, updating the value means the new value applies from the date of posting onward. If you change the value, you *overwrite* the old value. You need to enter *totals values* (such as number of telephone units) in every period. If you post the totals values twice, each record counts as a separate entry, and you may have double the number of telephone units. Before you start, check whether somebody else has already recorded the values in that period.

3.3.1 Statistical Key Figure Groups

Statistical key figure groups are much less commonly used than cost center groups and orders groups, but you can use them to help with selection in all allocation cycles. They're mainly useful if you want to plan several statistical key figures on one cost center or set up assessment cycles to read several statistical key figures as the basis for the equivalences in the allocation. The example shown in Figure 3.18 is used to select all relevant statistical key figures for planning equipment-related costs on a cost center. During planning the manager enters how many items of each he has on his cost center, and controlling uses this information to calculate the manager's equipment costs.

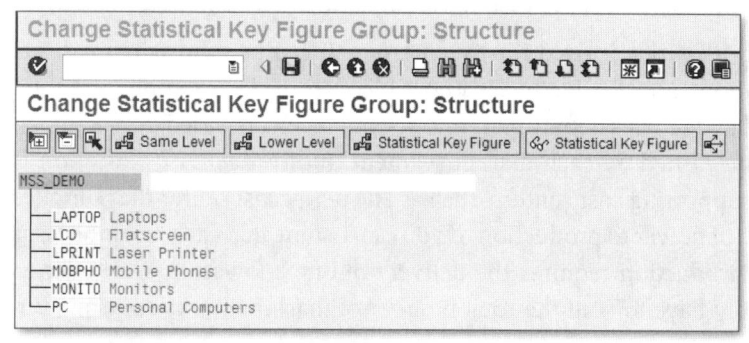

Figure 3.18 Statistical Key Figure Groups

Now that we've established the statistical key figures for the cost center, in other words, the number of employees that work there, the number of square feet it occupies, the number of telephones it has, and so on, it's time to establish the output of the cost center. This means defining activity types for the work performed by the cost center. This might take the form of machine hours, labor hours, kilowatt hours, and so on. Technically, these are all activity types, as explained next.

3.4 Activity Types

The cost center design is not complete until you define output measures for all operational cost centers in the form of *activity types*. SAP ERP distinguishes between direct activity allocation and indirect activity allocation.

- *Direct activity allocation* is used whenever a direct activity allocation is posted in CO using Transaction KB21N, working time is recorded in a time sheet in human resources, and operations are confirmed in Logistics. We'll see many examples of this kind of allocation in Chapter 6, where manufacturing work is performed for a production order or an employee's work time is posted to a project. This type of allocation is always performed in real time as the work is recorded. Think of this type of allocation as the equivalent of entering paper time sheets. It's usually possible to assign most of the work performed by blue-collar workers this way. For white-collar workers it depends whether their work lends itself to being recorded in a time sheet (such as consulting hours) or whether it's essentially overhead because employees are unwilling or unable to record it in such detail (you'll often find that this is the case for administrative tasks).

- *Indirect activity allocation* is used for two reasons. It can be used when a direct activity allocation is unfeasible but it's possible to split, for example, the total hours worked by the sales department into several receivers based, for example, on the revenue earned by each market segment. Indirect activity allocation is also used for supporting cost centers, such as an energy cost center that supplies kilowatt hours of power to production. If you can assume that each machine hour confirmed in production requires the delivery of one kilowatt hour of energy, then you simply have to read the total number of machine hours confirmed in production and have the system derive the amount of energy that must have been supplied if the machine ran for so long. Use this type of allocation when time recording is not possible and controlling has to start making business assumptions about how much work is being performed or how much energy is being supplied.

Activity types are first created without reference to a cost center but can only be used for direct activity allocations, time recording, order confirmations, or indirect activity allocations once they have been linked with the relevant cost center and an activity rate defined for the combination. The combination is created with reference to a fiscal year and contains control data for the activity allocation. We'll cover this combination and the calculation of the activity rate in more detail in Chapter 5.

You'll find the master data for the activity types using Transaction KL01 or by going to ACTIVITY TYPES in Figure 3.1. Alternatively, follow the menu path ACCOUNTING • CONTROLLING • COST CENTER ACCOUNTING • MASTER DATA • ACTIVITY TYPE •

INDIVIDUAL PROCESSING • CREATE. Figure 3.19 shows the master data for the activity type Wage Hours.

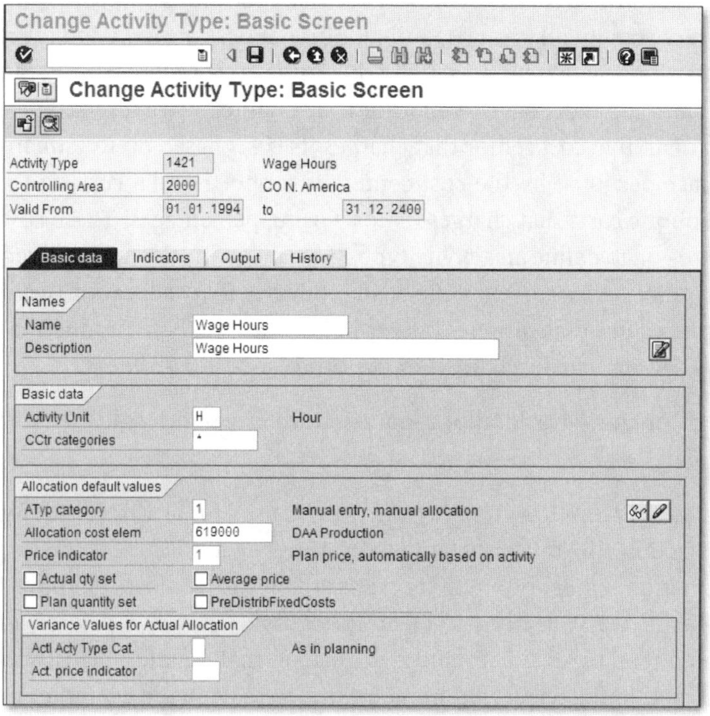

Figure 3.19 Activity Type Master Record

The first decision when defining the activity type is the choice of unit (in our example, we've used H for hours). This unit must harmonize with the units you plan to use to capture the *standard values* in your routings, recipes, and so on. It's perfectly acceptable to express standard values for machine time per operation in minutes in the routing and hours in the activity type since one unit can easily be converted into the other. It's not acceptable to maintain one in pieces and the other in hours.

The next decision is under which cost element the posting for the activity values will be recorded. The cost element will be visible in all cost center reports and provide the assignment to the cost component split, which is one of the major elements for reporting product cost estimates. We'll look at the cost element in more detail in Section 3.6.

3.4.1 Direct and Indirect Activity Allocations

As already mentioned, there are two main types of activity: those involved in *direct* activity allocations and those involved in *indirect* activity allocations. Some organizations use only direct activity allocations, and all other allocations take the form of assessments or distribution, where no activity quantity is recorded, but only the value of, for example, rent expenses are allocated. In Chapter 7 we'll look at an example of an administrative cost center that charges its costs based on the square footage of office space occupied by the cost centers it supports and a cost center used to capture telephone costs that charges its costs using percentages. These cost centers do *not* require you to define an activity type, since no quantities are involved and only the *costs* are allocated. As an example of an indirect activity allocation, we'll look at an energy cost center that supplies power in kilowatt hours to production. Here the *number of kilowatt hours* is charged to the production cost centers.

The various types of quantity-based allocation are differentiated by the activity type category.

- CATEGORY 1 (MANUAL ENTRY, MANUAL ALLOCATION) is used for all direct activity allocations (Transaction KB21N), recording work time via a time sheet (CATS), and order confirmation. Category 1 activity types are by far the most commonly used activity types in CO. You need to create category 1 activity types for all activity types you intend to include in routings, recipes, maintenance plans, and so on in Logistics and in time sheets in human resources. We'll see examples of this type of allocation when we confirm operations and perform time recordings in Chapter 6.

- CATEGORY 2 (INDIRECT DETERMINATION, INDIRECT ALLOCATION) is used when a direct activity allocation is not feasible, but the total activity usage can be inferred from the activity requested by other cost centers (sometimes called *backflushing* or *pull* allocation). In this scenario the receiver cost centers record the amount of activity they need from the sender cost center (activity input planning). This request is treated as the scheduled activity for the sender cost center, and it plans its costs and calculates the activity rate to supply the requested activity. We'll see an example in Chapter 7 where the total kilowatt hours provided by an energy cost center are calculated by looking at the machine time on the production cost centers served by this cost center.

- CATEGORY 3 (MANUAL ENTRY, INDIRECT ALLOCATION) is used when a direct activity allocation is not feasible, but a total activity can be manually entered based on experience from the previous period. So a quality cost center might record the total time worked by the quality staff and then allocate this quantity to the production cost centers based on a statistical key figure such as number of units produced.
- CATEGORY 4 (MANUAL ENTRY, NO ALLOCATION) is rarely used but records the activity quantity against the cost center without performing an allocation.

Note the second field in Figure 3.19 for the ACTUAL ACTIVITY TYPE CATEGORY. This is used when the method chosen for actual price calculation at period close is different from the method chosen to establish the standard rate. This might be the case for an energy cost center, where the actual activity is calculated as if the plan applies (this method is called *target = actual calculation*).

3.4.2 Settings for Activity Price Calculation

We'll calculate the activity price in Chapter 5, but it's important to choose the correct method of calculating the activity price when you define your activity types. This acts as a default but can be adjusted when you enter the settings for the activity rate during planning.

As organizations start to use activity prices, they typically start with a manual rate that is calculated by spreadsheet and manually updated to the price tables. This approach is easy enough for the controllers to follow but has the disadvantage that you cannot then break the activity price into its cost components (wages, salaries, depreciation, energy, and so on) and show these components in Product Costing and Profitability Analysis.

If your organization wants to have an activity rate with this level of detail, the choice is between calculating the planned rate based on the *activity* or on the *capacity*. If the activity type chosen is a fair representation of the cost center's output, it makes sense to calculate the rate based on the activity provided. Normally this is the best option, provided that the cost center output is fairly stable. But if the cost center output fluctuates wildly, it may be fairer to calculate the rate based on the output that the cost center has the capacity to produce rather than the output it's currently required to produce. This does mean, however, that the costs of the idle capacity, needed only at periods of peak demand, are passed on to the other cost centers.

The following price indicators exist:

- 1 (PLAN PRICE, AUTOMATIC BASED ON ACTIVITY)
  Use the activity as the basis when activity output is relatively stable and the rate can be calculated by dividing the cost of the resources used by the quantity of activity delivered.

- 2 (PLAN PRICE, AUTOMATIC BASED ON CAPACITY)
  Use the capacity as the basis when activity output is radically different from the cost center's capacity and the rate is best calculated by dividing the cost of the resources used by the quantity of activity that the cost center has the capacity to deliver.

- 3 (DETERMINED MANUALLY)
  Use manual prices in the early days, when an externally set price is the best way to get the project started.

Again, note the second field for the actual PRICE INDICATOR. Use this when the approach used for the standard rate calculated during planning is different from the approach used for the actual rate calculated at period close.

3.4.3 Activity Type Groups

Just as we created cost center groups and order groups, we can group activity types hierarchically. The activity type groups are much less commonly used than the other groups, since activity types are selected for reporting via the associated cost center. However, as we'll see when we look at planning in Chapter 5, it can be useful to group similar activity types to aid selection for planning. Maintenance uses the same set maintenance transactions, but the hierarchies are rarely as complex as the cost center hierarchy.

To create an activity type group, use the role COST CENTER ACCOUNTING and select the ACTIVITY TYPE GROUP folder, as shown in Figure 3.1 Alternatively, follow the menu path ACCOUNTING • CONTROLLING • COST CENTER ACCOUNTING • MASTER DATA • ACTIVITY TYPE GROUP • CREATE or use Transaction KLH1.

3.4.4 Reporting Activity Type Master Data

While the grouping of the activity type groups is generally little more than an aid to selection, a list of the existing activity types can be useful if you want to make a quick check of existing activity types and their main settings. You can access such a list in the Master Data Indexes folder in Cost Center Reporting or by using Transaction KL13. Figure 3.20 shows a sample list of the activity types used in an engineering project. These are referenced during planning and when the activities for the project are confirmed.

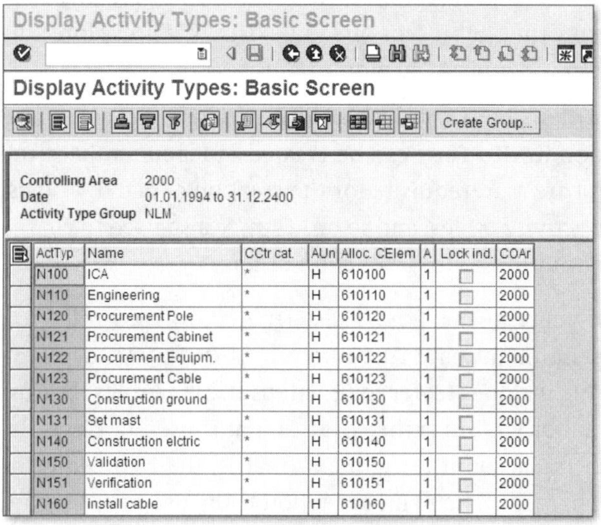

ActTyp	Name	CCtr cat.	AUn	Alloc. CElem	A	Lock ind.	COAr
N100	ICA	*	H	610100	1	☐	2000
N110	Engineering	*	H	610110	1	☐	2000
N120	Procurement Pole	*	H	610120	1	☐	2000
N121	Procurement Cabinet	*	H	610121	1	☐	2000
N122	Procurement Equipm.	*	H	610122	1	☐	2000
N123	Procurement Cable	*	H	610123	1	☐	2000
N130	Construction ground	*	H	610130	1	☐	2000
N131	Set mast	*	H	610131	1	☐	2000
N140	Construction elctric	*	H	610140	1	☐	2000
N150	Validation	*	H	610150	1	☐	2000
N151	Verification	*	H	610151	1	☐	2000
N160	install cable	*	H	610160	1	☐	2000

Figure 3.20 List of Activity Types

We've now covered the master data required for planning and operational use, but we won't be able to perform a single allocation until we've created the cost elements under which these allocations will be recorded. We saw our first cost element of this type in Figure 3.19, where we had to assign our activity type to a cost element.

3.5 Secondary Cost Elements

Cost elements are used to record transactions in CO. They can either replicate a profit and loss account (such as wages, salaries, depreciation, and material usage) or be used to record allocations in CO (such as assessments, activity allocations, and overhead). They're also used to record work in process on a production order or results analysis on a sales order or project as a basis for the balance sheet posting for work in process made during order settlement. We'll see many examples of such cost elements when we look at the postings that take place at period close in Chapter 7. We'll also need to ensure that they're in place before we embark on the planning process in Chapter 5, since the secondary cost elements record the flow of costs from sender to receiver within CO.

- The cost elements that represent profit and loss accounts are known as *primary cost elements* and are created using Transaction KA01. They can be created only if the profit and loss account they represent already exists. We'll explore this relationship in more detail in Chapter 4, Section 4.9.

- The cost elements for allocations in CO are known as *secondary cost elements* and are created using Transaction KA06. They can be created independently of the general ledger accounts and are a prerequisite for the creation of activity types, assessment cycles, indirect activity cycles, and so on. They're also used to charge overhead and to post work in process to production orders.

Figure 3.21 shows the master data in the COST ELEMENT ACCOUNTING role. You can access this by following the menu path ACCOUNTING • CONTROLLING • COST ELEMENT ACCOUNTING. This role includes fewer transactions than the roles for Cost Center Accounting and internal orders since the cost element is used not in isolation but in combination with the account assignment (that is, the cost center or order to which the costs are charged). The main exception is the use of the reconciliation ledger, which we discussed in the section on cost centers, but even this is redundant if you use the SAP ERP General Ledger. Generally, cost elements change much less frequently than cost centers and orders, because the chart of accounts is normally more stable. You're most likely to use this role or menu folder when your organization decides to revisit the structure of its chart of accounts. In some situations all that changes is the text for the cost element, but more often there's a major rethinking of the way costs flow in CO and how these flows are recorded. This puts the controlling department in the thick of the action.

The cost elements are a prerequisite for many of the steps performed in Customizing. These include:

- **Overhead calculation**
  Ensures that the correct cost elements are selected as the starting point for overhead calculation. We'll see this in Chapter 7, Section 7.2.1.

- **Order settlement**
  Ensures that the correct cost elements are selected for the sender object. We'll see this in Chapter 7, Section 7.2.4.

- **Cost component split for activity rate**
  Ensures that the cost elements are correctly assigned to components of the activity price, such as wages, salaries, depreciation, and so on, so they can then be mapped to the primary cost component split for the product cost estimate. We'll see this in Chapter 5, Section 5.1.2.

- **Cost component split for product cost estimate**
  Ensures that the cost elements are correctly assigned to the components of the cost of goods manufactured, such as material input, setup, labor, machine time, overhead, and so on. We'll see this in Chapter 5, Section 5.1.3.

- **Work in process calculation**
  Ensures that the costs are categorized properly during WIP calculation—in other words, for which cost elements WIP should be capitalized, for which cost elements there is an option to capitalize WIP, and so on. We'll see this in Chapter 7, Section 7.2.2.

- **Assets under construction**
  Ensures that the costs are categorized properly for capitalization during AUC calculation.

- **Value fields for Profitability Analysis**
  We'll see this in Chapter 6, Section 6.1.3.

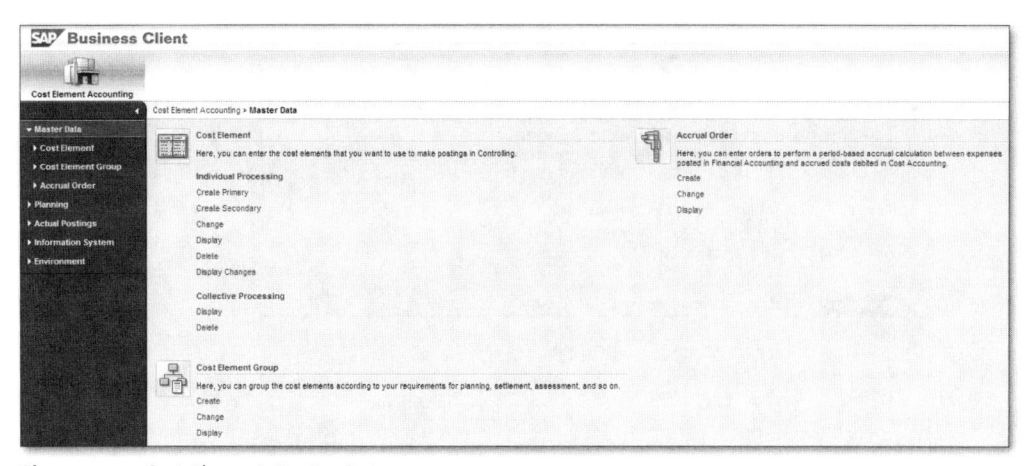

Figure 3.21 Cost Element Master Data

Many of the secondary cost elements will already have been defined in Customizing:

- **Overhead calculation**

  Used to document the assignment of overhead (category 41)

- **WIP calculation**

  Used to store the results analysis values before they're settled to FI (category 31)

- **Settlement**

  Used to store the offsetting entry for the settlement on the sender object (category 21)

For this reason, you may find that most of the cost elements you need have already been defined by the people who configured your system initially. However, you may need to create new cost elements in the following cases:

- To define how the costs for new activity types will be allocated (category 43). Usually you assign the costs of each activity type to a separate cost element, so you'll find yourself adding cost elements whenever you create new activity types.

- To define how the costs will be allocated in assessment cycles (category 42). Usually you assign the costs of each assessment cycle to a separate cost element, so you'll find yourself adding cost elements whenever you create new assessment cycles. We'll learn about this in Chapter 7, Section 7.1.3.

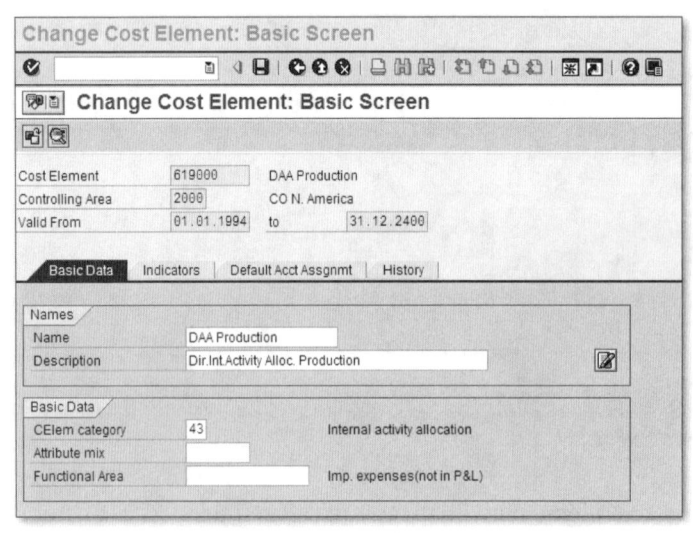

Figure 3.22 Cost Element Master Record

Figure 3.22 shows the cost element for the allocation of production activities. You can access this data by going to ACCOUNTING • COST ELEMENT ACCOUNTING • MASTER DATA • COST ELEMENT • INDIVIDUAL PROCESSING • CHANGE or Transaction KA02. To see how this cost element is used, refer back to Figure 3.19, where you can see how it's assigned to the activity type for wage hours.

3.5.1 Cost Element Groups

Cost element groups have two uses. One is as a mirror of the profit and loss statement and focuses mainly on the primary cost elements, though the structure can be extended to give a complete picture of all cost elements used. You're asked to enter the chart of accounts when you create your cost element group to ensure the link. This is something that tends to be handled centrally along with the chart of accounts, so controlling merely uses such a structure for reporting.

The other use is as a grouping to aid selection for planning and for allocations. Here controlling is in the lead, and you'll see examples of such cost element groups in use in all the allocation cycles we discuss in Chapter 7, Section 7.1.3. You'll also see them in use as selection parameters in planning in Chapter 5, Section 5.1.2. Generally, controlling defines hundreds of such cost element groups to provide just the right grouping for each planning requirement and allocation. Don't get too carried away defining cost element groups for every eventuality, or you'll find that they aren't much help. If you have a standard numbering convention for your cost elements, you can often get away with entering appropriate number ranges. So if all your assessment cost elements begin with 63XXXX, you don't need to create a special cost element group, provided you make sure that everybody follows the numbering convention when they create new cost elements. You can access this data by selecting ACCOUNTING • COST CENTER ACCOUNTING • MASTER DATA • COST ELEMENT GROUP • CHANGE or using Transaction KLH2.

Figure 3.23 shows the structure of a sample cost element group. By now the button bar for creating tree nodes and adding cost elements to the groups will be familiar from the cost center groups. Normally controllers check the cost element groups just before the period close, to make sure that all relevant cost elements are included in each group from which they intend to allocate.

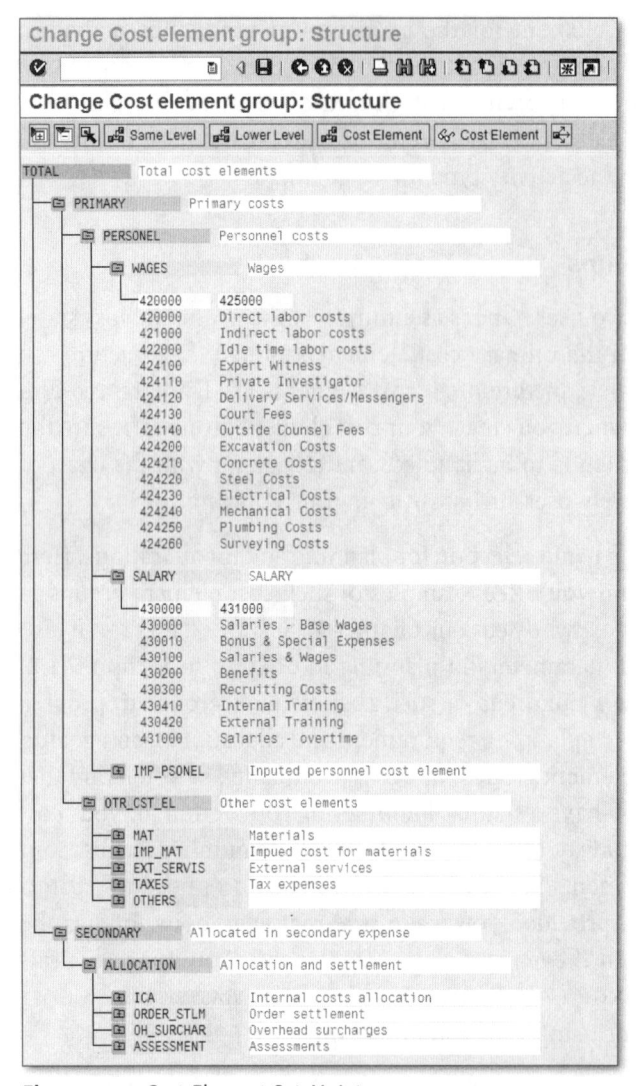

Figure 3.23 Cost Element Set Maintenance

3.5.2 Reporting on Cost Element Master Data

Whenever an organizational change occurs and allocation structures need to be revisited or there are changes to the chart of accounts, it can be useful to use the master data report of Transaction KA23 to list all cost elements, as shown in Figure 3.24. Notice that a COST CENTER field and an ORDER field are shown for the cost elements. These provide a default account assignment when costs are posted under

Secondary Cost Elements | **3.5**

a particular General Ledger account. So you might assign all price differences to one cost center, rather than assigning them to Profitability Analysis, as we'll see in Chapter 6, Section 6.1.1. The selection options for the cost element are fairly straightforward, since the cost element does not include a huge number of fields. You'll most likely use the COST ELEMENT CATEGORY option since this defines what sort of posting will be recorded under that cost element.

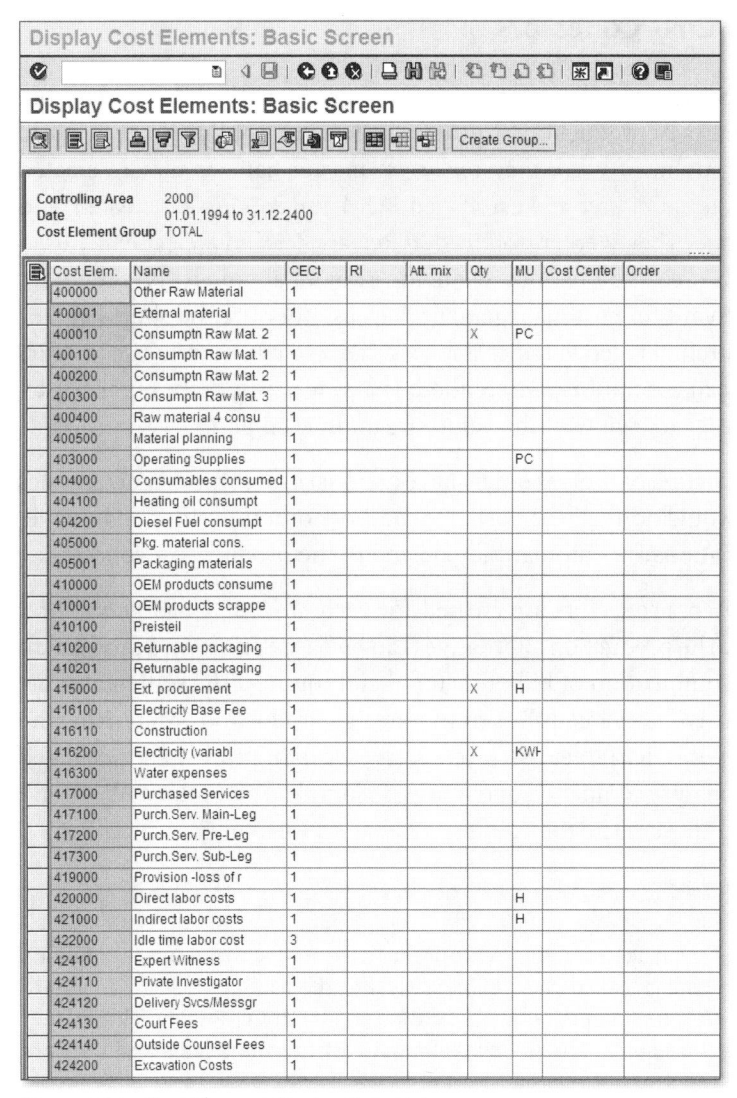

Cost Elem.	Name	CECt	RI	Att. mix	Qty	MU	Cost Center	Order
400000	Other Raw Material	1						
400001	External material	1						
400010	Consumptn Raw Mat. 2	1			X	PC		
400100	Consumptn Raw Mat. 1	1						
400200	Consumptn Raw Mat. 2	1						
400300	Consumptn Raw Mat. 3	1						
400400	Raw material 4 consu	1						
400500	Material planning	1						
403000	Operating Supplies	1				PC		
404000	Consumables consumed	1						
404100	Heating oil consumpt	1						
404200	Diesel Fuel consumpt	1						
405000	Pkg. material cons.	1						
405001	Packaging materials	1						
410000	OEM products consume	1						
410001	OEM products scrappe	1						
410100	Preisteil	1						
410200	Returnable packaging	1						
410201	Returnable packaging	1						
415000	Ext. procurement	1			X	H		
416100	Electricity Base Fee	1						
416110	Construction	1						
416200	Electricity (variabl	1			X	KWH		
416300	Water expenses	1						
417000	Purchased Services	1						
417100	Purch.Serv. Main-Leg	1						
417200	Purch.Serv. Pre-Leg	1						
417300	Purch.Serv. Sub-Leg	1						
419000	Provision -loss of r	1						
420000	Direct labor costs	1				H		
421000	Indirect labor costs	1				H		
422000	Idle time labor cost	3						
424100	Expert Witness	1						
424110	Private Investigator	1						
424120	Delivery Svcs/Messgr	1						
424130	Court Fees	1						
424140	Outside Counsel Fees	1						
424200	Excavation Costs	1						

Figure 3.24 Cost Element Master Data List

If you work for a public sector organization or a financial services company, you can skip from here to Section 3.10, since you'll have no use for product cost collectors or cost object hierarchies. If you work for a manufacturing company and want to look at options other than the classic work order approach to controlling, the next section will introduce the product cost collector.

3.6 Product Cost Collectors

We introduced product cost collectors in Chapter 2 as a special kind of order used for capturing the costs of production or process orders and settling them to stock. From a controlling point of view, they really are master data, as they're created once, when the material master and associated BOM and routing are created, and can then be left alone. They were introduced in Release 4.5 and are generally used for managing product costs by period, where the individual production orders are not considered relevant for cost management, because they are too short-lived or too similar to required detailed variance analysis. It's also common to use product cost collectors in lean accounting, where there is a move away from reporting by individual work order to a view of the value stream in each period.

The associated production or process orders have a special order type that determines that the costs that would normally be posted to the work orders during goods movements and confirmations are automatically posted to the product cost collector.

Generally, product cost collectors are created for each *production alternative* for a material and plant. The production alternatives can be based either on a production version or on the combination of bill of material and routing. The settlement rule assigns the costs to inventory but differs from a normal production order in that the settlement type is periodic. Target costs, scrap, and work in process are calculated in every period to analyze completed operations, incomplete operations (WIP), and scrap. We'll look at these calculations in more detail in Chapter 7, Section 7.2.2.

> **Product Cost Collectors and the Fiscal Period**
>
> One of the things that makes working with production orders and process orders a challenge for controlling is that they rarely fit neatly into the fiscal period and an input variance that occurs in the first period is only settled to FI and CO-PA when the order is completed in the subsequent period. Using product cost collectors can make it easier to reconcile FI and CO if you have production orders that extend over several periods, since the variance is always recognized in the period in which it occurs.

Generally, the COST OBJECT CONTROLLING menus don't support the creation of master data, since the assumption is that production orders, process orders, and so on are created on the shop floor in Logistics. The PRODUCT COST BY PERIOD menu is the exception, as the master data for product cost collectors and cost object hierarchies is maintained by the controlling department, in collaboration with production. Figure 3.25 shows the master data for PRODUCT COST BY PERIOD (see Chapter 2). Notice that you can create a product cost collector to collect the costs of the individual work orders and a cost object hierarchy to collect any costs that cannot be easily assigned to the work orders but belong to production (such as inventory variances).

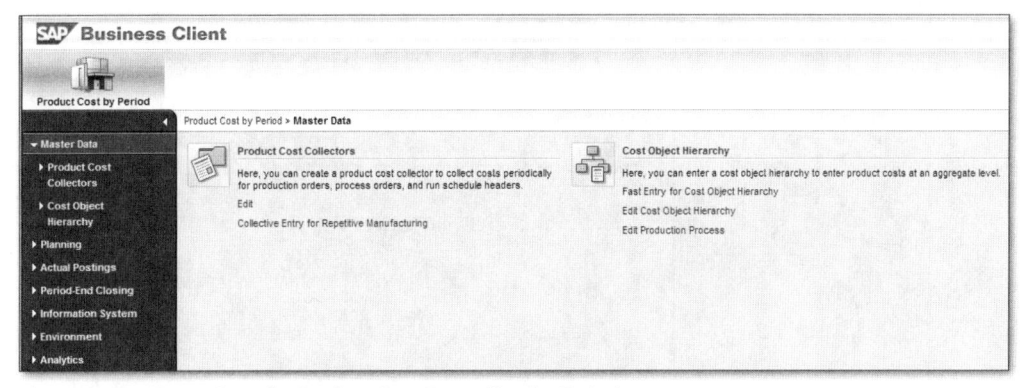

Figure 3.25 Master Data for Product Cost Controlling by Period

To create a product cost collector, go to ACCOUNTING • CONTROLLING • PRODUCT COST CONTROLLING • PRODUCT COST BY PERIOD • MASTER DATA • PRODUCT COST COLLECTOR • EDIT or Transaction KKF6N.

Figure 3.26 shows the master data for a product cost collector. Two production versions exist for the manufacture of material T-B400, on lines T-C00 and T-D00, and we've created a product cost collector for each version. The HEADER tab shows the link to the order number for each product cost collector (702645, in our example), and the link to the cost estimate, settlement rule, and production orders associated with the product cost collector are provided as buttons. We'll look at how to capture costs for a product cost collector in Chapter 6, Section 6.3.2, and how to calculate work in process, scrap, and variances in Chapter 7, Sections 7.2.2 and 7.2.3.

The product cost collector stores the costs associated with all the work orders created for a particular production alternative. If you're at a stage of the implementation where your routings are still in flux or it's not practical to track cost-relevant information by work order or product cost collector, then cost object hierarchies can represent a way of recording data for a production line or a part of the factory. We'll explore that next.

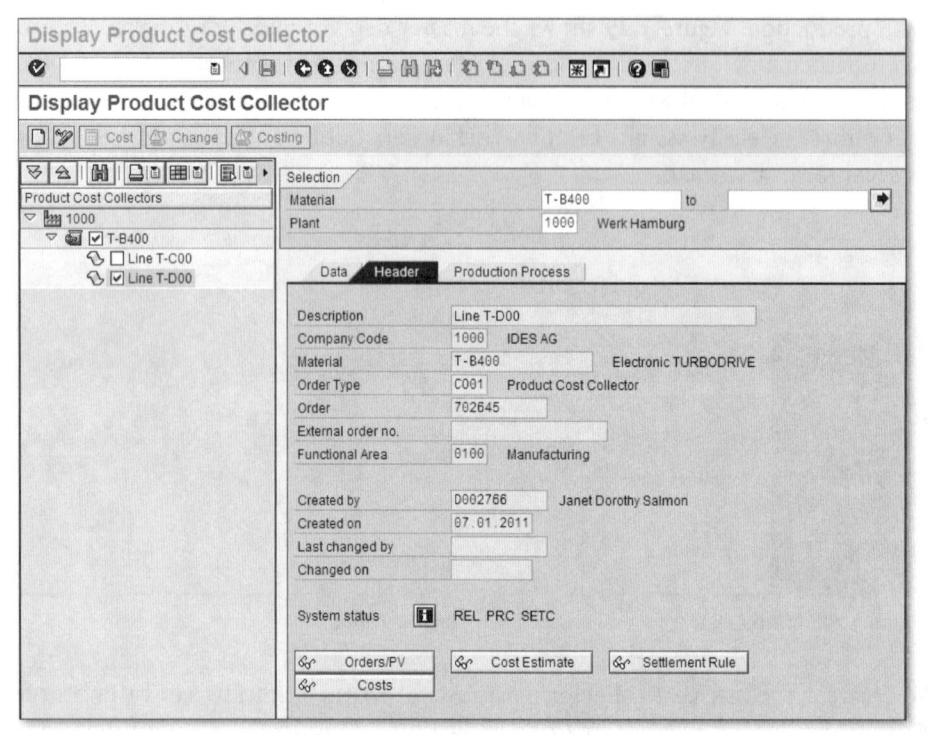

Figure 3.26 Master Data for Product Cost Collector

3.7 Cost Object Hierarchies

Cost object hierarchies are used where costs exist that cannot easily be assigned to production orders, process orders or product cost collectors. This can be the case when organizations have yet to define routings for their operations but only assign activity costs in total. They can also be used to capture certain types of costs, such as inventory differences or energy. Since the arrival of the distribution of usage variances function (see Chapter 6), the cost object hierarchy is no longer used for assigning inventory differences but can still be useful for capturing activity costs if your organization has yet to maintain accurate routings for all materials or to assign energy and other supporting costs to production.

The cost objects are account assignments to which actual costs can be assigned and typically represent plants and production lines. The bottom level of the hierarchy is the materials being manufactured on those lines.

To create a cost object hierarchy, go to ACCOUNTING • CONTROLLING • PRODUCT COST CONTROLLING • PRODUCT COST BY PERIOD • MASTER DATA • COST OBJECT HIERARCHY • EDIT COST OBJECT HIERARCHY or Transaction KKPHIE.

Figure 3.27 shows an example of a cost object hierarchy built to represent two production lines.

- This allows controlling to use a direct activity allocation (Transaction KB21N) to assign costs to the production line to capture, for example, the total machine time provided by that production line or the total hours worked by employees assigned to that production line, where the routings are incomplete. We'll look at how to perform a direct activity allocation in Chapter 6, Section 6.3.4. The important thing to know when working with cost object hierarchies is that you have to switch the screen variant from COST CENTER to SAP: COST CENTER/COST OBJECT to be able to enter the relevant node of the cost object hierarchy as a receiver of the allocation.

- It also allows controlling to use an indirect activity allocation (Transaction KSC5) to assign energy costs in kilowatt hours directly to the production line. We'll look at how to perform an indirect activity allocation in Chapter 7, Section 7.1.4. Here you'll proceed as described but enter the names of the cost object nodes rather than the operational cost centers as receivers of the allocation.

The master data includes the same assignments to the organizational entities as we saw for the cost center in Figure 3.2. In addition, we see the assignment to a variance key. This is important for variance calculation at period close. There are two ways of handling variances on a cost object hierarchy:

- You can *distribute* the costs collected on the hierarchy nodes to the associated product cost collectors or work orders. In this case, you don't need to enter a variance key, since all period close activities take place with reference to the product cost collector or attached work orders.

▶ You can *summarize* the costs collected on the assigned work orders or product cost collectors. In this case, you need the variance key, since the period close activities take place using the cost object hierarchy.

Now that we've discussed the master data elements in general that the controlling department is charged with keeping up to date, we'll discuss some of the more generic issues associated with master data maintenance.

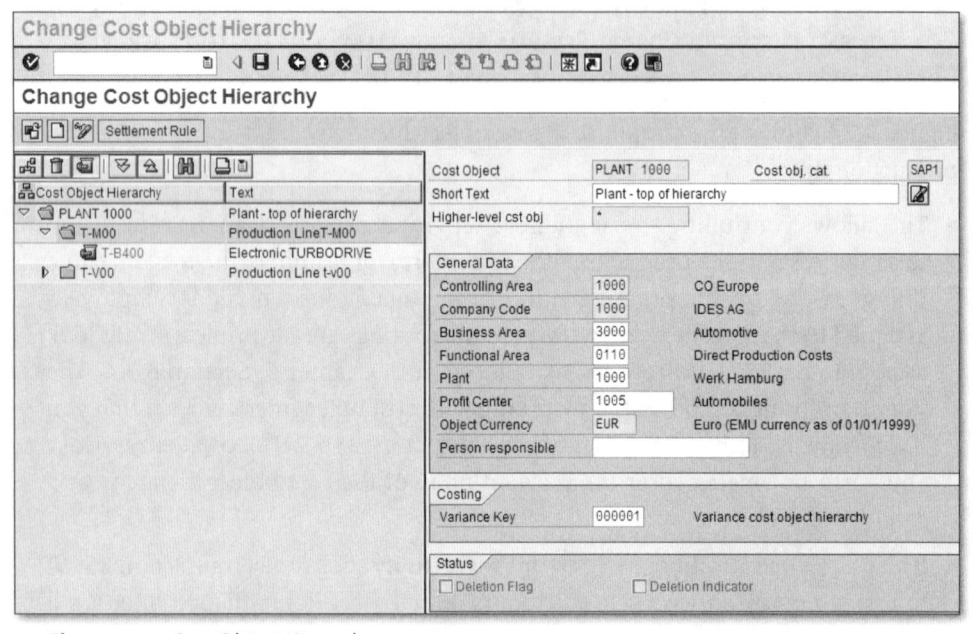

Figure 3.27 Cost Object Hierarchy

3.8 Maintenance Issues

As we discussed at the start of the chapter, compliance requirements affect the master data used in CO. Long before the Sarbanes-Oxley Act, any changes to the master data for cost centers, orders, cost elements, and activity types were documented in *change documents*. These are displayed in the HISTORY tab of each of these master data elements. This could document that the assignment of the cost center to a new profit center or the name of the cost center manager has changed. You need this information for retrospective reporting. Normally you analyze the situation for your cost centers at the current time, but for auditing purposes, you need to be able to view the situation on your cost centers in years past. Where the organization has undergone major restructuring, it's important to be able to document for the auditors when and why the change took place. Figure 3.28 shows the documents for all changes that have taken place on cost center 1000 (the Corporate Services cost center we used earlier).

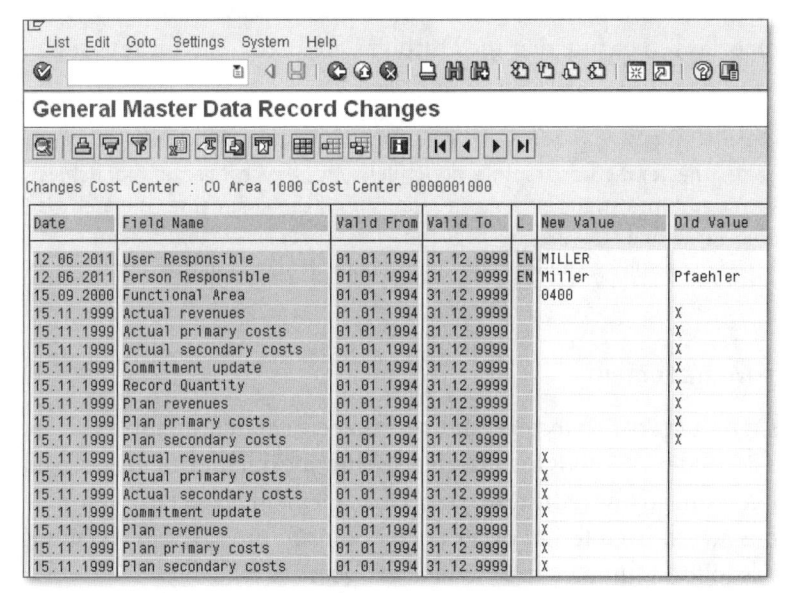

Figure 3.28 Change Documents for a Cost Center

3.8.1 Time-Dependent Fields

In our initial discussion of the different types of master data, we mentioned time-dependent fields for the asset but didn't mention the validity periods in the cost center header. If the master data never changes, the cost center validity will remain constant. However, for cost centers, cost elements, and activity types there is a concept of *data slices* in SAP ERP.

For a cost center, this might translate into the following data slices:

- From 01.01.2009 to 31.12.2009, assigned to profit center 1000
- From 01.01.2010 to 31.12.2010, assigned to profit center 1001
- From 01.01.2011 to 31.12.9999, new manager

Each time a major change is made, a new data slice is created to record the change. These slices are reflected in reporting, so calling up a report for the cost center in 2009 would show the assignment to profit center 1000 and in 2010 the assignment to profit center 1001. You see the slices when you display a cost center if you click on the DRILL-DOWN button (see Figure 3.2) and then select the data slice for the appropriate validity period.

This is also important if you're loading data into SAP NetWeaver Business Warehouse, as it's important to ensure that the attributes are up to date for reporting.

> **Caution**
>
> Since the cost center master records are time-dependent, but the cost center hierarchies are not, there are sometimes strange effects in reporting. If the cost center hierarchy is selected for a time frame that stretches over several years, cost centers that are not valid for the whole time frame will be shown with the message "No valid master record."

3.8.2 Status Management

Internal orders, product cost collectors, and cost object hierarchies don't use the concept of time-dependency. This is because they live for the duration of the task and are then completed and archived. Instead, status management is used to determine what transactions are allowed for an order at any point in time. The key statuses of an order are as follows, though many others are possible.

- **Created**
  Planned costs can be entered, but it's not possible to perform transactions that result in actual costs.

- **Released**
  Actual costs can be assigned. Usually this status covers the main lifespan of the order.

- **Technically Closed**
  This status implies that the order is complete and no more costs should be assigned to it. Any work in process or reserves created with respect to the order will be cancelled.

- **Closed**
  This status is required before an order can be deleted or archived.

For production and process orders, the other important status is Final Delivery. This status is a prerequisite for the calculation of variances and determines that any work in process for the orders is cancelled. We'll return to these statuses when we look at the period close activities for orders in Chapter 7.

While the functions we've just looked at have been around for many years, the business requirements concerning the documentation of organizational change have become considerably stricter since the Sarbanes-Oxley Act. For this reason, many organizations now have some kind of formal change request process in place for all master data changes.

3.9 Change Requests for a SOX-Compliant Master Data Process

In this chapter, we've discussed at length the need for consistent master data in CO. In practice, this often translates to authorization for the master data transactions being assigned to a few super users within an organization who are responsible for performing all the necessary data checks prior to changing a cost center or creating a new activity type.

Since the advent of the Sarbanes-Oxley Act, most organizations have some form of process in place to document why and on whose behalf a change has been made to master data, but this is often a matter of an email or phone call to initiate the request and a spreadsheet to document the nature of the change. Others use their own forms and Web services to document what changes need to be executed.

As of SAP ERP 6.0, SAP offers internal service requests to handle this kind of master data change. These include:

- A Web-based form that is filled out by the manager, requesting the change
- A workflow that documents who is to approve and who is to execute the change
- A link from the notification to the underlying transaction, allowing the controller to make the change

These are linked by a scenario that documents the technical settings required for the change request, including the link between the fields in the form and the fields in the underlying master data tables and the notification that is used to document each stage toward completion of the change request.

To illustrate the use of such forms, let's look at the cost center change request embedded in Express Planning, a Web-based planning application for cost center managers. We'll talk about Express Planning in more detail when we look at new options for planning in Chapter 10. For now, you need to understand that the first step is to have the manager confirm that the cost centers are actually his before proceeding with planning. Sometimes master data gets out of synch, and one of the good things about the planning process is that it forces the controlling department to bring the master data back up to date.

Express Planning differs from the applications we've looked at so far in that the most common way to start is to send the cost center managers an email with a link to the application (we'll look at how to set this process up in Chapter 10). The cost center manager clicks on this link and starts to update his plan. Alternatively, if you use Manager Self-Service (see the downloadable Appendix A at *www.sap-press.com*), the role includes a list of planning rounds, and you can click on the relevant planning round to access the application. Figure 3.29 shows the first step in Express Planning, where the cost center manager is asked to check whether the two cost centers currently assigned to him according to the information in the cost center master record are correct. If this is not the case, the manager can report a missing cost center or request a cost center change (see buttons in Figure 3.29). This initiates a change request.

Assuming you are the manager of these cost centers, place a request with your controlling department as follows:

1. To request a change, click on the COST CENTER CHANGE button shown in Figure 3.29. A form appears, as shown in Figure 3.30. This form displays information about you (derived from your user data in SAP ERP) and information about the selected cost center (the fields in the form are linked with the fields in the cost center master record).

2. Now document what needs to be done (in this example, you want to remove the cost center from the list) by choosing the action REMOVE FROM LIST and entering an explanatory text in this form.

3. Finally, submit the change request. When you submit the form the system generates a *notification* that routes the request to whoever must approve the change via workflow.

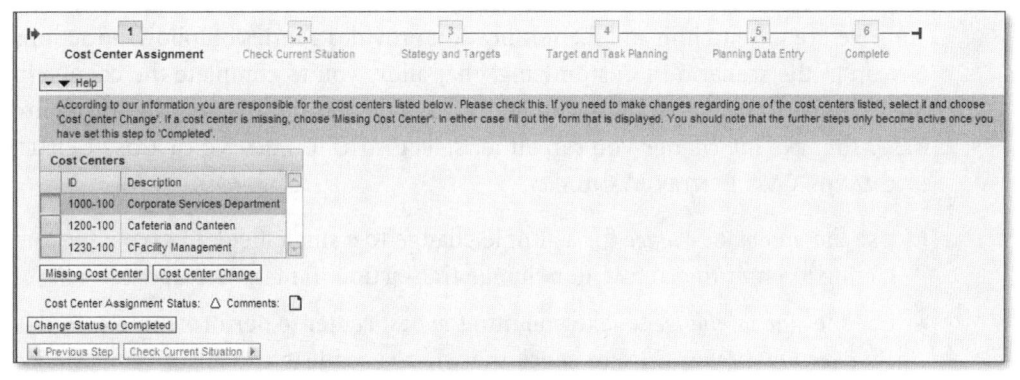

Figure 3.29 Buttons for Cost Center Change Requests in Express Planning

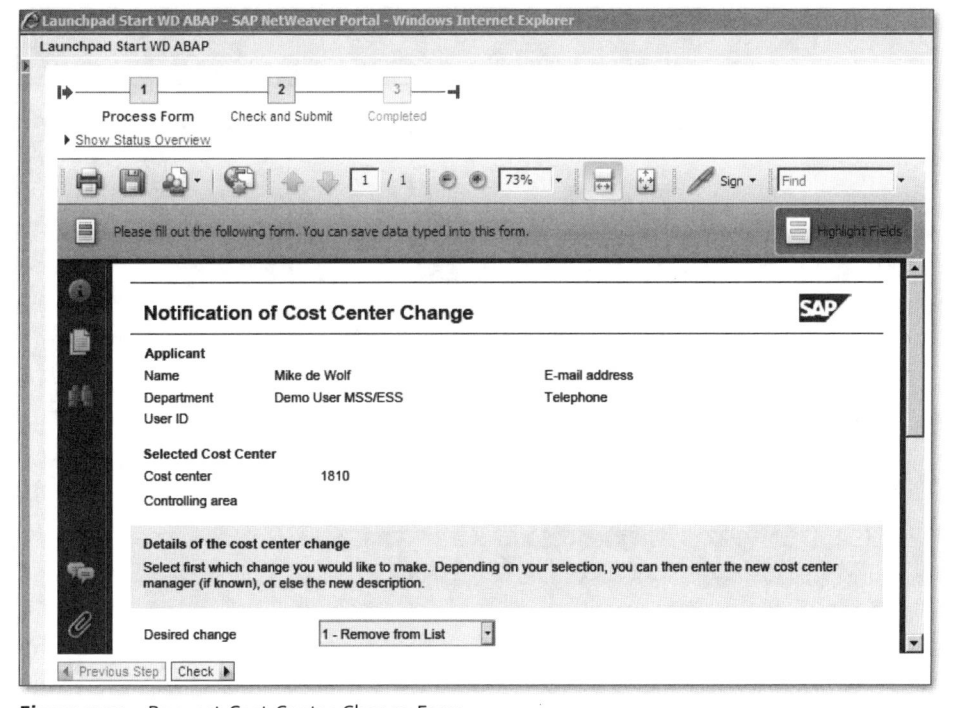

Figure 3.30 Request Cost Center Change Form

Figure 3.31 shows the notification for the change we submitted. Depending on how the workflow is configured, a manager will approve this request using a button in the notification.

It is now the controller's turn to act on the request. The workflow routes the approved request to him and the notification provides a series of follow-up actions (set up in the scenario in Customizing) that allow you to complete the change in the system. You can see these follow-up steps in the right-hand pane of Figure 3.31. To make the change you can either select Auto. Changing of Cost Center or Change Cost Center Manually.

- Use the *automatic change* for a simple change to a single field, to save you from having to enter the cost center change transaction to make the update.
- Use the *manual change* to take you into the cost center to perform more complex changes where you want to check the where-used lists and ensure consistency before making your change.

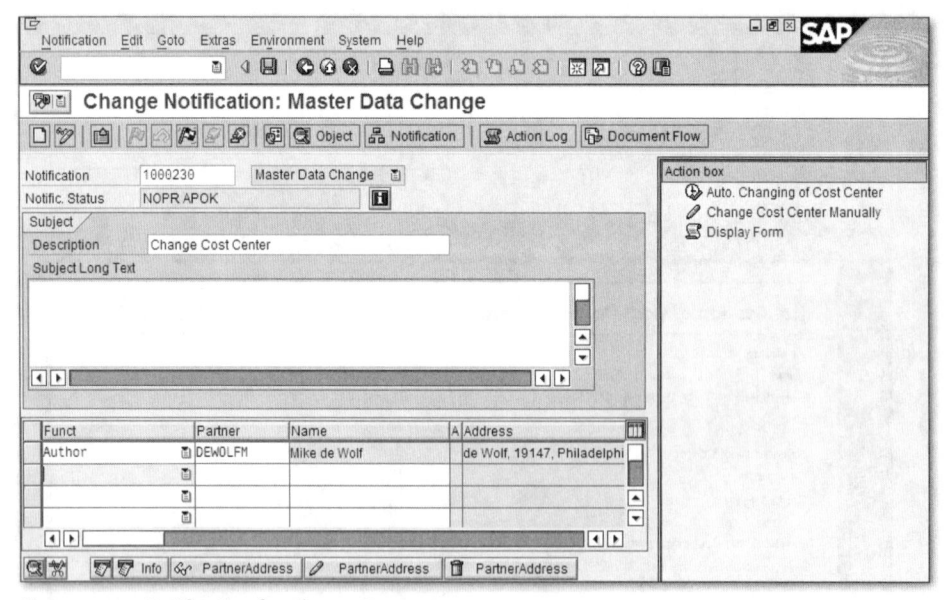

Figure 3.31 Notification for Change Request

The notification then serves as the record of the need for the change and who approved it in the system, supplementing the information in the change documents that we saw in Figure 3.28.

> **Change Requests in SAP ERP**
>
> We'll look at how to configure this change request in Chapter 9 and compare this approach with other types of change request available from enhancement package 5.

3.10 Summary

In this chapter we looked at the key elements of cost center design and the use of activity types and statistical key figures. We looked at the use of internal orders, product cost collectors, and cost object hierarchies and discussed the various groupings that exist in the system for reporting and allocations. You should now feel confident when you create and change this master data and understand the implications of any change in CO on other master data in SAP ERP. We also discussed compliance in this area and introduced the change request as a way of promoting compliance for master data control. We'll return to the subject of compliance in Chapter 9. But first, we'll look at master data that isn't owned by controlling, but where you have a custodial interest in ensuring its accuracy since wrong prices in Materials Management lead to wrong values in CO.

In this chapter we'll discuss the relevant fields for Product Costing and Profitability Analysis in the material master, customer master, work center, project, and investment program together with how they relate to the controlling processes, such as setting standard costs, calculating actual costs, cross-company costing, and so on.

4   Master Data Where Controlling Is a Stakeholder

In Chapter 3 we discussed the master data where the controlling department is in the lead, including cost centers and activity types. These are used in conjunction with work centers and routings in production to put a value on the activities performed in the course of the manufacturing process. To create an estimate of the costs to manufacture a product, this master data is combined with information in the bill of material to determine the quantities of materials used. Since the quantities in the bill of material and routing affect the standard costs, controlling has a shared responsibility with production for ensuring the accuracy of this master data. Technically it's possible to store two sets of BOMs and routings, one for controlling and one for production, and this can be a good way to get the controlling implementation off the ground while the production implementation is still in its infancy. In the long term, however, keeping separate structures in controlling is dangerous, because they can cease to reflect the reality on the shop floor. It's much better to work with production to have a single, accurate set of master data to determine what the material and activity input for each product is.

A material master must exist for all materials that are purchased, manufactured, or sold. The material master is the key element where the logistics requirements (size, weight, manufacturing approach, and so on) meet the requirements of the financials processes (standard price, future price, account determination, and so on). The material master is the single version of the truth. There can be only one material master for each material in each plant. Controlling must work with all the other stakeholders to ensure the accuracy of the master data. Since the same material may be acquired from multiple sources, we'll also look at how to set up procurement alternatives and establish mix relationships for Product Costing.

A customer master must exist before a sales order or an invoice can be created. Again, the requirements for the sales processes and for the handling of accounts receivable meet the controlling requirements in terms of key data for segmenting customers for Profitability Analysis. It's important to consider at an early stage to what extent customer-specific costs are relevant for controlling, since this will determine whether sales controlling takes place in Profitability Analysis alone or whether you have a requirement for sales order controlling, as we saw in Chapter 2.

We'll also look at projects and investment programs, where controlling is clearly a major stakeholder, but project or program management is in the lead. Here the role of controlling is to provide a basic structure for the projects (perhaps distinguishing investment projects from cost projects) and determine at what level the budget is set (for example, only for the top nodes of the project), for which work breakdown structure (WBS) elements actual costs can be captured (it may not make sense to capture costs for every WBS element in the structure), and for which WBS elements plan costs will be captured (it's common practice to plan at a much finer level of detail than actual costs are calculated). Finally we'll look at the profit and loss accounts and their relationship with the cost elements in the Controlling component of SAP ERP Financials (which we refer to as CO moving forward). Normally the role of controlling there is merely as a custodian of the data, ensuring that all follow-up processes are handled correctly. Controlling tasks might include the classification of these cost elements for overhead calculation, WIP calculation, or settlement.

As we discussed in Chapter 1, CO is highly reliant on the existence of standards in the form of standard prices. You might feel that the standard prices are not obviously master data, in the way that the weight and dimensions of a product clearly are, but they have to be in place before any of the goods movements can begin or planning can commence. So we'll look at the different methods of price setting in SAP ERP before we look at the planning process in the next chapter.

4.1 Material Masters

The material master is arguably the most important master record in Logistics. You'll need to create a material master for any material that is bought or sold on a commercial basis or is used, consumed, or created in production. Materials are distinguished by *material type*. Common material types include raw materials and trading goods for purchased materials and finished and semifinished materials for manufactured materials.

The material master is also the best example of shared master data, with each department having its own *view* of the material master.

- The basic view assigns the material to a *material group* and a *product hierarchy*, both of which are important for selecting the material for reporting. Most organizations have so many materials that controlling almost always makes a preliminary selection of the data using the material group or product hierarchy or another form of classification.

- The accounting view contains the valuation class that determines how the material costs are assigned to accounts and the price control indicator that determines whether the material is valued at a *standard price* or at a *moving or weighted average price*. Controlling has its part to play in recommending the price strategy for each type of material.

- The costing view contains the base data required for Product Costing, including the costing lot size (the standard output on which all targets are based) and key data affecting the costing process, such as the default production version or whether the material is a co-product. It also contains *planned prices* that can be used to set a standard price for the material in the future. Controlling "owns" these views, and it's their job to ensure that the correct prices and lot sizes are stored here.

- The MRP view contains additional data that's important for the costing process, including whether the material is make-to-stock or make-to-order, and settings that affect the allowance for planned scrap. Production owns these views, but it's important for controlling to understand which type of manufacturing is being performed, because this determines which will be the most appropriate form of Cost Object Controlling (product cost by order, product cost by period, or sales order controlling) as we saw in Chapter 2.

- The sales view contains key data for the sales process, including the assignment of the material to a division, which determines the business area to which the material is assigned. Probably the most important link from a controlling point of view is to the price conditions used to create the sales order, since these determine the degree of detail that's available for analyzing sales deductions in Profitability Analysis.

To access the material master, you can use Transaction MM03 or go to LOGISTICS • MATERIALS MANAGEMENT • MATERIAL MASTER • MATERIAL • DISPLAY • DISPLAY CURRENT and select the appropriate view(s). To display some of the views, you'll have to enter the appropriate organizational unit(s). The costing, accounting, and MRP views also require you to enter a plant, and the sales view requires you to enter a sales organization and a distribution channel.

> **Key Dates in the Material Master**
>
> It's possible to schedule changes to the material master for a key date in the future. But this doesn't apply to some data affecting costing, including configuration data, production versions, and co-products where changes cannot be scheduled.

4.1.1 Basic View

Let's start with the basic view. For controlling purposes the assignment to a material group and a product hierarchy are important for reporting and we'll see these fields showing up later as characteristics in CO-PA. For product costing the assignment of a base *unit of measure,* is critical because this determines the unit for the costing lot size. For a material like a pump, choosing the unit of measure is something of a nonevent, since it's easy to count units of such products. In other industries, the unit of measure presents more challenges. For foods, the physical quantity, such as a liter of milk or a pound of cheese tells you the volume but little about the value of the goods. In these industries, SAP Catch Weight Management is used to store two completely separate units of measure for each material—one referring to the physical quantity and the other to the valuation-relevant quantity. There has been significant development effort in this area in enhancement packages 4 and 5, so if you're in the food industry, it's probably worth taking a look at the latest developments, since they allow you to use the double quantity units within core SAP ERP.

Also notice that the basic view is not assigned to an organizational unit. This is master data in the true sense of the word: It applies to everybody. The same data is repeated in the sales view (product hierarchy, material group) and the purchasing view (material group). Figure 4.1 shows the basic data for a pump, material number P-100. Later you'll be able to enter a lot size for the pump in pieces and select it for reporting via the product hierarchy or the material group shown here.

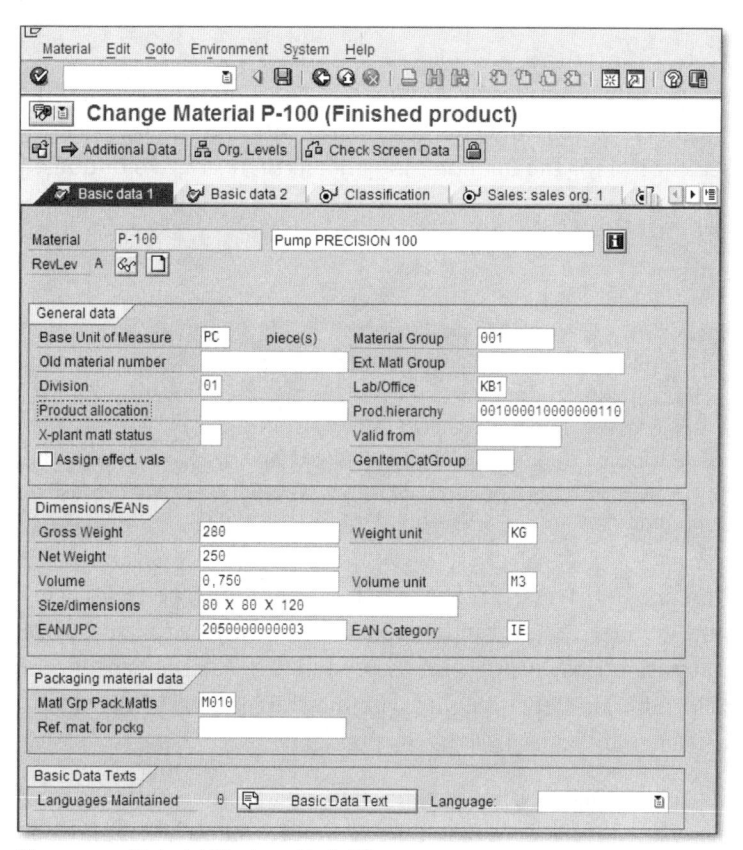

Figure 4.1 Material Master – Basic View

4.1.2 Accounting View

The accounting view assigns the material to a particular *valuation class*, which in turn determines to which *material account* the product costs will be assigned. The valuation class is derived from the material type. So it's possible to assign raw material costs to a different account from finished goods inventory. If your manufacturing involves make-to-order or engineer-to-order, you can also set up different valuation classes for sales order stock (inventory relating to a single sales order) or project stock (inventory relating to a single project), enabling you to separate such inventory values from inventory that has been made to stock and can be issued to any sales order. The accounting view assigns the material to a division, a characteristic used in Profitability Analysis to determine to which business area the material belongs.

The accounting view records the quantity of goods in stock and their value. It's updated every time a goods movement takes place. The value of the goods in stock depends on the price control for the material. In general, there are two options:

- Standard price (S)
- Moving average price (V)

> **Choosing the Correct Price Control Indicator**
>
> The moving average price is usually used for raw materials and the standard price for manufactured materials. SAP recommends that you don't use the moving average for manufactured materials because the moving average can become distorted as a result of the timing of cost postings, settlements, and the number of orders in progress for the same material (for more information, see SAP Note 81682).

From Release 4.6C the moving average price, which changes in response to every goods movement and invoice receipt, can be replaced by a *weighted average price*, which is calculated at period close using values stored in the Material Ledger. The accounting view looks different depending on whether the material is assigned to a plant in which the Material Ledger is active or not.

Figure 4.2 shows the accounting view for a material in a plant *without* the Material Ledger. The material is valued at standard costs (price control S), and a link is provided to the *standard cost estimate* that was used to calculate the standard costs. We'll look at how to set the initial standard price later in this chapter and how to calculate and update the standard price as part of the planning process in Chapter 5.

If you want to use a weighted average price rather than a moving average price, you should activate the Material Ledger for the relevant plants. This is a switch that's set in configuration for each plant.

Material Masters | 4.1

> **Activating the Material Ledger**
>
> Activating the Material Ledger has a considerable impact on your SAP ERP system. Before you embark on such a journey, read the detailed explanation in SAP Note 398949.

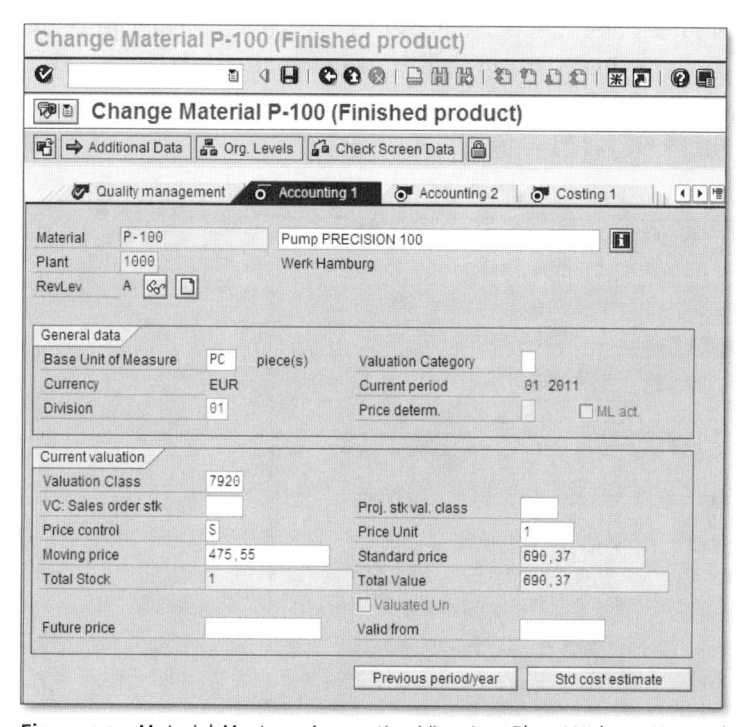

Figure 4.2 Material Master – Accounting View in a Plant Without Material Ledger

Activating the material ledger for the plant changes the look of the accounting view, creating additional tables to store the inventory values in multiple currencies and requiring an additional process at period close to calculate the periodic unit price for each material. Figure 4.3 shows the accounting view for a material in a plant *with* the Material Ledger. You reach this screen by the same route you take to get to Figure 4.2. The difference is that material ACT-DCD is in plant 6000, where we've activated the Material Ledger for demo purposes, whereas the pump was in plant 1000, where the Material Ledger isn't active. The PRICE DETERM. checkbox determines which form of Material Ledger postings you use for the material.

149

4 | Master Data Where Controlling Is a Stakeholder

▶ **Transaction-based**
Transaction-based simply means that a moving average price is created automatically in the currencies you've activated in the Material Ledger. It behaves exactly like the normal moving average price, but in multiple currencies.

▶ **Single-/multilevel**
Single-/multilevel price determination means that a weighted average price (or periodic unit price) is calculated using a costing run at period close.

We'll look at this process in more detail in Chapter 7.

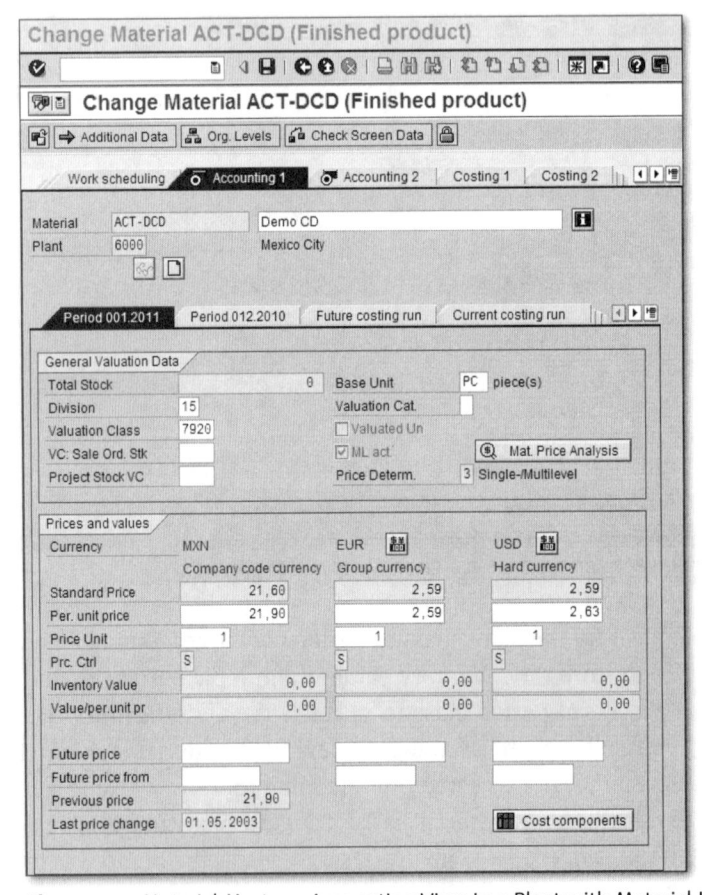

Figure 4.3 Material Master – Accounting View in a Plant with Material Ledger

In addition to storing the prices that are used for valuing goods movements, the accounting view includes a second set of prices that are used for balance sheet valuation at period close. There are various methods for valuing inventory, including LIFO (last-in, first-out), FIFO (first-in, first-out), and lowest of cost or market. German law also distinguishes between commercial law and tax law, so you'll see both commercial prices and tax prices in this screen. In the United States it's becoming common to distinguish between IFRS (which uses FIFO) and local GAAP. At the time of writing it's not yet a legal requirement for U.S. companies to store both, but there's undeniably a global trend toward IFRS reporting. We'll look at the options for balance sheet valuation later in this chapter.

4.1.3 Costing Views

The costing view (see Figure 4.4) contains control data for Product Costing, such as the costing lot size (the default quantity on which any cost estimate is based) and data to build up the quantity structure for Product Costing.

General Data

The GENERAL DATA section in the top section of the costing view has a control function.

- The WITH QTY STRUCTURE checkbox determines that the costs for the material are usually calculated using its bill of material and routing (its quantity structure). This is the default for all manufactured materials.

- The MATERIAL ORIGIN checkbox determines that the material costs include details of the material used and the assignment to the cost element. This is particularly important for *variance analysis* since it determines the level of detail stored on the production order (only the account information or details of the individual materials assigned to that account). If the checkbox is not already selected in your master data, use Report RKHKMAT0 to prepare your data. But be aware that setting the flag significantly increases the amount of data written to the database during each transaction.

- The ORIGIN GROUP field serves a similar purpose and predates the MATERIAL ORIGIN checkbox. Generally, if you work with the MATERIAL ORIGIN checkbox, you don't need to enter an origin group, unless you specifically need to distinguish between different groups of material assigned to one cost element when you're setting up your cost components for Product Costing. This can be useful if you want a simple way of classifying different types of material for costing.

- You use the OVERHEAD GROUP field if you need to calculate overhead percentages that are specific to certain groups of materials. In our example, the overhead group is SAP10. We'll use this overhead group in Chapter 7 to determine the percentage of overhead to be applied for all materials assigned to overhead group SAP10.
- The PROFIT CENTER field assigns the material to a profit center for Profit Center Accounting. It's copied into all purchase order items, production orders, sales order items, and so on created for this material, unless you define a substitution rule to invoke a different logic. As we saw when we looked at the cost center in the previous chapter, the profit center is one of the key ways of segmenting your business, so it's worth giving a lot of thought to how you want each material to be reflected in your Segment Reporting if you report according to IFRS 8 (International Financial Reporting Standards) or IAS 14 (International Accounting Standards).
- The variance key determines how variances are calculated and is copied into the production orders, process orders, and so on. We'll copy this variance key into a production order and then use it to calculate the variances for our production order in Chapter 7.

Quantity Determination

The costing view contains the costing lot size—the standard output quantity for the material and the basis for the standard costs. All other fields in this block are optional. You can specify that a particular bill of material and routing should be used as a basis for costing, though most customer sites use the configuration settings for quantity structure determination in the costing variant to determine which BOM and routing are used.

There are also several fields that overlap with fields in the MRP views, which include the following (also shown in Figure 4.4):

- The production versions are defined centrally and determine the BOM and routing used in each version. We saw these used when we looked at product cost collectors in Chapter 3, since you generally define a separate product cost collector for each production version. We'll also see them later in this chapter, when we define procurement alternatives for costing.

- The CO-PRODUCT and FXD PRICE checkboxes determine the handling of co-products (multiple outputs from the same production process). The JOINT PRODUCTION button determines how costs are split to the products. We'll return to these checkboxes when we look at the bills of material for such products. Selecting the CO-PRODUCT checkbox also affects how you perform Cost Object Controlling, since as we noted in Chapter 2, only product cost by order is possible for joint production.

- Finally, if your manufacturing process involves multiple plants, the special procurement key labeled SPEC. PROCUREMENT COSTING in Figure 4.4 can provide a link to the other plants for costing. So you can establish in Customizing that a special procurement key links an input material in plant A with an output material in plant B. When costing the input material in plant A, the system then reads or calculates the product costs for the output material in plant B and rolls them up through the costing structure. You can use transfer control in Customizing to determine whether a new cost estimate is created in the other plant or an existing cost estimate is copied from the other plant.

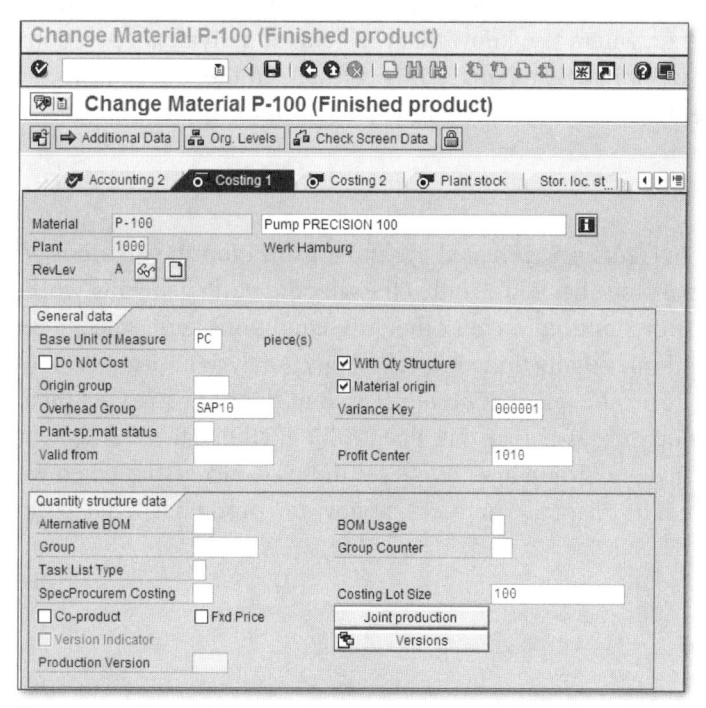

Figure 4.4 Material Master—Costing View

4.1.4 MRP View

Although not owned by the controlling department, the MRP views contain several fields that influence Product Costing.

When we talked about Cost Object Controlling in Chapter 2, we discussed the options for make-to-order and make-to-stock. The procurement type in the MRP 2 view controls whether the material is made in-house or procured externally or both. Depending on your configuration, the strategy group or the MRP class controls how the requirements category for the sales order item is determined. The requirements category determines whether the material is made to order or made to stock. The settings in the MRP 4 view control whether all dependent items are made to order (individual requirements) or whether standard items are made to stock (collective requirements).

The options for setting planned scrap are also covered here. You can enter component scrap, where you know that a given percentage of additional components are usually wasted during manufacture. Entering scrap results in the component requirements being raised accordingly when the material usage is calculated. You can also enter assembly scrap, where you know that problems at individual operations usually result in the assembly being damaged. This results in the order lot size or the costing lot size being raised accordingly to end up with the desired lot size.

4.1.5 Sales View

The sales view shown in Figure 4.5 is created by sales organization and distribution channels, organizational units that you'll find in the sales order. It's generally worth clicking on the CONDITIONS button to check the price conditions here, since these affect the revenues and sales deductions in Profitability Analysis. Normally, controlling has no control over the negotiation of price conditions but analyzes them and makes recommendations as part of sales controlling. Notice the assignment to a division and to a material group here. We'll see these characteristics when we create a sales order item in Chapter 6 and look at how the product is reflected in Profitability Analysis.

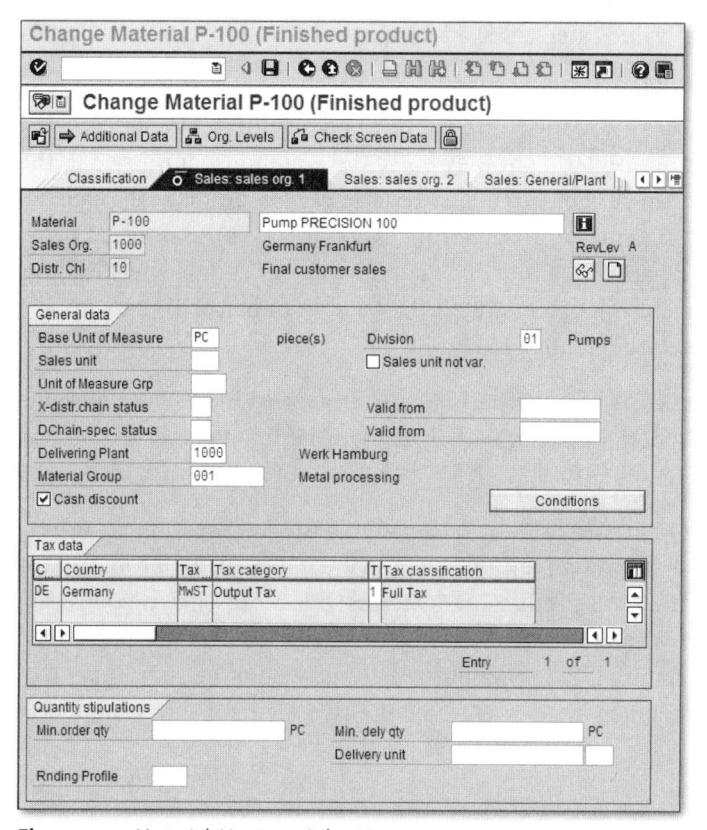

Figure 4.5 Material Master – Sales View

4.1.6 Batches

In the chemical, pharmaceutical, and food industries, materials have to be managed in *batches* to ensure traceability and ensure that the batch meets the specifications of the process (often determined via a quality control process). The batch quantity represents a nonreproducible unit with unique specifications. The batch is a subset of the material, and batches of a material are managed separately in stock. The specifications for the batch are set up using classification, so a batch might be identified, for example, by its viscosity and its color.

For accounting, the batch can be valued separately, especially if it includes active ingredients or other elements that significantly affect the value of a volume of material (such as the fat content in a liter of milk or a kilogram of cheese). This is achieved by setting the value category to allow split valuation in the ACCOUNTING 1 view.

Batch management may apply to the entire logistics chain, with raw materials being managed as batches from the moment they enter the warehouse until sale to the final customer. A batch can be allocated to a material at various points in the logistics process by creating a batch master record with a specific ID. For example, a batch ID may be created for a partial quantity of a material that has certain specifications as it leaves the manufacturing process, with the batch number or ID providing a unique identification of the quantity produced.

In Product Costing, the costs of individual batches are mixed to provide the value per material. In the Material Ledger, each batch can be handled as if it were a separate material.

We've now looked at the master data for each material that we might make or sell, but we cannot sell such a product until we've also created a customer master for the customer who will buy this product. In CO terms, this represents the transition from Product Costing, where all activities, whether make or buy, are performed with reference to the material, to Profitability Analysis, where the combination of customer and product comes into focus, since the two elements are captured in the sales order.

4.2 Customer Masters

In Chapter 2 we looked at an example of a report for Profitability Analysis. The key information for any kind of customer-based analysis is set up in the customer master, which is shared between the sales department and accounts receivable. For controlling there is significantly less information in the customer master than in the material master (which controls the whole procurement and production process). The main points of interest are the code for the customer (which is used to select the customer for analysis or as a receiver of an allocation) and the company code (which determines which company will carry the revenue for any sales to this customer). The customer master also includes the reconciliation account used to store details of the open item in the General Ledger. This reconciliation account stores the revenue earned with the customer and appears in account-based Profitability Analysis. This account is also linked with a value field for profitability reporting.

To create a customer master, you can use Transaction XD01 or go to LOGISTICS • SALES AND DISTRIBUTION • MASTER DATA • BUSINESS PARTNER • CUSTOMER • CREATE • COMPLETE. Figure 4.6 shows a sample customer and the assignment to the customer account. We'll see this account when we deliver goods to our customer in Chapter 6, Section 6.1.3. To understand the significance of the customer account, you need to understand how accounts receivable links with the General Ledger. The General Ledger stores the totals for this account, so that customer receivables in total can be displayed in the balance sheet. Accounts Receivable, on the other hand, stores details of the payments owed by every customer, so that each open item can be cleared when the customer makes the payment. The information shown here is sufficient to monitor any customer outside of your organization. We'll look at the fields relevant for monitoring sales between affiliated companies later in the chapter.

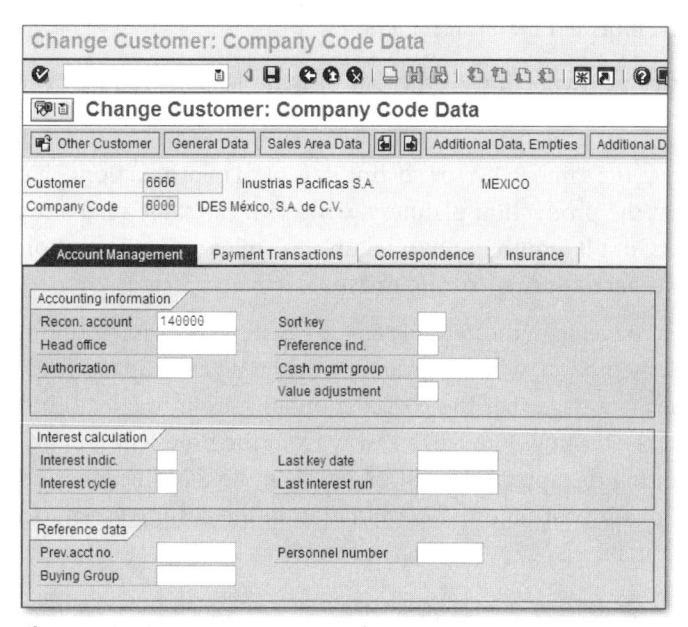

Figure 4.6 Customer Master Record

Because of the central nature of both the material master and the customer master, there has been a trend in recent years to take maintenance out of the hands of the individual departments and perform maintenance centrally. You might want to refer to Chapter 9 to find out how to handle material and customer masters centrally before moving on to the more local production master data, where it's still much more common for local plants to perform master data maintenance. We'll now look at the master data that needs to be in place before the product can be manufactured, namely, the bill of material, the routing, and the work centers where the operation is performed.

4.3 Bills of Material

In Chapter 2, we introduced the multilevel costed BOM as one of the key reports for Product Cost Planning. The BOM is a multilevel structure that describes which raw materials are used to make a quantity of semifinished product and which semifinished products are used to make a quantity of finished product. Before a material can be included in a bill of material, it must exist as a material master. The levels of the bill of material are then built up in stages, with a BOM existing for each finished and semifinished material.

There are two approaches to ownership of the bill of material for Product Cost Planning.

1. The first is simply to use the same BOM for costing as is used in production. This has the advantage that the production planners work with the same structures as the cost accountants, but it requires you to set up clear rules for collaboration so that any errors discovered during costing can quickly be corrected.
2. The other approach is to create dedicated BOMs for costing. This can be useful at the start of an implementation, where production may not yet be up to speed. The approach has the advantage that the cost accountants are in the lead, but it risks inaccuracies if the costing BOM drifts away from the production BOM. This is handled by setting the appropriate BOM usage in the BOM header and then configuring the quantity structure determination in the costing variant to select the most appropriate BOM for product costing.

> **Lean Accounting Tip**
>
> Lean accounting encourages the use of accurate BOMs and routings to allow you to backflush using the standard material and production costs. Having more than one BOM for any given product is wasteful. It's better to have one accurate set of BOMs than two different ones and spend time arguing about whose BOM represents the true material usage.

To display a bill of material, use Transaction CS03 or go to LOGISTICS • PRODUCTION PLANNING • MASTER DATA • BILLS OF MATERIAL • BILL OF MATERIAL • MATERIAL BOM • DISPLAY, and enter the material number, plant, and appropriate BOM usage.

Figure 4.7 shows a sample bill of material for the manufacture of the pump P-100. It consists mostly of materials of item category L for materials kept in stock. Items of category R have to be cut to size first, and the BOM contains directions for this process. Other BOMs may contain materials of category N for materials that have to be procured specially and text items. Figure 4.8 shows how this bill of material is used in costing. The left side of the screen shows the eight materials used to make the pump. Since the top five materials are assemblies, they have their own bills of material, which are also evaluated during costing. Clicking on the triangle icon takes you to the costed bill of material for each item. The process of rolling up the costs through the multilevel BOM structure is called a product roll-up.

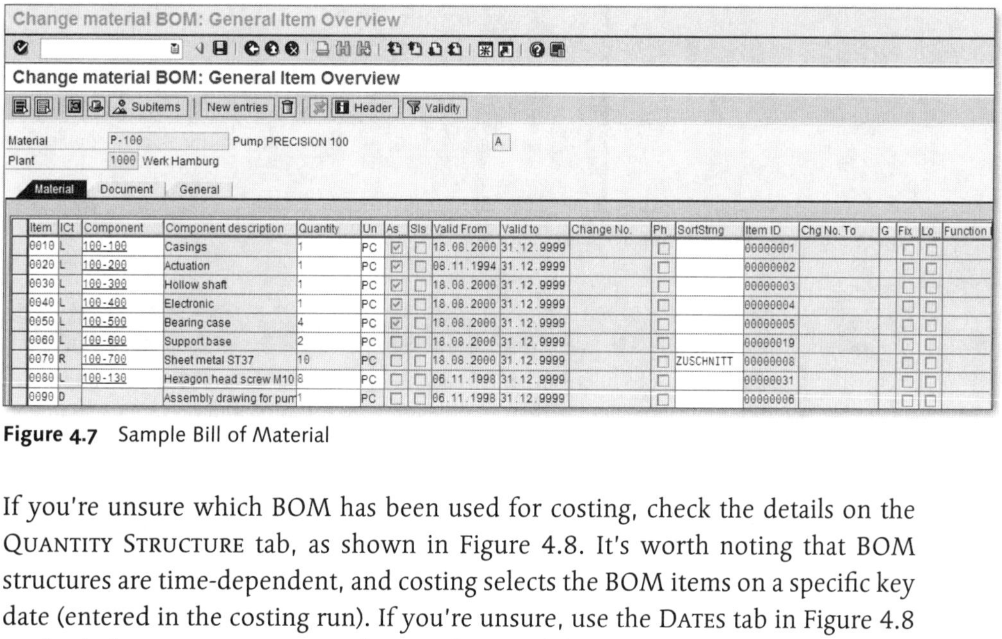

Figure 4.7 Sample Bill of Material

If you're unsure which BOM has been used for costing, check the details on the QUANTITY STRUCTURE tab, as shown in Figure 4.8. It's worth noting that BOM structures are time-dependent, and costing selects the BOM items on a specific key date (entered in the costing run). If you're unsure, use the DATES tab in Figure 4.8 to check the quantity structure date used to read the BOM.

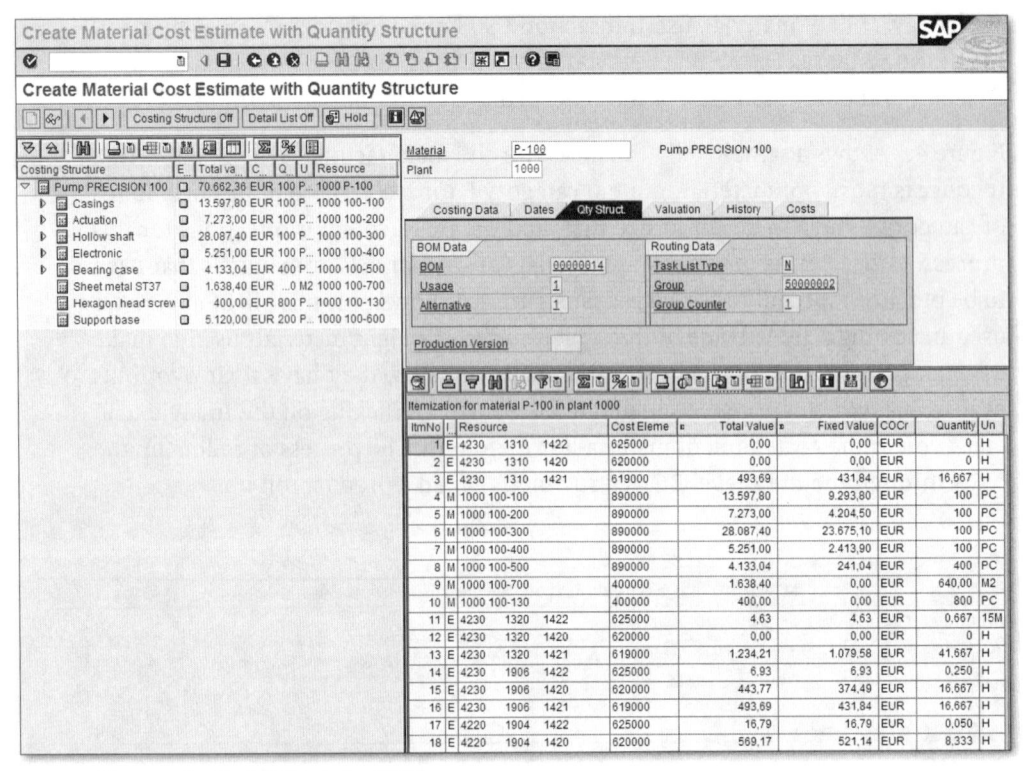

Figure 4.8 Cost Estimate for BOM

Lean Bills of Material

One trend you may want to be aware of here is the move toward simpler bills of material (the so-called pile of parts) rather than multilevel BOMs. For production, each triangle in Figure 4.8 represents a semifinished product that will be manufactured and delivered to stock. Each issue to and receipt from inventory interrupts the flow of production and can lead to piles of inventory building up, waiting for a sales order to request their usage. One way of getting around this is to use *order networks*, where each production order immediately picks up from the previous production order without waiting for the material to be delivered to and issued from stock. For controlling, however, this posting to and from stock is needed to ensure proper variance analysis. So if you work with order networks, you should ensure that your configuration team sets the flag in the order type for the plant that specifies that a goods receipt, and a simultaneous goods issue should be generated when each production order hands over to the next.

4.3.1 Quantity Definition

Generally, the quantities given in the BOM determine the quantities needed to manufacture a given lot size of the finished product. One exception is when spoilage is anticipated. Sometimes the manufacturing process is such that it's *never* possible to achieve the full output quantity in the order (computer chips are an obvious example). In other cases, experience tells that there will be some loss along the way. In either case, a planned scrap percentage can be defined in the bill of material. Entering 5% scrap for a component means that if 100 units are normally required to manufacture 100 units of the finished product, then 105 units are included in Product Costing to take account of the anticipated loss. This planned scrap is included in the scrap layout for the itemization (one of the layouts we saw when we looked at the product cost itemization in Chapter 2).

Another exception is the handling of components for inventory costing. In this case you can flag material costs as relevant, partially relevant, or not relevant. Partially relevant items are linked with a percentage in Customizing, allowing you to specify that, for example, only 60% of the packaging costs should be included in inventory costing for balance sheet purposes.

4.3.2 Co-Products and By-Products

In our pump example, multiple components were used to manufacture *one* finished product. In some industries, the bill of material is turned on its head, and *several* finished products may result from one production process (known as *joint production*). Meat production is an extreme example, where a single side of beef is processed to provide many different forms of meat product, but joint production is also common in the chemical and pharmaceutical industries, where several products may result from the same manufacturing process, some more valuable than others. SAP distinguishes between *co-products* and *by-products*. Both are included in the BOM with a negative quantity (see Figure 4.9), but co-products are flagged as such in the costing and MRP view of the material master.

- *Co-products* are considered equally valid outputs of the production process where manufacture is intentional (planned). During Product Costing they're shown in the itemization with item category A and negative costs. During order costing, an order item is created for each co-product. Each item is delivered to stock and has its own status. The order costs split to the order items in accordance with equivalence numbers during settlement. Variances can be calculated for each order item following settlement. The costs for the order items are then settled to stock. During reporting of the production or process order, you can view the details for the co-products by selecting EXTRAS • ORDER ITEMS • ON/OFF.

- *By-products* are considered incidental outputs of the production process, whose manufacture is incidental (unplanned). They differ from co-products in that a fixed price is set in the material master. They reduce the costs of the production process.

- A *fixed price co-product* (see Figure 4.4) is a mixture of the two. The order contains an order item for this co-product, but it's treated with a fixed price like a by-product.

Figure 4.9 shows the bill of material for the manufacture of paint. The manufacture of the paint also results in the manufacture of paste (a co-product). Contaminated water occurs as a by-product, and there's a catalyst that can be recovered from the process. All of these are shown with negative quantities in the BOM. Every material in this list is linked with the operation to which it will be issued. This assignment is important for the calculation of WIP and scrap per operation, a subject we'll return to in Chapter 7.

If you create a process order for material Z-300, order items are automatically created for each of the co-products. We'll see this in Chapter 6. Costs captured at the order level are then split to the order items based on equivalence numbers in the settlement rule. The equivalence numbers for the splitting are defined in the material master in the form of an apportionment structure. The simplest option is to split all the costs in the same way, such as 80% to the first co-product and 20% to the second product. But if the split is different depending on the type of costs incurred, you can use a *source structure* to separate the material costs, production costs, and so on and then define a different percentage split for each of the elements in the source structure.

Figure 4.10 shows the apportionment structure used for material Z-300. To see this, select the COSTING 1 view of the material master and then click on the JOINT PRODUCTION button.

Bills of Material | **4.3**

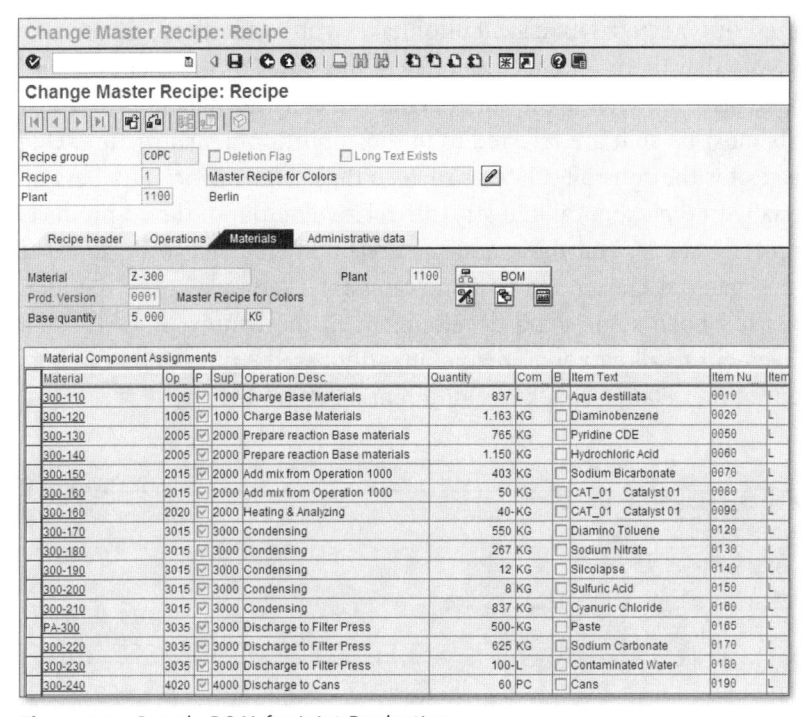

Figure 4.9 Sample BOM for Joint Production

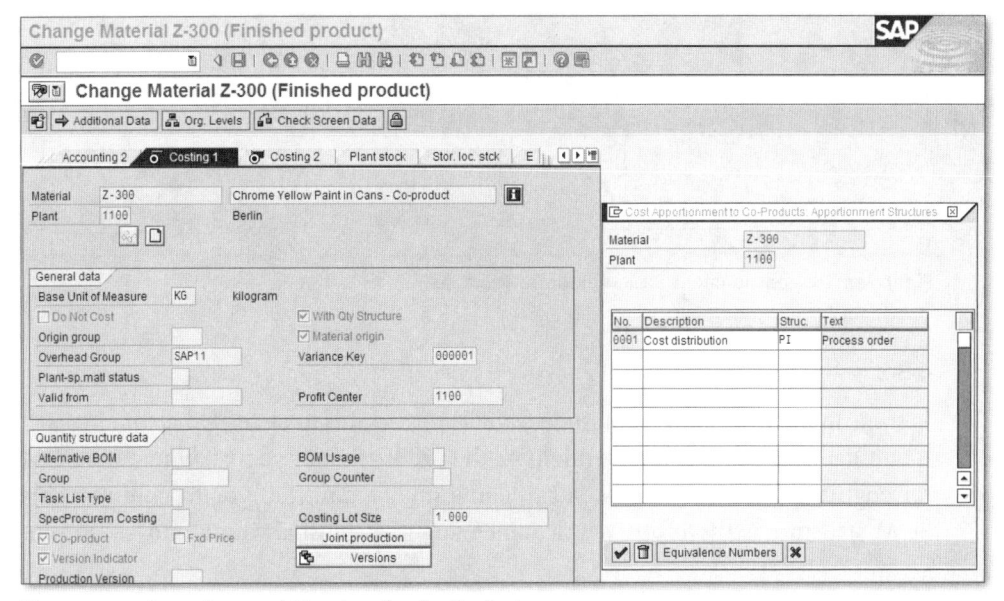

Figure 4.10 Apportionment Structure for Co-Products

163

Clicking on the EQUIVALENCE NUMBERS button takes you to the detail screen (see Figure 4.11). Note that there's no need to refer to the water or the catalyst, since they have a fixed price, entered in the material master. Only the materials to which the order costs must be split are referred to in the apportionment structure. One of the challenges for the controller here is to keep these equivalence numbers up to date. Especially in the chemical industry, the relative output of the co-products is rarely completely stable, and these equivalence numbers need to be adjusted regularly in the material master and in some cases for every order. For the food industry, there has been some extra development in the context of SAP Catch Weight Management to allow you to define quantity-based equivalence numbers to take account of the relative weights of different meat products.

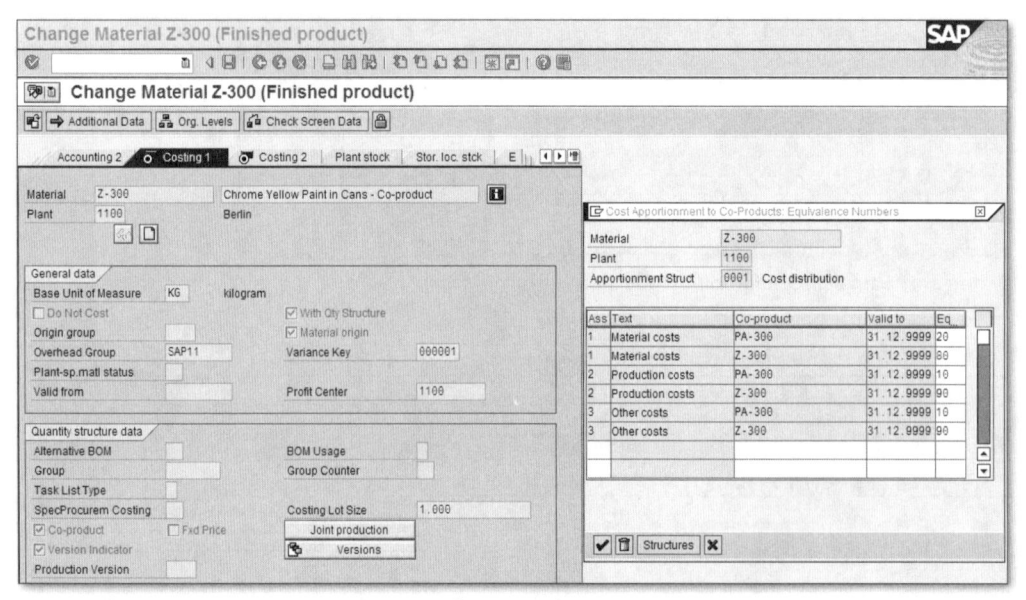

Figure 4.11 Apportionment Structure for Co-Products

4.3.3 Recursive BOMs

In some industries, it's also common for BOM structures to be recursive (or circular). A familiar household example might be the production of yogurt, where the BOM for yogurt might include milk, sugar, and a small amount of yogurt cultures. This BOM structure is therefore a cycle, since yogurt is both an input and an output.

During Product Costing each cycle has to be calculated separately, before the next costing level is handled. The materials within a cycle are costed iteratively until they converge. Only then is the next costing level in the bill of material costed.

4.3.4 Configurable BOMs

In the automotive industry, it's common for the final product to be heavily configurable, with the customer selecting the paint color, engine size, wheels, seats, stereo system, and so on as he places his order. To handle this variability, the bill of material for the vehicle includes all the possible options, together with certain rules that determine which combinations are technically feasible. Such materials that include all options are known as *configurable materials*. For the controlling department, it's not possible to set a standard price for the configurable material, since it contains all possible options that a customer might choose. The cost estimate is generally created in the sales order once the customer has selected his options and is in the process of placing his order. But for selected variants you can prepare a cost estimate in advance by defining certain "standard" options for costing. The other thing that characterizes this type of material is that it's always made to order (since we have to know what options the customer chose) before beginning manufacture. Depending on the configuration, however, it may be that the sales order is merely the carrier for the manufacturing information, but no additional costs will be captured for the sales order, or it may be that sales order controlling (see Chapter 2) is required, because additional costs, such as the costs associated with discussing the configuration with the customer, are captured on the sales order.

Figure 4.12 shows the material master for a configurable material. The important section is PLANT-SPECIFIC CONFIGURATION, which provides the link from the material that will be entered in the sales order and all possible variants of that material. In a typical automotive scenario, you might find about 2000 "standard" products and many thousands of configurations, since every car sold is potentially unique.

The BOM for this assembly contains all possible options, as we see in Figure 4.13. Compared to the normal BOM that is simply a list of the parts to be used, there's an extra tab, CLASS. The BOM itself contains several similar components (such as multiple choices of paint finishes). At the point of sale, the customer selects his chosen options, and the BOM is reduced to contain only those components that will be used in production. The technical variants that the customer is allowed are defined in the classification system, which is why the important data for a configurable BOM is in the CLASS tab.

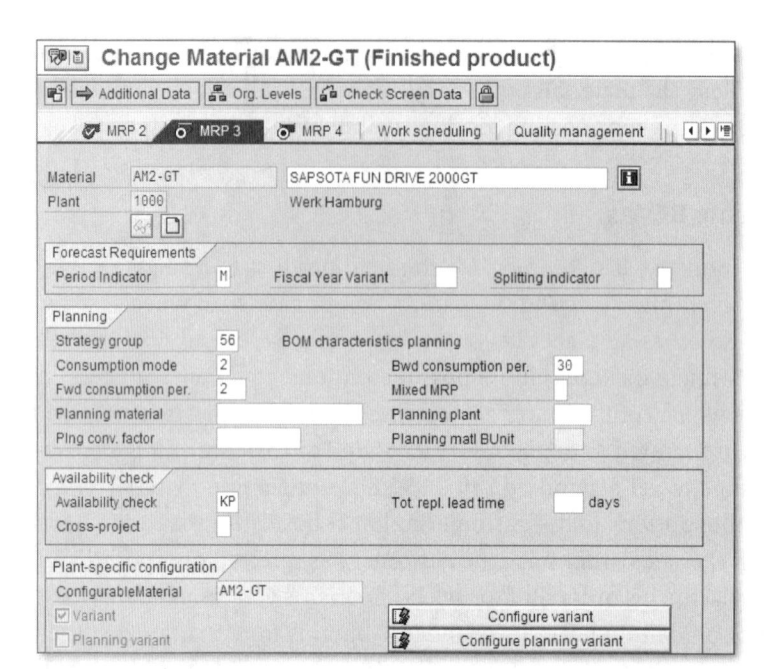

4 | Master Data Where Controlling Is a Stakeholder

Figure 4.12 Material Master for a Configurable Material

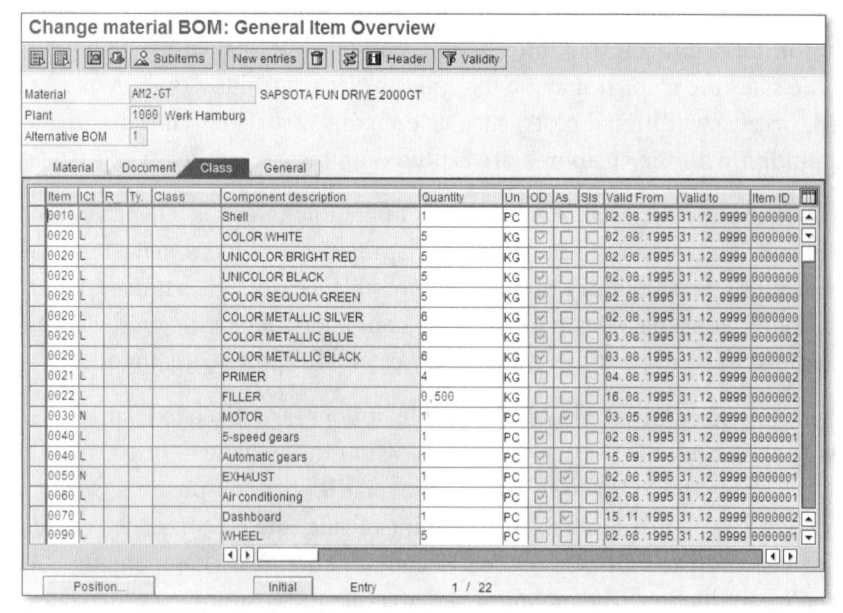

Figure 4.13 BOM for Configurable Material

For planning, it's also possible to define certain standard configurations from within the material master and to use these for planning. Such a configuration is shown in Figure 4.14. Here items with variants are represented as characteristics. Normally the process of picking the relevant characteristics doesn't take place until the customer places the order, but you can define certain plan variants in advance and store them in the MRP view of the material master. This information can then be used to set the standard costs for the standard product variant. Here you can see the characteristic value Paint, which determines the color picked from the BOM in Figure 4.13.

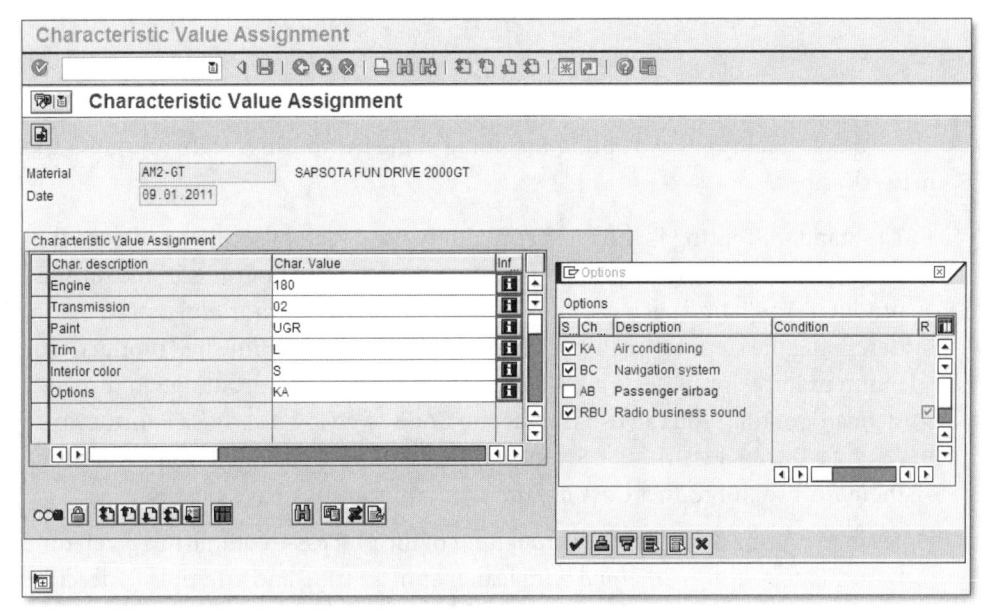

Figure 4.14 Choosing Options for a Planning Variant

The bill of material tells us what materials are required to manufacture the product. But this is not the whole story. We also have to know what manufacturing steps need to be performed to turn these components or ingredients into a finished product that the customer will buy. These steps are defined in the routing.

4.4 Routings

In Chapter 2 we introduced the itemization as one of the key reports for Product Cost Planning that shows the manufacturing operations performed according to the *routing*. It determines the processing steps to be performed in the manufacture of the material, the material components assigned to that step, and any planned scrap anticipated in the step.

We described how to set up activity types such as machine time, labor time, and so on in Chapter 3. These activity types must be linked with the operations in the routing or recipe for Product Costing.

4.4.1 Types of Routing

There are several types of routing including standard routings, rate routings, and master recipes.

- The standard routing is the most commonly used type of routing and describes the quantities of work required to create a given number of units of the finished products. You'll find such routings wherever there is batch-oriented production, describing the steps to create each finished product or semifinished product. Our pump example provides a classic use case for this kind of routing. To display a standard routing, you can use Transaction CA03 or go to LOGISTICS • PRODUCTION • MASTER DATA • ROUTINGS • STANDARD ROUTINGS • DISPLAY. If you're selecting them for use in Product Costing, the standard routings have type N.

- The rate routing describes the throughput of the process—volume in a given time frame. Rate routings emerged with lean manufacturing and attempts to describe production as a more or less constant flow, rather than as a series of disjointed batches with deliveries to inventory for each semifinished product. To display a rate routing, you can use Transaction CA23 or go to LOGISTICS • PRODUCTION • MASTER DATA • ROUTINGS • RATE ROUTINGS • DISPLAY. If you're selecting them for use in Product Costing, the standard routings have type R.

- The master recipe is used in the pharmaceutical and chemical industries and describes the production of one or more materials in one production run. From a costing point of view, master recipes are essentially a combination of a standard routing and a bill of material but include additional functions for material quantity calculation that are specific to these industries. Our paint example uses a recipe rather than a routing, so we saw that all items in the material list were linked with an operation. Operations may be broken down into phases. To display a master recipe, you can use Transaction C203 or go to Logistics • Production - Process • Master Data • Master Recipes • Recipes and material list • Display. If you're selecting them for use in Product Costing, the standard routings have type 2.

One thing to be aware of is that as we saw for the bill of material, it's possible to have routings and recipes that belong to production and routings and recipes that belong to controlling. Again, this may be a good way of getting started, but in the long term it's better to strive for one accurate set of recipes, rather than multiple versions of the truth.

Figure 4.15 shows a sample master recipe for the manufacture of paints, showing the operations and suboperations performed to manufacture the paint and the resources at which each operation is performed. On the far right of the screen are the base quantity (5000 kg) and the standard values—the number of minutes taken to perform the task to deliver the base quantity. This is needed to calculate the standard times for Product Costing.

If you refer back to Figure 2.14 in Chapter 2, you'll see the costs per operation in the cost estimate. While the controlling department does not own the recipes and routings, it must work with production to ensure that the values per operation are correct and that the correct materials are assigned to each operation. We'll see how important this is when we look at the calculation of WIP and scrap in Chapter 7.

- If the product has to be scrapped at the first operation, it's important that only those materials are included in the scrap value that has genuinely been issued from stock for this operation.
- If some of your components are very expensive, make sure they're issued at the correct operation to ensure that the WIP capitalized for each operation is correct.

Figure 4.15 Sample Recipe

4.4.2 Operation Values

Each operation in a routing or recipe contains a control key, which determines whether the operation is performed in-house or externally and whether costs are calculated for the operation. Figure 4.16 shows a sample operation with control key PI02. You can reach this screen by double-clicking on the correct line for the operation in Figure 4.15.

Each operation includes standard values for the manufacture of a particular base quantity of the product. As we learned for the BOM, it's also possible to flag operations as relevant for costing, partially relevant, or not relevant. In our example, to manufacture 5000 kg of the base quantity, 240 minutes (or 4 hours) of activity type 1420 would be required. The activity type is linked with the resource (since this is a process industry example) or a work center to determine the cost center supplying the activity and the activity price.

[Figure 4.16 screenshot: Change Master Recipe: Operation]

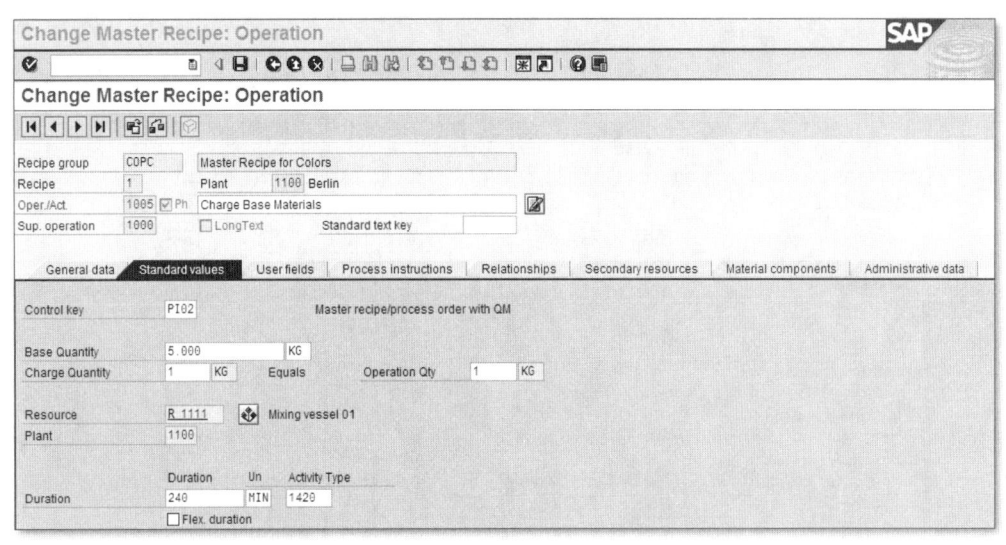

Figure 4.16 Sample Operation

If we now look at the cost estimate for material Z-300, we can display the itemization (in other words, the list of costing items from the BOM and routing) and the assignment of the items to the operations by selecting the layout OPERATIONS (see Chapter 2). Figure 4.17 shows the cost estimate for material Z-300. We looked at Operation 1005 (Charge Base Materials) in Figure 4.16. Line 1 is an item of category E (internal activity). Here we see the four hours of activity from the operation, work center R_1111, cost center 4240, and activity type 1420. Notice that two raw materials, aqua destillata (300-110) and diaminobenzene (300-120), are assigned to this operation (these costing items are shown above the totals line for the operation). This is important for when we calculate work in process and scrap in Chapter 7, since we want to be sure the material usage is recorded at the correct operation. Also notice that three costing items haven't been assigned to an operation. These are the percentage overheads applied to the cost estimate as a whole, rather than to individual operations. We'll look at how to set up the percentages for this allocation in Chapter 7, Section 7.2.

It's also possible to define planned scrap for an operation. This can be used to set the assembly scrap in the material master. You can see this in the cost estimate by selecting the layout for the scrap view.

Itm	I	Resource	Resource (Text)	¤	Total Value	Currncy	Quantity	Un
31	G	4130 655100	OHS Raw Material		185,35	EUR		
32	G	4130 655300	OHS Administration		0,00	EUR		
33	G	4130 655400	OHS Sales & Distrib.		0,00	EUR		
< not assigned >				■	185,35	EUR		
1	E	4240 R_1111 1420	Charge Base Materials		395,07	EUR	4	H
2	M	1100 300-110	Aqua destillata		1,62	EUR	167,400	L
3	M	1100 300-120	Diaminobenzene		288,42	EUR	232,600	KG
1005 Charge Base Materials				■	685,11	EUR		
4	E	4240 R_1111 1420	Analyze & Adjust		98,77	EUR	1	H
1010 Analyze & Adjust				■	98,77	EUR		
5	E	4240 R_1111 1420	Discharge to Reaction Ves		98,77	EUR	1	H
1020 Discharge to Reaction Vessel				■	98,77	EUR		
6	E	4240 R_1121 1420	Prepare reaction Base ma		395,07	EUR	4	H
7	M	1100 300-130	Pyridine CDE		163,71	EUR	153	KG
8	M	1100 300-140	Hydrochloric Acid		489,90	EUR	230	KG
2005 Prepare reaction Base materials				■	1.048,68	EUR		
9	E	4240 R_1121 1420	Add mix from Operation 10		395,07	EUR	4	H
10	M	1100 300-150	Sodium Bicarbonate		28,21	EUR	80,600	KG
11	M	1100 300-160	CAT_01 Catalyst 01		19,30	EUR	10	KG
2015 Add mix from Operation 1000				■	442,58	EUR		
12	E	4240 R_1121 1420	Heating & Analyzing		197,54	EUR	2	H
13	M	1100 300-160	CAT_01 Catalyst 01		15,44-	EUR	8-	KG
2020 Heating & Analyzing				■	182,10	EUR		
14	E	4240 R_1121 1420	Discharge to Condenser		197,54	EUR	2	H
2030 Discharge to Condenser				■	197,54	EUR		
15	E	4240 R_1131 1420	Receive mix from Operatio		98,77	EUR	1	H
3005 Receive mix from Operation 2000				■	98,77	EUR		
16	E	4240 R_1131 1420	Heating		98,77	EUR	1	H
3010 Heating				■	98,77	EUR		

Figure 4.17 Operations in the Cost Estimate

4.4.3 Operation-Level Costing

When you look at the reports in the standard cost estimate, you'll see the costs of each operation or suboperation. But if you look at the costs for an individual production order or process order, you'll see only the costs and quantities for each cost center/activity type combination, but no mention of the operation. This is because order costs are assigned at the order header level, and the operation does not exist as an account assignment object in Controlling.

The only exceptions to this rule are the operations for a maintenance or service order. The option to use the operation as an account assignment for a maintenance or service order was introduced in SAP enhancement package 5 for SAP ERP 6.0 with the business function LOG_EAM_OLC. Logistics, Controlling, and financial transactions were enhanced to allow the use of the operation as an account assignment object. At the time of writing, it's not possible to capture costs for production orders by operation.

The routings, recipes, and rate routings describe the steps required to manufacture a product, but they don't tell you *where* each step takes place. We need to know where the operation is performed to establish the link with the cost centers and activity types we defined in Chapter 3 to determine the value of the internal activity being supplied to production. In this way, we'll prepare the charge for the four hours of activity we saw in Figure 4.17.

4.5 Work Centers and Resources

Work centers and resources are used for capacity requirements planning and scheduling in Logistics. Every operation in a routing must be assigned to a work center (the place where the operation is performed). The work center includes formulas that determine how each standard value in the operation is interpreted (fixed in the case of setup time and varying with the lot size in the case of machine time and labor time). You can also include an efficiency rate to take account of different efficiencies in the operation.

- To display a work center, use Transaction CR03 or go to LOGISTICS • PRODUCTION • MASTER DATA • WORK CENTERS • WORK CENTER • DISPLAY.

- To display a resource, use Transaction CRC3 or go to LOGISTICS • PRODUCTION – PROCESS • MASTER DATA • RESOURCES • RESOURCE • DISPLAY.

For costing, every work center and resource must be assigned to a single cost center. This link is defined for a specified validity period. Figure 4.18 shows the resource used in the operation to manufacture the paint we showed earlier. You may recall that the activity type was 1420. The activity includes a formula key that determines how the activity quantities are calculated. For example, a set-up operation may require a fixed effort of 15 minutes regardless of what lot size is in the order or cost estimate. The example we looked at in Figure 4.16 referred to a base quantity that's referenced in the formula.

4 | Master Data Where Controlling Is a Stakeholder

The costing view in the work center determines the cost center that is linked with the work center and the activity types that can be performed at that work center.

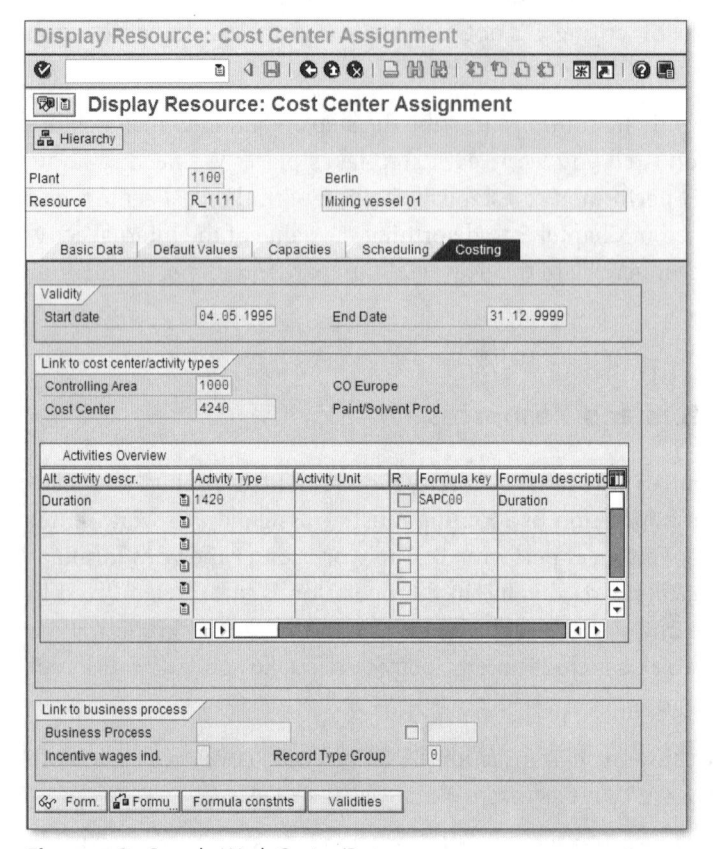

Figure 4.18 Sample Work Center/Resource

Activity Types per Work Center

Confusion frequently arises as to the limit of only six activity types at any work center. Why only six? The reason lies in SAP's understanding of the activity type as the *output measure* for the work center. The output measure is typically expressed in terms of drilling hours, welding hours, and so on. In other words, these are the outputs that are measured when order confirmation takes place.

> When people want to use more than six activity types, they're often confusing inputs and outputs. A work center may supply welding hours, but it often uses energy hours, maintenance hours, and so on. If what you're really trying to do by using more than six activity types is see the impact of increases in energy prices, higher wage costs, or changes in depreciation on product profitability, then you should consider activating the *primary cost component* split for your activity rates. Without the primary cost component split, energy costs, wage costs, and so on are subsumed in the activity price for the welding hours. With the primary cost component split, you can break out the activity rate into its cost components, which might be wages, salaries, operating supplies, depreciation, energy, maintenance, and so on. We'll look at this process in more detail in Chapter 5.

Looking at Figure 4.18, note the CAPACITIES tab in the resource. This is used during capacity requirements planning to determine how many units can be handled in each operation. When we look at Cost Center Planning in Chapter 5, we'll see that you can also enter a *capacity* for each cost center and activity type in a given period. This is sometimes a source of confusion, but the two are quite different.

- The *work center* capacity refers to the ability of a single machine to perform a given operation. It affects the activity quantity calculations in Product Costing because to produce a given lot size, the operation has to be performed a given number of times. For example, if the capacity of an oven is 100 units, to deliver a lot size of 200 units, the operation has to be performed twice.
- The *cost center/activity type* capacity refers to the whole period and can cover multiple work centers. It's used to define a standard quantity output over all machines assigned to the cost center in a given period.

In the early days of SAP R/3, product costing could handle one BOM and one routing, and it was the task of the Customizing settings to ensure that the correct BOM and routing were picked during costing. This was an overly simplistic view of the world. We'll now look at how to set up procurement alternatives to represent the different ways you can organize the manufacture or purchase of your materials.

4.6 Procurement Alternatives and Mixed Costing

Product costing can be based on a single BOM and routing for each material, but this does not take account of the complexities of a production process. These can be reflected by creating procurement alternatives for each option and then weighting the relative use of each alternative within the product costing. The procurement alternatives are also used in the Material Ledger to separate the data for each alternative. To create procurement alternatives, you can use Transaction CK91N or go to Accounting • Controlling • Product Cost Controlling • Product Cost Planning • Material Costing • Master Data for Mixed Cost Estimate • Edit Procurement Alternatives.

4.6.1 Internal Processing

Procurement alternatives for internal processing are needed where several BOMs or routings exist for the manufacture of the same material or when the product can be manufactured externally when there is insufficient capacity to manufacture the required volume in-house. This may be the case where several production lines can manufacture the same product, and capacity decisions determine which line is used. Figure 4.19 shows a sample procurement alternative for in-house production of ACT-DCD. This simply references the production version that stores the bill of material and routing used to manufacture material ACT-DCD in-house. We'll create a production order and manufacture this material according to this production version when we look at actual postings in Chapter 6.

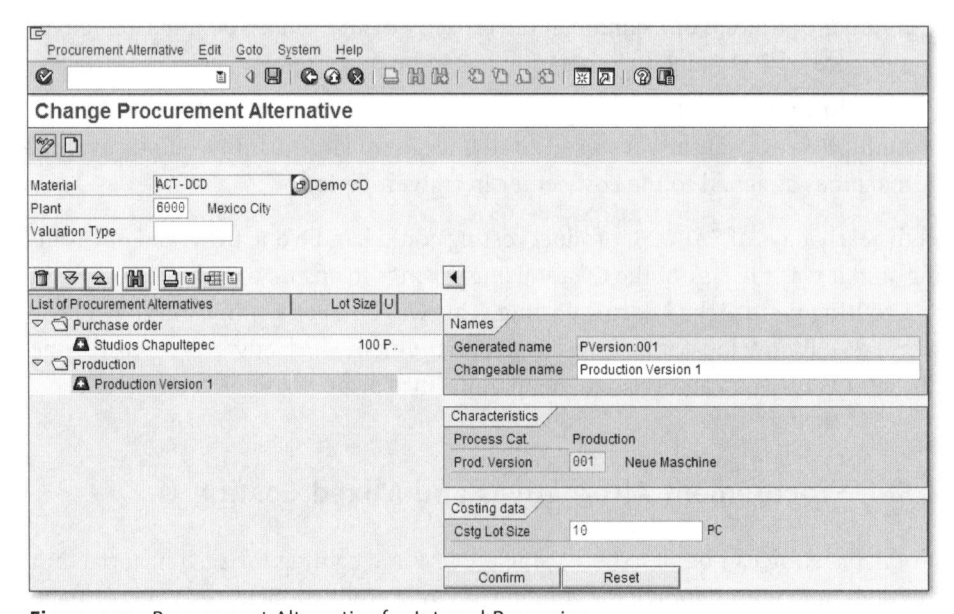

Figure 4.19 Procurement Alternative for Internal Processing

4.6.2 External Procurement

A procurement alternative by vendor is needed if the same material can be procured from several vendors or to support make-or-buy decisions for this material. A purchasing info record is maintained for each vendor. Figure 4.20 shows a procurement alternative for external procurement. Here we see the purchasing organization responsible for procurement and the vendor from whom material ACT-DCD is usually purchased. Instead of using a BOM and routing to perform costing, the information from the purchasing info record is read to determine the price conditions agreed with this vendor.

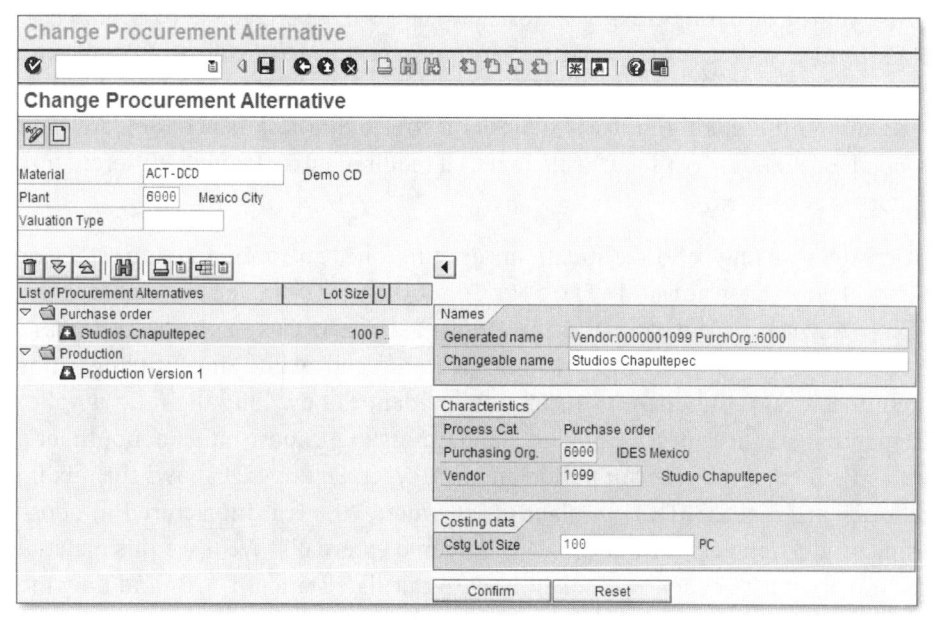

Figure 4.20 Procurement Alternative for External Procurement

4.6.3 Plant to Plant Transfer

Procurement alternatives for plant to plant transfer are needed if you manufacture the same material at multiple plants and transfer the semifinished products to a different plant for final assembly. In this case, you enter the name of the plant providing the stocks to be transferred. This corresponds to the use of the special procurement key in the costing view of the material master that we discussed earlier.

4.6.4 Subcontracting

Procurement alternatives are needed for subcontracting, when several vendors can take your material components and complete the finished product for you. For costing, the bill of material is used to determine the material components to be sent to the vendor(s) and a purchasing info record that defines the price charged for the work by each vendor.

4.6.5 Mixing Ratios

Before you can use any of these procurement alternatives to calculate standard costs, you must define mixing ratios that state what percentage of production is performed in-house and what percentage is performed externally. While the procurement alternatives are largely in the hands of production and procurement, maintaining the mixing ratios is typically a controlling task, since they are only needed for Product Costing. During material requirements planning, different mix factors may be used.

To create a mixing ratio or update an existing one, go to Transaction CK94 or Accounting • Controlling • Product Cost Controlling • Product Cost Planning • Material Costing • Master Data for Mixed Cost Estimate • Mixing Ratios • Create/Change and enter the material and plant. Since mixing ratios are not constant, the quantity structure type defines how long the ratio is valid. (Depending on the timescale of your standard costing, choose either a month, or a year.) Then enter the relevant period and fiscal year. Figure 4.21 shows the mixing ratio for material ACT-DCD in plant 6000, where 90% is manufactured in-house using production version 1 and 10% is procured externally. We'll see this material again in Chapter 5 when we look at how to calculate standard costs and how the two cost estimates are weighted against one another.

We have now looked at the main master data required to describe how to manufacture a product and can proceed to create sales orders or production orders. In addition to this master data, many organizations also use projects, either for complex make-to-order production or to manage internal investments, such as building a new production line.

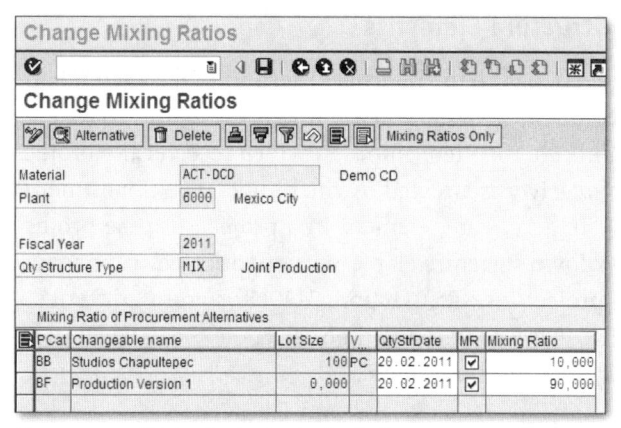

Figure 4.21 Mixing Ratio for Multiple Procurement Alternatives

4.7 Projects

In Chapter 3 we looked at internal orders as a means of capturing marketing costs, research costs, and so on. From a controlling point of view, a project is in essence an internal order with a hierarchical structure. A project definition defines the header data for the entire project. The activities to be performed within the project are defined as work breakdown structure elements. In an engineer-to-order scenario it's also common to assign networks and network activities to the work breakdown structure (WBS) elements. Responsibility for project master data varies depending on the organization.

- For engineer-to-order scenarios, the engineering department is generally in the lead, since they work with the customer to specify the technical details of each element of the project.

- For internal projects, however, it's common for controlling to establish rules for the upper WBS elements or even to create these in advance and to have the research departments, or whoever is executing the project, flesh out the lower-level detail of the work breakdown structure to describe the tasks they'll be performing.

- The same often applies to investment projects, where controlling establishes rules for the upper WBS elements and often creates the settlement rules to ensure that the values are capitalized correctly.

4.7.1 Work Breakdown Structure Elements

WBS elements have a certain overlap with the internal orders we looked at in Chapter 3. They also have a status (open, released, final billing, technically complete, complete, etc.) and a settlement rule that determines to which receiver the project costs are charged. The type of receiver is affected by the project type (investment, overhead, engineer-to-order). To access any element in a project, use the project builder that shows work breakdown structure elements, networks, network activities, and so on. To display a project, use Transaction CJ20N or go to LOGISTICS • PROJECT SYSTEM • PROJECTS • PROJECT BUILDER, and then select the project definition that represents the header for the project as whole.

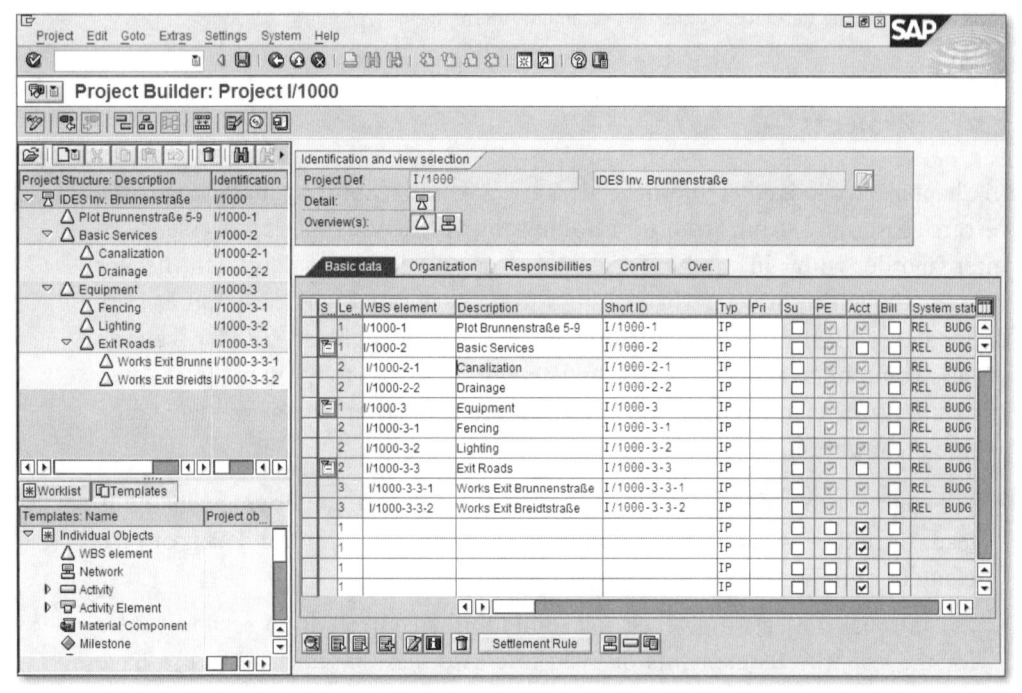

Figure 4.22 WBS Elements

Figure 4.22 shows a work breakdown structure comprising several WBS elements for the steps required to construct the site of a new plant. To see the basic data for each WBS element in the structure, click on the OVERVIEW icon (triangle). This takes you to a list of the control settings for each WBS element. You can issue materials to a WBS element, charge time to them, assign overheads, and so on, provided that the WBS element has the status REL (released). We'll look at examples of these postings in Chapter 6. The main difference with respect to an internal order is the hierarchical nature of the project, which becomes especially relevant when you assign the budget, since you may assign the budget at a much higher level than you plan or capture actual costs.

When looking at how a project is handled from a controlling point of view, three checkboxes are important:

- **Billing elements** (BILL column)
  This defines the level at which revenue is captured (this mainly applies for customer projects where the services are billed). The BILL checkbox is unselected in our example, since it's an internal project whose costs are not charged to a customer. We're simply using the project to provide cost transparency.

- **Account assignment elements** (ACCT column)
  This is the level at which costs are captured. All the lower-level nodes of our project are account assignment objects, but you can't assign costs to the elements Basic Services, Equipment, or Exit Roads, since the ACCT checkbox is unselected for these items. We'll look at how to assign costs to a WBS element in Chapter 6, Section 6.3.4.

- **Planning elements** (PE column)
  This is the level at which costs are planned (this can be at a more granular level than the account assignment elements). All elements in our structure are flagged as planning elements. We'll look at how to plan these elements in Chapter 5, Section 5.2.

4.7.2 Networks and Network Activities

When you need more accurate scheduling and deadline management, the work breakdown structure may also include networks and network activities. These also capture costs and have a status and settlement rule. To display networks or network activities, use the Project Builder as in the last example, but click on the NETWORK OVERVIEW icon and then select one of the networks in the list. Figure 4.23 shows a sample network. This looks almost exactly like the header data for a production order if you compare it with the examples in Chapter 6. Networks and network activities carry status information and are assigned to the organizational units in SAP ERP just like any other orders. The work they carry out is executed at work centers, so in this sense they are costed just like a production order.

> **Project Size**
>
> As you can imagine, the project structure in Transaction CJ20N can easily include a huge number of WBS elements, network activities, and activities if the project has any degree of complexity. If you're concerned that your projects will fall into this category (generally the problems start when you approach 10,000 WBS elements), take a look at the recommendations in SAP Note 206264.

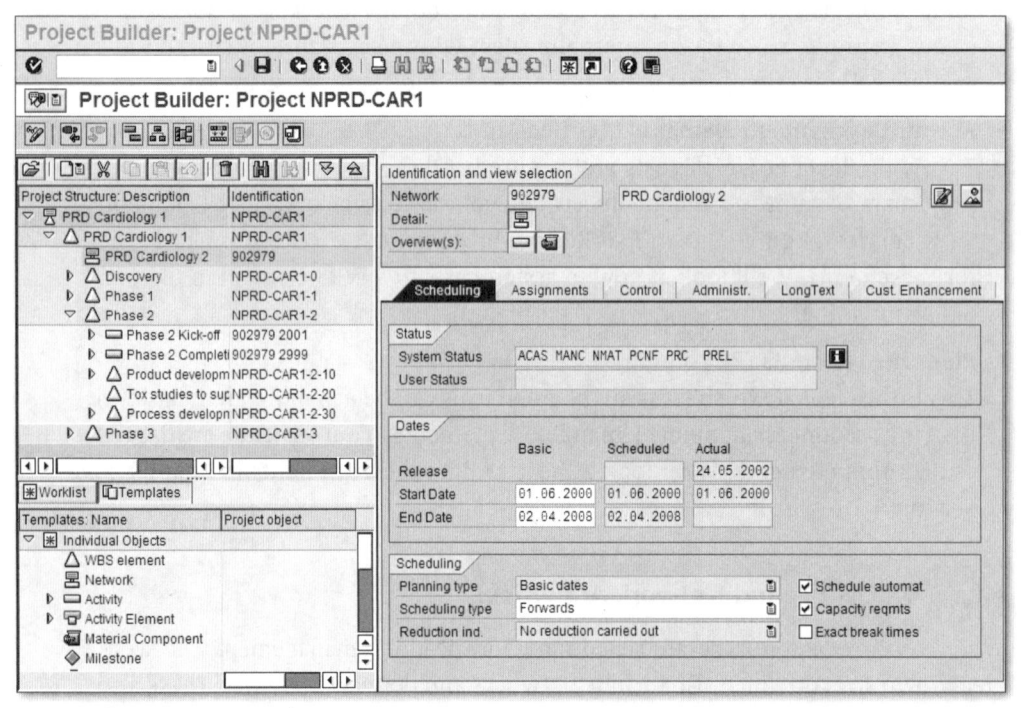

Figure 4.23 Network

If your organization only has a handful of investment projects running at any time, what we saw above will meet your purposes. But if you want to take a more structured approach to project management, you may want to link your projects with an investment program.

4.8 Investment Programs

In Chapter 3 we looked at investment orders as a type of internal order. If there are a large number of investment orders to be handled, more structure is often needed. If this is the case, you can create an investment program to structure the undertaking. This is particularly useful during planning and when assigning a budget to the individual nodes. Once approved, investment orders or investment projects may be created for the execution of the investment. The investment program itself cannot carry costs, so you won't find any transactions that include the investment program as an account assignment. Instead costs are assigned to the orders and WBS elements assigned to the investment program. These behave exactly like any other internal orders and WBS elements. The main difference is that they can be reported via the investment program and in isolation. To display an investment plan, use Transaction IM34 or go to ACCOUNTING • INVESTMENT MANAGEMENT • PROGRAMS • MASTER DATA • INVESTMENT STRUCTURE • DISPLAY and enter the program and approval year. The approval year is important in this context because investment programs are always created with reference to an approval year, even though the assigned projects or orders may take several years to complete. We'll look at how to move orders and projects between programs when we look at planning and budgeting in Chapter 5.

Figure 4.24 shows a sample investment program for 2010. You may recognize the structure from the cost center hierarchy we looked at in Chapter 3. This is just one way of structuring an investment program, with the investment taking place with reference to the associated cost centers.

If we now return to our project, we can display the link to the investment program by selecting the detail of a WBS element and selecting the INVESTMENTS tab. Figure 4.25 shows that WBS element I/1000-1 is linked to the Corporate Services item of our investment program. WBS elements I/1000-2 and I/1000-3 are assigned to the same item in the program. We'll see how this assignment affects the budget in Chapter 5, Section 5.2.4. The same link can be made for internal orders if you don't need quite as much structure as a project provides.

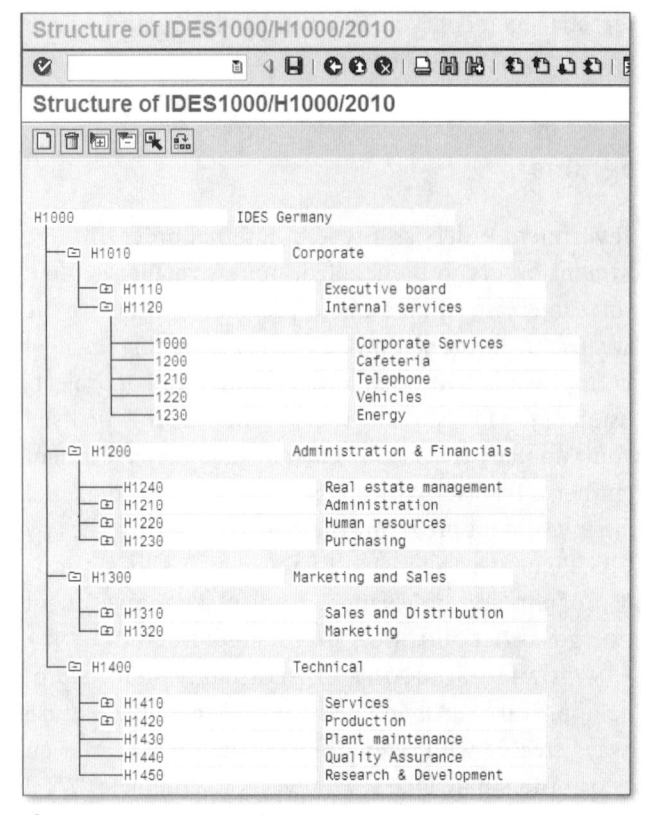

4 | Master Data Where Controlling Is a Stakeholder

```
Structure of IDES1000/H1000/2010

H1000                       IDES Germany
    ├─ H1010                Corporate
    │      ├─ H1110         Executive board
    │      └─ H1120         Internal services
    │              ├─1000       Corporate Services
    │              ├─1200       Cafeteria
    │              ├─1210       Telephone
    │              ├─1220       Vehicles
    │              └─1230       Energy
    ├─ H1200                Administration & Financials
    │      ├─ H1240         Real estate management
    │      ├─ H1210         Administration
    │      ├─ H1220         Human resources
    │      └─ H1230         Purchasing
    ├─ H1300                Marketing and Sales
    │      ├─ H1310         Sales and Distribution
    │      └─ H1320         Marketing
    └─ H1400                Technical
           ├─ H1410         Services
           ├─ H1420         Production
           ├─ H1430         Plant maintenance
           ├─ H1440         Quality Assurance
           └─ H1450         Research & Development
```

Figure 4.24 Investment Program

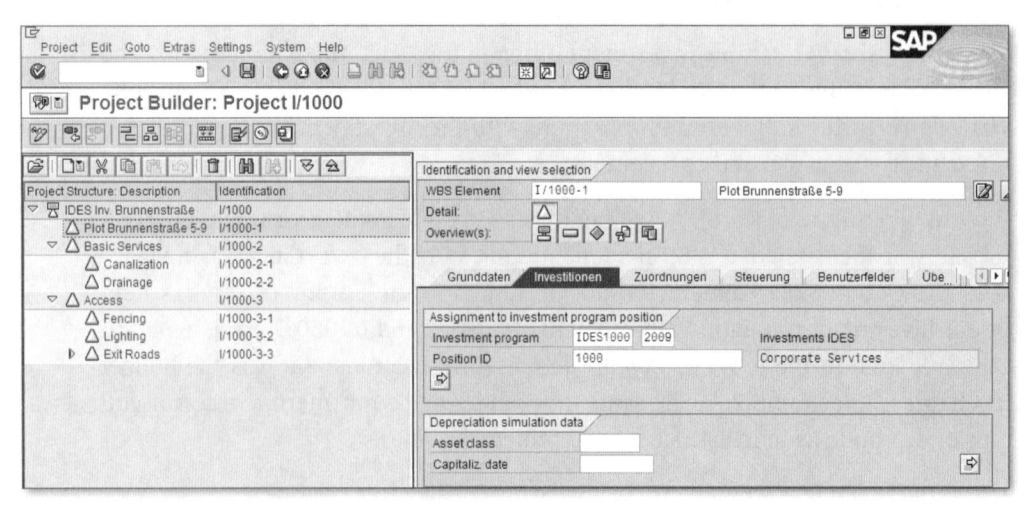

Figure 4.25 Link to Investment Program Item

184

4.8.1 Appropriation Requests

Appropriation requests are used to request investment as part of the investment program. The appropriation request contains details of the plan required to complete the investment. Several variants can be created that show the planning values, along with return on investment (ROI) values. Figure 4.26 shows a sample appropriation request, along with the estimate of the investment costs, overhead, and revenue submitted by the requester to support his request. To display the appropriation request, go to Transaction IMA11 or ACCOUNTING • INVESTMENT MANAGEMENT • APPROPRIATION REQUEST • EDIT APPROPRIATION REQUEST • INDIVIDUAL PROCESSING. To display the planned values, select the VARIANTS tab at the top and the PLANNED VALUES tab at the bottom.

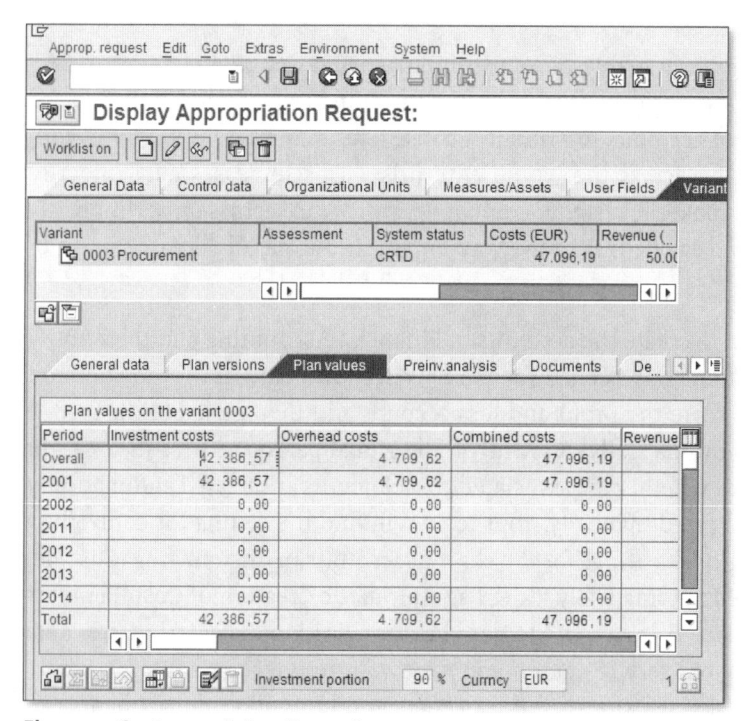

Figure 4.26 Appropriation Request

So far we've looked at the master data in Logistics and master data such as projects and investment programs that sit in Logistics and SAP ERP Financials. To complete the picture, we also need to look at the key master data for controlling in Financial Accounting. We need this to document the flow of costs from the financial accounts to controlling and from controlling back to the financial accounts.

4.9 Primary Cost Elements and P&L Accounts

In this chapter we've focused on the integration between CO and the master data in Logistics, touching on the subject of account assignment in terms of the material accounts to be updated during a goods movement or the reconciliation account to be used for a customer. As we discussed in Chapter 1, CO sits between Logistics and Financial Accounting, so it's also important to understand how the master data in Financial Accounting impacts CO.

The *chart of accounts* is arguably the most important master data element in SAP ERP Financials. In recent years, there's been a move in large organizations toward unifying the chart of accounts to provide a consistent account definition and consistent account usage across the whole enterprise. This increases data integrity across systems and makes it easier to compare performance across units. Implicitly this has also resulted in changes to the way organizations handle the definition of their cost elements.

Organizations used to create the accounts in Financial Accounting and then notify CO that a cost element was needed for the new account. Now it's more common to have one team create the profit and loss account and then generate the associated cost element automatically. A setting in the global parameters for the chart of accounts determines whether the associated cost elements are created automatically or continue to be created manually. Your team will find the setting for controlling integration in the global settings for the chart of accounts in Customizing. Cost elements are generated automatically if the flag Automatic Creation of Cost Elements is set here. Since there's also a trend toward having this kind of central master data maintained by a shared service center, you may want to refer to Chapter 9, where we'll look at the tasks of a shared service center and how other departments can raise requests to initiate the creation of a new account and its sister cost element centrally.

4.9.1 Chart of Accounts

Let's consider the different types of charts of accounts. SAP ERP includes three charts of accounts:

- **Operational chart of accounts**
  The operational chart of accounts contains the *operational accounts* used for recording financial transactions within a company code. The chart of accounts is included in the global parameters for the company code. These are the accounts we talked about in the context of material account assignment and the customer master, and it's these accounts that are linked with the primary cost elements for controlling purposes.

- **Group chart of accounts**
  The group chart of accounts contains all *group accounts* companies in the group use for consolidated financial reporting. The operational accounts are linked to the group chart of accounts in the account master record. Normally they're not relevant for CO, unless you're part of the team preparing group data for consolidation.

- **Country chart of accounts**
  Some countries have specific legislative requirements concerning the chart of accounts to be used to submit financial statements. The country chart of accounts is also included in the global parameters for the company code. These are defined as *alternative accounts* and are mapped to the operational accounts in the account master data at the chart of account level. They're not relevant for controlling unless they're used in isolation. In this case, the country chart of accounts is effectively the operational chart of accounts. This can be the case if you operate only in one country.

To display the accounts, use Transaction FSSO or go to ACCOUNTING • FINANCIAL ACCOUNTS • GENERAL LEDGER • MASTER RECORDS • GL ACCOUNTS • INDIVIDUAL PROCESSING • IN COMPANY CODE.

Figure 4.27 shows the master data definition for an inventory account. The main checkbox for our purposes is the P&L STATEMENT ACCOUNT TYPE checkbox, since only postings to P&L accounts are transferred to CO. You can also see the assignment to the group account, which is used for consolidation and group controlling. The EDIT COST ELEMENT button takes you to the master data for the associated cost element.

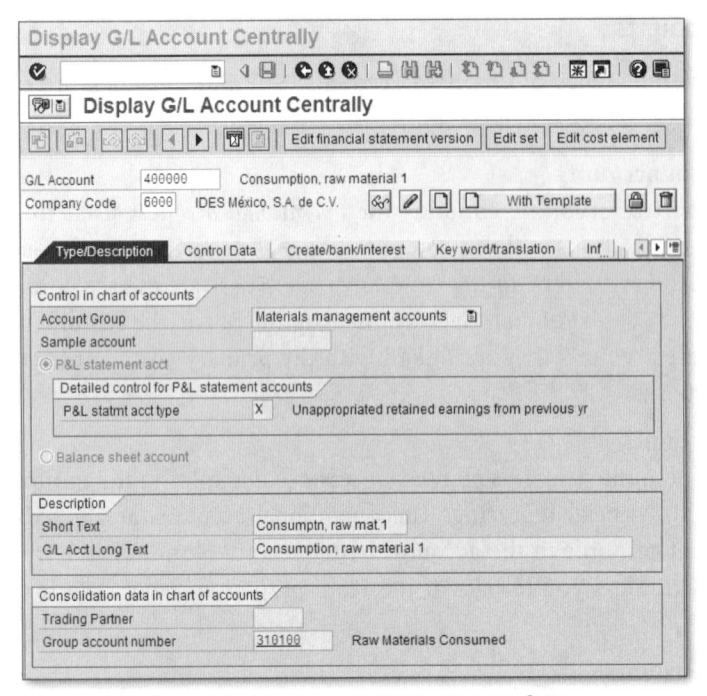

4 | Master Data Where Controlling Is a Stakeholder

Figure 4.27 General Ledger Account Master Data Definition

Figure 4.28 shows the associated cost element (which you can also reach using Transaction KA03). The definition is relatively simple (which is why the process can be automated). The important setting is the COST ELEMENT CATEGORY

- For costs, the cost element category is 1 (primary costs). You need cost elements of category 1 for all material accounts, asset accounts, wages, salaries, or for any profit and loss account whose costs you want to capture in CO.

- For revenues, the cost element category is 11 (revenue). You only need to create cost elements of category 11 for revenues that are assigned to projects or for make-to-order production with sales order controlling (see Chapter 2). All other revenues are captured as value fields in CO-PA and do not need to be recorded as cost elements.

Once a cost element has been created, it's important to ensure that it's properly assigned for overhead calculation, settlement, inclusion in work in process, and so on, as discussed in Chapter 3. We'll see this linkage again in Chapter 9 when we look at how to set up a dedicated system for master data governance, which is usually installed on the same client as the master customizing client, so that this kind of data can be maintained in one go.

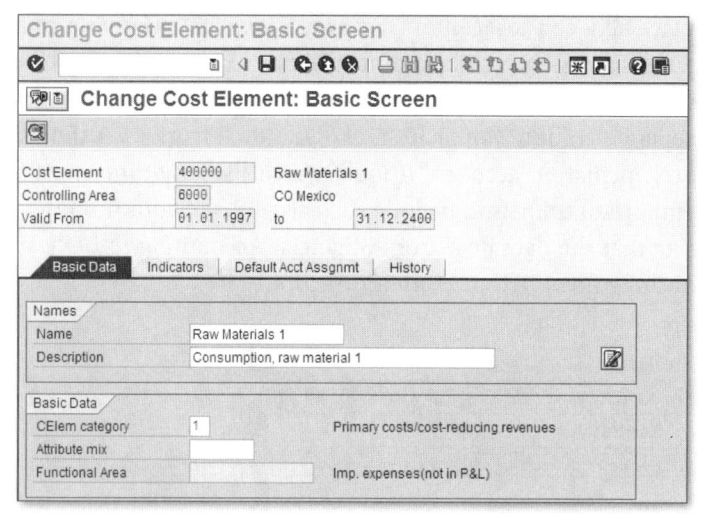

Figure 4.28 Primary Cost Element

4.9.2 Controlling and the Financial Accounts

The normal value flow is from the General Ledger account to the cost element. For example, whenever a goods movement is recorded, material account determination selects the correct accounts to be posted in the General Ledger for that business transaction, and a posting to CO is made under the appropriate cost element. We'll see lots of examples of this when we post goods movements in Chapter 6. Occasionally the flow is in the other direction.

Cross-Company Allocations

There is a flow of costs from CO to FI during allocations where the allocation crosses the boundary of the company code. An example of this might be a shared service center for controlling that works for multiple companies in a group and allocates its costs to these companies using an allocation cycle. In early releases of SAP ERP and SAP R/3 such postings were stored in a reconciliation ledger and transferred to the other company code at period close. One of the fundamental changes in SAP ERP is that the SAP ERP General Ledger allows the real-time integration of CO and Financial Accounting and can update such cross-company postings immediately.

4 | Master Data Where Controlling Is a Stakeholder

The SAP ERP update process affects not only postings that cross company codes, but also postings that cross business areas, profit centers, segments, and functional areas. Cross-company postings are generally quite rare, but it's much more common for allocations to take place between cost centers that are assigned to different profit centers or different business areas. So it's important to define *reconciliation accounts* in Financial Accounting to capture the results of each type of allocation you plan to use. You can define a separate account for each CO transaction. Figure 4.29 shows an example of such a reconciliation account. It looks much like any other profit and loss account. The important thing is to include such accounts in your thinking, since it's easy to imagine that the data flow from Financial Accounting to CO is a one-way street, with nothing flowing in the other direction.

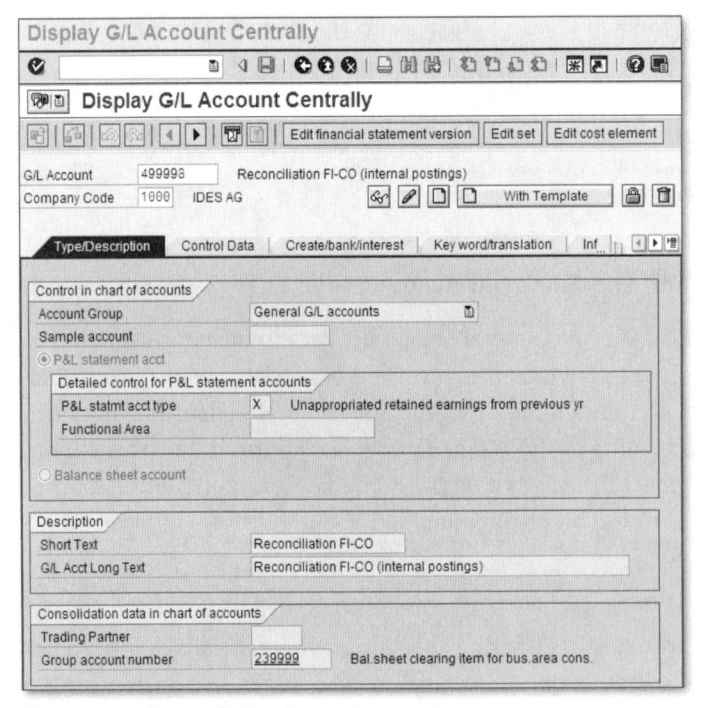

Figure 4.29 Reconciliation Account

Work in Process

If you calculate work in process, you must set up posting rules in Customizing that determine the balance sheet and profit and loss account to which the WIP is assigned. Typical postings in this context are for:

- Work in process (WIPR)
- Reserves for unrealized costs (RUCR)
- Revenue in excess of billings (POCI)
- Revenue surplus (POCS)

Figure 4.30 shows the posting rules for moving work in process and percentage of completion values back to Financial Accounting. The P&L accounts shown are unusual in that you're not allowed to create cost elements for them to stop WIP flowing back into CO, where they would run the risk of being counted twice.

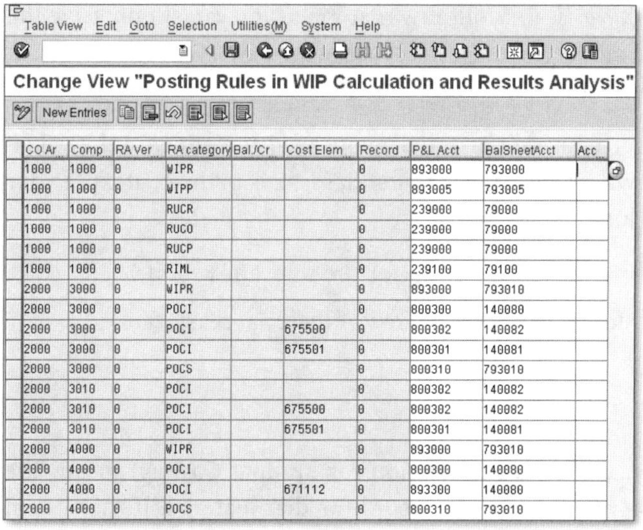

CO Ar	Comp	RA Ver	RA category	Bal./Cr	Cost Elem	Record	P&L Acct	BalSheetAcct	Acc
1000	1000	0	WIPR			0	893000	793000	
1000	1000	0	WIPP			0	893005	793005	
1000	1000	0	RUCR			0	239000	79000	
1000	1000	0	RUCO			0	239000	79000	
1000	1000	0	RUCP			0	239000	79000	
1000	1000	0	RIML			0	239100	79100	
2000	3000	0	WIPR			0	893000	793010	
2000	3000	0	POCI			0	800300	140080	
2000	3000	0	POCI		675500	0	800302	140082	
2000	3000	0	POCI		675501	0	800301	140081	
2000	3000	0	POCS			0	800310	793010	
2000	3010	0	POCI			0	800302	140082	
2000	3010	0	POCI		675500	0	800302	140082	
2000	3010	0	POCI		675501	0	800301	140081	
2000	4000	0	WIPR			0	893000	793010	
2000	4000	0	POCI			0	800300	140080	
2000	4000	0	POCI		671112	0	893300	140080	
2000	4000	0	POCS			0	800310	793010	

Figure 4.30 Posting Rules for WIP Calculation

Now that we've defined the accounts to be used to record the goods movements in Logistics and the cost elements to record the postings in CO, we're almost ready to start planning. The last step is to make sure the material masters contain the correct prices for costing.

4.10 Setting Prices for Product Costing

In Chapter 1 we introduced the concept of standard-setting as a key element of CO. We already discussed the two fundamentally different approaches to cost accounting—standard costs and actual costs—but we have yet to look at how prices get to the material master in the first place. One of the controlling department's most important jobs is to ensure that the material masters contain the correct standard costs at all times, since the planning process that we'll look at in Chapter 5 and the actual postings that we'll see in Chapter 6 rely on this data being accurate.

4.10.1 Setting Standard Costs for Raw Materials

Let's look first at how to determine the costs of the raw materials used to manufacture a product. Several options exist that go beyond the methods used for the real-time valuation of goods movements.

If you use the *moving average price* for your raw materials, you can simply have the system include the latest moving average price for each raw material in costing (this is configured in the valuation variant).

If you use *standard costs* for your raw materials, you need to configure the valuation variant to determine what constitutes the standard costs in the context of your business. The options include:

- Price from a purchasing info record (set up for the relevant vendor)
- PLANNED PRICE 1 (field in ACCOUNTING 2 view of material master)
- Standard price
- Moving average price

The logic of the valuation variant (configuration for Product Costing) means the system first searches for a purchasing info record for that material. If the system is unable to find a purchasing info record with a price agreement with a specific vendor for that material, it reads the planned price for the material, and so on.

> **Enhancements for Material Valuation**
>
> While the material valuation options available in Customizing will take you a long way, many organizations have requested the ability to apply their own logic to select material prices. If you find yourself involved in this kind of discussion, consider having your IT department implement one or more of the SAP Notes below:
>
> - SAP Note 1306588—Costing: BAdI for Valuation of Subcontracting
> - SAP Note 1326416—Costing: BAdI for Valuation of External Processing
> - SAP Note 1445940—Raw Material Cost Estimate: Origin Group for Delivery Costs

Whatever price you choose, marking and releasing the cost estimate (see Chapter 5) results in the cost estimate (either a material price or a purchasing info record) being updated to the material master as the new standard price.

Figure 4.31 shows a sample purchasing info record. This contains the pricing agreement for the material negotiated by your purchasing department. To display a purchasing info record, you can use Transaction ME13 or go to LOGISTICS • MATERIALS MANAGEMENT • MASTER DATA • INFO RECORD • DISPLAY, and then enter the relevant vendor, material, purchasing organization, and plant.

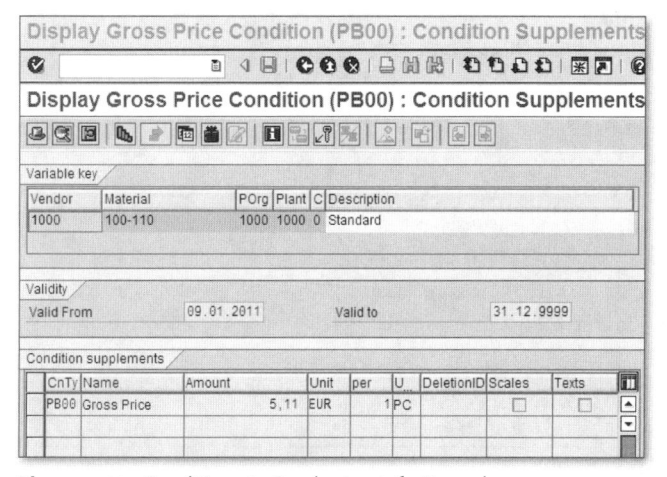

Figure 4.31 Conditions in Purchasing Info Record

You use the COSTING 2 view in the material master, shown in Figure 4.32, to set planned prices that will become the standard price in the future as part of the costing process. Many organizations automate the process of updating values to these fields with their own ABAP code. Note the link to the existing standard costs shown here, which enables you to check how realistic the new prices will be.

During Product Costing, you can always check which price has been used for a raw material by selecting the VALUATION tab in Transaction CK13N (see Figure 4.33). In this example, a value has been read from the purchasing info record. We've changed the layout (see Chapter 2) to show the vendor as well, to make it easier to check the conditions used in the purchasing info record.

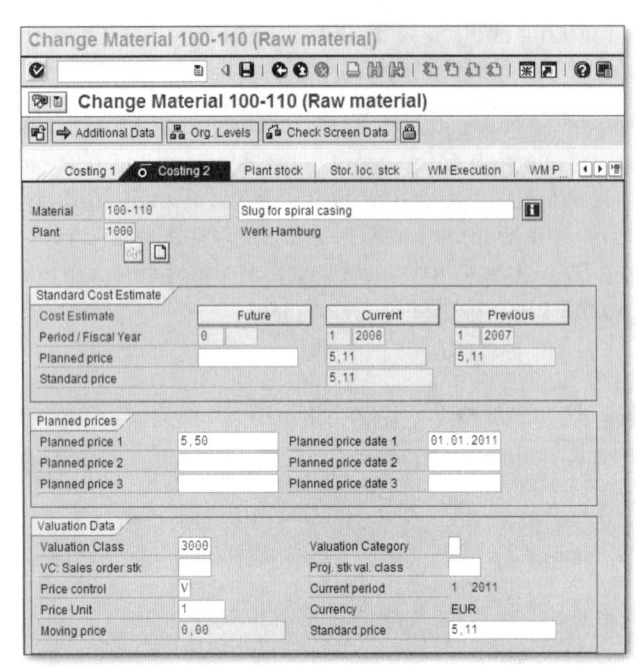

4 | Master Data Where Controlling Is a Stakeholder

Figure 4.32 Material Master – Costing 2 View

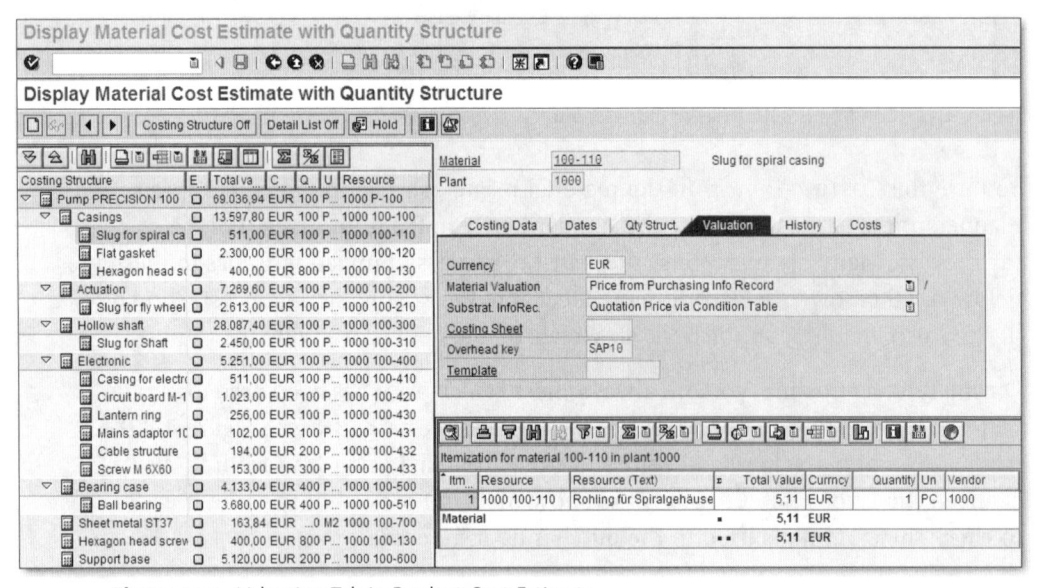

Figure 4.33 Valuation Tab in Product Cost Estimate

The VALUATION tab in Figure 4.33 shows that a substrategy for reading the info record has been used that reads the contents of a condition table. The purchasing info record in Figure 4.32 is fairly simple in that it only reads a material price. But it's common to include additional conditions for freight, duty, insurance, and other related costs in the info record. You can pull these conditions into the product cost estimate as well by mapping them to the origin groups we saw in the costing view of the material master. Since these conditions are not relevant for inventory valuation, you should flag them as not part of the cost roll-up and not relevant for inventory valuation during configuration of the cost components.

4.10.2 Balance Sheet Valuation

For balance sheet valuation, you can define tax and commercial prices in the ACCOUNTING 2 view of the material master. The same principle applies as for the calculation of standard costs. You can configure a valuation variant for inventory costing to select one of the commercial prices or one of the tax prices, shown in Figure 4.34. You can then transfer the results of this cost estimate to the material master for the finished product.

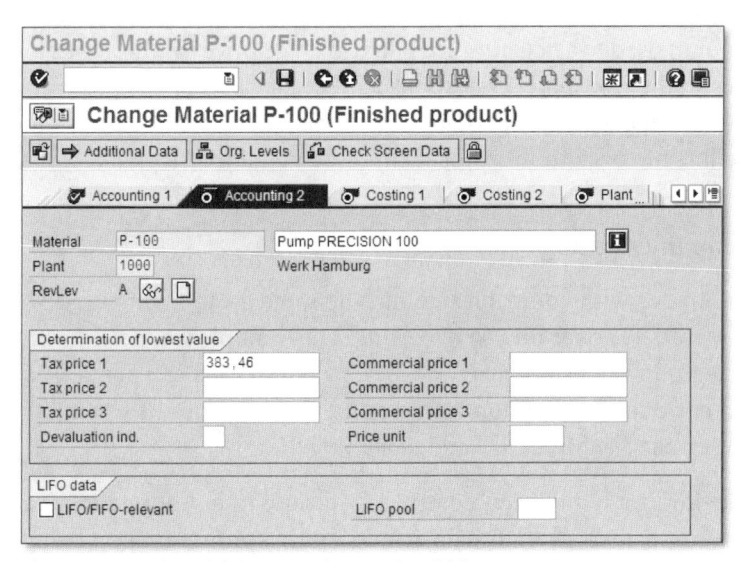

Figure 4.34 Material Master – Accounting 2 View

4.10.3 Calculating Actual Costs

Several business situations may require the calculation of actual costs in addition to standard costs.

- In some countries, it's a legal requirement to value at actual costs (common in South America and parts of Asia).
- It can also make sense to value at actual costs where raw material costs are volatile (this can be the case in the food industry) or where production structures are unstable (this can be the case in the chemicals industry).
- As accounting standards change, there's a requirement to value inventory according to multiple accounting standards (such as IFRS and local GAAP). This option is available from SAP enhancement package 5 for SAP ERP 6.0 and involves using the Material Ledger to calculate actual costs according to the alternative accounting principle. To use this function, you need to have your IT department activate the business function FIN_CO_COGM (parallel valuation of cost of goods manufactured).

If this is the case, all goods movements and transactions affecting prices (including invoice receipts and order settlement) are updated to the Material Ledger. At period close, this information is used to calculate a weighted average price for the goods in stock. Since changes in the raw material costs also affect the costs of the products manufactured, any differences are then assigned to the manufactured products and to cost of sales. We'll come back to this process in more detail in Chapter 7.

4.10.4 Cross-Company Costing

If your organization trades with companies within the same group, you may also consider using the Material Ledger for group costing. The example we looked at in Figure 4.3 stores the group values in Euros, the local values in Mexican pesos, and the dollar as a hard currency. In addition to the different currencies, it's possible to distinguish between the *legal valuation* and *group valuation*.

- In the legal valuation, trade between companies in the same group is treated as if the affiliated companies are external partners, with a profit mark-up being charged according to the price conditions. This is required to accommodate local tax regulations.
- In the group valuation, trade between companies in the same group is treated as if the movement is simply a stock transfer, with the cost of goods manufactured

being passed between the affiliated companies. This uses a special price condition, KW00, which selects the cost component split, rather than a selling price.

Affiliated companies are identified by the TRADING PARTNER field in the vendor and customer masters.

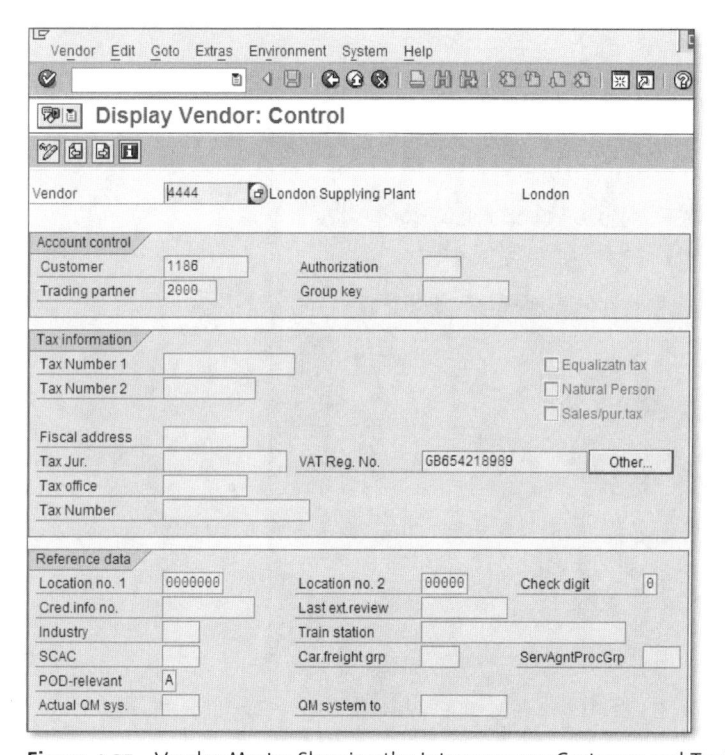

Figure 4.35 Vendor Master Showing the Intercompany Customer and Trading Partner

To create a vendor master, you can use Transaction XK01 or go to LOGISTICS • MATERIALS MANAGEMENT • PURCHASING • MASTER DATA • VENDOR • CENTRAL • CREATE. Enter the name of the vendor (e.g., 4444) and the company code for the supplying plant. In the GENERAL DATA section, click on the CONTROL checkbox. Figure 4.35 shows the vendor master for the supplying plant. The control data links the supplying plant to the receiving plant via the entry in the CUSTOMER field (e.g., 1186). The entry in the TRADING PARTNER field (e.g., 2000) identifies the company ID to which the plant belongs for consolidation purposes.

To create a customer master, use Transaction XD01 or go to LOGISTICS • SALES AND DISTRIBUTION • MASTER DATA • BUSINESS PARTNER • CUSTOMER • CREATE • COMPLETE.

Enter the name of the customer (e.g., 1186) and the company code for the receiving plant and select the CONTROL DATA tab. Figure 4.36 shows the customer master for the receiving plant. The control data links the receiving plant to the supplying plant via the entry in the VENDOR field (4444 here). The entry in the TRADING PARTNER field (1000 in this example) identifies the company ID to which the plant belongs for consolidation.

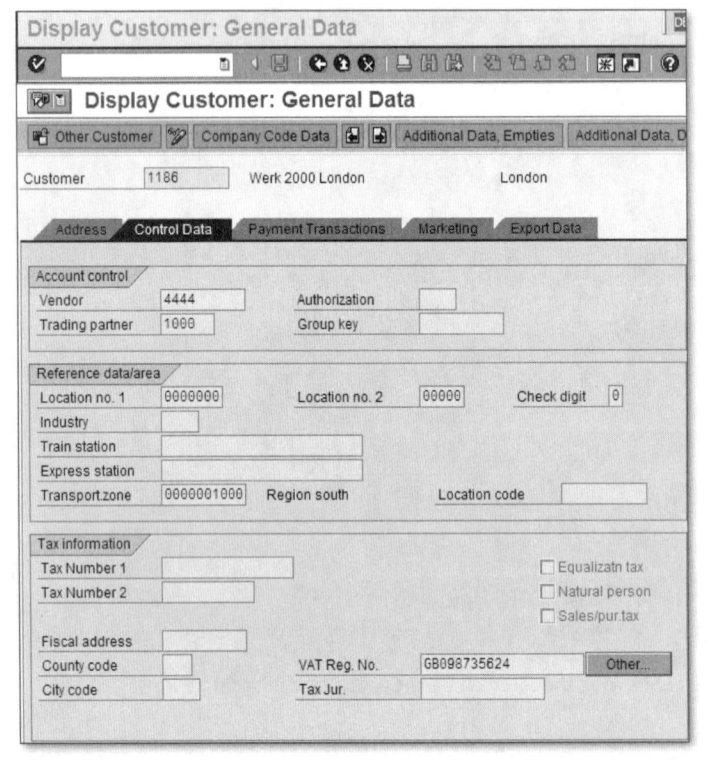

Figure 4.36 Customer Master Showing the Intercompany Vendor and Trading Partner

4.11 Summary

In this chapter, we looked at the master data that affects costing (material master, bill of material, routing, and work center) and profitability analysis (material master, customer master), together with the master data for projects and investment programs. We also looked at the links to the financial accounts and showed how to establish the initial prices for raw materials in the material master. This means we have pretty much all the information we need to embark on the planning process. This will pull together the assumptions documented in the master data throughout SAP ERP to tell us what it will cost to deliver on a given sales plan. We'll look at how to use this data in planning in the next chapter. We'll also return to our investment program and look at how to plan and budget for projects and orders assigned to an investment program.

This chapter discusses two forms of planning—one for a complete sales plan in a manufacturing environment and the other for the planning and budgeting of investment projects.

5 Planning and Budgeting

In Chapter 1 we discussed the importance of cost planning and standard-setting in the SAP approach to controlling. We also raised the terminology issue that SAP applications tend to refer to a *sales plan* and a *production plan*, whereas others might refer to a sales budget or a production budget. What is meant is the process of estimating future sales or production volumes and then determining the cost of delivering on this plan in terms of the *resources* to be used. Only when we look at projects and internal orders do we find SAP referring to a *project budget*. The budget refers to the *approved plan* that will act as a ceiling for spending on the project and not to the process of arriving at that figure by estimating the labor, time, materials, and so on required to complete the project.

So, terminology issues aside, why is planning so important for the controller? Beyond the need to establish targets and the resources required to achieve these targets, there's the business requirement to set *standard costs* for the materials to be manufactured. The standard costs are used to provide the initial valuation every time a goods movement is posted and as a basis for variance analysis at period close. The correct standard costs need to be in place before goods movements can take place, and ensuring that the standard costs are correct is one of the key responsibilities of controllers in any manufacturing organization. Similarly, since every shop floor worker who records a confirmation in Logistics and every employee who charges his work time to a project triggers a *direct activity allocation* in Controlling, an *activity price* needs to be in place before time can be charged this way, and ensuring that the activity price is correct is another key responsibility of the controller.

Both the standard costs and the activity price represent a "best guess" by the organization as to the costs to produce a given volume of product or supply a given amount of activity. These standards can be corrected as the actual costs for the period are known, and we'll look at that process in Chapter 7. Given the importance of planning and standards, we're sometimes asked if it's even possible to use the Controlling component of SAP ERP Financials (CO) without planning. You do need standard costs that remain fixed during the period even if you have the material ledger calculate the actual costs at period close. However, this "standard" can be set by selecting the actual costs from the previous period. The challenge here is the timing. The period close needs to have reached the stage when the actual costs for all materials are calculated and updated to inventory before the first goods movement is posted in the next period.

The other fundamental question a controller has to answer is the degree of variance analysis that's required or even relevant for the organization. The planning process is about setting targets in terms of what it should cost to manufacture a product or provide a service. There are arguments against using standard costs and variance analysis — mainly that it drives the wrong behavior in terms of encouraging large lot sizes and overproduction — but most organizations continue to use variances against plan to measure the efficiency of their organization, and the level of detail in your plan determines the level of variance analysis you can perform later.

These days, there's also the question of where to plan, and we'll explore the relationship between planning in SAP ERP and planning in SAP NetWeaver Business Warehouse (SAP NetWeaver BW) or SAP Strategic Enterprise Management (SAP SEM) in Chapter 10. For the moment, we'll focus on what determines the planning model in the two cases.

- In SAP ERP, it's the *output* of the sales plan, the production plan, or the activity requirements that drive the planning model. It's against these *volume or quantity assumptions* that the planning cycle in SAP ERP works, establishing the relationship between the proportional costs, which vary depending on the amount of goods sold or the amount of activity to be provided. The planning cycle uses the volumes and master data in SAP ERP and simulates the "pull" of the business transactions that ultimately execute the sales orders. In its most extreme form, it can try to capture the impact of all these business transactions, simulating allocations, order settlements, and all transfers of activities between units.

- In SAP NetWeaver BW and SAP SEM, the model is not so closely tied to the underlying business processes. It can be *freely modeled* in terms of the entities against which planning data is captured and the granularity of the plan. This can lead to some critical differences. The cost center plan in SAP ERP has to capture the plan by cost element, because this is the data structure used to capture actual costs, even if for planning purposes the individual accounts under which salaries and wage costs will be transferred from SAP HR are not relevant or even known. In SAP NetWeaver BW and SAP SEM you can enter data at the higher level of the cost element group (such as all salary and wage costs) and then have a planning function distribute this amount to the cost elements if you need that level of detail.

The idea of a quantity- or output-driven plan is at the heart of planning in SAP ERP, but we'll find the same approach when we look at activity-based budgeting in the context of SAP Profitability and Cost Management (SAP PCM) in Chapter 11.

5.1 Complete Sales Plan in a Manufacturing Environment

In this section we'll look at how to prepare the annual operating plan (AOP) or annual budget. This involves planning all aspects of the business—revenue, production, procurement, capacity, and product/overhead costs—and is an exercise typically started in the last quarter of each fiscal year. It's a process driven by the controller in collaboration with sales managers, production managers, cost center managers, plant controllers, and finance. Figure 5.1 provides an overview of the process. It's a highly collaborative process with a tacit assumption that the departments at each interface are prepared to share data and assumptions. We've drawn it as a linear process, but in practice there are iterations and changes at every intersection in the process as each department revisits its assumptions and adjusts its proposal.

Master Data (Materials, Customers, Cost Center, Activity Type, Cost Element, BOM, Routing, Work Center)
Sales Plan/Sales Quantities › Production Plan/Production Quantities › Cost Center Plan/Activity Quantities › Calculate Activity Price › Costing Run/ Standard Costs › Profitability Plan/ Contribution Margins

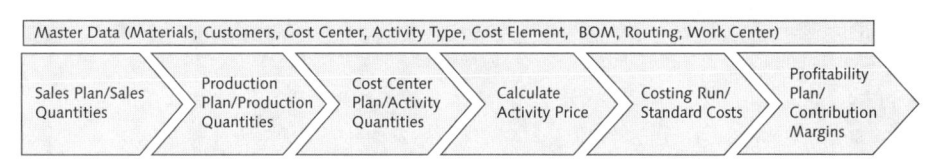

Figure 5.1 Planning Process Overview

The same basic flow can be used with some simplification to plan for a shorter time frame. It's possible to perform the same exercise on a quarterly or even a monthly basis, allowing you to provide a forecast or simply to develop standards that are more in keeping with the changing business conditions.

The different assumptions behind this process are usually modeled as *versions*. You'll see the option MAINTAIN PLANNED VERSIONS under CURRENT SETTINGS in

Figure 5.2. Normally there's an agreement concerning which version is the working version and which is the final approved version. Various copy functions allow the controller to copy data between different versions as required. When planning is complete, it makes sense to lock the version to prevent anybody from accidentally changing the plan. Don't be fooled by the term *version* into thinking you can save a version of your personal planning data as easily as you would save a new copy of a spreadsheet. Versions are created centrally and have a specific business purpose (annual plan, monthly forecast, and so on). As you save, you need to be clear whether you're saving data to the working version of the company plan or the final version. Once the data is saved, it's there for everyone with appropriate authorization to see. There's no "Janet's version" outside of test systems.

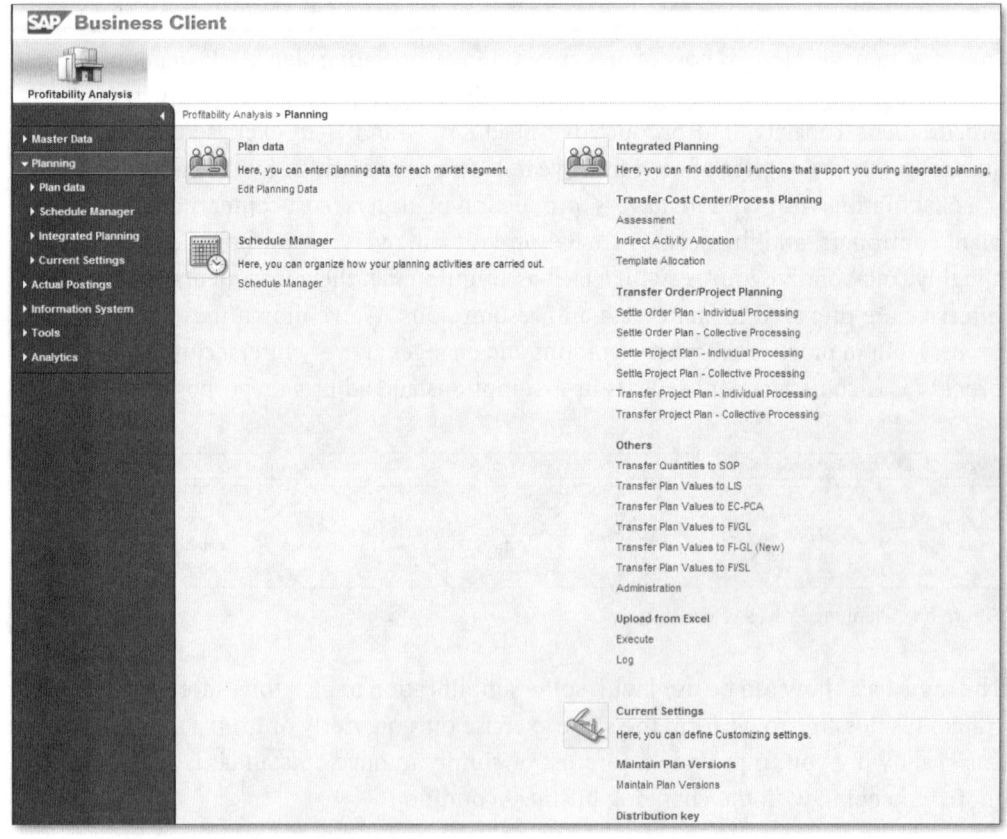

Figure 5.2 Planning Applications in Profitability Analysis

Since the planned volume or output drives the process it also makes sense to reflect on the meaning of the three main quantities we'll be planning:

- **Sales quantity**
  This is the basis for the sales plan and the profit plan and represents the volumes that each sales manager believes he can sell within the time frame.

- **Production quantity**
  This is the basis for the production plan and is derived from the sales plan but expanded to cover all semifinished products and raw materials and to take account of any materials in stock. It represents the quantity used by the production planners in their long-term planning assumptions.

  For the standard costs, the production quantity is the costing lot size in the material master, which is adjusted to reflect the planned sales volumes when the cost estimate is transferred to the profitability plan. Ensuring that these "ideal" lot sizes are in line with the typical lot sizes used in production is the controller's job.

- **Activity quantity**
  This can either be the capacity of the cost center that's set by the cost center manager, or it can be a dynamic quantity that responds to the pull of the production plan and the requests for activity from other cost centers. It's the controller's job to ensure that the capacity is a fair representation of the cost center's typical output.

5.1.1 Sales and Operations Planning

The planning exercise generally begins with forecasting the sales quantities and revenue for the coming fiscal year. Figure 5.2 shows the planning folder for PROFITABILITY ANALYSIS. This corresponds to following the menu path ACCOUNTING • CONTROLLING • PROFITABILITY ANALYSIS • PLANNING. Generally, it's the sales managers who enter their sales quantities and revenues under PLAN DATA • EDIT PLANNED DATA (Transaction KEPM), but controlling always checks and sometimes adjusts these figures to ensure that they're in line with company guidelines. These adjustments represent both the technical exercise of ensuring that the correct figures are entered and a business dialog where the controller questions the underlying planning assumptions and verifies the figures against historical actual data and the sales manager explains and justifies his decisions.

An additional folder, INTEGRATED PLANNING, provides many functions to transfer the plan to other applications, such as production and the general ledger, and to pull data from order planning, project planning, or cost center planning to get a complete picture of the likely profitability of the entire plan. We'll use functions in this folder to transfer the sales plan from CO-PA to the sales and operational plan in Logistics, where it will act as the starting point for requirements planning. These transactions are the domain of the controller, because they simulate the mass allocations and settlements that normally take place at period close. The data volumes can be similarly large, so you may have to schedule the planned allocations and calculations as carefully as those performed at period close (see Chapters 7 and 12).

Also note the SCHEDULE MANAGER folder. This allows you to define how any allocations, settlements, and so on required in the course of the plan are to be carried out and to automate the process of performing these tasks. We'll look at the Schedule Manager functions in more detail in Chapter 12.

> **Setting System Locks in Planning**
>
> Owing to the large data volumes involved, some of the transactions a controller uses during planning lock all related objects, to ensure that other applications cannot make changes while the planning application is running. For details of the locking procedure, refer to SAP Note 79634.

Create Sales Plan

There are many approaches to sales planning.

- One question is the level of detail to be captured in the plan. Does it make sense to capture data at the level of the product/customer or does it make more sense to capture it at a higher level, such as by product line, and then have the system break down the plan to the product/customer level using top-down distribution, a planning function in Profitability Analysis?

- Another question is whether to start from zero or refer to the past. Some organizations copy actual sales quantities from previous periods into a new planning version and have the sales managers adjust them. Others have the sales managers enter their data from scratch, believing this to provide a more rigorous basis for planning.

Clearly the first technical requirement of a planning application is flexibility, in terms of the granularity of the planning, the time frame for which data can be entered, and the sources from which data can be copied. Just like the reporting functions in Profitability Analysis, the planning applications are completely configurable. You can plan against any entity that exists in the operating concern, and part of the configuration effort is then to restrict what can be planned—the version to be used, the organizational units, the time frame, the level of detail, and so on.

Another central idea is *valuation*. This means using the values entered in the planning layout to derive further values. So if the sales manager enters sales of 100 units of a particular product as a planning assumption, the valuation function will select the product cost estimate and the cost components for that product and adjust the costs to reflect the lot size of 100 units. The valuation functions are set up in configuration and executed when the controller clicks on the appropriate button in the planning layout, as we'll do when we've completed the cost center plan and calculated the standard costs. We'll see the same function used at the end of the period close to pull the actual costs from the periodic costing run into Profitability Analysis.

Figure 5.3 shows the planning data in the sample operating concern S_GO, delivered to illustrate one approach to the implementation of Profitability Analysis in SAP ERP. This contains four sample planning levels for the planning of contribution margins, sales and marketing expenses, and other overhead and for the top-down distribution of costs from higher-level to lower-level characteristics. We've selected the planning package to show the parameters for which planned data can be entered for the contribution margins in this example. As we saw in Chapter 2, the record type F (billing documents) is used to establish that we're developing the planned *revenue stream*. The version provides the framework for the plan. You need to know the version when transferring data to the other applications. In this example, data can be entered for the customer group, distribution channel, and material group.

Figure 5.4 shows a sample data entry screen for the sales and profit plan. The sales quantities for the customer groups and material groups on the far right provide the output quantities against which the rest of the plan will be executed. Once the controller has checked the sales quantities for accuracy, the next stage is to transfer them to the production plan to determine how to manufacture the quantities that will be sold. We'll cover the use of the VALUATE button to complete the planning cycle later in this section.

5 | Planning and Budgeting

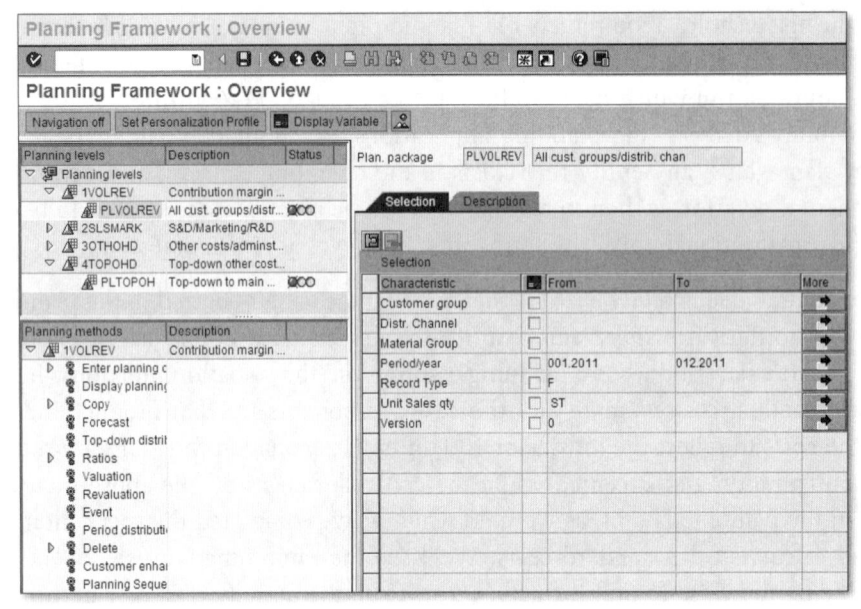

Figure 5.3 Planning Package for Sales and Profit Plan

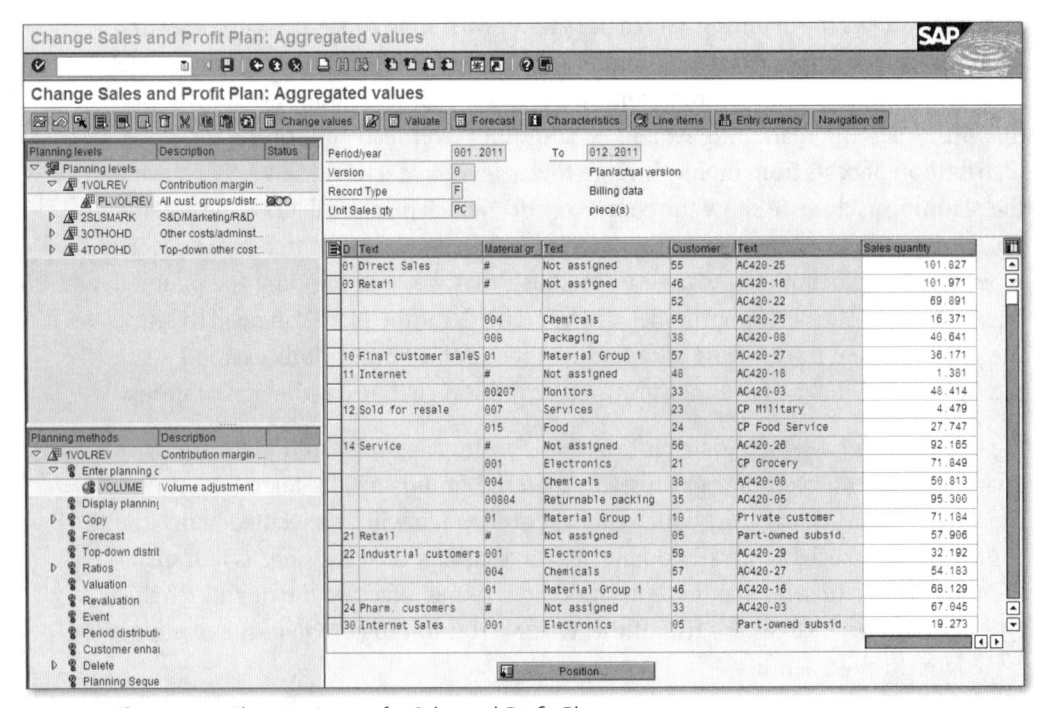

Figure 5.4 Planning Layout for Sales and Profit Plan

208

The controller initiates the transfer of the planning quantities from the sales and profit plan to the sales and operations plan by using the TRANSFER QUANTITIES TO SOP function (Transaction KE1E) in the PLANNING AIDS folder in Figure 5.2. Figure 5.5 shows the parameters for the transfer, particularly the version used to plan in Profitability Analysis and the receiving version in Long-Term Planning.

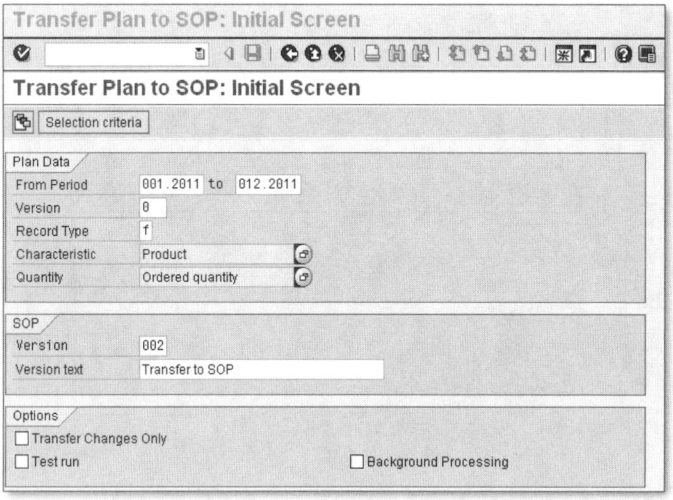

Figure 5.5 Transfer Sales and Profit Plan to Sales and Operations Plan

Create Production Plan

Once the controller has transferred the sales quantities to the sales and operations plan, the next step is for the production department to plan the semifinished products needed as intermediates and the raw materials that need to be purchased to enable delivery on the sales plan, using the bills of material for the finished products as a starting point.

Whereas the *plan version* provides the framework for the sales plan, the *planning scenario* provides the framework for the production plan. To define the planning scenario, go to Transaction MS31 or LOGISTICS • PRODUCTION • PRODUCTION • PLANNING • LONG TERM PLANNING • PLANNING SCENARIO • CREATE and give your scenario a name.

To bring the requirements from Profitability Analysis into the production plan, you need to link the plan version to the planning scenario by clicking on the PLANNED INDEPENDENT REQUIREMENTS button (see Figure 5.6). You also need to determine which plant(s) are affected by clicking on the PLANTS button before releasing and saving the scenario by clicking on the RELEASE AND SAVE button.

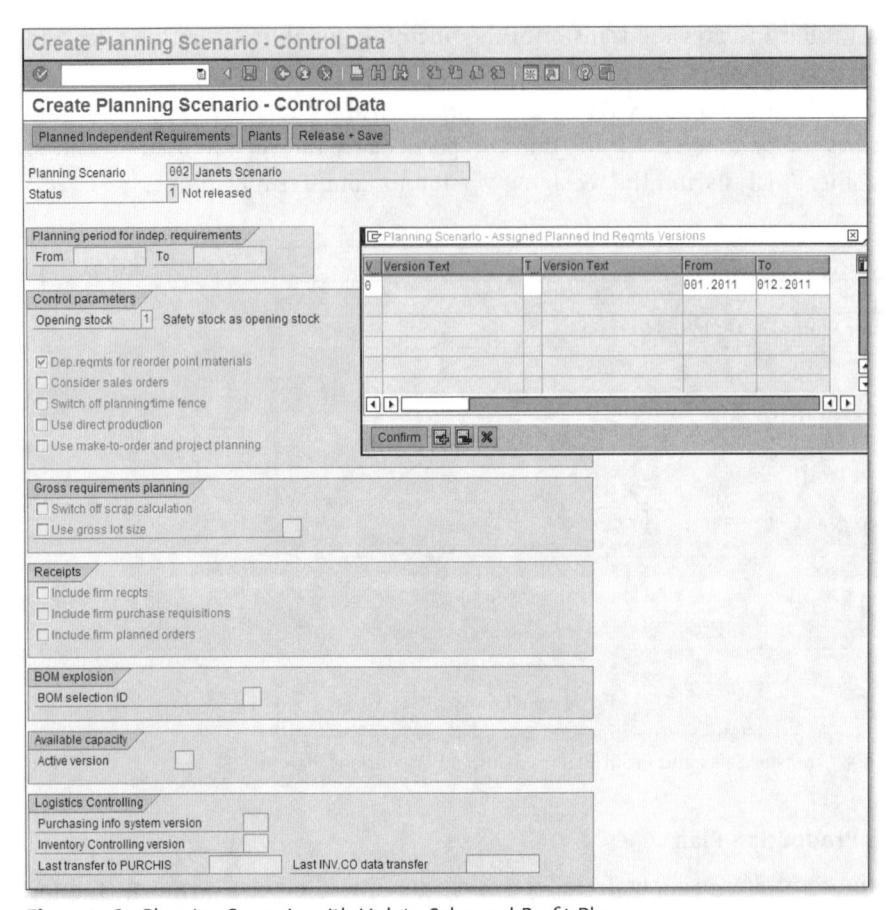

Figure 5.6 Planning Scenario with Link to Sales and Profit Plan

To create a long-term planning run, go to LOGISTICS • PRODUCTION • PRODUCTION PLANNING • LONG TERM PLANNING • LONG-TERM PLANNING • PLANNING RUN or Transaction MS01. Enter the planning scenario and plant and click on EXECUTE.

- Executing the long-term planning run reads the bill of material for each finished product to determine the dependent requirements (semifinished products and raw materials needed for the finished products).

- The long-term planning run also reads the routings for each of the materials to be manufactured to determine the machine time, labor time, and so on required. In controlling terms, this represents the scheduled activity that the production cost centers are required to produce. This is the quantity against which controlling is required to plan the cost center expenses.

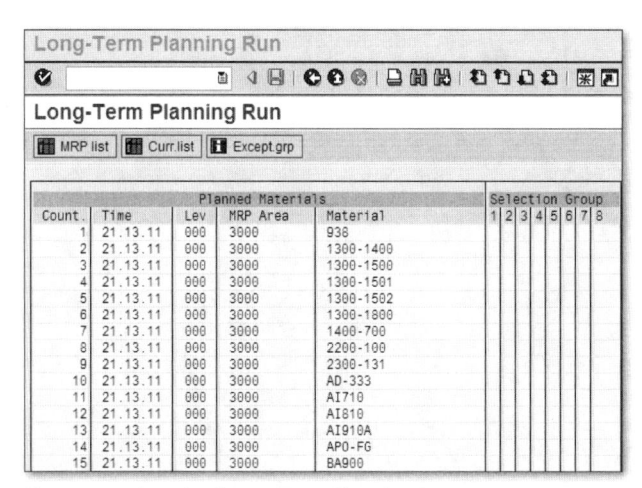

Figure 5.7 shows the result of the long-term planning run.

Figure 5.7 Result of Long-Term Planning Run

Once the production quantities have been checked, the next stage is to transfer them to the cost center plan, a task the controller performs.

5.1.2 Cost Center Planning

The next stage of the planning exercise involves the cost centers and their managers. Figure 5.8 shows the planning folder for COST CENTER ACCOUNTING. This corresponds to following the menu path ACCOUNTING • CONTROLLING • COST CENTER ACCOUNTING • PLANNING. Again, we see the planning applications used mainly by cost center managers and then checked by controlling under COST AND ACTIVITY INPUTS, ACTIVITY OUTPUTS/PRICES, and STATISTICAL KEY FIGURES and the transactions used only by controlling under PLANNING AIDS for copying data and transferring relevant data from other applications. The applications in this list illustrate how planning in SAP ERP mirrors the data flows during actual postings, with planned data being brought in from SAP ERP Human Capital Management (wages and salaries), Fixed Asset Accounting (depreciation), and Sales and Operations Planning (our production plan).

5 | Planning and Budgeting

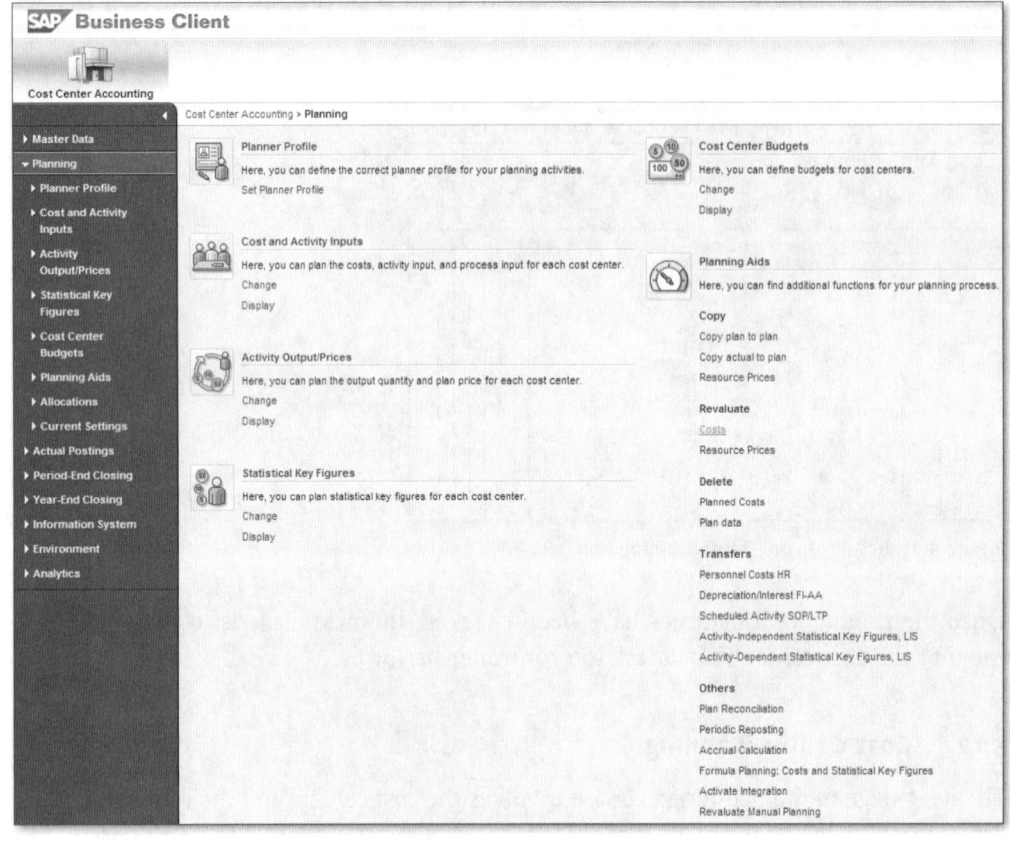

Figure 5.8 Planning Applications in Cost Center Accounting

> **Key Concept: Plan Integration**
>
> Plan integration ensures that any data you enter for one object or sender (such as a maintenance cost center) that affects another object or receiver (such as a production cost center) is updated on both the sender cost center and the receiver cost center. Before you start planning, it's worth checking whether the INTEGRATED PLANNING checkbox has been selected for the version and fiscal year you intend to use for your plan. To do this, select CONTROLLING • COST CENTER ACCOUNTING • PLANNING • CURRENT SETTINGS • MAINTAIN VERSIONS. Select your controlling area. Then select the relevant version and the SETTINGS FOR THE FISCAL YEAR folder. Ensure that the INTEGRATED PLANNING checkbox is selected for the year in question.

Activity Quantities

As we said at the beginning of this section, cost center planning in the SAP approach is driven by the activity quantities for the cost center. When we talked about the activity types in Chapter 3, we discussed the difference between calculating an activity price using the *capacity* or the *activity quantity*. The capacity behaves much like a costing lot size: It's set by the cost center manager or the controller as an "ideal" for the cost center. This can be the right approach if you have large seasonal variations or your planning process is still fairly raw. You can either enter the planned activity for each cost center manually or pull it from the requesting cost centers and production. The ACT SCHED. (Scheduled Activity) column in Figure 5.9 represents this pull or demand captured in other plans. If this pull is considered realistic, you can use the plan reconciliation function to transfer the scheduled activity into the PLANNED ACTIVITY column so it can be used to calculate the activity price.

To enter the capacities and output quantities, select ACTIVITY/OUTPUT PRICES and CHANGE in Figure 5.8. Alternatively, go to Transaction KP26 or ACCOUNTING • CONTROLLING • COST CENTER ACCOUNTING • PLANNING • ACTIVITY OUTPUT/PRICES • CHANGE and enter the cost center, the activity types, the version, and the planning time frame. To keep the data entry in this transaction manageable, it makes sense to revisit the section on activity type groups in Chapter 3. If you try to plan too many activity types in one session, it's easy to put the wrong figures in the wrong line.

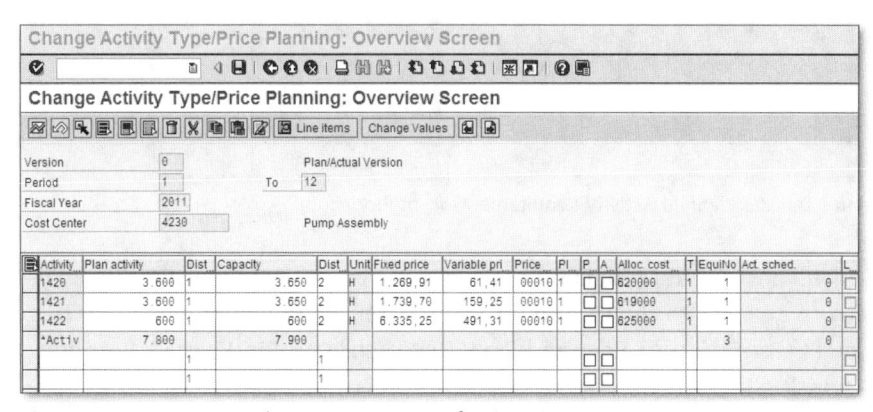

Figure 5.9 Capacities and Activity Quantities for Cost Center

Figure 5.9 shows the capacity of each cost center/activity type and the planned activity, but the scheduled activity (ACT. SCHED.) column is zero. Let's look at how to transfer the planned quantities based on the routings from our production plan to the cost center plan.

Transfer Production Requirements to Cost Center Plan

To link the cost center plan with the production plan, select the PLANNING AIDS folder in Figure 5.8 and SCHEDULED ACTIVITY SOP/LTP. Alternatively, go to Transaction KSPP or ACCOUNTING • CONTROLLING • COST CENTER ACCOUNTING • PLANNING • PLANNING AIDS • TRANSFERS • SCHEDULED ACTIVITY SOP/LTP and click on the TRANSFER CONTROL button. Figure 5.10 shows the link between the CO version and the planning scenario from the previous step. Remember that we fed data under a CO version from the sales plan to production, and now we're receiving data back from production under this same version.

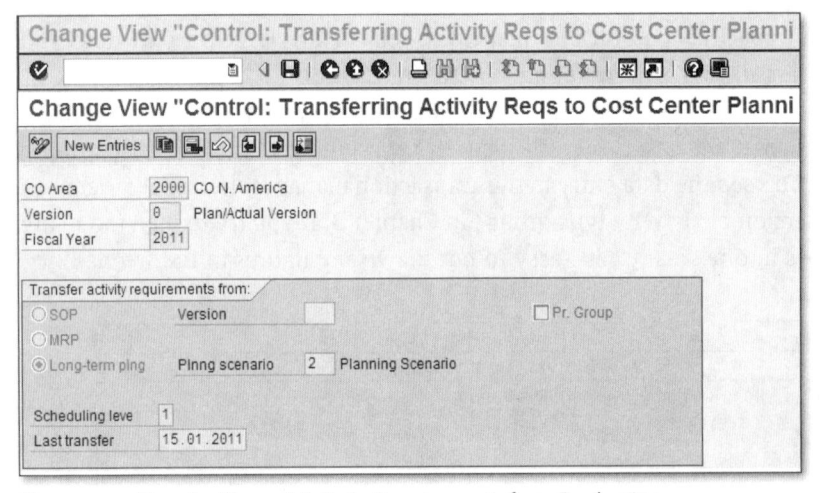

Figure 5.10 Transfer Planned Activity Requirements from Production

If you're only looking at production cost centers, you can now transfer the scheduled activity quantity to the PLANNED ACTIVITY column in Figure 5.9. To do this, select the PLANNING AIDS folder and PLAN RECONCILIATION in Figure 5.8 or go to Transaction KPSI or ACCOUNTING • CONTROLLING • COST CENTER ACCOUNTING • PLANNING • PLANNING AIDS • PLAN RECONCILIATION. Enter the version, the time frame, and whether you want to reconcile for all cost centers or just for a selection.

If you also want to include the activities from other cost centers (such as energy, repair, and quality cost centers) in this plan, you should wait until you've planned the activities required by the production cost centers from these cost centers before running plan reconciliation. We'll do that when we look at how to plan activity usage from supporting cost centers.

Plan Cost Center Costs

The controller now needs to work with the cost center managers to plan the costs required by each cost center to provide this level of output. There are various ways of working here:

- Some controllers sit down with their cost center managers and enter these values together.
- Others send out spreadsheets and have their cost center managers prepare the data for them to enter.
- Still others have the cost center managers enter this data. If you're in the last category, take a look also at the section on Express Planning in Chapter 10, which provides a Web-based application for this data entry.

To enter the planned costs for the cost center, select COST AND ACTIVITY INPUTS and CHANGE in Figure 5.8. Alternatively, go to Transaction KP06 or ACCOUNTING • CONTROLLING • COST CENTER ACCOUNTING • PLANNING • COST AND ACTIVITY INPUTS • CHANGE. The fields available for data entry in cost center planning are controlled by planning layouts configured in Customizing (we'll look at these settings in more detail in Chapter 10).

> **Finding Planning Layouts**
>
> The default planning layout for this type of planning is 1-101, but check that your organization has not configured its own. If you can't find planning layout 1-101, check whether it's been assigned to your planner profile. In the standard settings it's assigned to planner profile SAP101 rather than SAPALL. Refer to Figure 10.1 in Chapter 10 if you're not sure how to do this.

- Before you start, it's worth being absolutely clear about which cost elements are activity-dependent (such as external procurement and direct labor) and which are activity-independent (such as rent and facility costs) and making sure that you've set up cost element groups for each task that contain exactly these cost elements (see Chapter 3). If your cost elements were created using a standard numbering convention, you can dispense with cost element groups to a large extent and simply make you selection by entering cost elements 400000–415000 or whichever number ranges correspond to the type of cost elements for which you want to enter costs.
- It will also make life easier if you set up suitable activity type groups so you aren't handling too many activity types at any one time.

The selection screen in Transaction KP06 is the same for activity-independent and activity-dependent costs. You basically have to access the same transaction twice.

- Leave the activity type fields blank for activity-independent (or fixed) costs.
- Enter an activity type group for activity-dependent costs.

We'll first enter *activity-independent* costs to cover the fixed costs, such as rent and facilities costs. Select Transaction KP06 and enter the version, time frame, cost center, and your chosen cost element group, but leave the ACTIVITY TYPE field *blank*.

Before pressing Enter, choose between FREE and FORM-BASED planning (the default is FREE).

- If you select FORM-BASED PLANNING, you'll see a line for every cost element entered in the initial screen. This can be cumbersome if you have a large chart of accounts and are not careful with your initial cost element selection. However, you may find it easier to start with a form-based plan and a small cost element group or interval and then switch to free planning once you've captured your initial planning data. Since the form-based planning approach generates a line for every cost element in the interval or group for which active master data exists, this saves you from having to know exactly which cost element you want to plan for.
- If you select FREE PLANNING, you'll see a line for every line of planned data already entered. You can add new rows for additional cost elements as required. Once you've entered some data and are mainly adjusting the figures, free planning

gives you a better overview of what has already been entered. However, to add data you have to manually enter the number of each relevant cost element. If you choose free planning before any data has been entered, you'll see the message NO DATA HAS BEEN ENTERED YET. How easy you find entering your cost elements in free planning depends on how well you know your own chart of accounts.

Figure 5.11 shows the data entry screen with form-based planning selected. Here you see an empty line for each of the cost elements entered in the selection screen (and why it's worth creating lots of small specific cost element groups). You can go down this list entering a figure for each relevant cost element.

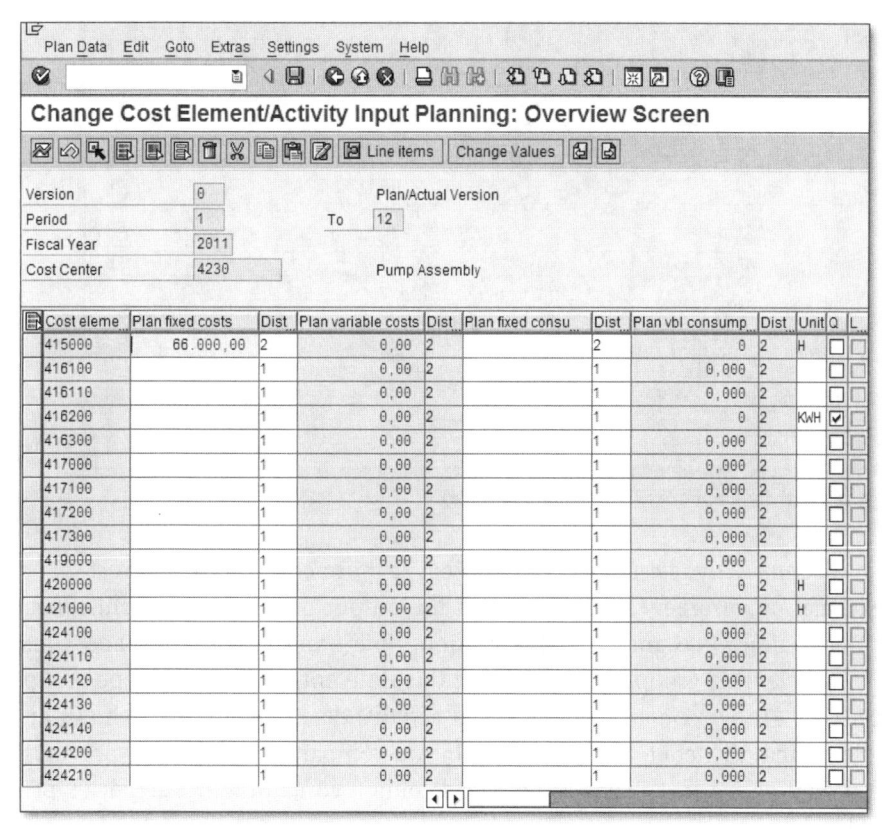

Figure 5.11 Activity-Independent Cost Planning (Form-Based)

5 | Planning and Budgeting

By comparison, in Figure 5.12 we chose free planning in the selection screen. Now we see only those lines for which data has been entered. Notice that a distribution key has been used to distribute the values from the years to the periods. In this example we're using distribution key 2 which uses any existing values as a guide for the distribution.

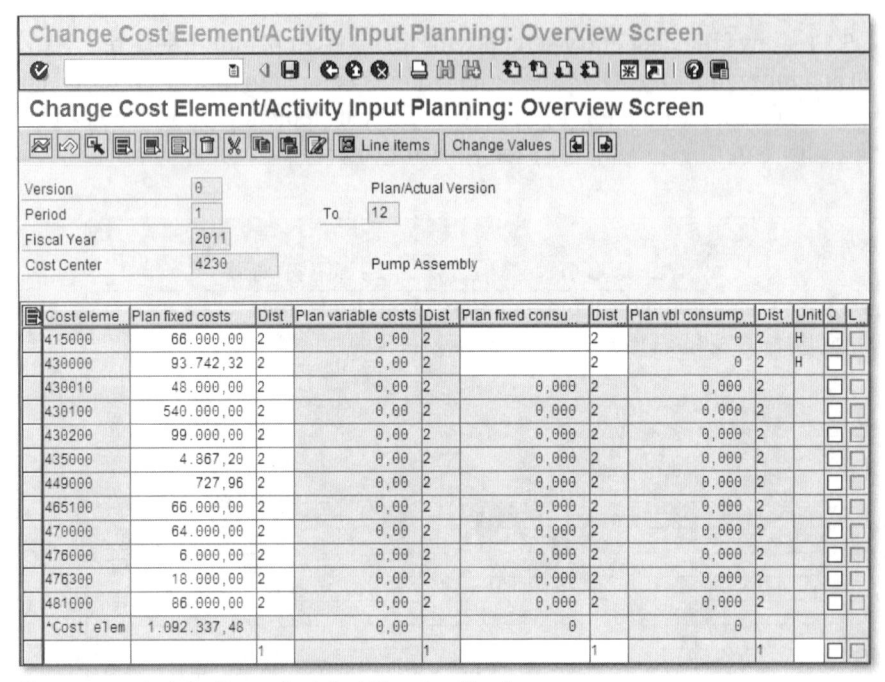

Cost eleme	Plan fixed costs	Dist	Plan variable costs	Dist	Plan fixed consu	Dist	Plan vbl consump	Dist	Unit	Q	L
415000	66.000,00	2	0,00	2		2	0	2	H	□	□
430000	93.742,32	2	0,00	2		2	0	2	H	□	□
430010	48.000,00	2	0,00	2	0,000	2	0,000	2		□	□
430100	540.000,00	2	0,00	2	0,000	2	0,000	2		□	□
430200	99.000,00	2	0,00	2	0,000	2	0,000	2		□	□
435000	4.867,20	2	0,00	2	0,000	2	0,000	2		□	□
449000	727,96	2	0,00	2	0,000	2	0,000	2		□	□
465100	66.000,00	2	0,00	2	0,000	2	0,000	2		□	□
470000	64.000,00	2	0,00	2	0,000	2	0,000	2		□	□
476000	6.000,00	2	0,00	2	0,000	2	0,000	2		□	□
476300	18.000,00	2	0,00	2	0,000	2	0,000	2		□	□
481000	86.000,00	2	0,00	2	0,000	2	0,000	2		□	□
*Cost elem	1.092.337,48		0,00		0		0				
		1		1		1		1		□	□

Figure 5.12 Activity-Dependent Cost Planning (Free)

We'll now enter *activity-dependent* costs to cover those costs, such as direct labor and external procurement, that vary with the output of the cost center. Again, go to Transaction KP06 and enter the version, time frame, cost center, and your chosen cost element group or interval, but this time enter an activity type group (see Chapter 3) that contains your chosen activity types. Figure 5.13 shows an example of activity-dependent planning. If you compare this with the previous screen, you'll notice that there's now a lead column containing the activity type. Proceed as before, this time entering the cost elements that refer to the delivery of a specific activity type.

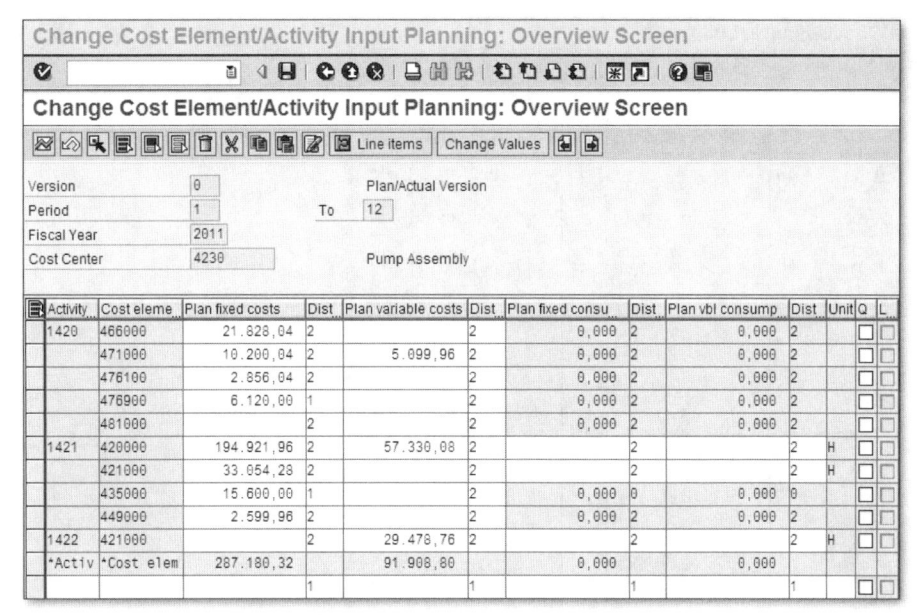

5.1 Complete Sales Plan in a Manufacturing Environment

Change Cost Element/Activity Input Planning: Overview Screen										
Version	0			Plan/Actual Version						
Period	1		To	12						
Fiscal Year	2011									
Cost Center	4230			Pump Assembly						

Activity	Cost eleme	Plan fixed costs	Dist	Plan variable costs	Dist	Plan fixed consu	Dist	Plan vbl consump	Dist	Unit	Q	L
1420	466000	21.828,04	2		2	0,000	2	0,000	2			
	471000	10.200,04	2	5.099,96	2	0,000	2	0,000	2			
	476100	2.856,04	2		2	0,000	2	0,000	2			
	476900	6.120,00	1		2	0,000	2	0,000	2			
	481000		2		2	0,000	2	0,000	2			
1421	420000	194.921,96	2	57.330,08	2		2		2	H		
	421000	33.054,28	2		2		2		2	H		
	435000	15.600,00	1		2	0,000	0	0,000	0			
	449000	2.599,96	2		2	0,000	2	0,000	2			
1422	421000		2	29.478,76	2		2		2	H		
*Activ	*Cost elem	287.180,32		91.908,80		0,000		0,000				
			1		1		1		1			

Figure 5.13 Activity-Independent Cost Planning

Notice again that a distribution key has been used to distribute the values from the years to the periods. In this example we're using equal distribution (distribution key 1). In other words, the USD 15,600 for cost element 435000 will be split across the periods such that each period receives USD 1,300. The split for the other lines is based on distribution key 2 and uses any existing values that have previously been entered as its guide. The controller can adjust the distribution key to select the method that best suits the business requirements in terms of seasonal variations.

Splitting Cost Center Costs

If the cost center provides more than one activity, such as machine hours, wage hours, and setup hours, as in our example, then the expenses captured at the cost center level (Figures 5.11 and 5.12) have to be "split" across the activity types before an activity price can be calculated. The split can use either equivalence numbers or a splitting schema. You define the approach in Customizing using a *splitting structure* and then assign it to the relevant cost centers. To perform splitting, go to Transaction KSS4 or ACCOUNTING • CONTROLLING • COST CENTER ACCOUNTING • PLANNING • ALLOCATIONS • SPLITTING. Enter the relevant version, periods, and fiscal year. Figure 5.14 shows the result of splitting. This is a fairly simplistic split, but it gives the general idea.

5 | Planning and Budgeting

Plan Cost Splitting: List				
Display status	Total for all periods			
Cost Object	Planned (COArCurr)	Crcy	TtlPlan(ObjCur)	ObCur
CTR 1000		EUR		EUR
ATY 1000/1510	2.127.402,27	EUR	2.127.402,27	EUR
CTR 1200		EUR		EUR
ATY 1200/1520	187.464,43	EUR	187.464,43	EUR
CTR 1210		EUR		EUR
ATY 1210/1530	99.513,46	EUR	99.513,46	EUR
ATY 1210/1540	99.513,07	EUR	99.513,07	EUR
CTR 1220		EUR		EUR
ATY 1220/1413	151.275,82	EUR	151.275,82	EUR
ATY 1220/1550	302.551,53	EUR	302.551,53	EUR
CTR 1230		EUR		EUR
ATY 1230/1232	165.121,92	EUR	165.121,92	EUR
CTR 2200		EUR		EUR
ATY 2200/1412	183.184,97	EUR	183.184,97	EUR
ATY 2200/1560	366.369,88	EUR	366.369,88	EUR
CTR 2300		EUR		EUR
ATY 2300/2426	688.106,63	EUR	688.106,63	EUR
CTR 3140		EUR		EUR
ATY 3140/1410	116.496,91	EUR	116.496,91	EUR
ATY 3140/2431	116.496,87	EUR	116.496,87	EUR
ATY 3140/5600	116.496,92	EUR	116.496,92	EUR
CTR 3200		EUR		EUR
ATY 3200/5600	303.074,59	EUR	303.074,59	EUR
CTR 4100		EUR		EUR
ATY 4100/1410	280.972,43	EUR	280.972,43	EUR
ATY 4100/1411	140.486,30	EUR	140.486,30	EUR
ATY 4100/1413	140.486,14	EUR	140.486,14	EUR
CTR 4110		EUR		EUR
ATY 4110/1410	270.301,03	EUR	270.301,03	EUR
CTR 4120		EUR		EUR
ATY 4120/1412	109.943,93	EUR	109.943,93	EUR
ATY 4120/2412	109.943,12	EUR	109.943,12	EUR
CTR 4130		EUR		EUR
ATY 4130/1421	103.514,44-	EUR	103.514,44-	EUR
ATY 4130/2423	103.514,43-	EUR	103.514,43-	EUR

Figure 5.14 Plan Price Splitting

Plan Direct Activity Allocation from Supporting Cost Centers

So far we've planned the direct costs, such as wages and rent, for the production cost centers. However, as we discussed when we looked at the cost center master data in Chapter 3, there are generally other cost centers and activity types that provide work to support the production cost centers. Figure 5.15 shows a report for a sample cost center hierarchy with two production cost centers and three supporting cost centers for energy, quality, and production. In this example, the quality cost center is selected, and we can see both the input for this cost center and the output, a planned activity of 150 hours for the month that will result in costs being charged to the two production cost centers (the credit line in the report). This plan was created using the same process as we used for the production cost center. In other words, we planned the cost elements salaries and office and building as activity-independent costs and the cost elements direct labor and external procurement as activity-dependent costs. We also used Transaction KP26

Complete Sales Plan in a Manufacturing Environment | 5.1

to plan the activity output (the 150 hours that the cost center plans to deliver to production). What are missing in Figure 5.15 are details of which cost centers will use quality hours from our cost center.

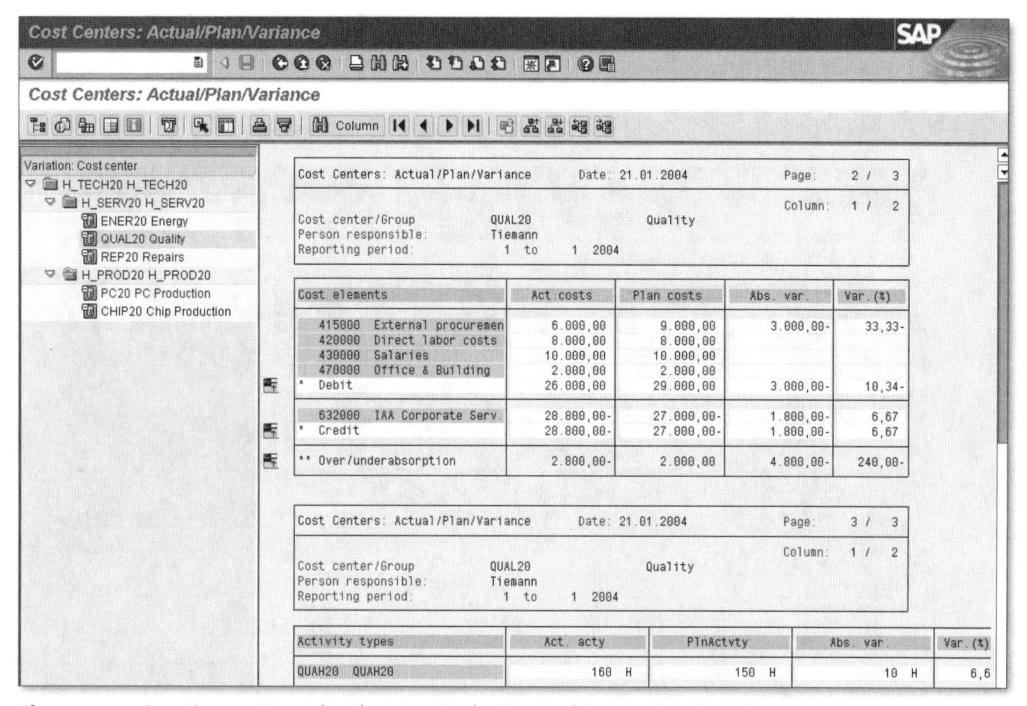

Figure 5.15 Cost Center Hierarchy Showing Production and Supporting Cost Centers

To plan the hours used by production, we need to plan the activity allocation for quality control—1200 hours to PC production and 600 hours to chip production. To plan activity input, go to Transaction KP06 or ACCOUNTING • CONTROLLING • COST CENTER ACCOUNTING • PLANNING • COST AND ACTIVITY INPUTS • CHANGE and select the appropriate planning layout (1-102 is the standard setting). This differs from the selection screen we saw previously in that you have to enter both the sender cost center (quality control) and activity types and the receiver cost centers (PC production and chip production) and activity types. Then plan for the PC production cost center and the chip production cost center the amount of quality hours they'll need in each period.

Figure 5.16 shows the planned costs (activity-dependent and activity-independent) for the quality cost center, the planned output (1500 hours), and the planned usage of this output in chip production and PC production for the *year*. You can reach this report from the Cost Center Reporting page shown in Chapter 2 or by going to ACCOUNTING • CONTROLLING • INFORMATION SYSTEM • REPORTS FOR COST CENTER ACCOUNTING • PLANNING REPORTS • COST CENTERS: PLANNING REPORT or Transaction KSBL.

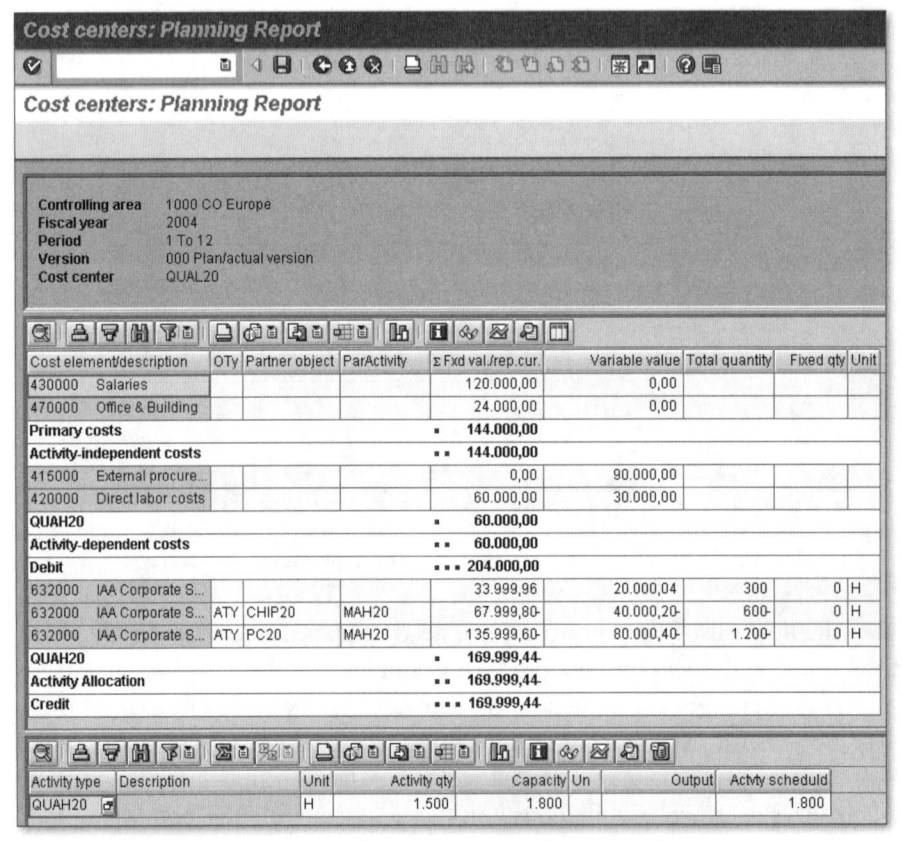

Cost element/description	OTy	Partner object	ParActivity	Σ Fxd val./rep.cur.	Variable value	Total quantity	Fixed qty	Unit
430000 Salaries				120.000,00	0,00			
470000 Office & Building				24.000,00	0,00			
Primary costs				▪ 144.000,00				
Activity-independent costs				▪▪ 144.000,00				
415000 External procure...				0,00	90.000,00			
420000 Direct labor costs				60.000,00	30.000,00			
QUAH20				60.000,00				
Activity-dependent costs				▪▪ 60.000,00				
Debit				▪▪▪ 204.000,00				
632000 IAA Corporate S...				33.999,96	20.000,04	300	0	H
632000 IAA Corporate S...	ATY	CHIP20	MAH20	67.999,80-	40.000,20-	600-	0	H
632000 IAA Corporate S...	ATY	PC20	MAH20	135.999,60-	80.000,40-	1.200-	0	H
QUAH20				▪ 169.999,44-				
Activity Allocation				▪▪ 169.999,44-				
Credit				▪▪▪ 169.999,44-				

Activity type	Description	Unit	Activity qty	Capacity	Un	Output	Actvty scheduld
QUAH20		H	1.500	1.800			1.800

Figure 5.16 Planning Report for Quality Cost Center (Before Reconciliation)

If you look closely at Figure 5.16, you'll see that the activity usage planned—1200 hours to PC production and 600 hours to chip production—is *higher* than the activity quantity (output) planned for the quality cost center (currently only 1500 hours). The time has come to use the *plan reconciliation* function that we discussed earlier to account for this discrepancy and adjust the planned cost center output from 1500 to 1800 hours to reflect the demand from the production cost centers. It also adjusts the activity-dependent costs accordingly. So the variable costs for external procurement are now EUR 108,000 instead of EUR 90,000, and the variable costs for direct labor are now EUR 36,000 instead of EUR 30,000. This is illustrated in Figure 5.17. If you don't run this transaction, plan reconciliation takes place automatically when you calculate activity prices.

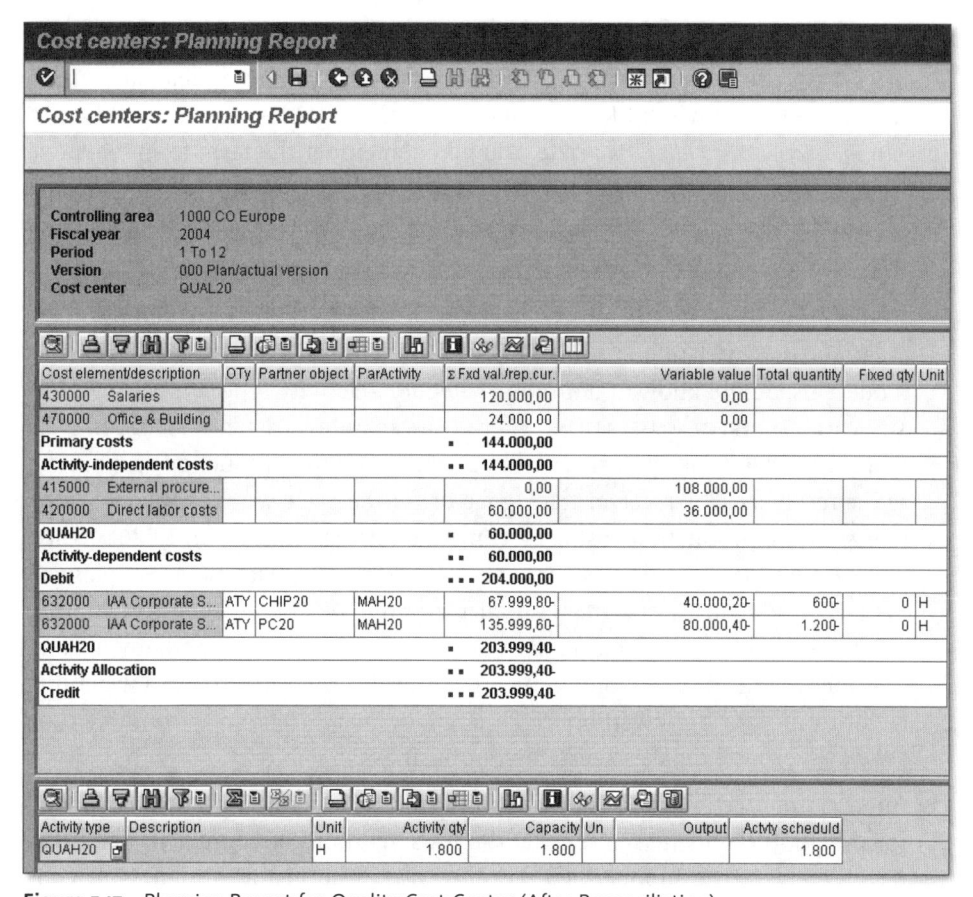

Cost element/description	OTy	Partner object	ParActivity	Σ Fxd val./rep.cur.	Variable value	Total quantity	Fixed qty	Unit
430000 Salaries				120.000,00	0,00			
470000 Office & Building				24.000,00	0,00			
Primary costs				▪ 144.000,00				
Activity-independent costs				▪▪ 144.000,00				
415000 External procure...				0,00	108.000,00			
420000 Direct labor costs				60.000,00	36.000,00			
QUAH20				60.000,00				
Activity-dependent costs				▪▪ 60.000,00				
Debit				▪▪▪ 204.000,00				
632000 IAA Corporate S...	ATY	CHIP20	MAH20	67.999,80-	40.000,20-	600-	0	H
632000 IAA Corporate S...	ATY	PC20	MAH20	135.999,60-	80.000,40-	1.200-	0	H
QUAH20				▪ 203.999,40-				
Activity Allocation				▪▪ 203.999,40-				
Credit				▪▪▪ 203.999,40-				

Activity type	Description	Unit	Activity qty	Capacity	Un	Output	Actvty scheduld
QUAH20		H	1.800	1.800			1.800

Figure 5.17 Planning Report for Quality Cost Center (After Reconciliation)

5 | Planning and Budgeting

> **Scope of Plan Reconciliation**
>
> The default setting for plan reconciliation and activity price calculation is ALL COST CENTERS. Since many organizations now have a single controlling area that spans the globe, many prefer to perform plan reconciliation and activity price calculation for a group of cost centers rather than all cost centers in the controlling area. To avoid accidental overwrites, consider implementing SAP Note 1399364 to set the default for Transactions KSPI and KPSI to cost center groups rather than all cost centers.

Plan Indirect Activity Allocation from Supporting Cost Centers

If you refer back to Figure 5.15, you'll see that one of the supporting cost centers is an energy cost center. You can plan kilowatt hours of energy manually using Transaction KP06 as we did for the quality hours. An easier way to do this is to use an *indirect activity allocation cycle*. You may remember the term from when we discussed the master data for the activity types in Chapter 3. Instead of making a direct activity allocation, as we did for the quality hours, we can make an indirect activity allocation, based on certain assumptions.

- One assumption might be that every hour of machine time provided by a production cost center requires one kilowatt hour from the energy cost center. To model this, define kilowatt hours as a category 2 activity type (INDIRECT DETERMINATION, INDIRECT ALLOCATION). Then create an indirect activity allocation cycle that contains the energy cost center as a sender and the production cost centers as the receivers. The receiver tracing factor for the cycle would be the machine hours on the production cost center (planned using Transaction KP26). When you execute the allocation cycle, the system reads the machine hours planned for each production cost center and calculates the total kilowatt hours that need to be provided to ensure this number of machine hours. It's worth knowing that this does not need to be a one-to-one relationship. You can also use a weighting factor to allocate 1 kilowatt hour of energy for every 10 hours of machine time or whatever factor makes sense in your business.

- Another approach might be to manually enter the total kilowatt hours supplied for the period. This makes sense if there's some kind of counter in place that records the energy supplied and you can use these historical figures in your plan. To model this, define kilowatt hours as a category 3 activity type (MANUAL ENTRY, INDIRECT ALLOCATION). The sender, receivers, and receiver tracing factor in the cycle would be the same as above. However, in this approach the manually planned total energy would be split to the production cost centers in proportion to the machine hours supplied by each cost center.

Since the same mechanisms are used to calculate planned costs as are used to allocate actual costs at period close, you'll find a more detailed description of how to set up indirect allocation cycles in Chapter 7. The only difference is the menu path (you'll find planned allocations in the ALLOCATIONS folder in Figure 5.8) and the fact that you have to include your plan version in the cycle.

Calculate and Settle Order Costs

Where orders are assigned to the cost centers to provide additional detailing (such as orders for marketing events assigned to the marketing cost center), you should also include these order costs in the cost center plan. Clearly, this plan only applies to a subset of the available orders, namely, those that exist for the whole planning period. Planning such orders can be the job of the individual manager (e.g., the person responsible for a particular marketing event), the cost center manager (if a research and development cost center performs many different R&D tasks), or even controlling (where the orders are for general administrative tasks).

The costs for production orders, process orders, and so on are captured when we calculate the standard costs for the manufactured materials, so we can ignore them here since we'll capture them in the next section. The costs of other logistics orders for maintenance activities and so on are usually planned via the cost center to which they settle their costs. We'll look at how to plan investment orders and projects later in this chapter.

Figure 5.18 shows the PLANNING folder for order planning. Unlike the PROFITABILITY PLANNING and COST CENTER PLANNING folders, only expenses and activity input are planned for the internal order, but there's no output quantity. Instead, order costs are settled or charged to the relevant market segment.

Plan Integration for Orders

The customizing settings for the version and order type include selecting the PLAN INTEGRATION checkbox. This checkbox is transferred to the CONTROL DATA tab of the internal order (see Chapter 3) and determines how the planned costs on the order (or WBS elements) are handled and whether a demand for activities from an order or project is treated the same way as a demand from another cost center.

5 | Planning and Budgeting

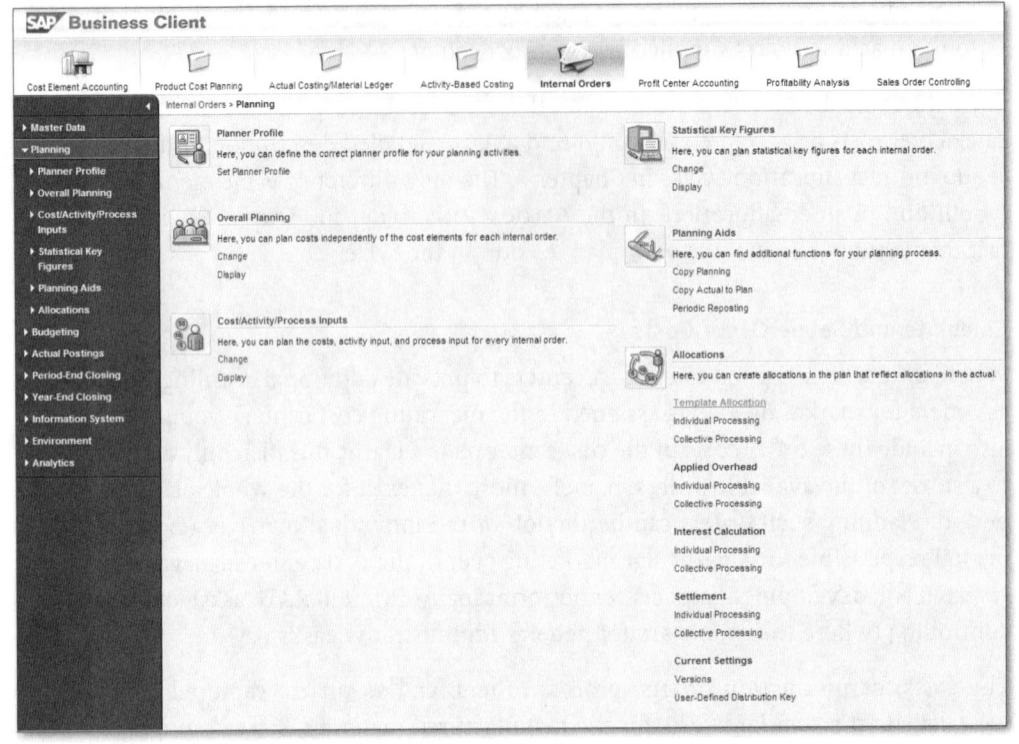

Figure 5.18 Planning Applications for Internal Orders

Figure 5.19 shows the order master data (Transaction KO01) and an order for which the PLAN-INTEGRATED ORDER checkbox has been selected. The value in the version is merely a default. It's the flag in the order itself that determines whether values planned for the order will be transferred or not, so make sure you're consistent in selecting this checkbox for order types whose values you want to include in planning.

The order planning application (Transaction KPF6) looks much the same as the cost center planning application. Figure 5.20 shows a sample order plan for a marketing event that will ultimately settle to the marketing cost center. This data is normally entered either by the manager of the Sapphire event or the cost center manager for the marketing cost center and then checked by controlling. We'll look at this same example in the context of Express Planning in Chapter 10, in case you want to compare the look of the two planning applications.

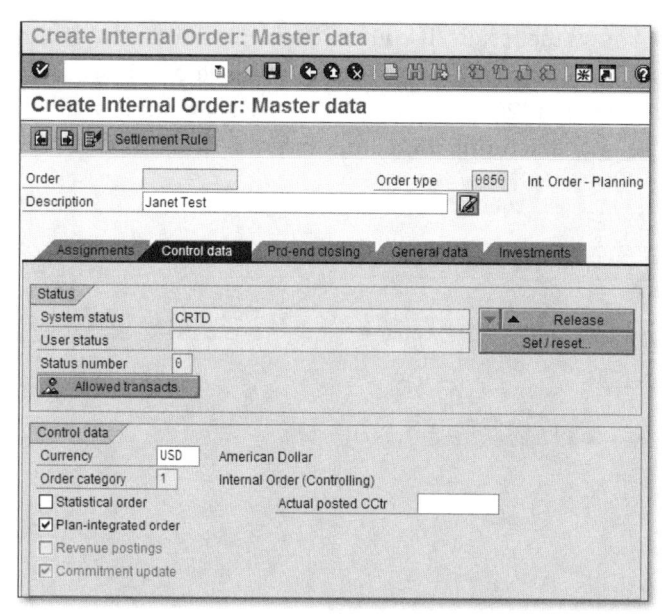

Complete Sales Plan in a Manufacturing Environment | **5.1**

Figure 5.19 Plan-Integrated Order Planning – Checkbox in Internal Order

Figure 5.20 Order Planning for a Marketing Order to Calculate Standard Price for Activity Types

When all the inputs to the cost centers are available, the final step in cost center planning is for the controller to calculate the activity prices. To do this, go to Transaction KSPI or Accounting • Controlling • Cost Center Accounting • Planning • Allocations and enter the version, the time frame, and whether you want to consider all cost centers. Figure 5.21 shows the results. If you search the result list, you'll find cost center 4230, which has been our sample cost center for much of this section, along with the three activity types 1420, 1421, and 1422. We'll use these activity prices to calculate the cost of manufacturing the pumps in the next section.

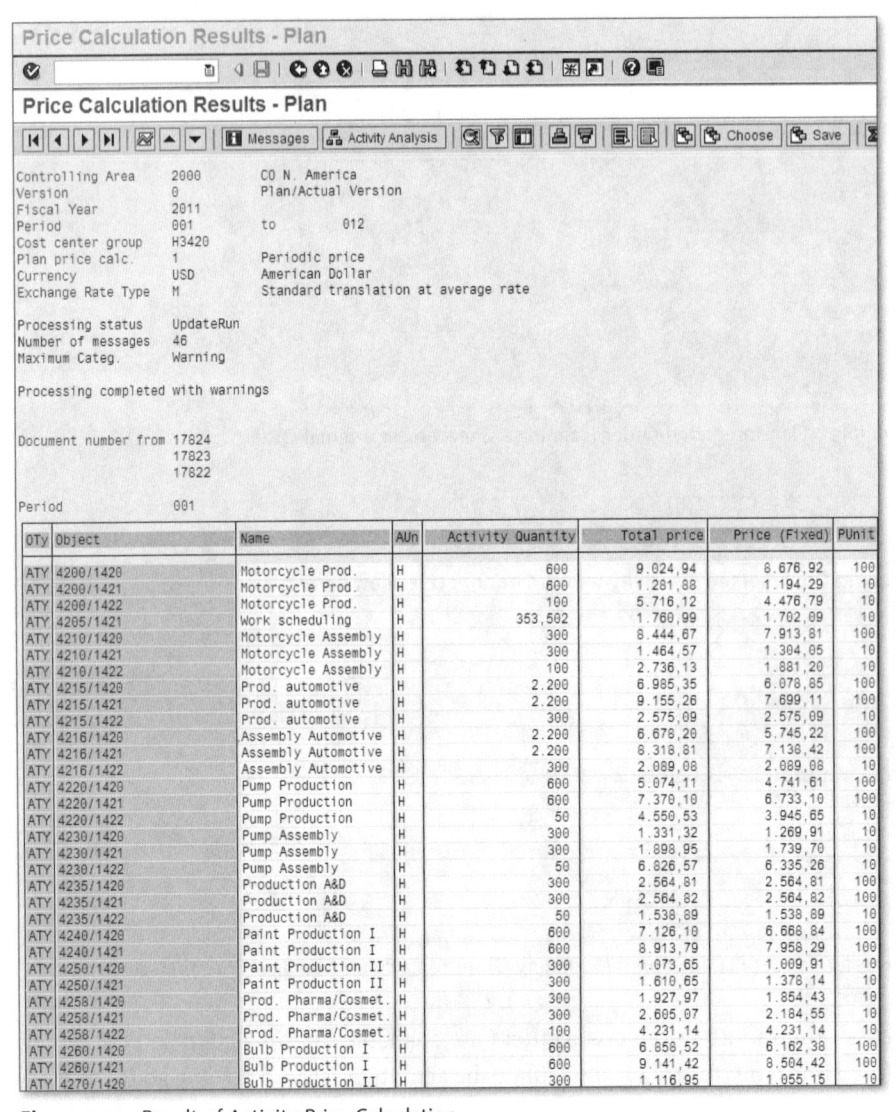

OTy	Object	Name	AUn	Activity Quantity	Total price	Price (Fixed)	PUnit
ATY	4200/1420	Motorcycle Prod.	H	600	9.024,94	8.676,92	100
ATY	4200/1421	Motorcycle Prod.	H	600	1.281,88	1.194,29	10
ATY	4200/1422	Motorcycle Prod.	H	100	5.716,12	4.476,79	10
ATY	4205/1421	Work scheduling	H	353.502	1.760,99	1.702,09	10
ATY	4210/1420	Motorcycle Assembly	H	300	8.444,67	7.913,81	100
ATY	4210/1421	Motorcycle Assembly	H	300	1.464,57	1.304,05	10
ATY	4210/1422	Motorcycle Assembly	H	100	2.736,13	1.881,20	10
ATY	4215/1420	Prod. automotive	H	2.200	6.985,35	6.078,85	100
ATY	4215/1421	Prod. automotive	H	2.200	9.155,26	7.699,11	100
ATY	4215/1422	Prod. automotive	H	300	2.575,09	2.575,09	10
ATY	4216/1420	Assembly Automotive	H	2.200	6.678,20	5.745,22	100
ATY	4216/1421	Assembly Automotive	H	2.200	8.318,81	7.138,42	100
ATY	4216/1422	Assembly Automotive	H	300	2.089,08	2.089,08	10
ATY	4220/1420	Pump Production	H	600	5.074,11	4.741,61	100
ATY	4220/1421	Pump Production	H	600	7.370,10	6.733,10	100
ATY	4220/1422	Pump Production	H	50	4.550,53	3.945,65	10
ATY	4230/1420	Pump Assembly	H	300	1.331,32	1.269,91	10
ATY	4230/1421	Pump Assembly	H	300	1.898,95	1.739,70	10
ATY	4230/1422	Pump Assembly	H	50	6.826,57	6.335,26	10
ATY	4235/1420	Production A&D	H	300	2.564,81	2.564,81	100
ATY	4235/1421	Production A&D	H	300	2.564,82	2.564,82	100
ATY	4235/1422	Production A&D	H	50	1.538,89	1.538,89	10
ATY	4240/1420	Paint Production I	H	600	7.126,10	6.668,84	100
ATY	4240/1421	Paint Production I	H	600	8.913,79	7.958,29	100
ATY	4250/1420	Paint Production II	H	300	1.073,65	1.009,91	10
ATY	4250/1421	Paint Production II	H	300	1.610,65	1.378,14	10
ATY	4258/1420	Prod. Pharma/Cosmet.	H	300	1.927,97	1.854,43	10
ATY	4258/1421	Prod. Pharma/Cosmet.	H	300	2.605,07	2.184,55	10
ATY	4258/1422	Prod. Pharma/Cosmet.	H	100	4.231,14	4.231,14	10
ATY	4260/1420	Bulb Production I	H	600	6.858,52	6.162,38	100
ATY	4260/1421	Bulb Production I	H	600	9.141,42	8.504,42	100
ATY	4270/1420	Bulb Production II	H	300	1.116,95	1.055,15	10

Figure 5.21 Result of Activity Price Calculation

Activity Price Calculation: Caution!

Calculating activity prices with Transaction KSPI sets the prices used to value production activities and work time throughout SAP ERP. If you run the calculation in test mode, you'll receive a message asking whether you want to save the results as you leave the transaction. Think before you save, especially if your plan data refers to the current year, since you don't want to overwrite your operative valuation.

One trick to use if you aren't sure your activity price calculation will be completely accurate is to copy all the relevant input data into a version other than 0 using Transaction KP97 (in the PLANNING AIDS folder) and run activity price calculation in a version that isn't going to be used for active valuation until you're satisfied with the results.

Only save results in version 0 that you really want to release for productive use. To ensure consistency, consider locking the plan version (under CURRENT SETTINGS) as soon as planning is complete.

Primary Cost Component Split for the Activity Price

When we discussed work centers in Chapter 4, we said there's often confusion around the fact that the maximum output of a work center is six activity types and many people feel that they need more. We argued that they're missing the distinction between inputs (wages, depreciation, energy, and so on) and outputs (machine hours, wage hours, and so on). Once your activity rates start to become stable, it's worth considering activating a primary cost component split for your activity types by defining a cost component structure and entering this in the planning version (these are Customizing activities).

The cost component structure takes the input cost elements (wages, depreciation, energy, and so on) from cost center planning and assigns them to cost components (these are configured the same way as the cost components we encountered when reporting on the product costs in Chapter 2). The same limit of 40 cost components applies as for the product cost component split.

Figure 5.22 shows an activity rate that has been broken out this way to show wages, salaries, employee benefits, material costs, imputed benefits, and external processing (primary cost elements) and energy and maintenance (secondary cost elements).

It's then possible to map the cost component split for the activity rate into the product cost estimate as a primary cost component split and to map these costs to value fields in Profitability Analysis to allow you to include these costs in your product and customer profitability reporting.

5 | Planning and Budgeting

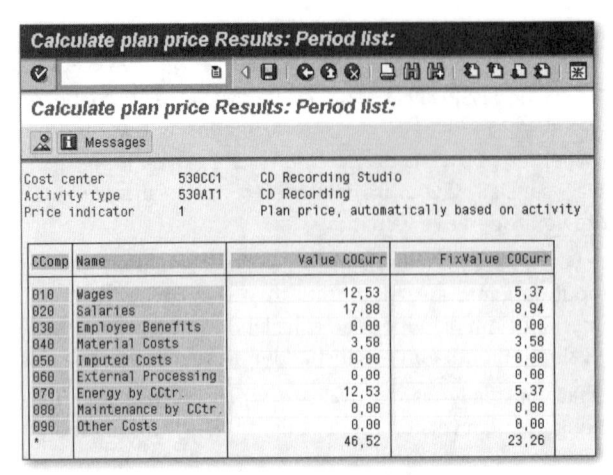

Calculate plan price Results: Period list:				
Cost center	530CC1	CD Recording Studio		
Activity type	530AT1	CD Recording		
Price indicator	1	Plan price, automatically based on activity		

CComp	Name	Value COCurr	FixValue COCurr
010	Wages	12,53	5,37
020	Salaries	17,88	8,94
030	Employee Benefits	0,00	0,00
040	Material Costs	3,58	3,58
050	Imputed Costs	0,00	0,00
060	External Processing	0,00	0,00
070	Energy by CCtr.	12,53	5,37
080	Maintenance by CCtr.	0,00	0,00
090	Other Costs	0,00	0,00
*		46,52	23,26

Figure 5.22 Primary Cost Component Split

The activity price calculation is the final step in cost center planning, but not the last step in planning. We can now use this rate per hour, broken down into its cost components, to calculate the standard costs for each of the materials we'll manufacture and apply these figures to the sales plan to calculate the contribution margin for the sales plan.

5.1.3 Calculate Standard Costs for Products to Be Manufactured

When we created the production plan, we used the bills of material and routings for each material to determine the *scheduled activity* required for production. We'll now use the same master data from production to determine the standard costs for all of our products. Figure 5.23 shows the planning applications for Product Cost Planning.

You use a *costing run* to calculate standard costs for all the materials in a plant or plants. This is a very different planning application from the sales and cost center planning applications in that it's largely automated and always performed by either central controlling or plant controlling, though individual managers may be called in to verify the results. The results of costing flow into profitability planning but are also used to set the standard costs in the material master (see Chapter 4). It's also possible to calculate the costs of individual materials using the Cost Estimate with Quantity Structure applications (Transaction CK11N), but this is mostly used for testing and for setting a standard price for new products, rather than for the mass calculation of standard prices for all materials as part of the annual operating plan.

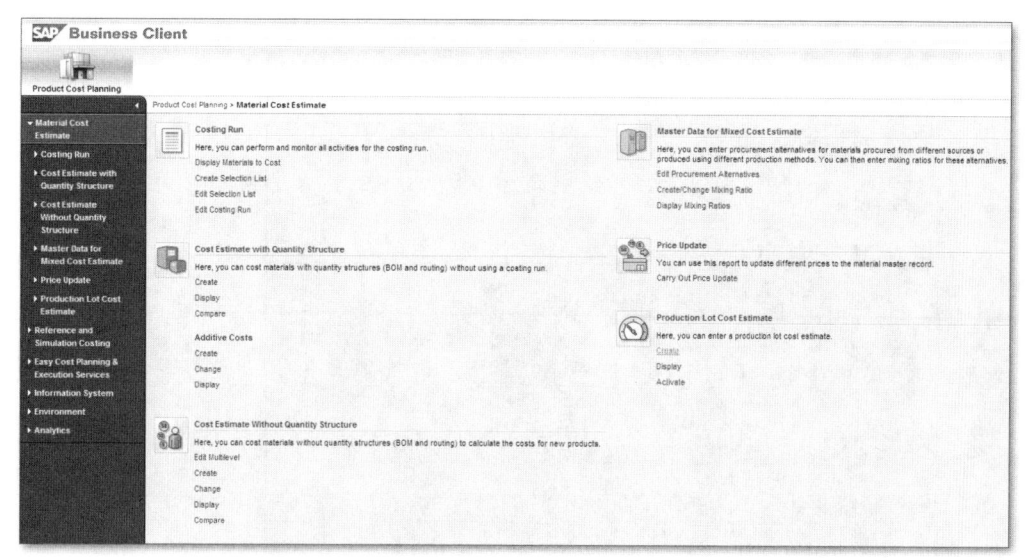

Figure 5.23 Planning Applications for Product Cost Planning

Create Costing Run

To create a costing run, select EDIT COSTING RUN in Figure 5.23, use Transaction CK40N, or follow the menu path ACCOUNTING • CONTROLLING • PRODUCT COST CONTROLLING • PRODUCT COST PLANNING • MATERIAL COSTING • COSTING RUN • EDIT COSTING RUN. Figure 5.24 shows the initial screen for a costing run on a specific key date. The costing run acts as the framework around the costing steps (selection, structure explosion, costing, analysis, marking, release) that are performed in the course of costing. The FLOW STEP column shows a line for each step. To perform the steps, proceed as follows:

1. To determine what information is used in each step, enter the selection parameters in the PARAMETER column (for example, the parameters for the SELECTION step are the finished products to be included in costing). You need to check the parameters before you enter each job.

2. To schedule the job (set it to start at a given time), click on the icon in the EXECUTION column. This icon is activated after you maintain the selection parameters.

5 | Planning and Budgeting

3. As each step is completed, you can monitor the status and the error logs in the other columns.

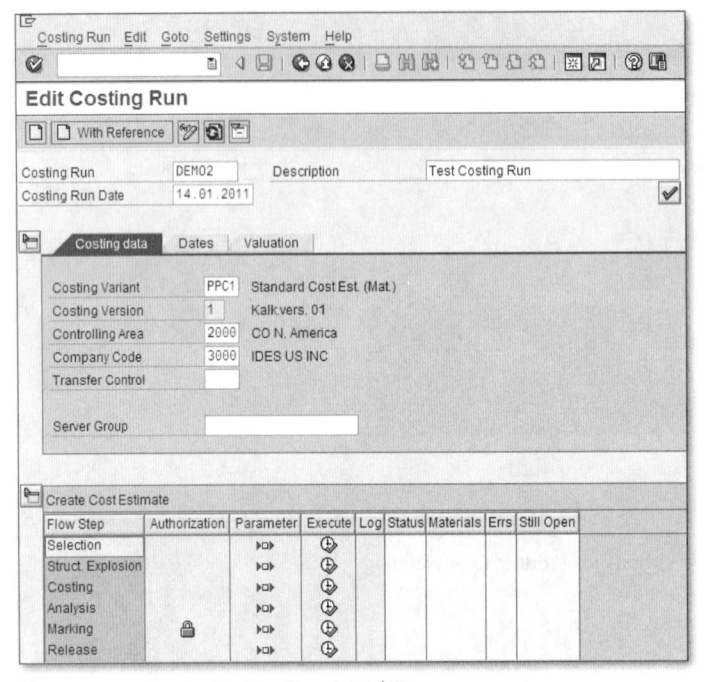

Figure 5.24 Create Costing Run: Initial Screen

As we discussed in Chapter 4, the underlying master data for the costing run is predominantly managed by the production department, so fixing the errors listed in the logs frequently requires collaboration between controlling and the other departments, especially if the cost estimates are based on shared master data.

Once each costing step has been completed, the costing results are shown in the bottom part of the screen. This allows you to view a list showing the details of what was selected or calculated in each step and to navigate from there to the individual cost estimate (the equivalent of calling Transaction CK13N for each material cost estimate). Because of the danger of errors, it's rare to schedule all costing jobs in one flow. At the latest, make sure that you have made a manual checks on the data before the mark and release steps, which initiate the inventory revaluation and thus can have a significant impact on the balance sheet.

> **Costing Run: Caution!**
>
> If you select more than 500 materials in your costing run, the material masters for all materials in the relevant plant will be locked while the costing step is performed. You'll find more information about this in SAP Note 1415153. Because of this, most organizations perform their costing runs overnight. You should also be careful if you have costing runs that cross several company codes that you don't encounter a deadlock. During the marking and releasing steps, the locks are set for the materials being updated in turn. If you have many tasks running in parallel, this can lead to an overrun of the lock tables.

The COSTING DATA tab contains the main organizational settings for the costing run. The *costing variant* provides the link to the configuration settings for Product Cost Planning and establishes:

- The purpose of costing, such as the calculation of standard costs for inventory valuation or the calculation of inventory costs based on methods such as FIFO and LIFO for balance sheet valuation. We're interested in calculating standard costs here, so select COSTING VARIANT PPC1, which has the correct costing type for standard costing.

- How the bills of material and routings/recipes for each material are selected. The relevant settings are combined in the quantity structure determination settings for the costing variant.

- Which prices are selected to value the raw materials and how overhead costs are applied. You may remember the purchasing info records and raw material prices that we looked at in Chapter 4. During costing these prices will be selected for each of the raw materials included in the costing run and added to the activity prices to determine the costs of the semi-finished and finished products in the costing run. The settings are combined in a valuation variant assigned to the costing variant.

- Proposals for the selection dates for selecting the items in the bills of material and routing and the material and activity prices. You can overwrite these in the DATES tab of the costing run. You may remember from Chapter 4 that bills of material and routings are time-dependent, so you want to be sure to select the correct key date.

Usually it's sufficient to enter costing version 1. You should enter a different version only in the following cases:

- If you're performing mixed costing to weight several cost estimates for different procurement alternatives (see Chapter 4).

5 | Planning and Budgeting

- If you're doing group costing to reference the data in the first costing run. In this case the quantity structure used as a basis for the standard costs in legal valuation is reused by the group valuation and profit center valuation to ensure that only the values but not the quantities change.

The CONTROLLING AREA and COMPANY CODE fields determine the framework within which the costing run takes place. Depending on the degree of centralization in the organization, a costing run may be performed by each plant in isolation, or a single costing run can cover all the materials in every plant in the world. As the use of a single controlling area becomes more widespread, the trend is toward a single global costing run.

> **Transfer Control and Costing Runs**
>
> If you create a costing run at a time other than during the annual operating plan, you can use the TRANSFER CONTROL field to have the system copy existing cost estimates for materials that have already been costed and only create new ones for materials that have been created since the last annual plan. This can significantly reduce the time it takes to perform a costing run. This can also be used where plants procure materials from one another, to ensure that the receiving plant copies the cost estimate from the supplying plant rather than creating a new cost estimate in the other plant.

Since the volumes of materials in the costing run can lock up system resources, you may also want to build packages of materials and run them on different server groups to spread the load.

Select Materials

If you want to make a fairly general selection, you can select the materials you want to include in the costing run by entering the appropriate plant and material type directly in the costing run. However, if you want to make a more specific selection, perhaps to exclude materials for which you have already created cost estimates, then you should consider using the separate selection list that was introduced in Release 4.7. You'll find the new transactions in the COSTING RUN folder under CREATE SELECTION LIST (Transaction CKMATSEL) and EDIT SELECTION LIST (Transaction CKMATCON), as shown in Figure 5.23.

Figure 5.25 shows the selection screen for such a selection list. This includes the same selections as in the costing run but also includes fields from the material master, such as BOM USAGE and the SPECIAL PROCUREMENT KEY, making it easier to be specific about the materials to be included and not waste system resources creating new cost estimates for materials that already have cost estimates.

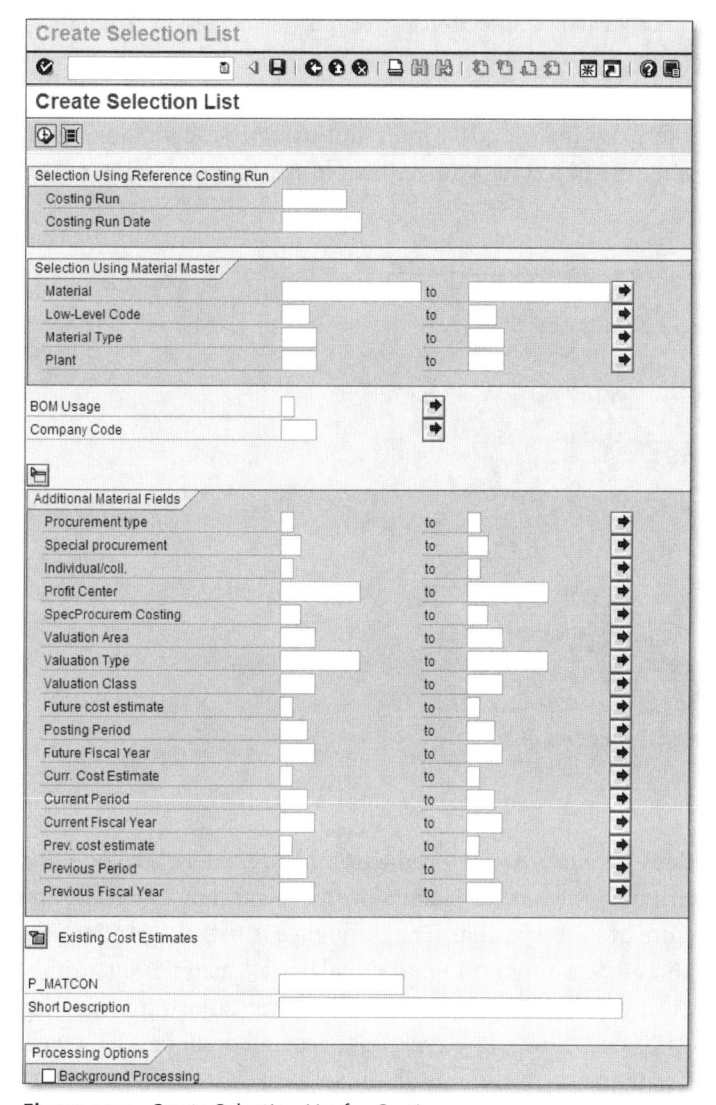

Figure 5.25 Create Selection List for Costing

5 | Planning and Budgeting

> **Enhancements to the Selection List**
>
> Some customers require even more sophisticated logic for selecting the relevant materials for costing. SAP Note 1019389 describes how to activate the BAdI MAT_SELECTION_CK to enable you to define your own logic for material selection.

Once you have a list, you may want to edit it further, to add additional materials manually or remove others, by marking the lines and using the icons shown in Figure 5.26. When you're satisfied with your selection list, you can move on to the next costing steps.

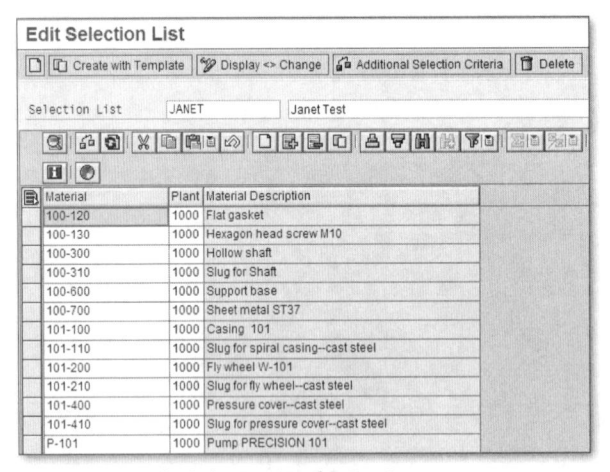

Figure 5.26 Edit Selection List for Costing

Structure Explosion

The next costing step does the same as the production plan, namely, explode the bills of material to determine which semifinished products and raw materials are needed in the manufacture of each material. The difference is that the production plan takes the sales plan as its starting point and calculates all material quantities and activity quantities using the sales quantities (with minor adjustments) as its starting point. The standard costs, however, have to take account of the cost behavior of the underlying cost elements (fixed or variable). So each cost estimate is created independently, taking the costing lot size as the "ideal" output and adjusting the input quantities in the BOM in line with this output quantity. This process is repeated for each level of the BOM.

Costing

The costing step creates a cost estimate for each material in the bill of material structure. For raw materials, it uses the valuation variant to determine how the initial costs will be calculated (the price from the purchasing info record or one of the prices in the material master (see Chapter 4)) and creates a cost estimate that contains the new price. For the semifinished products, it reads the routing and work center in combination to determine the activity usage and roll up the prices for the individual raw materials in the BOM to form a cost estimate for the semifinished product. Figure 5.27 shows a list of the materials costed as part of the costing run. To display the cost estimate for each material, click on the material in the list.

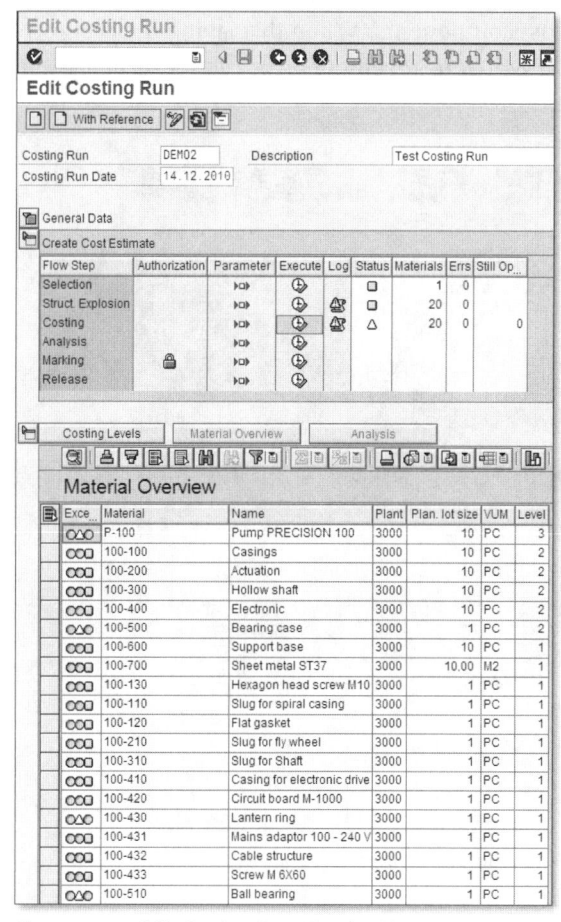

Figure 5.27 Edit Costing Run: Results List

5 | Planning and Budgeting

All cost estimates have the same basic structure: the cost component split that we introduced in Chapter 2. Figure 5.28 shows the cost component split for material ACT-DCD, comprising material components, production labor/setup, production machine, Logistics processes, material overhead, and other costs in this configuration. These are split into their fixed and variable parts based on the activity rates (for the labor, setup, and machine cost components) and the business process rates (for the Logistics processes cost component). All cost estimates are saved in this form: the *main cost component split*.

When we looked at the activity price, we saw that it's made up of wages, salaries, employee benefits, and so on (see Figure 5.21). Some organizations set up an additional *primary cost component split* that maps these primary costs from the activity rate into a second set of cost components. When displaying the cost estimate (Transaction CK13N), you can switch between the *main* and the *auxiliary cost component split* as shown in Figure 5.28.

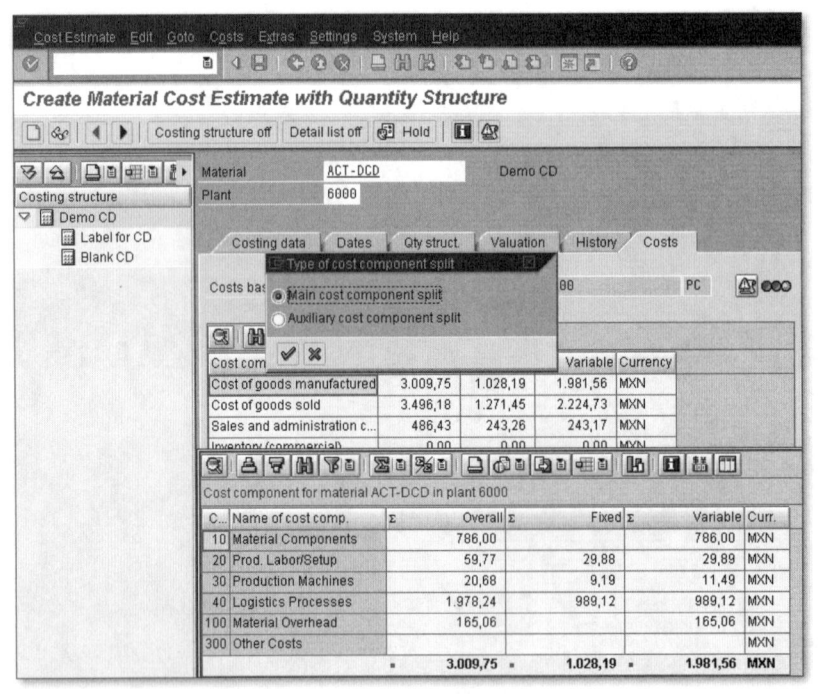

Figure 5.28 Cost of Goods Manufactured (Main Cost Component Split)

Figure 5.29 shows the primary cost component split for the material comprising material components, wages and salaries, energy, depreciation, and other costs in this configuration. Comparing the two screens, you'll see that the total product costs are the same, as are the lines for the material components, but in Figure 5.28 the cost elements in the activity rates from the routing determine to which cost components the costs are assigned (setup, labor, and machine), whereas in Figure 5.29 the underlying cost center costs determine the cost components (wages and salaries, energy, and depreciation).

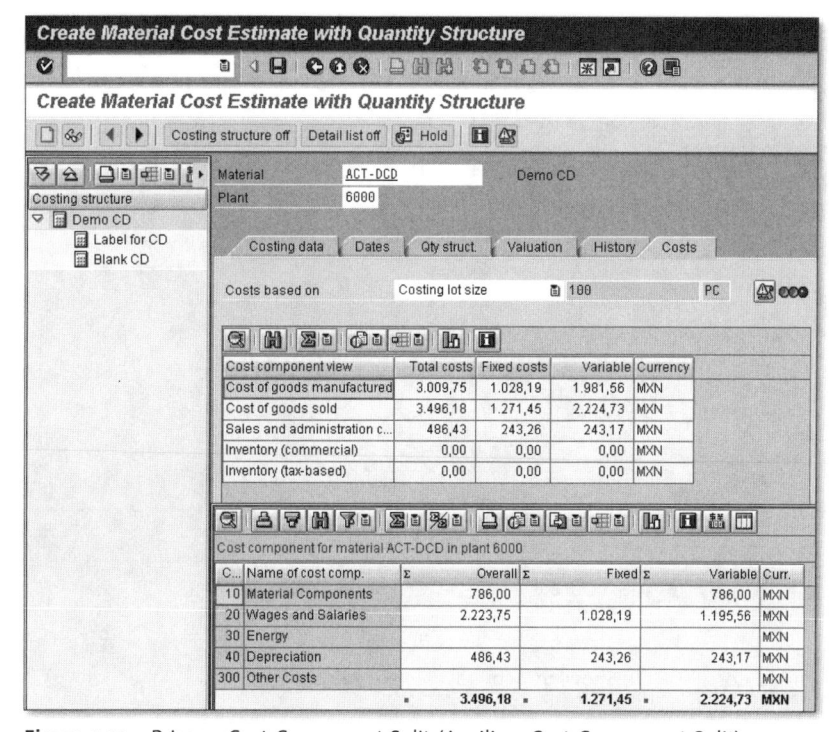

Figure 5.29 Primary Cost Component Split (Auxiliary Cost Component Split)

If multiple procurement alternatives exist for a single material (see Chapter 4), the costing step creates a separate cost estimate for each procurement alternative (manufacture according to production version 1, purchase from supplier A, and so on), and then reads the mixing ratios defined as master data for a mixed cost estimate and creates a mixed cost estimate.

5 | Planning and Budgeting

Figure 5.30 shows a sample cost estimate where 10% is externally procured (first line) and 90% is manufactured in-house (second line). The first cost estimate is based on the purchasing info record with the appropriate supplier, while the second cost estimate is based on the bill of material and routing. Notice that the itemization shows the cost estimate for each item. To see the info record for the supplier, click on the line for the first procurement alternative. To see the results of costing the BOM and routing for internal manufacturing, click on the line for the second procurement alternative.

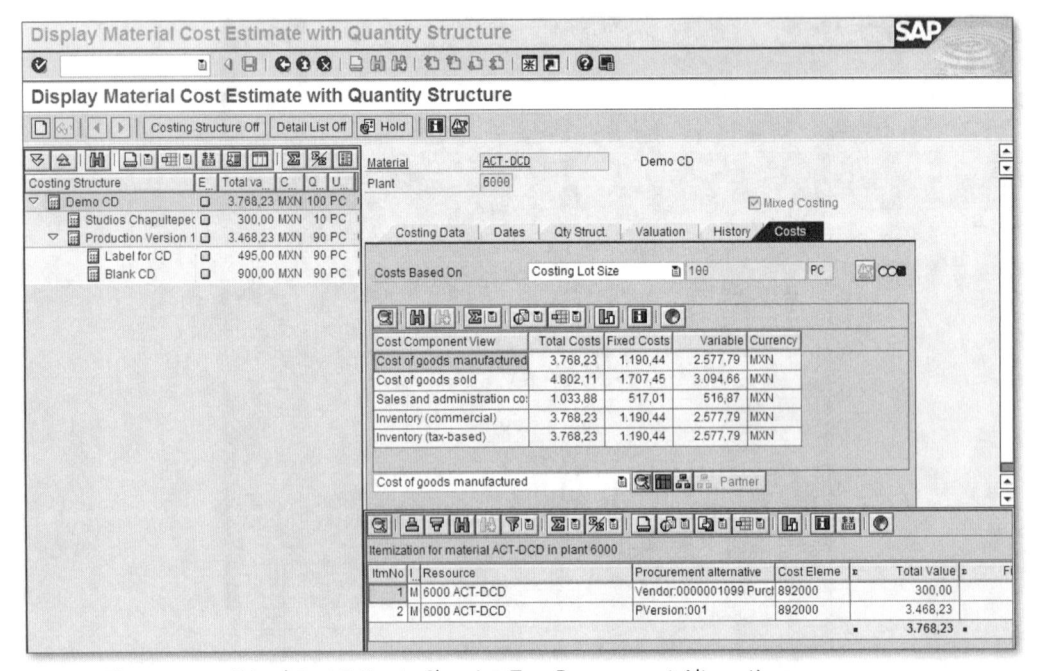

Figure 5.30 Mixed Cost Estimate Showing Two Procurement Alternatives

Analysis

Since the release of the cost estimate results in a stock revaluation that can have a significant impact on the balance sheet, it's is essential for the controller to run check reports that compare the result of the cost estimate with the current price in the material master (see Chapter 4). Figure 5.31 shows such a report from within the costing run. For several materials, including the final assembly, P-100, releasing the cost estimates would result in a huge revaluation, and the controller must

240

Complete Sales Plan in a Manufacturing Environment | 5.1

work to determine why these changes are so huge before moving on to the next steps in costing.

In such a situation, the controller repeats individual steps in the costing run using the selection list we discussed earlier to select exactly those materials that are causing errors and leaving untouched the materials that were costed successfully until the results are satisfactory.

Caution

Only when all the signal lights for the anticipated revaluation in Figure 5.31 are green should you move on to the next step, since the marking and releasing steps results in every costing result prepared during the costing run being taken and used to revaluate inventory. In our examples, you'll see that we've done some significant revaluations to the inventory in our demo system.

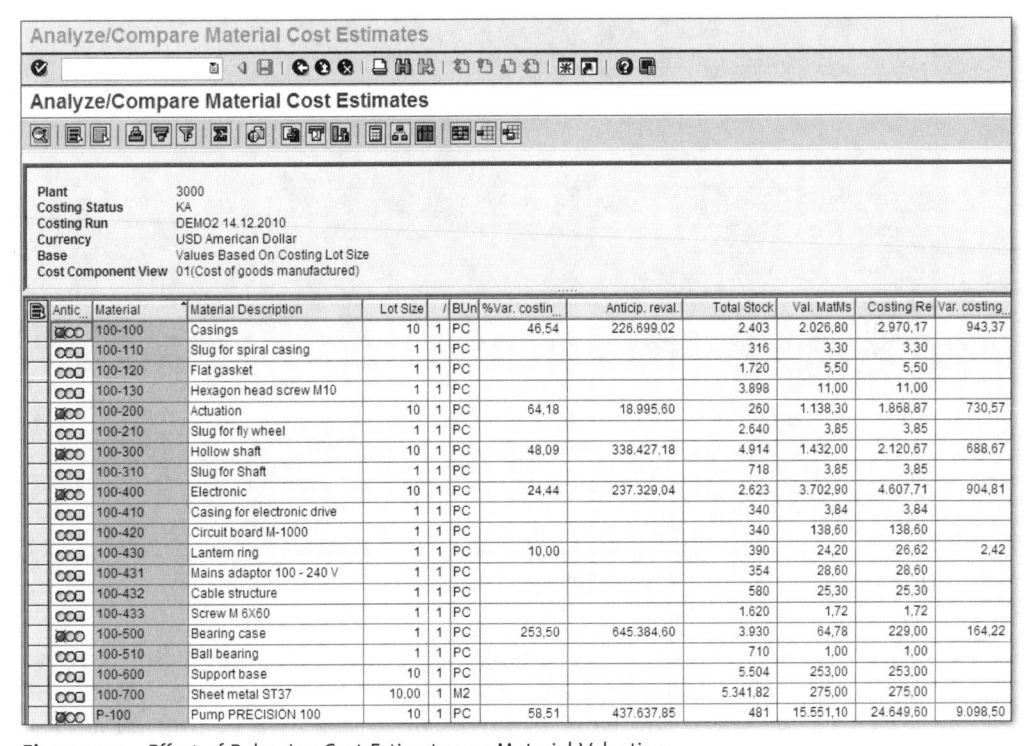

Analyze/Compare Material Cost Estimates

Plant	3000
Costing Status	KA
Costing Run	DEMO2 14.12.2010
Currency	USD American Dollar
Base	Values Based On Costing Lot Size
Cost Component View	01(Cost of goods manufactured)

Antic.	Material	Material Description	Lot Size	/	BUn	%Var. costin	Anticip. reval.	Total Stock	Val. MatMs	Costing Re	Var. costing
●○○	100-100	Casings	10	1	PC	46,54	226.699,02	2.403	2.026,80	2.970,17	943,37
○○○	100-110	Slug for spiral casing	1	1	PC			316	3,30	3,30	
○○○	100-120	Flat gasket	1	1	PC			1.720	5,50	5,50	
○○○	100-130	Hexagon head screw M10	1	1	PC			3.898	11,00	11,00	
●○○	100-200	Actuation	10	1	PC	64,18	18.995,60	260	1.138,30	1.868,87	730,57
○○○	100-210	Slug for fly wheel	1	1	PC			2.640	3,85	3,85	
●○○	100-300	Hollow shaft	10	1	PC	48,09	338.427,18	4.914	1.432,00	2.120,67	688,67
○○○	100-310	Slug for Shaft	1	1	PC			718	3,85	3,85	
●○○	100-400	Electronic	10	1	PC	24,44	237.329,04	2.623	3.702,90	4.607,71	904,81
○○○	100-410	Casing for electronic drive	1	1	PC			340	3,84	3,84	
○○○	100-420	Circuit board M-1000	1	1	PC			340	138,60	138,60	
○○○	100-430	Lantern ring	1	1	PC	10,00		390	24,20	26,62	2,42
○○○	100-431	Mains adaptor 100 - 240 V	1	1	PC			354	28,60	28,60	
○○○	100-432	Cable structure	1	1	PC			580	25,30	25,30	
○○○	100-433	Screw M 6X60	1	1	PC			1.620	1,72	1,72	
●○○	100-500	Bearing case	1	1	PC	253,50	645.384,60	3.930	64,78	229,00	164,22
○○○	100-510	Ball bearing	1	1	PC			710	1,00	1,00	
○○○	100-600	Support base	10	1	PC			5.504	253,00	253,00	
○○○	100-700	Sheet metal ST37	10,00	1	M2			5.341,82	275,00	275,00	
●○○	P-100	Pump PRECISION 100	10	1	PC	58,51	437.637,85	481	15.551,10	24.649,60	9.098,50

Figure 5.31 Effect of Releasing Cost Estimates on Material Valuation

Marking

Since the release results in a *revaluation* of all materials in stock and can cause a significant difference in the balance sheet, the revaluation step is split into two steps: marking and release.

- Marking the cost estimate takes the value in the cost estimate and updates it to the value in the FUTURE STANDARD PRICE field in the COSTING 2 view of the material master (see Chapter 4). You can still mark again if you discover that you have marked an incorrect cost estimate.

- Releasing the cost estimate takes the future standard price and supporting cost estimate and uses them to create a new standard price. Once this has happened, you cannot change the standard price until the next period—another reason to be sure to check the results before releasing.

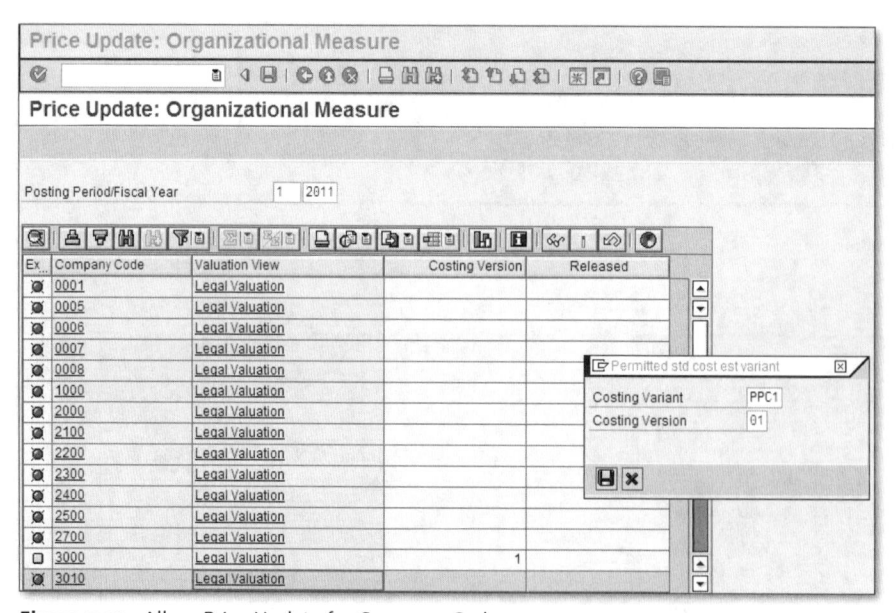

Figure 5.32 Allow Price Update for Company Code

Before you can perform either of these steps, you have to explicitly allow the price change in the relevant company code. Figure 5.24 shows the costing run. The marking step includes a lock icon in the AUTHORIZATION column. To allow marking, click on this icon and allow the price change for the relevant costing variant and costing version as shown in Figure 5.32. Be careful to enter the correct version (usually 1). Organizations are usually very restrictive about who has authorization to perform this step. Figure 5.33 shows the result of marking the materials contained in the costing run. Once marking has taken place, the cost estimates have the status VO (marked).

Ex	Material	Plant	Valuation Type	Costin	Fut. plnd price	Standard price
☐	100-100	3000		VO	297,02	202,68
☐	100-110	3000		VO	3,30	3,30
☐	100-120	3000		VO	5,50	5,50
☐	100-130	3000		VO	11,00	11,00
☐	100-200	3000		VO	186,89	113,83
☐	100-210	3000		VO	3,85	3,85
☐	100-300	3000		VO	212,07	143,20
☐	100-310	3000		VO	3,85	3,85
☐	100-400	3000		VO	460,77	370,29
☐	100-410	3000		VO	3,84	3,84
☐	100-420	3000		VO	138,60	138,60
☐	100-430	3000		VO	26,62	24,20
☐	100-431	3000		VO	28,60	28,60
☐	100-432	3000		VO	25,30	25,30
☐	100-433	3000		VO	1,72	1,72
☐	100-500	3000		VO	229,00	64,78
☐	100-510	3000		VO	1,00	1,00
☐	100-600	3000		VO	25,30	25,30
☐	100-700	3000		VO	27,50	27,50
☐	P-100	3000		VO	2.464,96	1.555,11

Figure 5.33 Using Marking to Create a Future Standard Price

Release

Figure 5.34 shows the result of completing the release step. Once release has taken place, the cost estimates have the status FR (released).

This process revalues inventory and results in price change documents being written that document the change. For auditing, you can always view the supporting cost estimate from the material master using Transaction MM03 (see Figure 5.35). Here you'll see that the standard price was created using a cost estimate created in January 2011.

5 | Planning and Budgeting

Ex	Material	Plant	Valuation Type	Costin	Standard price	Price Unit	Currency
☐	100-100	3000		FR	297,02	1	USD
☐	100-110	3000		FR	3,30	1	USD
☐	100-120	3000		FR	5,50	1	USD
☐	100-130	3000		FR	11,00	1	USD
☐	100-200	3000		FR	186,89	1	USD
☐	100-210	3000		FR	3,85	1	USD
☐	100-300	3000		FR	212,07	1	USD
☐	100-310	3000		FR	3,85	1	USD
☐	100-400	3000		FR	460,77	1	USD
☐	100-410	3000		FR	3,84	1	USD
☐	100-420	3000		FR	138,60	1	USD
☐	100-430	3000		FR	26,62	1	USD
☐	100-431	3000		FR	28,60	1	USD
☐	100-432	3000		FR	25,30	1	USD
☐	100-433	3000		FR	1,72	1	USD
☐	100-500	3000		FR	229,00	1	USD
☐	100-510	3000		FR	1,00	1	USD
☐	100-600	3000		FR	25,30	1	USD
☐	100-700	3000		FR	27,50	1	USD
☐	P-100	3000		FR	2.464,96	1	USD

Figure 5.34 Using the Release Step to Create a New Standard Price

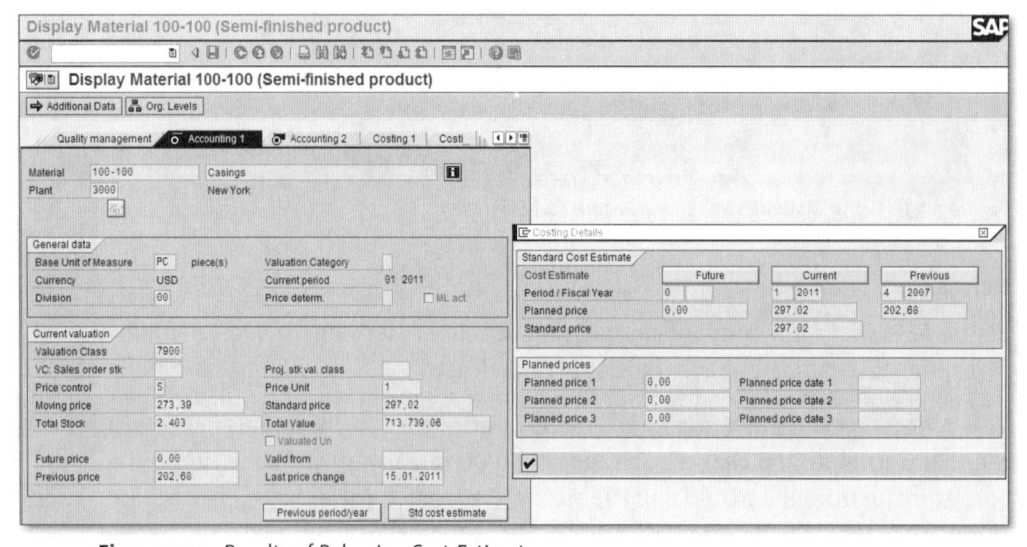

Figure 5.35 Results of Releasing Cost Estimate

5.1.4 Profitability Planning

Once the standard costs have been calculated and the cost centers and internal orders planned, the final stage of planning is to pull all the values together in Profitability Analysis. There are two parts to the completion of the plan:

- Click on the VALUATE button in the planning layouts to select the sales prices and deductions and the product cost estimates we just created. This allows you to forecast net revenue and the first and second contribution margin.
- Run assessment cycles, indirect activity allocation cycles, and order settlement to include the overhead. This allows you to forecast the final profit and contribution margin.

Figure 5.36 shows a sample profitability report including the planned data that will be used to assess the success of the actual data. This is based on the sample S_GO operating concern, so the figures are not necessarily realistic. The report was accessed using Transaction KE30 and selecting the appropriate report definition.

- To select the revenues and product costs, return to Transaction KEPM (see Figure 5.2) and click on the VALUATE button to read the sales prices and deductions and the product cost estimates.
- To run the planned assessment, indirect allocation cycles, and order settlement, use the transactions in the INTEGRATED PLANNING folder (see Figure 5.1). If you have planned costs on your cost centers, use the assessment function (Transaction KEUB) to allocate costs, such as planned sales and administration expenses. If you have planned costs on orders or projects, use the settlement functions to settle costs, such as planned research activities.

Once the plan is satisfactory to all parties, lock the plan version against changes to freeze the plan for future analysis. To lock the plan, select CURRENT SETTINGS • MAINTAIN PLAN VERSIONS in Figure 5.2.

While that wraps up the annual operating plan for the sales-driven processes, it does not cover investment plans or project plans, which many manufacturing companies plan to a greater or lesser extent. We'll now look at how investment plans fit in to the planning environment.

5 | Planning and Budgeting

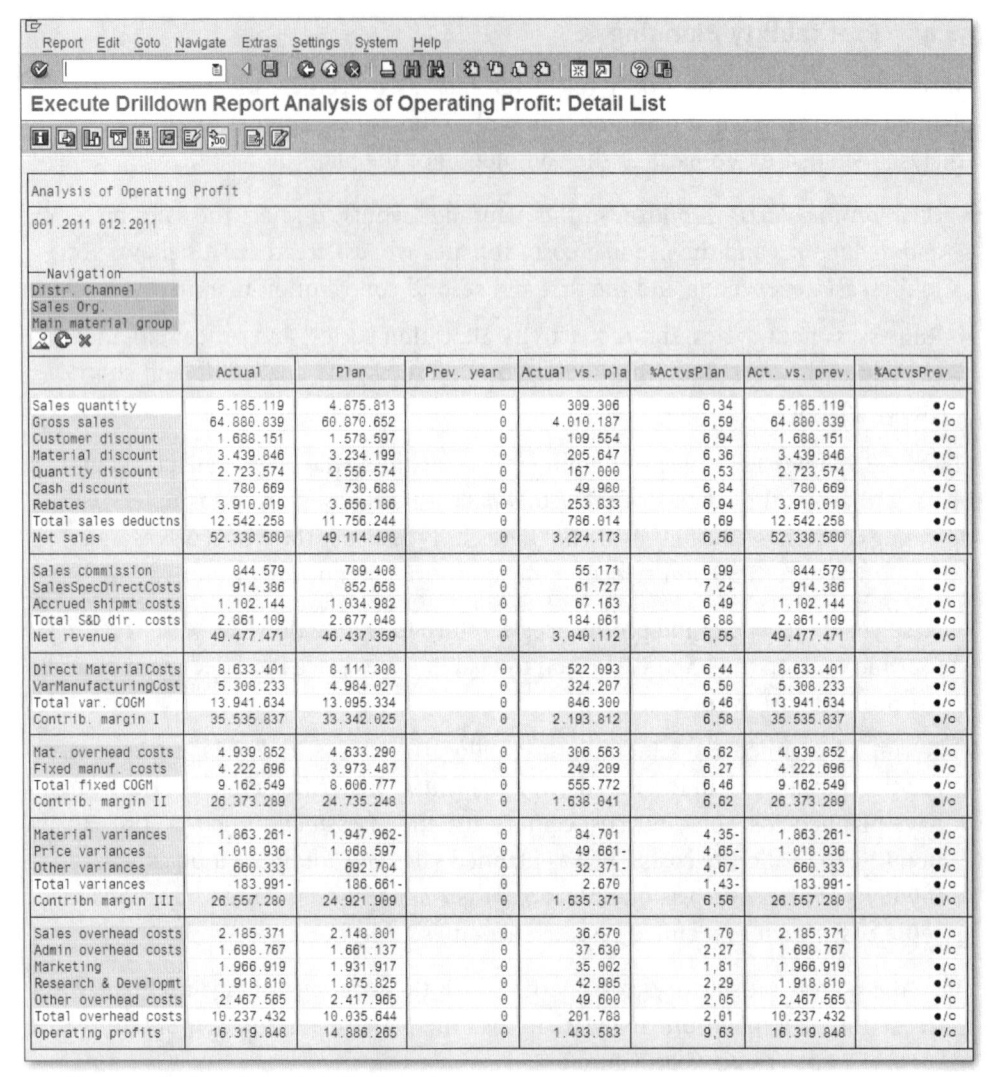

Figure 5.36 Sample Profitability Report

5.2 Planning and Budgeting For Investment Programs

In this section we'll look at investment planning. Investment programs describe the organization's targets in terms of capital investment projects to replace production equipment, prepare new products for launch, as we saw in Chapter 4. There's a link to the cost center plan in the sense that the same organizational structure (generally the cost center hierarchy) is often used to structure the investment program. In this type of plan, however, the controller plans the investment needed to ensure the cost center output in the long term, rather than the costs of providing the output in the immediate future. This plan is subject to much greater variability than the annual operating plan. While the costs incurred by a cost center in any period should be relatively stable, building a new production line is an inherently different undertaking. So SAP introduced the notion of a budget as a ceiling for such spending, a subject we'll return to in Chapter 6. Since the plan includes so much variability, it cannot be considered to represent a standard, so the variance analysis available for investment projects and orders is limited to a line by line comparison of plan and budget against actual costs and commitments.

5.2.1 Investment Program

Investment planning generally starts with the items of the investment program that we looked at in Chapter 4. These items provide the framework for the planning activities. However, if you don't use Investment Management, you can simply track your planning progress against a list of investment projects and orders and perform the same planning tasks on the individual objects. Before you start, check the budget settings for your program by going to Transaction IM03 or ACCOUNTING • INVESTMENT MANAGEMENT • PROGRAMS • MASTER DATA • INVESTMENT PROGRAM DEFINITION • DISPLAY and entering the program and approval year.

> **Linking Investment Program Budgets and the Underlying Orders/Projects**
>
> In the context of investment budget planning it's a good idea to select the BUDGET DISTRIBUTION ANNUAL checkbox so that any orders or projects assigned to the program position do not receive more annual budget for the fiscal year than is available for the program position to which they're assigned. This makes it easy to ensure that each project manager keeps to his allotted budget during the planning process.

5.2.2 Overall Plan

The high-level goals for investment planning are not determined by the sales, production and cost center output, but by the ability of the organization to make the investment at all. So the overall plan exists as a form of planning for orders and projects, but not for cost centers. The overall plan is used to document the progress from the high-level goal, such as the planned spending for a single project, to a level of detail appropriate for project approval. This documents the progress toward the final project structure, breaking down the total values to the individual work breakdown elements, and toward an understanding of the timing of the expenses: the years in which the costs will be incurred. To create an overall plan for a project, use Transaction CJ40 or follow the menu path ACCOUNTING • INVESTMENT MANAGEMENT • INVESTMENT PROJECTS • PLANNING • TOTAL COSTS • CHANGE or ACCOUNTING • PROJECT SYSTEM • FINANCIALS • PLANNING • COSTS IN WBS • OVERALL VALUES • CHANGE. Enter the project definition, the currency, and the version. If you already know which level of the project hierarchy interests you in a large project, you can also enter a WBS element.

Figure 5.37 shows a sample overall plan. You can toggle between this view (the element view), where the leading column shows the WBS elements, and the annual view, where the leading column shows the year, by clicking on the ANNUAL VIEW button.

- The process of breaking down the project plan structurally and across the time dimension is generally known as *top-down planning*. The DISTRIBUTABLE column gives an overview of the costs awaiting distribution to the lower levels. The costs that have been distributed are shown in the DISTRIBUTED column.

- Alongside this process, we often find planned data being entered for individual WBS elements when details are known (contracts with a supplier, agreements on the level of work required to perform the task, and so on). These are shown in the PLANNED TOTALS column and aggregated in a process known as *bottom-up planning*. At some point the two value flows should meet, but the essence of the planning application is in matching the detail against the target and understanding where compromises will be needed.

We'll use this overall plan later to prepare the budget for the project later.

5.2.3 Cost Element Planning

The overall plan also aggregates any other known planning data available for the project. Where assets under construction have to be capitalized for the project, it's is important to distinguish the type of costs in the project (direct, indirect, material, and so on). This forces the controller to plan at the same level of detail as the inputs in the cost center. To access the planning application shown in Figure 5.38, choose the ANNUAL OVERVIEW button shown in Figure 5.37 and then click on the PRIMARY COSTS button. This takes you into the form-based cost element plan, where you'll see a line for every cost element in your chart of accounts.

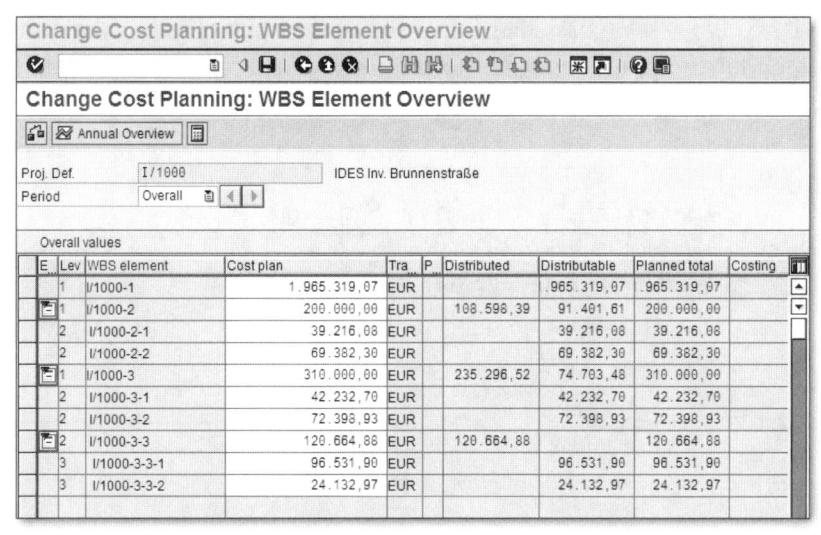

5.2 Planning and Budgeting For Investment Programs

Figure 5.37 Overall Plan for a Project

> **Including Your Own Planning Layouts in Project Planning**
>
> If you click on the PRIMARY COSTS button, a standard planning layout will be used that cannot be switched once you are in the planning transaction. If you want planners to be able to jump to the primary costs from the overall plan, but use a different planning layout, refer to the instructions in SAP Note 47207 for details of how to change the planning layout. Alternatively, use Transaction CJR2 with layout 1-701 or follow the menu path ACCOUNTING • INVESTMENT MANAGEMENT • INVESTMENT PROJECTS • PLANNING • COST AND ACTIVITY INPUTS • CHANGE or ACCOUNTING • PROJECT SYSTEM • FINANCIALS • PLANNING • COSTS IN WBS • COST AND ACTIVITY INPUTS • CHANGE. Enter the project definition, the currency, the version, and the cost element group or interval. If you choose this route, you can choose between free planning (where you'll only see data for the cost elements you've already captured) and form-based planning (where you'll see an empty line for every cost element in the group or interval you entered in the initial screen). Figure 5.38 shows the planning screen. This behaves exactly the same way as cost element planning on cost centers or on internal orders.

Alongside the primary costs (the purchased materials and contract work) that are required to complete the project, you can also plan the work required to complete the project in the form of activity input.

If these projects are assigned to an investment program, when you finish the detailed planning you can roll up the values captured on the assigned orders and projects by going to Transaction IM34 or ACCOUNTING • INVESTMENT MANAGEMENT • PROGRAM

249

5 | Planning and Budgeting

PLANNING • DEFAULT PLAN VALUES. Figure 5.39 shows the result of rolling the plan values captured for the project assigned to the research and development node into the investment program.

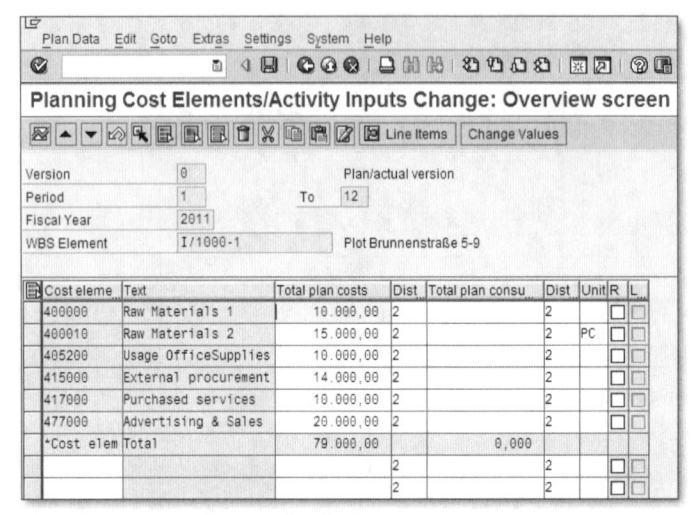

Figure 5.38 Cost Element Plan for a Project

Figure 5.39 Investment Program Planning

Normally we would continue planning for each item in the investment program, but we'll go straight to budgeting.

5.2.4 Budgeting

If we now assume that the project plan has been approved, the next task is the creation of the budget. Figure 5.40 shows the budgeting applications for an internal order, but the same applications are available for projects. The *original budget* is created using the approved plan as a guide. This budget is more than just a plan. It's an agreement with the organization about proposed spending levels. Changing circumstances can render this ceiling inappropriate. At this stage, you can either create a *return* to give back some of the original budget or a *supplement* to document the assignment of an additional budget.

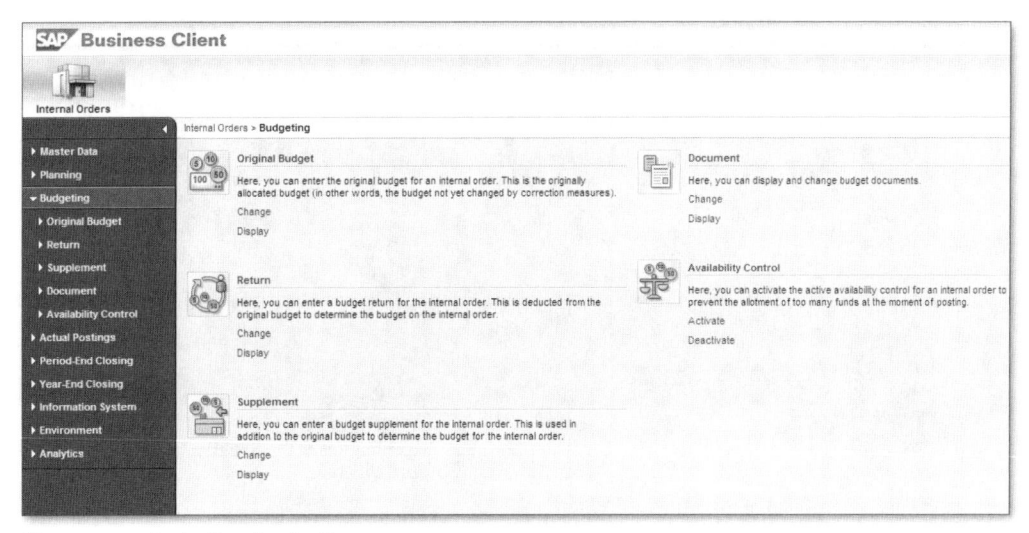

Figure 5.40 Budgeting Applications

If you use investment programs, it makes sense to start your budgeting process at the highest level, namely, in the investment program. You can prepare the budget using Transaction IM32 or by following the menu path ACCOUNTING • INVESTMENT MANAGEMENT • PROGRAMS • BUDGETING • EDIT ORIGINAL and entering data in much the same way as we saw for the overall plan. If you've already prepared plan data for the investment program, you can copy this data by selecting EDIT • COPY VIEW

5 | Planning and Budgeting

as shown in Figure 5.41. Once you have the rough values for the items, adjust these to meet your needs by selecting EDIT • REVALUATE. When you're satisfied with your budget at the program level, you can ensure that the budget set cannot be exceeded on the associated WBS elements, orders, and appropriation requests using Transaction IM52 or by following the menu path ACCOUNTING • INVESTMENT MANAGEMENT • PROGRAMS • BUDGETING • BUDGET DISTRIBUTION • EDIT.

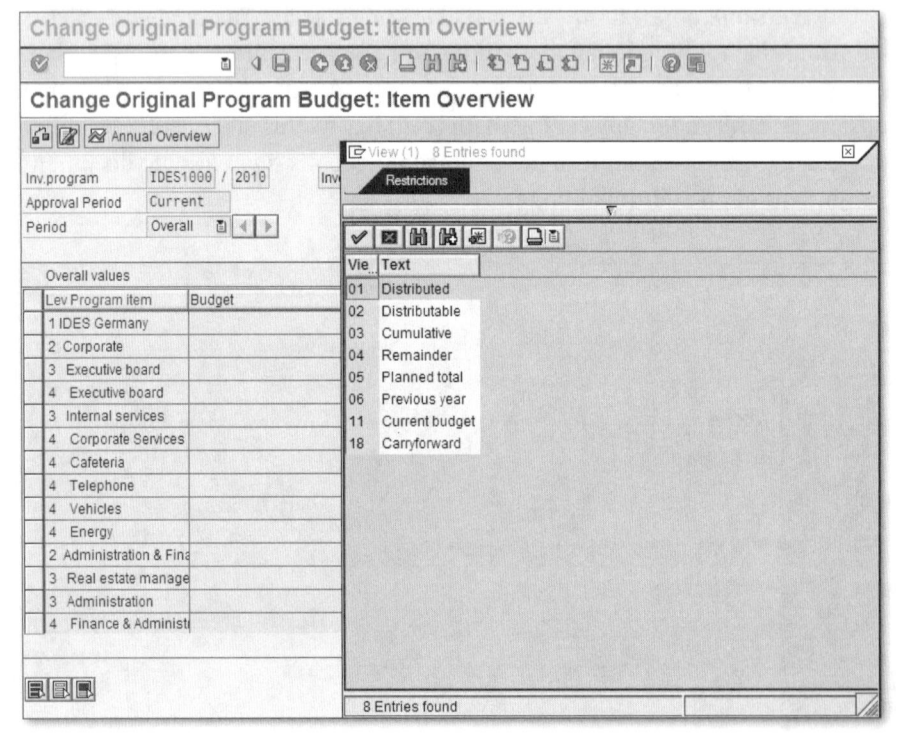

Figure 5.41 Change Investment Program

Figure 5.42 shows the original budget for a WBS element. You can enter the budget for a project using Transaction CJ30 or by selecting PROJECT SYSTEM • FINANCIALS • BUDGETING • ORIGINAL BUDGET • CHANGE. Notice that some of the lines in the BUDGET column don't allow entry. This is because we assigned the WBS elements to an investment program position in Chapter 4, and we specified that the budget for the investment program should not receive more annual budget for the fiscal year than is available for the program position by selecting the BUDGET DISTRIBUTION

ANNUAL checkbox for the investment program. If you want to check the connection between the WBS element and the investment program during budgeting, simply select EXTRAS • INVESTMENT PROGRAM.

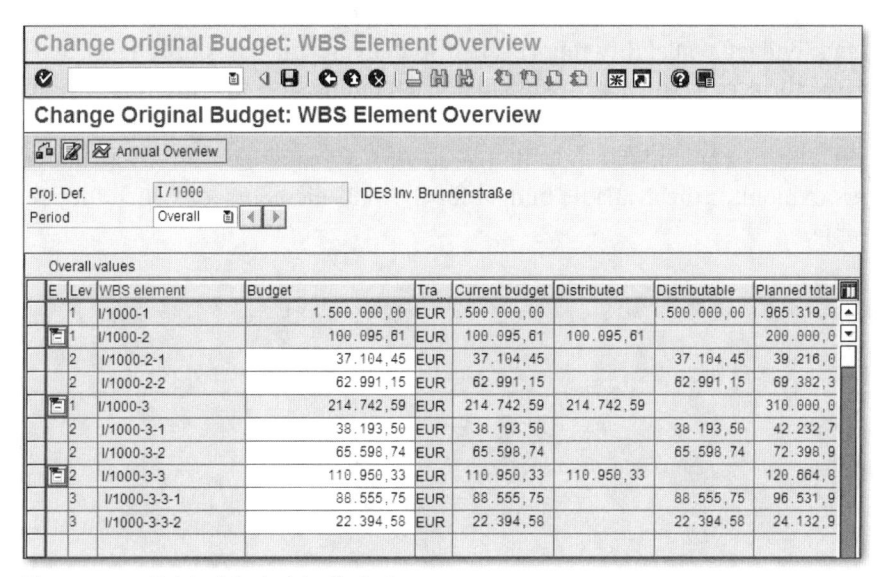

Figure 5.42 Original Budget by Project

Having planned your overall values and then broken them down per year, you may wonder what happens as you go into the next fiscal year. In Investment Management, you need to ensure that a new approval year is created and the budget from the old year carried through into the new. To open a new fiscal year, use Transaction IM27 or follow the menu path ACCOUNTING • INVESTMENT MANAGEMENT • PROGRAMS • PERIODIC PROCESSING • FISCAL YEAR CHANGE • OPEN NEW APPROVAL YEAR. You can then copy the existing program structure and carry forward the planned values, budget values, and measures (orders and projects).

> **Carrying Forward a Budget**
>
> Remembering what you need to do to correctly move an investment program into the next fiscal year can be tricky. SAP Note 444444 tells you exactly how to proceed and avoid any pitfalls.

5.2.5 Displaying and Changing a Budget

The management of these budgets is usually in the hands of controlling or a dedicated investment management department. However, it's equally important that project managers have the details of their available budget at their fingertips. For this reason, budget availability reports are also delivered as part of Manager Self-Service (see the accompanying downloadable appendices) so that the responsible managers can monitor the budget they still have at their disposal. Figure 5.43 shows the budget availability report delivered with Manager Self-Service to allow managers to monitor the available budget for the WBS elements for which they're responsible.

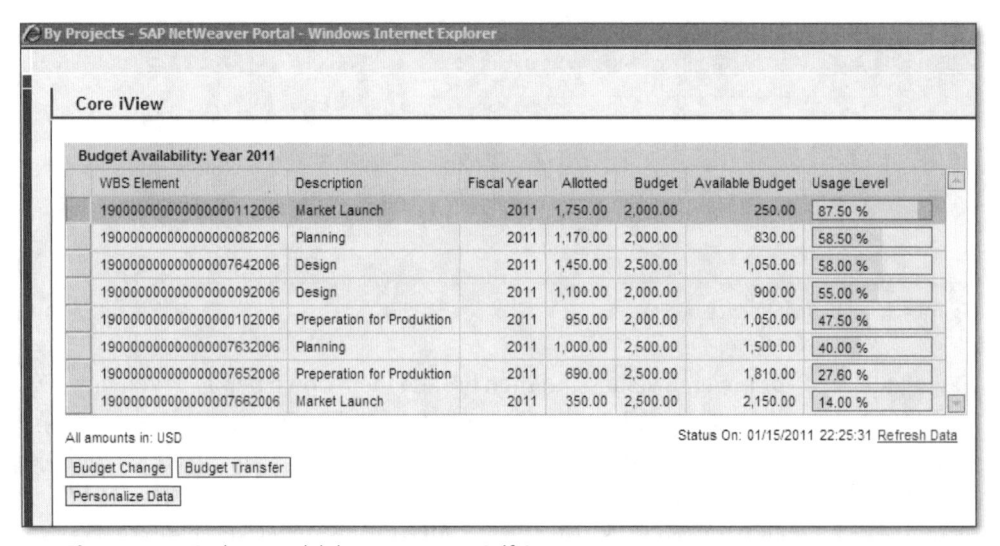

Figure 5.43 Budget Availability in Manager Self-Service

We looked at the subject of change requests for cost centers in Chapter 3. Since the need for a budget change normally arises in the field, the same mechanisms can be used to allow project managers to request budget changes and supplements and make returns. Figure 5.44 shows a sample budget transfer request form. To launch this form, click on the BUDGET CHANGE button in the budget availability report in Manager Self-Service (Figure 5.43).

ANNUAL checkbox for the investment program. If you want to check the connection between the WBS element and the investment program during budgeting, simply select EXTRAS • INVESTMENT PROGRAM.

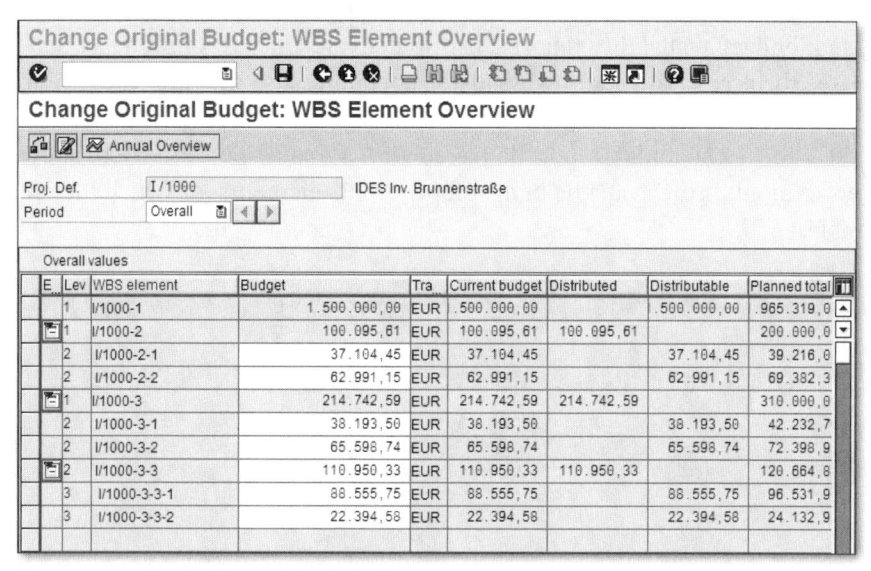

E	Lev	WBS element	Budget	Tra	Current budget	Distributed	Distributable	Planned total
	1	I/1000-1	1.500.000,00	EUR	500.000,00		500.000,00	965.319,0
	1	I/1000-2	100.095,61	EUR	100.095,61	100.095,61		200.000,0
	2	I/1000-2-1	37.104,45	EUR	37.104,45		37.104,45	39.216,0
	2	I/1000-2-2	62.991,15	EUR	62.991,15		62.991,15	69.382,3
	1	I/1000-3	214.742,59	EUR	214.742,59	214.742,59		310.000,0
	2	I/1000-3-1	38.193,50	EUR	38.193,50		38.193,50	42.232,7
	2	I/1000-3-2	65.598,74	EUR	65.598,74		65.598,74	72.398,9
	2	I/1000-3-3	110.950,33	EUR	110.950,33	110.950,33		120.664,8
	3	I/1000-3-3-1	88.555,75	EUR	88.555,75		88.555,75	96.531,9
	3	I/1000-3-3-2	22.394,58	EUR	22.394,58		22.394,58	24.132,9

Figure 5.42 Original Budget by Project

Having planned your overall values and then broken them down per year, you may wonder what happens as you go into the next fiscal year. In Investment Management, you need to ensure that a new approval year is created and the budget from the old year carried through into the new. To open a new fiscal year, use Transaction IM27 or follow the menu path ACCOUNTING • INVESTMENT MANAGEMENT • PROGRAMS • PERIODIC PROCESSING • FISCAL YEAR CHANGE • OPEN NEW APPROVAL YEAR. You can then copy the existing program structure and carry forward the planned values, budget values, and measures (orders and projects).

Carrying Forward a Budget

Remembering what you need to do to correctly move an investment program into the next fiscal year can be tricky. SAP Note 444444 tells you exactly how to proceed and avoid any pitfalls.

5.2.5 Displaying and Changing a Budget

The management of these budgets is usually in the hands of controlling or a dedicated investment management department. However, it's equally important that project managers have the details of their available budget at their fingertips. For this reason, budget availability reports are also delivered as part of Manager Self-Service (see the accompanying downloadable appendices) so that the responsible managers can monitor the budget they still have at their disposal. Figure 5.43 shows the budget availability report delivered with Manager Self-Service to allow managers to monitor the available budget for the WBS elements for which they're responsible.

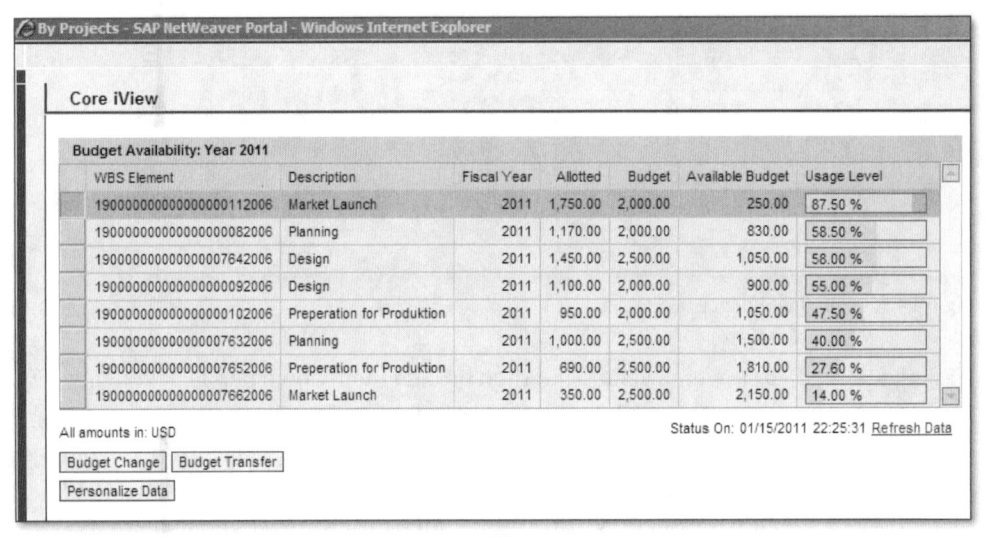

Figure 5.43 Budget Availability in Manager Self-Service

We looked at the subject of change requests for cost centers in Chapter 3. Since the need for a budget change normally arises in the field, the same mechanisms can be used to allow project managers to request budget changes and supplements and make returns. Figure 5.44 shows a sample budget transfer request form. To launch this form, click on the BUDGET CHANGE button in the budget availability report in Manager Self-Service (Figure 5.43).

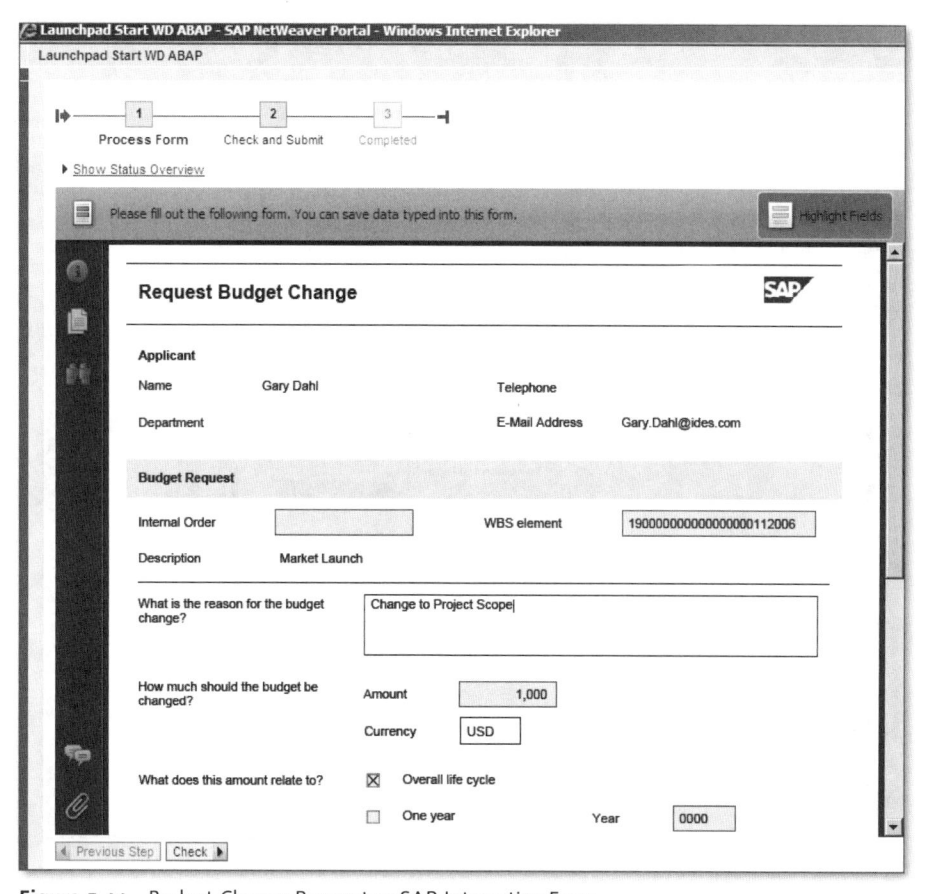

Figure 5.44 Budget Change Request as SAP Interactive Form

The form is linked with the fields in the project, so it can determine whether budget values refer to the whole lifecycle of the project or individual years and the currency used for budgeting. To enter the type of change required from controlling, scroll down the form and choose from the dropdown box shown in Figure 5.45. The controller can initiate these changes without a form by choosing the appropriate transactions under PROJECT SYSTEM • FINANCIALS • BUDGETING, but the change request provides a good way of documenting the rationale behind a change in a budget and including a workflow so the budget change can be approved properly.

5 | Planning and Budgeting

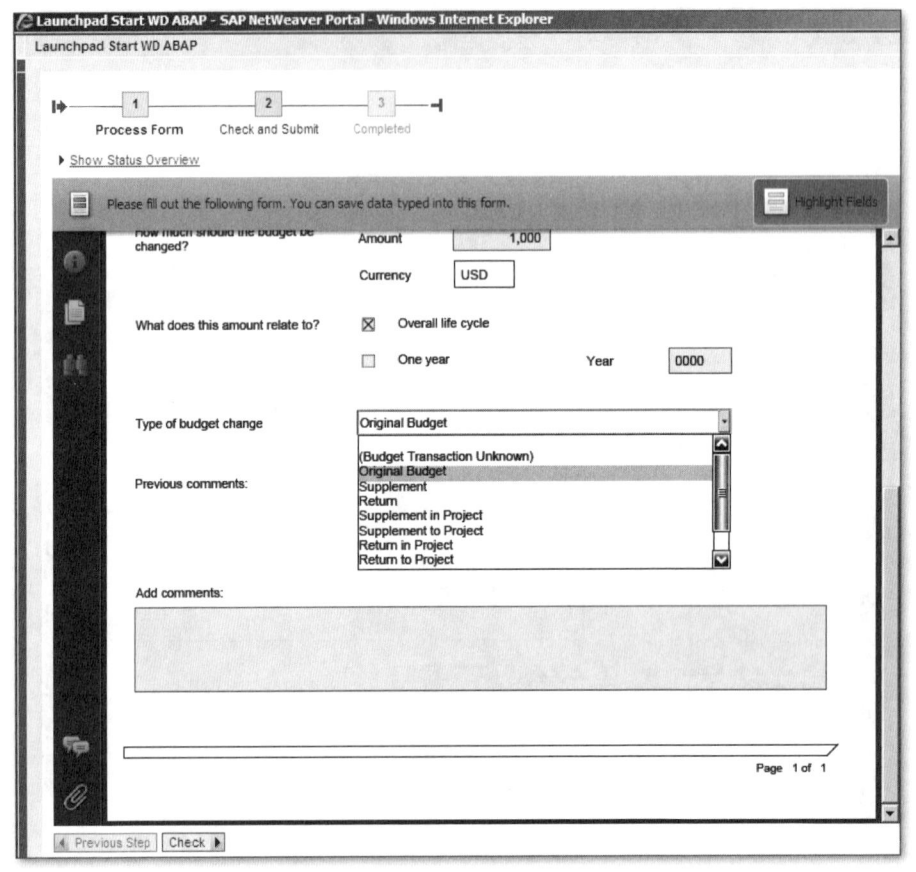

Figure 5.45 Types of Budget Change Request in SAP Interactive Form

5.3 Summary

We've have seen that planning in SAP ERP relies heavily on the existing master data we created in Chapters 3 and 4 and is a prerequisite for most of the actual postings we'll see in Chapter 6, since it's is needed to set standard costs as an initial valuation for all goods movements and standard activity rates for all confirmations in production and time recording in SAP ERP Human Capital Management. We'll now look at how our plan is used during the posting of actual costs. To find out how to set up forms like those we just displayed for a budget change request, please refer to Chapter 9.

This chapter looks at actual postings by following the costs incurred during procurement, production, and sales in various situations, including intercompany goods movements. It explains what happens if you find differences during an inventory count or need to make corrections.

6 Actual Postings

Because of the integrated nature of SAP ERP, it's rare for a controller to make a manual posting. In many cases the controller simply monitors the postings created in Logistics and Human Capital Management and anticipates their impact on the Controlling component of SAP ERP Financials (which we'll refer to as CO). The best way to get a feel for the nature of the actual postings is to follow a business process from end to end, showing what transactions initiate the postings and what data is then available for you to monitor in CO. In the first section of this chapter, we'll follow two raw materials from their initial purchase through the manufacturing process to their final sale to the customer and discuss the issues a controller monitors at each stage. When we looked at the master data in Chapter 4, we discussed how to backflush the goods movements and confirmations based on the information in the BOM and routing for our finished product. We'll do this here too and then look at how to handle any differences discovered during a physical inventory check. After that we'll return to the scenarios we discussed in Chapter 2 and look at the typical postings for product cost by order, product cost by period, product cost by sales order, and project controlling. We'll then discover how to make corrections and adjustment postings. Finally we'll look at how to post values in a logistics scenario involving two affiliated companies.

6.1 Integrated Process Flows: Buy, Make, and Sell

A controller in a manufacturing environment monitors the following key logistics processes:

- The *procurement process* and the impact of the price his buyers are able to negotiate on the product costs
- The *manufacturing process* and the impact of the value added during production on the product costs
- The *sales process* and the impact of the product costs on profitability

This section is based on a very simple example involving the sale of a finished product, ACT-DCD, to the final customer, looking at how the raw materials ACT-BCD and ACT-LCD are procured for use in the manufacture of this finished product and how these raw materials are issued to production and delivered to stock as the finished product for sale. In each step, we'll look at the logistics steps and then explain their impact on CO.

6.1.1 Procure to Pay

Let's start by looking at how CO works for a material purchased to stock for use in a manufacturing process. Figure 6.1 shows the basic flow of the procure-to-pay process.

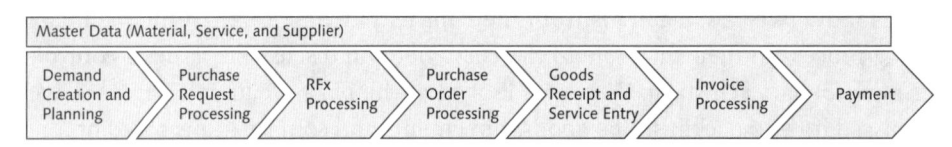

Master Data (Material, Service, and Supplier)
Demand Creation and Planning → Purchase Request Processing → RFx Processing → Purchase Order Processing → Goods Receipt and Service Entry → Invoice Processing → Payment

Figure 6.1 Procure-to-Pay Process

Usually a materials requirements planning (MRP) run like we saw in Chapter 5 and the creation of a purchase request precedes the creation of the purchase order, but we'll start with the purchase order since this is where the choice of account assignment (cost center, project, neutral stock, and so on) impacts how the values will be transferred to CO.

The purchase order is an agreement with a vendor to supply materials at a given price. As we saw in Chapter 4, this price is established in a purchasing info record that defines the agreement between the supplier/vendor and the buyer. This price can be used to set the standard price in the material master, but it may change depending on the business climate. The receipt of the materials into stock and the invoice reference this purchase order. The goods receipt is valued initially using the price in the purchase order, and the invoice may adjust this price. The controller's concern in this process is *purchase price variances*.

Creating a Purchase Order

The first step is to create a purchase order to request the supply of our two raw materials from a vendor. To create a purchase order, use Transaction ME21N or follow the menu path LOGISTICS • MATERIALS MANAGEMENT • PURCHASING • PURCHASE ORDER • CREATE • VENDOR/SUPPLYING PLANT KNOWN. Then enter the vendor, purchasing organization, and company code in the header and the material, plant, and quantity for each item (see Figure 6.2).

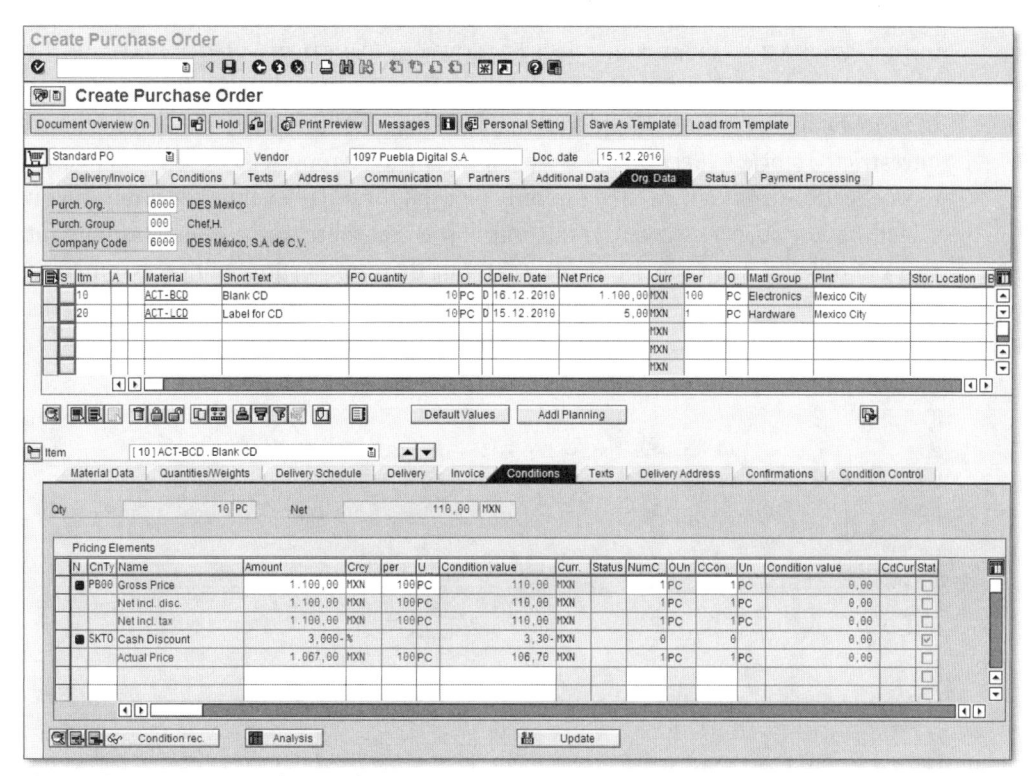

Figure 6.2 Creating a Purchase Order

To view the *price* of each item, select the item and select the CONDITIONS tab. Here we see that the first item for the blank CD costs 1100 Mexican pesos per 100 units. This may already be the source of a purchase price variance if the agreement with

6 | Actual Postings

the vendor is based on a different price than that currently in the material master. The controller might also check the *account assignment*. In our example, column A (Account Assignment Category) is blank, meaning the purchase order will be delivered to regular inventory and can be used by any production order that reserves it. In Section 6.3.4, we'll create a purchase order where the WBS element of a project is the account assignment and compare the postings.

The next step is to record the arrival of the goods into stock.

Posting a Goods Receipt

Now we'll create the goods receipt for the purchase order by referencing the purchase order and the prices contained in it. The easiest way to do this is to stay in the PURCHASING menu and select FOLLOW-ON FUNCTIONS • GOODS RECEIPT or Transaction MIGO. Enter the purchase order from Figure 6.2 as a reference. Figure 6.3 shows the two items we ordered and indicates that they're to be delivered into unrestricted stock. In Section 6.3.3 we'll look at what happens if goods are delivered to sales order stock, where they can only be used for the relevant sales order. If you select the ACCOUNT ASSIGNMENT tab, you'll see that there's no account assignment to a CO object (as we saw in Figure 6.2), but that the posting will be assigned to a profit center using the profit center entered in the material master for the items concerned. This is the standard process for the procurement of stock materials.

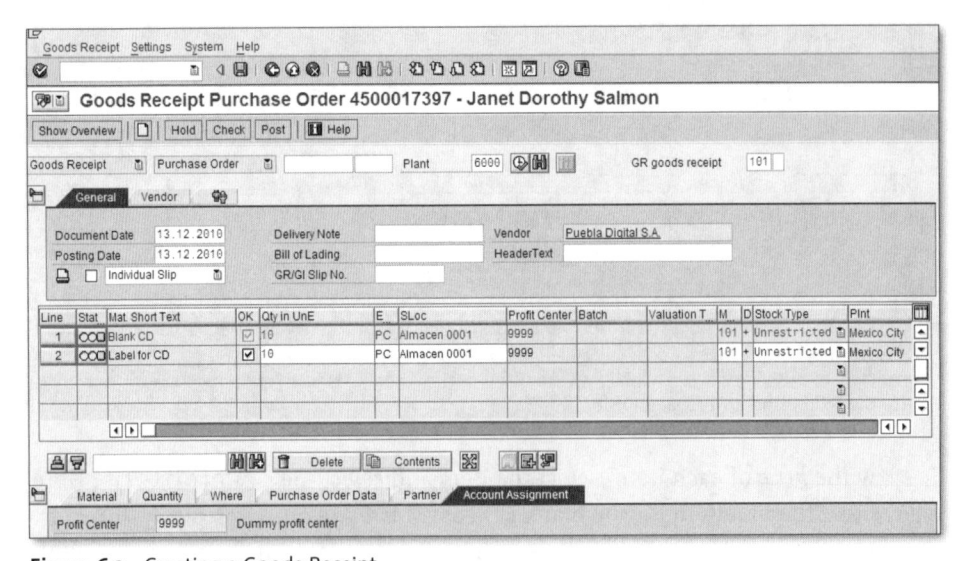

Figure 6.3 Creating a Goods Receipt

Goods receipts for stock materials don't show up as actual costs on a cost center or order until the material is issued to production later. However, if the MATERIAL LEDGER is active in the plant concerned, the goods receipt is recorded in the Material Ledger. To display the associated postings, use Transaction CKM3N or go to CONTROLLING • PRODUCT COST CONTROLLING • ACTUAL COSTING/MATERIAL LEDGER • INFORMATION SYSTEM • DETAILED REPORTS • MATERIAL PRICE ANALYSIS. Enter the material number for the blank CD, the plant, and the current period. Figure 6.4 shows that the price in the purchase order differs from the standard price for the raw material in the material master. The preliminary valuation is based on the standard price for the material (10 pesos per unit), whereas the price conditions in the purchase order item were 11 pesos per unit. This difference of 11 pesos for 10 units is recorded in the Material Ledger and will be included in the actual costs for the material when we use the *periodic costing run* to calculate the periodic unit price for the material as part of the period close in Chapter 7.

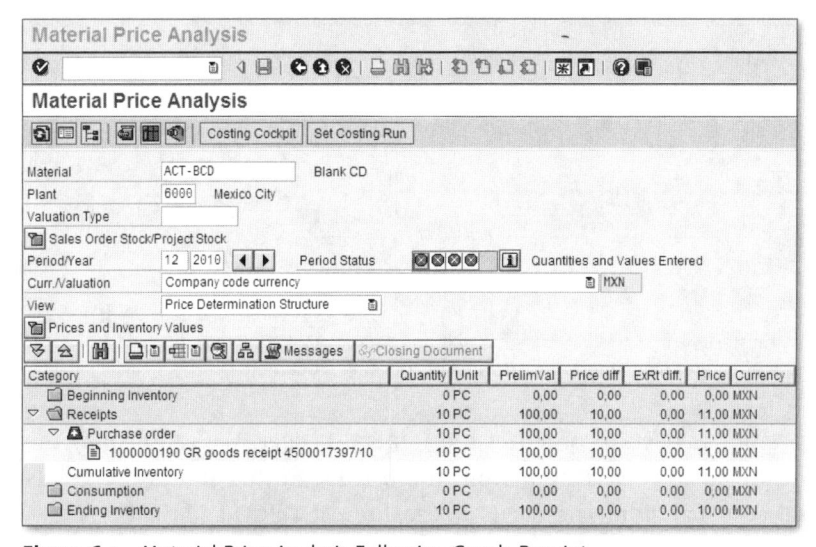

Category	Quantity	Unit	PrelimVal	Price diff	ExRt diff.	Price	Currency
Beginning Inventory	0	PC	0,00	0,00	0,00	0,00	MXN
Receipts	10	PC	100,00	10,00	0,00	11,00	MXN
▽ Purchase order	10	PC	100,00	10,00	0,00	11,00	MXN
1000000190 GR goods receipt 4500017397/10	10	PC	100,00	10,00	0,00	11,00	MXN
Cumulative Inventory	10	PC	100,00	10,00	0,00	11,00	MXN
Consumption	0	PC	0,00	0,00	0,00	0,00	MXN
Ending Inventory	10	PC	100,00	0,00	0,00	10,00	MXN

Figure 6.4 Material Price Analysis Following Goods Receipt

System Performance with the Material Ledger

When people first hear that the Material Ledger stores an extra document for each goods movement, invoice, and so on, they tend to worry that this will put an unnecessary burden on their system. The act of writing a material ledger document adds a couple of percent to the time it takes to post the goods receipt. If you want to find more information about system performance metrics, check the information in SAP Note 668170.

6 Actual Postings

The PURCHASE ORDER line in the MATERIAL PRICE ANALYSIS screen shows both the Material Ledger document number and the purchase order item that initiated the posting. To display the Material Ledger document created during the goods receipt, click on the document line in Figure 6.4. This takes you to the Material Ledger document shown in Figure 6.5. Since as the controller, you won't have created the goods receipt as we just did, normally on checking this list, you might click on the SOURCE DOCUMENT button to display the goods receipt document if you need to check the details of what we entered in Figure 6.3. To display all the accounting documents associated with the goods movement, click on the ACCOUNTING DOCUMENTS button, as shown in Figure 6.5.

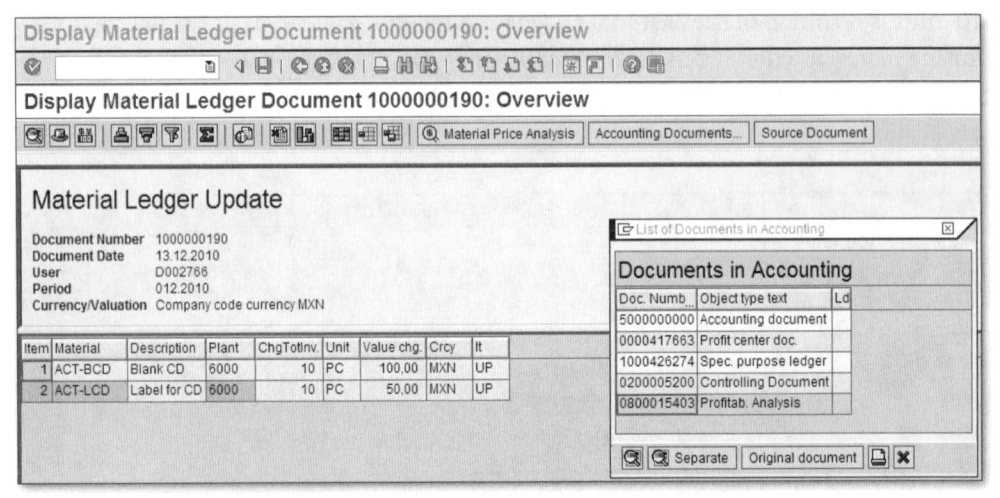

Figure 6.5 Material Ledger Document and Links to Accounting Documents

The goods receipt has been recorded in the General Ledger. We can display the accounting document by selecting it from the list. Figure 6.6 shows the goods valuation (100 pesos) and the variance (10 pesos) for ACT-BCD and the inventory valuation (50 pesos) for ACT-LCD. Our example predates the ability to include the profit center and the functional area in the General Ledger (see Chapter 3), so there are separate documents for Profit Center Accounting and the Special Ledger.

Now return to the list of accounting documents, where we see a CO document that records the posting to CO-PA in general and a CO-PA document. To display this document, select the PROFITABILITY ANALYSIS document in Figure 6.5.

6.1 | Integrated Process Flows: Buy, Make, and Sell

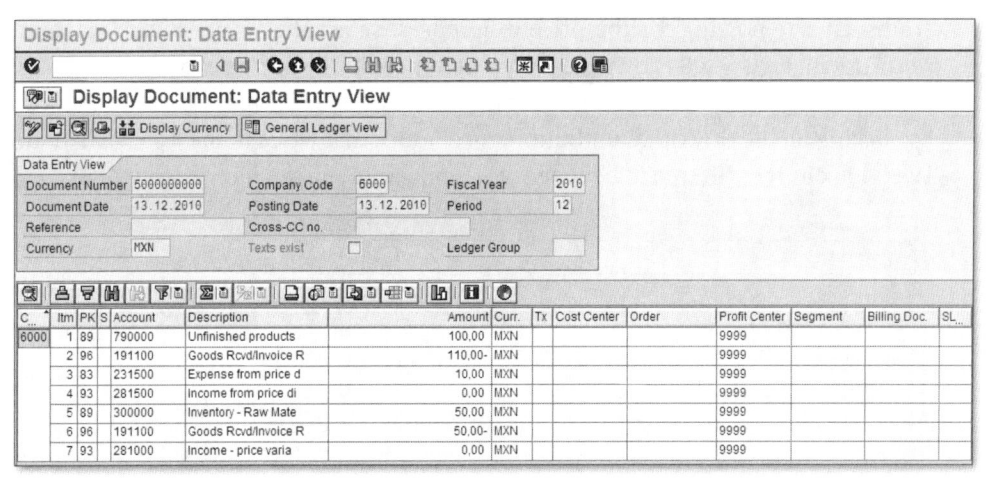

Figure 6.6 Accounting Document for Goods Receipt

Figure 6.7 shows the characteristics for the purchased material, including the material group, company code, and plant. Notice that the document is record type B (direct posting from FI) since it records the variances from the General Ledger and that only the material-related characteristics contain values. This is because at this stage we don't know which customer will purchase the product and to which sales organization he'll belong.

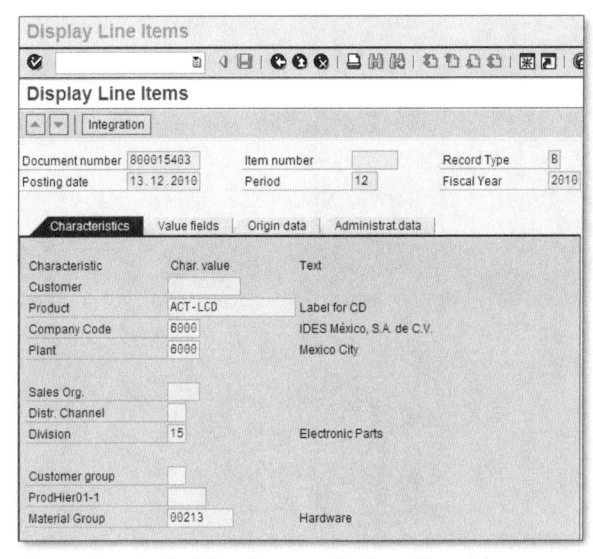

Figure 6.7 Profitability Segment for Raw Material

263

6 | Actual Postings

To display the posting for the price differences, select the VALUE FIELDS tab and scroll down. Figure 6.8 shows the price differences in the currency of the operating concern (here Euros). You can switch to the company code currency (Mexican pesos) by clicking on the CoCodeCrcy button. Also notice that we're in the legal valuation. We'll look at the difference between *legal* and *group valuation* in Section 6.5.

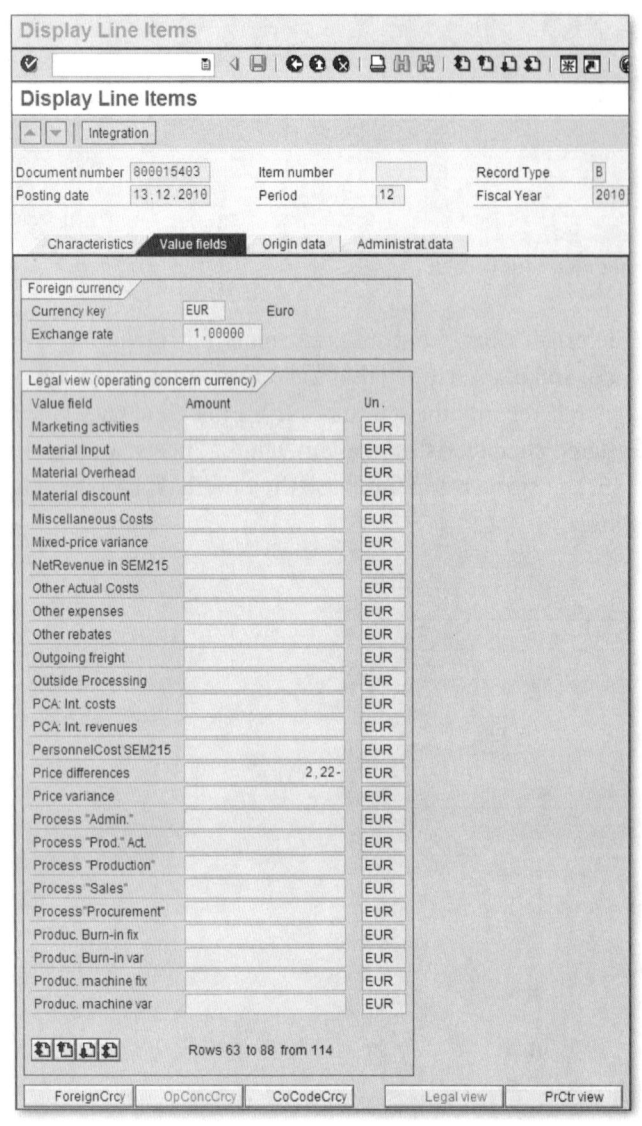

Figure 6.8 Value Fields Showing Price Differences for Raw Materials

The next step is to record the invoice from the vendor for these goods.

Entering an Incoming Invoice

Now we'll record the receipt of the invoice from the vendor for the delivery of the materials. To record the invoice, return to the PURCHASING menu and select FOLLOW-ON FUNCTIONS • LOGISTICS INVOICE VERIFICATION or Transaction MIRO. For invoices to be captured in the Material Ledger, it's important to use the Logistics Invoice Verification transaction (Transaction MIRO) rather than the Invoice Entry transaction (FB60) in Accounts Payable, since you need to ensure that the invoice is linked to the material purchased for the Material Ledger. Just as we saw for the goods receipt, the invoice also is created with reference to the initial purchase order (see Figure 6.9).

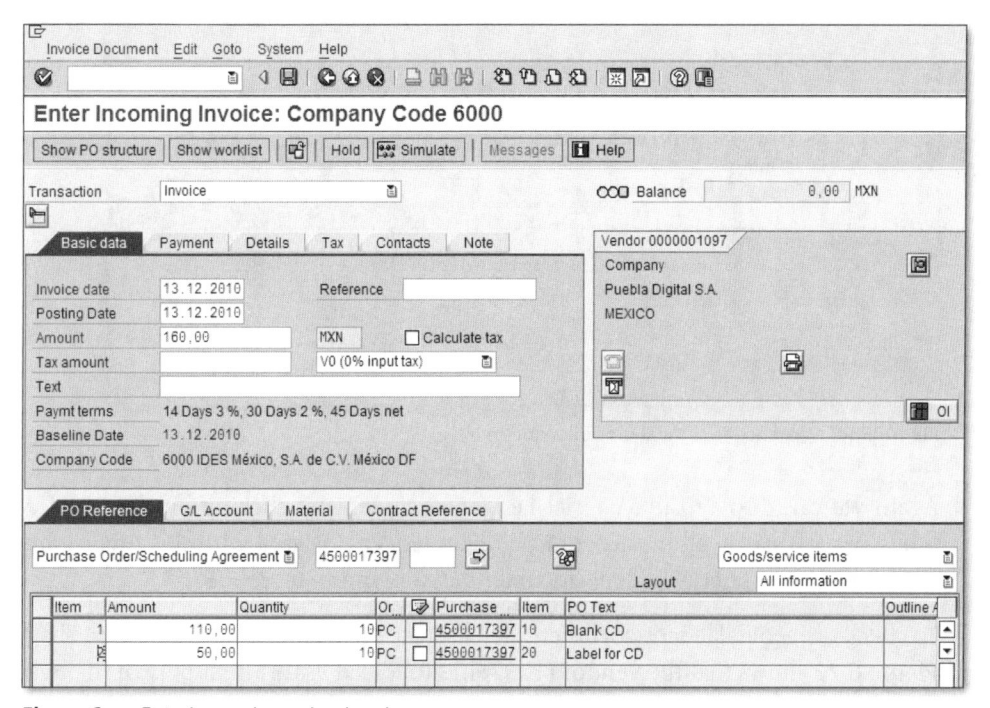

Figure 6.9 Entering an Incoming Invoice

Again, the controller's task is to monitor the values of such invoices in the Material Ledger. The Material Price Analysis report shown in Figure 6.10 now includes a second line for the invoice. In our example, the values are zero because the supplier invoiced for the amount in the initial purchase order. However, there are situations where a supplier invoices for a different amount. For example, it's common in the food industry for milk to be delivered by volume but for the invoice to be based on the fat content (the higher the cream content, the higher the price). This results in a purchase price variance that most manufacturers want to pass on to the cheese products made using that milk.

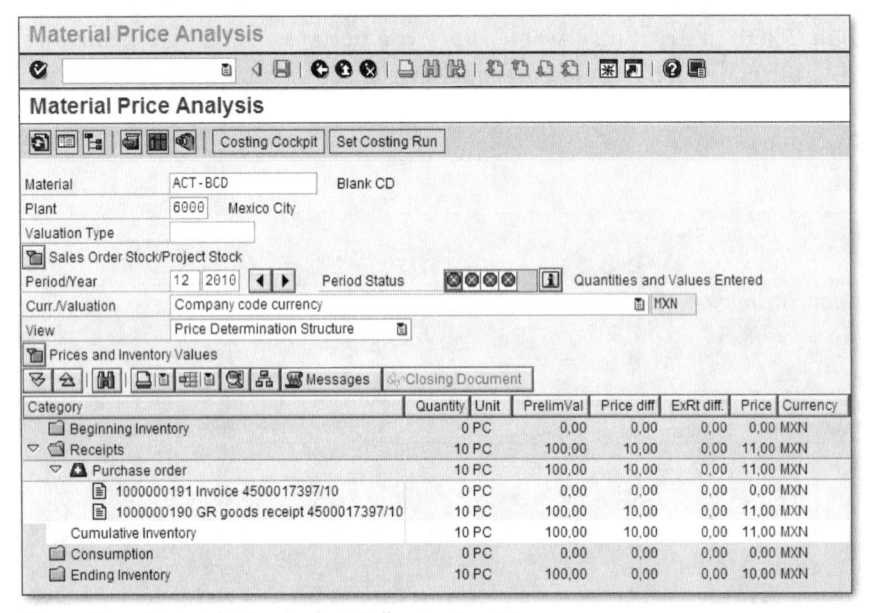

Category	Quantity	Unit	PrelimVal	Price diff	ExRt diff.	Price	Currency
Beginning Inventory	0	PC	0,00	0,00	0,00	0,00	MXN
▽ Receipts	10	PC	100,00	10,00	0,00	11,00	MXN
▽ Purchase order	10	PC	100,00	10,00	0,00	11,00	MXN
1000000191 Invoice 4500017397/10	0	PC	0,00	0,00	0,00	0,00	MXN
1000000190 GR goods receipt 4500017397/10	10	PC	100,00	10,00	0,00	11,00	MXN
Cumulative Inventory	10	PC	100,00	10,00	0,00	11,00	MXN
Consumption	0	PC	0,00	0,00	0,00	0,00	MXN
Ending Inventory	10	PC	100,00	0,00	0,00	10,00	MXN

Figure 6.10 Material Price Analysis Following Invoicing

Again we can display the Material Ledger document by clicking on the invoice line. We can display all the accounting documents associated with this invoice by clicking on the Material Ledger document as shown in Figure 6.11.

To check the general ledger document, select ACCOUNTING DOCUMENT from the list. Figure 6.12 shows that the vendor (1097) has invoiced us for the supply of the two materials. Normally the process would continue with an open item in Accounts Payable and a payment to the vendor that would clear that open item, but we'll move straight to the manufacturing process, since the processes in accounts payable have no impact on CO.

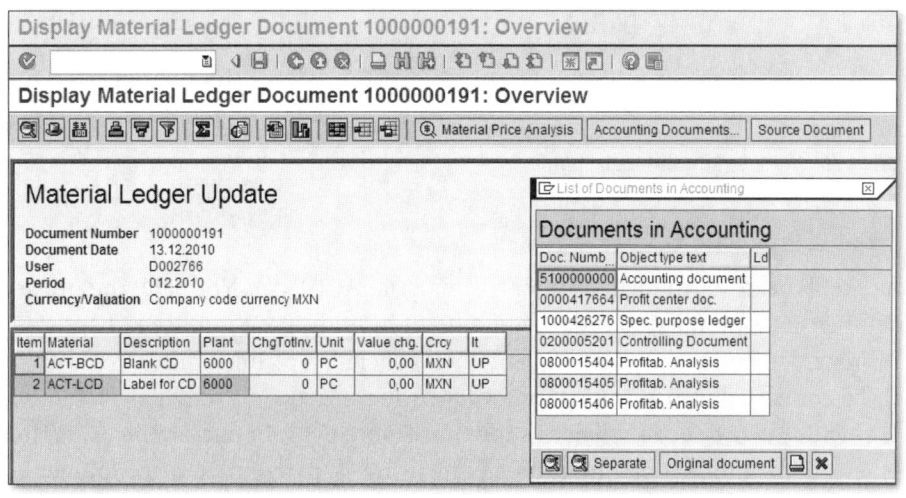

Figure 6.11 Material Ledger Document and Links to Accounting Documents

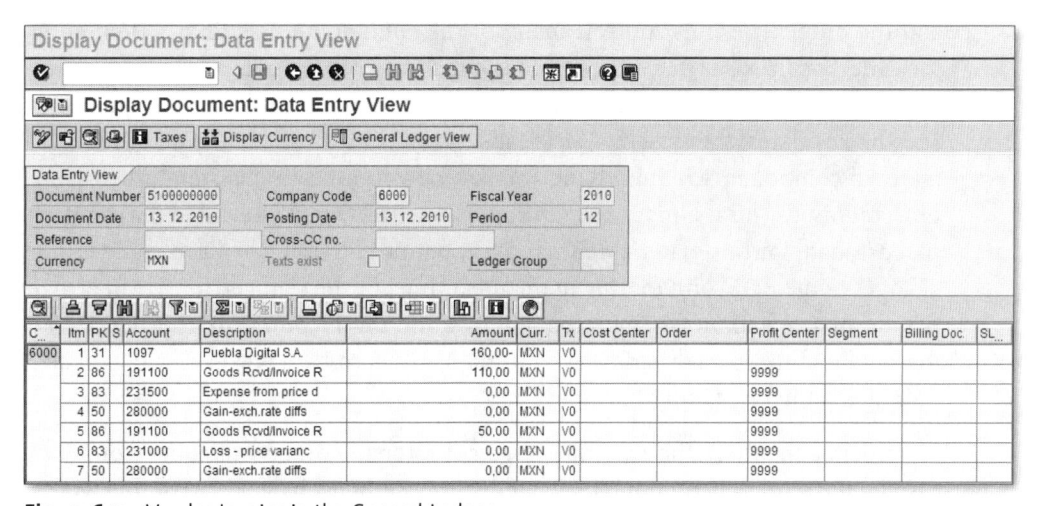

Figure 6.12 Vendor Invoice in the General Ledger

6.1.2 Plan to Manufacture

Now we'll look at how the materials we just purchased to stock are consumed in the manufacturing process and what information is available to CO in this process. Figure 6.13 shows the basic flow of the manufacturing process.

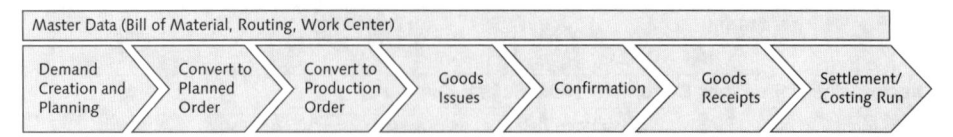

Figure 6.13 Make to Stock Manufacturing

Creating a Production Order

First, we'll create a production order for material ACT-DCD. Normally the procedure to create a production order would be to have the MRP run (see Chapter 5) determine demand for the material and then generate a planned order that would then be converted into a production order so the production activities would be linked with the production plan as shown in Figure 6.13. In our simple example, we'll create the production order directly by using Transaction CO01 or following the menu path LOGISTICS • PRODUCTION • SHOP FLOOR CONTROL • ORDER • CREATE WITH MATERIAL. Enter the material to be manufactured (ACT-DCD), the plant (6000), and the order type (this controls many of the configuration settings). Then enter the order lot size (this may differ from the costing lot size used in planning, giving rise to MRP variances) and the key dates for the order. Based on the quantities and the key dates, the system selects the relevant bill of material to determine the material components required and the relevant routing to determine the operations required. This is almost exactly what happened when we created the standard cost estimate for this material in Chapter 5, but production may have made minor changes to the BOM and routing in the meantime, or the changed lot size may give rise to lot-size variances. Figure 6.14 shows the production order header. Given the potential for lot-size variances, our major concern here is whether the lot size (here five units) is standard or not.

To understand where the material usage costs for the order will come from, let's display the material components copied from the BOM by clicking on the MATERIAL COMPONENTS icon in Figure 6.14. Figure 6.15 shows the component overview and the two materials (ACT-BCD and ACT-LCD) required to manufacture material ACT-DCD. When the production order is released, a reservation will be created for these materials.

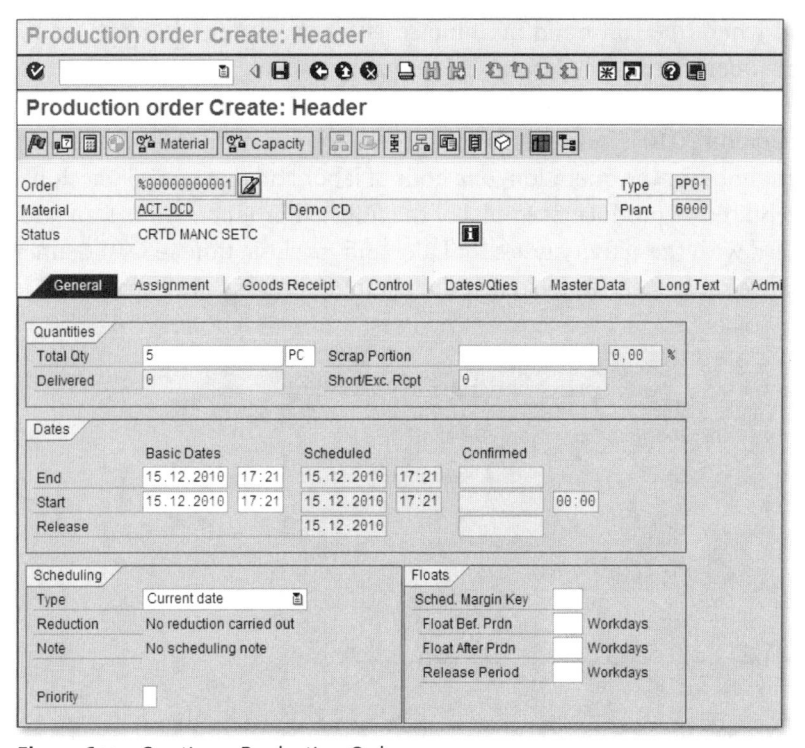

Figure 6.14 Creating a Production Order

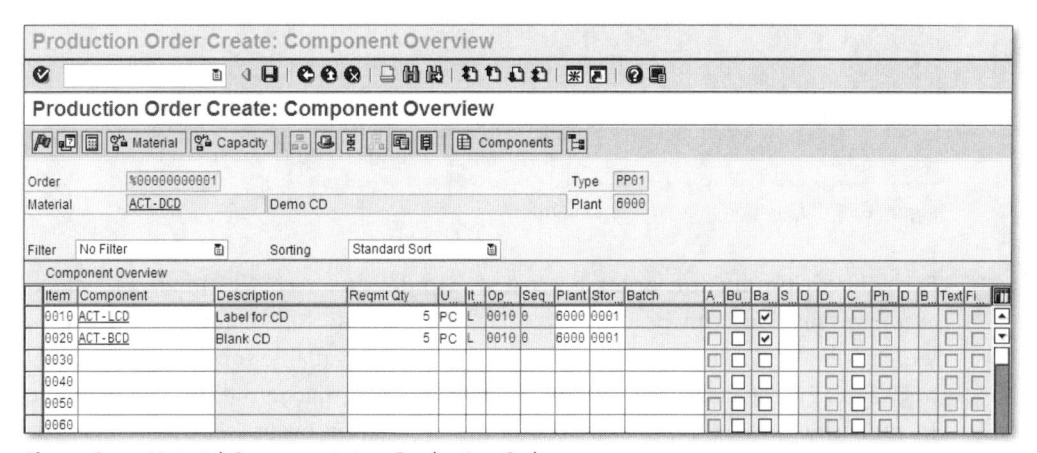

Figure 6.15 Material Components in a Production Order

To understand where the labor and machine costs for the order will come from, let's display the operations copied from the routing by clicking on the OPERATIONS icon in Figure 6.15 and then selecting the first operation. Figure 6.16 shows the first operation. Operation 0010 is being performed at work center WP530-00. According to the standard times for the operation, one hour of labor and one hour of machine time will be required to produce five units of the finished product. These standard values are linked with the activity types for labor and machine time in Cost Center Accounting as we saw when we looked at the planning process in Chapter 5.

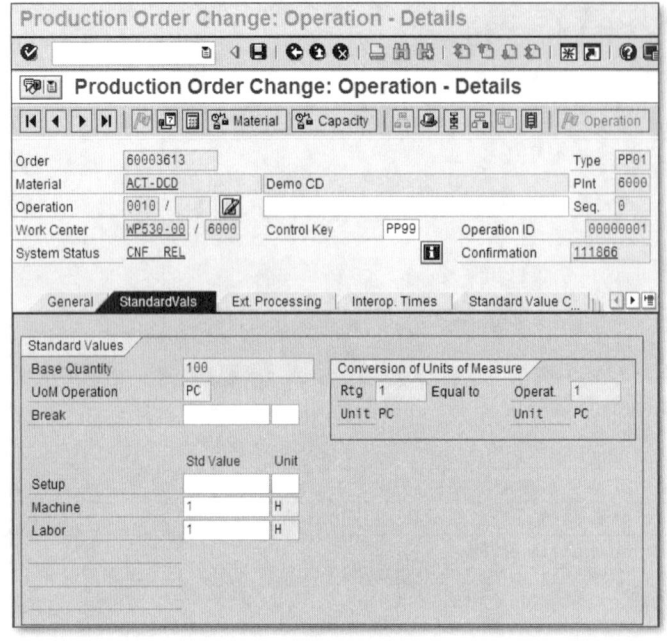

Figure 6.16 Operation in a Production Order

Each time a production order is created, a preliminary cost estimate is created automatically (this can be deactivated in Customizing for performance reasons, which will affect whether this cost estimate will be available for variance analysis in Chapter 7). You can display the result of the cost estimate either by following the menu path GOTO • COSTS • ANALYSIS in the production order (see Figure 6.17) or by selecting the appropriate detail report in the COST OBJECT CONTROLLING menu (see Chapter 2).

6.1 Integrated Process Flows: Buy, Make, and Sell

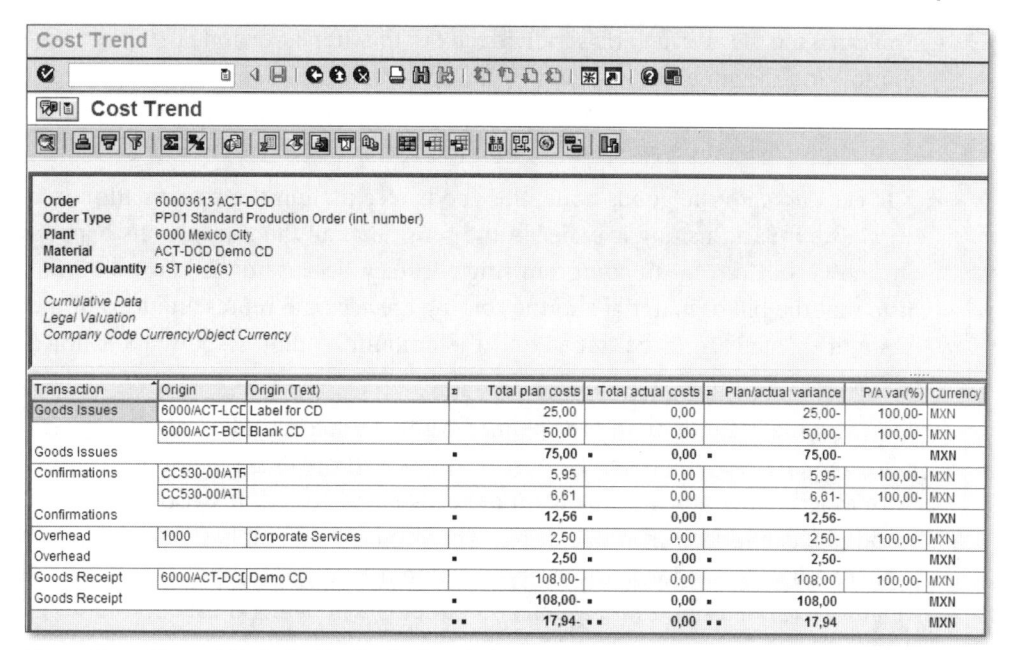

```
Cost Trend
```

Cost Trend

Order	60003613 ACT-DCD
Order Type	PP01 Standard Production Order (int. number)
Plant	6000 Mexico City
Material	ACT-DCD Demo CD
Planned Quantity	5 ST piece(s)

Cumulative Data
Legal Valuation
Company Code Currency/Object Currency

Transaction	Origin	Origin (Text)	Σ	Total plan costs	Σ Total actual costs	Σ Plan/actual variance	P/A var(%)	Currency
Goods Issues	6000/ACT-LCD	Label for CD		25,00	0,00	25,00-	100,00-	MXN
	6000/ACT-BCD	Blank CD		50,00	0,00	50,00-	100,00-	MXN
Goods Issues			•	75,00 •	0,00 •	75,00-		MXN
Confirmations	CC530-00/ATF			5,95	0,00	5,95-	100,00-	MXN
	CC530-00/ATL			6,61	0,00	6,61-	100,00-	MXN
Confirmations			•	12,56 •	0,00 •	12,56-		MXN
Overhead	1000	Corporate Services		2,50	0,00	2,50-	100,00-	MXN
Overhead			•	2,50 •	0,00 •	2,50-		MXN
Goods Receipt	6000/ACT-DCD	Demo CD		108,00-	0,00	108,00	100,00-	MXN
Goods Receipt			•	108,00- •	0,00 •	108,00		MXN
			••	17,94- ••	0,00 ••	17,94		MXN

Figure 6.17 Planned Costs for the Production Order

The goods issue line in the cost analysis report shows the two raw materials together with their standard costs. The confirmation line shows the standard values for the activities at each operation. A percentage overhead has been applied. In addition, the value of the goods receipt has been calculated, again using the standard price. This makes the preliminary cost estimate look slightly different from the standard cost estimate, since it simulates the effect of delivering the finished goods to stock, whereas the standard cost estimate only shows the inputs. Notice that there's a small variance, since the planned costs for the order are not identical to the standard costs for the material.

We'll now show how the costs of the goods issues and operations are assigned to the production order. Before you can perform these steps, you need to release the order by selecting FUNCTIONS • RELEASE (see Chapter 3) or choosing the RELEASE button shown in Figure 6.14.

Issuing Materials to a Production Order

For posting the goods issues for the raw materials, there are two fundamentally different approaches.

- You can issue the raw materials individually to the shop floor and post the confirmation and the goods receipt later. This approach is common in batch-oriented, discrete production where there's a focus on capturing as much detailed information as possible on the work order (in this case, the production order).

- You can *backflush* the goods issue, the goods receipt, and the confirmation in a single step. Backflushing is easier in the sense that all the transactions happen in one go but can mean compromising accuracy because of the tacit assumption that the bill of material and the routing are accurate representations of the amount of material to be issued and the amount of time to be worked for a given lot size.

Backflushing is common in the chemical and pharmaceutical industries, where it's often physically impossible to issue goods to individual operations or measure exactly how much of the component is being issued. It's also considered good practice in lean manufacturing, where there's an emphasis on removing unnecessary transactions. The entry in column B of the component overview (Figure 6.15) determines that both components will be backflushed.

To create the confirmation at the header level, follow the menu path Logistics • Production • Shop Floor Control • Confirmation • Enter • For Order or use Transaction CO15, and enter the order number (you'll find the transactions for confirmations at the operation level in the same folder). We confirmed the completion of five units of the finished product, resulting in the creation of a goods issue and a goods receipt. Figure 6.18 shows the materials issued (movement type 261) and the goods received (movement type 101). To check the account assignment for the movements, select the Account Assignment tab. Here we can see that the material costs have been assigned to the production order (unlike the situation we had for the goods receipt on the purchase order).

If we now display one of the raw materials (ACT-BCD) we purchased above in the Material Ledger using material price analysis (Transaction CKM3N), we can see that of the ten units we delivered to stock, five have been issued to the production order (see Figure 6.19). If the period close were to occur now, we would need to apply any purchase price variances to the five units in inventory and the five units that have been issued to production.

Integrated Process Flows: Buy, Make, and Sell | 6.1

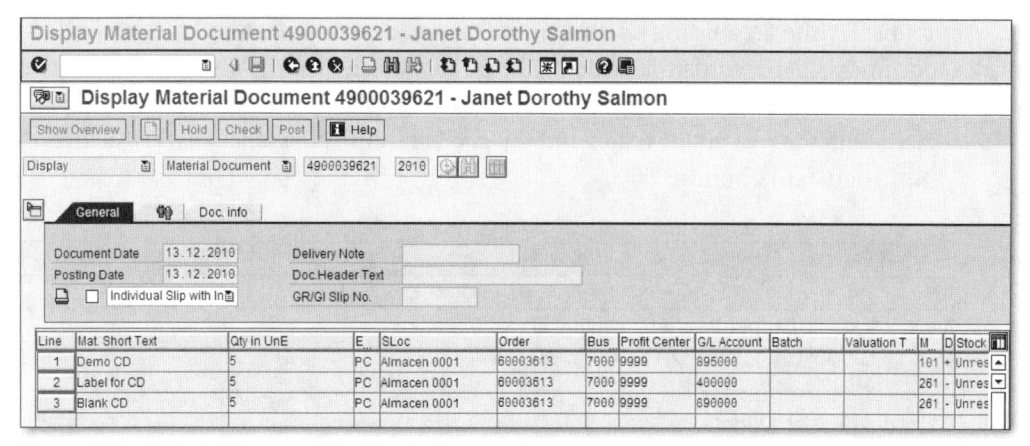

Figure 6.18 Material Document for Goods Movements

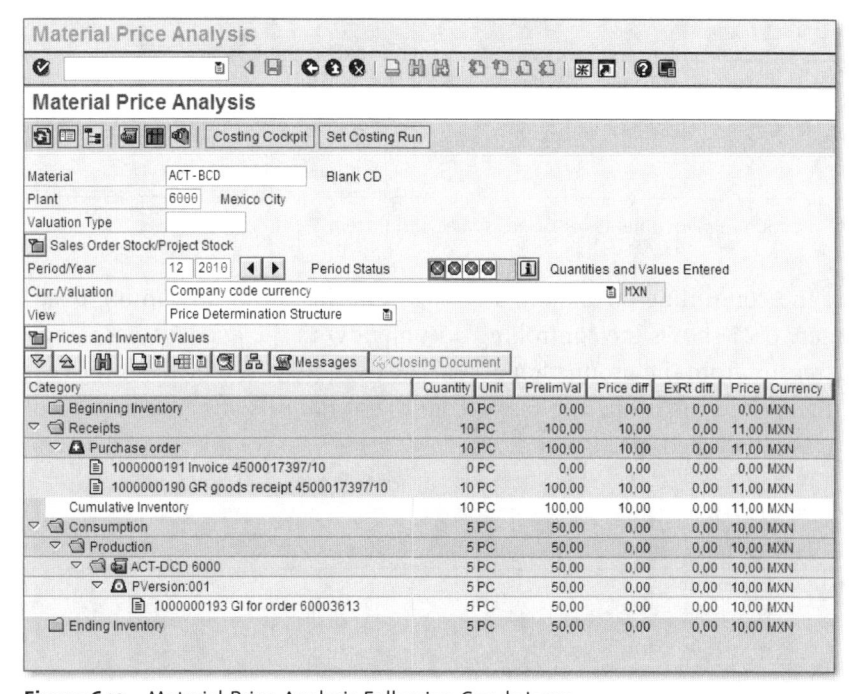

Figure 6.19 Material Price Analysis Following Goods Issue

273

6 | Actual Postings

To display the accounting document for the goods movement and the controlling document that records the issue of the goods to the production order, select the relevant document line in Figure 6.19. Figure 6.20 shows the material ledger document with the two goods issues and the goods receipt. Now click on the ACCOUNTING DOCUMENTS button.

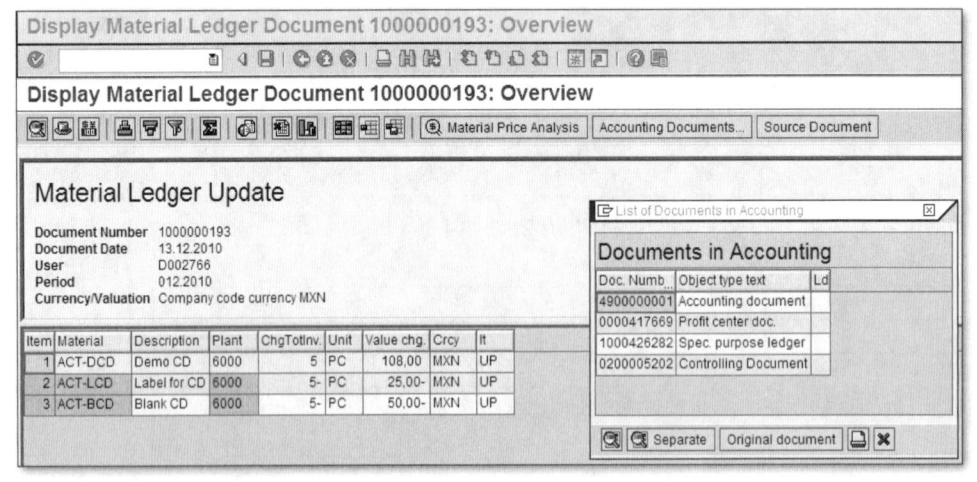

Figure 6.20 Accounting Documents for Goods Issues and Receipts

To display the controlling document, select it from the list of accounting documents. Figure 6.21 shows the controlling document with the goods issues to and the goods receipt from the production order. The document also includes the cost element (the link to the profit and loss account) and the offsetting balance sheet account, as we discussed in Chapter 4.

Figure 6.21 Controlling Document for Goods Issues and Receipts

274

Confirming a Production Order

Now let's return to the confirmation document by selecting ENVIRONMENT • SOURCE DOCUMENT in Figure 6.21. This will take us to the confirmation document shown in Figure 6.22. Again, it's possible to post either the finished quantity and have the system calculate the actual hours based on the standard values in the routing or to record the hours worked on each operation as separate transactions. The industry tends to determine which approach is more common. In the discrete industry, operation-based confirmation prevails. In the chemical industry, such detail can be virtually impossible to achieve, and the assumptions in the routing must be assumed to apply. In our case, you can see that five units of finished product have been confirmed. The confirmation results in a charge to the production order for the production activities performed.

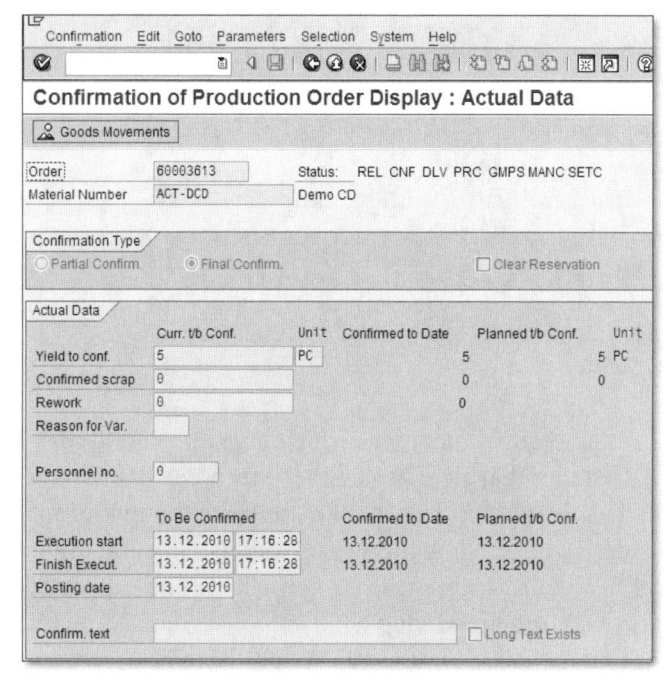

Figure 6.22 Confirming a Production Order

When we discuss scrap calculation in Chapter 7, note that the confirmation is also used to record scrap either by operation or for the whole order (as we see here). Also notice the field for entering rework. We'll look at the impact of rework in Section 6.3.1.

6 | Actual Postings

Since the activity confirmation is not material-related, you won't find it in the Material Price Analysis report. To display the activity usage for the finished product, use the Valuated Quantity Structure report by following the menu path CONTROLLING • PRODUCT COST CONTROLLING • ACTUAL COSTING/MATERIAL LEDGER • INFORMATION SYSTEM • DETAILED REPORT • VALUATED QUANTITY STRUCTURE or using Transaction CKMLQS. Enter the finished material (ACT-DCD), the plant, and the period. Note that this transaction was introduced in Release 4.7.

In Figure 6.23 we see the finished product, the two raw materials, and the two operations together with the relevant quantity information.

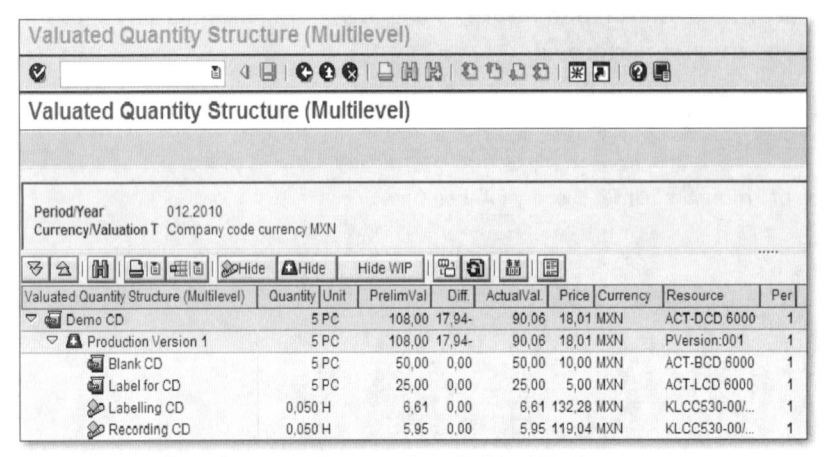

Valuated Quantity Structure (Multilevel)	Quantity	Unit	PrelimVal	Diff.	ActualVal.	Price	Currency	Resource	Per
Demo CD	5	PC	108,00	17,94-	90,06	18,01	MXN	ACT-DCD 6000	1
Production Version 1	5	PC	108,00	17,94-	90,06	18,01	MXN	PVersion:001	1
Blank CD	5	PC	50,00	0,00	50,00	10,00	MXN	ACT-BCD 6000	1
Label for CD	5	PC	25,00	0,00	25,00	5,00	MXN	ACT-LCD 6000	1
Labelling CD	0,050	H	6,61	0,00	6,61	132,28	MXN	KLCC530-00/...	1
Recording CD	0,050	H	5,95	0,00	5,95	119,04	MXN	KLCC530-00/...	1

Figure 6.23 Valuated Quantity Structure for a Finished Product

To display the actual costs in the production order, follow the menu path GOTO • COSTS • ANALYSIS. Figure 6.24 shows that all costs have been recorded to plan (see TOTAL ACTUAL COSTS column), since we backflushed the materials and activities and used the same standard values as in the preliminary cost estimate for the order. All that's missing is the overhead calculation, which is normally applied at period close (see Chapter 7, Section 7.2). When working with a report like this one, the goal of the controller is to monitor *production variances*. We posted to plan, so there are no variances.

One source of confusion is the term *actual costs* in a report like the one shown in Figure 6.24. These costs are not actual costs, in the full sense of the word, since they are determined by multiplying the *actual quantities* recorded during backflushing with the *standard costs* for the materials and activities. At this point, any purchase price variances may not be known, since the vendor may not have submitted his invoice. We saw in the first section that the values in the purchasing info record differed from the standard price for one of the raw materials. The real *actual costs* for the material will only be calculated when we use the *periodic costing run* to transfer any purchase price variances for the raw materials to production as part of the period close in Chapter 7.

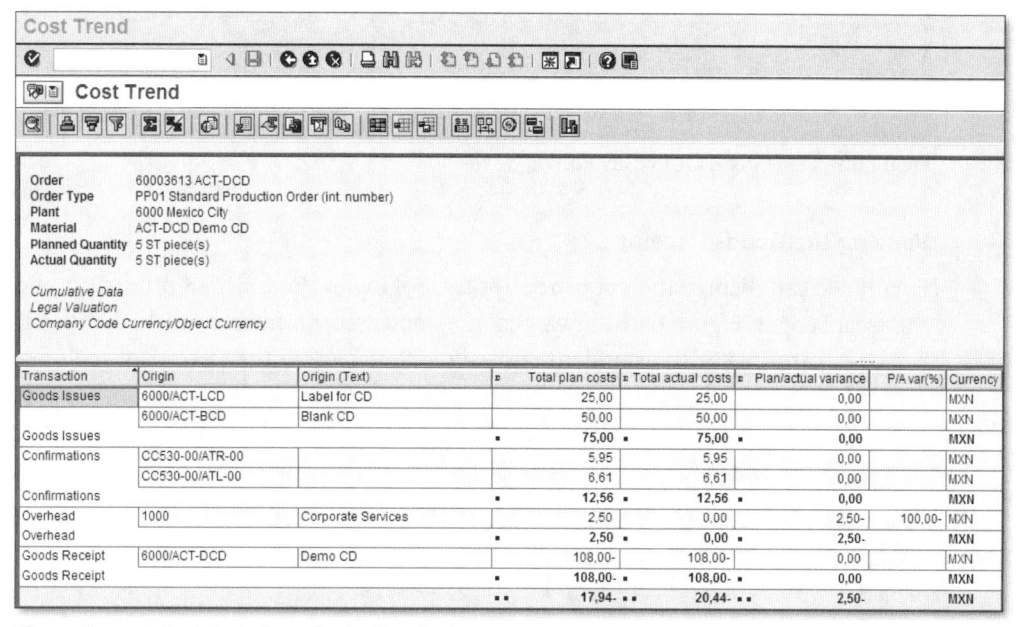

Transaction	Origin	Origin (Text)		Total plan costs	Total actual costs	Plan/actual variance	P/A var(%)	Currency
Goods Issues	6000/ACT-LCD	Label for CD		25,00	25,00	0,00		MXN
	6000/ACT-BCD	Blank CD		50,00	50,00	0,00		MXN
Goods Issues				75,00	75,00	0,00		MXN
Confirmations	CC530-00/ATR-00			5,95	5,95	0,00		MXN
	CC530-00/ATL-00			6,61	6,61	0,00		MXN
Confirmations				12,56	12,56	0,00		MXN
Overhead	1000	Corporate Services		2,50	0,00	2,50-	100,00-	MXN
Overhead				2,50	0,00	2,50-		MXN
Goods Receipt	6000/ACT-DCD	Demo CD		108,00-	108,00-	0,00		MXN
Goods Receipt				108,00-	108,00-	0,00		MXN
				17,94-	20,44-	2,50-		MXN

Figure 6.24 Actual Costs for a Production Order

The cost posting to the production order has also credited the cost center that provided the machine time and labor time to production. You can display this activity by going to Transaction KSB1 or ACCOUNTING • CONTROLLING • COST CENTER ACCOUNTING • INFORMATION SYSTEM • REPORTS FOR COST CENTER ACCOUNTING • LINE ITEM REPORTS • DISPLAY LINE ITEMS and entering the name of the cost center (CC530-00), the cost elements under which the confirmation posting was made, and the relevant time frame. Figure 6.25 shows the line item for the posting to the cost center. Again, this is based on a *standard* activity rate, since we don't yet know how much energy the cost center used to supply this activity, how much overhead

6 | Actual Postings

it absorbed, and so on. At period close, we'll be able to calculate the *actual* activity price and adjust the values on the production order to take account of this.

Figure 6.25 Line Items for Activity Posting

Viewing the Goods Receipt

Finally we can display the goods receipt by looking at the finished product in the Material Ledger. Figure 6.26 shows that the goods receipt for the finished material has been captured at the standard cost, since the value in the PRICE DIFF column is zero.

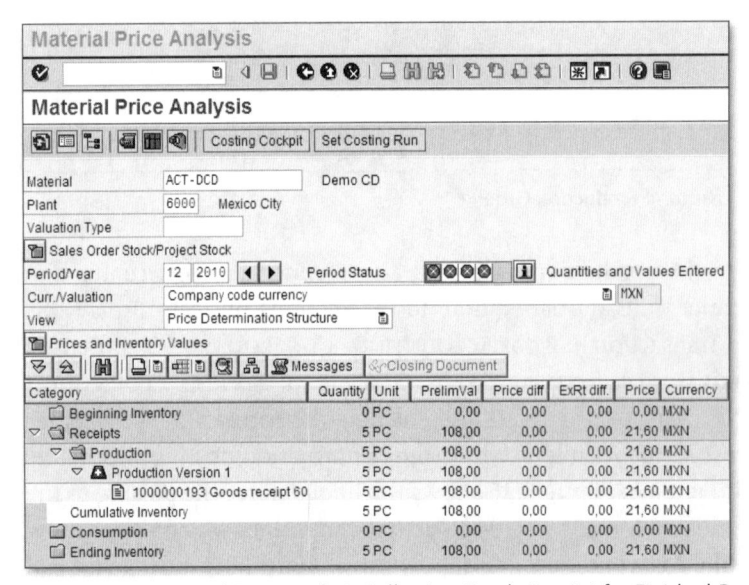

Figure 6.26 Material Price Analysis Following Goods Receipt for Finished Product

To display the material ledger document, click on the goods receipt line and then the ACCOUNTING DOCUMENTS button, as shown in Figure 6.27.

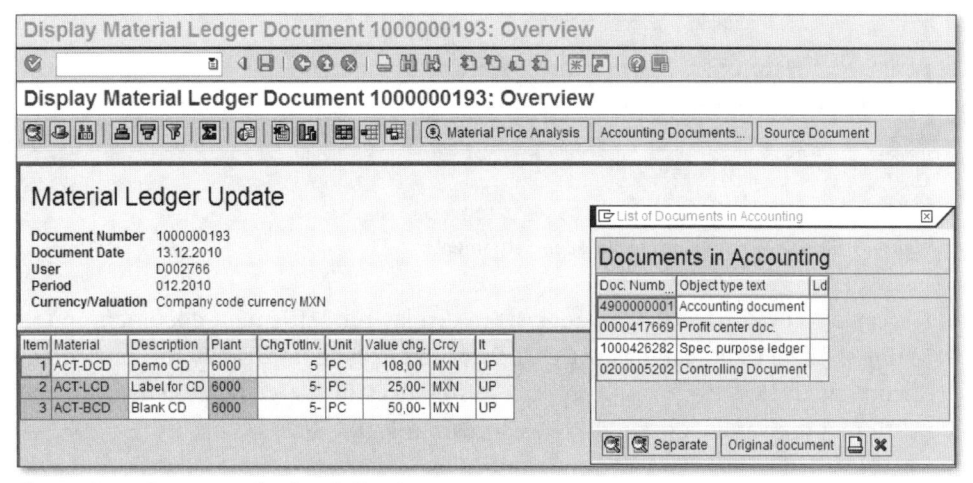

Figure 6.27 Documents for Goods Receipt

From here, we can display the accounting document that documents the goods movement in the General Ledger and the controlling document that documents the goods movements on the production order that we looked at in Figure 6.21.

Settling the Production Order

The final step in our process usually takes place at period close, when overhead is applied to the production order and any variances are settled. Variances are always settled to a stock account, where depending on the price control for the material (see Chapter 4), they may either affect the material price (moving average price) or be assigned to a variance or price difference account (standard price). If you're using CO-PA they'll also be settled to the profitability segment there so that the complete product costs are available for analysis. In this example, we can see the settlement document showing how the variances on our production order were settled to the finished material ACT-DCD and to the profitability segment for that material (see Figure 6.28). We'll look at settlement rules in more detail in Chapter 7, Section 7.2.

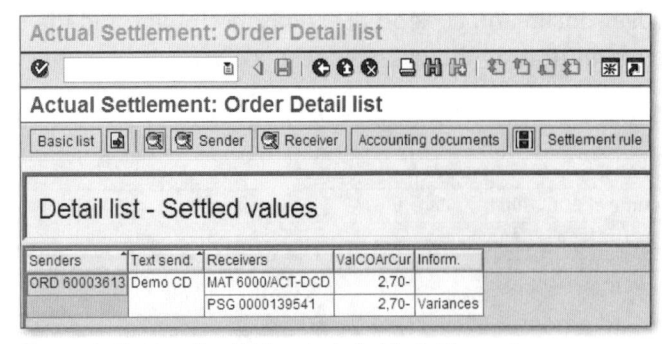

Figure 6.28 Details of Values Included in Settlement

We can also use material price analysis to display the settlement document in the Material Ledger and can again use the document links to display the settlement document in CO, the posting to price differences in the General Ledger, or the posting of the variances to CO-PA, as shown in Figure 6.29.

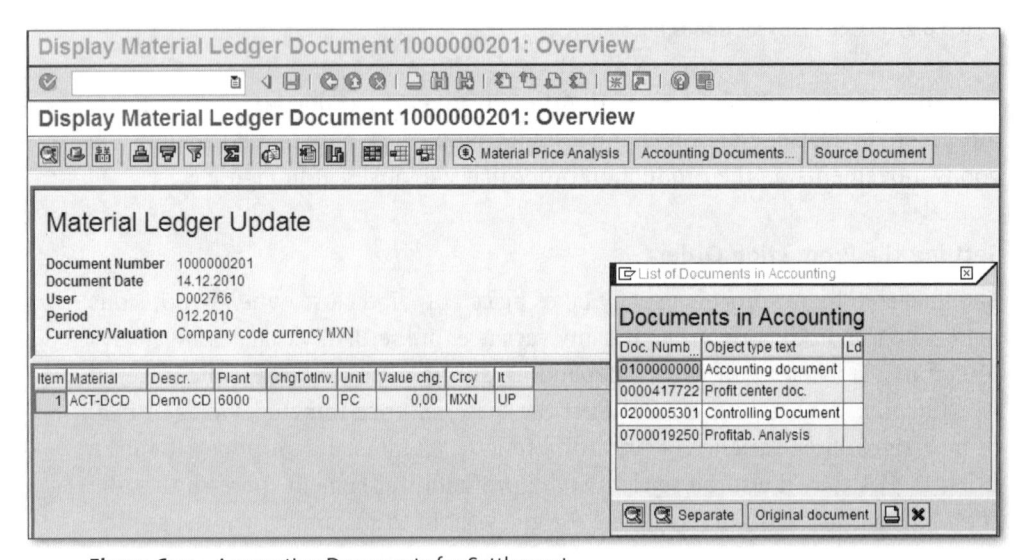

Figure 6.29 Accounting Documents for Settlement

Of course, the production process does not have to be only single level. Another production process could now consume the semifinished product and perform further activities to manufacture a finished product, but the process would be exactly the same from a controlling point of view, so we'll now look at how to sell our finished product.

6.1.3 Order to Cash

Now we'll look at how the material we just delivered to stock is issued to the sales process and what information is available to CO in this process. Figure 6.30 shows the basic flow of the sales process.

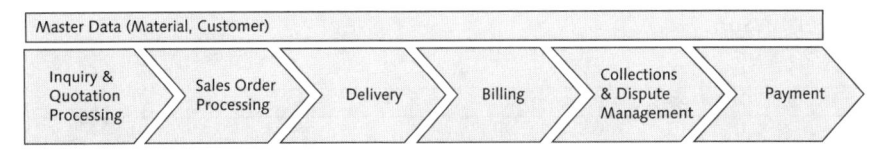

Figure 6.30 Order-to-Cash Process

Creating a Sales Order

Sometimes an inquiry or quotation precedes the sale, but let's start by creating a sales order for the product ACT-DCD that we manufactured in the previous step. The sales order records the agreement by the organization to supply the customer with a particular product. The main focus from a controlling perspective is on the price conditions and the assignment to CO-PA. This is because, as we discussed in Chapter 2, every sales order item generates a preliminary valuation in CO-PA. The profitability segment is derived from the customer, product, and other organizational information in the sales order.

To create a sales order, go to Transaction VA01 or LOGISTICS • SALES AND DISTRIBUTION • SALES • ORDER • CREATE and enter the order type, the sales organization, the distribution channel, the division, the sales office, and the sales group. Then enter the name of the sold-to party (customer) in the order header and the material and quantity in the order item. From a controlling perspective, these are the characteristics that will form the basis of your sales controlling activities in Profitability Analysis. Figure 6.31 shows the characteristics that will be recorded in Profitability Analysis for the sales order. To check them, once you've created your sales order, select the ITEM DETAILS on the initial entry screen and then the ACCOUNT ASSIGNMENT tab. Now click on the PROFITABILITY SEGMENT button. Here you can see that in addition to the information we entered when we created the order (order type, sales organization, distribution channel, division, sales office, sales group, customer, and product) the system has selected additional characteristics including billing type, business area, company code, material group, plant, and profit center using a process known as *derivation*. To simulate this step, when you're creating an order, click on the DERIVATION button shown in Figure 6.31 to check the assignments. The program logic for performing such a derivation is set up in Customizing with the goal of deriving additional data about the product, such as the material group or the product hierarchy from the fields in the material master, and additional data about the customer, such as the billing type from the customer master.

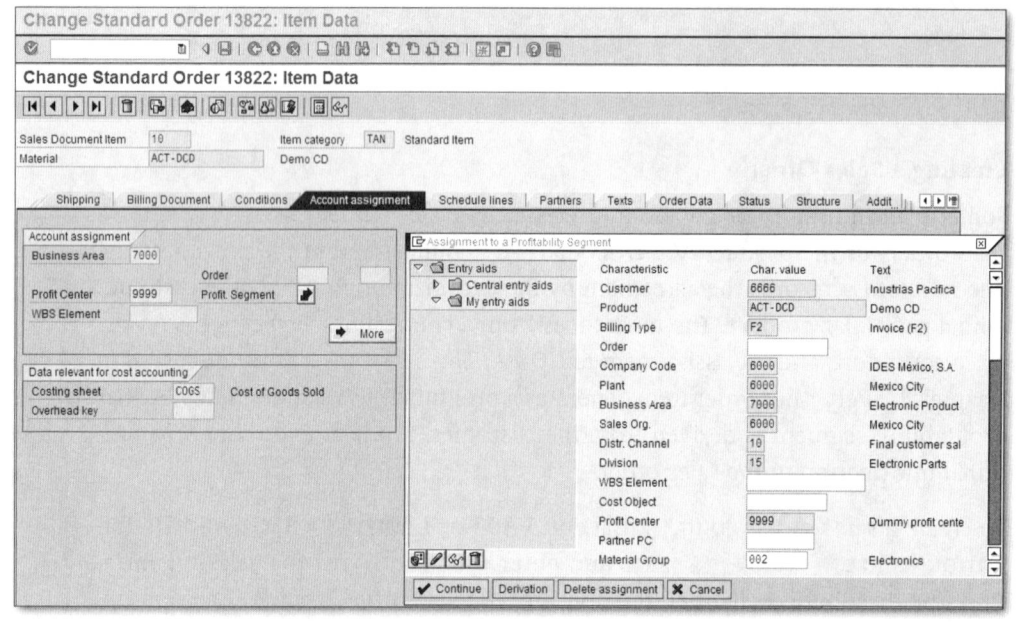

Figure 6.31 Sales Order Item and Associated Profitability Segment

When you've saved the sales order, display the line item in CO-PA by following the menu path CONTROLLING • PROFITABILITY ANALYSIS • INFORMATION SYSTEM • DISPLAY LINE ITEM LIST • ACTUAL or using Transaction KE24. Line items derived from the sales order are recorded as record type A (sales order entry). Figure 6.32 shows the characteristics for the sales order. Here you can see many more characteristics than we saw in the previous screen, including the customer group, country, region, and so on.

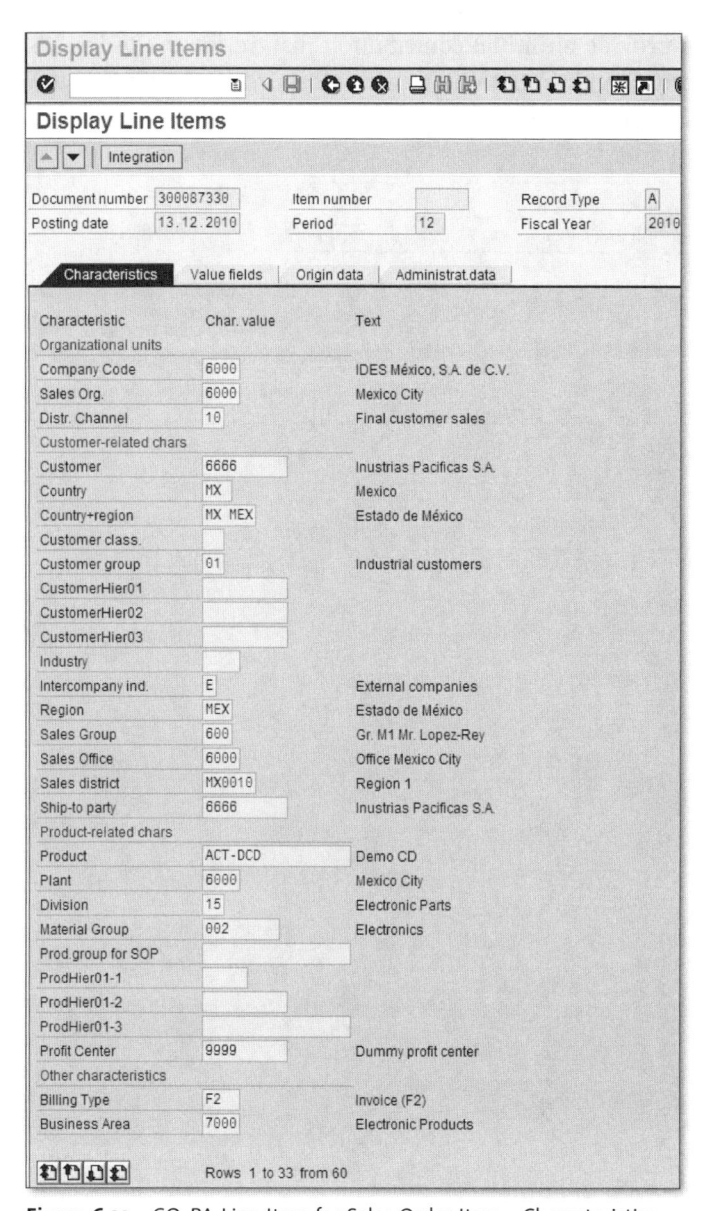

Figure 6.32 CO-PA Line Item for Sales Order Item—Characteristics

Figure 6.33 shows the value fields for the sales order item. In this case, revenue (EUR 11.34) and cost of goods manufactured (EUR 8.17) have been transferred to

Profitability Analysis to provide an initial contribution margin for the order. It's also common for the price conditions to be transferred in more detail; this is a matter for configuration, as we discussed in Chapter 2.

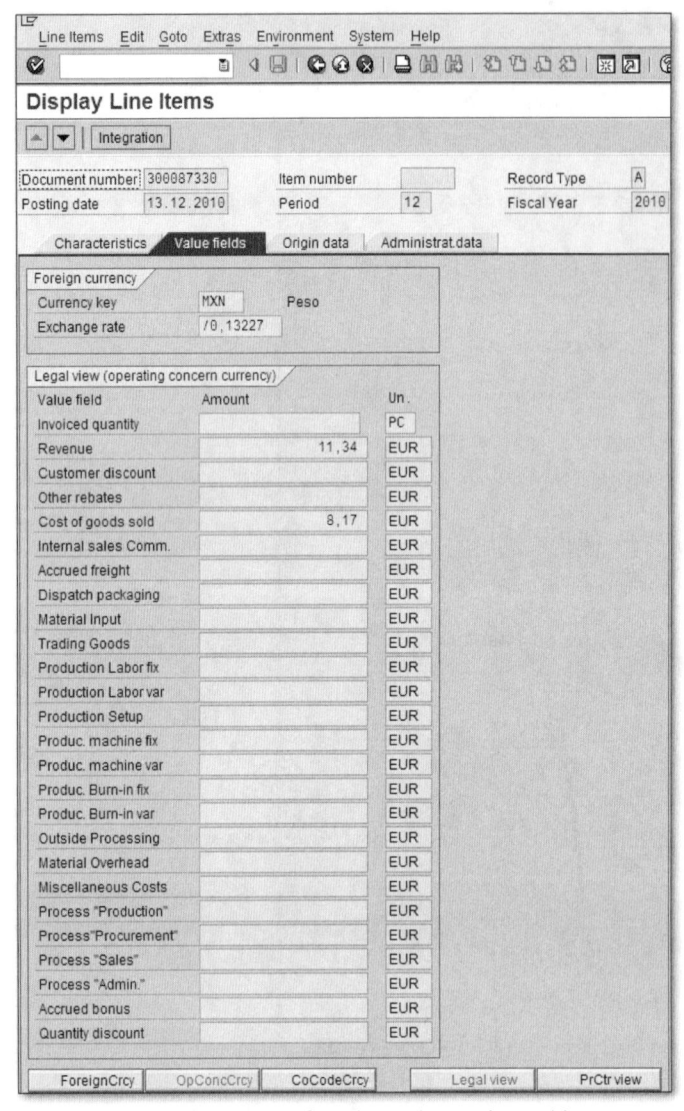

Figure 6.33 CO-PA Line Item for Sales Order – Value Fields

Delivering the Sales Order

We'll now record the delivery of the finished product to the customer. In the SALES ORDER menu, select SUBSEQUENT FUNCTIONS • OUTBOUND DELIVERY and enter your sales order number. Then enter the quantity to be delivered as the picking quantity and post the goods issue as shown in Figure 6.34.

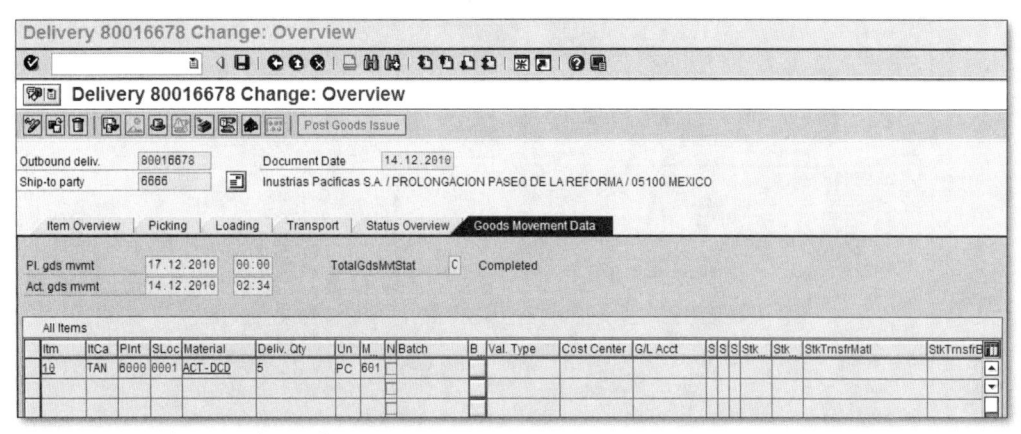

Figure 6.34 Delivery with Goods Issue

Figure 6.35 shows the goods movement in the Material Price Analysis report following the delivery. Here we can see the goods issue of five units to the customer account. What is shown here is not the customer number we saw in the profitability segment, but the reconciliation account for the customer (entered in the customer master) that records the goods movement in the General Ledger.

Figure 6.36 shows the accounting documents again, with a posting to the General Ledger and a controlling document. Notice that there's no PROFITABILITY ANALYSIS document. The delivery is recorded in the financial accounts as the goods movement is posted. The revenue is recorded in Profitability Analysis when the invoice is posted. The cost of sales is determined using condition type VPRS and reading the price from the goods receipt on the date of the goods receipt. You can also configure the invoice posting to CO-PA to read the cost component split to provide more detail on the cost of goods sold. However, if the delivery takes place in one period and the invoice in the next, the values in the profit and loss statement won't reconcile with the values in Profitability Analysis. In this case, you'll want to use the reports listed under ACCOUNTING • CONTROLLING • PROFITABILITY ANALYSIS • TOOLS • ANALYZE VALUE FLOWS to find such differences.

6 | Actual Postings

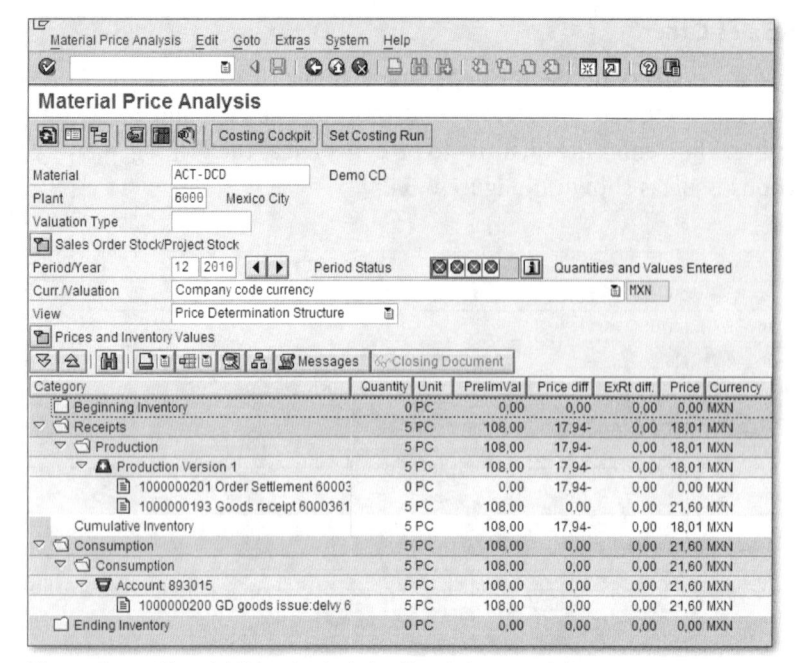

Figure 6.35 Material Price Analysis for Goods Issue to Sales

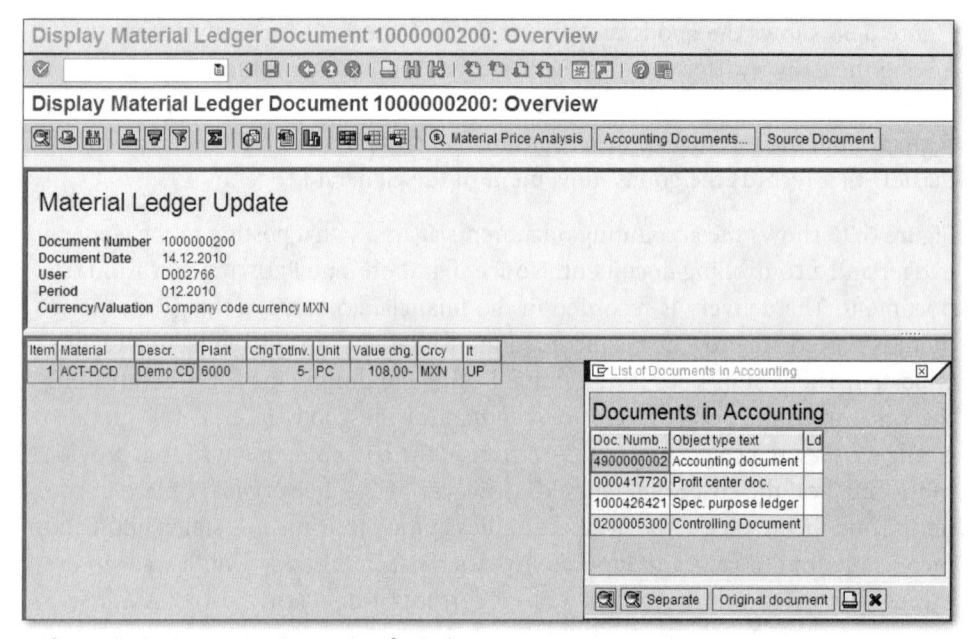

Figure 6.36 Accounting Documents for Delivery

Billing the Customer

Finally the customer is invoiced for receipt of the goods, again triggering a posting to Profitability Analysis. To trigger the invoice, select SUBSEQUENT FUNCTIONS • BILLING DOCUMENT in the SALES ORDER menu and enter the delivery document number. Figure 6.37 shows the customer invoice document for the demo CD.

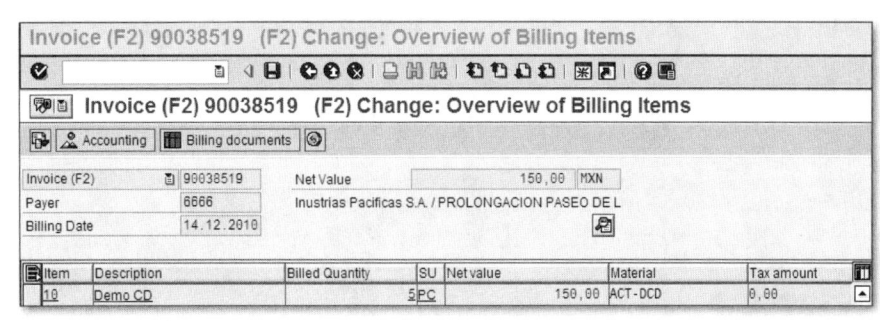

Figure 6.37 Billing Document

Again we can display the line item in Profitability Analysis using Transaction KE24 and selecting record type F for billing. The value fields are the same as we saw before. Figure 6.38 shows the characteristics for the invoicing document.

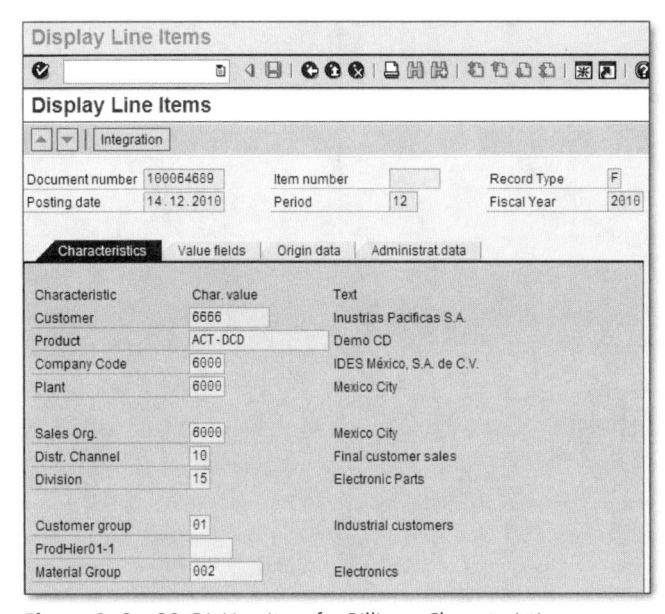

Figure 6.38 CO-PA Line Item for Billing – Characteristics

6 | Actual Postings

To show the value fields, select the VALUE FIELDS tab, as shown in Figure 6.39. The revenue (150 Mexican pesos) and the cost of goods sold (108 Mexican pesos) are the same as we saw for the sales order document. This time, however, we see that the system has been configured to capture the cost components in more detail. The standard costs are broken down into their cost components, so we can see raw material costs, labor costs (fixed and variable), machine costs (fixed and variable), and overhead from the cost estimate.

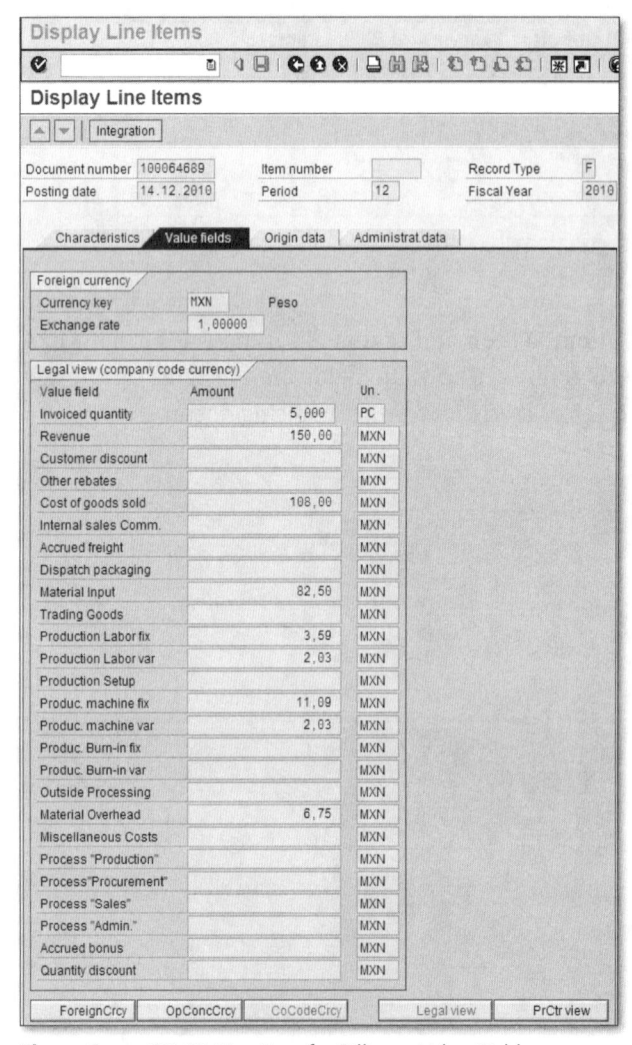

Value field	Amount	Un.
Invoiced quantity	5,000	PC
Revenue	150,00	MXN
Customer discount		MXN
Other rebates		MXN
Cost of goods sold	108,00	MXN
Internal sales Comm.		MXN
Accrued freight		MXN
Dispatch packaging		MXN
Material Input	82,50	MXN
Trading Goods		MXN
Production Labor fix	3,59	MXN
Production Labor var	2,03	MXN
Production Setup		MXN
Produc. machine fix	11,09	MXN
Produc. machine var	2,03	MXN
Produc. Burn-in fix		MXN
Produc. Burn-in var		MXN
Outside Processing		MXN
Material Overhead	6,75	MXN
Miscellaneous Costs		MXN
Process "Production"		MXN
Process "Procurement"		MXN
Process "Sales"		MXN
Process "Admin."		MXN
Accrued bonus		MXN
Quantity discount		MXN

Figure 6.39 CO-PA Line Item for Billing – Value Fields

The process would normally continue with the open item being monitored in accounts receivable and then in a receipt of payment or collection activities. At period close, the cycle would be closed by settling the production variances to PROFITABILITY ANALYSIS and running allocations to transfer cost center expenses to Profitability Analysis. Since we've been collecting all the relevant data in the Material Ledger, it is also possible to calculate the periodic unit price for each of the raw materials and include the variances in the raw materials inventory at period close. We can then roll the variances up to the finished goods inventory and finally to the cost of sales, to provide a complete picture of the cost impact of the whole process. We'll also be able to use the revaluation function to pull the actual cost component split for the material into CO-PA. We'll walk through this whole process in Chapter 7.

In the previous example, we used *backflushing* to record the goods issues, goods receipt, and confirmation for the production order in a single step. We'll now look at how to correct any data concerns following backflushing by using the *distribution of usage variances* function.

6.2   Distribution of Usage Variances

One of the concerns when organizations consider using backflushing is the tacit assumption that the standard values from the bill of material and the routing were accurate and thus a fair basis for cost accounting. Controllers instinctively believe it's better to confirm operations manually to have full control of the process. Here we're covering the same ground as in Chapter 4 when we discussed whether to use a costing BOM and routing or share data with production. Anybody involved in lean manufacturing will advice you that it's better to invest time and effort in high-quality BOMs and routings up front rather than trying to ensure accuracy as the orders are processed. Let's also not forget that plenty of chemical processes refuse to submit to operation-based confirmations.

Whatever your views, sometimes when inventory counts are performed for the goods in stock, the physical inventory reveals that the material movements recorded in the system don't tally with the number of goods in stock. Controllers working with actual costs definitely want to take account of the inventory differences and include them in the material valuation, and even controllers working with standard costs want to be aware of the variances.

There was a time when plants stopped work to perform a physical inventory, but now regular cycle counts are the order of the day for reasons of efficiency, and physical inventory can be performed daily, weekly, or monthly. More importantly for controllers, you can distribute the inventory differences recorded using a function called *distribution of usage variances*, which you'll find in the MATERIAL LEDGER menu, although it does not require use of the Material Ledger. This function was introduced in Release 4.7. If you can't find the relevant entries in your menu, check with your IT department to see whether the Enterprise Extension EA_FIN is activated (see Appendix C found at *www.sap-press.com*).

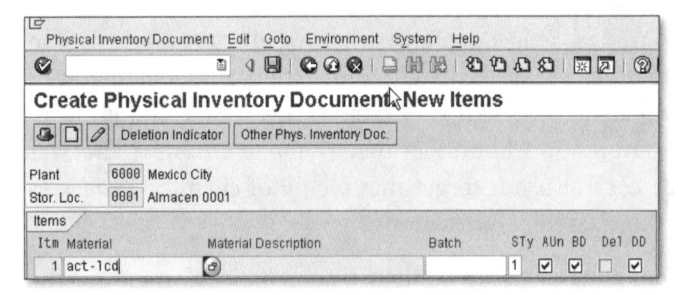

6.2.1 Capturing Physical Inventory Documents

A physical inventory requires whoever performs the check to create a physical inventory (PI) document to act as the header for all activities associated with the count for the auditors. To create a PI document, use Transaction MI01 or follow the menu path LOGISTICS • MATERIALS MANAGEMENT • PHYSICAL INVENTORY • PHYSICAL INVENTORY • DOCUMENT • CREATE. Enter the document date, plant, and storage location and the materials you intend to include in the count, which takes place per storage location. For controlling purposes, it's important to ensure that all relevant materials in the physical inventory documents are flagged as relevant for the distribution of physical inventory differences (DD field). Figure 6.40 shows a physical inventory document for a count of material ACT-LCD (one of the raw materials we used in the previous example).

Figure 6.40 Physical Inventory Document

The next step is to enter the difference in the inventory counts for the material in question. This extends the PI document to record exactly how much material is missing or in excess. To do this, go to Transaction MI04 or LOGISTICS • MATERIALS

MANAGEMENT • PHYSICAL INVENTORY • INVENTORY COUNT • ENTER. Enter the number of the PI document from the previous step and then the inventory count for each of the materials in the PI document. Note that this document does not impact the financial accounts. Again, make sure that whoever records the inventory count sets the DD flag for material ACT-LCD as shown in Figure 6.41.

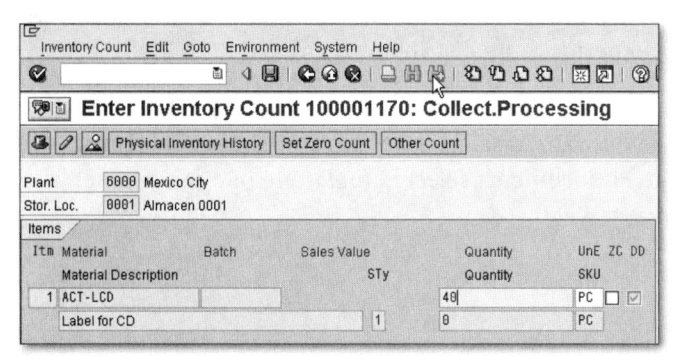

Figure 6.41 Recording Inventory Differences

Finally, to post the inventory differences to FI, go to Transaction MI07 or LOGISTICS • MATERIALS MANAGEMENT • PHYSICAL INVENTORY • DIFFERENCES • POST, as shown in Figure 6.42. This posting adjusts the stock level and posts the costs associated with the missing materials to the profit and loss from PI differences account. It also makes the inventory count available for CO so you can assign the value of the materials recorded in the count to the production orders that consumed the missing raw materials.

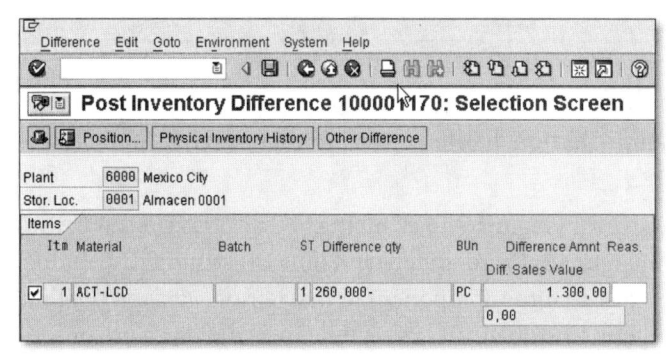

Figure 6.42 Posting Inventory Differences

6.2.2 Distribution of Usage Variances

Once the physical inventory differences have been captured for the storage location, the controller distributes them to the production orders that used that material in the period. To do this, use Transaction CKMATDUV or follow the menu path ACCOUNTING • CONTROLLING • PRODUCT COST CONTROLLING • ACTUAL COSTING/MATERIAL LEDGER • ACTUAL COSTING• DISTRIBUTION OF USAGE VARIANCES • DISTRIBUTION OF INVENTORY DIFFERENCES. To perform the distribution, proceed as follows:

1. Enter either the range of physical inventory documents (if you know them) or the materials for which you want to select differences, as shown in Figure 6.43. You can see a list of the PI documents selected (only one in our example), the quantity, and the status NEW.

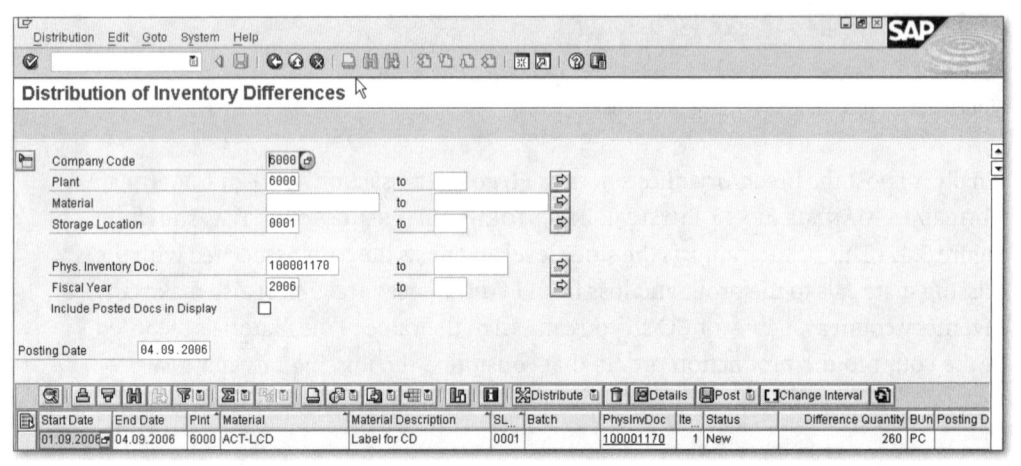

Figure 6.43 Selection of PI Document for Distribution

2. Now click on the DISTRIBUTE button, located in the button bar above the selected document(s).

3. This results in the status NEW in Figure 6.43 changing to the status DISTRIBUTION COMPLETED as shown in Figure 6.44. To understand how the system distributed that value to the orders that used the component in that period, click on the line containing the PI document. The quantities of material withdrawn to the orders were 100, 50, and 50 (shown in the WITHDRAWN QUANTITY column), and the system proposal for the distribution of the 260 units is 130, 65, and 65 (shown in the DEFAULT QUANTITY column). Generally you accept the system's proposal and select POST. However, if you know one order has caused particularly high

variances, you can correct the proposal by overwriting the figure proposed and entering a different figure in the QUANTITY column.

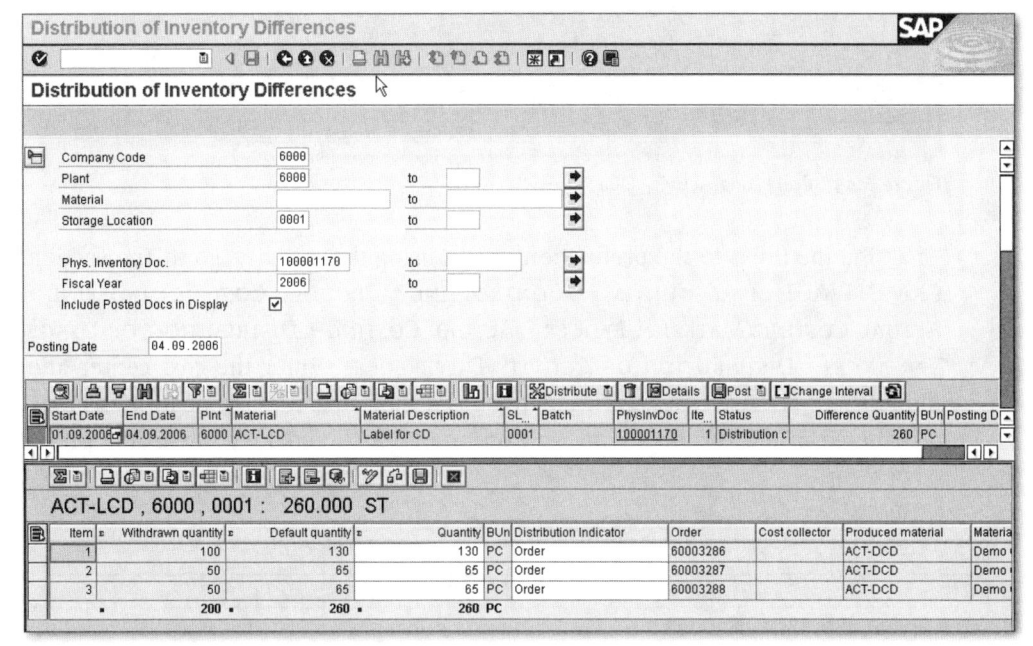

Figure 6.44 Distribution of Inventory Differences

6.2.3 Distribution of Activities

If you want to correct the machine or labor time from the routing, you can use the same mechanism to assign differences to the production orders. This might be the case if you're posting standard time to your orders but have found that the machine ran for more hours than the sum of the standard values suggests. This information might come from workers' time sheets, machine hour counters, or electricity consumption meters. To record the initial differences, use Transaction CKMDUVREC or follow the menu path ACCOUNTING • CONTROLLING • PRODUCT COST CONTROLLING • ACTUAL COSTING/MATERIAL LEDGER • ACTUAL COSTING • DISTRIBUTION OF USAGE VARIANCES • ENTER ACTUAL ACTIVITY QUANTITIES. Enter values for cost center CC530-00 and activity types ATL-00 and ATR-00, as shown in Figure 6.45. Note that the system only saves the data if you select the ITEM OK checkbox on the far left.

6 | Actual Postings

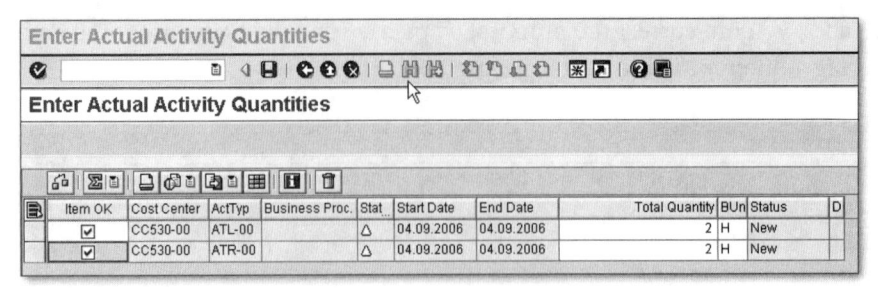

Figure 6.45 Correcting Activity Quantities

To assign the times to the production orders using that activity, go to Transaction CKMDUVACT or ACCOUNTING • CONTROLLING • PRODUCT COST CONTROLLING • ACTUAL COSTING/MATERIAL LEDGER • ACTUAL COSTING • DISTRIBUTION OF USAGE VARIANCES • DISTRIBUTION OF ACTIVITY DIFFERENCES. Enter the cost center and the relevant activity types. Figure 6.46 shows the actual activity quantities being distributed instead of the quantities from the PI documents we saw in the previous example.

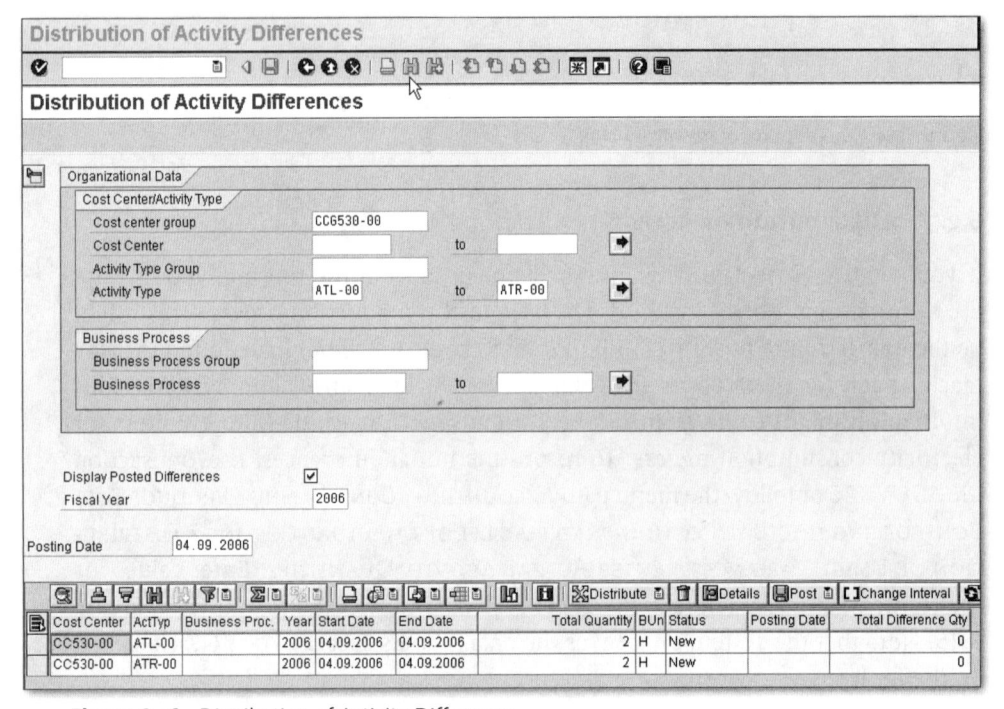

Figure 6.46 Distribution of Activity Differences

If we were a manufacturer of demo CDs, we could now move on to the period close in Chapter 7, having captured all relevant data. Before we do that, however, we'll look at some of the process variants you might find for each of the cost object controlling approaches we discussed in Chapter 2.

6.3 Integrated Process Flows: Other Logistics Scenarios

In this section we'll look at product cost by order, product cost by period, product cost by sales order, and project controlling to take us a little deeper than the simple demo CD example.

6.3.1 Product Cost by Order

The difference between using production orders, as we described in Section 6.1, and process orders is minimal, and you'll be able to follow the flow quite successfully. The process looks slightly different if you have co-products, as we discussed when we looked at master data in Chapter 4.

In Section 6.1 we assumed that everything went perfectly; we didn't initiate rework or split an order because something had gone wrong. As a controller it's important to understand what can happen in Logistics and what effect the measures taken will have on the data you analyze.

Process Orders with Joint Production

If multiple products are manufactured in a single production process as we discussed in Chapter 4, then the costs that are assigned to the work order have to be split to the order items using settlement at period close. If you use the Material Ledger, the same split is used when distributing any variances to the co-products.

In this example, we'll use a process order instead of a production order. To create a process order, go to Transaction COR1 or LOGISTICS • PRODUCTION – PROCESS • PROCESS ORDER • PROCESS ORDER • CREATE. Enter material Z-300, the plant, the order type, and the quantity for the leading product. The material list selected for Z-300 includes co-product PA-300. To display the material list, click on the MATERIALS button. Figure 6.47 shows the material list for Z-300, which includes the input materials and the output materials. Both the leading product and the other co-product are flagged as co-products. Notice small amounts of catalyst and contaminated water being recovered from the process.

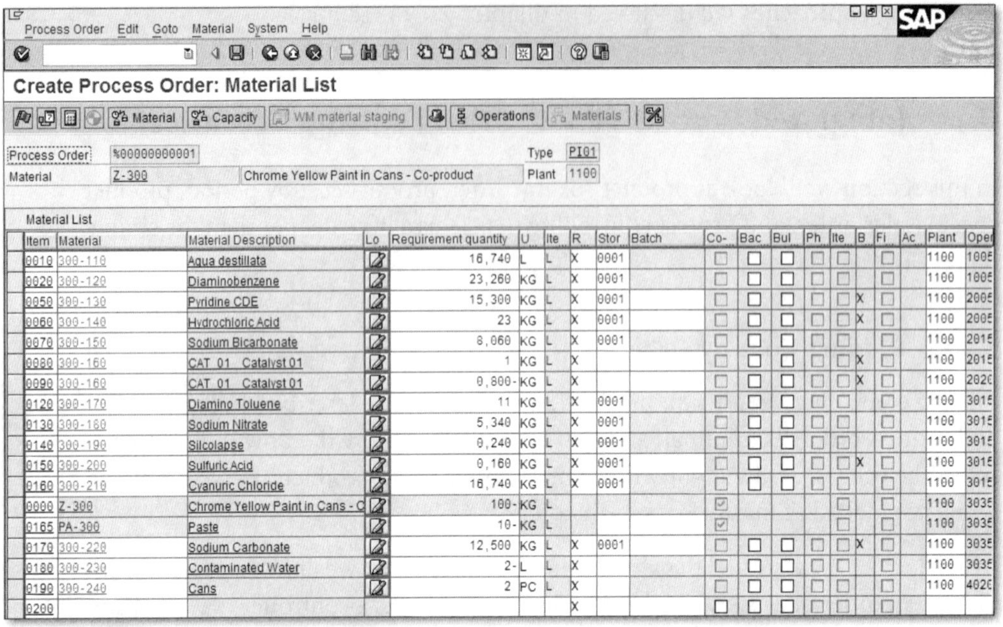

Item	Material	Material Description	Lo	Requirement quantity	U	Ite	R	Stor	Batch	Co-	Bac	Bul	Ph	Ite	B	Fi	Ac	Plant	Oper
0010	300-110	Aqua destillata		16,740	L	L	X	0001										1100	1005
0020	300-120	Diaminobenzene		23,260	KG	L	X	0001										1100	1005
0050	300-130	Pyridine CDE		15,300	KG	L	X	0001							X			1100	2005
0060	300-140	Hydrochloric Acid		23	KG	L	X	0001							X			1100	2005
0070	300-150	Sodium Bicarbonate		8,060	KG	L	X	0001										1100	2015
0080	300-160	CAT_01 Catalyst 01		1	KG	L	X								X			1100	2015
0090	300-160	CAT_01 Catalyst 01		0,800-	KG	L	X								X			1100	2020
0120	300-170	Diamino Toluene		11	KG	L	X	0001										1100	3015
0130	300-180	Sodium Nitrate		5,340	KG	L	X	0001										1100	3015
0140	300-190	Silcolapse		0,240	KG	L	X	0001										1100	3015
0150	300-200	Sulfuric Acid		0,160	KG	L	X	0001							X			1100	3015
0160	300-210	Cyanuric Chloride		16,740	KG	L	X	0001										1100	3015
0000	Z-300	Chrome Yellow Paint in Cans - C		100-	KG	L				✓								1100	3035
0165	PA-300	Paste		10-	KG	L				✓								1100	3035
0170	300-220	Sodium Carbonate		12,500	KG	L	X	0001							X			1100	3035
0180	300-230	Contaminated Water		2-	L	L	X											1100	3035
0190	300-240	Cans		2	PC	L	X											1100	4020
0200							X												

Figure 6.47 Material List Showing Co-Products

The structure of the process order includes a header to which all costs are posted and order items for each co-product. We discussed the assignment of the order costs to the order items in Chapter 4, Section 4.3.2. To display the cost split in the settlement rule, select HEADER • SETTLEMENT RULE. Figure 6.48 shows the settlement rule for the process order with two settlement receivers, item 0001 (material Z-300) and item 0002 (material PA-300). The apportionment structure in the material master specifies that when splitting the costs to the order items, the different cost elements are treated differently. The values in the EQUIVALENCE NUMBERS column have been derived from the apportionment structure and can be adjusted manually in the order.

Figure 6.49 shows the cost report for the process order. You can display this by selecting GOTO • COSTS • ANALYSIS in the order. This shows two planned goods receipts, one for Z-300 and one for PA-300. It also includes negative costs for the contaminated water and the part of the catalyst that can be recovered from the process, since these are by-products.

6.3 | Integrated Process Flows: Other Logistics Scenarios

Maintain Settlement Rule: Overview

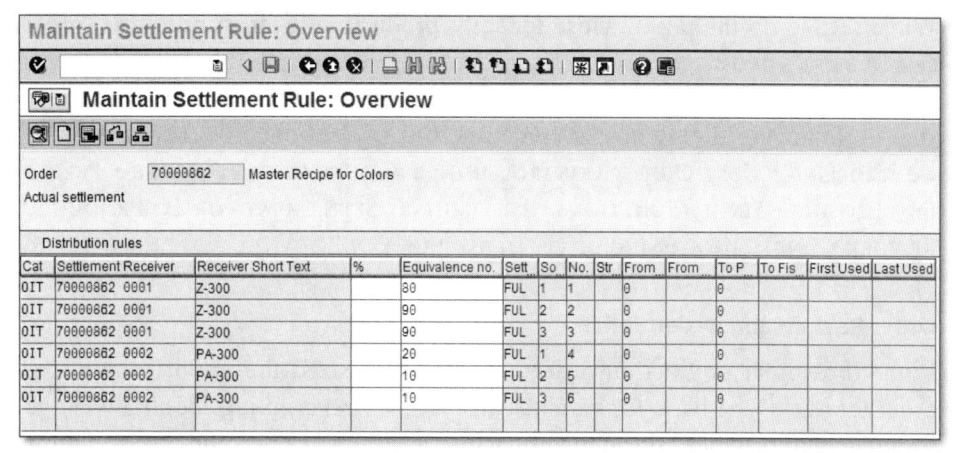

Order: 70000862 Master Recipe for Colors
Actual settlement

Distribution rules

Cat	Settlement Receiver	Receiver Short Text	%	Equivalence no.	Sett	So	No.	Str	From	From	To P	To Fis	First Used	Last Used
OIT	70000862 0001	Z-300		80	FUL	1	1		0		0			
OIT	70000862 0001	Z-300		90	FUL	2	2		0		0			
OIT	70000862 0001	Z-300		90	FUL	3	3		0		0			
OIT	70000862 0002	PA-300		20	FUL	1	4		0		0			
OIT	70000862 0002	PA-300		10	FUL	2	5		0		0			
OIT	70000862 0002	PA-300		10	FUL	3	6		0		0			

Figure 6.48 Settlement Rule for Joint Production

Create Process Order: Material List

Plant: 1100 Berlin
Material: Z-300 Chrome Yellow Paint in Cans - Co-product

Transaction	Cost Elem.	Origin	Origin (Text)	Total plan	Total act.costs	Plan qty	Actual Qty	Plan/act. var.	P/A var(%)	Curre
Goods Issues	400000	1100/300-110	Aqua destillata	0,09	0,00	16,740	0	0,09-	100,00-	EUR
	400000	1100/300-120	Diaminobenzene	17,91	0,00	23,260	0	17,91-	100,00-	EUR
	400000	1100/300-130	Pyridine CDE	7,80	0,00	15,300	0	7,80-	100,00-	EUR
	400000	1100/300-140	Hydrochloric Acid	52,90	0,00	23	0	52,90-	100,00-	EUR
	400000	1100/300-150	Sodium Bicarbonate	5,16	0,00	8,060	0	5,16-	100,00-	EUR
	400000	1100/300-160	CAT_01 Catalyst 01	0,26	0,00	1	0	0,26-	100,00-	EUR
	400000	1100/300-170	Diamino Toluene	2,86	0,00	11	0	2,86-	100,00-	EUR
	400000	1100/300-180	Sodium Nitrate	12,55	0,00	5,340	0	12,55-	100,00-	EUR
	400000	1100/300-190	Silcolapse	0,06	0,00	0,240	0	0,06-	100,00-	EUR
	400000	1100/300-200	Sulfuric Acid	0,38	0,00	0,160	0	0,38-	100,00-	EUR
	400000	1100/300-210	Cyanuric Chloride	2,18	0,00	16,740	0	2,18-	100,00-	EUR
	400000	1100/300-220	Sodium Carbonate	38,38	0,00	12,500	0	38,38-	100,00-	EUR
	400000	1100/300-240	Cans	1,22	0,00	2	0	1,22-	100,00-	EUR
	895000	1100/300-160	CAT_01 Catalyst 01	0,21-	0,00	0,800-	0	0,21	100,00-	EUR
	895000	1100/300-230	Contaminated Water	0,02-	0,00	2-	0	0,02	100,00-	EUR
Goods Issues				▪ 141,52 ▪	0,00 ▪	115,800 14,740 2	▪	141,52-		EUR
Confirmations	620000	4240/1420	Paint/Solvent Prod. / Machine Hours	3.205,75	0,00	33	0	3.205,75-	100,00-	EUR
Confirmations				▪ 3.205,75 ▪	0,00 ▪	33	▪	3.205,75-		EUR
Overhead	655100	4130	Warehouse	14,18	0,00			14,18-	100,00-	EUR
Overhead				▪ 14,18 ▪	0,00		▪	14,18-		EUR
Goods Receipt	895000	1100/Z-300	Chrome Yellow Paint in Cans - Co-prd	466,00-	0,00	100-	0	466,00	100,00-	EUR
	895000	1100/PA-300	Paste	74,40-	0,00	10-	0	74,40	100,00-	EUR
Goods Receipt				▪ 540,40- ▪	0,00 ▪	110-	▪	540,40		EUR

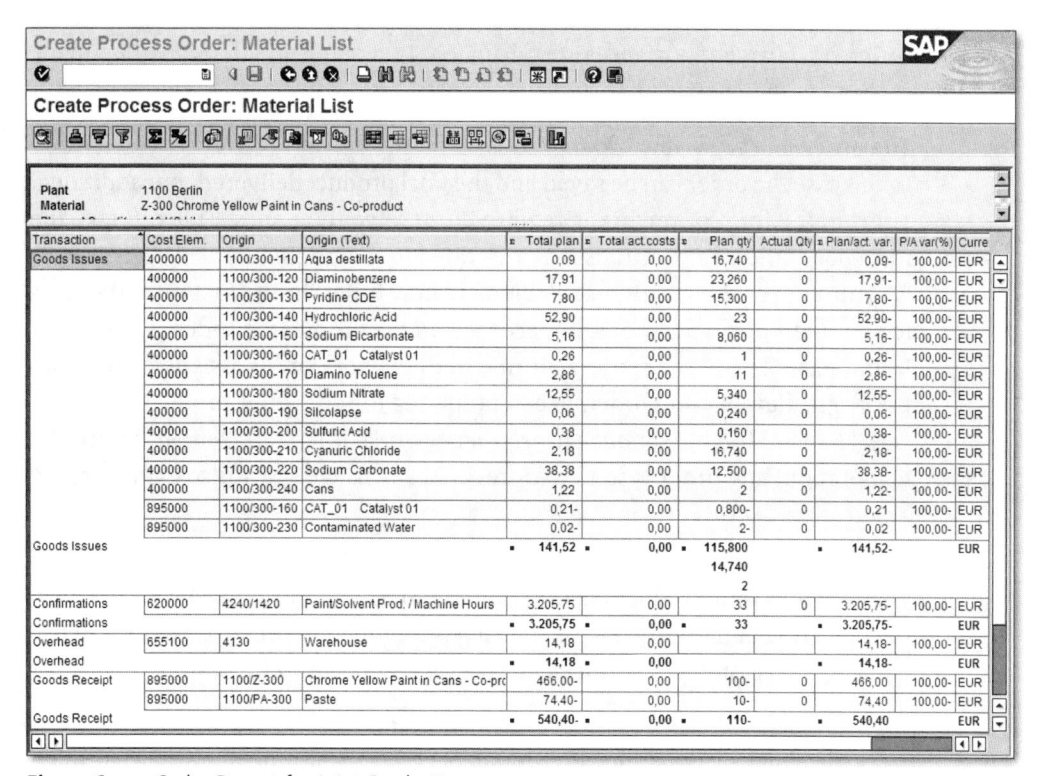

Figure 6.49 Order Report for Joint Production

When setting up the period close for joint production, bear in mind that order settlement is a two-stage process. The order costs are first split into the order items and then settled to stock for the relevant co-product. You'll find this extra close step by following the menu path ACCOUNTING • CONTROLLING • PRODUCT COST CONTROLLING • COST OBJECT CONTROLLING • PRODUCT COST BY ORDER • PERIOD END CLOSING • SINGLE FUNCTIONS • PRELIMINARY SETTLEMENT FOR CO-PRODUCTS/REWORK • SINGLE PROCESSING or via Transaction CO8B.

Order Rework and Order Split

When looking at production orders, we've emphasized the importance of the order lot size as the basis for variance analysis. However, things don't always go completely to plan, and during manufacture it sometimes becomes clear that the order cannot be completed in the form intended. Sometimes it's impossible to save the order, and the entire quantity has to be scrapped. In this case, all costs are considered scrap when variances are calculated. Two other situations are potentially interesting to the controller.

- **The order has to be reworked.**
  In this case the order can be saved and the final product delivered, but additional effort in the form of rework is required to resolve the issues. This can take the form of additional operations that are added to the original order when rework is confirmed or the creation of a complete new order. In the first case, the costs for the additional operations are recorded on the production order as variances. In the second case, the settlement rule in the rework order assigns the costs to the original production order. When preparing to settle your production orders (see Chapter 7), you should ensure that rework orders are settled before the main production order is settled to stock. Again, as we saw for co-products, use Transaction CO8B.

- **The order has to be split.**
  The ability to split production and process orders was introduced with the business function enhancements for splitting of production order (LOG_PP_PROD_ORDER_SPLIT) in SAP enhancement package 4 for SAP ERP 6.0.

  Several business reasons can make an order split necessary.

  - The customer changes his requirements, and the production order has to be adjusted to reflect this.

- Part of the quantity manufactured is faulty and has to be reworked or used to manufacture a different product.
- The priorities of the production plan are changed, and production orders have to be postponed.
- The necessary machines or tools are defective.

The order split means that a child order is created either for the new materials (if the customer changes his order or the product specifications change) or for the original material (if the dates or production resources change significantly). It can also mean that the part of the semifinished product completed to date is delivered to stock.

For the controller, what matters is how the planned costs are apportioned between the parent and child orders. This is based on the proportion of the quantities up to the operation at which the split took place, so that a meaningful comparison of planned and actual costs is still possible.

Outsourced Manufacturing

Alongside production orders and process orders, you'll also find that the PRODUCT COST BY ORDER menu references something called a *CO production order*. This is a more like an internal order than a production order in that it's created in CO to capture manufacturing costs (goods issues, goods receipts, and so on) when production planning is not implemented in SAP ERP. While the original CO production order dates back to the early days of SAP R/3, it has come back into focus as a means of collecting costs in external manufacturing scenarios with the introduction of business function LOG_MM_OM_1 (Outsourced Manufacturing in SAP ERP Operations) in SAP enhancement package 4 for SAP ERP 6.0.

Outsourced manufacturing involves the subcontracting of the manufacturing work to an external supplier who takes delivery of the material components, performs the necessary work, and then ships the finished product back to the requesting organization and bills for his services. The purchase order that requests the subcontracting work creates a CO production order automatically. You cannot create confirmations for these orders (since the assumption is that the work is being performed by a subcontractor), but you can apply overhead and calculate work in process, meaning that the costs associated with these orders can be included in the financial statements earlier. It's also possible to transfer status information from the external supplier to these orders.

6.3.2 Product Cost by Period

In Chapter 3 we showed how to create a product cost collector to collect costs by period rather than on the individual production orders. This is a way of moving away from the strong work order focus of traditional accounting systems and toward a lean accounting approach, where the focus is on the direct costs incurred for the value stream in the period.

Before manufacturing begins, you must ensure that you create product cost collectors for all relevant materials and production versions (see Chapter 3). You can then create the production orders as described in Section 6.1, but using an order type that supports working with product cost collectors (order type PP08 in the standard configuration). For the people working on the shop floor, the production order looks completely normal, allowing scheduling, material reservations, and so on. The difference is that the order has no settlement rule, and the costing functions and cost reports are inactive.

To display a list of all associated production orders and the relevant production version, click on the ORDERS/PV button, as shown in Figure 6.50. You can use this list to navigate to the individual production orders if you need to check details of what quantities were recorded on the order.

When you create the master data for a product cost collector, you're asked if you want to create a cost estimate for each production version. You don't have to create a cost estimate, since you can use the standard cost estimate to determine the target costs for each operation to calculate the work in process and the scrap. However, if your production version includes a BOM or routing with a different structure than that used to set the standard costs, it makes sense to create a new cost estimate for the product cost collector using the BOM and routing in your production version as a starting point. Figure 6.51 shows the cost estimate for material T-B400. You can access it by clicking on the COST ESTIMATE button in Figure 6.50. If you compare this cost estimate with the cost estimates we looked at in Chapters 4 and 5, you'll notice that it's based on the bill of material and the routing but also includes a link to the production version, the procurement alternative (since multiple production versions have been assigned to the product cost collector), and the special procurement key. The actual process of costing follows the same logic as the calculation of standard costs.

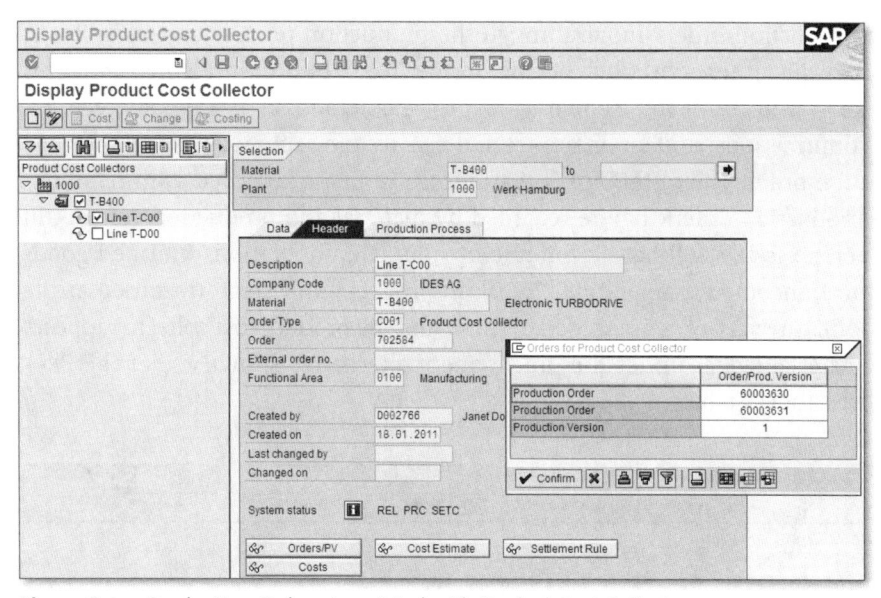

Integrated Process Flows: Other Logistics Scenarios | **6.3**

Figure 6.50 Production Orders Associated with Product Cost Collector

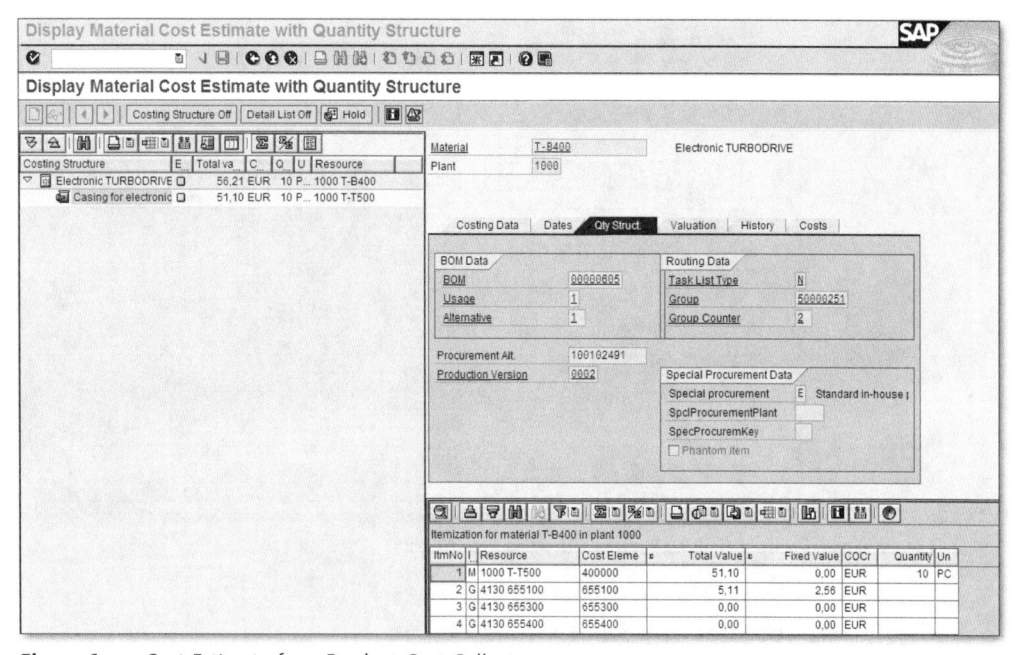

Figure 6.51 Cost Estimate for a Product Cost Collector

As the production orders move through the production process and incur costs, you can display these costs by clicking on the COSTS button in Figure 6.50. This will take you to the report shown in Figure 6.52. Goods issues, goods receipts, order confirmations, and so on are treated exactly the same way as for a normal production order. The difference is that instead of being recorded with reference to the production order, they're recorded by material and production version. In any given period, you'll have a mixture of completed operations (finished goods inventory), incomplete operations (work in process), and scrap (recorded at the operation). Any variances are settled to stock, and the product cost collector appears in the material ledger under the procurement alternative shown under the PRODUCTION PROCESS tab.

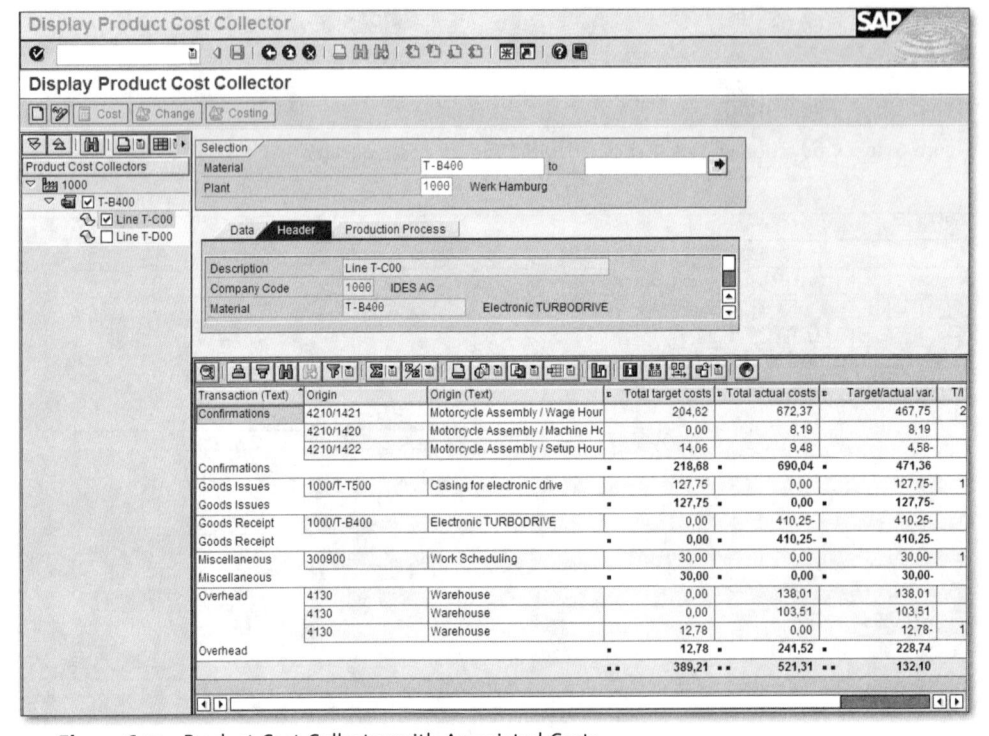

Figure 6.52 Product Cost Collector with Associated Costs

6.3.3 Product Cost by Sales Order

In Chapter 2 we discussed the difference between sales controlling in profitability analysis and product costs by sales order. In Section 6.1 all sales controlling activities took place in Profitability Analysis and the delivery for the sales order involved picking goods from neutral stock to ship to the customer. It's also possible to configure your sales order process to initiate a production process to manufacture the goods to order (make-to-order).

The most common reason to initiate make-to-order production is that the product requested is configurable and the customer has made certain selections that will affect the parts needed in manufacturing and sometimes the operations to be performed. You have two options in a make-to-order scenario.

- The production order is triggered from the sales order and delivers its completed product to sales order stock, from where it will be shipped to the customer. If there are no customer-specific costs for the delivery, there's no need to configure the sales order item as an account assignment and set up revenue cost elements for the revenues. The main difference compared to what we saw in Section 6.1 is that the production order settles its costs to sales order stock. Reporting and variance analysis can still take place by production order as in Section 6.1. However, the sales order stock is *valued*, meaning the system is configured to pick a price for the sales order stock using a sales order cost estimate, the production order cost estimate, or occasionally the standard cost estimate (if one exists) rather than the standard price we used to value the receipt to stock in Section 6.1.

- The sales order initiates make-to-order production, and production costs are collected on the production order. However, the cost of performing customer-specific configuration or special delivery costs needs to be charged to the sales order. In this case, the sales order item needs to be configured as an account assignment, and sales revenue is captured as a cost element. You'll also have to perform results analysis at period close.

Let's look at the process flow for the first option. To illustrate this process, we'll create a sales order for configurable material DPC1. The procedure to create a sales order is the same as before, except that we entered a configurable material as the product. As soon as you create the sales item, the system directs you to the Configuration screen. Figure 6.53 shows the selection screen for the characteristics that represent the different configuration options. You may remember these from when we looked at the configuration settings in the material master in Chapter 4. The sales manager maintains these in collaboration with the customer, or they can be transferred from an external application, such as a Web order entry screen.

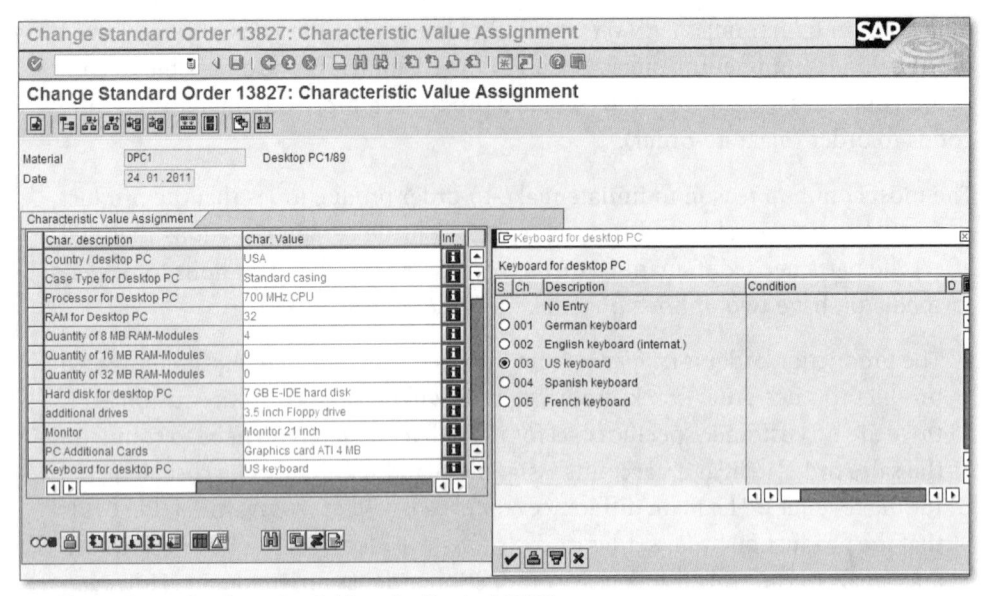

Figure 6.53 Configuration Settings for Product DPC1

The sales order item for this material has a special requirements type (see Figure 6.54) that controls the fact that the production order will be created with reference to the sales orders, so that the customers' requirements can be taken into account during production. To check the requirements type for a sales order, select the Procurement tab in the order overview. This requirements type also determines that the goods will be delivered to and issued from sales order stock—in other words, the inventory that belongs to the sales order rather than the general finished goods inventory. This raises the issue of how the sales order item will be valued, since no standard cost estimate exists for the customer-specific configuration. Again, this is customizable. Usually either a cost estimate is created for the sales order or the production order cost estimate is used to provide an initial valuation. It's also the requirements type that determines whether the sales order item exists as an account assignment in CO or not. In both cases, the costs for the sales order item flow into Profitability Analysis.

The MRP run links the production order with the sales order item that triggered the order, or you can manually create a production order with reference to a sales order item. When we display a production order for make to order using Transaction CO03, we see a link to the sales order item and the ordering party in the General tab for the production order (see Figure 6.55).

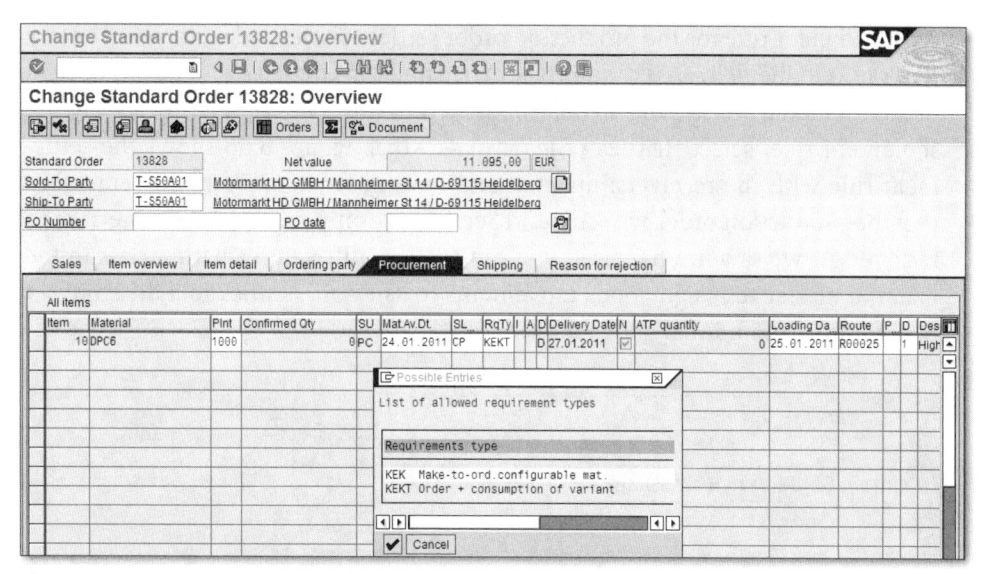

6.3 | Integrated Process Flows: Other Logistics Scenarios

Figure 6.54 Requirements Type of Sales Order

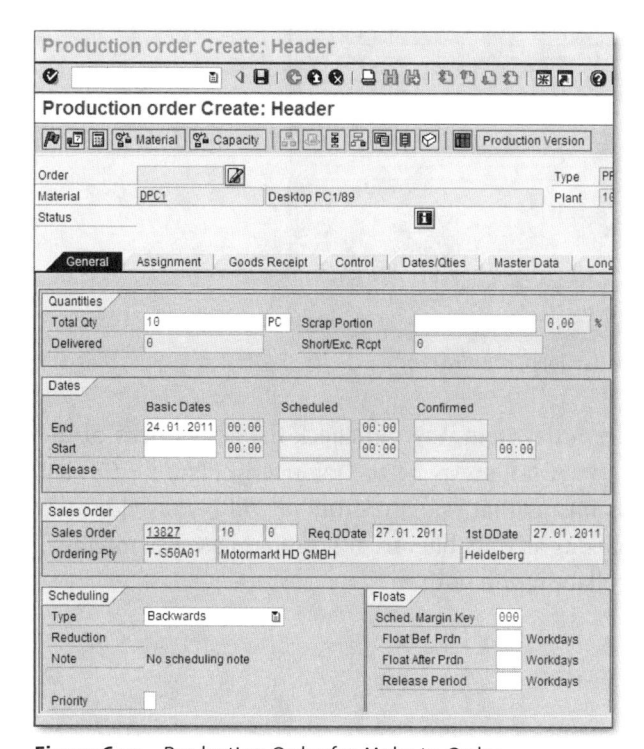

Figure 6.55 Production Order for Make to Order

The settlement rule for the production order settles to sales order stock (inventory that can only be delivered to the customer named in the sales order), rather than neutral material stock (which could be issued to any sales order). To display the settlement rule, select HEADER • SETTLEMENT RULE. Figure 6.56 shows the settlement rule with the receivers: material and sales order item. You may remember that the production order we settled in Section 6.1 only included the material as a receiver. As we saw in Chapter 4, you can set up a different valuation class in the material master to assign goods movements to sales order stock to a different set of accounts from normal goods movements.

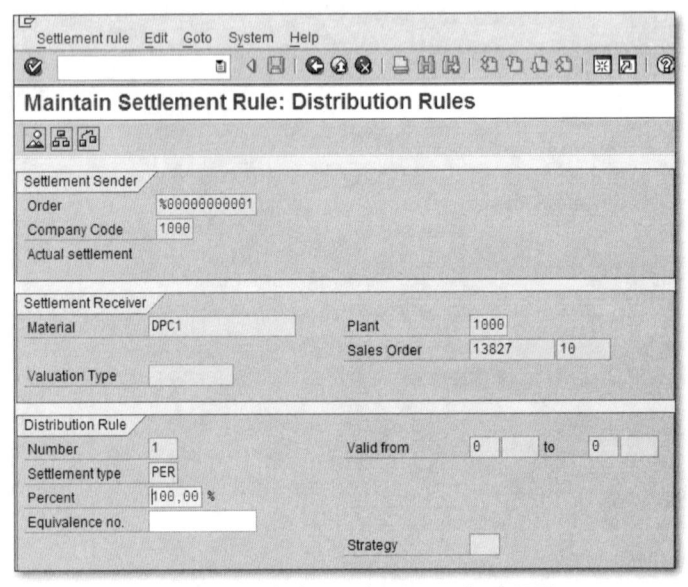

Figure 6.56 Settlement Rule for Production Order (MTO)

Finally if we return to the sales order item, we can check the assignment of the sales order item to PROFITABILITY ANALYSIS as before. Notice in Figure 6.57 that the material is still DPC1. This means that sales controlling will be based on the configurable material (encompassing all possible variants) rather than the individual configuration worked out in collaboration with the final customer.

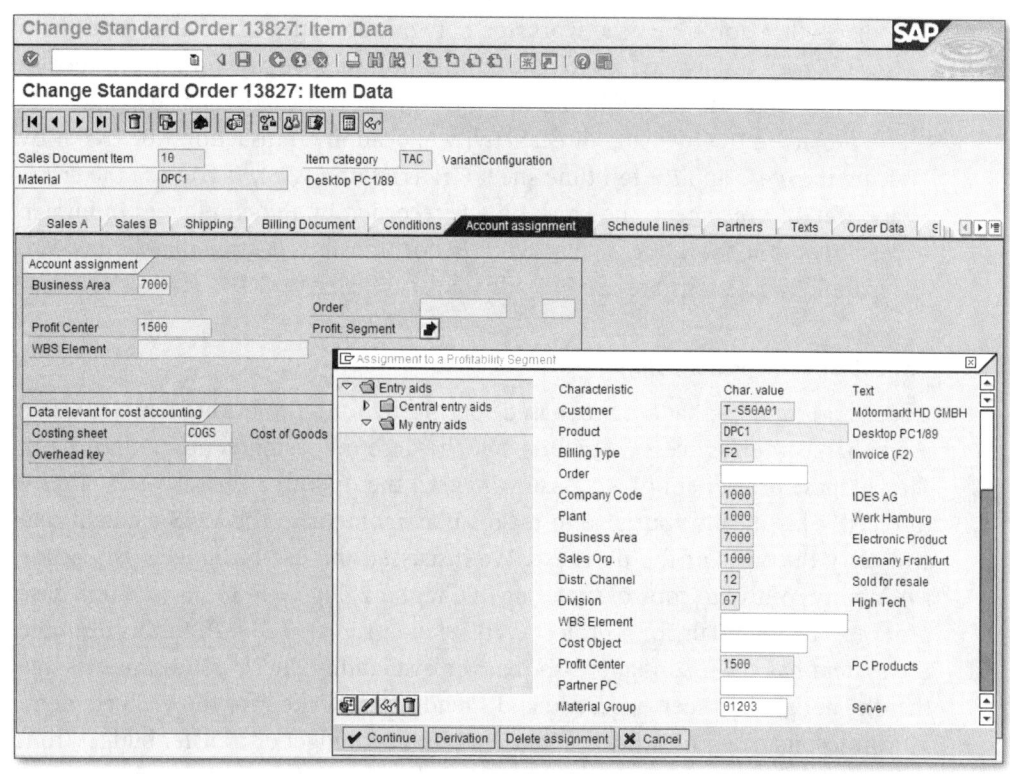

Figure 6.57 Profitability Segment for Make to Order

6.3.4 Project Controlling

Essentially project controlling is similar to order controlling, with several notable exceptions.

- Whereas we procured the blank CDs and labels for production of our CDs with no reference to a cost center, order or project, goods or services procured specifically for the project include the WBS element as an *account assignment* in the purchase order item. The costs are expensed to the WBS element immediately rather than when the goods are issued from raw materials inventory to the project/order.

- In addition to monitoring expenses on projects, it's also common to monitor future expenses that are known, since purchase orders have been created to buy materials or services for the project. Such known future expenses are called *commitments*.

► Projects that don't have networks or network activities associated with them (see Chapter 4) have no link to the confirmation step we saw for the production order. Instead, the cost of doing work for the project can either be assigned to the project in CO by using direct activity allocation (Transaction KB21N) or by using the cross-application time sheet (Transaction CATS). If you use the cross-application time sheet, the work time is recorded by the employees in human resources, but the value of that work is not transferred immediately. Instead, separate transactions are used to initiate the transfer to CO.

Project-Specific Purchasing

Goods and services that are purchased specifically for a project are handled using a purchase order as we saw before, but the account assignment (column A) in the purchase order item or AccAssCat field in the ACCOUNT ASSIGNMENT tab is P (project). This means you have to make an assignment to the WBS element that will carry the costs of the purchase. We discussed the use of budgets and active availability control to control spending in Chapter 2. Figure 6.58 shows a purchase order to buy materials for a project (WBS element I/1000-3-3-2). In this example the system has been configured so that the availability check issues the message that the budget has been exceeded and spending is blocked for the WBS element. The project manager now has to request additional budget or transfer budget from another WBS element (see Chapter 5) before he can complete his purchase.

> **Scope of Availability Checks**
>
> It's only possible to activate availability checks for projects and internal orders. We're often asked whether such a function is also available for cost centers, but this is not possible at the time of writing. SAP Note 68366 describes a workaround using statistical orders to represent each cost center.

The check above is a hard check against the existing budget prior to making any expense or commitment posting to the project. The budget and spending to date is shown in several reports to enable managers to monitor where they stand prior to making a purchase. Figure 6.59 shows the current spending for the project in question. We've accessed this from Manager Self-Service (see Appendix A found at www.sap-press.com) and clicked on the PERSONALIZE DATA button to enter the project in question.

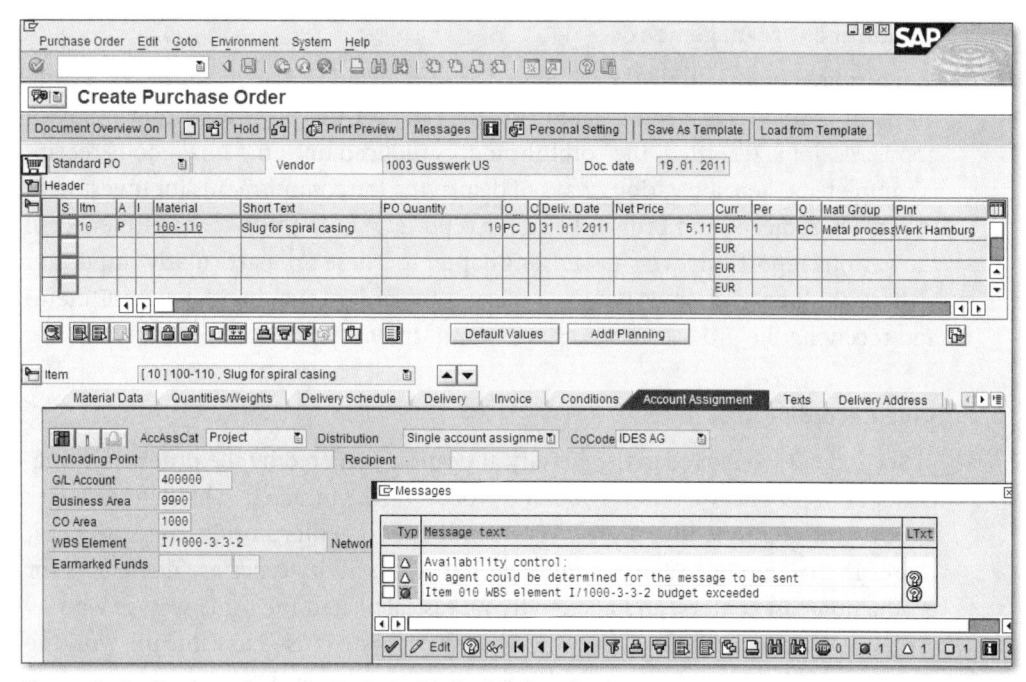

6.3 Integrated Process Flows: Other Logistics Scenarios

Figure 6.58 Purchase Order for Project with Availability Check

Figure 6.59 Plan/Actual Comparison for Project

Commitment Management

If in our previous example the manager had succeeded in placing his order, a commitment would have been created for the value of the purchase order. As each goods receipt is recorded, the commitment is reduced until the final goods receipt is completed. There are various ways of displaying the commitments for investment programs, projects, and orders. Look for reports with the title "commitments" in the various report lists we showed in Chapter 2. These are particularly important if there are long lead times between placing the order (opening the commitment) and receiving the order (cancelling the commitment).

Time Recording

In Section 6.2 we looked at the activity allocation triggered by the order confirmation for our production order. The same process can be initiated in human resources to post working time to a project. The sending cost center in this case is the cost center in the employee's organizational unit. The activity types are defined as for production cost centers, and an activity rate is calculated the same way as we saw for production activities in Chapter 5. This activity rate is used to value the working time entered by the employee for his work on a particular project.

To post working time to a project, go to Transaction CAT2 or HUMAN RESOURCES • TIME MANAGEMENT • TIME SHEET • CATS CLASSIC • RECORD WORKING TIME, and select the relevant data entry profile and a personnel number. The data entry profiles are configured to determine what account assignments the employee is allowed to record time against. Then enter the working times as shown in Figure 6.60. The time sheet includes the employee's cost center and the activity type wage hours as the sender of the allocation and the WBS element as the receiver of the allocation.

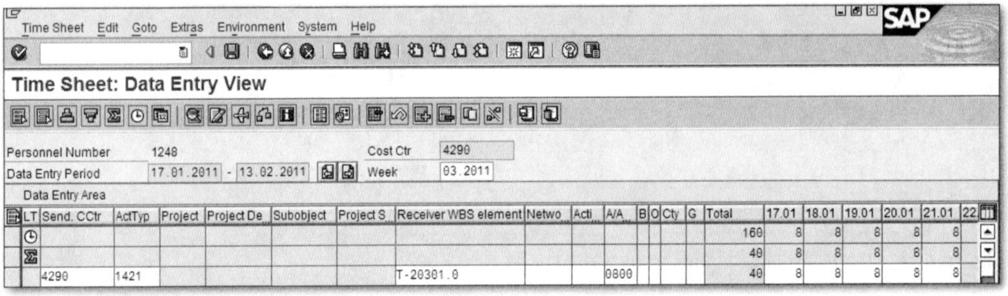

Figure 6.60 Time Recording

The attendance type in HR is 0800 (attendance hours). From a controlling point of view, the relevant fields are the sender cost center and activity type, the receiver WBS element, and the hours entered.

The main difference between a confirmation in Logistics and time recording in human resources is that the activity allocation does not take place immediately. Instead, a transfer has to be scheduled to transfer the working time recorded from human resources to CO. To make the transfer, use Transaction CAT5 or follow the menu path HUMAN RESOURCES • TIME MANAGEMENT • TIME SHEET • TRANSFER • PROJECT SYSTEM • TRANSFER. Similar transactions exist for transfers to cost centers and plant maintenance or customer service orders. Figure 6.61 shows the transfer log, with an item for each time record transferred.

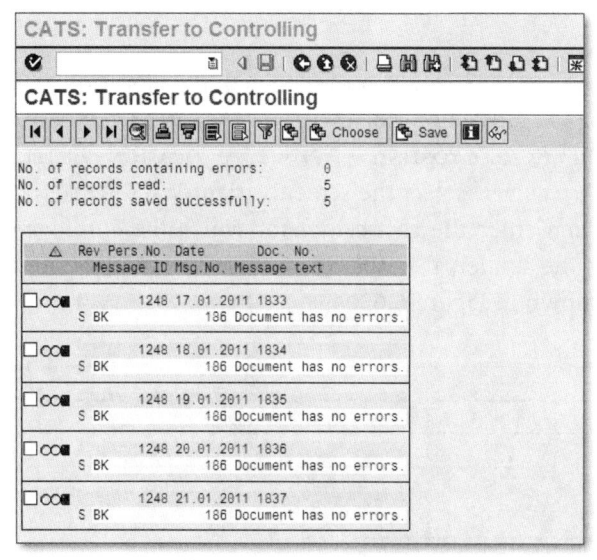

Figure 6.61 Transfer Work Times to Controlling

Figure 6.62 shows the line item for the activity allocation once the data transfer is complete (see Chapter 2). You can display the project line item by using Transaction CJ13 or following the menu path ACCOUNTING • PROJECT SYSTEM • INFORMATION SYSTEM • FINANCIALS • LINE ITEMS • ACTUAL COSTS/REVENUES and entering the relevant project, WBS number, cost element, and time frame. Just as we saw for the production activities, you can also see this work time on the cost center by using Transaction KSB1 (see Chapter 2, Section 2.1) to view the line items on the cost center.

6 | Actual Postings

Figure 6.62 Direct Activity Allocation for Time Sheet

If you don't use Time Recording in CATS, you can post an activity allocation to a WBS element directly, by going to Transaction KB21N or ACCOUNTING • CONTROLLING • COST CENTER ACCOUNTING • ACTUAL POSTINGS • ACTIVITY ALLOCATION • ENTER. To enter the WBS element as a receiver, select the screen variant WBS ELEMENT/ NETWORK (see Figure 6.63). Then enter the cost center for which the employee works and the activity type as the sender, the WBS element as the receiver, and the appropriate quantities as shown in Figure 6.63.

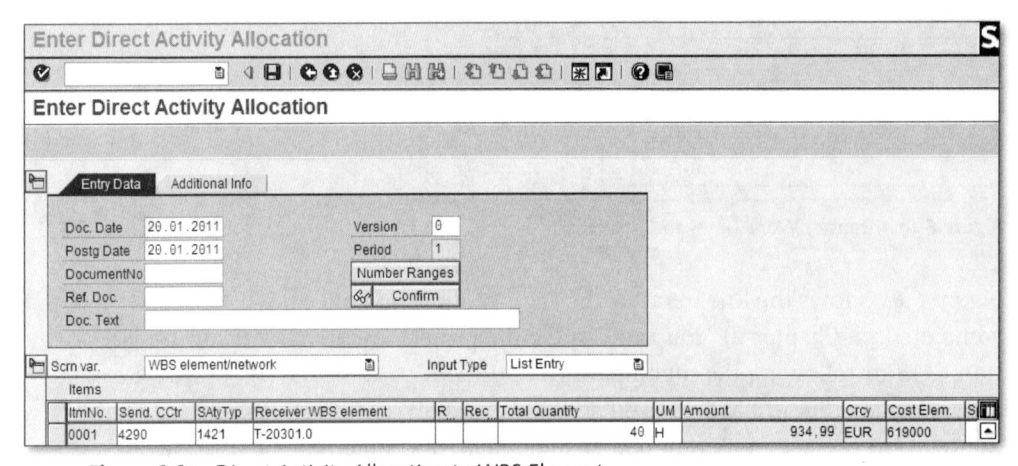

Figure 6.63 Direct Activity Allocation to WBS Element

312

We've looked at actual postings in many of the Logistics processes and in human resources and at how to make direct activity allocations in CO. If these are wrong for any reason, it's common to correct the working time in human resources or the confirmation in Logistics, but you should also know how to make correction postings in CO for when it's not possible or practical to reverse the original document.

> **Prior Year Rates for Projects**
>
> A development for the public sector in SAP enhancement package 4 for SAP ERP 6.0 may be of interest to controllers. Since federal agencies allow timesheet corrections in the 13 months preceding the document date, there was a need to value the changed working time not with the activity price valid on the key date for the change, but when the work was originally performed. Follow-up functions, such as overhead calculation, should also be based on the values used for time recording. While most industries don't allow such a long period for corrections to time recordings, many will be interested to learn that it's possible to calculate overhead in real time when the time sheet transfer from HR takes place or the activity allocation in CO is posted. You can activate this process can be activated using the business function CO_ALLOCATIONS.

6.4 Corrections or Adjustment Postings

Our examples showed complete flows that took place without a hitch, but the controller is occasionally called upon to make a correction. Sometimes a complete *reversal* is required, which acts as a documented "undo" of the original posting. Sometimes a posting is made using the wrong account assignment (for example, travel expenses are charged to the wrong cost center or order) or the controller must move a direct activity allocation from one account assignment to another (for example, work posted to one WBS element must be moved to a different WBS element).

Figure 6.64 shows the ACTUAL POSTINGS folder for Cost Center Accounting, but the same applications are available in the INTERNAL ORDERS, PRODUCT COST BY ORDER, PRODUCT COST BY PERIOD, SALES ORDER CONTROLLING, and ACTIVITY-BASED COSTING folders. Here you'll see the transactions for time recording and direct activity allocation that we talked about in the previous section. We'll now look at the other actual posting transactions.

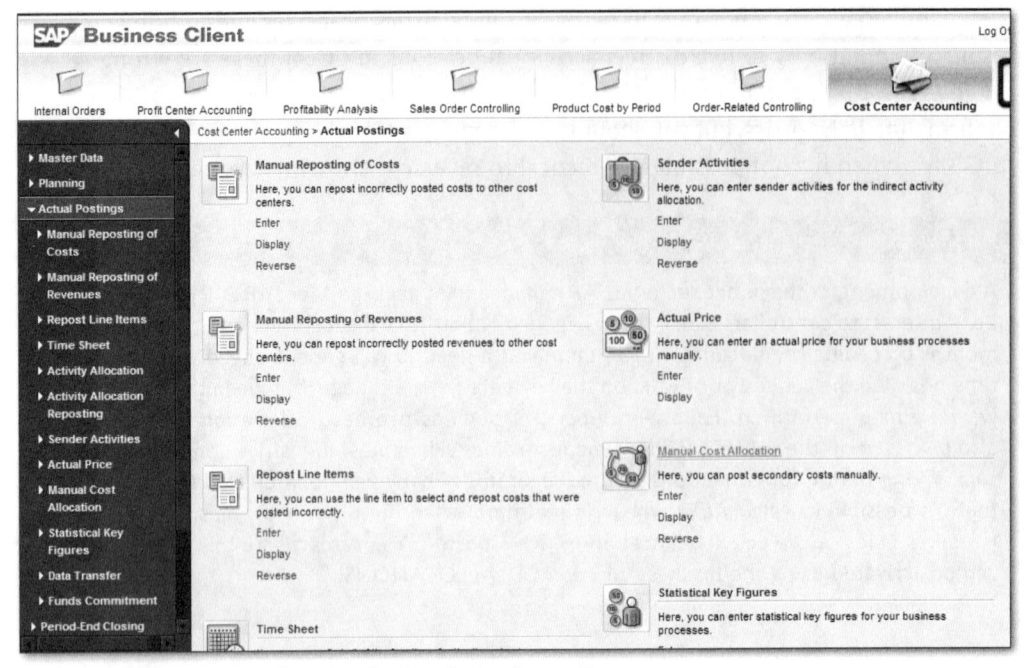

Figure 6.64 Actual Postings in Cost Center Accounting

6.4.1 Reposting Line Items

Let's assume that one of the employees on a cost center has just moved to another cost center, but his travel expenses from the previous period have been posted to the old cost center. To move these costs to the correct cost center, we need to *repost* the line item that recorded the original expense posting by using Transaction KB61 or following the menu path ACCOUNTING • CONTROLLING • COST CENTER ACCOUNTING • ACTUAL POSTINGS • REPOST LINE ITEM • ENTER. In an ideal world, you know the document number under which the travel expenses were posted and can enter it in the selection screen shown on Figure 6.65. Usually, however, the biggest challenge of reposting a line item is finding the document you want to repost in the first place. If you don't enter a document number in the selection screen, the system will select all documents that meet your selection criteria (all travel postings to the sales cost center in 2010, in our example). If this will result in too many documents being selected for reposting, click on the CHANGE SELECTION PARAMETERS button.

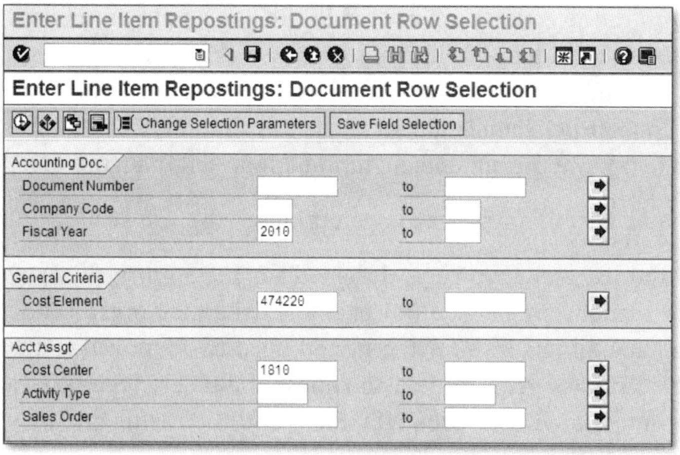

Corrections or Adjustment Postings | 6.4

Figure 6.65 Selection Screen for Reposting

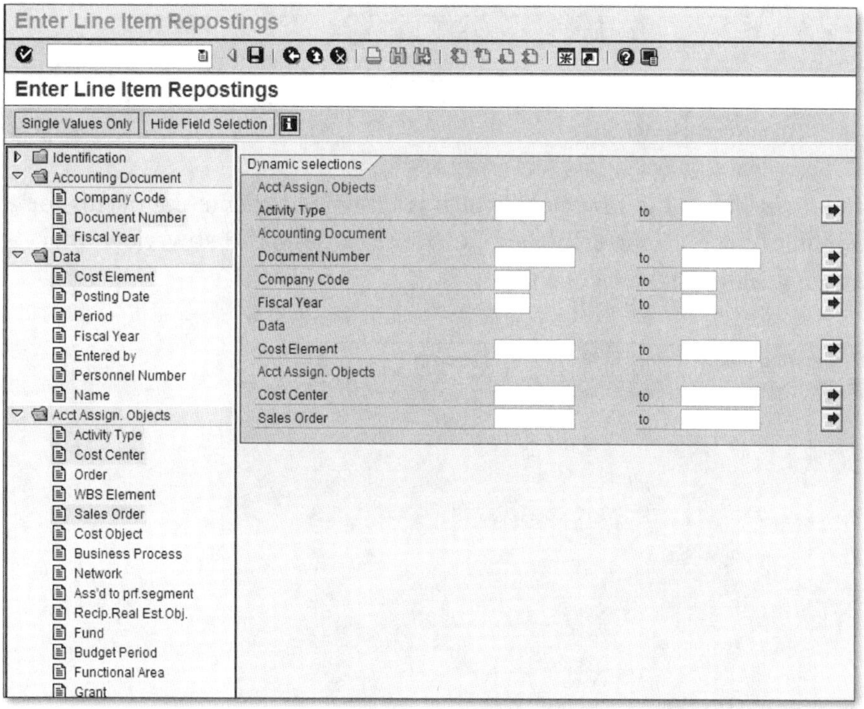

Figure 6.66 Selection Parameters for Line Item Reposting

Figure 6.66 shows all selection parameters for a line item reposting, and as we discovered in Chapter 2, the cost center line item includes a lot of fields. To include

315

6 | Actual Postings

additional parameters on the selection screen, double-click on a field on the left, such as PERSONNEL NUMBER, to identify the employee who changed cost center. This field then appears on the right as a dynamic selection parameter. When you save the dynamic selection, the personnel number appears as an additional selection parameter to help you locate the correct document to be reposted in Figure 6.66.

Once you have made your selection, you have two options.

- Figure 6.67 shows the list view, which is designed for mass entry of many items when mass corrections are needed (for example, when the organization is being restructured and all postings for the period need to be moved to the new cost center. The list view requires you to choose the object type (OTYPE column) for the account assignment using [F4] help and then enter the new account assignment.

Figure 6.67 Reposting: List View

- Figure 6.68 shows the row view, which is designed for entering details for a single item (such as our employee's travel expenses). The ROW view offers a separate field for each object type.

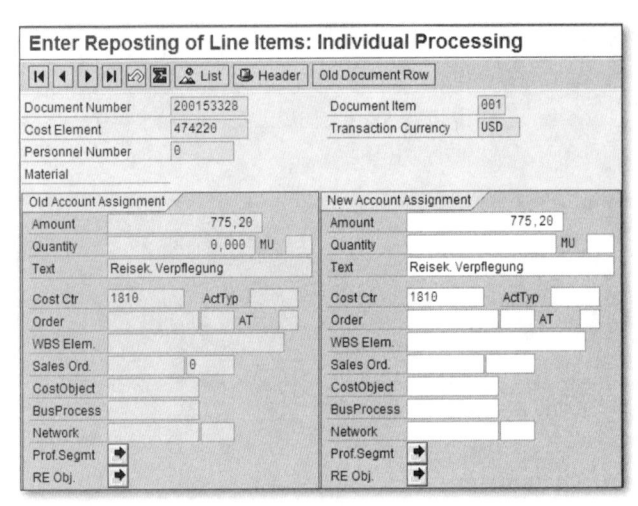

Figure 6.68 Reposting: Row View

You can switch to the row view by clicking on the Row button in the list view and to the list view by clicking on the LIST button in the row view.

In both cases you can easily enter the correct cost center or another account assignment, such as a WBS element, for the document. You can identify the reposting documents for auditing by entering Transaction RKU3 as a dynamic selection in the line item report. Figure 6.69 shows a line item report for the sales cost center, where the December travel costs have been reposted to another cost center, and the fields BUSINESS TRANSACTION, PARTNER OBJECT TYPE, and PARTNER OBJECT have been added to the report layout so that you can see to which cost center the costs have been reposted, as we explained in Chapter 2.

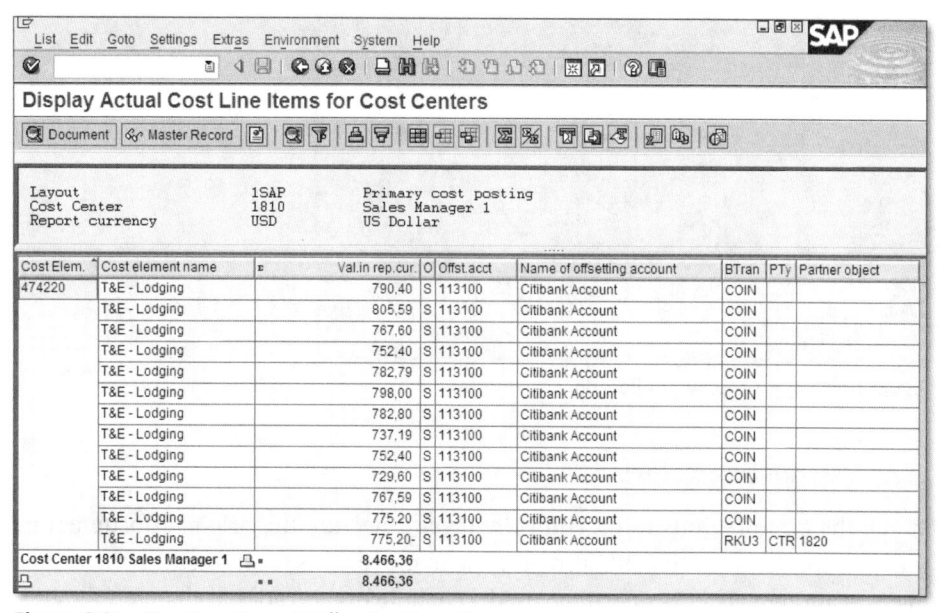

Cost Elem.	Cost element name	Σ	Val.in rep.cur.	O	Offst.acct	Name of offsetting account	BTran	PTy	Partner object
474220	T&E - Lodging		790,00	S	113100	Citibank Account	COIN		
	T&E - Lodging		805,59	S	113100	Citibank Account	COIN		
	T&E - Lodging		767,60	S	113100	Citibank Account	COIN		
	T&E - Lodging		752,40	S	113100	Citibank Account	COIN		
	T&E - Lodging		782,79	S	113100	Citibank Account	COIN		
	T&E - Lodging		798,00	S	113100	Citibank Account	COIN		
	T&E - Lodging		782,80	S	113100	Citibank Account	COIN		
	T&E - Lodging		737,19	S	113100	Citibank Account	COIN		
	T&E - Lodging		752,40	S	113100	Citibank Account	COIN		
	T&E - Lodging		729,60	S	113100	Citibank Account	COIN		
	T&E - Lodging		767,59	S	113100	Citibank Account	COIN		
	T&E - Lodging		775,20	S	113100	Citibank Account	COIN		
	T&E - Lodging		775,20-	S	113100	Citibank Account	RKU3	CTR	1820
Cost Center 1810 Sales Manager 1			8.466,36						
			8.466,36						

Figure 6.69 Line Item Report Following Reposting

6.4.2 Correcting an Activity Allocation

If an employee has posted time to the wrong order or WBS element, you can correct the line item for the direct activity allocation in much the same way, by using Transaction KB65 or following the menu path ACCOUNTING • CONTROLLING • COST CENTER ACCOUNTING • ACTUAL POSTINGS • ACTIVITY ALLOCATION REPOSTING • ENTER.

Figure 6.70 shows the ROW view for the correction. The difference is that the line item now contains the sender cost center and activity type, rather than the cost center and the travel cost element. You'll effectively be posting time in the form of an activity type rather than expenses to the new cost object.

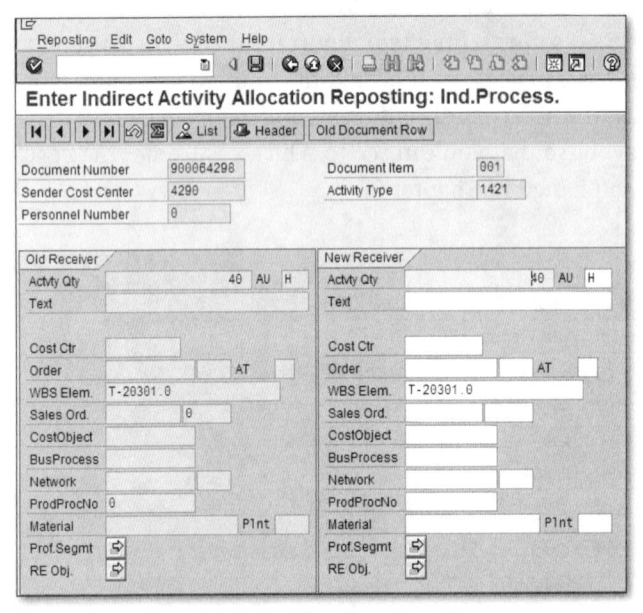

Figure 6.70 Repost Activity Allocation: Row View

6.4.3 Reposting Values

While the two previous transactions involved selecting the original document as the basis for the reposting, it's also possible to move costs from one account assignment to another. This again can be used to handle organizational changes, moving costs from one cost center to another. To repost from one cost center to another, use Transaction KB11N or follow the menu path ACCOUNTING • CONTROLLING • COST CENTER ACCOUNTING • ACTUAL POSTINGS • MANUAL REPOSTING OF COSTS • ENTER. To access the relevant account assignments in this transaction, select the appropriate screen variant (as we did for the direct activity allocation). Then enter the document date, the cost element, and the amount together with the old cost center and the new cost center (or whichever account assignment you're moving costs from and to) as shown in Figure 6.71.

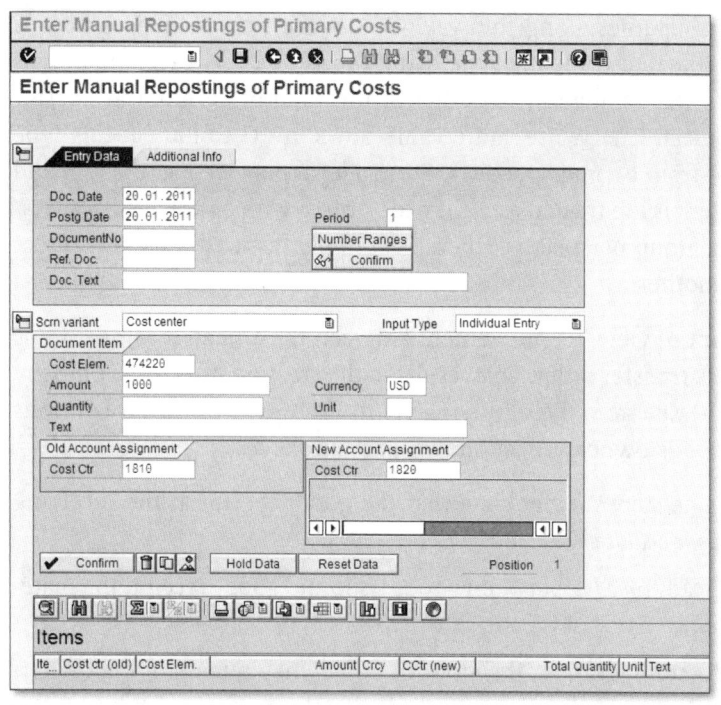

Figure 6.71 Manual Cost Reposting

The actual postings we've looked at so far have all been within the same company code. We'll now look at what happens when goods move from one affiliated company to another in the same group and at your options for cost accounting in such a situation.

6.5 Cross-Company Postings

We've looked at actual postings within a single company, but in today's global supply chains, it's common for several plants to be involved in manufacturing a single product and for these plants to belong to different legal entities. It's also common for organizations to have a central distribution center that's supplied by multiple plants that belong to different legal entities. In this case, as well as there being an initial purchase of the raw material from an external supplier and a final sale of the finished product to the end customer, there will be a sale and purchase of materials between affiliated companies along the way. One of the first challenges here is to make sure both affiliated companies are using the same code for the materials they're buying from and selling to each other. If this kind of harmonized master data is in place, you activate two separate value flows in CO to look at this type of goods movement from two perspectives. From a legal perspective, the sale and purchase of the materials are treated as if they took place with external customers/vendors, but from a group perspective, there has simply been a goods movement from one plant to another.

From a logistics point of view, the movement between the affiliated companies is handled using a stock transfer order. This results in the creation of a cross-company delivery and a goods issue from the supplying plant. There are a number of options for the transfer of goods ownership, as shown in Figure 6.72.

- There may be a one-step transfer such that the goods receipt at the receiving plant is recorded *immediately*.
- If there is a significant *time lag* between goods issue and goods receipt, the material may be posted to stock in transit.
- Depending on the configuration, the stock in transit may remain in the ownership of the supplying company or move immediately to the ownership of the receiving company
- The stock in transit may be transferred en route.

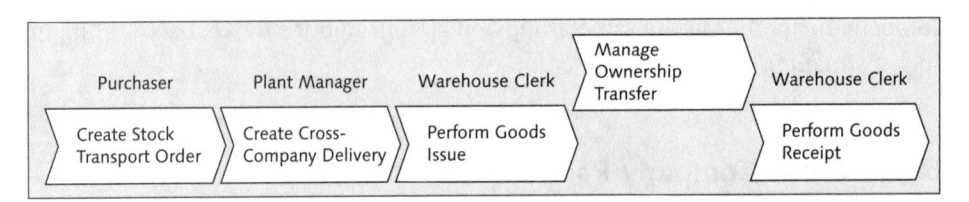

Figure 6.72 Cross-Company Stock Transport Order

From a financial point of view, there are two points to consider. One is the *legal transfer* of goods from one company to another. This takes place using pricing conditions just as if the materials were purchased from and sold to a nonaffiliated company (sometimes called *arm's length trading*). The other point is the group controlling view, where the intercompany markups can be eliminated and the flow treated as if it were taking place within the same company. This dual flow is enabled in the Material Ledger from SAP enhancement package 5 for SAP ERP 6.0 by activating the business function Cross-Company Code Stock Transfer & Actual Costing (LOG_MM_SIT).

We'll now look at an example of such a goods flow. Plant 2000 (Heathrow Hayes) in the United Kingdom has supplied material RH-3S-02 to plant 1000 (Hamburg) in Germany. Let's look first at the situation in the *supplying* plant, 2000 (Heathrow Hayes), by using Transaction CKM3N or following the menu path CONTROLLING • PRODUCT COST CONTROLLING • ACTUAL COSTING/MATERIAL LEDGER • INFORMATION SYSTEM • DETAILED REPORTS • MATERIAL PRICE ANALYSIS. Figure 6.73 shows the legal valuation (company code currency). Here we see a folder, PURCHASE ORDER (GROUP), which includes two goods transfers for the consumption or issue of 6 kg and 5 kg of material RH-3S-02 (the bottom two lines). Make a note of the document numbers for these two lines, since we'll need them later.

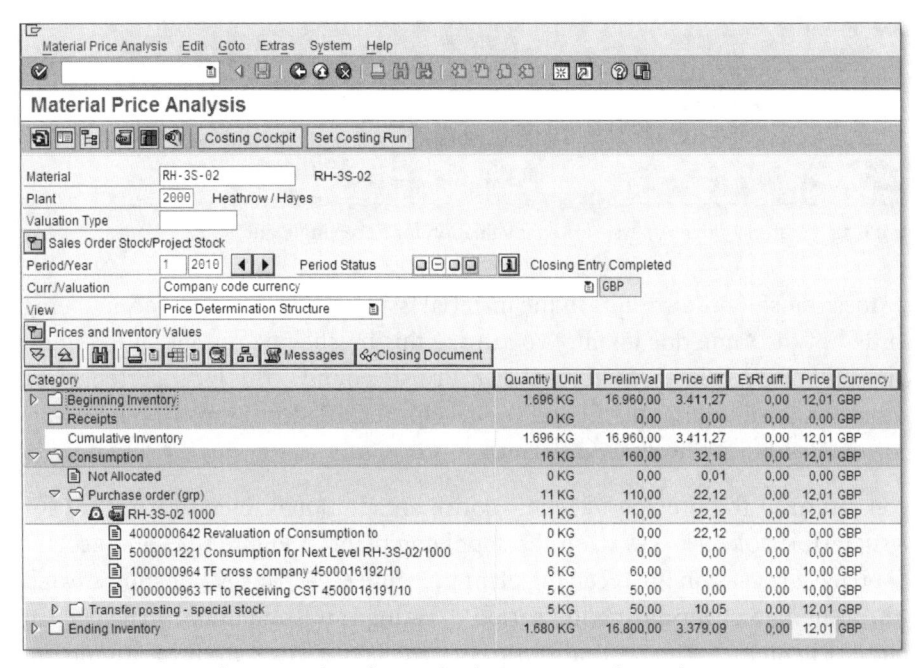

Figure 6.73 Material Price Analysis for Legal Valuation in Supplying Plant

Now let's look at the stock situation for the same material in plant 1000 (Hamburg). Figure 6.74 shows that the same materials have been *received*. The bottom lines show the same two document numbers as in Figure 6.73, but this time they appear in the RECEIPTS folder. We can also see that the receiving plant has been invoiced by the supplying plant.

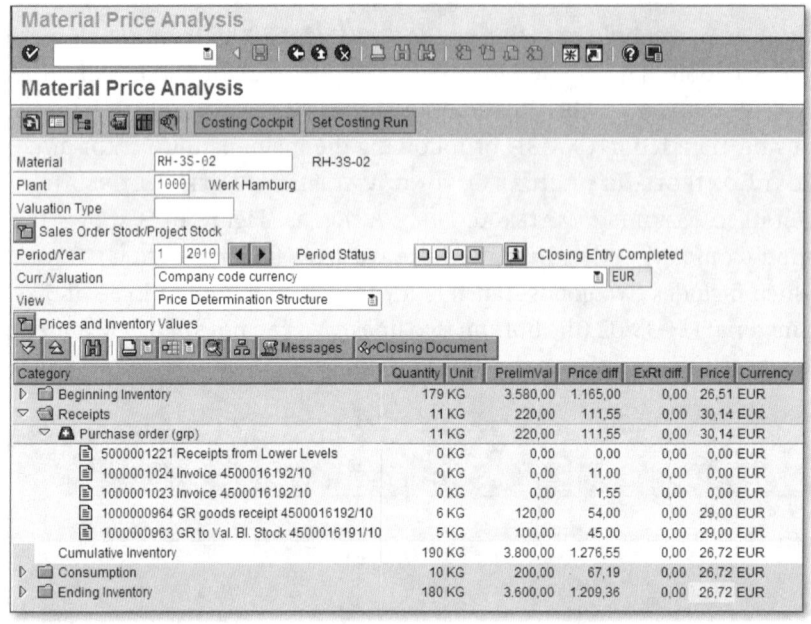

Category	Quantity	Unit	PrelimVal	Price diff	ExRt diff.	Price	Currency
▷ Beginning Inventory	179	KG	3.580,00	1.165,00	0,00	26,51	EUR
▽ Receipts	11	KG	220,00	111,55	0,00	30,14	EUR
▽ Purchase order (grp)	11	KG	220,00	111,55	0,00	30,14	EUR
5000001221 Receipts from Lower Levels	0	KG	0,00	0,00	0,00	0,00	EUR
1000001024 Invoice 4500016192/10	0	KG	0,00	11,00	0,00	0,00	EUR
1000001023 Invoice 4500016192/10	0	KG	0,00	1,55	0,00	0,00	EUR
1000000964 GR goods receipt 4500016192/10	6	KG	120,00	54,00	0,00	29,00	EUR
1000000963 GR to Val. Bl. Stock 4500016191/10	5	KG	100,00	45,00	0,00	29,00	EUR
Cumulative Inventory	190	KG	3.800,00	1.276,55	0,00	26,72	EUR
▷ Consumption	10	KG	200,00	67,19	0,00	26,72	EUR
▷ Ending Inventory	180	KG	3.600,00	1.209,36	0,00	26,72	EUR

Figure 6.74 Material Price Analysis in Legal Valuation for Receiving Plant

The stock transfer order results in the material issue and the material receipt being recorded in the same document. We can see this by clicking on one of the lines. Figure 6.75 shows the issue recorded in British pounds (the local currency for Heathrow, the supplying plant) and the receipt recorded in Euros (the local currency for Hamburg, the receiving plant).

If you return to the previous screens, notice an additional line at each plant for CONSUMPTION FOR NEXT LEVEL on the supplying plant in Figure 6.73 and RECEIPT FROM LOWER LEVELS on the receiving plant in Figure 6.74. This is a posting created by the Material Ledger during the periodic costing run (something we'll cover in detail in Chapter 7). The costing run passes the actual costs from the supplying plant to the receiving plant. In Figures 6.73 and 6.74 the value passed is zero, because we're looking at the legal valuation, which keeps the two companies at "arm's length." From a legal perspective Hamburg does not receive follow-on costs from Heathrow.

Cross-Company Postings | 6.5

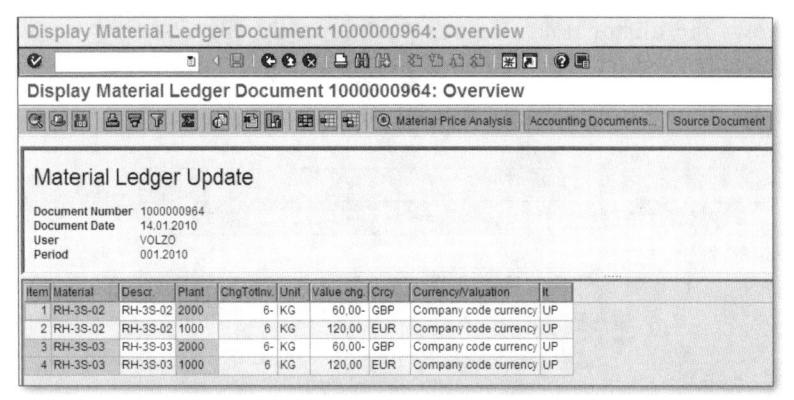

Figure 6.75 Material Ledger Document Showing Both Plants

However, a corporate controller expects to see this flow in its entirety. This can be done by switching to the *group view*. Usually, access to this view is restricted, and only corporate controllers with appropriate authorization can see the actual costs that have been passed between the companies during the costing run.

Figure 6.76 shows the same materials in group valuation. This time we can see that the CONSUMPTION FOR NEXT LEVEL line includes price differences of EUR 33.06 that were passed from Heathrow (supplying plant) to Hamburg (receiving plant).

Figure 6.76 Material Price Analysis in Group Valuation in Supplying Plant

Figure 6.77 shows the mirror image of this posting in the line RECEIPTS FROM LOWER LEVELS, where we can see the same EUR 33.06 being assigned to the receiving plant.

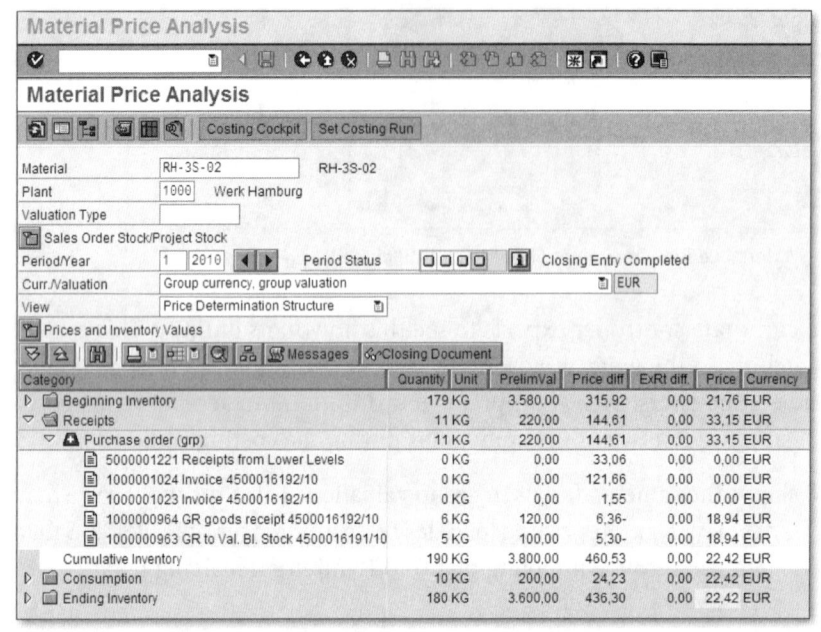

Figure 6.77 Material Price Analysis in Group Valuation in Receiving Plant

6.6 Summary

In this chapter we walked through the full process of buying, making, and selling goods and how to assign inventory variances. We looked at a number of process variants, including joint production, rework, and order splits, and different forms of product cost controlling (by order, by period, by sales order). We also looked at project controlling and integration with Time Management. Finally we looked at the options to repost costs in CO and how cross-company flows are captured in the Material Ledger. We'll now look at how these postings are handled in the period close and what adjustments are made to reflect the actual costs for the period completed in order to have a complete view of the costs and revenues in the organization.

This chapter provides an overview of the main allocations and calculations that take place at period close. It also shows you the tasks that make up multilevel actual costing and how to bring all data into CO-PA.

7   Period Close

In Chapter 1 we discussed the difference between postings that take place in *real time*, such as goods movements, and time recording and postings that take place at *period close*, such as allocations and order settlement. This is a significant change if you're moving from a legacy system where all of cost accounting effectively happens at period close after all relevant data has been loaded from the operational systems. The tasks themselves generally sound familiar enough, once you have mapped the SAP terminology to the terms you know. The other significant change is that in the SAP approach costs are not simply moved about within the Controlling component of SAP ERP Financials (CO), but postings to Financial Accounting are generated for work in process, revaluation of inventory, cost of goods sold, and so on.

This is because during the period SAP ERP uses the *standards* that were established in the planning process (see Chapter 5) to value all goods movements, confirmations, and time recording, since these assumptions are the most reliable source of data *at the time of posting*. As goods are issued from stock to production or sales, the supplier may not yet have submitted his invoice. As an operation is confirmed in production, the amount of energy used by the cost center in the period may not yet be known. The period close is the time to *adjust* these assumptions to reflect the reality of the business situation. You'll see the term *variance calculation* several times in the sections that follow. The difference between the original planning assumptions and reality is a *variance,* and it is the controlling department's job to work with the cost center managers and production managers to explain these variances and identify the root cause of any problems that have caused variances.

There are several approaches to variance analysis.

- If the raw material prices are stable and the production structures don't vary significantly, the organization tends to use *standard costs* and analyze its variances by department (purchasing, production, sales) but not adjust the value of inventory or cost of goods sold. The rationale is that if the planning assumptions were reliable, there's no need to make adjustments to the balance sheet.

- If the raw material prices are volatile or the production structures are constantly in flux, the organization tends to use *actual costs* and to push the variances through the production process, adjusting inventory values and cost of goods sold to reflect the variances.
- If the organization is presenting its financial statements according to multiple accounting principles, you may find both approaches in the same organization.

One frequently asked question is how often to close the books. For almost all CO processes, the close is identical in each fiscal period. For fast-moving orders, it's possible to run actual costing more frequently than once per period so you can react quickly to changing cost situations. This function is available from SAP enhancement package 4 for SAP ERP 6.0. However, inventory revaluation and other processes affecting Financial Accounting are only supported once per period.

The good news is that much of the closing process can be automated. We'll look at how to manage and automate the close in Chapter 12. In this chapter we'll focus on what happens in each closing step to help you understand the implications of performing each step. We'll start by looking at the different forms of allocations.

7.1 Allocations

An allocation is simply a movement of costs from one cost center to another, from a cost center to an order or project or from a cost center to the relevant market segment to allow profitability analysis.

- In the SAP approach some of the allocations have *already* happened. The costs to convert raw materials into products have already been assigned to the production orders when the orders or operations were confirmed or backflushed. The costs to perform maintenance operations have already been charged to the relevant receivers when the maintenance orders were confirmed. Any process with a time recording is already allocated. If you refer back to the activity type master data in Chapter 3, any category 1 (manual entry, manual allocation) activity type has probably already been allocated. Here the question is whether an *adjustment* needs to be made because the standard activity rates were not accurate enough or if the difference will simply be treated as a cost center variance.

- In addition allocations are used to move sales, administration, and marketing expenses from the departments where the expenses were originally captured to the relevant market segments, in other words from Cost Center Accounting to CO-PA.
- Other allocations are used to move the costs on supporting cost centers, such as rent and energy, to the operational cost centers.

This can require the creation of a more or less complex network of allocation cycles to move costs around the organization. While the controller could sit back and watch as the real-time allocations were posted, at period close he's in the driver's seat, ensuring that the allocation cycles are correctly prepared and that all relevant data is available. In this context, it's also worth bearing in mind that one of the guiding principles of lean accounting is that costs should be assigned directly to the value stream and not allocated in endless wasteful iterations.

Figure 7.1 provides an overview of all tasks to be performed in Cost Center Accounting. This is the equivalent of following the menu path ACCOUNTING • CONTROLLING • COST CENTER ACCOUNTING • PERIOD-END CLOSING. One folder contains the Schedule Manager, which can be used to manage the period close. We'll look at this tool in more detail in Chapter 12. Another folder includes tasks such as activity price calculation and variance calculation that are used to calculate whether an adjustment is needed (activity price calculation) and to analyze the difference between the planning assumptions and the actual postings.

Before we look at the contents of the ALLOCATIONS folder, you should be aware of the meaning of the CURRENT SETTINGS folder.

- For consistency, some organizations maintain their allocation cycles in their Customizing system and then transport them to the productive system, making only emergency changes in the productive system (the one where you execute the close).
- Others maintain the allocation cycles only in the productive system.

Either way, if you need to make a change, use the CURRENT SETTINGS folder that contains a list of all allocation cycles.

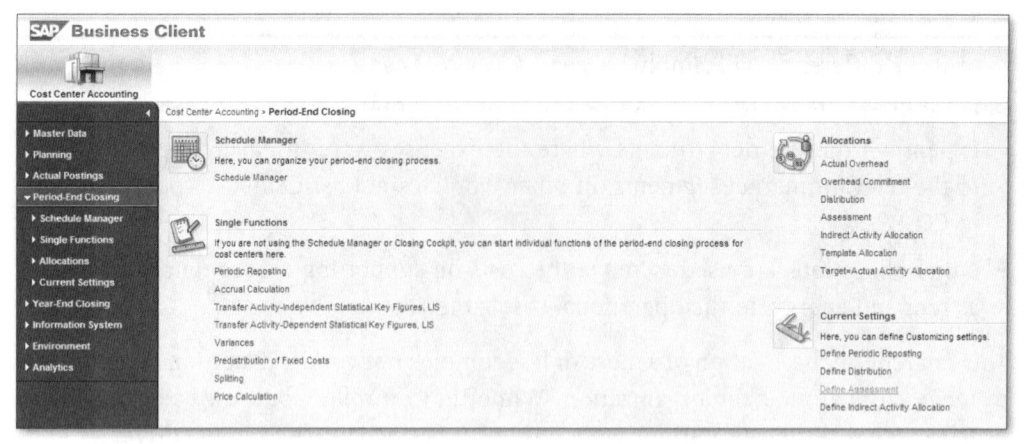

Figure 7.1 Period Close Tasks in Cost Center Accounting

7.1.1 Steps Prior to the Start of the Period Close

Before we talk about the closing tasks in detail, it makes sense to ensure that all relevant data will be available before close can commence. Billing and payroll are typical tasks that take place in the days running up to the end of the month. Billing brings revenue into CO-PA and assigns revenue to commercial projects and orders. It's especially important in industries with contract accounting (such as utilities and telecommunications), where most of the billing is done once a month. Payroll brings wage and salary costs to the relevant cost centers. It's not always a monthly process, but it makes sense to ensure that all payroll-related expenses are available in CO before embarking on the steps described below.

7.1.2 Depreciation of Fixed Assets

The costs of fixed assets (property, plant, and equipment) have to be matched against the revenues earned by their use. The asset is acquired at a given time via purchase or production. This one-off cost must be spread over the useful life of the asset. This spreading process is known as *depreciation* and is used to transfer the costs of the fixed assets to the periods in which the assets are used. All assets contain a link to the cost center, though they can be linked with an order or WBS element. Usually the asset depreciation run is executed by an asset accountant, but a controller often checks the asset-cost center assignment to ensure consistency. Figure 7.2 shows the master data for the property on which the cost center for pump assembly 4230 is located. To display the fixed asset, follow the menu path ACCOUNTING • FINANCIAL ACCOUNTING • FIXED ASSETS • ASSET • DISPLAY • ASSET or use Transaction AS03. Enter the name of the asset and the company code. The link between the asset and cost center is valid for a specified time period. To display the cost center assignment, select the TIME-DEPENDENT tab. There can be many methods of depreciation for the same asset, so it's a good idea to also check the entries on the DEPRECIATION AREAS tab.

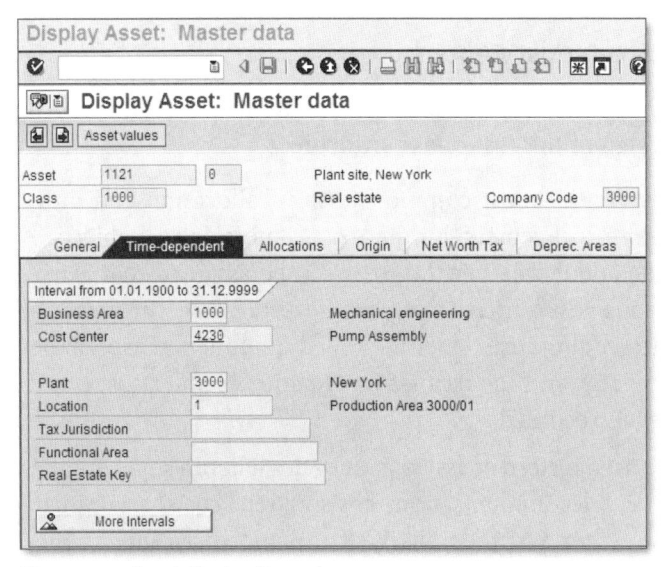

Figure 7.2 Asset Master Record

For cost accounting purposes only one method of depreciation was reflected in COST CENTER ACCOUNTING until the latest release of SAP ERP. This transfer involved linking one depreciation area with the leading ledger. SAP enhancement package 5 for SAP ERP 6.0 introduced the business function Parallel Valuation of Cost of Goods Manufactured (FIN_CO_COGM). This allows you to link more than one depreciation areas with Cost Center Accounting, taking each set of values into a different *version*. We'll see the term *version* time and time again in our discussions on the period close. Whereas the versions we encountered in planning represented different planning assumptions (optimistic, pessimistic, and so on), the versions for the actual values are used to separate value flows according to different accounting principles in CO. So one version might represent values under IFRS and another could represent values under local GAAP.

- Whenever you perform a step in the period close, you store the appropriate allocation, calculation, settlement, or whatever in version 0. In Customizing version 0 is flagged as relevant for legal valuation.
- Some steps of the period close can also store data in another version so that the data is available for valuation according to the alternative GAAP. This version is flagged as relevant for parallel cost of goods manufactured in Customizing. Going forward, we'll mention this additional version whenever it's relevant.

7.1.3 Allocations Between Cost Centers

As shown in Figure 7.1, there can be many forms of allocations between cost centers, depending on the design of the cost center structure.

- *Assessment cycles* are by far the most common form of allocation and move *amounts* from one or more cost centers to other cost centers or cost objects. A decision has to be made about whether the costs can be assigned to a *market segment* or from supporting cost centers to productive *cost centers*. The details of all cost elements on the sending cost center are rolled up under an assessment cost element (see Chapter 3), and the partner information (sender cost center and receiver cost center) is recorded.
- *Distribution cycles* can be used instead of assessment cycles where a small number of cost elements (such as telecommunications costs or rent costs) are initially posted to a single cost center and then charged to many cost centers. They work according to the same basic principle as assessment cycles but transfer the original primary cost element to the receiving cost center. Because of the data volumes, it makes sense to use them where the sender cost center only has a few cost elements.
- *Reposting cycles* provide a more compact way of allocating costs than distribution cycles since they don't update the sender cost center as a partner in the totals record. This information can only be viewed in the line items.
- *Indirect activity allocation cycles* are used to move activity quantities between cost centers. They work in much the same way as assessment cycles, but a quantity (such as the total number of labor hours worked by a call center or the total number of kilowatt hours supplied to a group of production cost centers) is allocated rather than the costs of the call center or energy cost center. This quantity is valued with the activity price (calculated during planning).

Before we compare the different types of allocation, you might want to check what's already active in your system. The overview is slightly hidden, but if you select any of the allocation types (for instance, ACCOUNTING • CONTROLLING • COST CENTER ACCOUNTING • PERIOD-END CLOSING • CURRENT SETTINGS • DEFINE ASSESSMENT) and then EXTRAS • CYCLE • DISPLAY OVERVIEW, you can then choose the type of allocations you're interested in by selecting the relevant checkboxes under CYCLE TYPE and then clicking on the EXECUTE button to see all the cycles in your controlling area.

Figure 7.3 shows all the allocation cycles active in controlling area 2000 in our demo system. Many controllers keep a list like this in spreadsheets to remind them of the structure of the cycles they use.

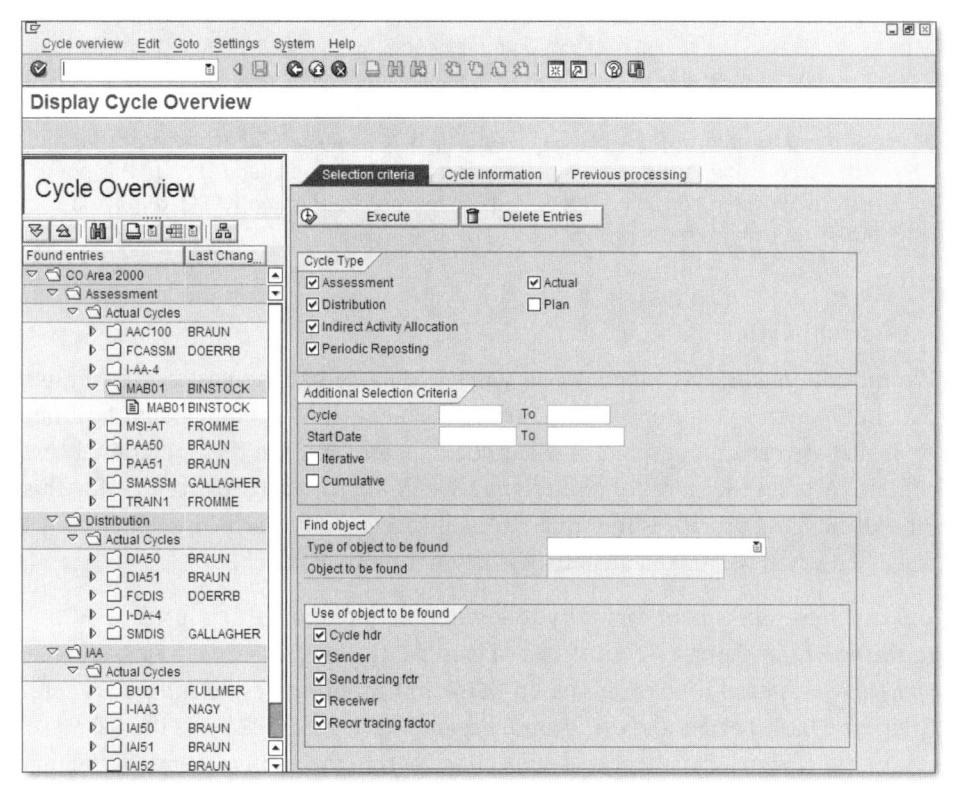

Figure 7.3 Cycle Overview

One of the most useful functions in the overview is the FIND OBJECT function, since there will inevitably be some cost center that has been locked and needs to be removed from the cycles in the run up to the period close. To select the object you're looking for, make a selection in the TYPE OF OBJECT TO BE FOUND field and then select, for example, COST CENTER, enter the cost center in question, and click on EXECUTE. Once you've identified the cycle you're interested in, you can display the details of each segment by selecting the CYCLE INFORMATION tab or details of the previous allocations by selecting the PREVIOUS PROCESSING tab.

> **Real-Time Integration of CO with Financial Accounting**
>
> When you're building up allocation cycles it's easy to become so focused on finding the right senders and receivers that you forget the impact of allocations on other areas. With this in mind, refer back to Chapter 3, Section 3.1.3, where we discussed the impact of the assignment of the cost center to a company code, functional area, and profit center. When you perform an allocation, it's more than likely that in moving costs between cost centers you'll also move them between profit centers, functional areas, or even company codes. If you use the SAP ERP General Ledger, this means you generate a posting in Financial Accounting at the same time. If you use the classic General Ledger, this posting is stored in the reconciliation ledger until you use Transaction KALC to move it to the other company code.

Assessment Cycles

We introduced the assessment cycle when we looked at the cost center master data in Chapter 3. A common business requirement is the need to assign facilities costs that are usually captured on a supporting cost center to the operational cost centers. A good measure for the relative weighting of each cost center for this kind of charging process is the square footage occupied by each cost center, as we discussed when we looked at statistical key figures in Chapter 3.

You can view assessment cycles by following the menu path ACCOUNTING • CONTROLLING • COST CENTER ACCOUNTING • PERIOD-END CLOSING • CURRENT SETTINGS • DEFINE ASSESSMENT or via Transaction KSU2 and choosing a cycle and a start date. Each cycle has a header and one or more segments. Figure 7.4 shows the SEGMENT HEADER tab for an assessment cycle that allocates rent to various other departments according to the statistical key figure square feet.

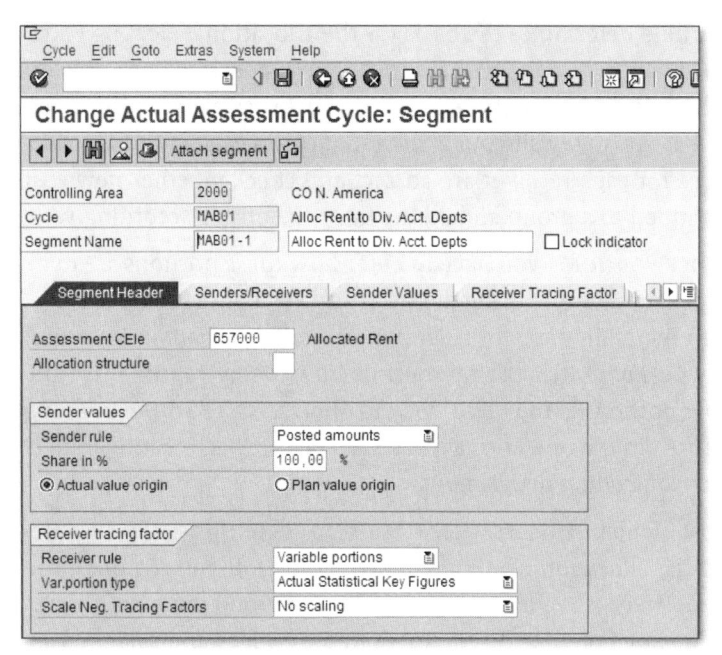

Figure 7.4 Segment Header for Assessment Cycle

One of the things that make assessment cycles tricky at first is that the screen layout is highly dynamic. Changing the type of sender rule or receiver rule can result in new fields appearing on the screens and the tabs changing to reflect the different inputs needed.

- The SENDER RULE field determines whether you're simply going to allocate all the costs on the cost center (POSTED AMOUNTS) or a fixed amount or fixed rate. Posted amounts is by far the most common approach and requires no work in preparation for the period close, since the costs on the sender cost centers are read during allocation. Fixed amounts and fixed rate require you to update the cycle prior to allocation but can be useful if you want to calculate the amounts for an allocation in an external system or spreadsheet and then load them to the assessment cycle. This might be the case if you want to calculate the work performed for different departments by a shared service center and then enter these manually as sender values in the segment.

- The Receiver Rule field determines the basis for the allocation. Selecting Fixed Amounts, Fixed Percentages, or Fixed Portions might seem like the easiest way to get started because it's an easy rule for everyone to understand. However, this type of rule forces you to revisit your assessment cycles each month to make sure the percentages for each receiver are correct and check whether new cost centers have been added to a group and adjust the percentages accordingly.

    If you select Variable Portions, you have to enter how these portions are to be determined. In our example we're using the statistical key figure square footage, which we'll have to maintain once for each cost center (see Chapter 3, Section 3.3). Generally, if you know that the relevant detail is being captured for the cost center, variable portions is the better way to allocate since you're building on data being captured in the operational processes rather than creating unnecessary work for the controlling department.

- The assessment cost element (Assessment CEle field) determines the cost element under which the allocation posting will be recorded. If you require more detail than this, you can enter an allocation structure to group the costs according to their origins, allowing you to see, for example, wages and salary costs, material costs, and depreciation separately.

The next step is to define the partners in the allocation, in other words, which cost center is sending costs and which cost centers will be receiving costs, by navigating to the Senders/Receivers tab. Figure 7.5 shows the sender cost center MB1300 (Administration) and the sender cost element 470000 (Office and Building). The receivers are all cost centers in group MGTACCTG. If you're not sure which cost centers are assigned to the receiver group, select the Receiver Weighting Factors tab on the far right, where you'll see all cost centers in group MGTACCTG. The entries in this cost center group will be expanded during the allocation. If new cost centers are added to the group, they'll automatically be included in the allocation, provided you ensure that the statistical key figure square footage is maintained for the new cost centers.

Before you can perform an allocation with the sender rule variable portions, you must define the key figure to be used to establish the ratio between the cost centers. To do this, select the Receiver Tracing Factor tab. Figure 7.6 shows that the rule type is Actual Statistical Key Figures (transferred from Figure 7.3), and the key figure is SQFT.

7.1 Allocations

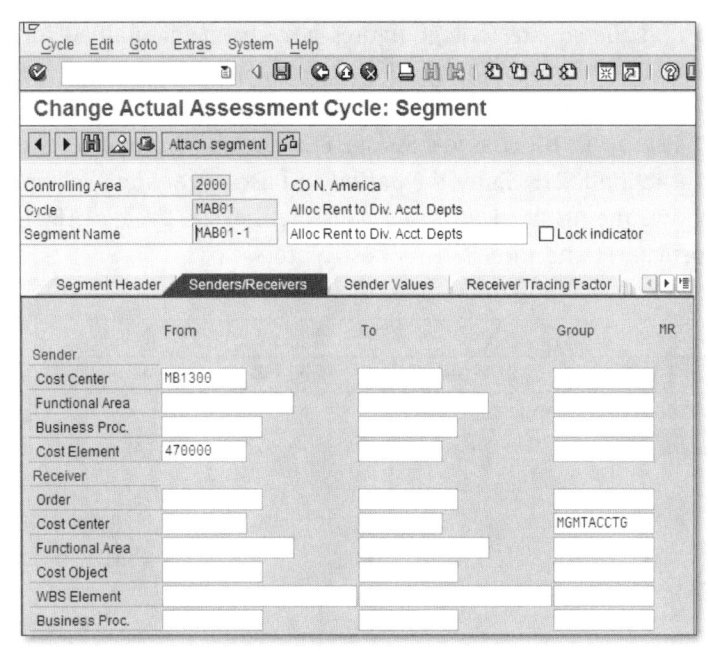

Figure 7.5 Sender/Receivers for Assessment Cycle

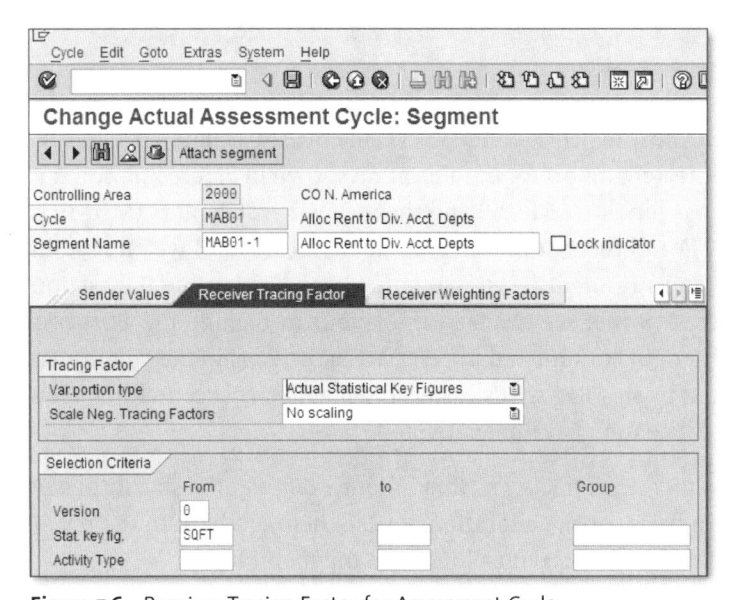

Figure 7.6 Receiver Tracing Factor for Assessment Cycle

7 | Period Close

Once you've checked that the square footage figures have been maintained for each cost center (we explained how to do this in Chapter 3, Section 3.3), execute the allocation by following the menu path ACCOUNTING • CONTROLLING • COST CENTER ACCOUNTING • PERIOD-END CLOSING • SINGLE FUNCTIONS • ALLOCATIONS • ASSESSMENT or via Transaction KSU5. Enter the period and fiscal year and click on EXECUTE. Figure 7.7 shows the results list for this assessment cycle. Cycle MAB01 contains one *sender* cost center and three *receiver* cost centers.

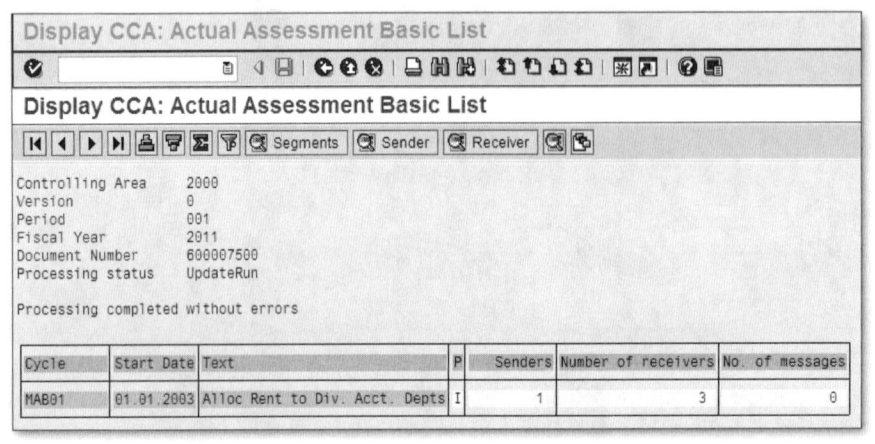

Figure 7.7 Result of Assessment Cycle

To display details of the posting, click on the CYCLE line (MAB01) in the results list. This takes you to the line item report for the allocation shown in Figure 7.8. You can see both the sender cost center (MB1300) and the receiver cost centers (MB1391, MB2391, and MB3391) and the assessment cost element (657000) we entered in the segment header. You can identify assessments for auditing with Transaction RKIU. Notice in Figure 7.8 that we changed the layout to include the BUSINESS TRANSACTION in the far right column and the DEBIT/CREDIT flags in the column on the left. We then sorted by this flag so it's easier to see which cost center has been credited and which cost centers have been debited.

This report does not show what tracing factors (in our example, the statistical key figures) were used as a basis for the allocation. To see them, go back to the result list (Figure 7.7) and click on the RECEIVER button in the menu bar.

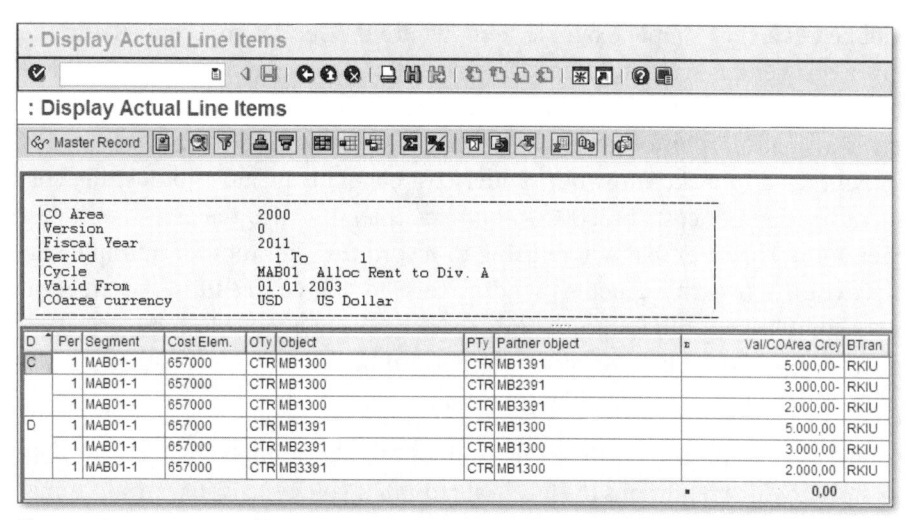

Figure 7.8 Line Items Following Execution of Assessment Cycle

Figure 7.9 shows the tracing factors on the receiver cost centers that were used for the allocation. In our example, cost center MB1391 had 50 square feet, cost center MB2391 had 30 square feet, and cost center MB3391 had 20 square feet. The rent costs have been split in this ratio: 5,000 to 3,000 to 2,000. In both reports notice the assessment cost element 657000 that we entered in the segment header. You'll see this as a line in your cost center reports, recording the credit to the sender and the debit to the receiver cost centers.

Figure 7.9 Tracing Factors on Receiver Cost Centers

We looked at a very simple example here, where the sender cost centers and the receiver cost centers were different. Assessment cycles often involve cyclical relationship where one cost center passes its costs to "all" cost centers and by definition receives a small portion of its own costs back. If you want to create this sort of cycle, you need to make sure your sender cost elements include not just the cost element for the rent costs (470000 in our example), but also the assessment cost element (657000 here) that you're using to record the allocation. If multiple segments exist where each segment is sending costs to "all" cost centers, the situation is more complicated still. In recent years there has been a move in some organizations to unravel such iterative cycles since it can be difficult to trace their results reliably, but they are still relatively common.

If you use other reports to analyze the result of this allocation, you'll find the data in version 0 (which represents the legal valuation). If you've activated an additional version for the parallel valuation of cost of goods manufactured, a second set of values will be used in the allocation. To view these values in reporting, you have to select the other version as you execute the report.

Using Cycle Run Groups for Allocations

All allocation cycles are defined at the controlling area level and automatically assigned to Cycle Run Group 0000. Because of the iterative nature of many cycles, only one assessment cycle can run at a time to ensure consistency. If you want to run assessment cycles in parallel, for example, because you want to allocate the costs from all cost centers in company code A and all cost centers in company code B at the same time, create two cycle run groups, one for company code A and one for company code B. To create a cycle run group, select Goto • Cycle Run Group from within the cycle. If you use cycle run groups, be careful to ensure that the cycles really are independent of each other, since the system will no longer check this.

Distribution Cycles

Once you understand the basic principles of working with assessment cycles, you'll find that the other types of cycle are similar. The proper term for what happens during the execution of a distribution cycle is *primary cost distribution*. These cycles make sense when you use a supporting cost center to capture a few very specific primary costs (such as telephone costs) and then want to distribute these over many cost centers. The main visual difference between an assessment and a distribution cycle is that you don't need to enter an assessment cost element. This is because the original cost element (whatever account was used to record the telephone costs) will be used in the posting. You should also be careful when defining the senders to only include primary cost elements as senders when you choose the cost element group. Most organizations have a numbering scheme that makes it easy to identify cost elements tied to accounts (primary) and cost elements used to record allocations (secondary).

You can view distribution cycles by following the menu path ACCOUNTING • CONTROLLING • COST CENTER ACCOUNTING • PERIOD-END CLOSING • CURRENT SETTINGS • DEFINE DISTRIBUTION or using Transaction KSV2 and entering the cycle. Figure 7.10 shows the segment header for a distribution cycle. This distributes the telephone costs to several operational cost centers based on the square footage of office space entered for those cost centers.

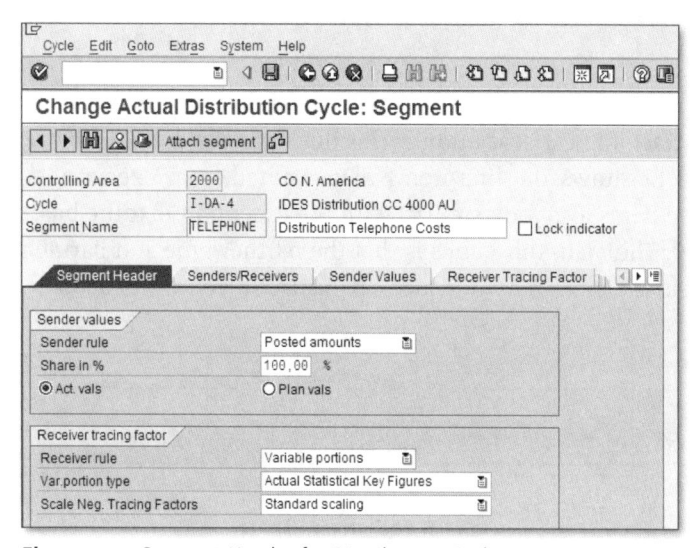

Figure 7.10 Segment Header for Distribution Cycle

To execute the distribution, follow the menu path ACCOUNTING • CONTROLLING • COST CENTER ACCOUNTING • PERIOD-END CLOSING • SINGLE FUNCTIONS • ALLOCATIONS • DISTRIBUTION or use Transaction KSV5. Enter the period and fiscal year and click on EXECUTE. Figure 7.11 shows the line items created during the distribution. If you compare this list with Figure 7.8, you'll see that the cost element is the primary cost element under which the telephone costs were captured. The sender cost center is 4-1210, and the receiver cost centers are 4-1000, 4-1110, and 4-1200. The business transaction is RKIV.

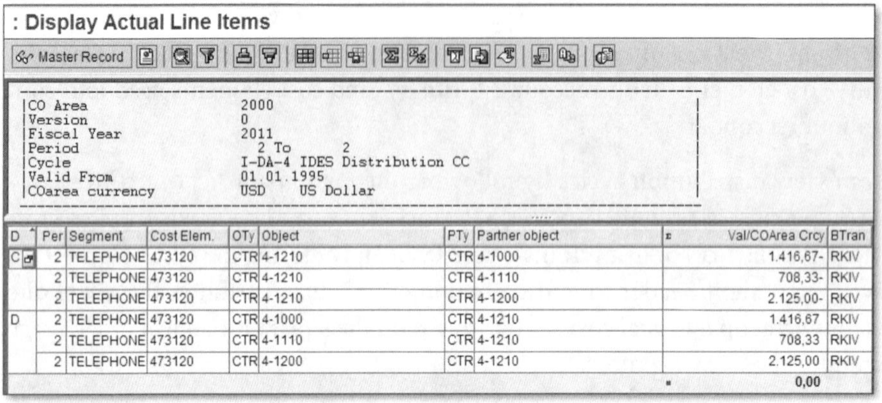
: Display Actual Line Items

CO Area	2000
Version	0
Fiscal Year	2011
Period	2 To 2
Cycle	I-DA-4 IDES Distribution CC
Valid From	01.01.1995
COarea currency	USD US Dollar

D	Per	Segment	Cost Elem.	OTy	Object	PTy	Partner object	Val/COArea Crcy	BTran
C	2	TELEPHONE	473120	CTR	4-1210	CTR	4-1000	1.416,67-	RKIV
	2	TELEPHONE	473120	CTR	4-1210	CTR	4-1110	708,33-	RKIV
	2	TELEPHONE	473120	CTR	4-1210	CTR	4-1200	2.125,00-	RKIV
D	2	TELEPHONE	473120	CTR	4-1000	CTR	4-1210	1.416,67	RKIV
	2	TELEPHONE	473120	CTR	4-1110	CTR	4-1210	708,33	RKIV
	2	TELEPHONE	473120	CTR	4-1200	CTR	4-1210	2.125,00	RKIV
								0,00	

Figure 7.11 Line Items Following Execution of Distribution Cycle

Reposting Cycles

Reposting cycles look exactly like distribution cycles but store the data in a more compact way. Figure 7.12 shows the line items that resulted from executing a reposting cycle. The line items also look similar, with the exception that the business transaction is RKIB. The main difference is that the partner type and partner object are not included in the totals record, which saves space if you won't actually be reporting on these.

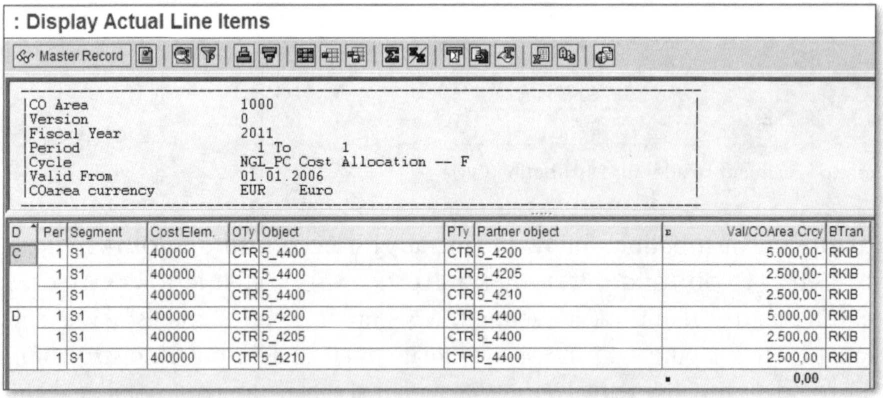
: Display Actual Line Items

CO Area	1000
Version	0
Fiscal Year	2011
Period	1 To 1
Cycle	NGL_PC Cost Allocation -- F
Valid From	01.01.2006
COarea currency	EUR Euro

D	Per	Segment	Cost Elem.	OTy	Object	PTy	Partner object	Val/COArea Crcy	BTran
C	1	S1	400000	CTR	5_4400	CTR	5_4200	5.000,00-	RKIB
	1	S1	400000	CTR	5_4400	CTR	5_4205	2.500,00-	RKIB
	1	S1	400000	CTR	5_4400	CTR	5_4210	2.500,00-	RKIB
D	1	S1	400000	CTR	5_4200	CTR	5_4400	5.000,00	RKIB
	1	S1	400000	CTR	5_4205	CTR	5_4400	2.500,00	RKIB
	1	S1	400000	CTR	5_4210	CTR	5_4400	2.500,00	RKIB
								0,00	

Figure 7.12 Line Items Following Execution of a Reposting Cycle

Indirect Activity Allocation Cycles

The main difference between an assessment and an indirect activity allocation cycle is that the sender is not a cost center but is the combination of a cost center and an activity type (see Chapter 3). You should use an indirect activity allocation cycle whenever the quantity (such as kilowatt hours) rather than the amount is important. So a quality cost center might record the total *time in hours* worked by the quality staff and then allocate this quantity to the production cost centers based on a statistical key figure such as number of units produced, or an energy cost center might allocate the *kilowatt hours* provided to the production cost centers based on the machine hours confirmed by the production cost centers. Since it's the *quantity* rather than the amount that's allocated, you also need to define an activity price before you execute such allocations. You can view indirect activity allocation cycles by following the menu path ACCOUNTING • CONTROLLING • COST CENTER ACCOUNTING • PERIOD-END CLOSING • CURRENT SETTINGS DEFINE INDIRECT ACTIVITY ALLOCATION or using Transaction KSC2 and choosing a cycle.

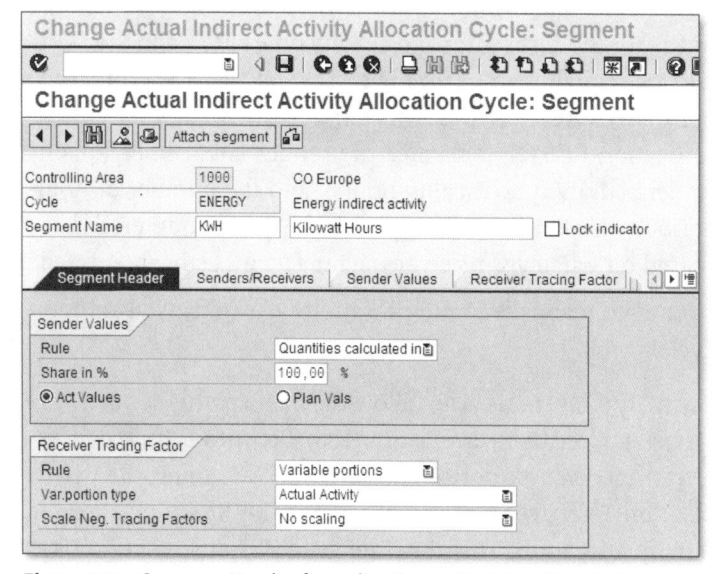

Figure 7.13 Segment Header for Indirect Activity Allocation Cycle

Figure 7.13 shows the SEGMENT HEADER tab for an indirect activity allocation cycle. The main difference compared to the assessment cycle is in the sender rule, where you have the options POSTED QUANTITIES, FIXED QUANTITIES, and QUANTITIES CALCULATED INVERSELY since you're sending activity quantities rather than amounts. At this stage, it makes sense to check the master data of the activity type you intend to use (see Chapter 3).

- The QUANTITIES CALCULATED INVERSELY option is used in combination with category 2 activity types (indirect determination, indirect allocation). The inverse calculation reads the quantity entered under RECEIVER TRACING FACTOR (in our example, this is the ACTUAL ACTIVITY option) to determine how much energy has been supplied. The underlying assumption is that the more production activity the production cost centers have provided, the more kilowatt hours of energy they will have used. If the relationship between machine time and kilowatt hours of energy is not 1:1, you need to tab to the far right in Figure 7.13 and change the receiver weighting factor from 100 (the default) to a factor that better reflects your business needs.

- The POSTED QUANTITIES option is used in combination with category 3 activity types (manual entry, indirect allocation). To use this option, every month you need to enter a quantity for the cost center and activity type entered in the SENDERS/RECEIVERS tab. To enter quality hours for the cost center, go to ACCOUNTING • CONTROLLING • COST CENTER ACCOUNTING • ACTUAL POSTINGS • SENDER ACTIVITIES • ENTER or Transaction KB51N and enter the sender cost center (quality cost center), the sender activity type (quality hours), and the number of hours performed in the period. The allocation then spreads the quantity entered to the selected receivers based on whatever receiver tracing factor has been entered.

- Fixed quantities are entered manually in the allocation cycle (like fixed amounts in an assessment cycle).

To execute an indirect activity allocation cycle, follow the menu path ACCOUNTING • CONTROLLING • COST CENTER ACCOUNTING • PERIOD-END CLOSING • SINGLE FUNCTIONS • INDIRECT ACTIVITY ALLOCATION or use Transaction KSC5. Enter the period and fiscal year and click on EXECUTE. Figure 7.14 shows the line items created during the indirect activity allocation. This time the sender is an activity (OTYPE ATY) rather than a cost center, and the receivers are the production cost centers that have performed work in the period. The amounts are calculated by multiplying the number of kilowatt hours by the activity price for one kilowatt hour. The business transaction is RKIL.

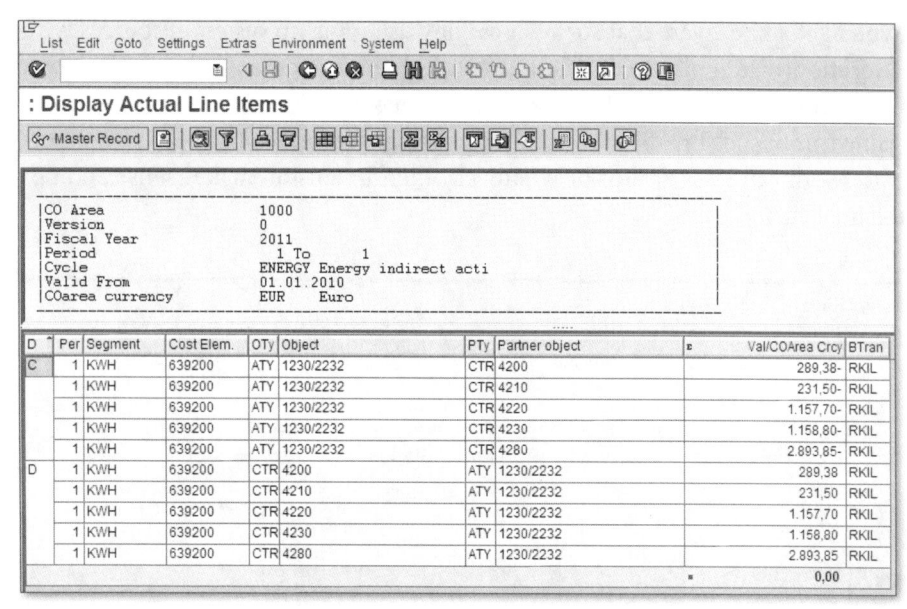

Figure 7.14 Line Items Following Execution of Indirect Activity Cycle

7.1.4 Allocations to Profitability Analysis

The allocations we've discussed so far were all initiated in Cost Center Accounting. As we saw when we looked at the planning process in Chapter 5, there are also allocations that are initiated in Profitability Analysis. Figure 7.15 provides an overview of the period-close activities in PROFITABILITY ANALYSIS. Note that only assessment and indirect activity allocation cycles are supported. Distribution cycles are redundant since for costing-based CO-PA the values on the cost centers are always mapped to value fields. Generally, allocation cycles in PROFITABILITY ANALYSIS tend to be created in Customizing to ensure consistency, so you won't find a CURRENT SETTINGS folder here, as we had in Cost Center Accounting.

Allocations to PROFITABILITY ANALYSIS follow a pattern similar to allocations in Cost Center Accounting. The main difference is that the senders are the cost centers but the receivers can be any characteristic in Profitability Analysis (see Chapter 2). One of the main decisions to be made in the context of allocating costs to CO-PA is whether you want to take the costs down to the lowest level of detail—to charge costs to individual customers and products—or whether a higher level of detail, such as a product group or sales region is sufficient. It can be tempting to charge all expenses to customers and products to see the full costs on these dimensions, but you need to be aware that such allocations risk tying up system resources with an allocation that applies a couple of cents to each customer. Break down costs to the product and customer level only when there's sufficient business insight to be gained from such an allocation. It's completely acceptable to apply some costs only to regions or sales groups or whatever other dimension makes sense and not to the final customer.

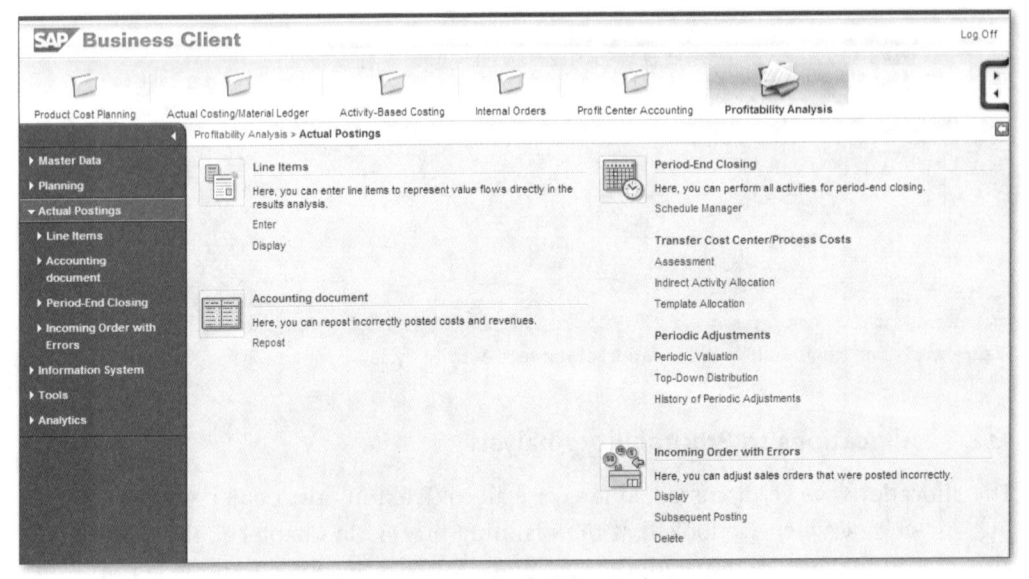

Figure 7.15 Period-End Close Activities in Profitability Analysis

To display an assessment cycle, follow the menu path ACCOUNTING • CONTROLLING • PROFITABILITY ANALYSIS • ACTUAL POSTINGS • PERIOD END CLOSING • ASSESSMENT and then EXTRAS • CYCLE • CHANGE or use Transaction KEU2. Figure 7.16 shows the segment header for the allocation of research and development costs to the company's divisions. Again it's important to consider the practicality of your cycles in terms of the receiver rules. If you select FIXED PORTIONS as the receiver rule, you'll have to manually enter the split to each of the company's industries, customer groups, divisions, and sales organizations—a tedious manual effort each month. If, instead, you select the sender rule VARIABLE PORTIONS, you simply enter the value field to be used to determine the ratio for each characteristic. In our example, the allocation will be based on the cost of goods sold recorded for each division.

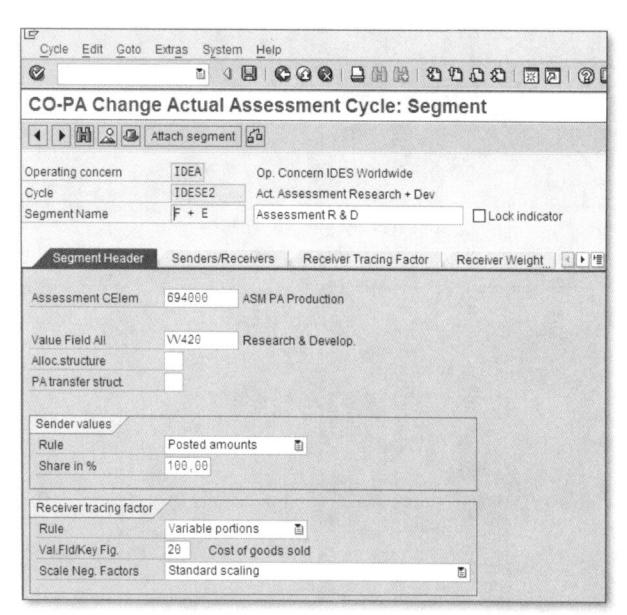

Figure 7.16 Segment Header with Receiver Rule "Variable Portions"

Figure 7.17 shows the SENDERS/RECEIVERS tab for this segment. Since it's possible to allocate costs to any characteristic in Profitability Analysis (there can be up to 50 different characteristics), you almost always need to scroll down the receiver list to see all relevant receivers. Here the sender cost center is a research and development cost center (not on the screen), whose costs are going to be charged to the divisions for which it works. You can also assign the values to more than one characteristic, so you might assign the R&D costs not just to the divisions supported, but also to other organizational units associated with those divisions. As we mentioned earlier, it makes sense to consider performance issues when defining which characteristics should be the receiver of an allocation and to stop at the level of detail that makes sense from a business perspective. If you try to assign all overhead to the lowest-level characteristics, product, or customer, tiny amounts will inevitably be assigned to all customers or products, adding no real business insight.

Now all you have to do is define which record types will be read from Profitability Analysis as a basis for the allocation. Figure 7.18 shows that we'll use record type F (for billing data) to determine the cost of goods sold. As we said for the cost center allocations, basing your allocations on data that the system records anyway is much preferred over fixed percentages, because it saves preparatory work checking the tracing factors in the run-up to the period close.

7 | Period Close

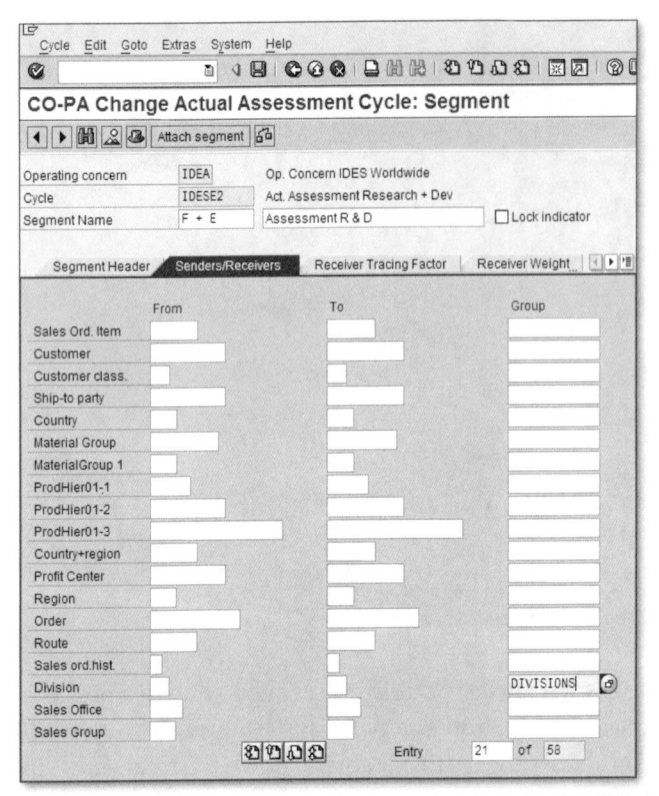

Figure 7.17 Senders/Receivers in Assessment Cycle to Profitability Analysis

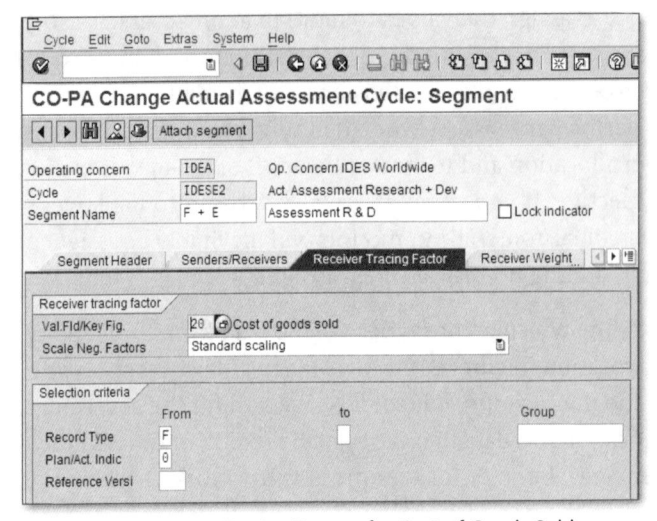

Figure 7.18 Receiver Tracing Factors for Cost of Goods Sold

To perform an allocation, follow the menu path ACCOUNTING • CONTROLLING • PROFITABILITY ANALYSIS • ACTUAL POSTINGS • PERIOD END CLOSING • ASSESSMENT or use Transaction KEU5.

7.1.5 Target Costs and Variances on Cost Centers

When all the allocations for the period have been completed, the following tasks remain for the cost centers.

- For cost centers *without* activity types, check that the balance on the cost center is zero (all costs have been allocated) and analyze any variances between planned costs and actual costs.

- For cost centers *with* activity types, check the balance on the cost center. This is rarely zero because the activity allocations were performed using a standard rate that does not include any variances that occurred during the period. However, this kind of cost center has an output quantity (the amount of machine hours supplied, the amount of kilowatt hours supplied, and so on). This quantity is used to adjust the plan to calculate the *target costs,* in other words, the costs that should have been incurred to provide that level of activity. In this case, variance calculation is not a line-by-line comparison of plan against actual but a system-supported process that suggests the source of the variance (price changes, quantity changes, and so on). Note that variance calculation only takes place in legal valuation (version 0), so it's worth being clear which accounting approach you want to use for your management reporting when you prepare your design.

- Finally, if you want to include these variances in your production costs, calculate new activity rates and include these either in your production orders or in the Material Ledger. You can use the Material Ledger to include values in legal valuation and for the parallel valuation of cost of goods manufactured.

Target Costs

If you refer back to Chapter 5, you'll see that our quality cost center *planned* to provide 150 hours of quality checks, but *actually* provided 160 hours. If we compare Figures 5.15 and 7.19, we can see that the total *planned costs* were EUR 29,000 and the total *target costs* were EUR 29,800. All cost elements containing activity-dependent costs (in our case, external procurement and direct labor) have been affected by switching from planned costs to target costs. So the planned/actual comparison shows a variance of EUR 3,000 for external procurement and no variance for direct labor, whereas the target/actual comparison shows a variance of EUR 3,600 for external procurement and EUR 200 for direct labor. Only the activity-independent costs (salaries and office and building) remain the same. However, this variance is offset by the fact that the higher output quantity means the cost center was also able to charge more of its costs to the production cost centers. This kind of analysis can help you understand the effect of the amount of work provided on the amount of resources used by your cost center.

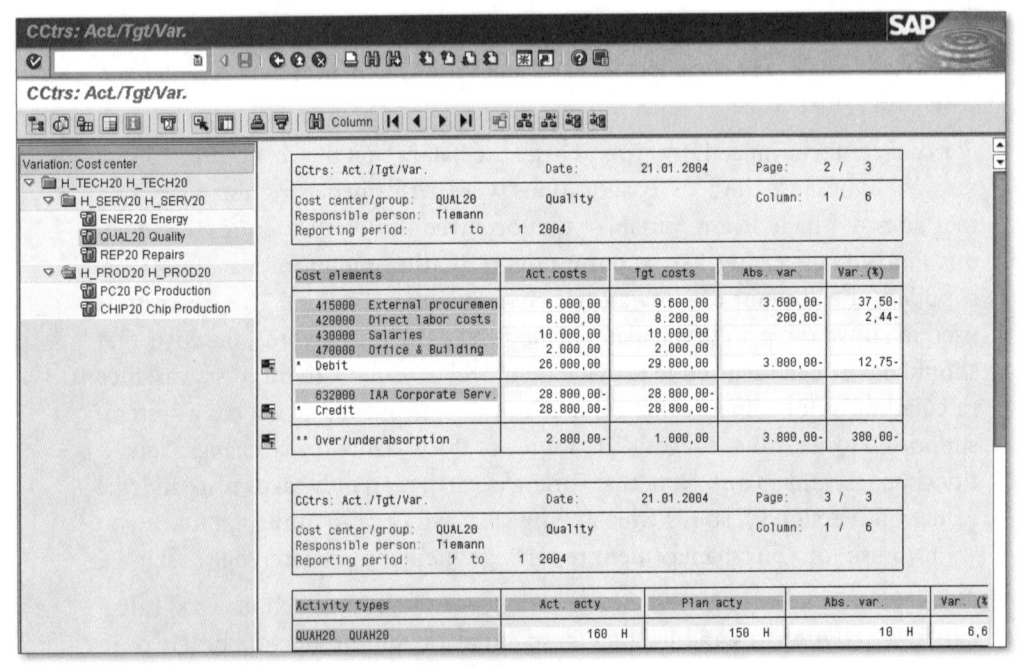

Figure 7.19 Target/Actual Cost Report

Running variance analysis will give us an even more powerful explanation of the source of each variance. By double-clicking on each report line, you can see the categories of variance for each activity type. Figure 7.20 shows the operating rate, the planned quantity, and the actual quantity.

- The control costs are the actual costs assigned to the cost center for the period. (We'll see the same screens in Product Cost Controlling, where this field is needed to cleanse the actual costs of any scrap or work in process. In Cost Center Accounting the control costs include all input costs).

► The target costs are the planned costs adjusted to reflect the operating rate (in our case 106.67%).

► The actual costs allocated are the costs assigned from repairs to production using the planned activity price for the cost center.

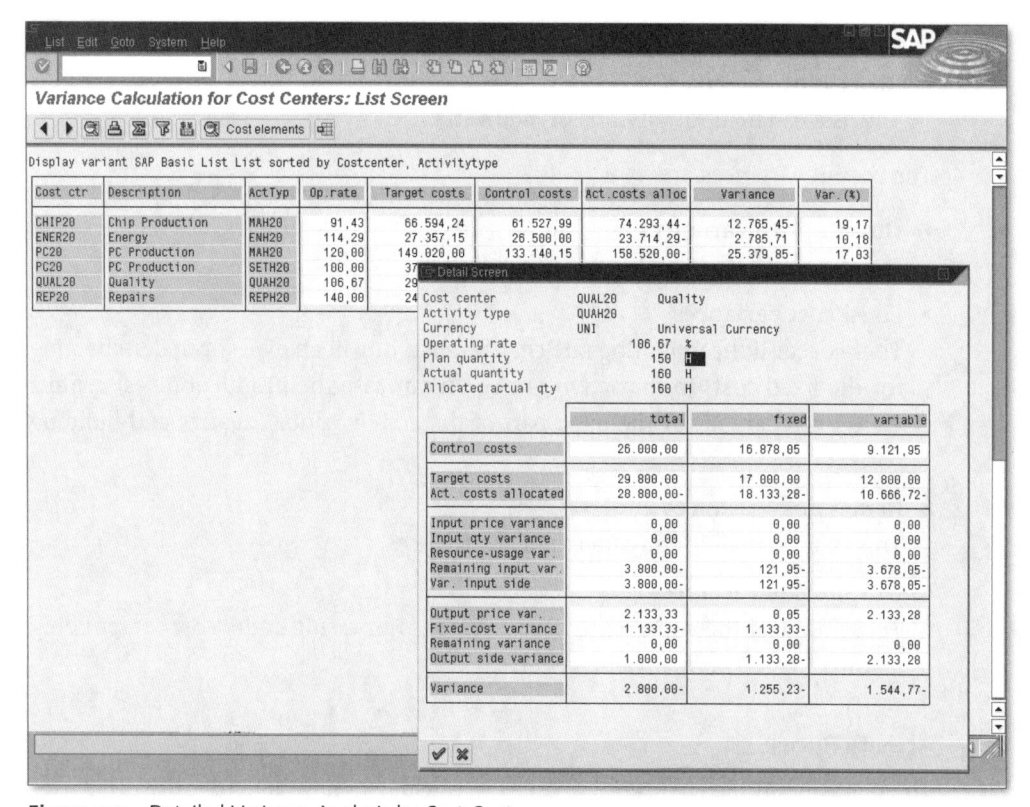

Figure 7.20 Detailed Variance Analysis by Cost Center

In variance analysis we distinguish between *input variances* (those resulting from changes in the costs coming on to the cost center) and *output variances* (those resulting from changes to the output of the cost center or the activity price).

The input variances are:

► **Input price variances**
These occur as a result of changes to the activity prices for other cost centers or material price changes.

▶ **Input quantity variances**
These occur as a result of using a different quantity of activity from other cost centers.

▶ **Resource-usage variances**
These occur if an activity is used from a different cost center than was originally planned.

▶ **Remaining variances**
This is a catch-all for any unassigned variances.

The output variances are:

▶ **Output price variances**
These occur if the activity price changes for any reason.

▶ **Fixed cost variances**
These occur if the operating rate changes resulting in an over- or under-charging for the fixed costs in the activity price. In our case the production cost centers were overcharged for the fixed part of the activity price (salaries and building costs).

▶ **Remaining variances**
This is a catch-all for any unassigned variances.

▶ **Output side variances**
These occur if the chosen activity price does not result in the cost center being credited to give a final value of zero.

Activity Prices

The final step in the cost center close is to calculate a new activity price. This uses exactly the same mechanisms as we saw during activity price planning in Chapter 5 and can also give you an actual cost component split. To execute activity price calculation, follow the menu path ACCOUNTING • CONTROLLING • COST CENTER ACCOUNTING • PERIOD-END CLOSING • SINGLE FUNCTIONS • PRICE CALCULATION or use Transaction KSII.

If you use the business function Parallel Valuation of Cost of Goods Manufactured (FIN_CO_COGM), available from SAP enhancement package 5 for SAP ERP 6.0, two sets of input values are available in Cost Center Accounting to reflect the different accounting principles governing the approach to calculating depreciation in Asset Accounting. These are used to calculate two activity prices, stored as separate versions.

To check the results of price calculation, follow the menu path ACCOUNTING • CONTROLLING • COST CENTER ACCOUNTING • INFORMATION SYSTEM • REPORTS FOR COST CENTER ACCOUNTING • PRICES • COST CENTERS: ACTIVITY PRICES or use Transaction KSBT and enter the cost center, activity types, version, and time frame. Figure 7.21 shows three activity prices for each activity type on the cost center. The PRICE INDICATOR column shows the following.

- 1 — planned activity price based on the planned quantity
- 5 — actual activity price based on the actual quantity
- 8 — purely iterative price (normally this is the same as 5)

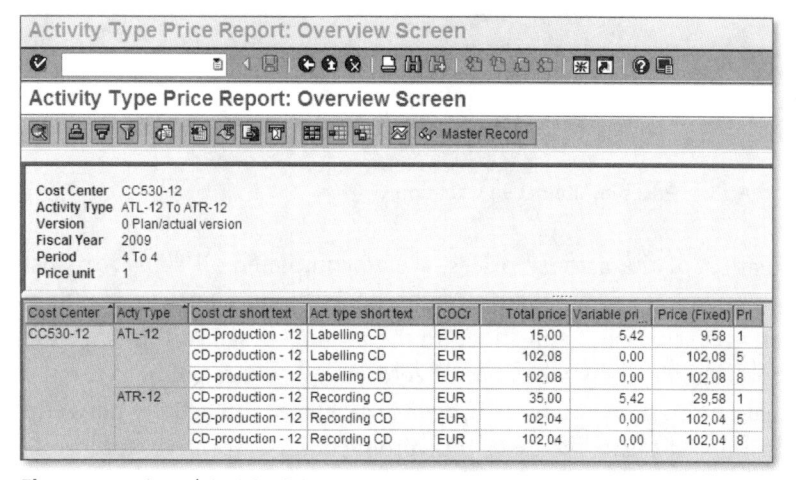

Figure 7.21 Actual Activity Prices in Version 0

Figure 7.22 shows the activity price according to a different accounting principle, which means different depreciation expenses have been included in the calculation. Notice that the activity price in version 0 is slightly higher than the activity price in the other version.

If you want to assign the new activity prices to your production orders, process orders, and so on, every menu for the period close in Cost Object Controlling includes the step REVALUATE AT ACTUAL PRICES (Transaction CON2) that updates the orders with the newly calculated prices. If you use the Material Ledger, you can leave out this step and use the alternative valuation run to determine the activity rates for the materials and pass them on to the materials produced in the course of the period. We'll look at this in Section 7.3. Alternatively, you can simply consider the difference as a cost center variance and use an assessment cycle to allocate it to PROFITABILITY ANALYSIS.

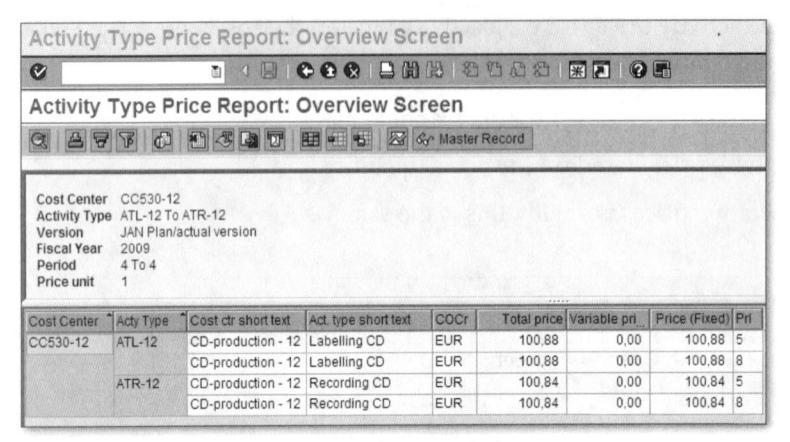

Figure 7.22 Actual Activity Prices in Alternative Valuation

With the calculation of the activity prices, we've completed all steps for Cost Center Accounting and are now ready to move on to Product Cost Controlling, where these activity prices can be included in the product costs. At this stage the cost center reports should show a balance of zero, unless you're going to use the alternative valuation run in the Material Ledger to calculate your activity rates and clear the cost centers. If this is the case, your production cost centers still have a value awaiting clearing.

7.2 Calculations and Settlement

The period close tasks for Product Cost Controlling are slightly different depending on whether you work with product cost by period, product cost by order, or sales order controlling (see Chapter 2). Since there's a degree of overlap between the three approaches, we'll look at the whole flow for product cost by order and then at the differences in the other two approaches.

Figure 7.23 gives an overview of the period close activities for product cost by order, some of which we encountered when we followed a production order in

Chapter 6. You'll find the same activities under SHOP FLOOR CONTROL in the PRODUCTION menu, since some plants perform these tasks locally. In the menu, notice that all tasks have an entry for INDIVIDUAL PROCESSING and COLLECTIVE PROCESSING. In this chapter we'll discuss the individual processing of a single production order so we can focus on the value flows and the details of what happens in an individual order. We'll come back to collective processing in Chapter 12, when we discuss your options for efficiently processing multiple orders.

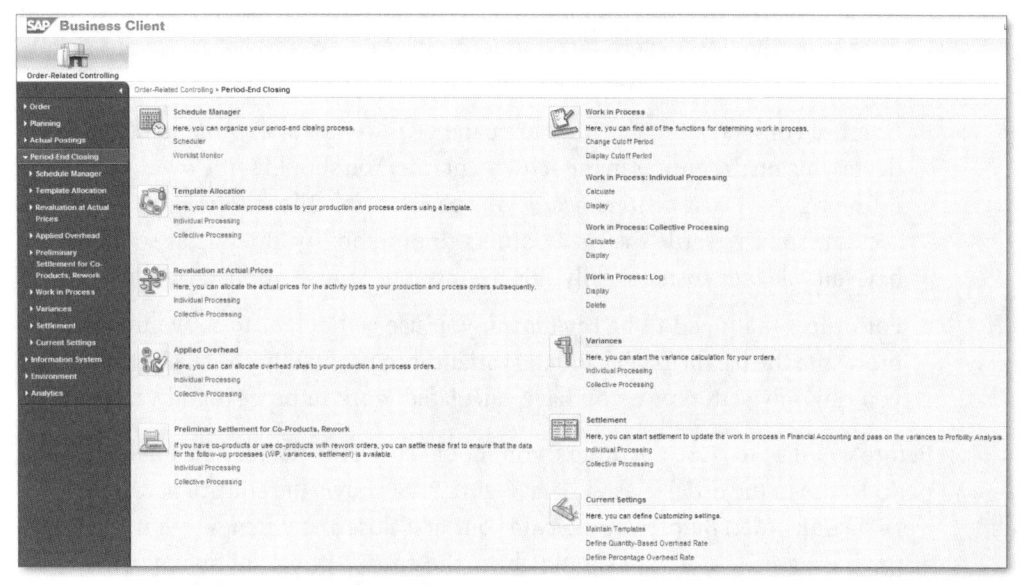

Figure 7.23 Period Close Activities for Production Orders

The following tasks are included:

- Template allocation is used in the context of Activity-Based Costing. We'll look at this in more detail in Chapter 11.
- Revaluation at actual costs allows you to update the production orders with the activity prices you calculated in the previous step.
- Applied overhead allows you to charge a percentage or quantity-based overhead to your production orders, as we saw in Chapter 6.
- We discussed preliminary settlement for co-products and rework when we looked at the handling of co-products and rework orders in Chapter 6.

- Work in process is required for all production orders that are open at the time of the period close. If you use product cost collectors (see Chapter 3), you also need to calculate work in process for any incomplete operations.
- The VARIANCES folder allows you to calculate production variances and scrap for all completed production orders. If you use product cost collectors, it allows you to calculate production variances for all completed operations.

  Your use of the SETTLEMENT folder depends on your type of orders, in other words, on whether the expenses collected have to be capitalized (investment orders, production orders carrying work in process, and so on) or are simply overhead (research and development orders and so on).
- Overhead orders can settle either to a parent cost center or to profitability analysis, depending on the entries in the settlement rule. You should settle overhead orders to their parent cost centers *before* you perform the allocations in the previous section. You can settle overhead orders to profitability analysis as soon as they have all relevant costs (usually this means after you've applied overhead).
- For orders that need to be *capitalized*, you use settlement to move the work in process to the balance sheet and the variances to profitability analysis. This means you can only settle once you have calculated work in process and variances.

Before you start to close the orders, you should check the parameters relevant to the period close in the order master data. Figure 7.24 shows the control parameters for a production order. Before you execute your first close and whenever you encounter errors during the close, you should check the entries in the following fields.

- COSTING SHEET
  Contains all parameters relating to the calculation of overhead (Section 7.2.1).
- OVERHEAD KEY
  Used to calculate material-specific overheads. This is linked with the overhead group in the costing view of the material master (see Chapter 4).
- RESULTS ANALYSIS KEY
  Used to determine how work in process is calculated. The default is set by order type and plant (Section 7.2.2).
- VARIANCE KEY
  Used to determine how variances are calculated. The default is set in the costing view of the material master (Section 7.2.3).

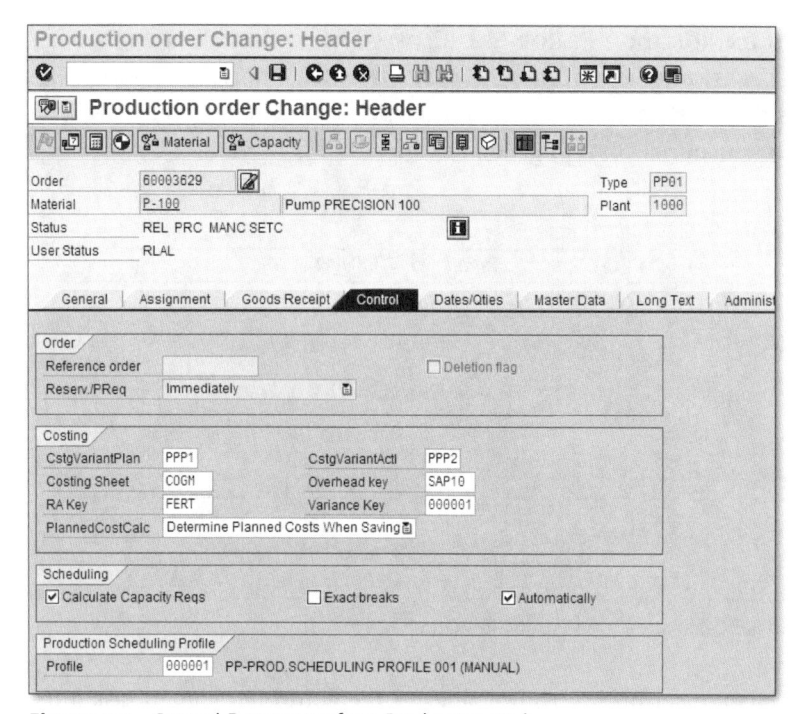

Figure 7.24 Control Parameters for a Production Order

7.2.1 Overhead Calculation

The purpose of overhead calculation is to charge the costs, for example, of storing materials in the warehouse, to the production orders. The costing sheet links together several condition types that determine the following:

- The basis for the calculation (such as all relevant raw material costs)
- The conditions under which overhead is applied (such as within a particular plant or when manufacturing a certain material)
- The percentage to be applied (such as 10% on all raw material costs)
- The cost center that's the sender of the charge (such as the warehouse cost center)

While you might calculate overheads for individual orders during testing, the normal procedure is to schedule a job that selects all relevant production orders in the plant and assigns overhead to each one in turn based on the conditions in the costing sheet. To calculate overheads, follow the menu path ACCOUNTING • CONTROLLING •

PRODUCT COST CONTROLLING • PERIOD-END CLOSING • PRODUCT COST BY ORDER • OVERHEAD CALCULATION • INDIVIDUAL PROCESSING or use Transaction KGI2. Figure 7.25 shows the overheads for a single production order. Ten percent has been applied to the raw material costs to give an overhead of EUR 55.22.

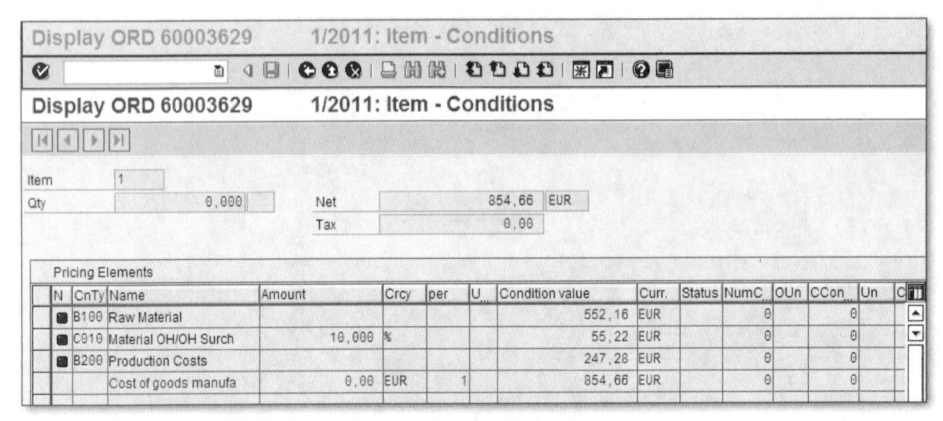

Figure 7.25 Overhead Calculation for a Production Order

The costing sheets are set up in Customizing, so the controller's main task after implementation is to make sure the percentage rates are still correct. You'll find this activity under CURRENT SETTINGS (see Figure 7.23). Figure 7.26 shows the percentages used to calculate the overhead in our example. Our production order (see Figure 7.24) contained the costing sheet COGM, which applied overhead under condition type C010. Condition C010 calculates overhead by overhead type (planned or actual) and overhead key. Our production order included overhead key SAP010, so a 10% overhead was applied.

> **Template Allocation**
>
> If you think this type of percentage overhead is too simplistic for your business needs or you're having trouble calculating a percentage that will result in all costs being charged to the production orders, consider using Template allocation for some of your overhead. This will allow you to calculate overhead using much more complex drivers and to clear all costs on the cost center at the end of the period. It's especially useful if you need to make sure that the outstanding balance on your cost centers is zero at the end of the period (a legal requirement in some parts of the world). We'll look at this in more detail in Chapter 11.

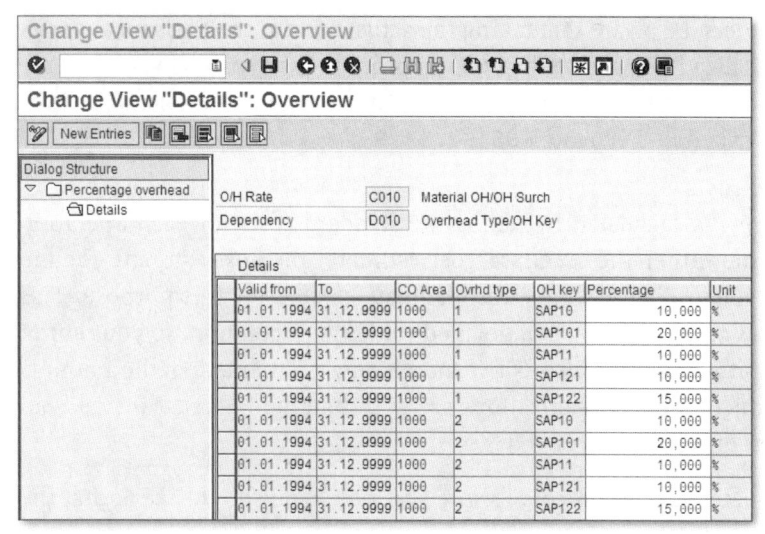

Figure 7.26 Overhead Percentages in the Costing Sheet

7.2.2 Work in Process

As we discussed in Chapter 1, work in process is a source of much confusion. In any multilevel bill of material, there are raw materials, semifinished products, and finished products. Production orders are created for each step that results in a product being delivered to *inventory*. During production, all values on the production order are considered as an *expense* until we move this expense to the balance sheet as *work in process* at period close. There are two basic ways of handling work in process:

- **WIP at actual costs**

    Work in process is calculated by subtracting the value of any deliveries to stock from the actual costs. Some organizations configure the work in process by cost element type and capitalize only part of the conversion costs. Work in process is calculated until the order has the status Final Delivery or Technically Completed (see Chapter 3, Section 3.8.2). When you calculate the WIP in the next period, the last WIP is cancelled.

    You have to use this method if you have co-products, but cannot use it with product cost collectors or cost object hierarchies. If you have very long-running production orders, be aware that taking the actual costs as the basis means variances are capitalized along with the work in process. If substantial variances are included in WIP, you should consider using the additional functions for WIP valuation described in SAP Note 608162.

- **WIP at target costs**
  Work in process is calculated by taking the standard costs for each operation completed from either the standard cost estimate, the cost estimate for the product cost collector, or another cost estimate created for this purpose. This approach relies on the existence of detailed values per operation, so you cannot use this method with co-products (since there's only a settlement of the amounts to the co-products). Some organizations prefer this method because it avoids an overstatement of work in process.

Before you calculate work in process for the first time, you should check that the production orders contain a results analysis key (see Figure 7.24). The settings are Customizing activities and cannot be adjusted for reasons of consistency. When you calculate WIP, you'll be required to enter a results analysis version. Normally, you only need to enter version 0 for the legal valuation of your work in process. You may find that your organization has additional versions if you use group valuation or transfer price valuation or if you have activated parallel valuation of cost of goods manufactured. In such cases, it makes sense to calculate WIP for all results analysis versions.

To execute work in process, follow the menu path ACCOUNTING • CONTROLLING • PRODUCT COST CONTROLLING • COST OBJECT CONTROLLING • PRODUCT COST BY ORDER • PERIOD-END CLOSING • SINGLE FUNCTIONS • WORK IN PROCESS • INDIVIDUAL PROCESSING • CALCULATE or use Transaction KKAX. Enter the order number, the period, the fiscal year, and the results analysis version(s) and click on EXECUTE. Figure 7.27 shows the result of WIP calculation for a production order. The figure in the WIP (CUMULATED) column is the work in process for the complete lifecycle of the order. The figure in the WIP (PERIOD) column is the increase/decrease in work in process in that period. In our example, the production order was created in the same period as the WIP calculation, so the two figures are identical. This process of calculating the additional work in process in each period continues until the order is complete (in other words, has the status Final Delivery or Technically Complete). When you calculate work in process in the period that follows, the work in process is cancelled.

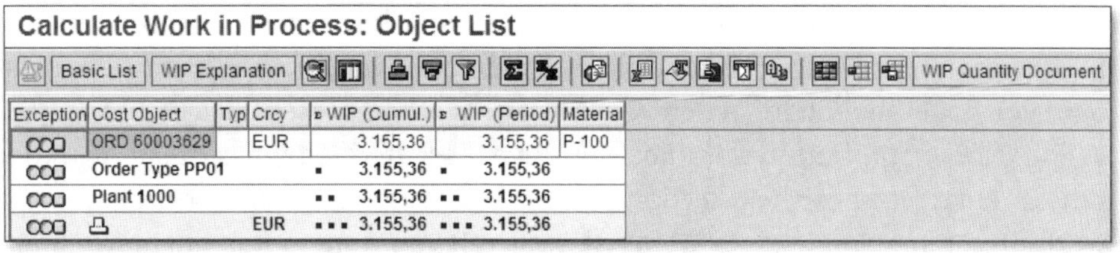

Calculations and Settlement | 7.2

Calculate Work in Process: Object List						
Exception	Cost Object	Typ	Crcy	Σ WIP (Cumul.)	Σ WIP (Period)	Material
◌◌◌	ORD 60003629		EUR	3.155,36	3.155,36	P-100
◌◌◌	Order Type PP01			3.155,36	3.155,36	
◌◌◌	Plant 1000			3.155,36	3.155,36	
◌◌◌			EUR	3.155,36	3.155,36	

Figure 7.27 WIP Calculation for a Production Order

Depending on your configuration, the work in process can be separated and stored under different results analysis cost elements depending on the underlying costs, such as raw material costs, production costs, and overhead. To check how your WIP has been stored, follow the menu path ACCOUNTING • CONTROLLING • PRODUCT COST CONTROLLING • COST OBJECT CONTROLLING • PRODUCT COST BY ORDER • INFORMATION SYSTEM • REPORTS FOR PRODUCT COST BY ORDER • DETAILED REPORTS • FOR ORDERS or use Transaction KKBC_ORD. Enter the order number and switch the layout to 1SAP03 (work in process). Figure 7.28 shows the results analysis cost elements that store these values in CO. Notice that these all begin with 672 as distinct from the original cost elements under which the costs were first recorded in CO.

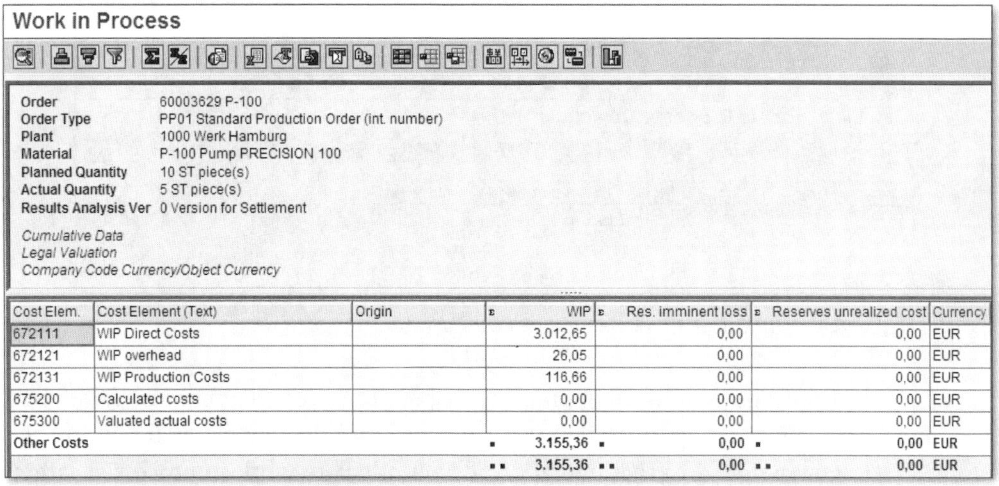

Work in Process

Order: 60003629 P-100
Order Type: PP01 Standard Production Order (int. number)
Plant: 1000 Werk Hamburg
Material: P-100 Pump PRECISION 100
Planned Quantity: 10 ST piece(s)
Actual Quantity: 5 ST piece(s)
Results Analysis Ver: 0 Version for Settlement

Cumulative Data
Legal Valuation
Company Code Currency/Object Currency

Cost Elem.	Cost Element (Text)	Origin	Σ WIP	Res. imminent loss	Σ Reserves unrealized cost	Currency
672111	WIP Direct Costs		3.012,65	0,00	0,00	EUR
672121	WIP overhead		26,05	0,00	0,00	EUR
672131	WIP Production Costs		116,66	0,00	0,00	EUR
675200	Calculated costs		0,00	0,00	0,00	EUR
675300	Valuated actual costs		0,00	0,00	0,00	EUR
Other Costs			3.155,36	0,00	0,00	EUR
			3.155,36	0,00	0,00	EUR

Figure 7.28 Work in Process: Detail Report

359

You can also access this report by selecting the order line and clicking on the WIP REPORT button in Figure 7.27 and then changing the layout to WORK IN PROCESS once you get in the report. When you calculate work in process at actual costs, the WIP EXPLANATION button does not work (we'll see it when we calculate work in process at target in the next section). The WIP QUANTITY DOCUMENT button only works in conjunction with the Material Ledger. If you want to find out more about this solution, read SAP Note 608162.

But first, let's calculate work in process for production orders that don't carry their own costs but have been created with reference to a product cost collector (see Chapters 3 and 6). To calculate work in process, follow the menu path ACCOUNTING • CONTROLLING • PRODUCT COST CONTROLLING • COST OBJECT CONTROLLING •PRODUCT COST BY PERIOD • PERIOD-END CLOSING • SINGLE FUNCTIONS • WORK IN PROCESS • INDIVIDUAL PROCESSING • CALCULATE or use Transaction KKAS. Enter the material, plant, and if multiple production versions exist for the material, the production process along with the period, fiscal year, and results analysis version and click on EXECUTE. Figure 7.29 shows the result of WIP calculation for a product cost collector. To view the details by operation, select the product cost collector line and click on the WIP EXPLANATION button.

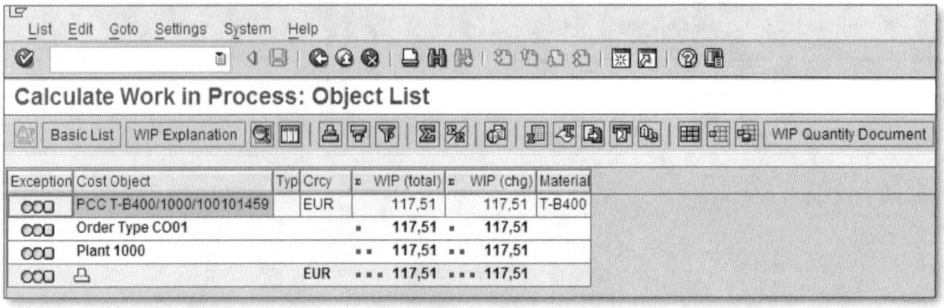

Figure 7.29 WIP Calculation for a Product Cost Collector

Figure 7.30 shows the work in process by operation. Note that because of the way the routing was set up, operation 0010 also includes the raw material costs for the BOM item assigned to that operation. If you calculate work in process at target, it's important to ensure that the BOM items are linked to the correct operations, since the costs for the raw material are automatically included in the WIP and scrap costs for the relevant operation (see Chapter 4).

Calculate WIP: Explanation

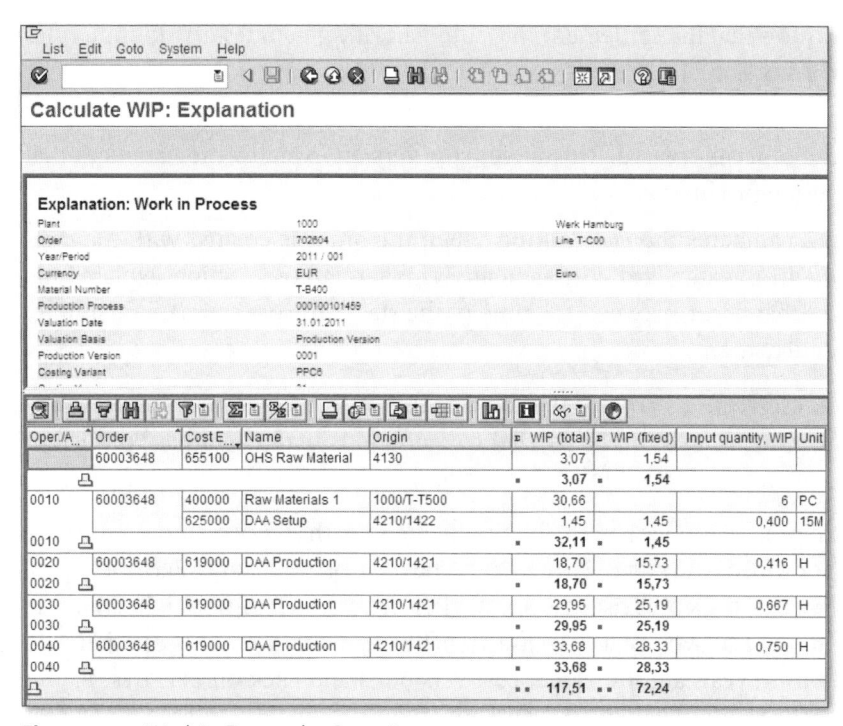

Explanation: Work in Process

Plant	1000		Werk Hamburg
Order	702604		Line T-C00
Year/Period	2011 / 001		
Currency	EUR		Euro
Material Number	T-B400		
Production Process	000100101459		
Valuation Date	31.01.2011		
Valuation Basis	Production Version		
Production Version	0001		
Costing Variant	PPC6		

Oper./A	Order	Cost E	Name	Origin	WIP (total)	WIP (fixed)	Input quantity, WIP	Unit
	60003648	655100	OHS Raw Material	4130	3,07	1,54		
					3,07	1,54		
0010	60003648	400000	Raw Materials 1	1000/T-T500	30,66		6	PC
		625000	DAA Setup	4210/1422	1,45	1,45	0,400	15M
0010					32,11	1,45		
0020	60003648	619000	DAA Production	4210/1421	18,70	15,73	0,416	H
0020					18,70	15,73		
0030	60003648	619000	DAA Production	4210/1421	29,95	25,19	0,667	H
0030					29,95	25,19		
0040	60003648	619000	DAA Production	4210/1421	33,68	28,33	0,750	H
0040					33,68	28,33		
					117,51	72,24		

Figure 7.30 Work in Process by Operation

7.2.3 Target Costs and Variances in Production

We already discussed how to calculate target costs and variances for each activity type on the cost centers. You take the same approach for the production orders, but this time the *order quantity* provides the basis for the calculation of target costs. If you're working with product cost by order, you generally cancel the work in process and then calculate target costs and variances on completion of the order. You're also required to enter one or more target cost versions. These are configured in Customizing, and the usual settings are as follows:

▶ Version 0 compares the *actual costs* on the order with the *standard costs* in the standard cost estimate. This target cost version explains the difference between the standard costs used to valuate inventory when the goods are delivered to stock with the actual costs. These values will be settled, meaning they'll be included in the Material Ledger and CO-PA. The settlement profile for your production order ensures that the settlement rule automatically generates distribution rules to the correct senders.

- Version 1 compares the *actual costs* on the order with the *planned costs* calculated when the order is created. This target cost version explains the variances that occur during production.
- Version 2 compares the *planned costs* when the order is created with the *standard costs* in the standard cost estimate. This target cost version explains the variances that occur between the time of the standard cost estimate (planning) and order creation.

Note that these versions are not the same as the versions that store group valuation, profit center valuation, or parallel cost of goods manufactured. Production variances are only calculated in legal valuation.

To calculate production variances, follow the menu path ACCOUNTING • CONTROLLING • PRODUCT COST CONTROLLING • COST OBJECT CONTROLLING • PRODUCT COST BY ORDER • PERIOD-END CLOSING • SINGLE FUNCTIONS • VARIANCES • INDIVIDUAL PROCESSING • CALCULATE or use Transaction KKS2. Enter the order number, the period and fiscal year, and the target cost version(s) and click on EXECUTE. Figure 7.31 shows the result of variance calculation on the production order in target cost version 0. To see the details, we selected the order line and clicked on the COST ELEMENTS button. What we're looking at is a comparison of the actual costs for the order with the standard costs to produce the delivered quantity. Since the order is complete, there's no work in process.

Just as we saw earlier for the activity quantities on the cost center, the production variances are assigned to variance categories. To display the variance categories, switch the layout for the report in Figure 7.31 to VARIANCE CATEGORIES. Figure 7.32 shows the variance categories for our production order.

The input variances are:

- **Input price variances**
  These occur as a result of changes to the material prices and activity prices.

- **Input quantity variances**
  These occur as a result of using a different quantity of material or activity.

7.2 Calculations and Settlement

- **Resource-usage variances**
  These occur if an operation has to be performed at a different work center or a material replaced as a result of material shortages.

- **Remaining variances**
  This is a catch-all for any unassigned variances.

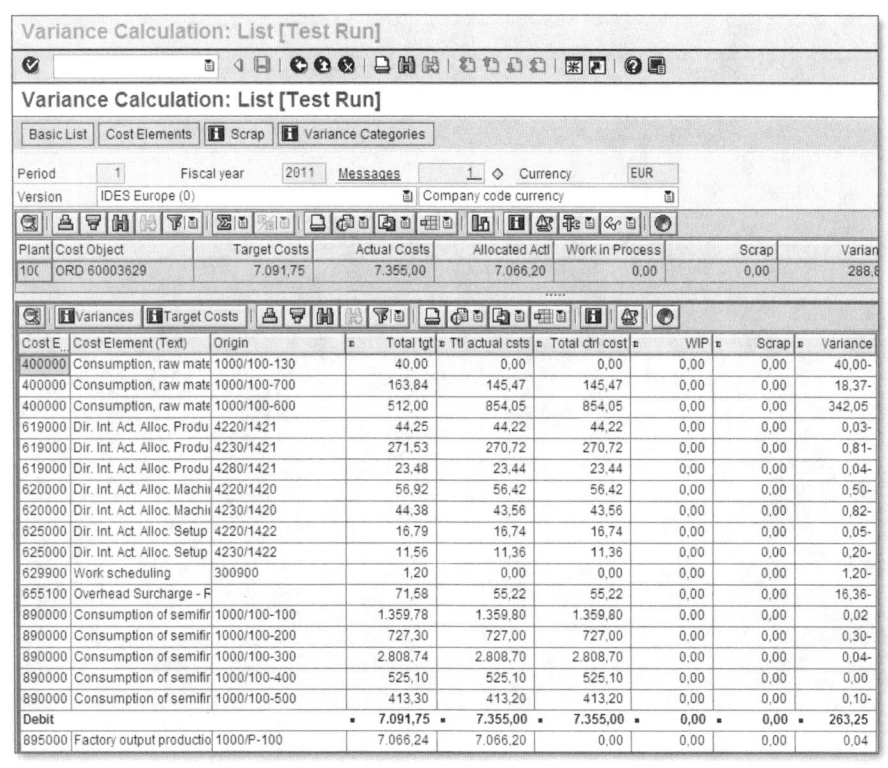

Plant	Cost Object	Target Costs	Actual Costs	Allocated Actl	Work in Process	Scrap	Varian
100	ORD 60003629	7.091,75	7.355,00	7.066,20	0,00	0,00	288,8

Cost E.	Cost Element (Text)	Origin	Total tgt	Ttl actual csts	Total ctrl cost	WIP	Scrap	Variance
400000	Consumption, raw mate	1000/100-130	40,00	0,00	0,00	0,00	0,00	40,00-
400000	Consumption, raw mate	1000/100-700	163,84	145,47	145,47	0,00	0,00	18,37-
400000	Consumption, raw mate	1000/100-600	512,00	854,05	854,05	0,00	0,00	342,05
619000	Dir. Int. Act. Alloc. Produ	4220/1421	44,25	44,22	44,22	0,00	0,00	0,03-
619000	Dir. Int. Act. Alloc. Produ	4230/1421	271,53	270,72	270,72	0,00	0,00	0,81-
619000	Dir. Int. Act. Alloc. Produ	4280/1421	23,48	23,44	23,44	0,00	0,00	0,04-
620000	Dir. Int. Act. Alloc. Machi	4220/1420	56,92	56,42	56,42	0,00	0,00	0,50-
620000	Dir. Int. Act. Alloc. Machi	4230/1420	44,38	43,56	43,56	0,00	0,00	0,82-
625000	Dir. Int. Act. Alloc. Setup	4220/1422	16,79	16,74	16,74	0,00	0,00	0,05-
625000	Dir. Int. Act. Alloc. Setup	4230/1422	11,56	11,36	11,36	0,00	0,00	0,20-
629900	Work scheduling	300900	1,20	0,00	0,00	0,00	0,00	1,20-
655100	Overhead Surcharge - F		71,58	55,22	55,22	0,00	0,00	16,36-
890000	Consumption of semifin	1000/100-100	1.359,78	1.359,80	1.359,80	0,00	0,00	0,02
890000	Consumption of semifin	1000/100-200	727,30	727,00	727,00	0,00	0,00	0,30-
890000	Consumption of semifin	1000/100-300	2.808,74	2.808,70	2.808,70	0,00	0,00	0,04-
890000	Consumption of semifin	1000/100-400	525,10	525,10	525,10	0,00	0,00	0,00
890000	Consumption of semifin	1000/100-500	413,30	413,20	413,20	0,00	0,00	0,10-
Debit			7.091,75	7.355,00	7.355,00	0,00	0,00	263,25
895000	Factory output productio	1000/P-100	7.066,24	7.066,20	0,00	0,00	0,00	0,04

Figure 7.31 Variances on a Production Order

The output variances are:

- **Output price variances**
  These occur if the standard cost is not used for stock valuation.

- **Mixed price variances**
  These occur if the standard costs were calculated by weighting several cost estimates (see Chapter 5).

▶ **Lot size variances**
These occur if the lot size for the order differs from the lot size in the standard cost estimate.

▶ **Remaining variances**
This is a catch-all for any unassigned variances.

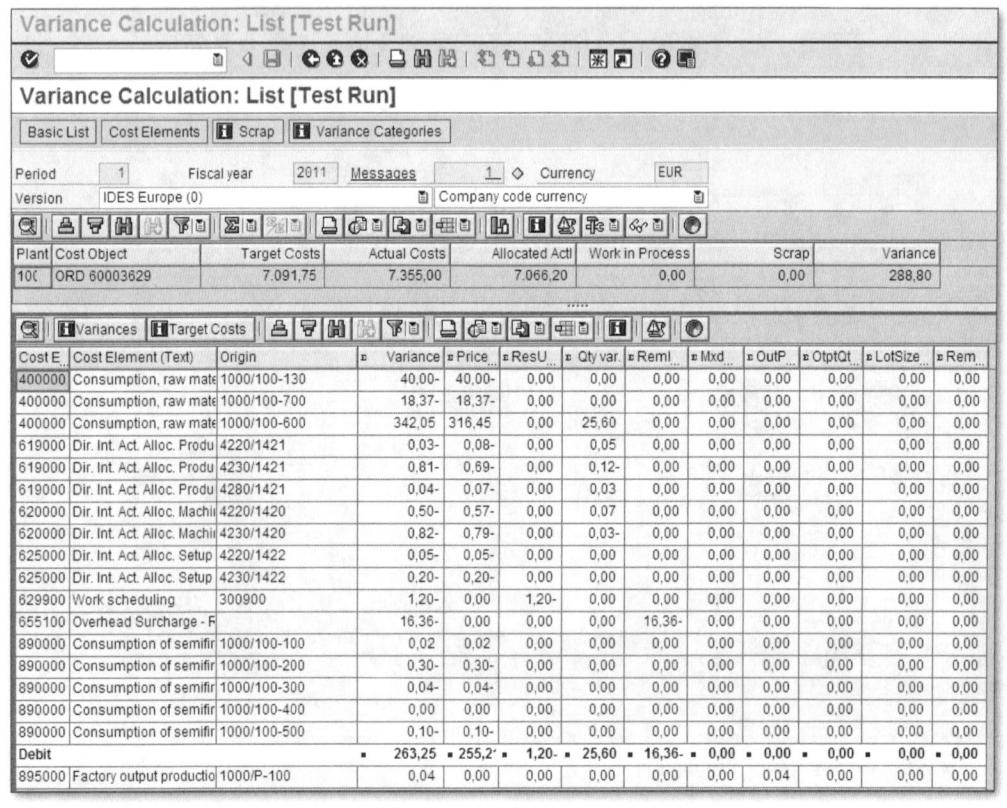

Plant	Cost Object	Target Costs	Actual Costs	Allocated Actl	Work in Process	Scrap	Variance
100	ORD 60003629	7.091,75	7.355,00	7.066,20	0,00	0,00	288,80

Cost E	Cost Element (Text)	Origin	Variance	Price	ResU	Qty var.	Reml	Mxd	OutP	OtptQt	LotSize	Rem
400000	Consumption, raw mate	1000/100-130	40,00-	40,00-	0,00	0,00	0,00	0,00	0,00	0,00	0,00	0,00
400000	Consumption, raw mate	1000/100-700	18,37-	18,37-	0,00	0,00	0,00	0,00	0,00	0,00	0,00	0,00
400000	Consumption, raw mate	1000/100-600	342,05	316,45	0,00	25,60	0,00	0,00	0,00	0,00	0,00	0,00
619000	Dir. Int. Act. Alloc. Produ	4220/1421	0,03-	0,08-	0,00	0,05	0,00	0,00	0,00	0,00	0,00	0,00
619000	Dir. Int. Act. Alloc. Produ	4230/1421	0,81-	0,69-	0,00	0,12-	0,00	0,00	0,00	0,00	0,00	0,00
619000	Dir. Int. Act. Alloc. Produ	4280/1421	0,04-	0,07-	0,00	0,03	0,00	0,00	0,00	0,00	0,00	0,00
620000	Dir. Int. Act. Alloc. Machi	4220/1420	0,50-	0,57-	0,00	0,07	0,00	0,00	0,00	0,00	0,00	0,00
620000	Dir. Int. Act. Alloc. Machi	4230/1420	0,82-	0,79-	0,00	0,03-	0,00	0,00	0,00	0,00	0,00	0,00
625000	Dir. Int. Act. Alloc. Setup	4220/1422	0,05-	0,05-	0,00	0,00	0,00	0,00	0,00	0,00	0,00	0,00
625000	Dir. Int. Act. Alloc. Setup	4230/1422	0,20-	0,20-	0,00	0,00	0,00	0,00	0,00	0,00	0,00	0,00
629900	Work scheduling	300900	1,20-	0,00	1,20-	0,00	0,00	0,00	0,00	0,00	0,00	0,00
655100	Overhead Surcharge - F		16,36-	0,00	0,00	0,00	16,36-	0,00	0,00	0,00	0,00	0,00
890000	Consumption of semifir	1000/100-100	0,02	0,02	0,00	0,00	0,00	0,00	0,00	0,00	0,00	0,00
890000	Consumption of semifir	1000/100-200	0,30-	0,30-	0,00	0,00	0,00	0,00	0,00	0,00	0,00	0,00
890000	Consumption of semifir	1000/100-300	0,04-	0,04-	0,00	0,00	0,00	0,00	0,00	0,00	0,00	0,00
890000	Consumption of semifir	1000/100-400	0,00	0,00	0,00	0,00	0,00	0,00	0,00	0,00	0,00	0,00
890000	Consumption of semifir	1000/100-500	0,10-	0,10-	0,00	0,00	0,00	0,00	0,00	0,00	0,00	0,00
Debit			263,25	255,2'	1,20-	25,60	16,36-	0,00	0,00	0,00	0,00	0,00
895000	Factory output productio	1000/P-100	0,04	0,00	0,00	0,00	0,00	0,04	0,00	0,00	0,00	0,00

Figure 7.32 Variance Categories for a Production Order

The third line in the list (consumption of material 100-600) shows an exceptionally high variance. To analyze this in more detail, select the line and click on the VARIANCES button. Figure 7.33 shows the details of this variance. Again, we see the input price variance and the input quantity variance, but now we have a full explanation of how variance calculation performed the calculation. You can use this button to perform spot checks on any lines that seem to be unreasonably high.

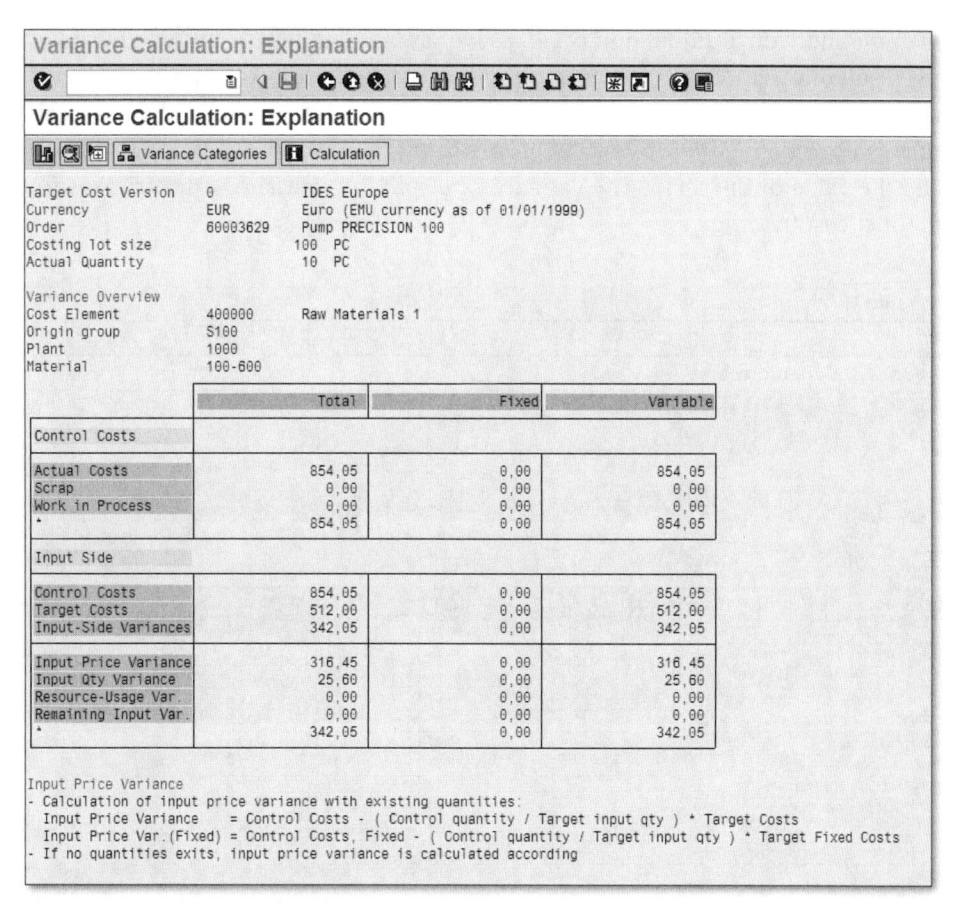

Figure 7.33 Explanation of Production Variances

If you're working with product cost collectors, you'll generally find work in process, variances, and scrap in the same period, since for any given production version some orders are in process and some complete in that period. To calculate variances, follow the menu path ACCOUNTING • CONTROLLING • PRODUCT COST CONTROLLING • COST OBJECT CONTROLLING • PRODUCT COST BY PERIOD • PERIOD-END CLOSING • SINGLE FUNCTIONS • VARIANCES • INDIVIDUAL PROCESSING • CALCULATE or use Transaction KKS6. Enter the material, plant, and if multiple production versions exist for the material, the production process along with the period, fiscal year, and target cost version(s) and click on EXECUTE. The only difference compared to product cost by order is that the planned costs are calculated for the product cost collector rather than the individual production order, as we saw in Chapter 6. Figure 7.34 shows the result of variance calculation for a product cost collector. Again, we've selected the product cost collector line and clicked on the COST ELEMENTS button. This time, we see the figure for work in process from the previous step, the variances, and the value of the scrap. The variances are split into variance categories, as for product cost by order.

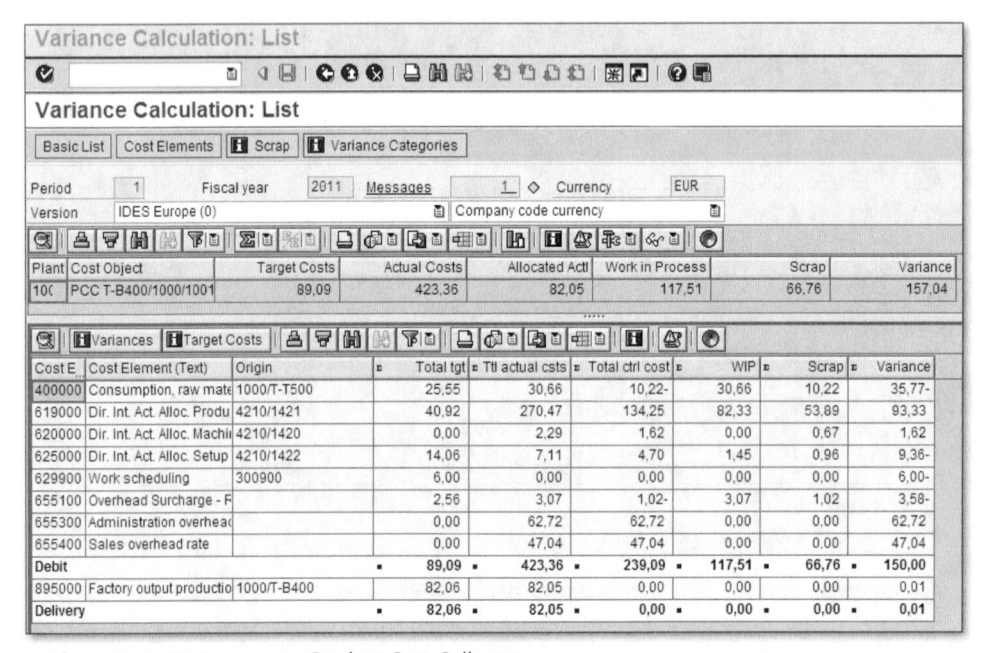

Plant	Cost Object	Target Costs	Actual Costs	Allocated Actl	Work in Process	Scrap	Variance
100	PCC T-B400/1000/1001	89,09	423,36	82,05	117,51	66,76	157,04

Cost E	Cost Element (Text)	Origin	Total tgt	Ttl actual csts	Total ctrl cost	WIP	Scrap	Variance
400000	Consumption, raw mate	1000/T-T500	25,55	30,66	10,22-	30,66	10,22	35,77-
619000	Dir. Int. Act. Alloc. Produ	4210/1421	40,92	270,47	134,25	82,33	53,89	93,33
620000	Dir. Int. Act. Alloc. Machi	4210/1420	0,00	2,29	1,62	0,00	0,67	1,62
625000	Dir. Int. Act. Alloc. Setup	4210/1422	14,06	7,11	4,70	1,45	0,96	9,36-
629900	Work scheduling	300900	6,00	0,00	0,00	0,00	0,00	6,00-
655100	Overhead Surcharge - F		2,56	3,07	1,02-	3,07	1,02	3,58-
655300	Administration overhead		0,00	62,72	62,72	0,00	0,00	62,72
655400	Sales overhead rate		0,00	47,04	47,04	0,00	0,00	47,04
Debit			89,09	423,36	239,09	117,51	66,76	150,00
895000	Factory output productio	1000/T-B400	82,06	82,05	0,00	0,00	0,00	0,01
Delivery			82,06	82,05	0,00	0,00	0,00	0,01

Figure 7.34 Variances on a Product Cost Collector

To see details of the value of the scrap, select the product cost collector line and click on the SCRAP button. Figure 7.35 shows that a scrap quantity was confirmed at operation 0060. In our example, there was no planned scrap, so the whole scrap quantity is valued with the standard costs for that operation. However, sometimes a planned scrap quantity is included in the cost estimate. If this is the case, the planned scrap quantity is subtracted from the actual scrap quantity and the *difference* used to value the scrapped items. The scrap will also be updated to the balance sheet as a production variance when the product cost collector is settled.

Variance Calculation: List

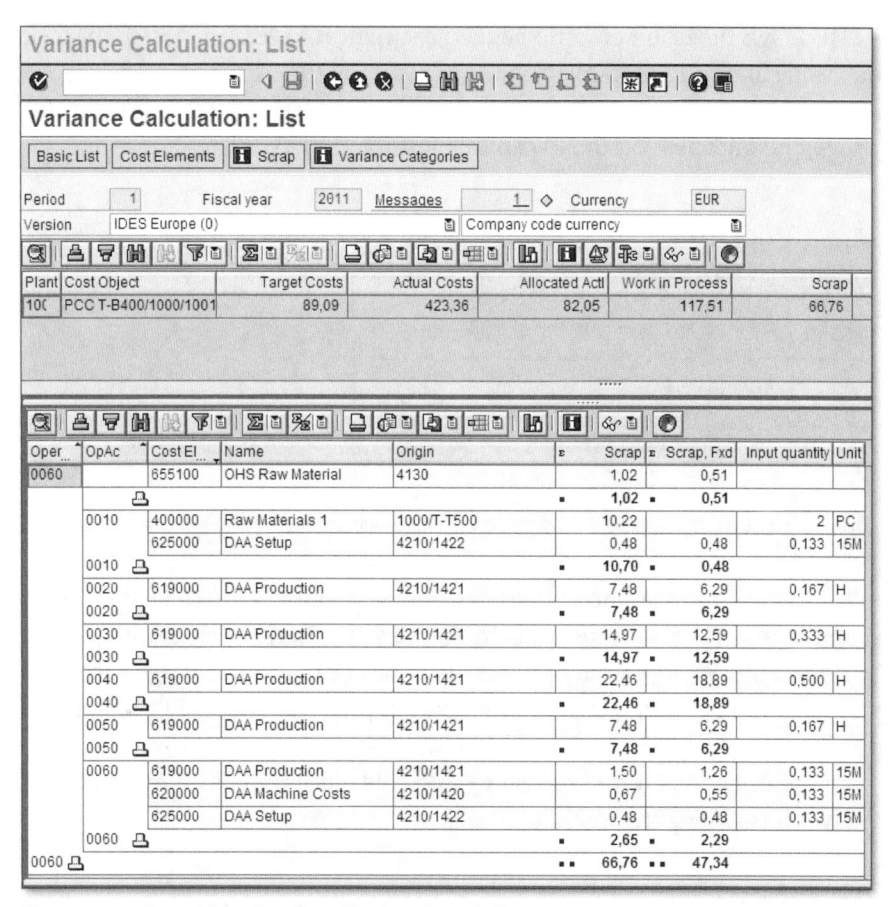

Plant	Cost Object	Target Costs	Actual Costs	Allocated Actl	Work in Process	Scrap
100	PCC T-B400/1000/1001	89,09	423,36	82,05	117,51	66,76

Oper	OpAc	Cost El	Name	Origin	Σ	Scrap	Σ	Scrap, Fxd	Input quantity	Unit
0060		655100	OHS Raw Material	4130		1,02		0,51		
					■	1,02	■	0,51		
	0010	400000	Raw Materials 1	1000/T-T500		10,22			2	PC
		625000	DAA Setup	4210/1422		0,48		0,48	0,133	15M
0010					■	10,70	■	0,48		
	0020	619000	DAA Production	4210/1421		7,48		6,29	0,167	H
0020					■	7,48	■	6,29		
	0030	619000	DAA Production	4210/1421		14,97		12,59	0,333	H
0030					■	14,97	■	12,59		
	0040	619000	DAA Production	4210/1421		22,46		18,89	0,500	H
0040					■	22,46	■	18,89		
	0050	619000	DAA Production	4210/1421		7,48		6,29	0,167	H
0050					■	7,48	■	6,29		
	0060	619000	DAA Production	4210/1421		1,50		1,26	0,133	15M
		620000	DAA Machine Costs	4210/1420		0,67		0,55	0,133	15M
		625000	DAA Setup	4210/1422		0,48		0,48	0,133	15M
0060					■	2,65	■	2,29		
0060					■■	66,76	■■	47,34		

Figure 7.35 Scrap Valuation for a Product Cost Collector

7.2.4 Settlement

The final step in cost object controlling is to settle the orders and product cost collectors. We looked at this process for production orders when we settled during the plan-to-manufacture process in Chapter 6. We'll now complete the process for our production cost collector and look at the postings in detail. To run settlement, follow the menu path ACCOUNTING • CONTROLLING • PRODUCT COST CONTROLLING • COST OBJECT CONTROLLING • PRODUCT COST BY PERIOD • PERIOD-END CLOSING • SINGLE FUNCTIONS • SETTLEMENT • INDIVIDUAL PROCESSING or use Transaction KK87. Enter the material, plant, and if multiple production versions exist for the material, the production process along with the period and fiscal year and click on EXECUTE.

Figure 7.36 shows the result of settlement. The variances have been posted to stock as a total value and to PROFITABILITY ANALYSIS split by the variance categories. To see the breakdown by variance category in more detail, select the PSG line (profitability segment) and click on the RECEIVERS button.

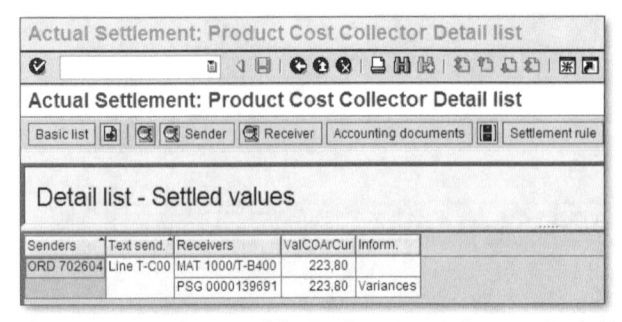

Figure 7.36 Settlement of the Product Cost Collector – Settled Values

Figure 7.37 shows the variance categories on our product cost collector. These correspond to the variance categories in Figure 7.32. Here we're settling input price variances (PRIV), input quantity variances (QTYV), resource usage variances (RSUV), remaining input variances (INPV), output price variances (OPPV), lot size variances (LSFV), remaining variances (REMV), and scrap (SCRP). This will apply these variance categories to the relevant value fields in Profitability Analysis (the PSG receiver lines in Figure 7.37).

Figure 7.37 Settlement of the Product Cost Collector – Receiver Debits

7.2.5 Product Cost by Sales Order

The period close activities for sales order controlling are dominated by the results analysis activities (see Figure 7.38). This is essentially a variant on WIP calculation for orders that also carry revenue (which production orders and product cost collectors do not). The basic idea is to look at the costs and revenues on the sales order and determine what part of that cost is *work in process* and what part is *cost of goods sold*.

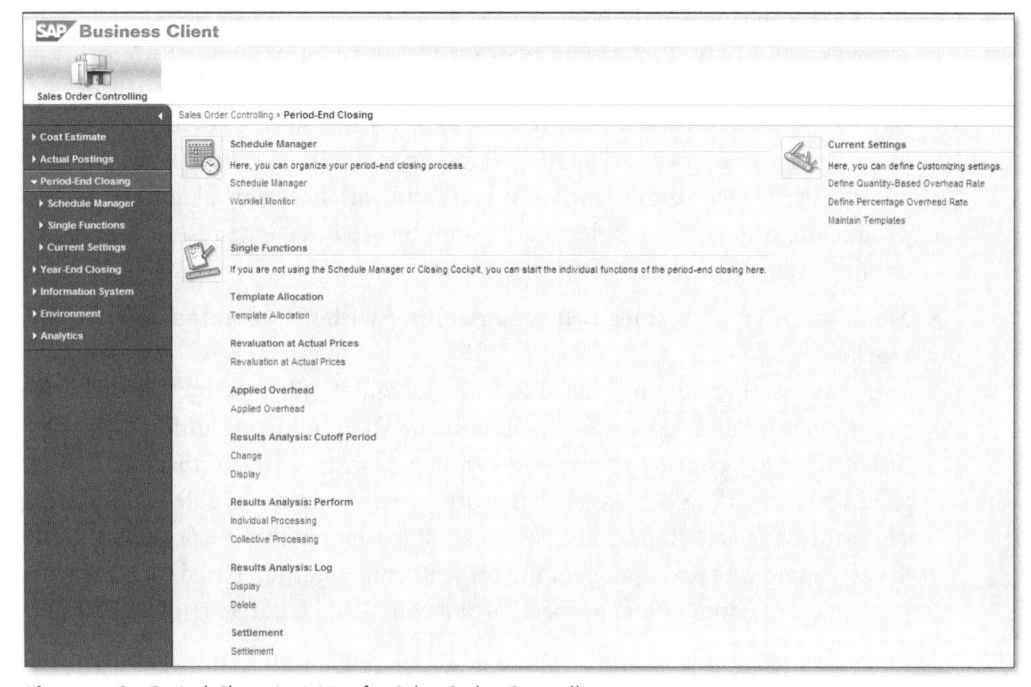

Figure 7.38 Period Close Activities for Sales Order Controlling

In releases prior to Release 4.0, you had to perform results analysis for all sales orders with make-to-order production. From Release 4.0 the approach varies depending on whether you're using sales order stock or not and whether the sales order carries costs over and above the manufacturing costs being captured on the assigned production orders (see Chapter 6). Currently the following options exist.

- **Make-to-order without sales order controlling**
 Here the production order is created with reference to the sales order item, as we saw in Chapter 6, Section 6.3.3. All costs are captured on the production order, and WIP and variance calculation take place for the production order. Sales controlling takes place in Profitability Analysis. The only difference from the process described in Section 7.2.2 is that the final delivery is made to sales order stock rather than neutral stock.

- **Make-to-order with sales order controlling and valuated sales order stock**
 If there's a business requirement to capture special sales or marketing costs by sales order item or calculate reserves or the value of goods in transit, the requirements type for the sales order item can be configured to allow the sales order item to carry costs. In this case, you also need to define a revenue element for your revenue postings (see Chapter 3). The production orders still deliver to sales order stock and WIP, and variances are calculated for the production orders, but results analysis can be used to create reserves or value goods in transit.

- **Make-to-order with sales order controlling without valuated sales order stock**
 This was the only option prior to Release 4.0 and is still used by some companies even after an upgrade. Since all costs on the production orders and sales order items are considered expenses (rather than inventory), there is a need to capitalize work in process. You perform results analysis by sales order item. This process selects all revenues and costs associated with the sales order item. Several approaches exist, depending on your configuration, based on either the percentage of completion approach or the completed contract approach.

 In the *percentage of completion* approach, the costs incurred or the quantity completed is used to determine the degree of completion of the sales order item. The revenue appropriate to this degree of completion is then calculated and compared with the billing for the sales order item. If the calculated revenue is higher, a posting is made for *revenues in excess of billing*. If the calculated revenue is lower, a posting is made for *revenue surplus* (a type of reserve).

 In the *completed contract* approach, the revenue invoiced for is taken as the degree of completion for the sales order item. Some of the costs incurred are taken to be associated with that revenue and are treated as cost of goods sold, and the rest are treated as *work in process*. If costs appear to be missing in view of the revenue, *reserves for unrealized costs* are created.

Postings to Financial Accounting are made for revenues in excess of billing, revenue surplus and/or work in process, and reserves for unrealized costs. We discussed the posting rules and the accounts associated with these postings when we looked at the accounting master data for work in process in Chapter 4.

Once you've settled all your production orders, product cost collectors, and sales orders, you've completed the closing steps in Cost Object Controlling. At this stage there are still costs on your open production orders and sales orders, but you'll have created the necessary postings in your balance sheet to account for work in process. If your organization works with *standard costs*, you can skip the next section and go straight to the next section on PROFITABILITY ANALYSIS to complete your close. If you use the Material Ledger, the next step is to perform your periodic costing run.

7.3 Multilevel Actual Costing in Material Ledger

If your organization works with *actual costs*, the next stage is to pull together all the cost information gathered in the Material Ledger to provide the actual costs for all materials bought and sold in the period. Figure 7.39 shows the period close activities for actual costing. We discussed distribution of usage variances in Chapter 6, Section 6.2. This does not need to be a period close activity, especially if you perform cycle counts on a more regular basis, but if you haven't included inventory differences until now, the period close is the time to make sure that you've captured any known differences and assigned them to production. The costing run is always performed as part of the period close. You may remember the term from Chapter 5 when we looked at the process of calculating standard costs. There are a lot of similarities between the two costing runs. The main differences are that in planning you're working with planning data in the form of bills of material and routings, whereas at period close you're working with the actual goods movements and confirmations that took place in the course of the period, all of which were stored in the Material Ledger as we saw in Chapter 6. In planning, the prices are selected from the material master, whereas at period close the values come from the invoices, goods movements, and settlement that were stored in the Material Ledger over the course of the period.

7 | Period Close

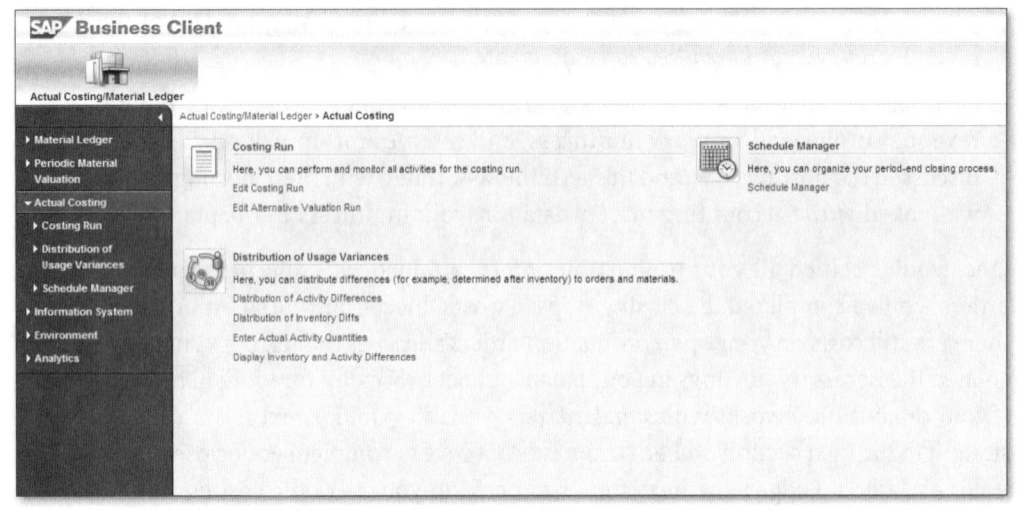

Figure 7.39 Actual Costing in the Material Ledger

7.3.1 Types of Costing Run

There are two types of costing run within the material ledger.

- The *periodic costing run* is used to calculate the periodic unit price, sometimes known as a weighted average price. It takes place once per period and is used to calculate the prices for the period just completed.

- The *alternative valuation run* is used where material or activity prices are subject to seasonal variances that need to be smoothed, to reduce the effect of work in process and beginning and ending inventory on the prices, or when material prices are subject to balance sheet adjustments (FIFO, LIFO, and so on). It's an *additional* costing run, taking as its starting point the quantity structure built up on the basis of the goods movements during the periodic costing run.

7.3.2 Periodic Costing Run

To create a costing run, follow the menu path ACCOUNTING • CONTROLLING • PRODUCT COST CONTROLLING • ACTUAL COSTING/MATERIAL LEDGER • ACTUAL COSTING • EDIT COSTING RUN or use Transaction CKMLCP.

Figure 7.40 shows the steps in a periodic costing run. These are as follows.

- SELECTION

    This step specifies which plants are to be included in the costing run. Because of the multilevel nature of the costing, it's is not possible to exclude particular materials from a costing run as you can in standard costing. To perform actual costing for the cross-company example we looked at in Chapter 6, Section 6.5, you need to ensure that all relevant plants in the supply chain are included in the selection.

- DETERMINE SEQUENCE

    This step checks the material inputs and outputs of each production process and determines the number of levels in the quantity structure. This step is needed to build the quantity structure for actual costing dynamically each period, especially for cyclical production structures and co-products. It corresponds to the structure explosion step for standard costing and effectively determines the sequence that the multilevel price determination uses to roll actual costs through the structure.

- SINGLE-LEVEL PRICE DETERMINATION

    This step calculates the periodic unit price for each material, taking account of price differences, revaluation differences, and exchange rate differences. It also determines the difference to be rolled through the quantity structure during the multilevel settlement. This step results in a new period status being set: single-level price determination (column S in Figure 7.40).

- MULTILEVEL PRICE DETERMINATION

    This step takes the difference calculated during the single-level settlement and passes it on to each material and procurement alternative in the quantity structure in turn. Note that this step handles goods movements arising from external procurement, subcontracting, and stock transfers as well as in-house production. After the multilevel settlement, you'll see a new material price and the cumulated price differences from the subordinate materials (multilevel price difference) for each material. In our cross-company example, this step also transfers the variance to the other company code, where you'll see the difference in the group valuation and as a delta in the legal valuation. This step results in a new period status being set: multilevel price determination (column M in Figure 7.40).

- REVALUATION OF CONSUMPTION

    This step was added in Release 4.7 and is activated using the enterprise extension EA_FIN (see Appendix C at *www.sap-press.com*). If you activate the appropriate movement type groups in configuration, it will update either the cost of goods sold account used to record the material movement or the sales order in a make-to-order scenario. This step results in a new period status being set: revaluation of consumption completed (column R in Figure 7.40).

- POST CLOSING

    When you create closing entries, the system switches the price control in the material master from S (standard price) to V (periodic unit price) for the period closed, writes the price calculated to the material master as a new V price and adjusts the balance sheet for the period closed. This step results in a new period status, closing entry, and must be completed before you start posting goods movements in the next period.

- MARK MATERIAL PRICES

    When we discussed the planning process in Chapter 5, we said you can use the prices calculated in the Material Ledger as the standard costs for the next period, provided you could complete your closing activities quickly enough to have the new standard costs in place before the first goods movement was posted. The costing run can transfer the new prices to the material master (see Chapter 4) and set the status to Marked. The mechanism for picking these prices from the material master is then the same as for releasing the standard cost estimate.

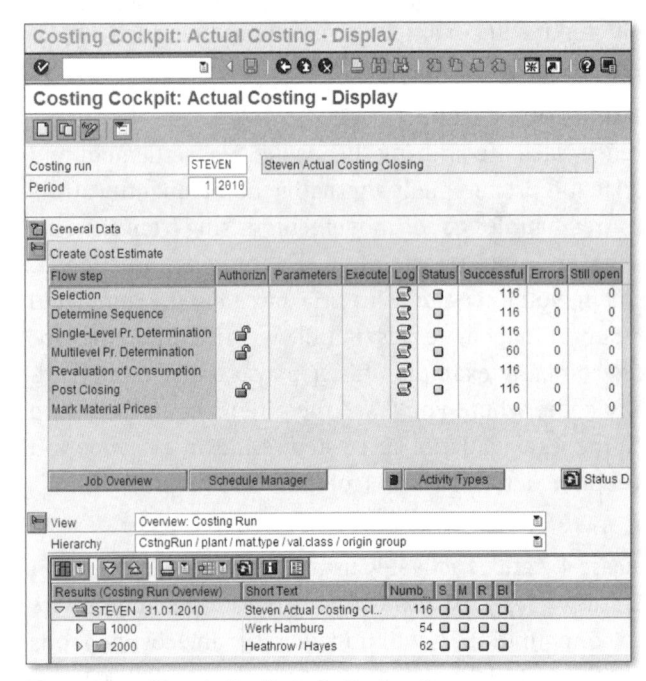

Figure 7.40 Steps in the Periodic Costing Run

Also notice lock icons for the price calculation steps and the post closing step. Since these steps can have a significant impact on the balance sheet, you need to have rules in place about who can perform these steps and under what circumstances, as we discussed when we talked about process controls in Chapter 1.

As we saw for the standard costing run in Chapter 5, the EXECUTE icon only appears when you've maintained the parameters for the step. On completion you'll see an error log and a status for each step.

The name Material Ledger might lead you to think that only material movements are updated, but there's also an ACTIVITY TYPES button in the costing run. Some countries have legal requirements for all production cost centers to be cleared at the end of each period. So the material ledger stores the activity prices for each cost center/activity type combination in the period and can then clear the individual cost centers that have supplied production activities in the course of the period.

To check the materials processed in each level, click on the line for the whole costing run or the line for one of the plants. A report as shown in Figure 7.41 will appear. This shows the current standard price for the material, the new periodic unit price, and the variance. You can also see special stocks. The T in our example refers to stock in transit, a stock type that can be valued since SAP enhancement package 5 of SAP ERP 6.0, removing the need for manual accrual postings to handle the cost of goods that are in transit between storage locations in one country and another. The sum of the price variances tells you the impact of performing the post closing step on your balance sheet.

> **System Performance for a Costing Run**
>
> Because of the volume of materials handled in a periodic costing run, it's good to be aware of the sort of factors that affect the speed with which your costing run can execute. Generally, it's the number of materials and not the number of Material Ledger documents that affect how long each step takes. In this context, a "material" is considered a material and plant (entry in table MBEW); a material, plant, sales order, and sales order item (entry in table EBEW); or a material, plant, and work breakdown structure element (entry in table QBEW). If you need to discuss system requirements with your IT department, you'll find details in SAP Note 668170.

7 | Period Close

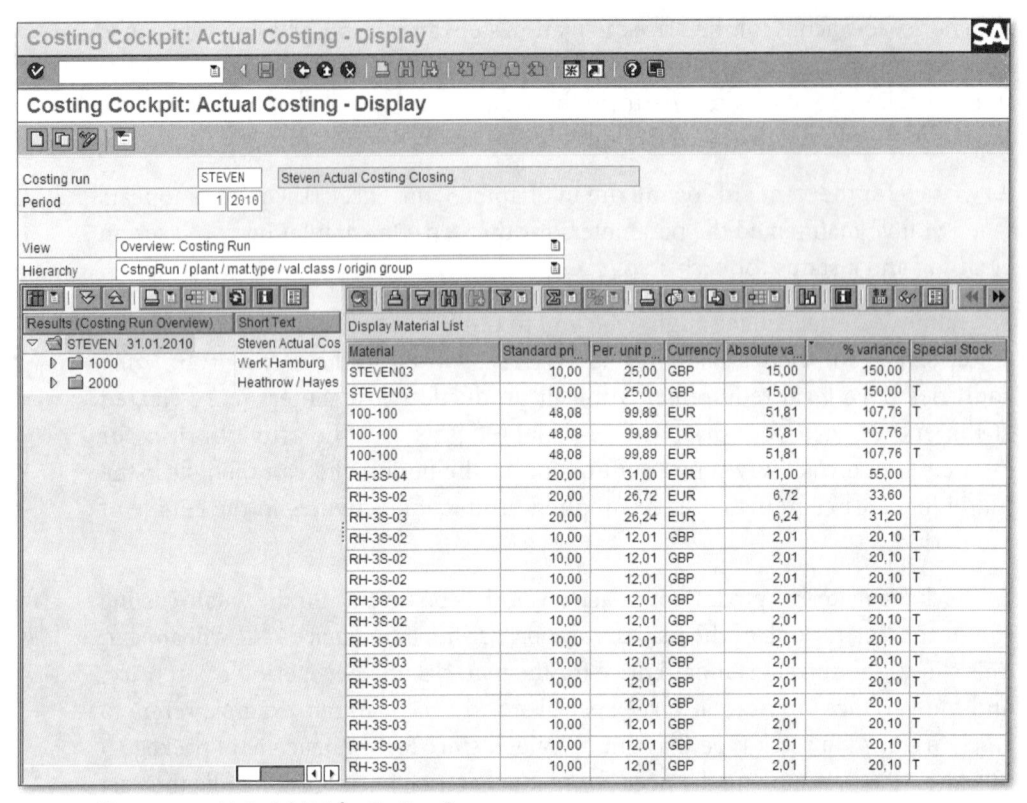

Costing Cockpit: Actual Costing - Display						
Costing run	STEVEN	Steven Actual Costing Closing				
Period	1 2010					
View	Overview: Costing Run					
Hierarchy	CstngRun / plant / mat.type / val.class / origin group					

Results (Costing Run Overview)	Short Text	Material	Standard pri	Per. unit p	Currency	Absolute va	% variance	Special Stock
▽ STEVEN 31.01.2010	Steven Actual Cos							
▷ 1000	Werk Hamburg	STEVEN03	10,00	25,00	GBP	15,00	150,00	
▷ 2000	Heathrow / Hayes	STEVEN03	10,00	25,00	GBP	15,00	150,00	T
		100-100	48,08	99,89	EUR	51,81	107,76	T
		100-100	48,08	99,89	EUR	51,81	107,76	
		100-100	48,08	99,89	EUR	51,81	107,76	T
		RH-3S-04	20,00	31,00	EUR	11,00	55,00	
		RH-3S-02	20,00	26,72	EUR	6,72	33,60	
		RH-3S-03	20,00	26,24	EUR	6,24	31,20	
		RH-3S-02	10,00	12,01	GBP	2,01	20,10	T
		RH-3S-02	10,00	12,01	GBP	2,01	20,10	T
		RH-3S-02	10,00	12,01	GBP	2,01	20,10	T
		RH-3S-02	10,00	12,01	GBP	2,01	20,10	
		RH-3S-02	10,00	12,01	GBP	2,01	20,10	T
		RH-3S-03	10,00	12,01	GBP	2,01	20,10	T
		RH-3S-03	10,00	12,01	GBP	2,01	20,10	T
		RH-3S-03	10,00	12,01	GBP	2,01	20,10	T
		RH-3S-03	10,00	12,01	GBP	2,01	20,10	T
		RH-3S-03	10,00	12,01	GBP	2,01	20,10	T
		RH-3S-03	10,00	12,01	GBP	2,01	20,10	T

Figure 7.41 Material List for Costing Run

Occasionally, the controller discovers some errors in the costing run that need to be corrected before he makes the closing entries. He can do this by making manual changes to the cost component split. To do this, select Transaction CKMCCD or ACCOUNTING • CONTROLLING • PRODUCT COST CONTROLLING • ACTUAL COSTING/ MATERIAL LEDGER • MATERIAL LEDGER • SET PRICES • MANUAL CHANGE OF COST COMPONENT SPLIT (this transaction is only active if enterprise extension EA_FIN is active; see Appendix C at www.sap-press.com). Figure 7.42 shows the initial screen once you have entered the relevant material, plant, and period. It looks almost identical to material price analysis (or Transaction CKM3N), except that there are change icons. To change the base quantity, select USER ENTRY in the BASE QUANTITY field. To adjust the values for the beginning inventory or the receipts via purchase order, position the cursor on the relevant line and click on the CHANGE icon.

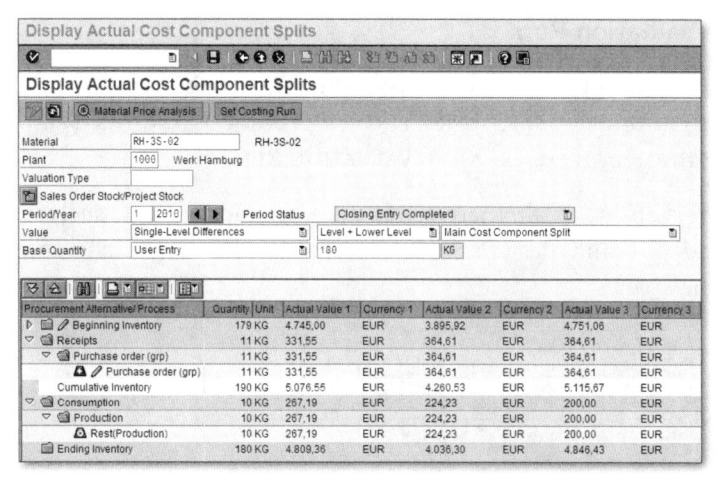

7.3 Multilevel Actual Costing in Material Ledger

Figure 7.42 Cost Component Split for Material Following Costing Run

Figure 7.43 shows a full cost component split for the chosen material. You can enter figures to correct data as required. You can make corrections until the closing entries are made. To ensure consistency, after the status Closing Entries Completed has been set, the system will not allow you to make changes to the cost component split.

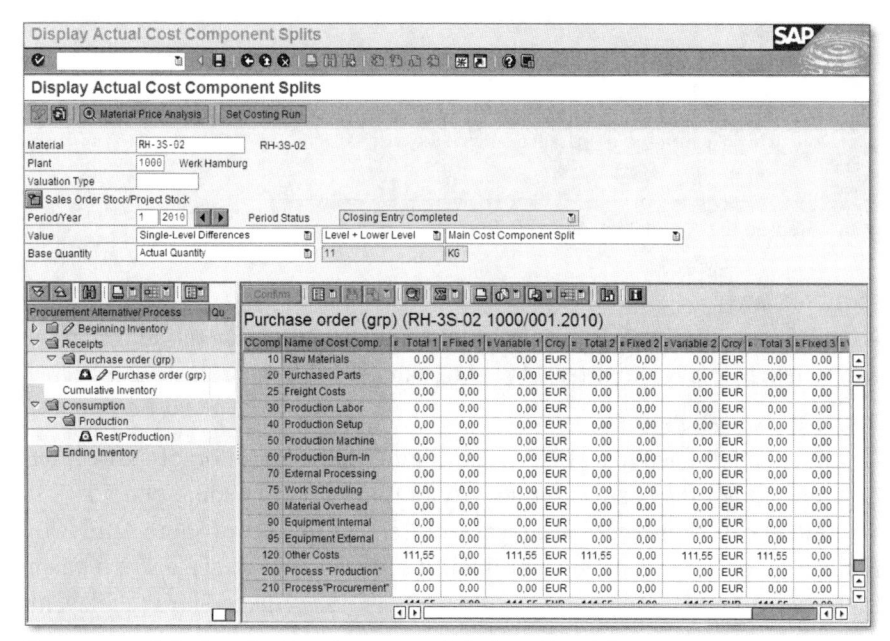

Figure 7.43 Adjusting the Cost Component Split for a Material

377

7.3.3 Alternative Valuation Run

To create an alternative valuation run, select Transaction CKMLCPAVR or ACCOUNTING • CONTROLLING • PRODUCT COST CONTROLLING • ACTUAL COSTING/MATERIAL LEDGER • ACTUAL COSTING • EDIT ALTERNATIVE VALUATION RUN.

Figure 7.44 shows the steps in an alternative valuation run. Some steps, such as selection, are the same for both types of costing run, but the alternative valuation run includes several new steps:

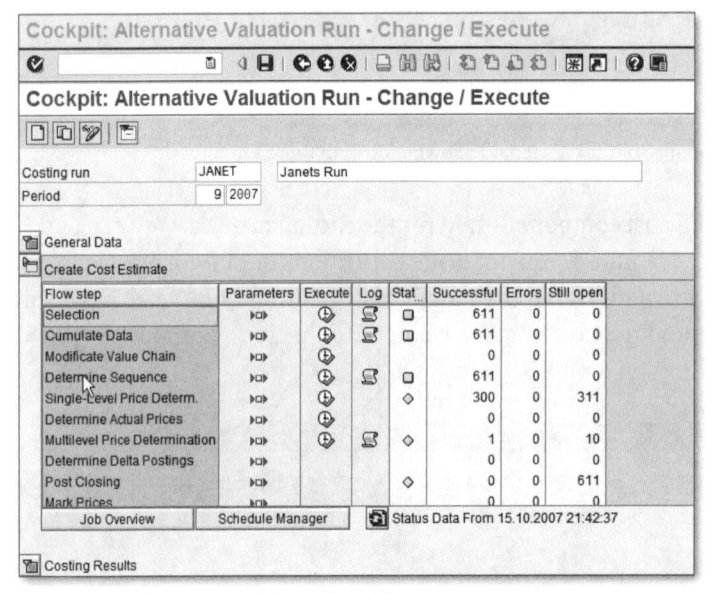

Figure 7.44 Steps in the Alternative Valuation Run

- CUMULATE DATA
  This step takes actual data from the original costing runs for the longer time frame, whether this is a quarter or year to date.
- DETERMINE ACTUAL PRICES
  This step cumulates activity prices, ensuring the full absorption of cost center costs even though the cost center activity output is zero in some periods (full absorption of cost center costs is a legal requirement in parts of South America). This step will only appear if the checkbox ACTIVITY UPDATE RELEVANT TO PRICE DETERMINATION was set when the material ledger was activated for the relevant

plant and replaces the use of Transaction CON2 to bring the activity prices into the inventory values.

- DETERMINE DELTA POSTINGS
  This step only applies if you flag the alternative valuation run as a posting run. The results of the alternative valuation run are compared with the current material valuation material by material. The difference is posted to a delta stock account that must be different from the normal stock to keep the new valuation separate from the operative valuation. The posting is automatically reversed with a key date in the next period.

> **Periodic Costing Runs and Alternative Valuation Runs**
>
> Before creating an alternative valuation run, it's a good idea to check that a periodic costing run has been performed for the periods you want to use before proceeding. Otherwise, the alternative valuation run won't find the beginning inventory, ending inventory, quantity structure, single-level price differences, and activity prices it needs as its starting point.
>
> The next thing to be aware of is that you can create a chain of alternative valuation runs by entering the previous valuation run and clicking on the CREATE FOLLOWING RUN button. In a productive environment this ensures that the ending inventory recorded by the first run is transferred to the follow-up run as the beginning inventory. If you don't enter a previous run, the system will take the beginning inventory for the first period you include in the valuation run as its starting point.

To create a new alternative valuation run, proceed as follows:

1. First, enter a name and description for the costing run together with the initial period (such as January if you're trying to cumulate values for the fiscal year) and the current period.

2. Select the PLANT ASSIGNMENT tab and enter the plants to be included in the calculations. If your aim is to smooth out price variances by taking a longer time frame, you should include the same plants here as you used in the original costing run. If your aim is to apply different valuation approaches, the company codes will probably be your guide. There may be legal obligations to apply alternative valuation approaches in only some of the countries in which the Material Ledger is active.

3. Select the SETTINGS tab to enter the system settings for your alternative valuation run. You should only make entries in this tab after you've completed the entries

under Period Data and Plant Assignment since the checks performed by the system are dependent on the plants and periods entered in these screens.

If may help to view the Settings screen (see Figure 7.45) as having three distinct parts:

- The upper part of the Settings screen (see Figure 7.45) determines what ultimately happens to the results of the costing run. If you select the Posting Run checkbox, you'll have to establish the link to the account assignment for the inventory accounts by making an appropriate entry in the Acc. Modification field. The system only allows you to update one inventory account per plant and period and issues an error if you try to update the same account twice with alternative valuation runs. If you're reporting according to multiple accounting principles, such as IFRS and local GAAP, you should also specify which accounting principle you're following. You can also update the cost of goods sold if you select the Revaluate Consumption checkbox. You can make the results available for use in the standard cost estimate (see Chapter 5) by selecting the Relevant for Costing checkbox. Whether the Credit Cost Center checkbox is selected depends on your configuration settings for the material ledger in each plant.

- The middle part of the screen (from Provisional Price downwards) determines which prices will be used for the valuation of the activities. The first field, Provisional Price, determines whether the initial activity price will be the standard activity price from the first period included in the alternative valuation run or the last period. This price is calculated in Cost Center Accounting using Transaction KSPI (see Chapter 5).

    The next field, Price, determines which price will be used to revalue the activities during the alternative valuation run. If you enter the actual price, this ensures that the actual price is calculated in the Material Ledger and not in Cost Center Accounting, so you should remove Transaction KSII (actual price calculation) from your period closing activities. You should also enter the version under which this price will be updated in the Price for Cumulation.: Legal field. If your configuration settings also cover group and profit center valuation, the system will provide additional fields for the version used in group valuation and in the profit center valuation. By doing this, we're following the same principles as for the standard cost estimate, where the quantity structure stays the same, but different prices are applied to the structure in each valuation approach.

- The lower part of the screen determines which prices will be used to value the raw materials. Your entry in the VALUATION ALTERNATIVE field will determine which of the values from balance sheet valuation the system will apply to the quantity structure. The options include the FIFO valuation, the LIFO valuation, and the lowest value prices. These valuations are performed in Logistics via the menu path LOGISTICS • MATERIALS MANAGEMENT • VALUATION • BALANCE SHEET VALUATION • DETERMINATION OF LOWEST VALUE / LIFO VALUATION / FIFO VALUATION. You have to ensure that the appropriate balance sheet valuation has been performed and the data updated to the material master as physical inventory prices *before* you run the alternative valuation run.

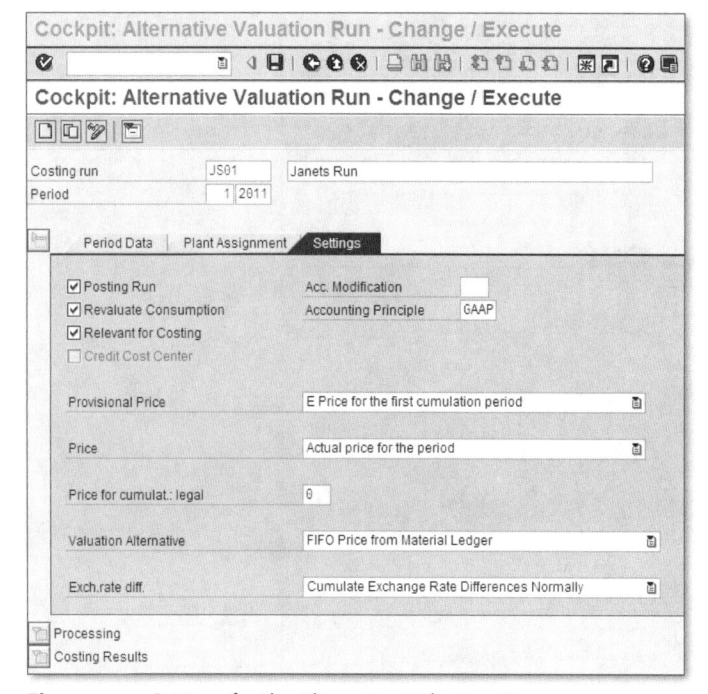

Figure 7.45 Settings for the Alternative Valuation Run

Alternative Valuation Run for Parallel Valuation of Cost of Goods Manufactured

Since SAP enhancement package 5 for SAP ERP 6.0 there's been a special form of alternative valuation run, used specifically for inventory valuation. This is activated using the business function Parallel Valuation of Cost of Goods Manufactured (FIN_CO_COGM). The alternative valuation run looks slightly different, in that it is flagged as being relevant for the calculation of the cost of goods manufactured in the PERIOD DATA tab, and the SETTINGS tab is slightly different (see Figure 7.46). Notice that there's no account modification field, since the inventory valuation can update to the same pair of accounts as the periodic costing run.

- The periodic costing run updates the accounting principle IFRS.
- The alternative valuation run updates the accounting principle local GAAP.

The version entered in the PRICE field is the version used to store the second set of activity prices in CO. There are no settings for group valuation or transfer price valuation, since these are always updated in the leading ledger/leading valuation.

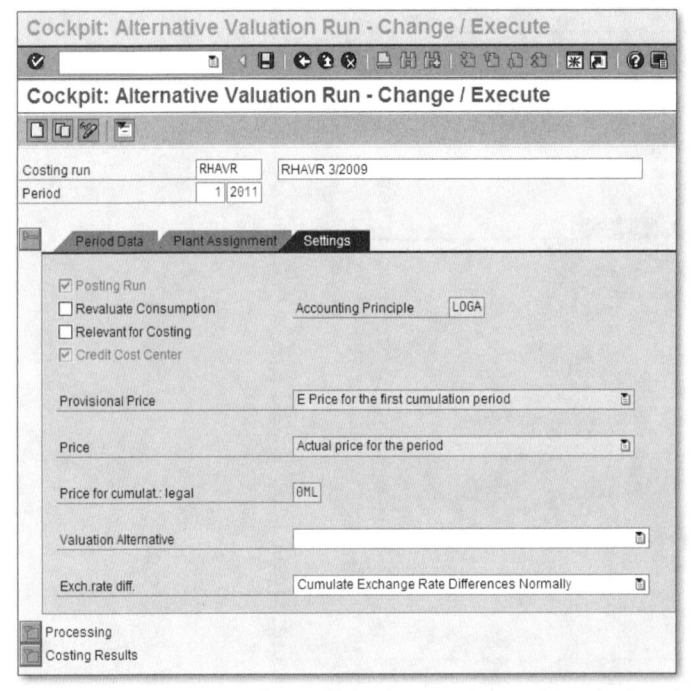

Figure 7.46 Settings Tab for Parallel Valuation of Cost of Goods Manufactured

Figure 7.47 shows the effect of completing the alternative valuation run on a production cost center (we're using the cost center line item report we discussed extensively in Chapter 2, Section 2.1). Notice that this report shows the valuation view PARALLEL COST OF GOODS MANUFACTURED rather than the legal valuation, since we've cleared the activity costs in the second GAAP. Working through the report from top to bottom, you'll see:

- Primary cost postings for the depreciation of the fixed assets. Blank lines are for depreciation according to the leading valuation and would be visible if we switched to the legal valuation by selecting EXTRAS • ACTUAL VALUATION in the selection screen.

- Primary cost postings for pension reserves (from Payroll Accounting).

- Secondary costs for machine costs. There's one line for the posting made at the time of confirmation (10 hours) and an additional line for the correction made when the final activity rate was calculated and applied (business Transaction KSII in the report).

- Primary cost postings to clear the cost center made by the alternative valuation run.

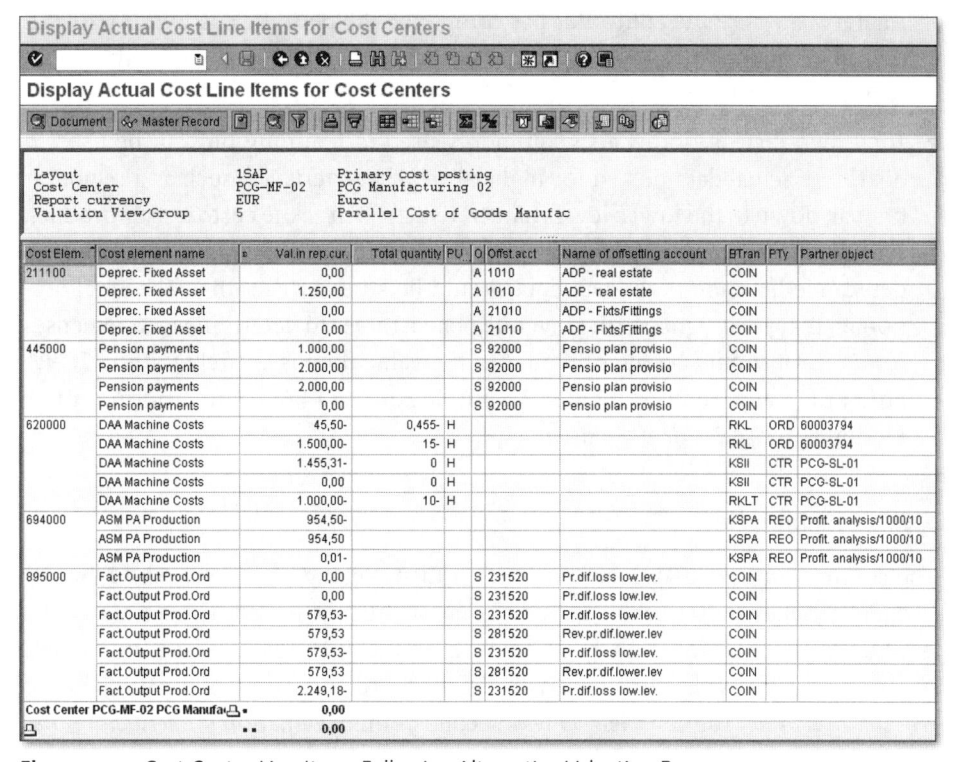

Cost Elem.	Cost element name	Val.in rep.cur.	Total quantity	PU	O	Offst acct	Name of offsetting account	BTran	PTy	Partner object
211100	Deprec. Fixed Asset	0,00			A	1010	ADP - real estate	COIN		
	Deprec. Fixed Asset	1.250,00			A	1010	ADP - real estate	COIN		
	Deprec. Fixed Asset	0,00			A	21010	ADP - Fixts/Fittings	COIN		
	Deprec. Fixed Asset	0,00			A	21010	ADP - Fixts/Fittings	COIN		
445000	Pension payments	1.000,00			S	92000	Pensio plan provisio	COIN		
	Pension payments	2.000,00			S	92000	Pensio plan provisio	COIN		
	Pension payments	2.000,00			S	92000	Pensio plan provisio	COIN		
	Pension payments	0,00			S	92000	Pensio plan provisio	COIN		
620000	DAA Machine Costs	45,50-	0,455-	H				RKL	ORD	60003794
	DAA Machine Costs	1.500,00-	15-	H				RKL	ORD	60003794
	DAA Machine Costs	1.455,31-	0	H				KSII	CTR	PCG-SL-01
	DAA Machine Costs	0,00	0	H				KSII	CTR	PCG-SL-01
	DAA Machine Costs	1.000,00-	10-	H				RKLT	CTR	PCG-SL-01
694000	ASM PA Production	954,50-						KSPA	REO	Profit. analysis/1000/10
	ASM PA Production	954,50						KSPA	REO	Profit. analysis/1000/10
	ASM PA Production	0,01-						KSPA	REO	Profit. analysis/1000/10
895000	Fact.Output Prod.Ord	0,00			S	231520	Pr.dif.loss low.lev.	COIN		
	Fact.Output Prod.Ord	0,00			S	231520	Pr.dif.loss low.lev.	COIN		
	Fact.Output Prod.Ord	579,53-			S	231520	Pr.dif.loss low.lev.	COIN		
	Fact.Output Prod.Ord	579,53			S	281520	Rev.pr.dif.lower.lev	COIN		
	Fact.Output Prod.Ord	579,53-			S	231520	Pr.dif.loss low.lev.	COIN		
	Fact.Output Prod.Ord	579,53			S	281520	Rev.pr.dif.lower.lev	COIN		
	Fact.Output Prod.Ord	2.249,18-			S	231520	Pr.dif.loss low.lev.	COIN		
Cost Center PCG-MF-02 PCG Manufa		0,00								
		0,00								

Figure 7.47 Cost Center Line Items Following Alternative Valuation Run

7 | Period Close

Now that we've calculated actual costs for all materials in the Material Ledger, we're ready to move to the final stage of the close and complete the valuations in Profitability Analysis.

7.4 CO-PA Processes

We looked at allocations from Cost Center Accounting to Profitability Analysis in Section 7.1.4. The other main processes in CO-PA are periodic valuation and top-down distribution.

- In Chapter 5 we used the valuation function to pull the results of the cost estimates into Profitability Planning. The periodic valuation works on the same principle. If you performed the revaluation of consumption step in the Material Ledger, you'll want to see these values not just on the COGS account in Financial Accounting, but also in the value fields for cost of goods sold in Profitability Analysis. So once the controller has completed the periodic costing run, he can use the periodic revaluation function to update the value fields with the actual costs from the Material Ledger.

- Top-down distribution is also commonly used in planning but can be used to distribute actual data posted for higher-level characteristics, such as a region or branch, down to the lower-level characteristics, such as the customer or product. This process involves using reference data for the lower-level characteristics to determine how the high-level data should be spread. It's rather like an allocation, in that you might use the revenue per customer to determine how expenses for a region should be distributed, but the value flow is entirely within CO-PA rather than between Cost Center Accounting and CO-PA. Another term for this kind of approach is *decomposition*.

7.4.1 Revaluation

The settings for revaluation are covered in Customizing. If you use the Material Ledger, it makes sense to link the cost component split under which your actual product costs are stored with value fields in profitability analysis. The initial sales order and invoice will be valued with the standard cost component split during *real-time valuation*. You can then set up a second point of valuation for *periodic revaluation of actual data* to bring the latest actual costs into Profitability Analysis from the revaluation of consumption step in the Material Ledger. To perform revaluation, select Transaction KE27 or ACCOUNTING • CONTROLLING • PROFITABILITY ANALYSIS • ACTUAL POSTINGS • PERIOD-END CLOSING • PERIODIC ADJUSTMENTS • PERIODIC VALUATION and select the PERIODIC VALUATION checkbox as shown in Figure 7.48. The result will be the update of the value fields with the actual costs from the cost component split in the Material Ledger.

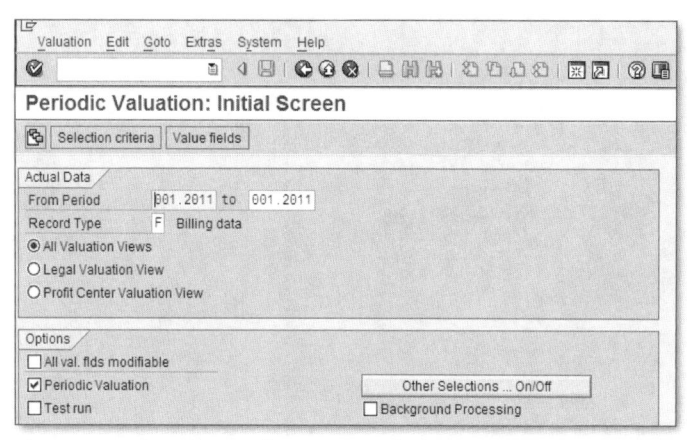

Figure 7.48 Periodic Revaluation in Profitability Analysis

7.4.2 Top-Down Distribution

The most important task in defining how top-down distribution should take place is the entry of reference data, since this tells you the basis for the distribution. The reference is always a value field (such as revenue or cost of goods sold) and can be either an actual value from a previous time period or a planned value.

To enter the relevant values for top-down distribution, select Transaction KE28 or ACCOUNTING • CONTROLLING • PROFITABILITY ANALYSIS • ACTUAL POSTINGS • PERIOD-END CLOSING • PERIODIC ADJUSTMENTS • TOP-DOWN DISTRIBUTION. Figure 7.49 shows the selection screen.

From here you can click on the relevant buttons to maintain the following settings prior to execution.

- PROCESSING INSTRUCTIONS
- SELECTION CRITERIA
- VALUE FIELDS

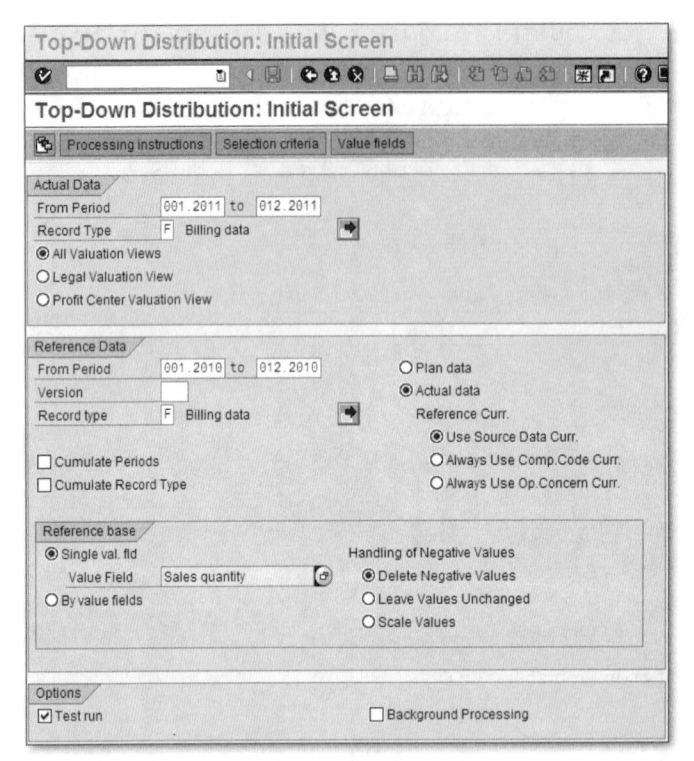

Figure 7.49 Initial Screen for Top-Down Distribution

Currently, the selection criteria and value fields are fairly technical in nature, but there will be enhancements in this area in the future.

7.5 Summary

We've covered what happens in the main steps of the period close for controllers, and in so doing completed our journey through the basic controlling functions. We'll now return to the reporting functions we discussed in Chapter 2 and discuss how to work with high volumes of data and the newer options for reporting. To find out more about managing and automating the period close, skip to Chapter 12.

This chapter looks at how to handle large data volumes both in SAP ERP and in SAP NetWeaver Business Warehouse. It shows various examples of cost center reporting and explains how the BW Query is also the basis for reporting in the SAP BusinessObjects tools.

8 Reporting in SAP NetWeaver BW and SAP BusinessObjects

When we discussed reporting in Chapter 2, we focused on list reporting for cost centers, internal orders, production orders, and so on and explained how to use SAP List Viewer to build your own layouts for the individual reports. This was partly because we wanted to introduce the data structures in SAP ERP before we looked at the operative processes in more detail, but it was also because list reporting is a task best performed in SAP ERP, since the data structures the controller uses for analysis are similar to the data structures in the underlying tables. For the most part, such reporting is simply a matter of selecting the data set that interests you and then performing simple operations such as totaling and sorting on the results shown in your report. However, most controllers will agree that there's more to reporting than neatly sorted lists.

In Chapter 2 we made the assumption that the reports were being run *online*. If it's not essential to have the very latest data in your reports, you can also work with *extracts*, where the data in the report is preselected and stored as an extract to accelerate access. This is especially useful when you're looking at large structures, such as the costs for an entire cost center hierarchy or all the items in a balance sheet, and has the twofold effect of providing you with quicker access to the data in your report since it has been preselected and reducing strain on your system since the preparation of the extracts can be performed at night when system load is generally lower.

When we looked at the line items for CO-PA, we were looking at the characteristics and value fields recorded for each data record, which is clearly useful for performing a spot check on the integrity of the data. However, most controllers want to select *all data records* relating to a particular customer, customer group, product, product group, region, sales organization, and so on. Likewise, a report that shows an individual production order, as we saw in Chapters 6 and 7, is interesting once you've determined that there are issues with that production order, but you're unlikely to want to analyze thousands of production orders in turn. You'll want to select *all production orders* in a particular plant or in a particular product group and then drill down to the problem orders, so in this chapter, we'll also look at your options for drill-down reporting in SAP ERP. In case these options still aren't enough to meet your reporting requirements we'll then discuss when to introduce SAP NetWeaver BW as a dedicated data warehouse, your reporting options with SAP BusinessObjects tools, and finally the very latest technology, the High Performance Analytic Appliance, or SAP HANA™ for short.

8.1 Reporting on Large Data Volumes in SAP ERP

In this section we'll look at your options for accelerating Report Writer reports and your drill-down reports in SAP ERP.

8.1.1 Using Extracts to Accelerate Cost Center and Internal Order Reports

One way the controlling department can speed up cost center and internal order reporting is to prepare extracts of the data and encourage your cost center managers to work with these extracts rather than querying the live tables to speed up the selection and ease general system performance. This option works for any report built using Report Writer. If you refer back to Figure 2.1 in Chapter 2, you'll see that this option covers reports such as Cost Centers: Actual/Plan Variance, Cost Centers: Actual/Target Variance, Cost Centers: Quarterly Comparison, and so on. The same applies to most of the reports shown for internal orders in Figure 2.9. You'll recognize these reports by the DATA SOURCE button in the selection screen, as shown in Figure 8.1. Choosing this button allows you to switch between live data (NEW SELECTION) and an extract (DISPLAY EXTRACT). The result of executing the report is the same, but if you try it with your own data, you should notice an improvement.

If nobody has prepared an extract for you, you'll first need to create one. To find the settings for creating extracts, switch to expert more by selecting ENVIRONMENT • OPTIONS and selecting the EXPERT MODE checkbox. This results in several new buttons appearing on the selection screen, as shown in Figure 8.2. We'll now look at the purpose of the VARIATION, OUTPUT PARAMETERS, and EXTRACT PARAMETERS buttons. To maintain the settings for your extracts, click on EXTRACT PARAMETERS, select CREATE EXTRACT, give your extract a name, and enter an expiry date, as shown in Figure 8.2.

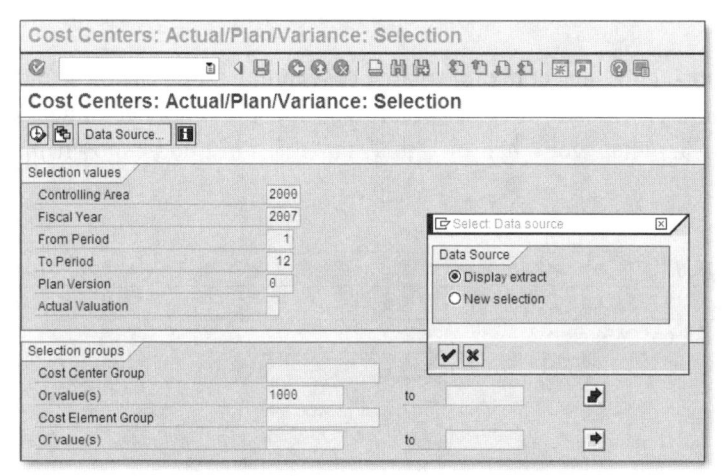

Figure 8.1 Using an Extract for a Cost Center Plan/Actual Report

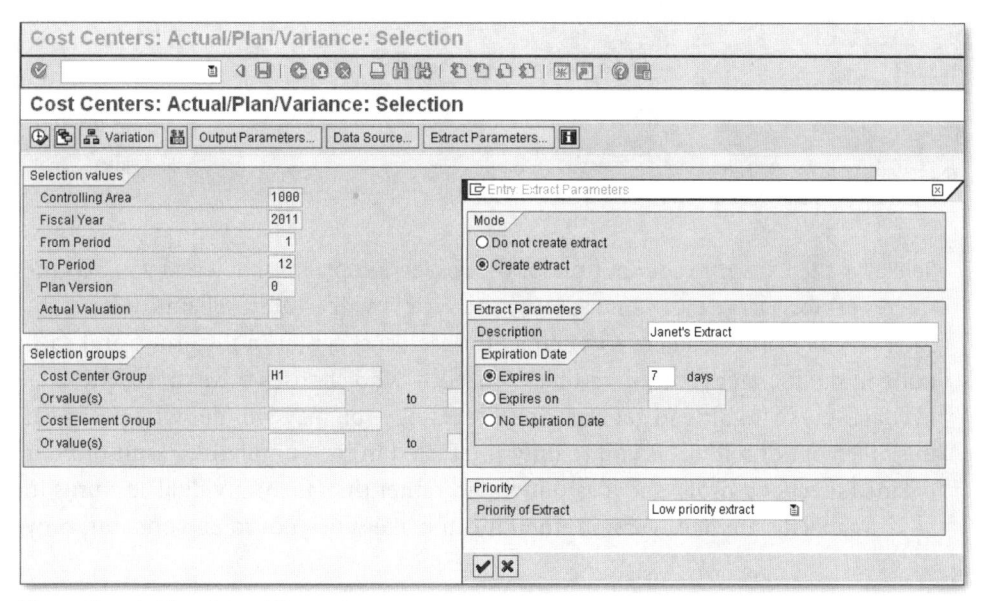

Figure 8.2 Setting Extract Parameters

Caution: Use of Extracts

When you see the expiry dates in the extract parameters, it's easy to imagine that you've found the perfect solution for storing the contents of your report for safe keeping until the next audit. This only works as long as the structure of your report does not change. If your report structure changes, your extracts may become unusable. Don't rely on the extract for long-term auditing.

If you're planning to execute the report for a large cost center group or even the whole cost center hierarchy, make sure that before you run the report you check the settings that appear when you click on the VARIATION button, as shown in Figure 8.3.

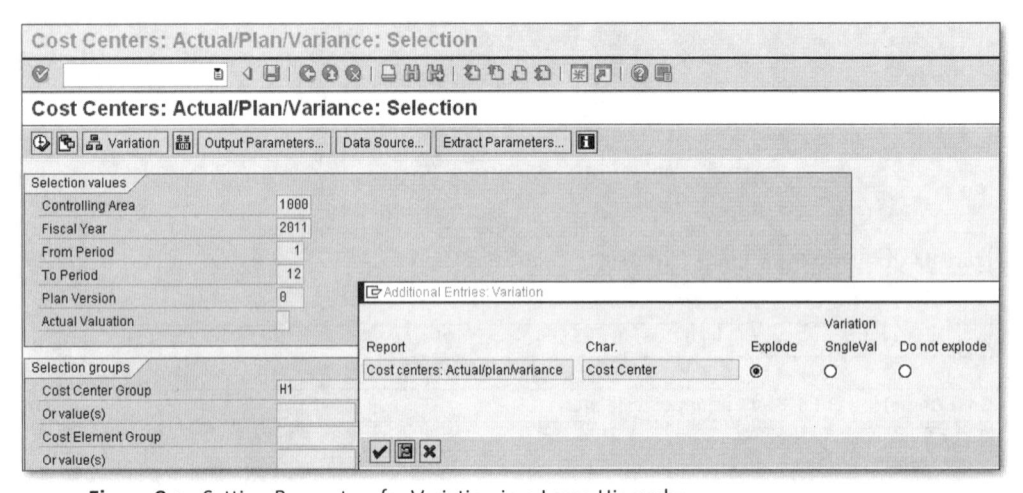

Figure 8.3 Setting Parameters for Variation in a Large Hierarchy

Selecting the EXPLODE radio button for the cost center means that when you execute the report for a large cost center group, the system will create a separate extract for each *variation*. This results in an extract for each cost center in the group and each node in the hierarchy, meaning that everybody who chooses the extract option as his data source is going to get faster report results. You may wonder why you need the other options at all. If you're only interested in the cumulative result of your balance sheet and profit and loss statement, rather than the individual accounts in your financial statement version, then it can make sense not to explode, but only to view the totals. However, in the Controlling component of SAP ERP Financials (CO) you almost always want to explode for each cost center, each order, each project, and so on in your chosen group to provide a report for each cost center manager and project manager.

Before you execute a report in the background, you should also check the output parameters, as shown in Figure 8.4. It may seem at odds with common sense, but what you should do now is set the OUTPUT MEDIUM to NO OUTPUT. This means that instead of writing to a spool or a printer, the contents of the list are only written to the extracts. If you have no plans to use the spool list, this is another way to ease the load on your system. You're now ready to execute the report, either by selecting PROGRAM • EXECUTE or if you want to schedule it at night, by selecting PROGRAM • SCHEDULE JOB. It's good practice to execute this type of mass report in the background once all the relevant steps of the period close are complete. Many organizations include the preparation of these extracts in the Closing Cockpit or Schedule Manager so they can be scheduled automatically, as we'll discuss in Chapter 12.

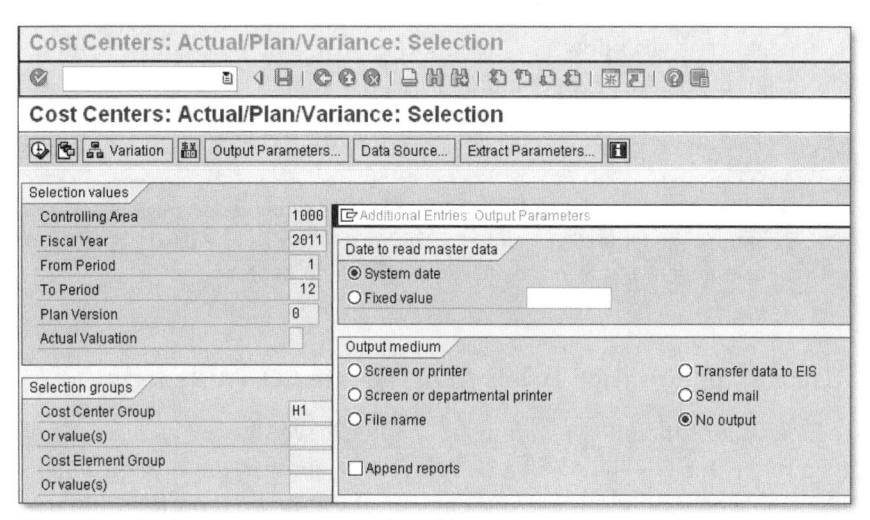

Figure 8.4 Setting Output Parameters for a Report

Once the extract has been prepared, you'll see the extract when you select DISPLAY EXTRACT, as shown in Figure 8.1, and you can then choose your extract, as shown in Figure 8.5.

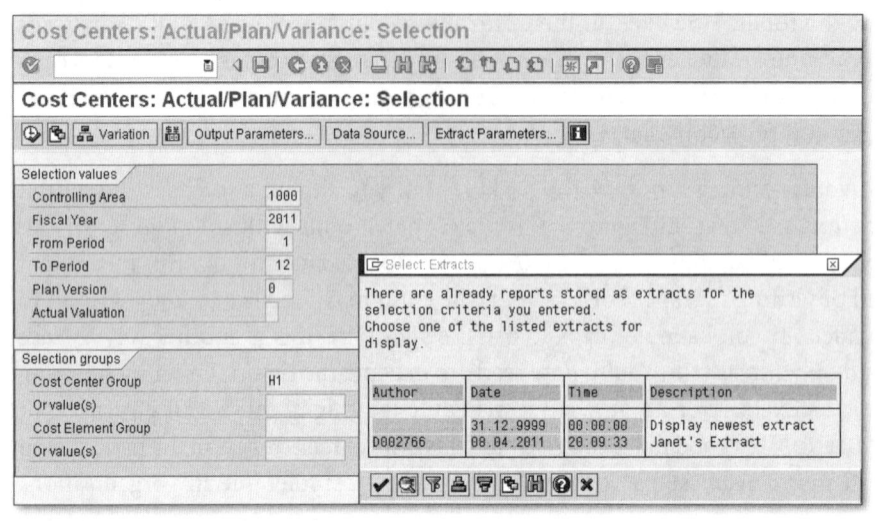

Figure 8.5 Choosing a Prepared Extract

Once you're working with the data in your report, you have exactly the same options to navigate and drill down in the report as with live data. Only the initial selection is different, reading *extracted* rather than live data.

> **Creating Extracts for Line Items**
>
> If you're interested in creating extracts for line items for scheduled jobs, consider asking your IT Department to implement SAP Note 1572806. This can also be used to prepare extracts for the line items we saw in the allocation cycles in Chapter 7.

8.1.2 Using Summarization Levels to Accelerate CO-PA Reports

When we looked at profitability planning in Chapter 5, we showed an example of a drill-down report for CO-PA in SAP ERP. Figure 5.36 showed the results of planning for the whole operating concern presented in a drill-down report. Within this report you could drill down to see the same key figures by distribution channel, sales organization, and material group. There are many different types of drill-down reports you can build to display the data in your operating concern. One way to ease performance concerns if you're working with huge sets of data is to use *summarization levels* to preselect and summarize data for dimensions you know you'll be reporting on regularly. Your implementation team will define the dimensions for which summarization levels are created when they configure your operating concern, but you should use the refresh function to extract the latest data to these summarization levels on a regular basis. To prepare the summarization levels, follow the menu path ACCOUNTING • CONTROLLING • PROFITABILITY ANALYSIS • TOOLS SUMMARIZATION LEVELS • REFRESH and fill out the selection shown in Figure 8.6. If you don't do this, the system has to select new data each time you drill down to a new characteristic, which can mean long wait times as the system performs a new selection each time you click and a lot of frustration.

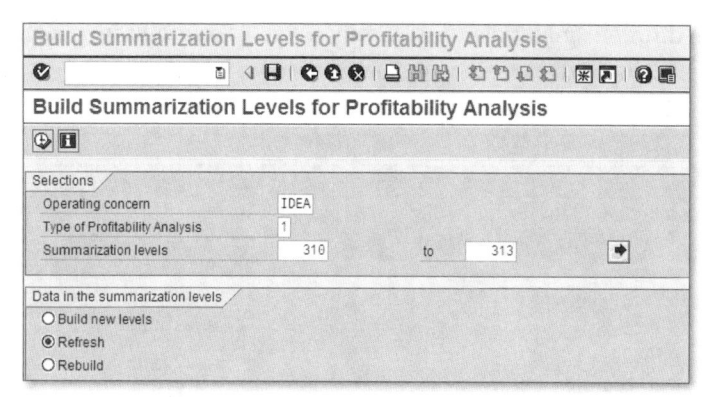

Figure 8.6 Building Summarization Levels for Profitability Analysis

8.1.3 Using Summarization in Product Cost Reports

You'll also find drill-down reports in Cost Object Controlling. These options are listed in Chapter 2, Figure 2.16 under SUMMARIZED ANALYSIS • WITH PRODUCT DRILL-DOWN. Technically, these are very similar to the CO-PA reports, though you don't have to build them from scratch when you implement. However, while not filling the summarization levels in CO-PA gives you a tedious wait when you run the report, in Cost Object Controlling you *must* run a special transaction (KKRV) to fill the summarization levels prior to executing the reports. If you don't, the report will indicate that no data is available. You'll also find that the summarization levels are set by SAP, so you can only summarize by plant, product group, product, and period. To prepare the data for these reports, select Transaction KKRV or ACCOUNTING • CONTROLLING • PRODUCT COST CONTROLLING • COST OBJECT CONTROLLING •

PRODUCT COST BY ORDER • INFORMATION SYSTEM • TOOLS • DATA COLLECTION • FOR PRODUCT DRILLDOWN and enter the relevant plant(s) and time frame. It's common to consider this transaction as part of the period close (See Chapter 7) since it requires you to have calculated work in process, variances, and so on prior to data collection. To display the report, follow the menu path FINANCIALS • CONTROLLING • PRODUCT COST CONTROLLING • COST OBJECT CONTROLLING • PRODUCT COST BY ORDER • INFORMATION SYSTEM • REPORTS FOR PRODUCT COST BY ORDER (OR PRODUCT COST BY PERIOD) • SUMMARIZED ANALYSIS • WITH PRODUCT DRILLDOWN • ACTUAL COSTS • CUMULATIVE and enter the relevant plant and time frame. Figure 8.7 shows the results of such a report. We've drilled down by product to show the product costs for four different materials (this is only a small example; in a real system there would be far more data records in such a view).

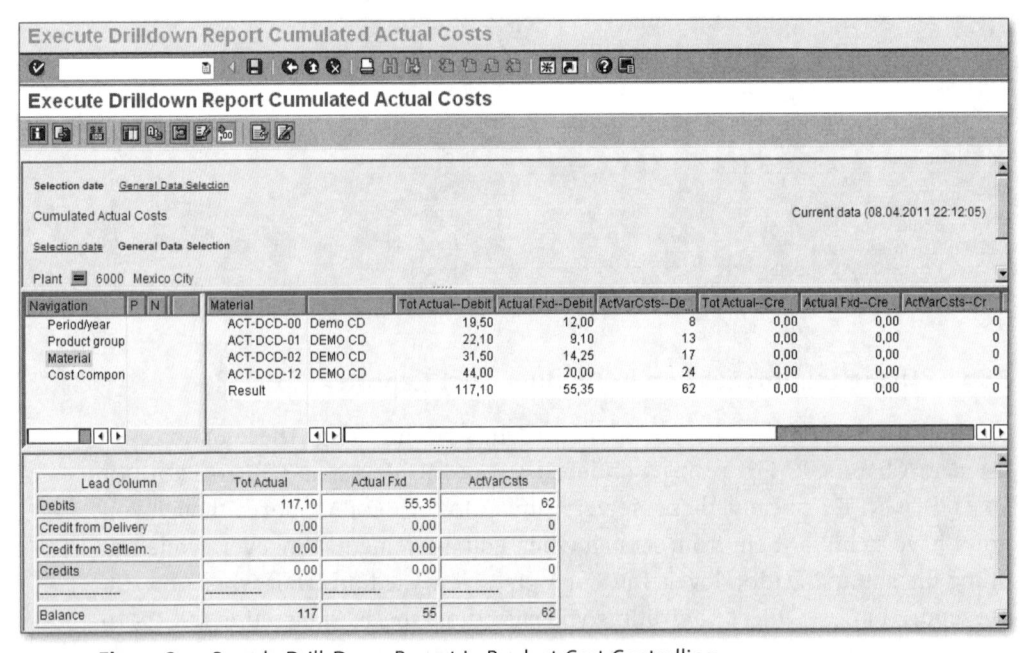

Figure 8.7 Sample Drill-Down Report in Product Cost Controlling

If you explore the Investment Management reports, you'll find that they also use the drill-down techniques but don't require you to perform a preliminary collection run for the data. Now that we've looked at the options for summarized reporting in SAP ERP, let's consider what might affect a decision to move your reporting tasks to SAP NetWeaver BW.

8.2 How to Decide Whether You Need SAP NetWeaver BW for Reporting

If your organization has yet to make the move to SAP NetWeaver BW or another data warehouse, you should ask several questions. It may be that the decision has been made for you or that you're already using SAP NetWeaver BW, but we'll look at some of the questions you might ask from a controlling perspective.

> **SAP NetWeaver BW for Controllers**
>
> The next 30 pages won't turn you into an SAP NetWeaver BW expert. They will tell you where SAP NetWeaver BW provides options that don't exist in SAP ERP and help you understand what sort of reports you can build in SAP NetWeaver BW. As power users, controllers are frequently asked for their requirements in the early days of a reporting project, but they can find it difficult to provide an adequate answer because they don't know what can and can't be done in SAP NetWeaver BW, leading to frustration on both sides.

8.2.1 Performance Concerns

When we looked at the order-to-cash process in Chapter 6, we saw how CO-PA records sit behind every sales order and invoice. In Chapter 7 we went on to allocate general expenses to CO-PA, settle production orders to CO-PA, and finally to perform top-down allocations in CO-PA, generating yet more data records. It's easy to imagine just how huge the data volumes in the CO-PA tables can become and how the apparently simple act of selecting all the invoices in an operating concern can become a potential performance headache. The same applies to Cost Object Controlling. If you're capturing data for every production order and then aggregating this data for analysis by product group or plant, the data volumes can be large.

Moving data to a dedicated data warehouse is an extension of the extraction process we just discussed, but instead of simply preparing data extracts for analysis, you move all relevant data to an environment designed specifically for reporting. As far as CO is concerned, SAP delivers a series of extractors that a system administrator can use to pull the data from the CO tables into SAP NetWeaver BW. The process of moving data from SAP ERP to SAP NetWeaver BW is handled by setting up *InfoPackages* that parcel the data to be selected from SAP ERP and then schedule the data load. The load intervals can range from hourly to daily to once a month, where the relevant data is only calculated as part of the period close. Think of it simply as an extension of the extraction process we discussed at the beginning of the chapter, where you need to prepare your selection parameters and then schedule the timing of the load.

DataSources provide the link between the operational system and the reporting system. SAP delivers DataSources for all areas of CO and Investment Management. Your administrator can display and test the DataSources in your SAP ERP system using Transaction RSA3, provided that your SAP ERP system is on the correct release level (you can check the minimum release level for each DataSource in the SAP documentation for the BW content).

Once the SAP NetWeaver BW system is installed, the first step is for a system administrator to activate the relevant business content (the DataSources, Info-Providers, and so on that you plan to use). Once this infrastructure is installed, you can display the delivered InfoProviders by logging on to SAP NetWeaver BW and selecting SAP BUSINESS INFORMATION WAREHOUSE • ADMINISTRATION • DATA WAREHOUSING WORKBENCH ADMINISTRATION and then MODELING • INFOPROVIDER. To display the InfoProviders delivered for CO, select FINANCIAL MANAGEMENT AND CONTROLLING • CONTROLLING • OVERHEAD COST CONTROLLING or PRODUCT COST CONTROLLING or PROFITABILITY ANALYSIS in the right-hand part of the screen, as shown in Figure 8.8.

To work with the workbench, you need to understand three terms.

- Each application menu in CO is mapped to an *InfoArea*. The InfoAreas are simply a set of folders that group the relevant applications, so the InfoArea for overhead cost controlling includes InfoAreas for Activity-Based Costing, Cost Center Accounting, Overhead Projects, and Overhead Cost Orders.

- If you select the InfoArea Cost Center Accounting, you'll see a series of *InfoProviders*. The InfoProviders, as the name implies, provide the data to be analyzed to the query when the user executes a report. You load data from the CO tables to the InfoProviders for activity types and prices, costs and allocations, statistical key figures, and so on. If you find the term *InfoProvider* off-putting, it may help to think of InfoProviders simply as the tables where the transactional data is stored once it has been extracted from SAP ERP and that are read when you execute a query.

▶ Finally, SAP delivers *queries* that select data from these InfoProviders and display the costs per cost center, the activity prices per cost center, and so on. These are the equivalent of the reports in SAP ERP.

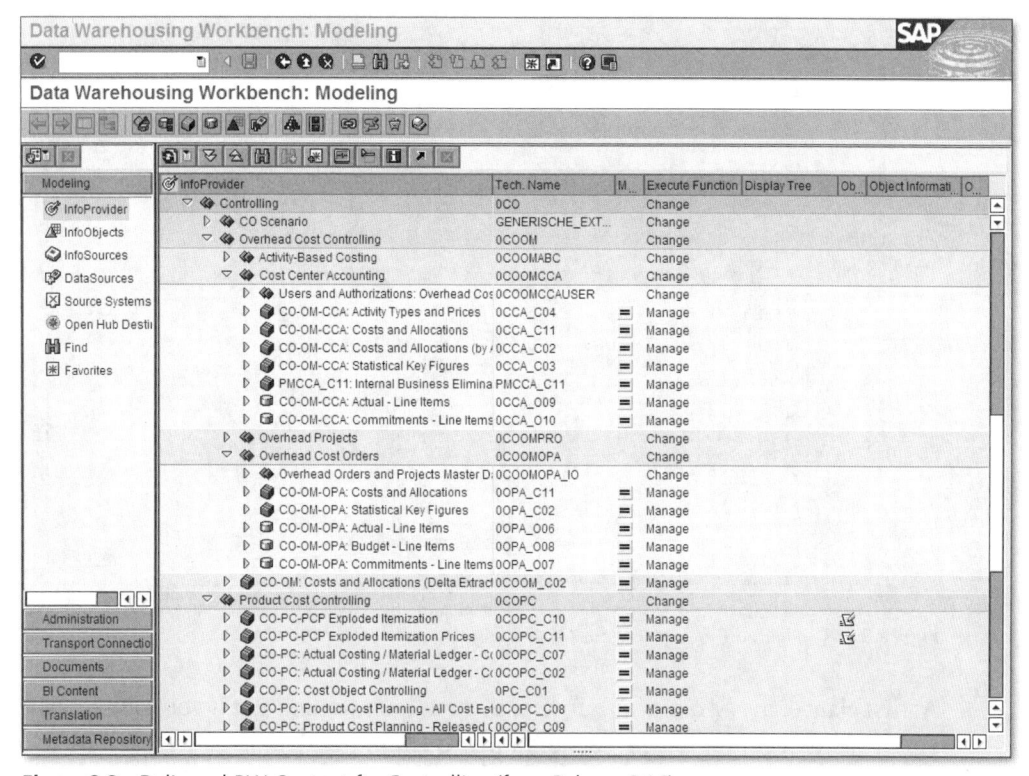

Figure 8.8 Delivered BW Content for Controlling (from Release 2.1C)

If you're using a newer version of SAP NetWeaver BW, you might want to consider using a newer set of InfoProviders that were delivered to take advantage of changes to the SAP NetWeaver BW architecture in Release 7.0. Your administrator will find the business content for Simplified Reporting by following the menu path above but selecting the InfoArea FINANCIAL MANAGEMENT AND CONTROLLING • REPORTING FINANCIALS (EhP3) • COST CENTER REPORTING • OVERHEAD COST ORDERS or PRODUCT COST CONTROLLING as shown in Figure 8.9. Enhancement package 4 included additional new content for PROFITABILITY ANALYSIS and Investment Management.

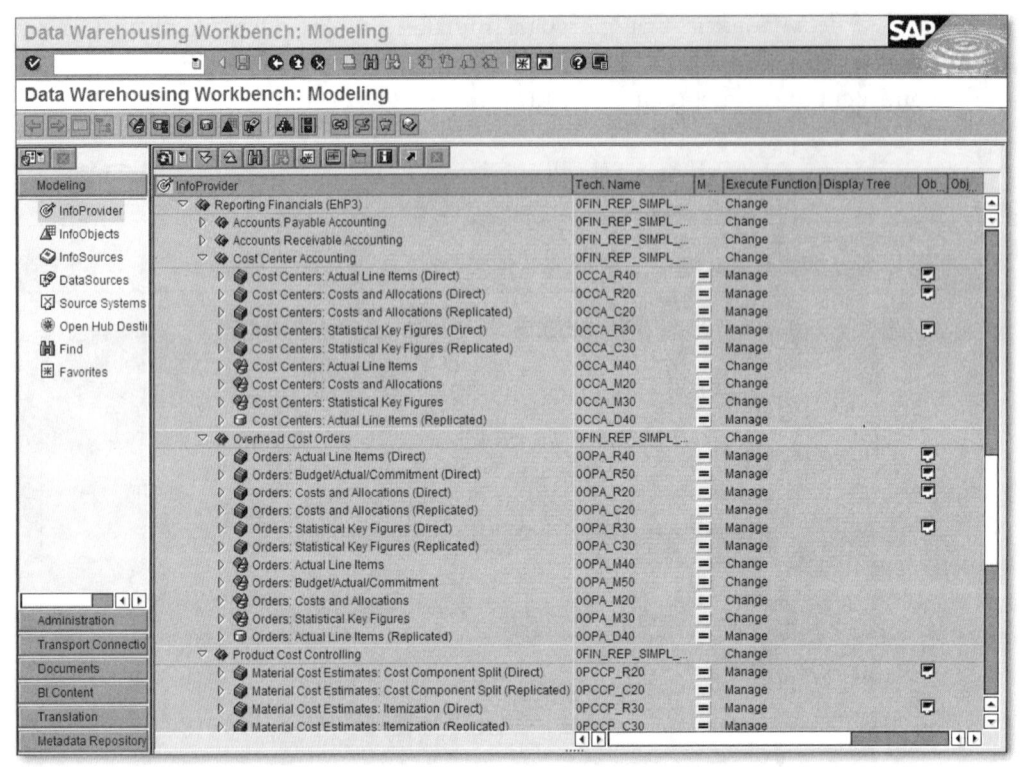

Figure 8.9 Delivered BW Content for Controlling (from Release 7.0)

At first glance, the two sets of business content look similar, but if you look closely you'll see that in the newer version a pair of InfoProviders is delivered for each application, one labeled Replicated and the other labeled Direct. This is because the new InfoProviders offer you a choice between working with *replicated* data (in other words, data that has been extracted or copied to SAP NetWeaver BW from SAP ERP) or working with live data in SAP ERP that is selected when the query is executed (*direct access* in SAP NetWeaver BW terms).

If your data volumes are not excessively large, direct access means you can dispense with the process of performing regular loads of data to the SAP NetWeaver BW tables but can enjoy the benefits of the modeling options to look at the data in ways that are not currently possible in SAP ERP alone. Whichever version of SAP NetWeaver BW you use, the link between the information in the SAP ERP tables and SAP NetWeaver BW is established using a DataSource. You can check this mapping by choosing any of the InfoProviders shown above and clicking on the DATASOURCE icon, as shown in Figure 8.10. This allows you to display the mapping of the fields from the SAP ERP tables that we used for our list reports in Chapter 2 and the DataSources that are the basis for SAP NetWeaver BW reporting.

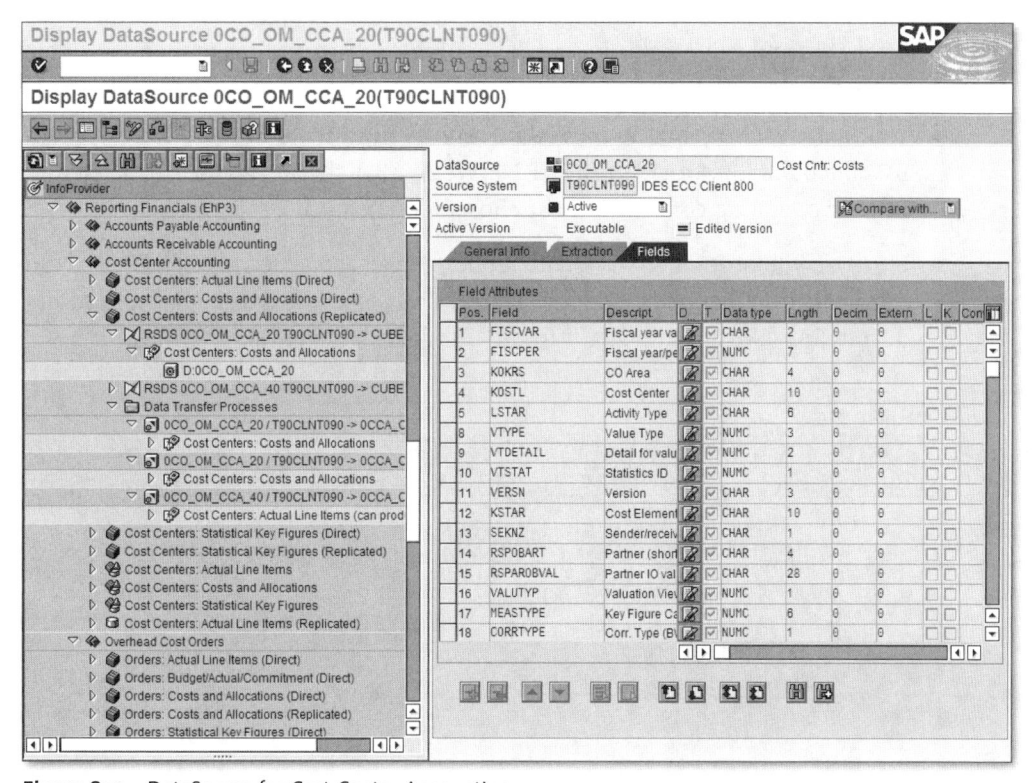

Figure 8.10 DataSource for Cost Center Accounting

While you can easily move data from Cost Center Accounting, Internal Orders, and Product Cost Controlling into SAP NetWeaver BW since the underlying table structures are the same in all organizations, remember from Chapter 2 that Profitability Analysis is based on *generated* tables, so there's no standard BW content for CO-PA. Instead, your administrator will find an implementation guide in SAP ERP that will guide him through the process of creating DataSources that read the structure of the operating concern configured for your business and move this structure into SAP NetWeaver BW. Your administrator will find this implementation guide in SAP ERP by selecting INTEGRATION WITH OTHER MYSAP.COM COMPONENTS • DATA TRANSFER TO SAP BUSINESS INFORMATION WAREHOUSE • SETTINGS FOR APPLICATION

SPECIFIC DATASOURCES (PI) • PROFITABILITY ANALYSIS or Transaction SBIW, as shown in Figure 8.11. This guide will provide your administrator with detailed instructions on how to set up the replication model to transfer the operating concern to SAP NetWeaver BW in the PROFITABILITY ANALYSIS folder.

- This process involves setting up transactional data sources that read the characteristics and value fields in your operating concern and make them available for use in SAP NetWeaver BW.

- You then need to replicate these data sources from SAP ERP to SAP NetWeaver BW and build InfoProviders in SAP NetWeaver BW that assign the characteristics in your operating concern to your chosen dimensions.

- Finally, if you're going to work with replicated data, you need to establish the load mechanism so that a system administrator can schedule a data load to read the data in SAP ERP and transfer it to the InfoProviders in SAP NetWeaver BW.

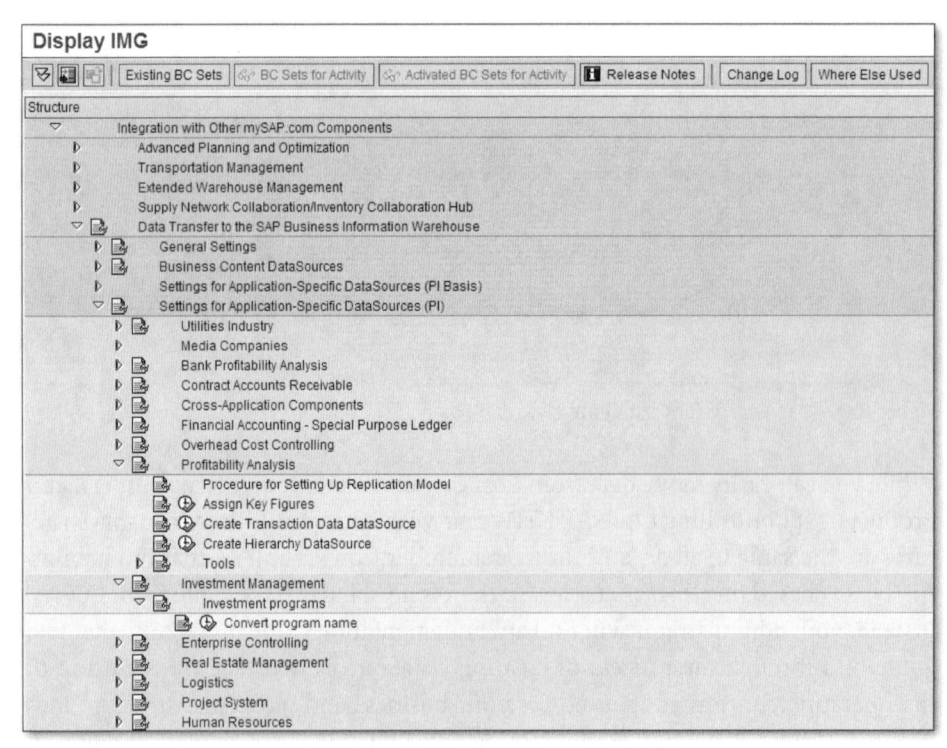

Figure 8.11 Implementation Guide for SAP NetWeaver BW in SAP ERP

8.2.2 Multidimensionality

Simply moving the data out of SAP ERP and into SAP NetWeaver BW is not the whole answer to any performance issues you might have been experiencing. When we talk about a dedicated reporting environment, what we often mean is one that is architected to support *multidimensional* analysis. The data in an operating concern is inherently multidimensional, meaning that any sales order or invoice can be queried to display the value fields by customer, by product, by sales organization, by region, and so on.

Profitability Analysis

In SAP ERP, the underlying data for a profitability report is stored in a single dimension, meaning that the characteristics (product, customer, sales organization, and so on) are stored in table CE4XXXX, and the value fields (sales quantity, gross sales, customer discount, and so on) are stored in table CE3XXX (where XXXX stands for your operating concern). When you run a report in SAP ERP, the query accesses tables CE4XXXX and CE3XXXX to select the data required. To determine whether data exists for a specific customer or a specific product, every data record has to be read.

In SAP NetWeaver BW, CO-PA is modeled to provide a central fact table, containing all the value fields, and separate dimensions for the product, the customer, the sales organization, and time. This means that to determine whether data exists for a specific customer, the customer dimension is read. This subset of data is then read to determine whether a specific product was purchased. The use of a *star schema* (the technical term for this multidimensional model) is substantially more efficient than reading the CO-PA tables directly. Figure 8.12 shows the dimensions for the S_GO operating concern. You can access this view of the InfoCube by selecting the correct InfoProvider from the list shown in Figures 8.8 and 8.9 and then selecting the INFOPROVIDER icon.

Notice that the material-related characteristics we saw when we looked at the material master in Chapter 4 (division, profit center, material group, and so on) are all assigned to the PRODUCT dimension, while the order-related characteristics we saw when we created sales orders in Chapter 6 (distribution channel, sales organization, customer group, sales office, and so on) are all assigned to the CUSTOMER dimension. You'll find organizational units under ORGANIZATIONAL STRUCTURE and general selection criteria such as currency type and valuation view under MANDATORY CHARACTERISTICS.

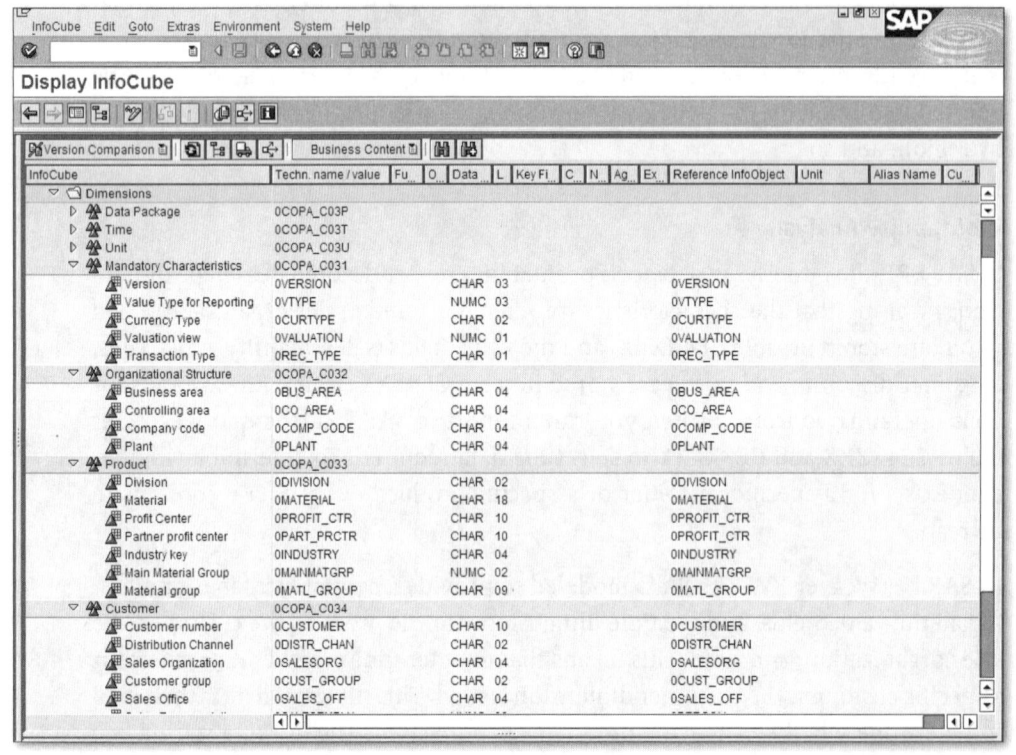

Figure 8.12 Dimensions of the S_GO InfoCube for CO-PA

This brings us to one of the most frequently asked questions since the advent of SAP NetWeaver BW, namely, whether you need Profitability Analysis in SAP ERP at all or whether all modeling can take place in SAP NetWeaver BW. As a general rule, it still makes sense to configure and activate CO-PA even if you intend to do all your reporting in SAP NetWeaver BW, since the purpose of CO-PA is not just to provide drill-down reporting on your sales orders and invoices but also to collect cost center costs during an allocation and order costs or production variances during settlement. If you refer back to Chapter 7, you'll see that CO-PA is usually the final step for your period close activities. In this context, the profitability segments behave as an account assignment, and you can always report on the partner relationship between the sender cost center and the receiver profitability segment, giving you a complete basis for an audit. You'll find that a properly configured CO-PA gives you much for free that you would otherwise have to build rules for in SAP NetWeaver BW.

- We saw the *derivation* function when we created sales orders in Chapter 6 (see Figure 6.31) and watched how the system used the information we entered to derive further characteristics for analysis.

- We used the *valuation* function to determine the product cost component split for the article we had just invoiced the customer for (see Figure 6.39).

- We used allocations, settlement, and top-down distribution in Chapter 7 to ensure that all costs ultimately ended up assigned to the appropriate profitability segment.

Cost Center Accounting

While CO-PA is the obvious example of a multidimensional data structure, you'll also need multidimensional analysis in Cost Center Accounting. All the reports we looked at in Chapter 2 selected the relevant data set using the cost center (or cost center group) and then additional information such as the time frame, version, and (sometimes) a cost element group. This is because it's relatively easy to select data for all production cost centers, all sales cost centers, all marketing cost centers, and so on, because the cost center is a *key field* in the underlying tables (COSPA, COSSA, and so on). If you need to turn the question around and determine salary and wage costs across all cost centers, it's a different story. This is because to provide such a report, every data record has to be selected to determine whether salary and wage costs were incurred for the cost center in that time frame, since the cost element under which the posting was recorded is not a key field. Moving the cost element data to a separate dimension from the cost center data when you set up your InfoProviders for SAP NetWeaver BW immediately resolves this issue, by making it immaterial whether you query by cost center or by cost element from a performance point of view.

Figure 8.13 shows the InfoCube delivered for Cost Center Accounting, where the cost center, cost element, and origin are modeled as separate dimensions to support just such reporting questions. Since the Cost Center Accounting tables (COSPA, COSSA, and so on) are also used to store the data for internal orders, production orders, WBS elements, sales order items, and so on, you'll find that exactly the same benefits apply to the InfoCubes for Internal Orders, Projects, and Cost Object Controlling.

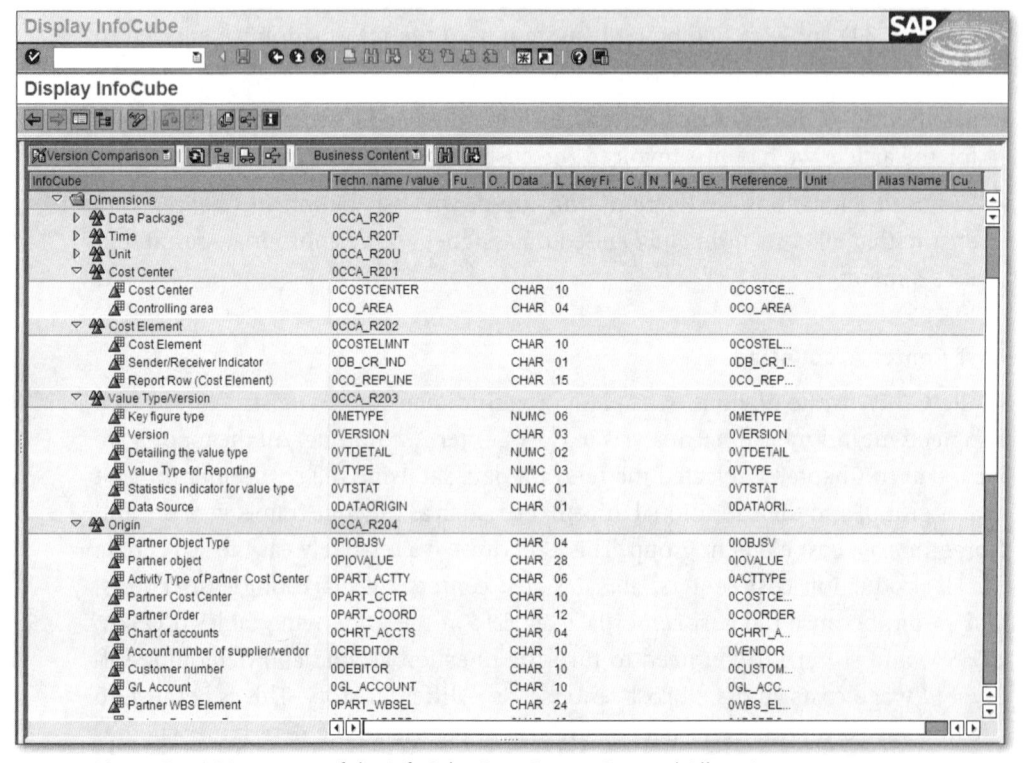

Figure 8.13 Dimensions of the InfoCube Cost Center: Cost and Allocations

8.2.3 Navigation Attributes

In addition to the data included in the operational tables, you'll often find yourself wanting to use additional data for drill-downs that wasn't included in the original table. An easy example is the drill-down in a cost center hierarchy that shows the person responsible for each cost center alongside the cost center key (see Chapter 3).

In this case you would create the attribute cost center manager for the characteristic cost center and use this to navigate within the query.

It's worth noting that while you never need to worry about the master data for reporting in SAP ERP, in SAP NetWeaver BW you have to make sure that you replicate not just the costs for each cost center (the contents of COSPA, COSSA, and so on), but also the master data for each cost center: in other words, the cost center hierarchy, the texts, and the attributes for the cost center.

Each piece of master data in SAP NetWeaver BW is modeled as an *InfoObject*, so if you refer back to Figure 8.13 you'll see InfoObjects for the cost center, the controlling area, the cost element, and so on. If you double-click on InfoObject 0COSTCENTER, you can check the master data for the cost center as shown in Figure 8.14. One thing to be aware of is that while we talk about replicating master data to SAP NetWeaver BW, by no means do all the fields that we saw in the cost center master data in Chapter 3 need to be included in SAP NetWeaver BW. One of the challenges is to decide which attributes you will want to report on for each master data element.

Reading the tabs in Figure 8.14 from left to right, you see an extractor to read the cost center texts (MASTER DATA/TEXTS), an extractor to read the cost center hierarchy (HIERARCHY), an extractor to read the attributes—in this case business area, company code, and so on—and a tab called COMPOUNDING that ensures that the cost center is always read in combination with the controlling area. Remember that we saw in Chapter 2 that all data in CO is associated with a controlling area. Before you can run a cost center report, an administrator has to load the contents of each of these tabs to make sure you have the relevant cost center master data, cost element master data, and so on in your reports.

If you prefer, you can adjust your settings to determine that instead of preloading your *master data* from SAP ERP, it should be read at run time. Figure 8.15 shows the MASTER DATA/TEXTS tab for the cost center master data. The usual setting for the MASTER DATA ACCESS field is DEFAULT (which means access to replicated data), but in recent versions of SAP NetWeaver BW you can switch this to DIRECT ACCESS to read data directly from the SAP ERP tables. Discuss with your system administrator whether this option makes sense in the context of your data volumes.

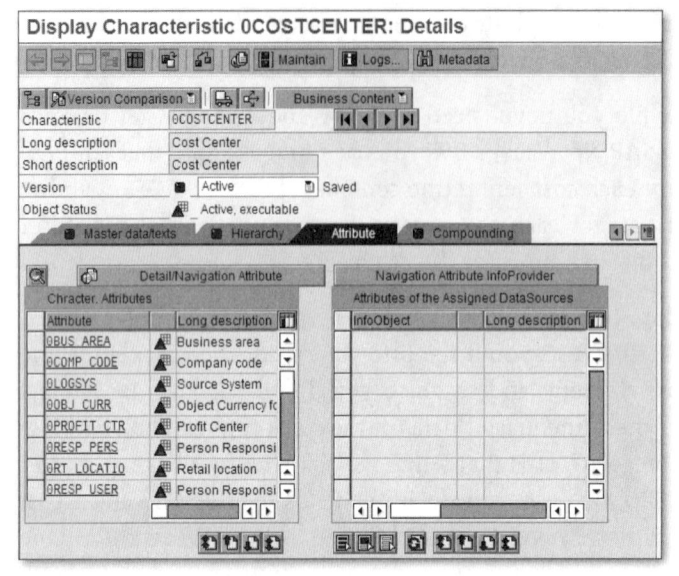

Figure 8.14 Master Data for Cost Center in SAP NetWeaver BW

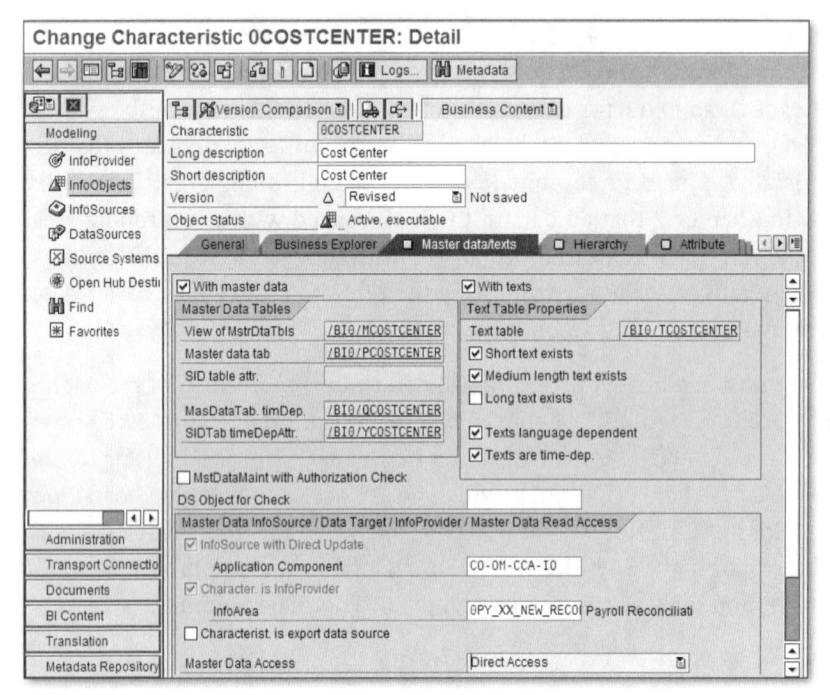

Figure 8.15 Master Data Access Options for Cost Center

8.2 How to Decide Whether You Need SAP NetWeaver BW for Reporting

When we compare your options for reporting in Cost Object Controlling in SAP NetWeaver BW with those we just looked at in SAP ERP, the master data attributes provide the most powerful options for building new reports. Figure 8.16 shows the delivered InfoCube for Cost Object Controlling. You can flag any attribute of the InfoObject Material as a navigation attribute by clicking on the DETAIL/NAVIGATION ATTRIBUTE button (see Figure 8.14). Defining attributes such as division, material type, product hierarchy, profit center, and so on as navigation attributes allows you to build queries that select by these attributes, giving you substantially more options than we saw in the SAP ERP-based drill-down report in Figure 8.7. If you refer back to Chapter 4, it's clear that one of the reporting challenges is to decide which information you've entered in the material master you're going to require for selection in your reports.

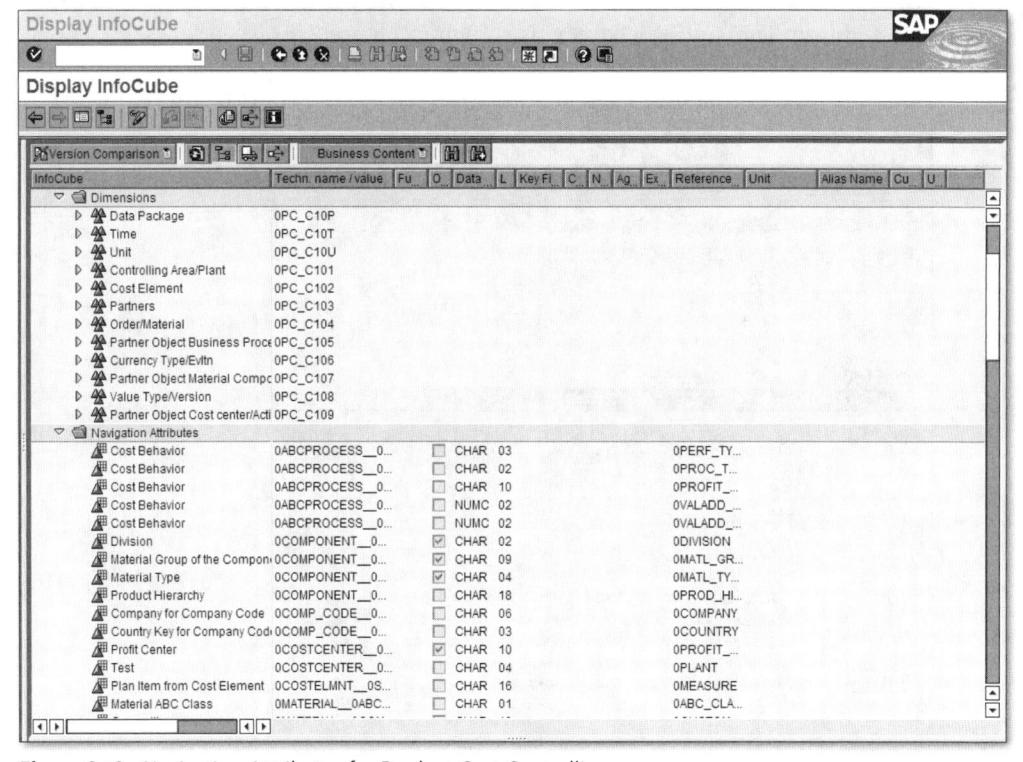

Figure 8.16 Navigation Attributes for Product Cost Controlling

407

8.2.4 Inclusion of Non-SAP Data

As a general rule, SAP ERP reports show data from SAP ERP. However, there are countless cases when you may need to mix data from SAP ERP and data from another system. One example is for reporting customer profitability. Profitability Analysis provides all the data you need to tell you the contribution margins per customer. However, if you're looking at retail customers, marketing people are likely to want to mix this information with demographic data about these customers to decide which customers to address in their next advertising campaign. Another example might be the use of data from a credit rating agency such as Dun and Bradstreet to include the customer's likelihood to pay alongside his profitability. To see an example of this, let's return to the CO-PA InfoCube and select the master data for the customer number. This includes attributes for the account group, city, and region that are being read from SAP ERP and additional attributes that are being selected from Dun and Bradstreet, as shown in Figure 8.17.

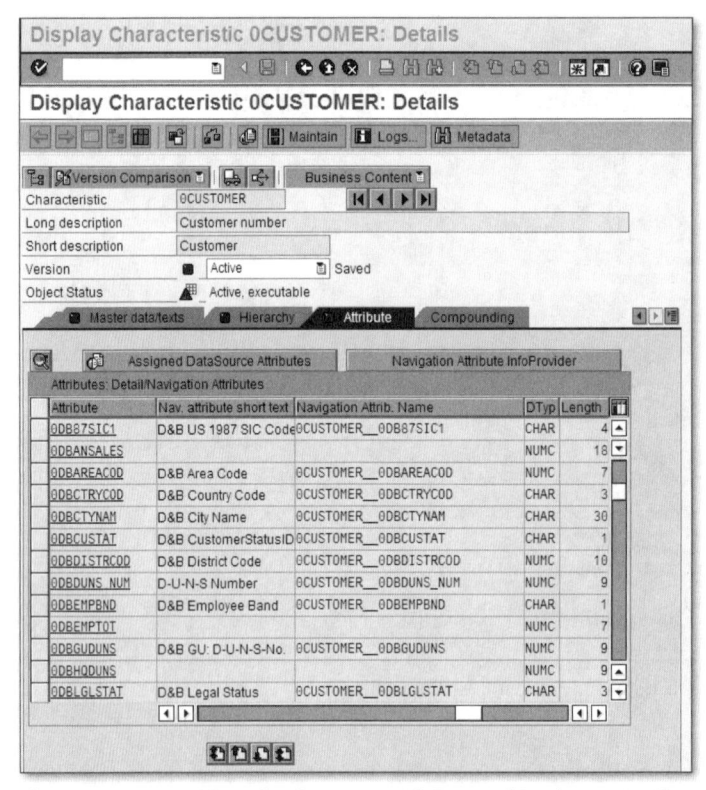

Figure 8.17 Master Data for Customer with Dun and Bradstreet Attributes

And not every organization runs all its business processes on SAP ERP. There are plenty of examples of mixed system landscapes where only part of the relevant data is captured in SAP ERP and the rest is mapped from other systems, but since this book focuses on CO, we'll ignore those options. They're generally well covered in books dedicated to SAP NetWeaver BW reporting.

8.2.5 Building Queries

Once you have your InfoProviders in place, you need queries to access the data. While SAP delivers many queries for use in CO, it's worth knowing how to check the settings for an existing query and, if necessary, create a new one. You'll find the toolsets for query creation on your desktop. Follow the menu path START • PROGRAMS • BUSINESS EXPLORER • QUERY DESIGNER, as shown in Figure 8.18. The system will then require you to log on to the required SAP NetWeaver BW system.

Figure 8.18 Finding the Query Designer on Your Desktop

Once you have filled out the logon credentials, select either QUERY • NEW or QUERY • OPEN. In either case you'll need to establish a link with the InfoProvider that contains the data you want to display in your query. Figure 8.19 shows the InfoAreas for Financial Management and CO. These correspond to the folders containing

8 | Reporting in SAP NetWeaver BW and SAP BusinessObjects

the BW content that we saw in Figure 8.9. Within this list, select the InfoArea that includes your InfoProvider. In our example, we'll select REPORTING FINANCIALS (EHP4) and then PROFITABILITY ANALYSIS to take us to a query to display data for the InfoCube we looked at in Figure 8.12.

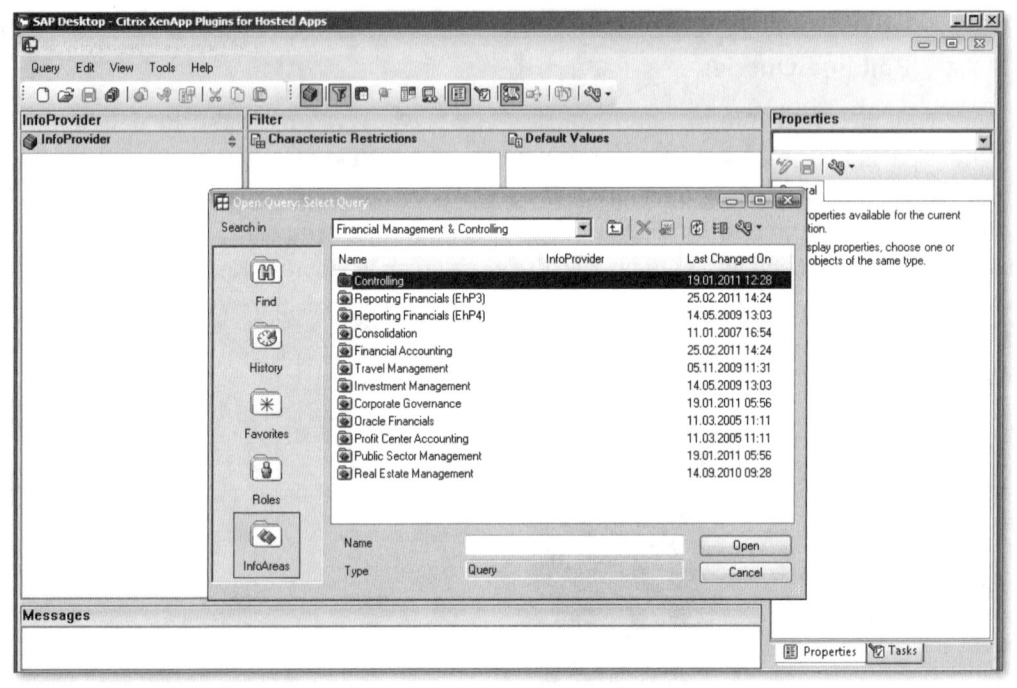

Figure 8.19 Choosing an InfoProvider for Your Query

All queries have the same basic structure, regardless of the underlying InfoProvider. Figure 8.20 shows the initial screen for a query.

- The area on the left provides the link to the InfoProvider. Here we're looking at the InfoProvider linked with the operating concern S_GO. In the case of our CO-PA cube, the structure of the InfoProvider gives us a list of key figures and the dimensions. The *key figures* are the value fields from SAP ERP plus several calculated key figures that are used to calculate the various contribution margins that characterize CO-PA reporting. The *dimensions* provide a grouping of the characteristics (product, customer, and so on). For each characteristic, you have two options. You can either use a variable to select, for example, the relevant

410

customer group by choosing the relevant customer group as you run your report or you can "hard code" your query by selecting one of the customer groups that have been loaded to SAP NetWeaver BW from SAP ERP. You will not then be able to change this selection as you run the report.

▶ The area in the middle contains the characteristic restrictions, in other words, the filters that apply to the whole query. These are the fields in the selection screen that allow you to select the time frame, material group, sales organization, and distribution channel you're interested in by choosing a variable for these characteristics. Other restrictions can be hard-wired for the query, such as the record types (transaction type) you want to view in this particular query. If you know you're only going to work with either live data or replicated data, you can also hard-wire the access method.

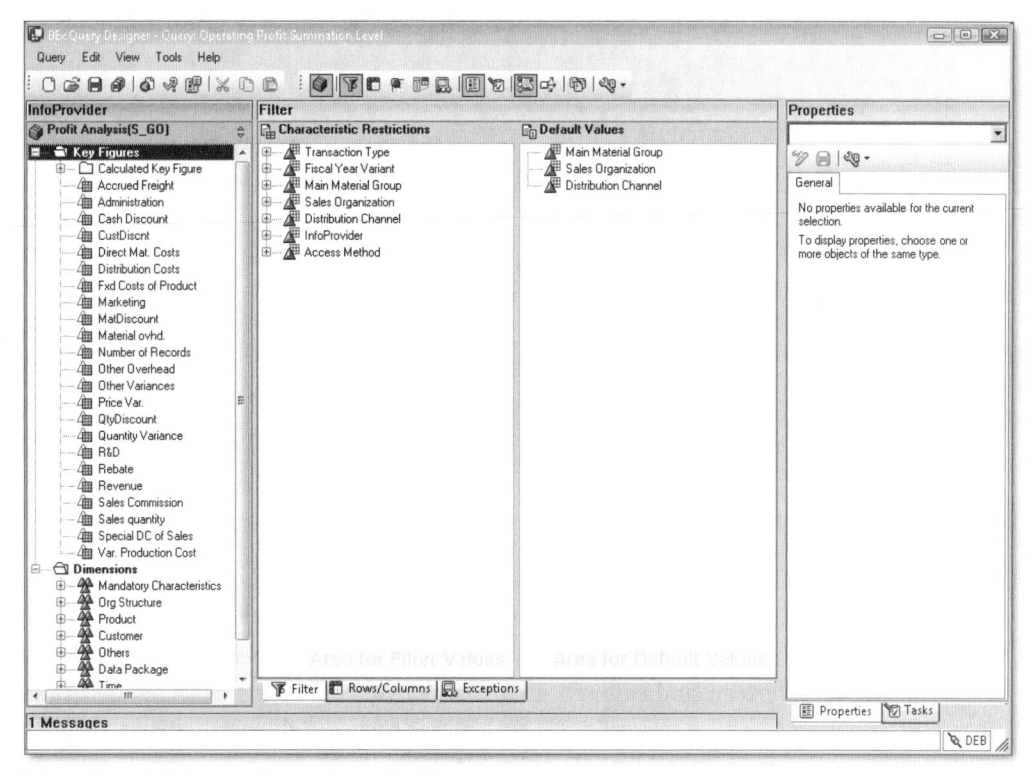

Figure 8.20 Building a Query – Characteristics

8 | Reporting in SAP NetWeaver BW and SAP BusinessObjects

The next step is to define what should be shown in the lines of your report by selecting the ROWS/COLUMNS button. Figure 8.21 shows a simple query that displays a row for each value field and actual costs, planned costs, and so on in the columns. To execute this query in test mode, select QUERY • EXECUTE. This will start the SAP BEx Web analyzer tool, and a URL will appear that contains the selection screen for your query.

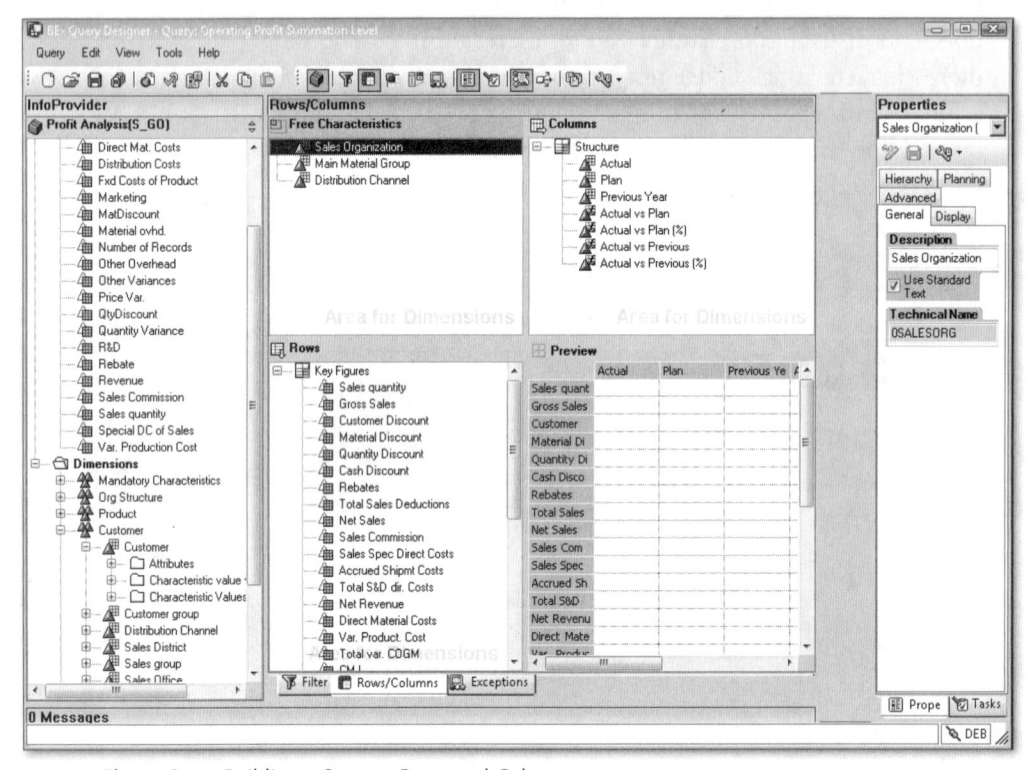

Figure 8.21 Building a Query – Rows and Columns

So far, we've looked at the general architecture of SAP NetWeaver BW, how data is selected from the SAP ERP system (data provisioning is the technical term for this process), and how to build a query to display the data once it's in SAP NetWeaver BW. We'll now use the example of a cost center report to illustrate the options for displaying your data in SAP NetWeaver BW.

8.3 Cost Center Reporting in SAP NetWeaver BW

In this section we'll look at different approaches to Cost Center Reporting to illustrate the different ways of using the latest version of SAP NetWeaver BW. We'll use the same basic report—cost center expenses with variances—to illustrate the different ways of accessing data from the cost center tables. You can access this report using the report launchpad we showed in Chapter 2, Figure 2.8 and selecting the line Cost Centers: Actual/Plan/Variance - Cost Elements (Analysis). This starts the SAP BEx Web Analyzer. To find out how to check the settings for this report and configure the launchpad to include your own reports, refer to Appendix B at *www.sap-press.com*.

Figure 8.22 shows the selection options for the Cost Centers: Actual/Plan/Variance—Cost Elements (Analysis) report. Most of the parameters will be familiar from SAP ERP reporting. The only thing that might be unfamiliar is the Insert Row button. You'll need this if you want to enter more than one cost center group or cost element group, if you have not defined the perfect group to cover your selection requirements.

> **Hierarchies and Groups**
>
> In SAP ERP it's easy enough to refer to cost center groups and cost center hierarchies as if they were synonyms for a cost center tree structure. In SAP NetWeaver BW, the cost center *hierarchy* is the root node that's entered in the controlling area (H1 in our examples), whereas a cost center *group* is any group that refers to this hierarchy. In SAP NetWeaver BW, the cost element *hierarchy* is the chart of accounts set for the controlling area (INT in our examples), whereas the cost element *group* is any group that refers to this hierarchy. In SAP ERP, you never need to enter the hierarchy in the selection screens because it can be derived from the settings for the controlling area in which you are working. In SAP NetWeaver BW, you need to include both fields in the selection parameters for your reports.

The other thing to notice is the Access Method option that's used in all queries built using the InfoProviders we saw in Figures 8.9 and 8.10. This allows you to switch between access method C (access to operative data) and access method R (direct access to replicated data).

- Access method C allows you to use the SAP NetWeaver BW data structures to select the data you need from SAP ERP when you execute the query. This uses the InfoProviders labeled Direct in Figures 8.9 and 8.10. Another term used here is *virtual InfoProviders*.

- Access method R represents the traditional use of a data warehouse where data is first loaded from SAP ERP to SAP NetWeaver BW and then reported on. This uses the InfoProviders labeled REPLICATED in Figures 8.9 and 8.10. These are also known as *physical InfoProviders*.

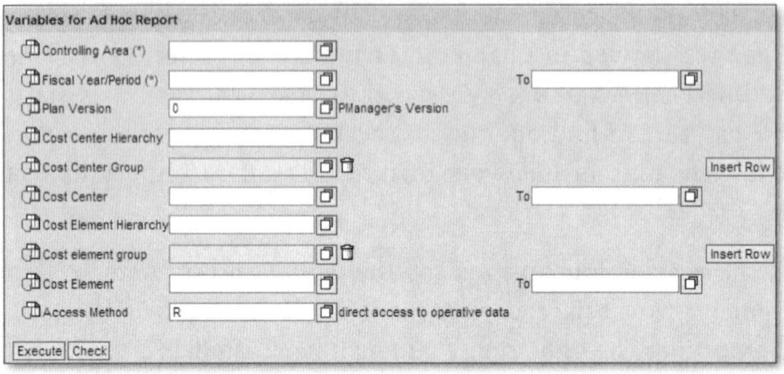

Figure 8.22 Selection Screen for Simplified Reporting

The result of executing the query is shown in Figure 8.23. If you compare this report with the cost center report we looked at in Chapter 2, Figure 2.8, the main difference you'll see is the block on the left, which allows you to *drill down* by selected dimensions. Choosing which dimensions you want to use for drill-down is a key part of building your queries. You can then use these drill-down dimensions to create and save various *views* of the data contained in a single report.

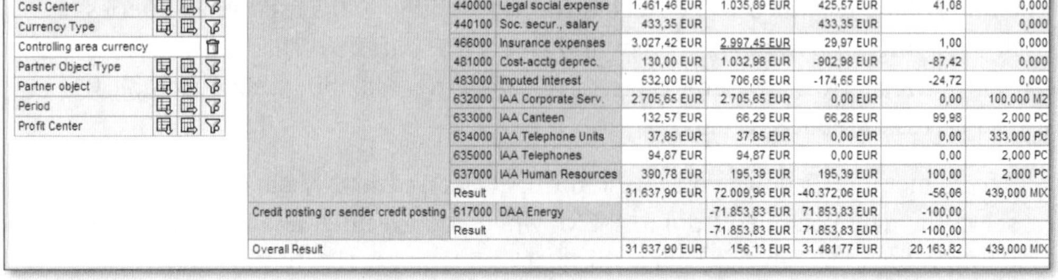

Senders/receivers	Cost Element		Actual Costs	Planned Costs	Difference	Difference (%)	Actual Quantity
Debit posting or receiver debit posting	211100	1000/211100	1.063,00 EUR		1.063,00 EUR		0,000
	261000	1000/261000	-130,00 EUR		-130,00 EUR		0,000
	416100	Electricity Base Fee	2.065,93 EUR	2.086,80 EUR	-20,87 EUR	-1,00	0,000 PC
	416200	Electricity Usage	10.974,29 EUR	56.670,07 EUR	-45.695,78 EUR	-80,63	0,000 KWH
	420000	Direct labor costs	6.366,78 EUR	4.380,07 EUR	1.986,71 EUR	45,36	0,000
	430000	Salaries	2.351,95 EUR		2.351,95 EUR		0,000
	440000	Legal social expense	1.461,46 EUR	1.035,89 EUR	425,57 EUR	41,08	0,000
	440100	Soc. secur., salary	433,35 EUR		433,35 EUR		0,000
	466000	Insurance expenses	3.027,42 EUR	2.997,45 EUR	29,97 EUR	1,00	0,000
	481000	Cost-acctg deprec.	130,00 EUR	1.032,98 EUR	-902,98 EUR	-87,42	0,000
	483000	Imputed interest	532,00 EUR	706,65 EUR	-174,65 EUR	-24,72	0,000
	632000	IAA Corporate Serv.	2.705,65 EUR	2.705,65 EUR	0,00 EUR	0,00	100,000 M2
	633000	IAA Canteen	132,57 EUR	66,29 EUR	66,28 EUR	99,98	2,000 PC
	634000	IAA Telephone Units	37,85 EUR	37,85 EUR	0,00 EUR	0,00	333,000 PC
	635000	IAA Telephones	94,87 EUR	94,87 EUR	0,00 EUR	0,00	2,000 PC
	637000	IAA Human Resources	390,78 EUR	195,39 EUR	195,39 EUR	100,00	2,000 PC
	Result		31.637,90 EUR	72.009,96 EUR	-40.372,06 EUR	-56,06	439,000 MIX
Credit posting or sender credit posting	617000	DAA Energy		-71.853,83 EUR	71.853,83 EUR	-100,00	
	Result			-71.853,83 EUR	71.853,83 EUR	-100,00	
Overall Result			31.637,90 EUR	156,13 EUR	31.481,77 EUR	20.163,82	439,000 MIX

Figure 8.23 Sample Cost Center Report—Initial View

Figure 8.24 shows the same report, but with a drill-down by partner type and partner, which we created by selecting the icon to the right of the free characteristics partner type and partner. This drill-down shows the activity types that charged costs to the power cost center and the operational cost centers and activity types that received costs from the energy cost center when the indirect activity allocation cycles were executed at period close (for how to perform these allocations, refer to Chapter 7, Section 7.1). You may remember that partner postings like this only exist for secondary costs occurring as a result of allocations and so on. One thing to get used to in SAP NetWeaver BW reporting is the use of the # symbol to mean "not assigned." Since the incoming electricity costs have been transferred from FI (primary costs), there's no partner dimension to be displayed for these lines, so SAP NetWeaver BW shows a # symbol for these costs.

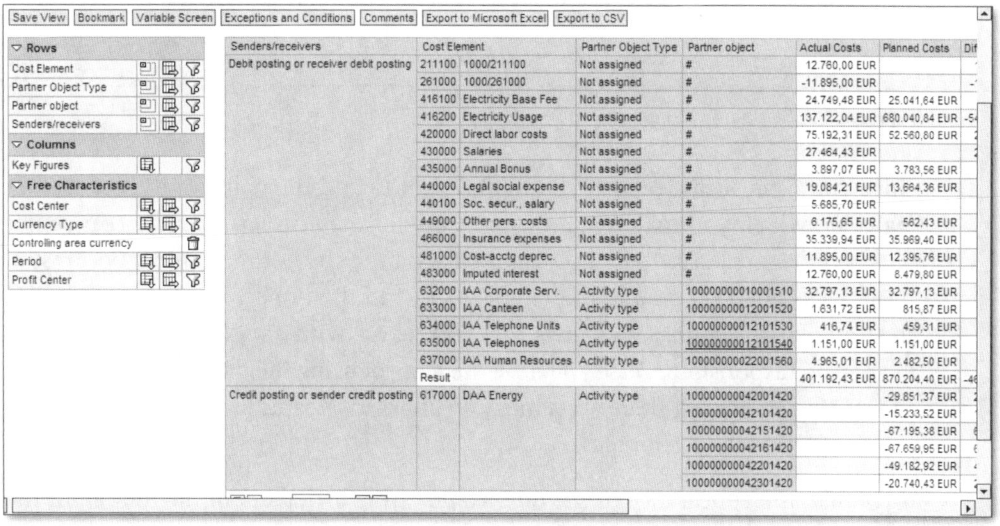

Senders/receivers	Cost Element		Partner Object Type	Partner object	Actual Costs	Planned Costs
Debit posting or receiver debit posting	211100	1000/211100	Not assigned	#	12.760,00 EUR	
	261000	1000/261000	Not assigned	#	-11.895,00 EUR	
	416100	Electricity Base Fee	Not assigned	#	24.749,48 EUR	25.041,64 EUR
	416200	Electricity Usage	Not assigned	#	137.122,04 EUR	680.040,84 EUR
	420000	Direct labor costs	Not assigned	#	75.192,31 EUR	52.560,80 EUR
	430000	Salaries	Not assigned	#	27.464,43 EUR	
	435000	Annual Bonus	Not assigned	#	3.897,07 EUR	3.783,56 EUR
	440000	Legal social expense	Not assigned	#	19.084,21 EUR	13.664,36 EUR
	440100	Soc. secur., salary	Not assigned	#	5.685,70 EUR	
	449000	Other pers. costs	Not assigned	#	6.175,65 EUR	562,43 EUR
	466000	Insurance expenses	Not assigned	#	35.339,94 EUR	35.969,40 EUR
	481000	Cost-acctg deprec.	Not assigned	#	11.895,00 EUR	12.395,76 EUR
	483000	Imputed interest	Not assigned	#	12.760,00 EUR	8.479,80 EUR
	632000	IAA Corporate Serv.	Activity type	100000000010001510	32.797,13 EUR	32.797,13 EUR
	633000	IAA Canteen	Activity type	100000000012001520	1.631,72 EUR	815,87 EUR
	634000	IAA Telephone Units	Activity type	100000000012101530	416,74 EUR	459,31 EUR
	635000	IAA Telephones	Activity type	100000000012101540	1.151,00 EUR	1.151,00 EUR
	637000	IAA Human Resources	Activity type	100000000022001560	4.965,01 EUR	2.482,50 EUR
	Result				401.192,43 EUR	870.204,40 EUR
Credit posting or sender credit posting	617000	DAA Energy	Activity type	100000000042001420		-29.851,37 EUR
				100000000042101420		-15.233,52 EUR
				100000000042151420		-67.195,38 EUR
				100000000042161420		-67.659,95 EUR
				100000000042201420		-49.182,92 EUR
				100000000042301420		-20.740,43 EUR

Figure 8.24 Sample Cost Center Report—Drill-Down by Partner Object and Type

Once you understand the drill-down options in the query, you can begin to switch the dimensions around and really explore the data. In Figure 8.25 we've called up the same report but selected the entire cost center hierarchy rather than a single cost center and switched the drill-down to display the values first by cost center group and then by cost element. Because such a report can easily include many lines of data, you'll also want to explore the options you get when you click on the EXCEPTIONS AND CONDITIONS button to try to focus on what records are really important for you. In Figure 8.25, we've created an exception condition for the report that shows variances over a certain threshold in red and variances under a certain threshold in green.

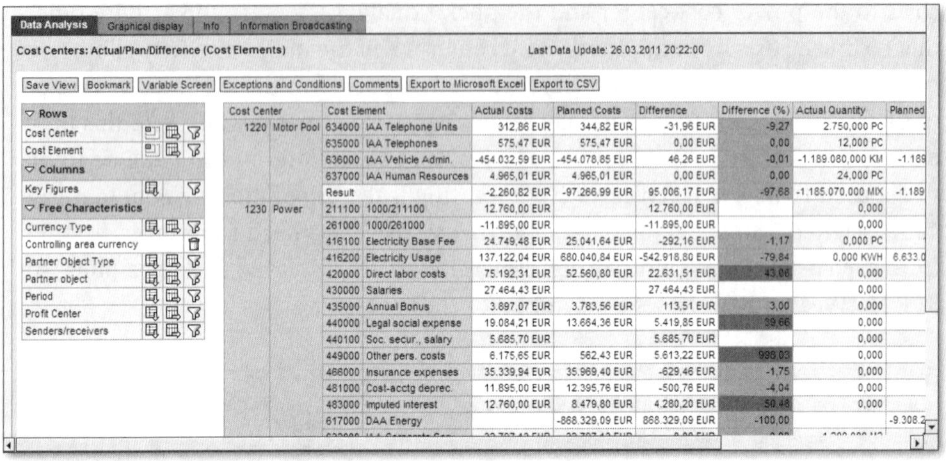

Figure 8.25 Sample Cost Center Report – Exceptions

Once you have such a report, you might want to add the name of the cost center manager, which you may remember was one of the *attributes* for the cost center we saw in Figure 8.14. To do this, right-click on the cost center in the report result, select ENHANCED MENU and then PROPERTIES and then select the PERSON RESPONSIBLE attribute. Figure 8.26 shows the new report with an additional column for the person responsible. Once you have the hang of using the drill-down parameters and adding attributes, there are almost no limits to the number of potential views you can build for such a report.

If you like the appearance of the queries but are worried about the burden of the infrastructure of InfoSources, InfoProviders, and so on, one option to consider from SAP enhancement package 5 for SAP ERP 6.0 is *transient InfoProviders*. This allows you to have all the query options we just talked about, but there's no InfoProvider behind the query. The transient InfoProvider, as the name implies, only exists at run time when you execute your query. Technically the BW query calls an InfoSet query in SAP ERP to perform the data selection. Let's have a look at these options.

To display the available InfoSet queries in SAP ERP, call up Transaction SQ01 and search for the InfoSet queries that include CO_OM_CCA in their key, as shown in Figure 8.27. Notice that there are also InfoSet queries for Product Cost Controlling in the same list.

8.3 Cost Center Reporting in SAP NetWeaver BW

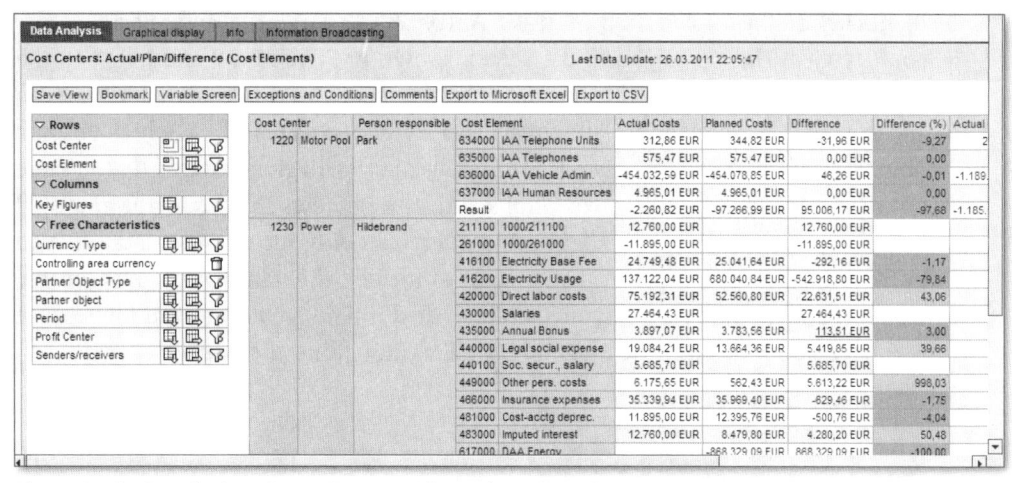

Figure 8.26 Sample Cost Center Report with Attribute Cost Center Manager

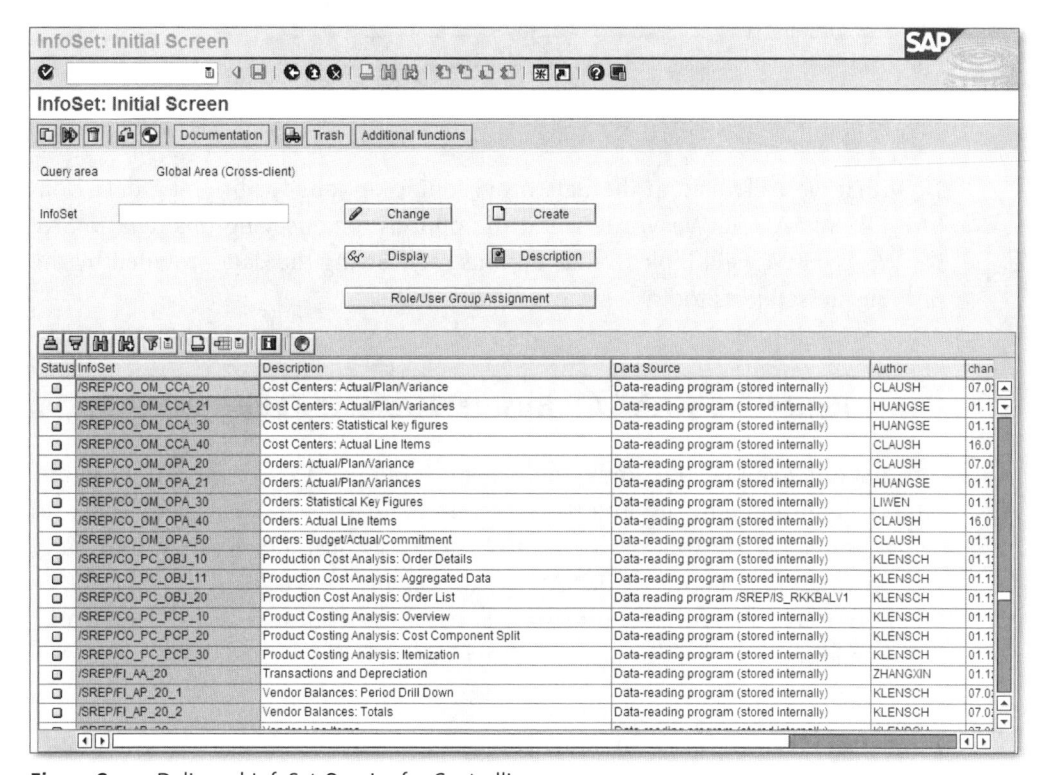

Figure 8.27 Delivered InfoSet Queries for Controlling

417

Right-click on the InfoSet COST CENTERS: ACTUAL/PLAN/VARIANCE and select QUERIES FOR INFOSET. This takes you to the screen shown in Figure 8.28 and tells you the name of the BW query for this InfoSet query. Armed with this knowledge, you can add the query to your report launchpad as described in Appendix B (which you can download at *www.sap-press.com*). Running this query will give you exactly the same options in terms of building exceptions and storing views as we saw for a normal BW query. The difference is that such a query can only include the data selected in the original InfoSet query. If you want to include the name of the responsible manager and the InfoSet query doesn't include this field, you cannot add it because you have no modeled InfoObject 0COSTCENTER behind the query.

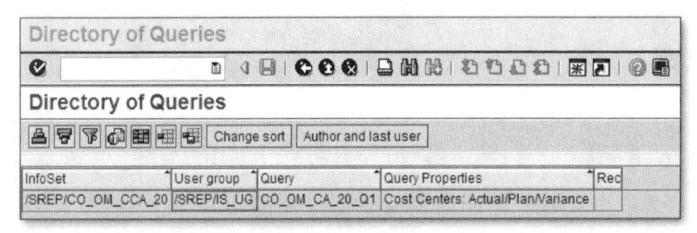

Figure 8.28 Link from InfoSet Query to BW Query

Now that we've looked at the data provisioning options for bringing data from SAP ERP to SAP NetWeaver BW and the options for querying this data in SAP NetWeaver BW, we'll look at your options for viewing the data provided by the SAP BusinessObjects tools.

8.4 Reporting with SAP BusinessObjects Tools

The first thing you need to know in the context of CO is that all the SAP BusinessObjects reporting tools use queries to access the data to be displayed. They can call an InfoSet query (the transient InfoProvider we just looked at), a BW query that provides direct access to the SAP ERP data (sometimes called a virtual InfoProvider), or a BW query that reads data that has been replicated to SAP NetWeaver BW (sometimes called a physical InfoProvider).

8.4.1 Crystal Reports for Controlling

You can use Crystal Reports to build a formatted report on top of any InfoSet query, ABAP Query, or transparent table in SAP ERP or any BW query, InfoCube, Virtual

Cube, or ODS (operational data store) in SAP NetWeaver BW. Figure 8.29 shows Crystal Reports (which is installed on the user's desktop) and the link to the BEx query that will be used to select the data from SAP NetWeaver BW.

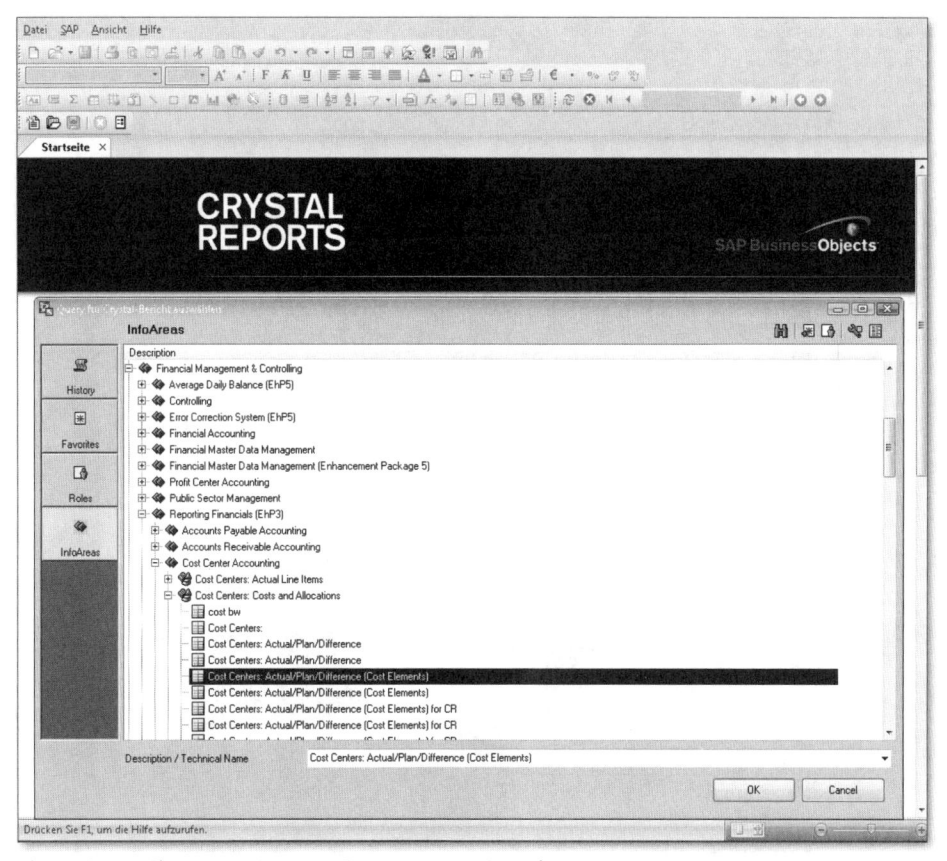

Figure 8.29 Choosing a Query to Provision Your Crystal Report

To create a report that shows cost center data, open the Crystal Reports Designer from your desktop, select SAP • CREATE NEW REPORT USING QUERY (top right), and log on to SAP NetWeaver BW. Then select the InfoArea FINANCIAL MANAGEMENT AND CONTROLLING • REPORTING FINANCIALS (EhP3) • COST CENTER ACCOUNTING • COST CENTERS: COSTS AND ALLOCATIONS (as we saw in Figure 8.9) and select the query COST CENTERS: ACTUAL/PLAN/DIFFERENCE (COST ELEMENTS). Then you can use the Crystal Reports Designer to format the data in this query to create a report like the sample report shown in Figure 8.30. This was built in one of the test systems to provide a taste of what the cost center reports we explored in Section 8.3

8 Reporting in SAP NetWeaver BW and SAP BusinessObjects

could look like with the improved *formatting* offered by Crystal Reports instead of the SAP BEx Web analyzer tool we used to display the queries shown in Figures 8.22 to 8.26.

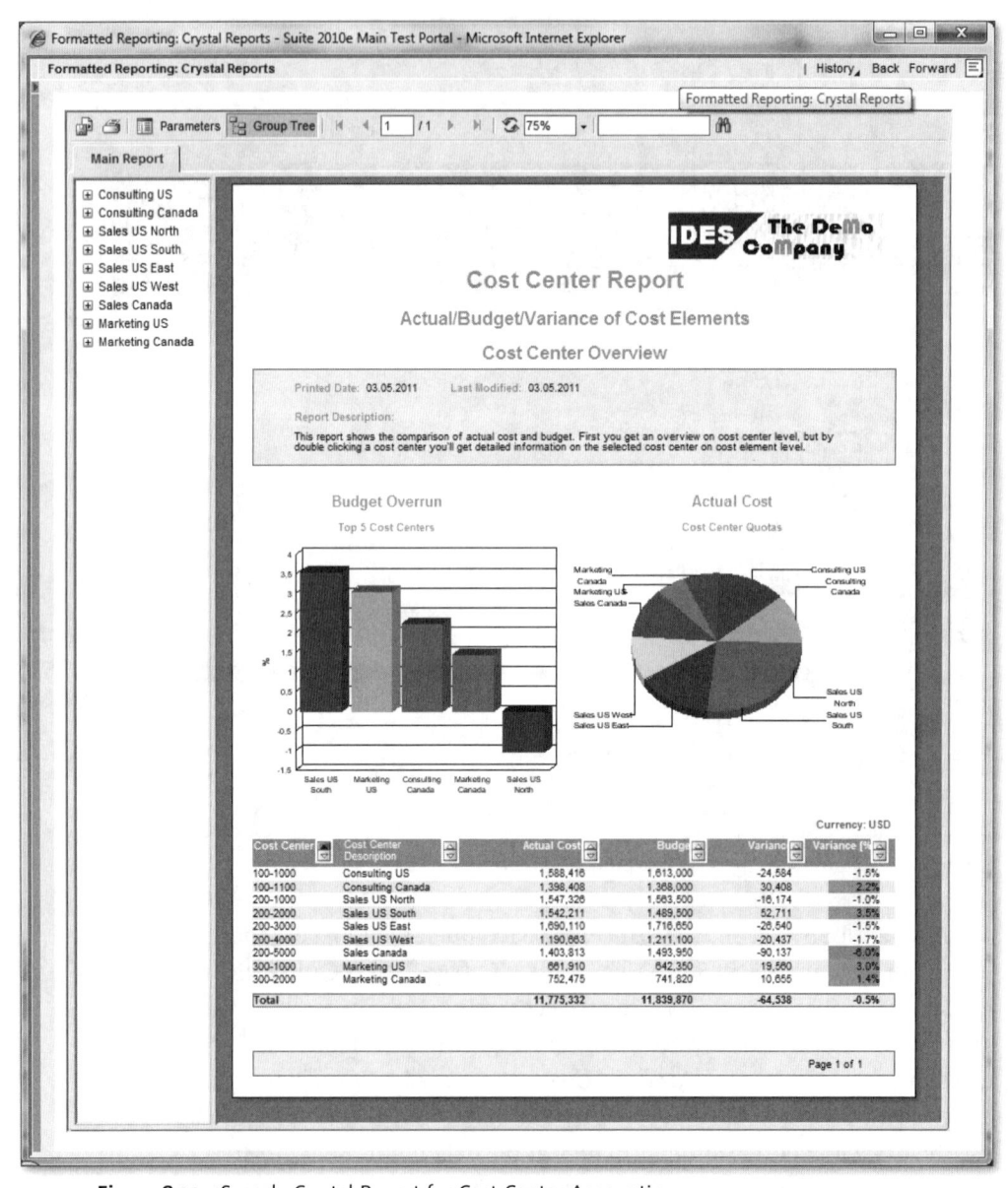

Figure 8.30 Sample Crystal Report for Cost Center Accounting

This approach requires you to license Crystal Reports. In addition, a handful of Crystal Reports are delivered as part of SAP enhancement package 5 for SAP ERP 6.0 and are covered by the SAP ERP license costs. These reports are listed in the report launchpads we showed in Chapter 2 (Figures 2.6, 2.11, and 2.25). You'll recognize them by the term *Crystal Report* in the report title. Enhancement package 5 includes sample Crystal Reports for Cost Center Accounting, Internal Orders, and CO-PA.

Starting with SAP enhancement package 5 for SAP ERP 6.0, there's also a generic function for all SAP List Viewer reports that lets you use Crystal Reports as an alternative to the table view. The Crystal Viewer is available for download according to a procedure described in SAP Note 1353044.

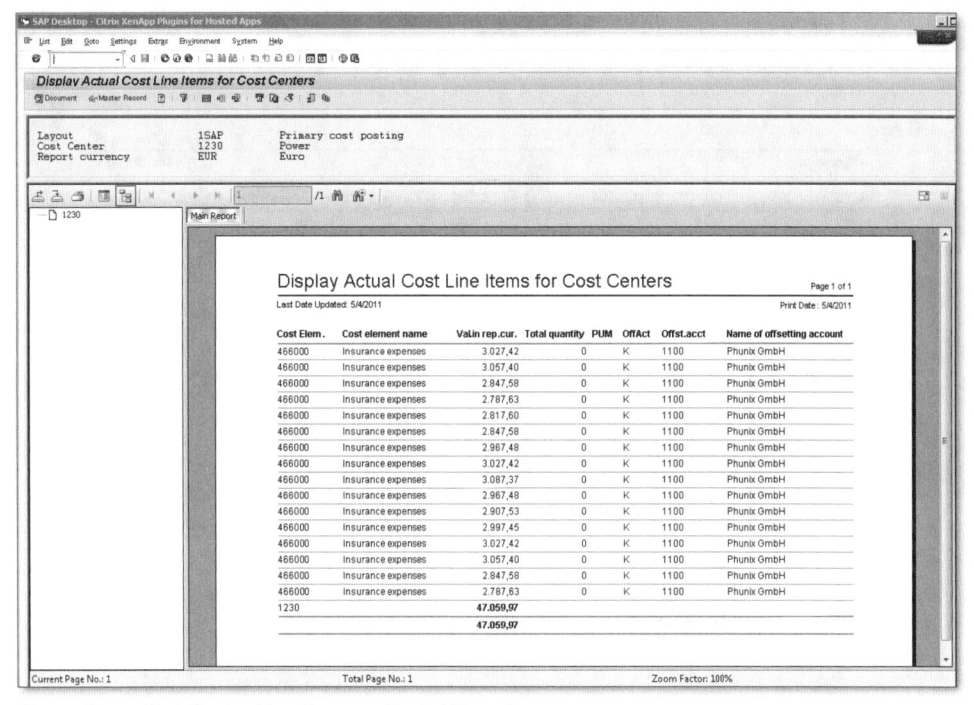

Figure 8.31 Cost Center Line Items as Crystal Report

Figure 8.31 shows the cost center line item report that we looked at in the first section of Chapter 2. To switch to the Crystal Report, select CHANGE LAYOUT and select the DISPLAY tab shown in Figure 2.5. Then switch to CRYSTAL REPORTS and save the display settings for your layout. Every time you execute the report using this layout, Crystal Reports will be used as a default. Notice that the SAP List Viewer toolbar is still shown in this view, meaning that all the functions we discussed in Chapter 2 are still available. We've simply changed the look of the report.

We can do the same if we return to the cost center master data report we showed in Figure 3.7 and switch from Show as Table to Show as Crystal Report, as shown in Figure 8.32. If you then choose the icon in the top-right corner of the Crystal Report, you can switch to full screen to show the whole report.

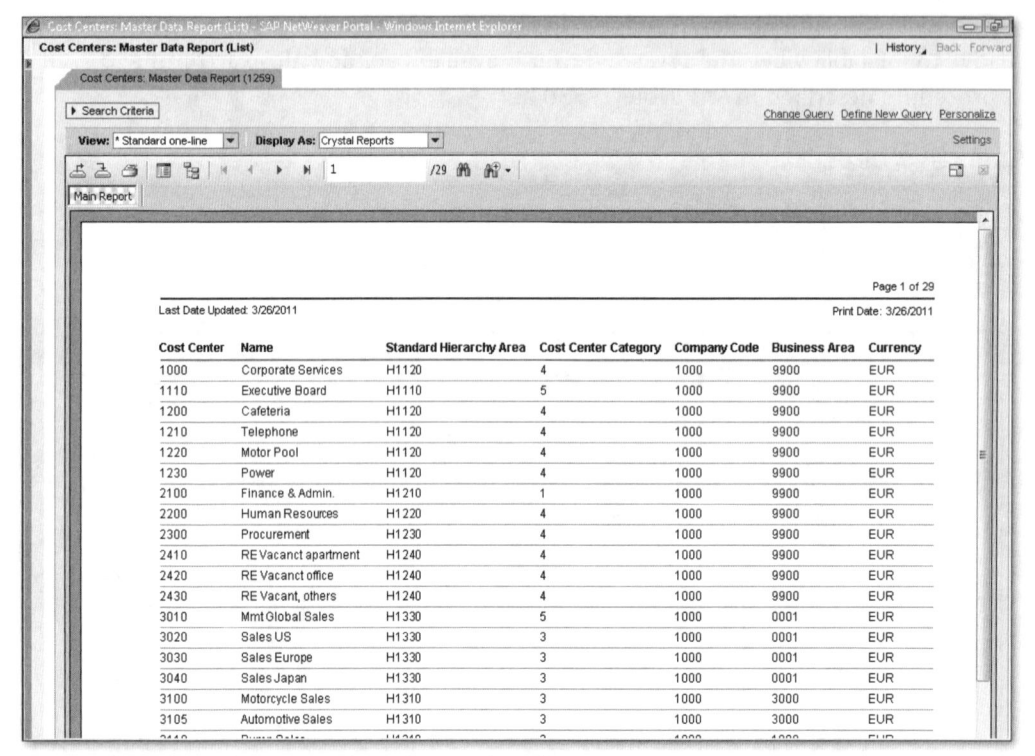

Figure 8.32 Cost Center Master Data as Crystal Report

8.4.2 Dashboards for Controlling

If the purpose of a Crystal Report is to provide a standard format for a report that will be delivered in a familiar, stable form to every cost center manager, the case for an xCelsius dashboard is to provide highly interactive dashboards that invite exploration. Here the focus is on a highly visual, intuitive representation of the data with lots of graphical elements, dials, and so on, as illustrated in the dashboard shown in Figure 8.33. This was built in one of the test systems to provide a taste of what the cost center reports we explored in Section 8.3 could look like if displayed as a dashboard.

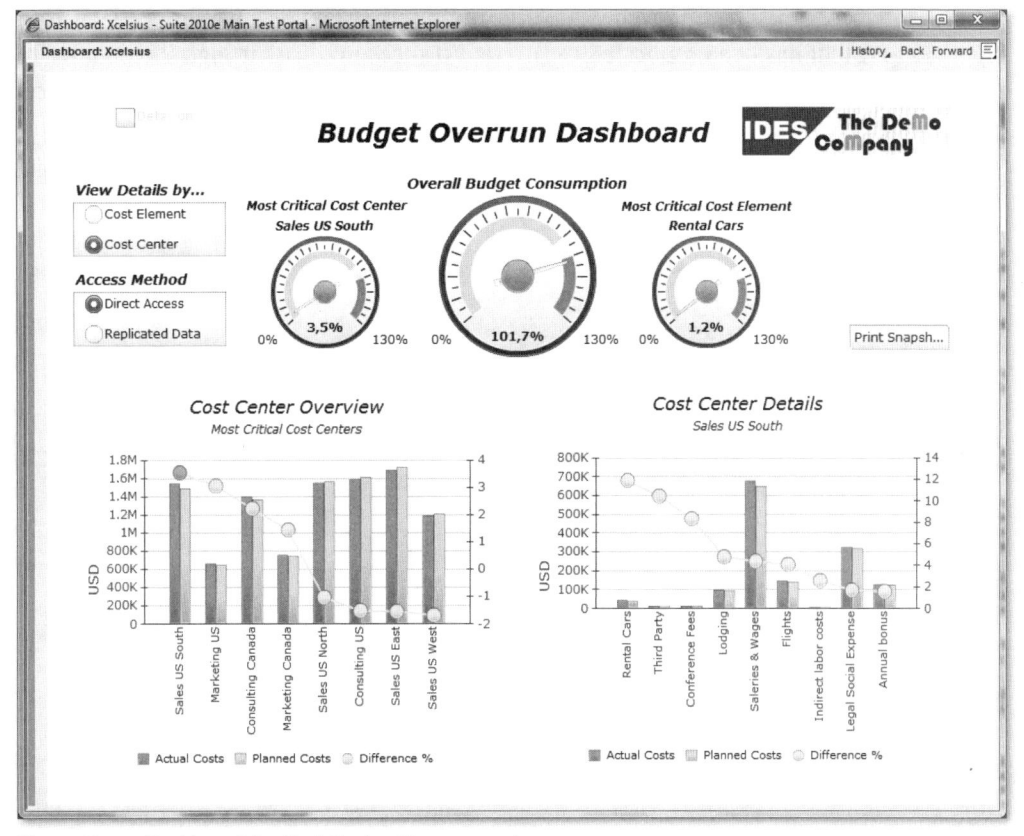

Figure 8.33 Dashboard for Cost Center Management

While Crystal Reports and xCelsius dashboards build on the queries available in SAP NetWeaver BW, whether transient, virtual, or replicated, SAP BusinessObjects Explorer uses a slightly different approach, as the name implies, to search and explore data.

8.4.3 SAP BusinessObjects Explorer for CO-PA Reporting

One of the biggest changes in reporting technologies at the time of writing is the introduction of the High Performance Analytic Appliance (or SAP HANA™). While we've discussed the balancing act between using replicated data and accessing data directly, HANA works with replicated data but performs the replication not once a day or once an hour, but every few seconds. This speed makes it particularly suited to the sort of sales reporting that characterizes CO-PA, where new sales orders or invoices may be entering CO-PA by the minute. Figure 8.34 shows data from CO-PA that has been replicated to HANA. To slice and dice through the data we're using the SAP BusinessObjects Explorer. Having logged on to SAP BusinessObjects Explorer, we entered the name of the query (ACT-IDES). The initial results are shown in Figure 8.34. In the top-right corner you'll see the number of documents that have been read to provide the information shown in the report.

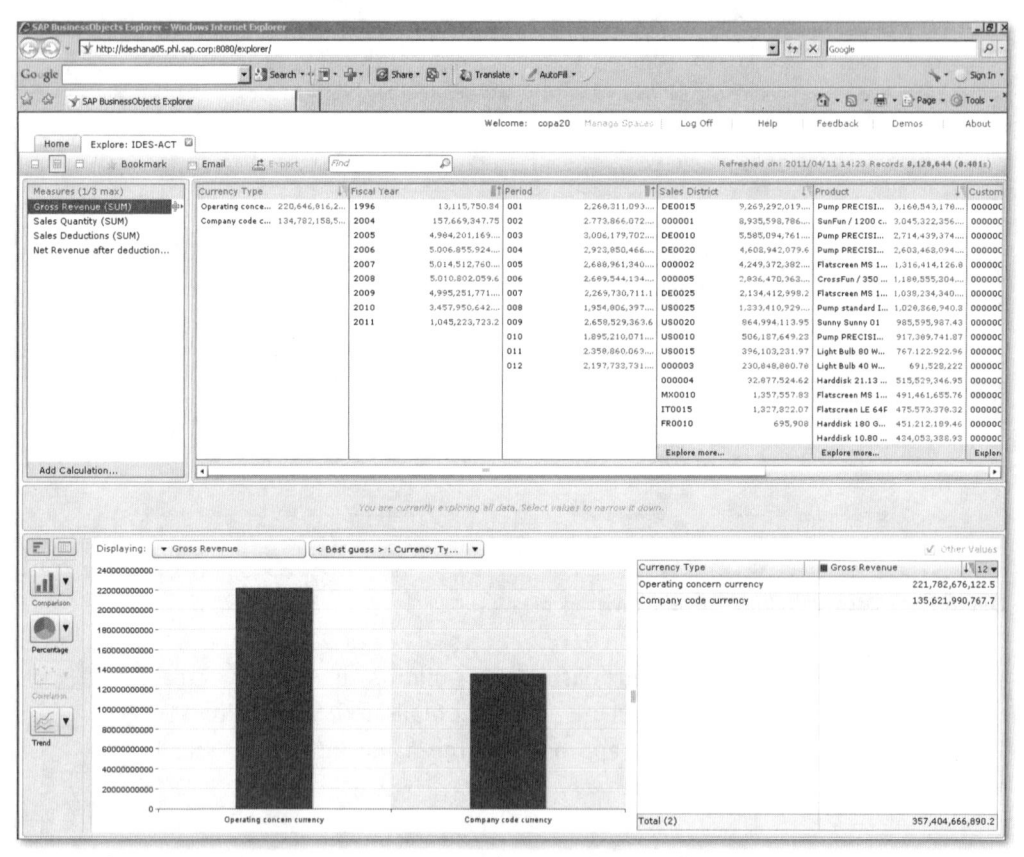

Figure 8.34 CO-PA Data in SAP BusinessObjects Explorer—Full Data Set

To drill down through this information, we'll select data from a single year (2010) and a single sales district. Figure 8.35 shows the result of setting this filter. You can see that a filter has been set by the two boxes for the filter conditions above the chart. Again, look at the number of records that meet these selection criteria along with the total records read in the top-right corner. It's hard to convey just how quickly such a selection is performed in a screenshot, but you can see that both screen captures were taken at 14:23.

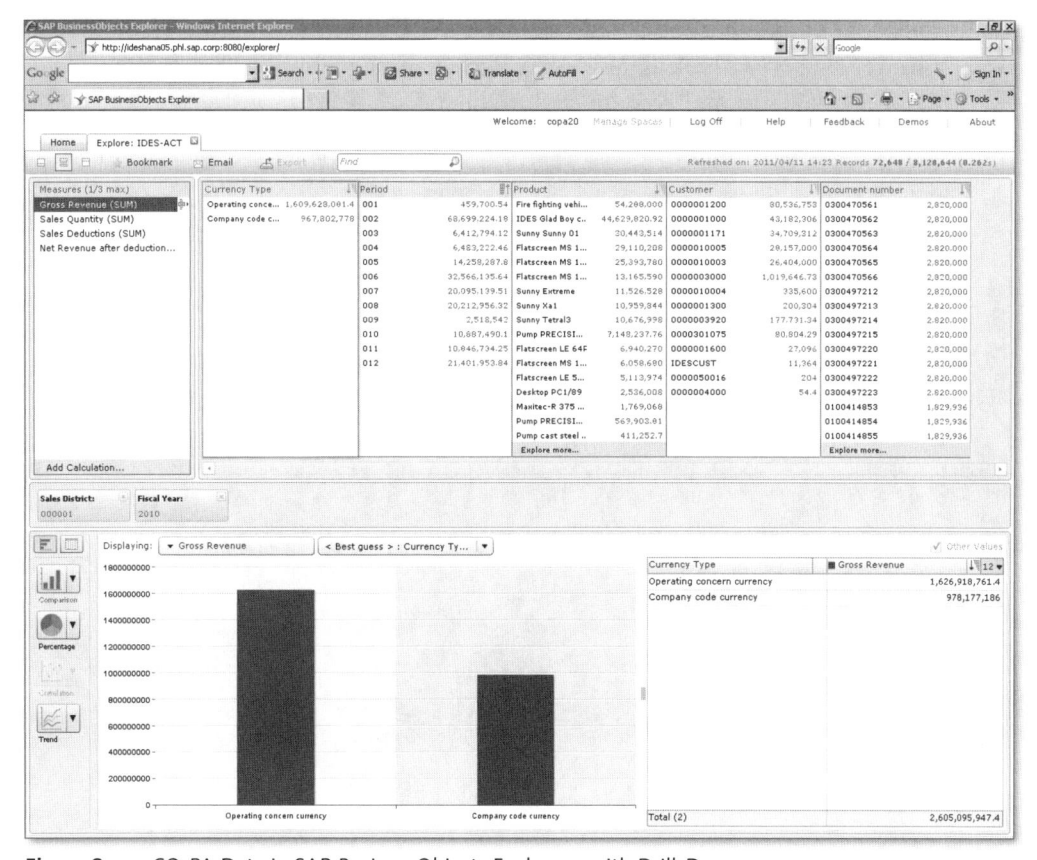

Figure 8.35 CO-PA Data in SAP BusinessObjects Explorer—with Drill-Down

To implement a report like this one, remember Figure 8.11 and the replication model for bringing an operating concern into SAP NetWeaver BW. For HANA too, there is a mapping between the characteristics and value fields of the operating concern and the data store in HANA. The replication then transfers the data from the operating concern tables to the in-memory tables.

8.5 Summary

In this chapter we looked at your options for reporting in SAP ERP and SAP NetWeaver BW and showed how to display the data from your query in Crystal Reports and dashboards and in a traditional query. We also introduced brand new tools for CO-PA reporting based on HANA. We'll return to SAP NetWeaver BW in Chapter 9 when we look at how to use it for planning purposes, but first we'll look at master data in a multisystem environment.

This chapter gives details of change requests in SAP ERP. It introduces new solutions for handling master data in a multisystem environment with full governance requirements and in a shared service environment.

9 Master Data in a Multisystem/ Shared Service Environment

In Chapters 3 and 4 we discussed the need for consistent master data as a basis both for the planning and budgeting tasks we discussed in Chapter 5 and for the actual postings we performed in Chapter 6. Agreeing on the master data can be one of the first challenges of an implementation. To prepare the material master, the purchasing, production, sales, accounting, and controlling departments have to come together and agree on a common code for each material. If several plants handle the material, there needs to be a consensus on the common fields, but also agreement about where plants can go their own way and set parameters that make sense for them only. As you start to think about cross-company goods movements of the kind we looked at in Chapter 6, then both companies have to use the same code for the material bought and sold to establish a stock transfer process that moves materials from plant A to plant B. So long as everybody is working on the same ERP system, the system enforces consistency because there's a single master record for each material. However, in larger implementations it's common to split production activities to several different ERP instances. When we start to cross systems, this consistency becomes more important, because it may only become clear that individual companies are using disparate codes for the same material when you report or consolidate. At the latest, when you start moving your costs into a data warehouse, you'll need consistent master data or your reports will be of little use. This can take place via consolidations as you move the data into the data warehouse, but many companies try to establish consistent rules for master data creation up front rather than trying to consolidate inconsistent data afterward.

9   Master Data in a Multisystem/Shared Service Environment

The need for consistent master data is by no means limited to the material master. A consistent chart of accounts will make consolidating your General Ledger accounts for group reporting substantially easier. Business requirements often result in the separation of the SAP ERP Human Capital Management system and the Financials and Logistics system. Here again, if your payroll run is going to transfer data from human resources to Financials, you have to make sure your cost center structure is consistent in both systems. The same applies to the time recording we saw in Chapter 6. If you're going to assign time to a project or an order, your human resources system is going to have to know which cost centers, activity types, projects, and orders have been created in your Finance system.

Many organizations have already solved the technical side of master data management by establishing a separate master data server as a central hub where they maintain their master data (and often customizing settings as well) and then transfer the data from their master data server to the local ERP systems at regular intervals, usually using ALE (application link enabling) or similar technologies. It's also common to use SAP Solution Manager as a central repository for configuration settings and to replicate from there. While this sounds sensible enough, there's still a challenge to decide which part of the master data is truly global and which is more local in nature and to set up your authorizations to support this division.

Along with the technical challenges of consistent data, recent years have seen changes in responsibility for executing a master data change and changes to the whole process of creating and changing master data. The main *business* reason for the change is the move toward treating the finance and controlling functions as a *shared service*. Where once every company in a large group had its own team of accountants and controllers, along with a group controlling function at headquarters, quests for efficiency resulted in a split, with many of the more routine tasks (including some controlling tasks) being handled by a shared service center that can monitor receivables, collect payments, handle disputes, and so on, not just for a single company but for multiple companies in the same group.

For the controller, this means the definition of new processes for requesting master data changes and new roles for approving and updating master data. These processes usually include some kind of ticketing to initiate a change request and use workflow to move the ticket through approval and execution. In such an environment, the controller may initiate a request for a new cost element or cost center and comment

Master Data in a Multisystem/Shared Service Environment | 9

on or approve such a change, but the creation of the master data as such is likely to be handled by an agent working in a shared service center, while the controller is only authorized to use the display transactions for the master data we discussed in Chapters 3 and 4. In this chapter we'll look at two solutions introduced recently to support these business requirements.

- SAP introduced *SAP Master Data Governance for Financials* (SAP MDGF) in enhancement package 4 for SAP ERP 6.0 to handle chart of account data, including the group chart of accounts, operational and local charts of accounts, and their hierarchies. We discussed these accounts when we looked at accounts and primary cost elements in Chapter 4. If you have global, operational, and country-specific charts of accounts, don't be afraid that a central hub means that headquarters makes all the rules. You can set up central workflows for the global and operational charts of accounts and local workflows for country-specific charts of accounts in the same environment. In enhancement package 5, the entities cost element, cost center, profit center, group companies, materials, and vendors were added. Work continues and SAP plans to add customers in the future. From enhancement package 5 it's also possible to add your own master data entities if you decide that you want to use the same mechanisms to handle, for example, the creation of an activity type.

- SAP introduced the *SAP Shared Service Framework* in enhancement package 5 for SAP ERP 6.0 to provide support for multiple business functions through one central shared service hub. In this solution shared services for initiating master data changes and starting processes, such as a leave request in human resources, sit alongside business processes in the Finance (FI) and Controlling (CO) components of SAP ERP Financials. Since the focus here is on efficiency, the shared service framework supports both the process of handling, for example, a payment dispute or a change to the vendor master, but also provides functions that allow you to monitor the level of service of the shared service center—tracking the time it takes from receiving the request to the delivery of a solution. If you're the controller, you can then use these metrics to find out how long the shared service center took from the moment you requested a cost center change to the completion of your ticket.

Before we look at either of these solutions, let's return to the change request we discussed at the end of Chapter 3 as a simple way of providing a SOX-compliant ticketing solution if you're working with a single SAP ERP system.

9 Master Data in a Multisystem/Shared Service Environment

9.1 Change Requests in SAP ERP

We ended Chapter 3 with a discussion of the use of change requests to initiate a cost center change and described the approval workflow triggered by this request and how the notification provides a follow-up action to allow the controller to call the transaction and make the relevant change in SAP ERP. Let's now take a look behind the scenes to understand the mechanisms controlling the change request.

To view the settings for the change request in the IMG, follow the menu path CROSS-APPLICATION COMPONENTS • INTERNET/INTRANET SERVICES • INTERNAL SERVICE REQUEST (ISR) • SCENARIO DEFINITION • DEFINE SCENARIO. You might want to take a look at these settings with your system administrator to help you decide whether such a change request would meet your compliance needs or whether you need the more sophisticated options we'll cover later in the chapter.

Figure 9.1 shows some of the scenarios delivered in SAP ERP (there are too many to fit on one screen). To cover the master data we looked at in Chapter 3, you should explore the following scenarios:

- Create cost center (SMC1)
- Change cost center (SMC2)
- Create internal order (SM01)
- Change internal order (SM02)
- Request to change project (SPS1)
- Request to change WBS element (SPS2)
- Create WBS element (SPS3)
- Change WBS element (extended) (SPS4)
- Notification about missing cost center (SREA)
- Notification about cost center change (SREB)
- Notification about missing internal order (SREC)
- Notification about change of internal order (SRED)

If you're interested in the change requests we discussed for budget changes in Chapter 5, you might also want to take a look at the following scenarios.

- Budget request (SRB1)
- Budget request with approval (SRB2)
- Budget change (SRB3)
- Budget change with approval (SRB4)
- Budget transfer (SRBA)
- Budget transfer with approval (SRBB)

In Chapter 3, Section 3.10 we used scenario SREB to initiate a cost center change in the course of our planning activities. We'll now look at this scenario in more detail.

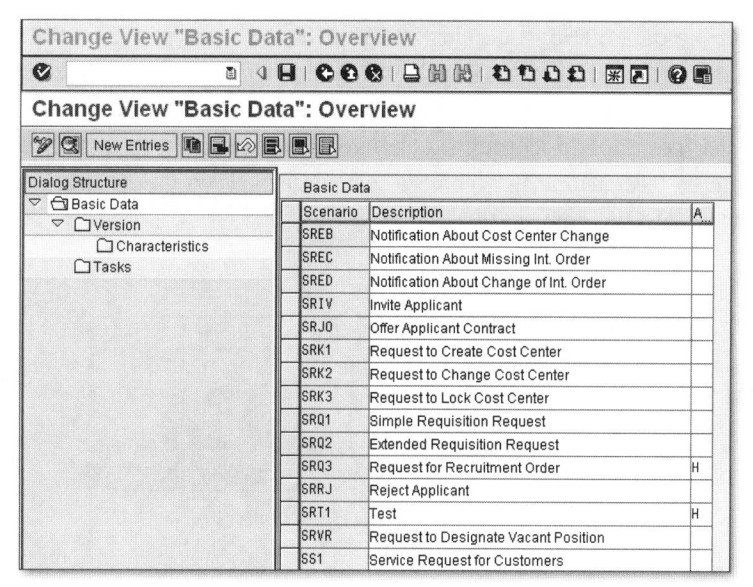

Figure 9.1 Change Request Scenarios in SAP ERP

To view the scenario details, select scenario SREB (NOTIFICATION OF MISSING COST CENTER) from the list in Figure 9.1. In the BASIC DATA screen (Figure 9.2) notice that the scenario includes a version and characteristics. The characteristics provide the link to the data in SAP ERP by linking the request scenario with the underlying data structure of the cost center in SAP ERP.

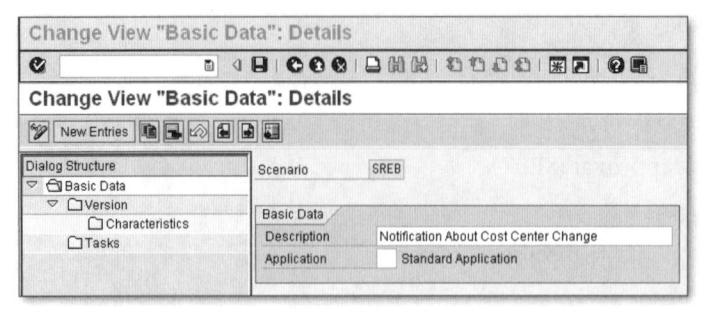

Figure 9.2 Basic Data for a Change Request

To take a look at these fields, select the VERSION folder (on the left) and then the CHARACTERISTICS folder. This takes you to the link between the characteristics in the change request and the data dictionary fields in SAP ERP as shown in Figure 9.3. We'll come to the meaning of the scenario and instance when we look at Express Planning in more detail in Chapter 10. The fields are specific to the scenario. The Express Planning change simply documents a change of cost center responsibility (see Chapter 3), whereas scenario SMC2 (change cost center) allows you to initiate more extensive changes to the cost center.

Figure 9.3 Characteristics of the Change Request

Let's now have a look at the settings for the change request as a whole by selecting the VERSION folder. This takes you into the screen shown in Figure 9.4.

9.1 Change Requests in SAP ERP

[screenshot of SAP "Change View 'Version': Details" screen showing Basic Data > Version with Characteristics and Tasks; scenario SREB, version 0, active; Description: Notification About Cost Center Change; Application: Standard Application; Notification Type: 90 Master Data Change; requires approval; contact SAP; Entry Type in Web: Entry Using Adobe PDF; Form: Z_ISR_FORM_SREB; Interface: ISR_IF_SREB; New Business Add-In selected]

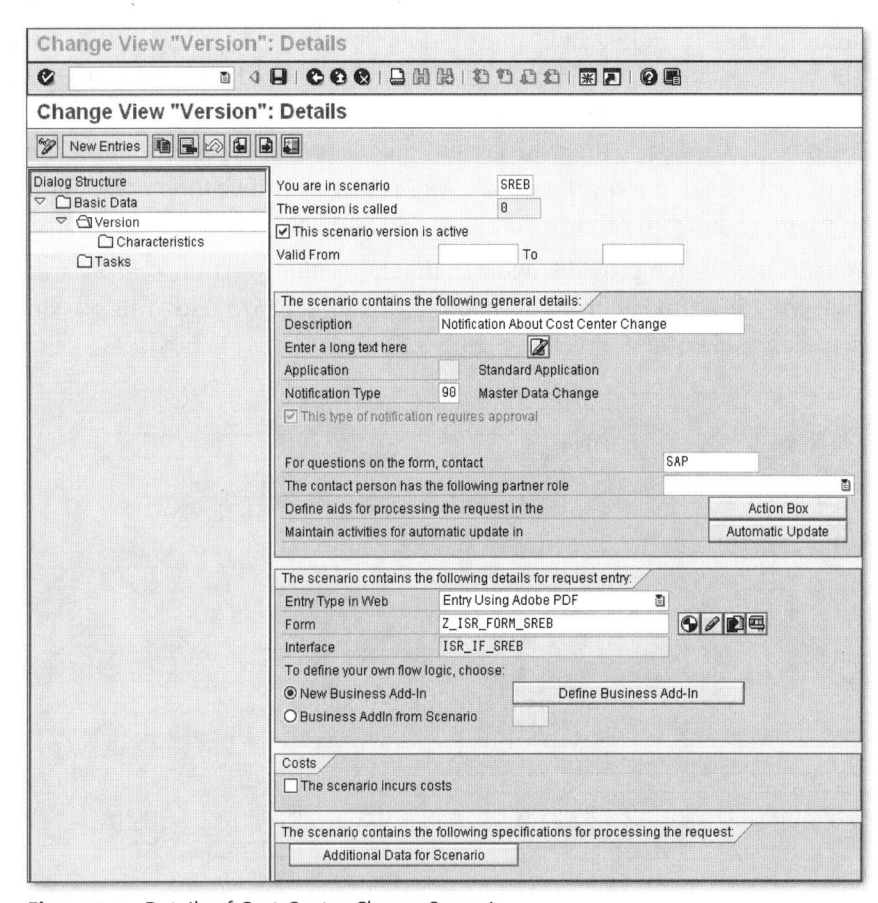

Figure 9.4 Details of Cost Center Change Scenario

The version provides the link to the three elements that characterize a cost center change request.

- The notification type indicates the type of notification that will be created with reference to the change request in SAP ERP. You may want to refer back to the notification we showed in Chapter 3, Figure 3.31 to remind yourself what a notification document looks like. As far as the change request is concerned, it's main feature is that it can record status information. Also notice that this scenario is flagged as requiring approval. In other words, the change request cannot be completed until the notification has the status Approved.

433

9   Master Data in a Multisystem/Shared Service Environment

- The form settings include a link to the Adobe form (Z_ISR_FORM_SREB) we saw the manager fill out in Figure 3.30. This form is linked with fields in SAP ERP so that the relevant checks on the existence of the cost center and related fields can be performed as the manager fills out his form. You can use the icons beside the form field to access this form. We're using an Adobe Interactive Form in this example, but you can use other form technologies instead.

- The ACTION BOX button provides a link to the transactions that the processor of the form will use to update the cost center information in SAP ERP. This was on the right-hand side of the screen in Figure 3.31.

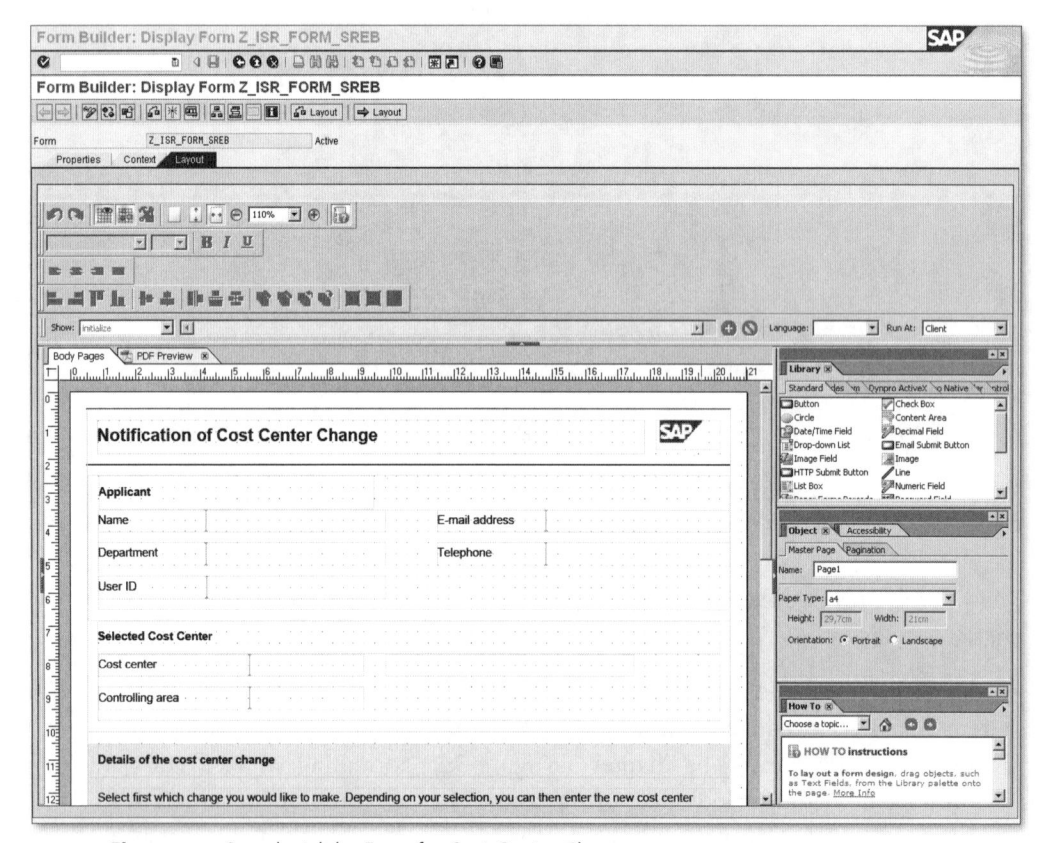

Figure 9.5   Sample Adobe Form for Cost Center Change

Let's first look at the form (Figure 9.5). If you don't have developer authorization, switch to DISPLAY mode and then click on the DISPLAY button next to the form field. Organizations can tailor these forms to include different data, formatting, and so

Change Requests in SAP ERP | **9.1**

on. You won't incur any additional license costs if you use the Adobe Interactive Forms as they are, but you'll need to change your license agreement if you want to build new forms (a similar agreement to the one we saw for Crystal Reports in Chapter 8).

To display the related actions, click on the ACTION BOX button shown in Figure 9.4. Figure 9.6 shows all the master data change actions. The context of the form tells the system to offer cost center change actions from the notification. If you refer back to Figure 3.31, you'll see that you can either select AUTO. CHANGING OF COST CENTER or CHANGE COST CENTER MANUALLY.

- In the first case, the data entered in the form is used to generate the master data automatically without the processor entering the master data transaction.
- In the second case, the data from the form is passed to the master data change transaction but the processor can make adjustments if necessary.

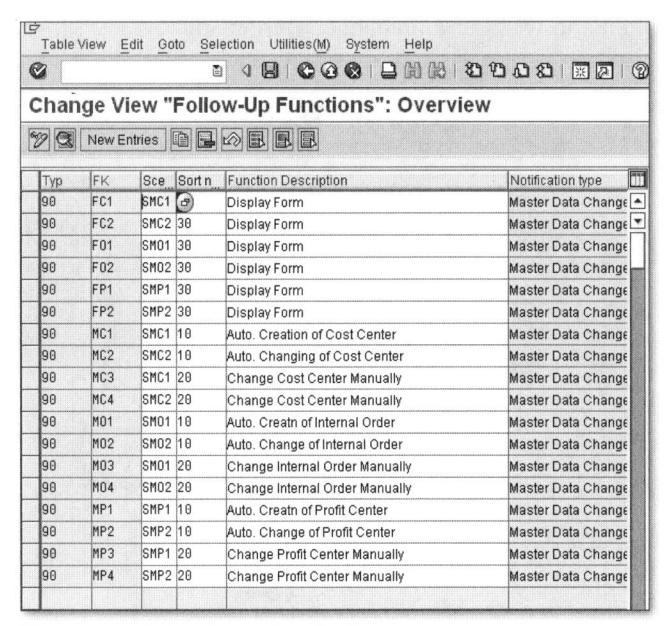

Figure 9.6 Follow-Up Actions for Form

Now that we've looked at a simple change request that initiates a notification to approve a master data change in SAP ERP, we'll look at a more complex scenario to introduce the new functions for SAP Master Data Governance in Financials.

435

9.2 New Solutions for Handling Master Data in a Multisystem Environment

The primary aim of SAP Master Data Governance for Financials is to ensure that consistent master data is prepared in a central hub and then made available across *multiple* systems. Figure 9.7 shows one example of the use of SAP Master Data Governance for Financials with chart of account data being maintained centrally and then transferred (for reporting, it's common to talk about the data being *replicated)* to the SAP ERP systems and the consolidation system to ensure that the financial results from the entities performing their operations in SAP ERP can easily be submitted to the group system for consolidation. This means that all companies will be using the same group and operational chart of accounts and ensures consistent mapping between the operational and corporate chart of accounts. Arrows indicate a change request process along the top, since governance is a key part of the approach, with proper approvals of all changes being recorded in the system, providing documentation to auditors about when and why certain changes were made.

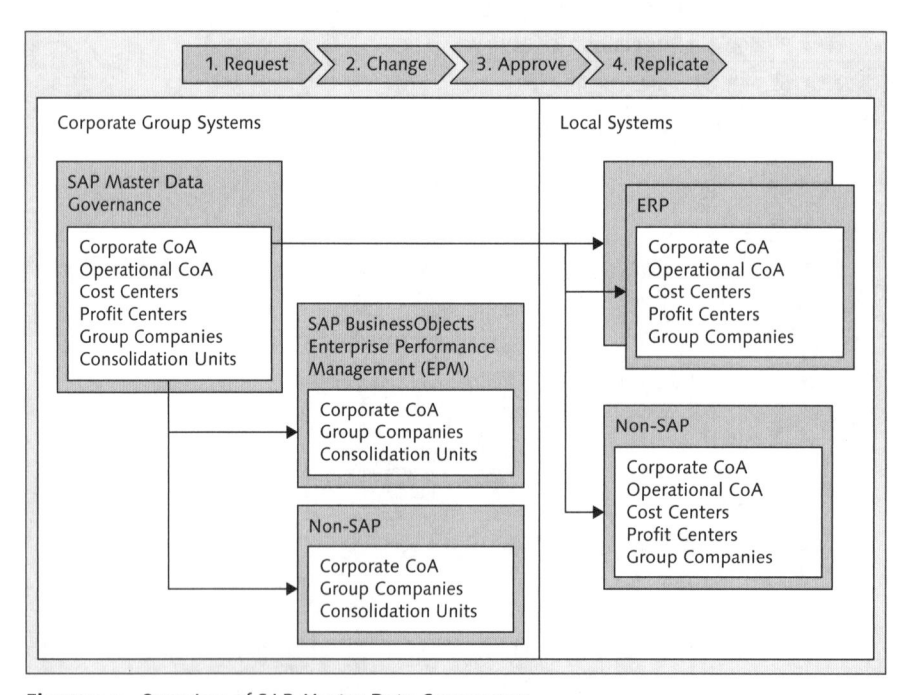

Figure 9.7 Overview of SAP Master Data Governance

9.2.1 Data Modeling in SAP Master Data Governance for Financials

In terms of data modeling, the master data governance requirements are similar to the requirements for master data reporting in SAP NetWeaver BW. Whereas in SAP NetWeaver BW we discussed a data model that included different InfoObjects for cost centers, customers, materials, and so on, in SAP MDGF we find a data model that comprises multiple entity types and includes such information as their attributes, whether they can be viewed in a hierarchy, how groups are handled, and so on. SAP delivers several data models for master data governance, which your administrator can activate via the IMG. You'll find the settings under CROSS APPLICATION COMPONENTS • PROCESSES AND TOOLS FOR ENTERPRISE APPLICATIONS • MASTER DATA GOVERNANCE • GENERAL SETTINGS • DATA MODELING • EDIT DATA MODEL. The delivered data models include the following. Again, take a look at these options with your administrator.

- **Chart of Accounts and Org. Units (0G)**
  This model was delivered in enhancement package 5 for use in combination with the business function Master Data Governance for Financials, Organizational Units (FIN_MDM_ORG). The data model includes companies, profit centers, and cost centers, in addition to charts of accounts and cost elements . If you plan to implement in enhancement package 5, use this data model rather than 0F.

- **Chart of Accounts (0F)**
  This model was delivered in enhancement package 4 for use in combination with the business function Financial Master Data Management: Charts of Accounts (FIN_MDM_ACC). The data model supports the central definition of global and local charts of accounts. This model has been superseded by data model 0G.

- **Business Partner (BP)**
  This covers the master data for the supplier and is available from enhancement package 5.

- **Material Maintenance (MM)**
  This covers the master data for the central part of the material master (MARA) and is available from enhancement package 5.

Figure 9.8 shows the entity types included in the master data model Chart of Accounts and Org. Units (0G). The entity types of most interest to the controller are the cost elements (CELEM), cost element groups (CELEMG), cost element hierarchies (CELEMH), cost centers (CCTR), cost center groups (CCTRG), and cost center hierarchies (CCTRH). If you're concerned about the difference between a group and a hierarchy, refer back to the note in Chapter 8, Section 8.3. In Figure 9.8 notice two fundamental aspects of master data governance.

- The controlling entity types are flagged as being changeable via a *change request*. This means that we'll find the change request used as both a ticketing mechanism to notify the relevant stakeholders that something is to be done and as a data store for the various approvals needed before the change can be executed. We'll look at the change process in more detail when we discuss governance requirements in Section 9.3.

- The entity types are linked with an *edition*. An *edition* typically refers to a specific time frame, such as the second quarter of 2011, and groups together all changes to the master data requested within that time frame. Many change requests can be assigned to a single edition, and once all these requests have been processed, the data in the edition can be replicated to the local systems.

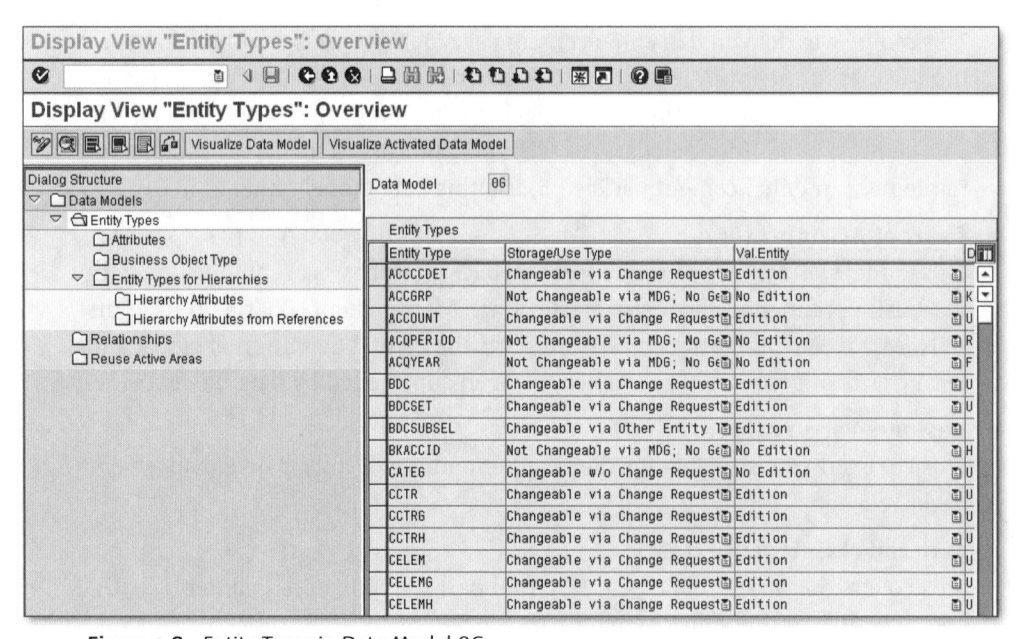

Figure 9.8 Entity Types in Data Model 0G

9.2.2 Editions in SAP Master Data Governance for Financials

Now that we've looked at the data model, let's have a look how that data is replicated to the local systems. As we already mentioned, one of the other central ideas of SAP Master Data Governance in Financials is the *edition,* which acts as a collector for all change requests raised within a given time frame.

Before you can create editions or change requests in SAP Master Data Governance in Financials, you need to ask your administrator to assign your user to the role SAP_FIN_MDM if you're are working in the SAP NetWeaver Business Client or the business package Financial MDM if you're are working in the SAP NetWeaver Enterprise Portal (see Appendix A, which you can download at *www.sap-press.com*). Once your user is assigned to this role, you'll see the work center shown in Figure 9.9 when you log on to the SAP NetWeaver Business Client.

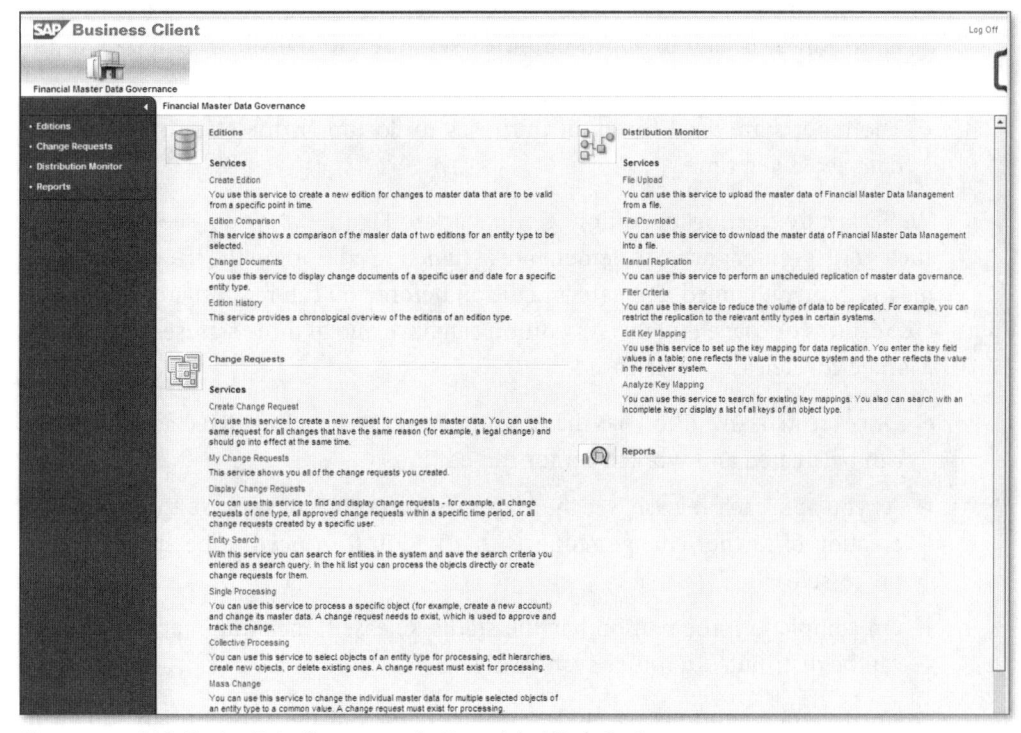

Figure 9.9 SAP Master Data Governance in Financials: Work Centers

The role structure for SAP Master Data Governance is familiar from the SAP ERP roles we've looked at throughout the book. However, this time we can't give you a menu path and transaction code for each of the applications listed because the links call Web Dynpro applications that are not included in the SAP Easy Menu. There are four main work areas: EDITIONS, CHANGE REQUESTS, DISTRIBUTION MONITOR, and REPORTS.

- The edition provides the framework around the master data update (e.g., all changes for the first quarter).
- Change requests are created with respect to this edition to document in detail what has to be done (which cost centers are to be changed, how the groups are to be restructured, and so on). The change request is attached to a workflow that routes the request through the various approval steps until each request has been processed and is ready for transfer to the local systems.
- The distribution monitor documents the replication to the local systems, providing an overview of which editions were used to transfer which data to the operational systems.
- The reports are used for audit purposes to document the state of the master data at a given time.

We'll start by creating an edition. Going back to Figure 9.8, you'll see that entities such as cost center and cost element are assigned to editions in the data model. This means that you'll need to create an edition before you can request any changes to cost centers or cost elements. An edition can have one of three statuses: In Process, Marked for Release, or Released.

- Once created, an edition has the status IN PROCESS, meaning that change requests can be created and worked on for the edition.
- As you approach release, set the status to MARKED FOR RELEASE to prevent the creation of further change requests that will in turn need to be approved and processed.
- On completion, the edition has the status Released, meaning that the changes can be distributed to other systems.

To create a new edition, select CREATE EDITION from the service map shown in Figure 9.9. This is a fairly simple application giving the edition a name, linking it to the data model via the type, and stating when it will become valid. Figure 9.10 shows the CREATE EDITION application. This will be the point of reference for all change requests and for all data replications. Two fields are worth discussing in more detail.

- Type field

  The type is set up in Customizing and defines the entities that can be handled in a single change request. So you might create one type for cost centers, profit centers, and their groupings and another for accounts, cost elements, and their groupings if you want to separate the distribution of your account structures from the distribution of your organizational structures.

- Immediately Distribute Change Requests checkbox

  If you're in the middle of your period close activities when you realize that you need a new account, you want a quick way to report and implement the change. This checkbox allows you to bypass the usual edition logic and effect a change immediately.

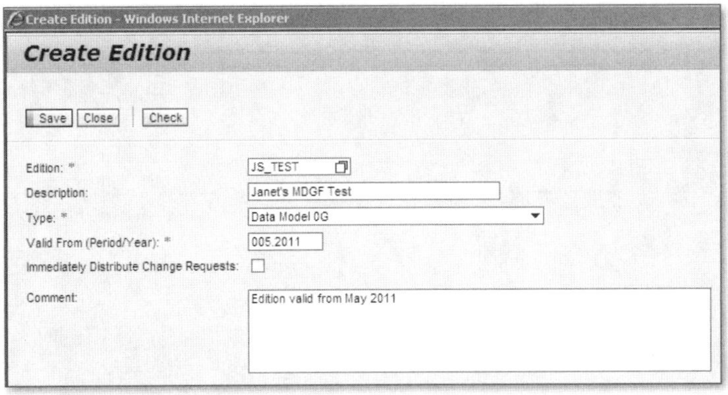

Figure 9.10 Create Edition

Once you've created your edition, it will appear in the list shown in Figure 9.11.

- To display this list, select Editions in the left-hand navigation panel. Notice a series of inactive buttons above the entry in the list. If you select an entry, these buttons will become active and you'll be able to display any change requests created with respect to the edition. You can also run validations and change the status of the edition from In Process to Released.

- As always with a list like these, if you can't see your edition, click on the Show Quick Criteria Maintenance button to access the selection parameters for this list.

9 Master Data in a Multisystem/Shared Service Environment

▶ If you know the name of your edition but can't find it in a long list, click on the FILTER icon to quickly find your edition, as we've done in Figure 9.11.

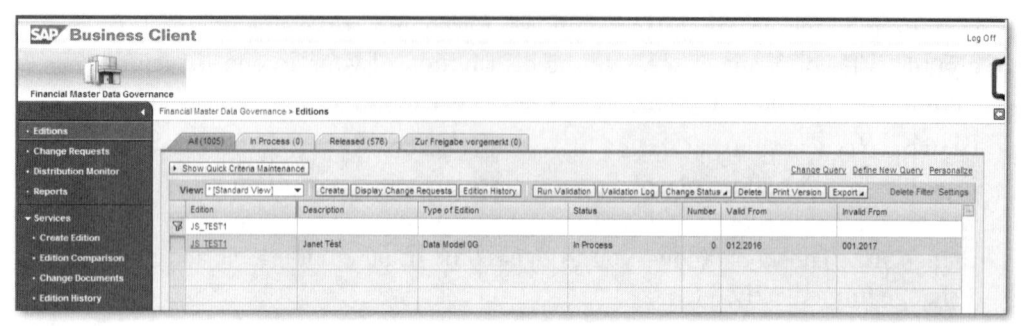

Figure 9.11 Overview of Editions

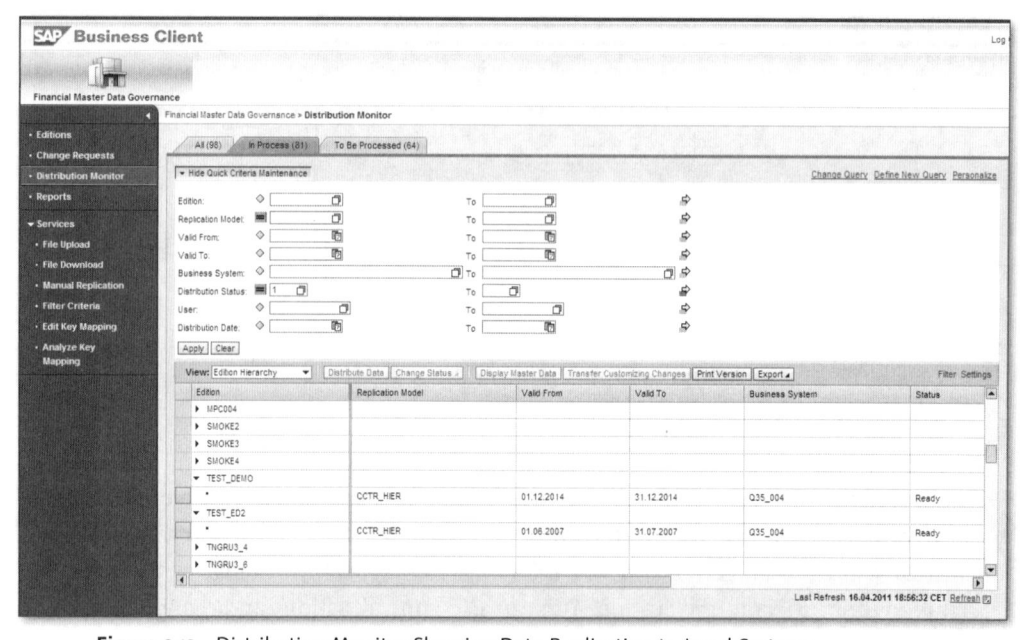

Figure 9.12 Distribution Monitor Showing Data Replication to Local Systems

Once all change requests have been gathered and completed, you can release the edition. The edition provides the framework for the transfer of data to the underlying ERP systems. This transfer takes place using SOA services or ALE. To activate these services, your administrator has to activate the business functions FIN_MDM_SOA_CU and FIN_MDM_SOA_ORG in the receiving systems. Figure 9.12 shows the result of running a data transfer for the selected editions to the underlying ERP system. Notice that this list has the same basic structure as the previous list, except that this time the HIDE QUICK CRITERIA MAINTENANCE button is toggled open so that you can see the selection criteria.

With the exception of terminology changes, most existing approaches to master data management that use a central master data server can handle the basic requirement to define the data centrally and then transfer it to the local systems. However, records of why and for whom a request was initiated are often stored as mail or in spreadsheets on local file servers, representing a potential compliance risk. What makes SAP Master Data Governance for Financials different is the use of change requests to handle all requirements relating to governance in this process, so let's now have a look at the options for handling change requests to ensure proper governance in the master data creation process.

9.3 Governance Requirements for Master Data

SAP Master Data Governance for Financials is essentially a more sophisticated version of the change request we looked at in Section 9.1, providing the ability to attach multiple objects to one request and link related requests via the edition. There's also the proviso that you have to license this solution, whereas the internal service request is covered by the normal SAP ERP license.

9.3.1 Creating a Change Request

The SAP MDGF change request is handled as a roadmap that walks you through the steps of describing the changes you want to make and including supporting documentation to justify your request. To create a change request, select CREATE CHANGE REQUEST in Figure 9.9. Figure 9.13 shows the GENERAL DATA screen for the change request. Notice the link to the edition, which will allow us to find all related change requests prior to release of the edition for transfer to the underlying systems, and later when we present our changes to the auditors. It's important to choose the correct change request type, since this will determine the entity types that can be included in the change request.

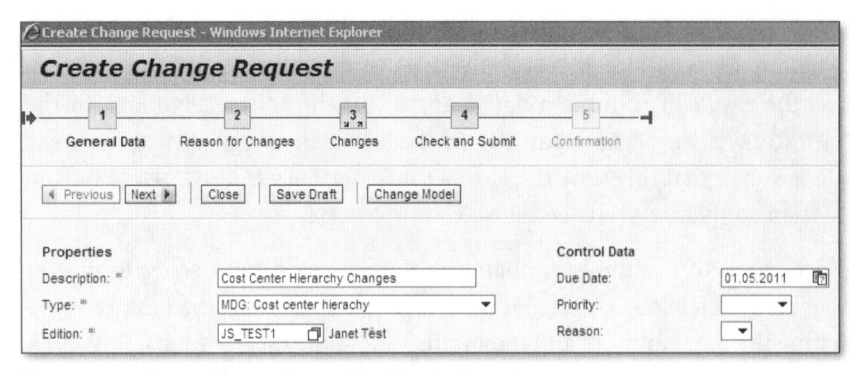

Figure 9.13 Create Change Request in Master Data Governance

Fill out the change request form as follows:

1. Under GENERAL DATA, enter the name of the edition that will provide the umbrella for all your change requests in the current time frame in the EDITION field, select the type of change request you want (this determines the entity types you can handle in the request), and enter the due date and the priority of the request.

2. Under REASON FOR CHANGES, explain why the change is needed and upload any attachments and notes that provide supporting evidence of the need for the change. This is especially important for major changes where there's large-scale restructuring.

3. Under CHANGE, describe the data change to be made. Depending on the type you picked in Figure 9.13, this information will appear as either an Adobe form, like the one we looked at earlier in the chapter, or a Web Dynpro application.

4. Under CHECK AND SUBMIT, make one last check prior to submitting the request for approval and execution.

There are some significant differences between this change request and the internal service request we looked at earlier.

- You can change *multiple* objects using a single change request.
- You can create hierarchies or groups using the collective processing function and include them in your change request.
- You can perform mass changes, for example, to lock many cost centers in one go and include this in your change request.

Figure 9.14 shows a list of cost centers for which a change is being requested. You can add further cost centers using the ADD OBJECTS or ADD ROW buttons. If a major structural reorganization is in process, hundreds of cost centers may be affected, and there's a clear audit requirement.

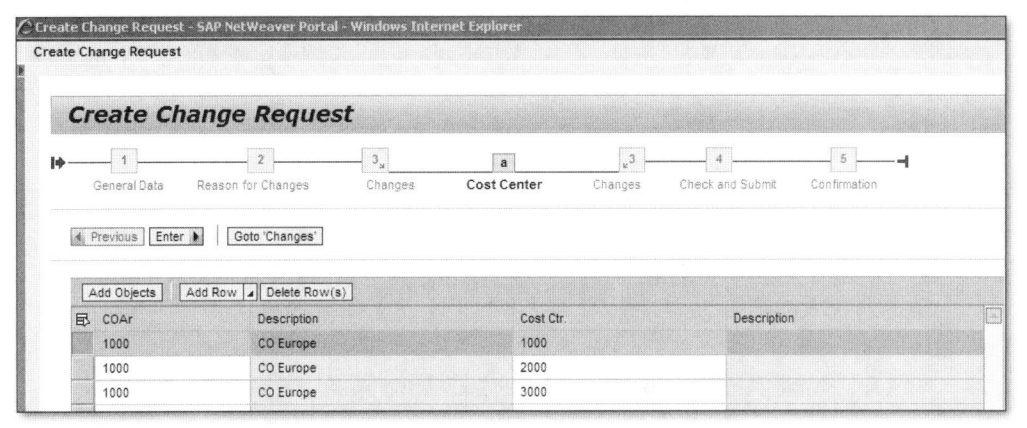

Figure 9.14 Including Multiple Cost Centers in a Change Request

To handle multiple objects, proceed as follows.

1. First, create a change request to provide the framework for the change.
2. Then use collective processing to prepare the list of the objects you want to change. Here you can also adjust the groupings of your objects within the hierarchy. Essentially you're adding and removing nodes just as we did for cost center groups in Chapter 3.
3. Link this list with the change request.
4. Finalize processing of the change request.

Figure 9.15 shows the initial screen for commencing collective processing of a particular cost center group or even an entire hierarchy.

To make changes to the hierarchy or group, select START. Figure 9.16 shows a cost center hierarchy like those we looked at in Chapter 3. You can use this application to add, remove, and reposition nodes and add and remove cost centers. This makes it quite different from the change request we looked at earlier, which simply provided a ticketing mechanism for changing a single object.

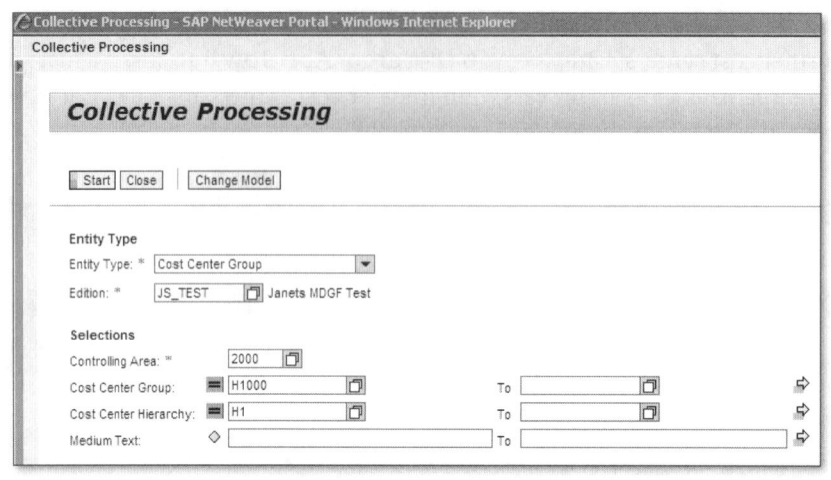

Figure 9.15 Collective Processing

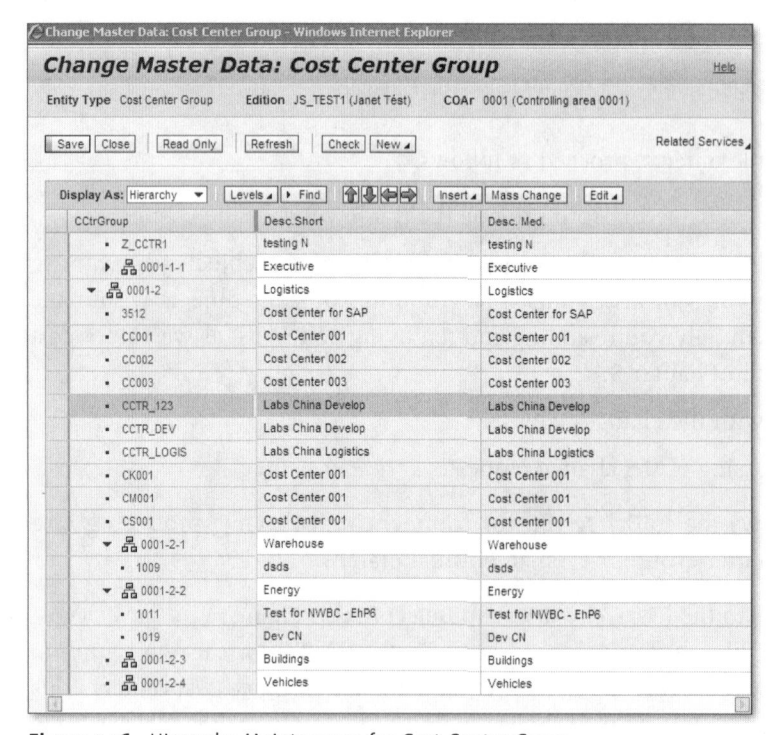

Figure 9.16 Hierarchy Maintenance for Cost Center Group

To perform mass changes, select MASS CHANGE in Figure 9.9. Figure 9.17 shows the roadmap that guides you through the steps required to make mass changes.

1. Select the relevant entity type and make the link to the edition again.
2. Select the objects for which you want to perform the mass change. You might enter the range of cost centers to be changed.
3. Refine the selection of your objects for the change operation.
4. Enter the data you want to be changed.
5. Confirm your changes.

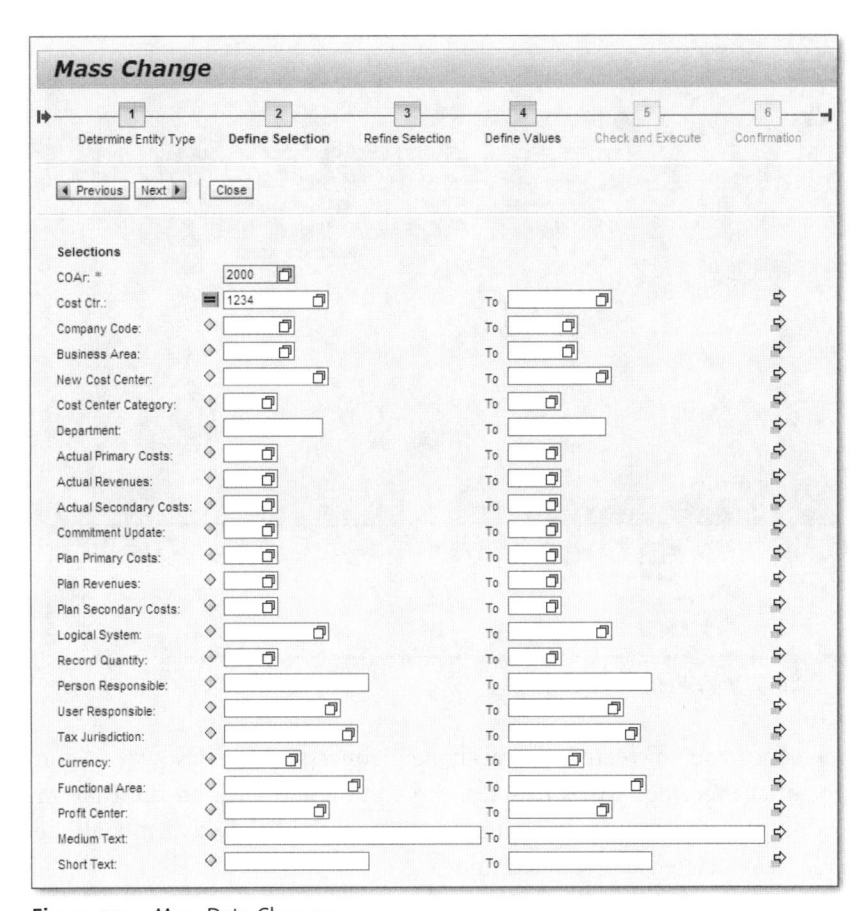

Figure 9.17 Mass Data Changes

9 | Master Data in a Multisystem/Shared Service Environment

Again, you'll have to link this change to a change request to be able to replicate your changes.

9.3.2 Finding Change Requests

Once you've created a change request, you can find it by selecting MY CHANGE REQUESTS in Figure 9.9. Figure 9.18 shows a list of the change requests that I am currently working on.

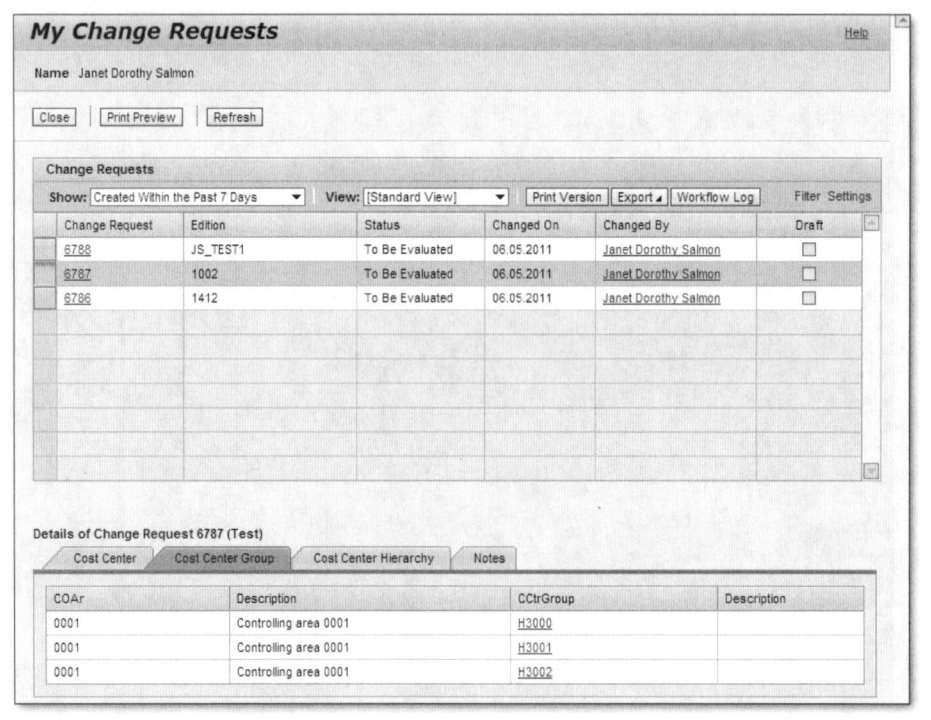

Figure 9.18 List of Change Requests

Alternatively, once you've created several change requests, the easiest way to find all the relevant change requests is to select the edition and click on the DISPLAY CHANGE REQUESTS button shown in Figure 9.11. Figure 9.19 shows a list of all the change requests associated with one edition.

Governance Requirements for Master Data | 9.3

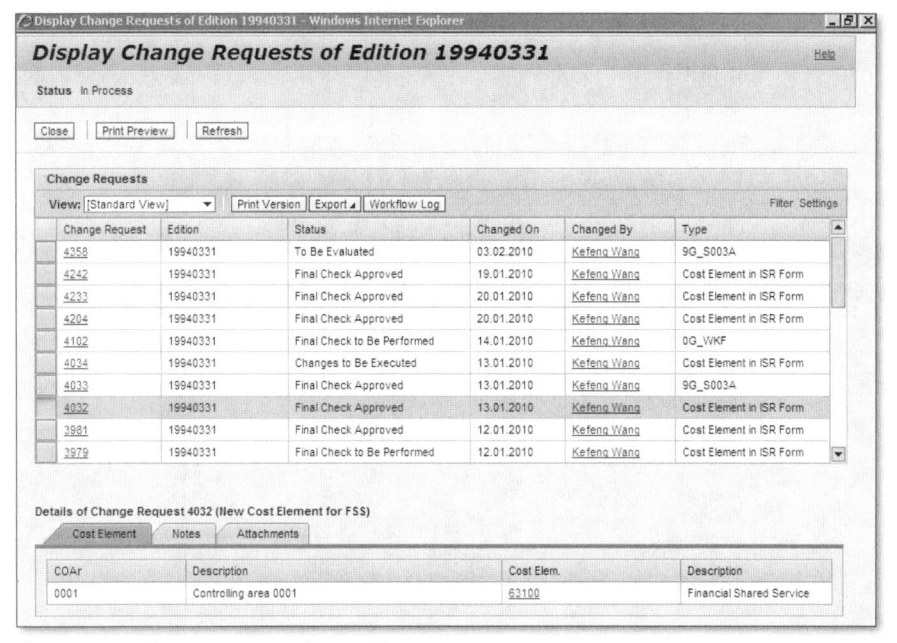

Figure 9.19 Change Requests for an Edition

9.3.3 Workflow Steps for a Change Request

In the change request we looked at initially, the approval is based on a notification and uses a classic SAP GUI user interface. In SAP MDGF the approvers, reviewers, and processors all see a Web application. Who does what with the change request is determined via a workflow linked to the request. Figure 9.20 shows some sample steps and processors. You can maintain these settings by following the menu path CROSS APPLICATION COMPONENTS • PROCESSES AND TOOLS FOR ENTERPRISE APPLICATIONS • MASTER DATA GOVERNANCE • MASTER DATA GOVERNANCE FOR FINANCIALS • WORKFLOW • ASSIGN PROCESSOR TO WORKFLOW STEP NUMBER. Figure 9.20 shows data model 0G, which has the following workflow steps:

- Evaluation
- Consideration and approval
- Processing
- Final check and approval

449

- Revision
- Consider in committee

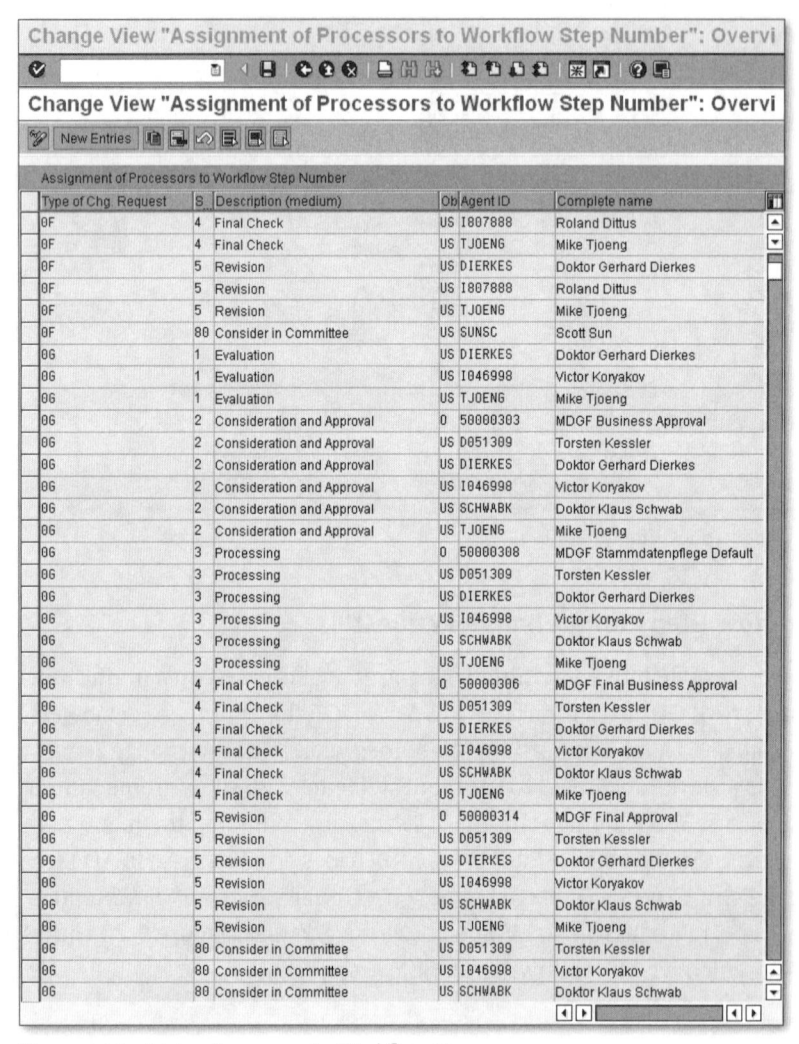

Figure 9.20 Assign Processors to Workflow Step

Each of these workflow steps is assigned to an agent or processor. When the change request is first created, it has the status To Be Evaluated. The next person in the workflow chain considers the suggestion and approve (or reject) the change. This results in the request being passed on to the next person in the workflow chain, who processes the request, maintaining the relevant entries in SAP MDGF. On completion of this step, the request moves to another party, who makes a final check and again approves the change. This process continues until all steps are complete.

If you're assigned to any tasks for a change request, you can see your requests by selecting MY CHANGE REQUESTS in Figure 9.9. In the example shown in Figure 9.21 you can see that several change requests are currently assigned to Alan Bradley. These have been approved but are awaiting execution in SAP MDGF. Once Alan has made the appropriate changes, the requests will be routed to the next person in the chain.

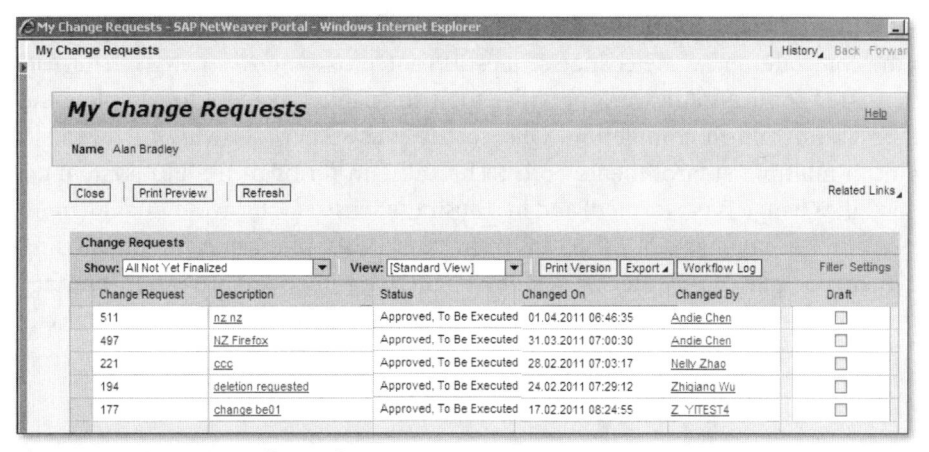

Figure 9.21 Approving a Change Request

When all change requests are complete, the edition can be released and an administrator can replicate the changes to the relevant systems. Now that we've walked through a master data change process in a multisystem environment, we'll compare the process with the change requests in a shared service center.

9.4 Creating Change Requests in a Shared Service Center

One of the biggest business changes in recent years has been the move of parts of the finance function to shared service centers. Many organizations embarked on their implementations of SAP ERP with a view to standardizing core processes, such as accounts payable, accounts receivable, and so on to later shift the function from the local organization to a shared service center. As far as CO is concerned, it's fairly common to handle routine correction postings or master data changes in a shared service center. Some organizations go further and execute many of their closing activities and routine reconciliation tasks in such an environment rather than performing them locally. In this section we'll focus on ticket handling for master data changes in a shared service center using the shared service framework, available from enhancement package 5.

Figure 9.22 shows the how a manager requests a master data change and an agent in the interaction center handles the change and then informs the manager that the change has been completed. The difference between this process and the change request we looked at in Chapter 3 is that instead of the change request being routed to the controller, now the change request is routed to a *shared service center agent*. The shared service framework provides tools to enable the agent to complete the request and confirm completion. One goal is consistency, allowing the agent to work in multiple environments both technically (in terms of the ERP system on which the change is performed) and in a business sense (so the agent might handle internal service requests but also calls from external suppliers questioning missing payments or calls from external customers querying invoices). The user interface for the request is similar, as is the connection to the underlying SAP ERP Financials system to perform the requested task.

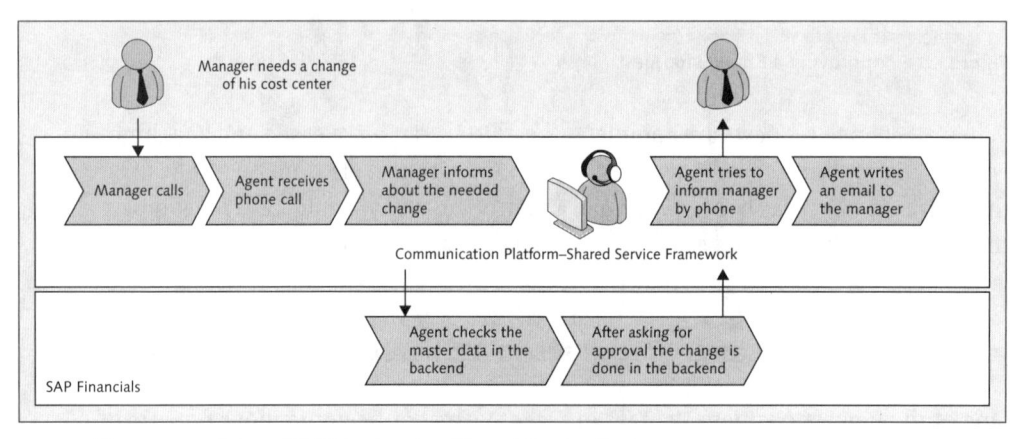

Figure 9.22 Internal Self-Services in a Shared Service Center

Shared Service Framework and SAP MDGF

You might wonder why there appear to be two solutions for master data change requests in SAP enhancement package 5, aside from the internal service request, which is somewhat older. Technically, the self-services for master data changes offered in the shared service framework use the SAP MDGF framework that we've just been looking at, even though approved changes are immediately updated in the corresponding backend system. This means that you have a central maintenance and governance process but are not initially forced to harmonize your master data. Later you can migrate to a central master data approach as described in Sections 9.2 and 9.3 if your business requires this.

Before you can use an internal self-service, you have to activate business function FIN_SSC_ISS_1 (Internal Self Services, Enablement for Fin. Shared Services) and have your administrator assign the role SAP_FIN_INT_SELF_SERVICE to your user (see Appendix A, found at *www.sap-press.com*). Figure 9.23 shows the internal self-services delivered in enhancement package 5. Whereas the assumption for SAP Master Data Governance in Financials was that the change request and master data model resided in a central master data system and data was replicated to *multiple* local systems when the change had been approved, the shared service framework assumes that the manager makes the request from his local system and the change is completed in that system (and only that system).

Figure 9.23 Financial Self-Services – List of Internal Services

Notice the MASTER DATA SERVICES folder and the DOCUMENT POSTING SERVICES folder, which allow you to request a correction posting like we saw in Chapter 6. The framework itself is configurable, so you can extend the list of services included in this list if need be. To view all master data services, select the DIRECTORY tab. Figure 9.24 shows the result.

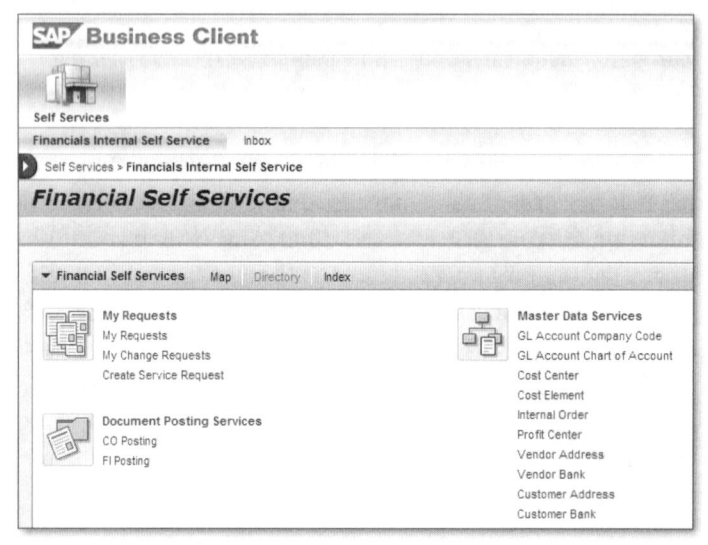

Figure 9.24 List of Financial Self-Services

To create a request for a new cost center, select the COST CENTER link under MASTER DATA SERVICES. Compared to Figure 9.14, where the cost center change request potentially triggered a major change affecting multiple systems, the request shown in Figure 9.25 will only affect the system in which the manager is working.

As we saw for master data governance, the manager can add notes and attachments to support his request by entering data on the relevant tabs (see Figure 9.26). Once the manager has placed the change request, he can see the request by selecting MY REQUESTS in Figure 9.23. This takes him to the same screen as we saw for SAP MDGF in Figure 9.17.

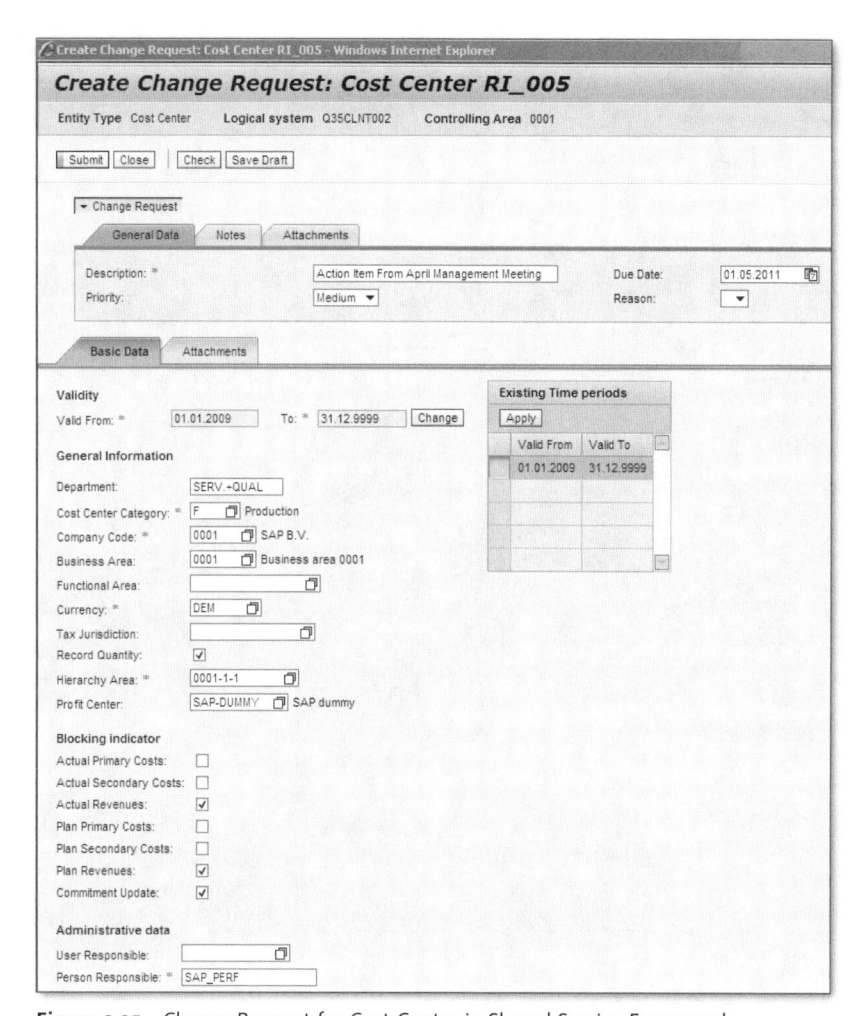

Figure 9.25 Change Request for Cost Center in Shared Service Framework

Again, the change request will be routed for approval and processing via workflow. Once the change has been approved, it can be implemented immediately in the underlying backend system since there's no replication process.

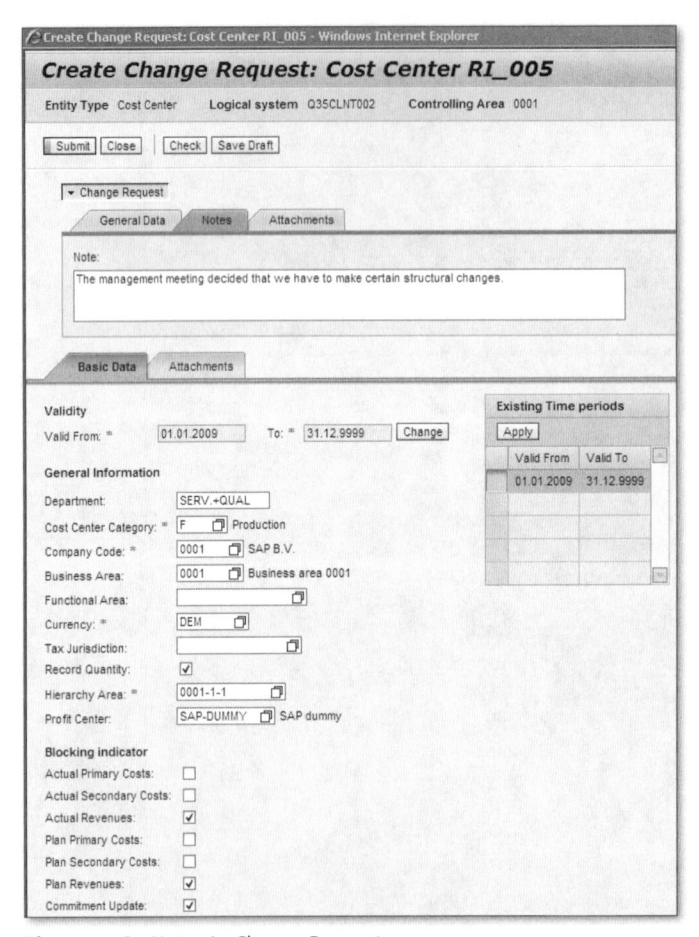

Figure 9.26 Notes in Change Request

9.5 Summary

In this chapter we looked at internal service requests for master data changes, SAP Master Data Governance for Financials, and the shared service framework. It's worth being aware that these two solutions both went to market in enhance package 5, so there are likely to be more changes to come in terms of scope. However you handle your master data, it's clear that consistency is essential both for the operative processes we looked at in Chapter 6 and for planning. And now, we'll return to planning to explore newer solutions for a modeled form of planning like those we previously discussed for reporting.

This chapter compares the planning options in SAP ERP with other options outside of SAP ERP. It introduces the latest options in enhancement package 6 and Express Planning as a framework for initiating and monitoring the planning process.

10   Planning in SAP NetWeaver BW or SAP SEM

When we looked at the subject of planning in Chapter 5, we focused on the flow of the planning process through the various applications. This sort of approach leverages the master data stored in SAP ERP, pulling together the information from the material masters, bills of material, routings, work centers, cost centers, and activity types along with prices, capacities, existing inventory, and so on to derive the annual operational plan on the basis of the planning assumptions stored in SAP ERP.

Alongside this detailed annual operational plan, there are almost always other plans that look at the likely performance of the same operations over a longer time frame (up to five years) or under changing circumstances (for example, taking account of increases or decreases in demand or capacity or changes to raw material prices). Such plans are rarely modeled in SAP ERP. They typically work not with individual products and customers but at a higher level, such as product groups and customer groups. There's a link with the master data in SAP ERP, but it's not a prerequisite that master records exist for every cost center and account included in the plan.

In the shorter term there's usually another plan that allows the supply chain to react to fluctuations in customer demand or to prepare for changes in consumption patterns due to trade promotion campaigns. Often this plan is at a much finer level of detail—not by product and customer but by SKU (stock keeping unit)—and covers a much shorter time frame. This plan may then be the basis for material requirements planning leading into the process of creating planned orders and production orders that we walked through in Chapter 6.

The two approaches to planning are most apparent when we look at the investment plan. If the organization plans to open a new plant or bring a new product to market, such a plan starts at a high level that has almost no relation to the master data in SAP ERP. It may also start at the corporate level and then be broken down to the local company codes whose controllers elaborate on the details of the local investment plan. Gradually such a plan is broken down to the individual measures to be executed. At this stage the project managers start to submit their plans by order and project. The bottom-up plan for the individual orders and projects supplied by the project managers is mapped against the top-down plan for the whole investment supplied by the corporate controllers. In the process of investment planning we see the cross-over from the detailed SAP ERP plan that we looked at in Chapter 5 and the higher-level corporate plan that's generally outside of SAP ERP.

It's common to talk about strategic plans, tactical plans, and operational plans in this context, but such definitions are rarely helpful when deciding what form of plan is best created where. Some organizations have a single operational plan stored in one plan version to provide the basis for their variance analysis and budget control in SAP ERP and prepare all other plans outside of SAP ERP. At the other extreme are organizations with multiple project plans that represent different planning assumptions and a complete investment plan in SAP ERP and only a corporate investment plan outside of SAP ERP.

Outside of SAP ERP generally means a plan based on SAP NetWeaver BW, though over the years there have been several planning tools that are based on SAP NetWeaver BW including:

- SAP SEM-BPS (Strategic Enterprise Management—Business and Planning Simulation)
- SAP Netweaver BW (Business Warehouse—Business and Planning Simulation)
- SAP NetWeaver BW-IP (Business Warehouse—Integrated Planning)
- SAP BusinessObjects Business Planning and Consolidation

You'll also find several partner products on the market that allow you to create plans in spreadsheets that then use BAPIs to write data back to SAP ERP. To understand the difference between a planning approach based on SAP ERP and a planning approach based on SAP NetWeaver BW, we'll look at the planning architecture in each case. This will help you understand what makes sense for you.

10.1 New Options for Planning

To understand the new options for planning, it's worth taking a few minutes to consider the underlying architecture of the planning transactions in Chapter 5.

> **SAP Planning Solutions for Controllers**
>
> Just as the reporting chapter merely scratched the surface, the next few pages won't turn you into a planning expert in SAP NetWeaver BW. What we'll try to show you is where SAP NetWeaver BW provides options that don't exist in SAP ERP and to help you understand what sort of planning applications you can potentially build in SAP NetWeaver BW and how these differ from those available in SAP ERP.

10.1.1 Structure of Planning Applications in SAP ERP

To help us to do this, let's go back to some of the transactions we looked at in Chapter 5 and consider them from a more technical perspective. The *planner profile* determines which planning applications you see when you select the planning transactions. In our example we were using the planner profile SAPALL. This includes all standard planning applications delivered by SAP, but you may find you use a different planner profile that includes a subset of the delivered applications and perhaps some others that your organization has configured for you.

- To find out which planner profile you've have been using, select Transaction KP04 or ACCOUNTING • CONTROLLING • COST CENTER ACCOUNTING • PLANNING • SET PLANNER PROFILE in SAP ERP.

- To display the settings associated with your chosen planner profile, select ACCOUNTING • CONTROLLING • COST CENTER ACCOUNTING • PLANNING • CURRENT SETTINGS • CREATE USER-DEFINED PLANNER PROFILES (Transaction S_ALR_87005852).

Figure 10.1 shows the planning areas associated with the planner profile SAPALL.

- In Chapter 5, Section 5.1.2 we looked at the cost center plan (Transaction KP06) that uses the planning area Cost Centers: Cost Elements/Activity Inputs.

- In Chapter 5, Section 5.1.2 we looked at the activity prices for the cost center (Transaction KP26) that uses the planning area Cost Centers/Activity Prices.

- In Chapter 5, Section 5.1.2 we looked at the order plan (Transaction KPF6) that uses the planning area Orders: Cost Elements/Activity Inputs.

10 | Planning in SAP NetWeaver BW or SAP SEM

- In Chapter 5, Section 5.2.3 we looked at the project plan (Transaction CJR2) that uses the planning area WBS Elements: Cost Elements/Activity Inputs.

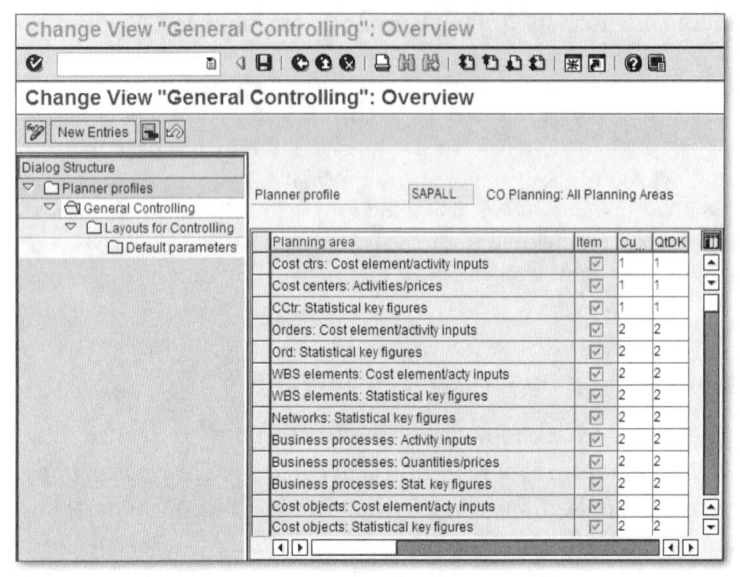

Figure 10.1 Planning Areas Assigned to the Planner Profile

Each planning area contains a series of planning layouts that determine the data you can plan. Let's look at the first one in the list (used in Transaction KP06).

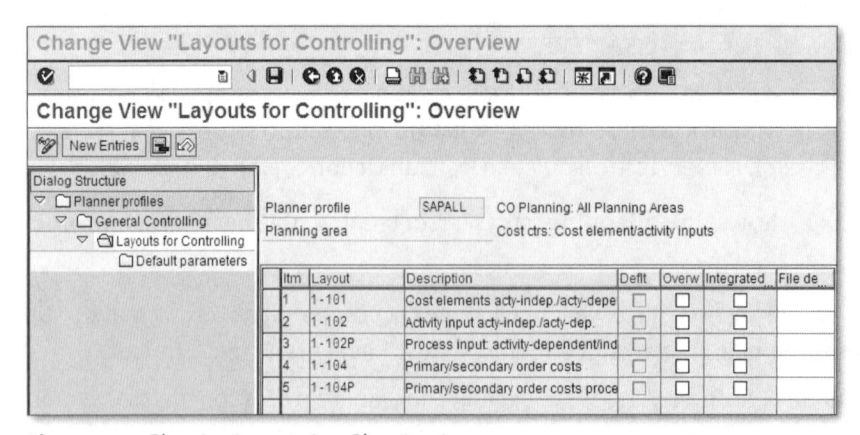

Figure 10.2 Planning Layouts in a Planning Area

460

Figure 10.2 shows the five planning layouts offered for cost and activity input planning. You can scroll through these layouts from the selection screen when you first call up the transaction and in the overview and period screens when you're entering plan data (see Figures 5.11 to 5.13). We used the following layouts.

- Layout 1-101 to plan the activity-dependent and activity-independent costs on our production cost centers. Remember that in the one we entered the activity type in the selection screen and in the other we left the activity type field blank.
- Layout 1-102 to plan the activities that the production cost center would use from the repair cost center.

The planning layouts are Customizing settings, so you may not have authorization to change them. You should be able to use Transaction KP67 to display the settings. Figure 10.3 shows the settings for the first planning layout in our list (1-101). The layout determines the technical settings in the planning transaction, including the variables you're required to enter in the selection screen and the fields available for data entry.

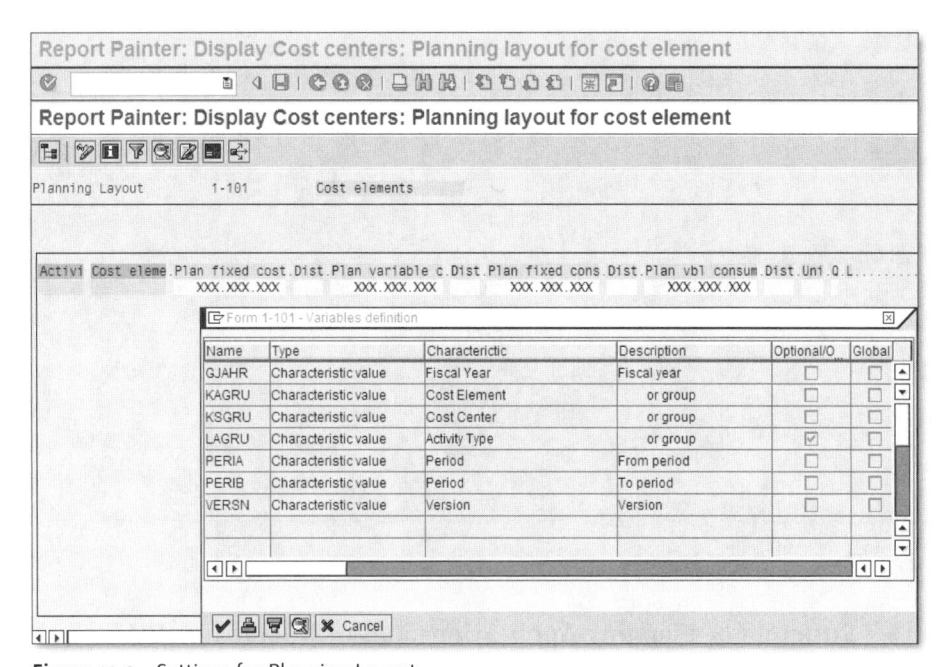

Figure 10.3 Settings for Planning Layout

In addition there are dedicated transactions for copying planned data, such as Transaction KP97 for copying cost center plan data (usually in the PLANNING AIDS folders we saw for each application).

Things are slightly different in profitability planning (Transaction KEPM), shown in Figure 10.4. Here there's more flexibility, since the underlying data structure is that of the operating concern, and planning layouts are created that capture data for the dimensions in the operating concern. You'll see a range of planning methods on the bottom-left of the screen representing the various methods possible in the planning processor. The presentation layer (the right-hand part of the screen) can use either the SAP GUI (as we see here) or Excel-in-place, depending on the planning layout your configuration team has prepared for you.

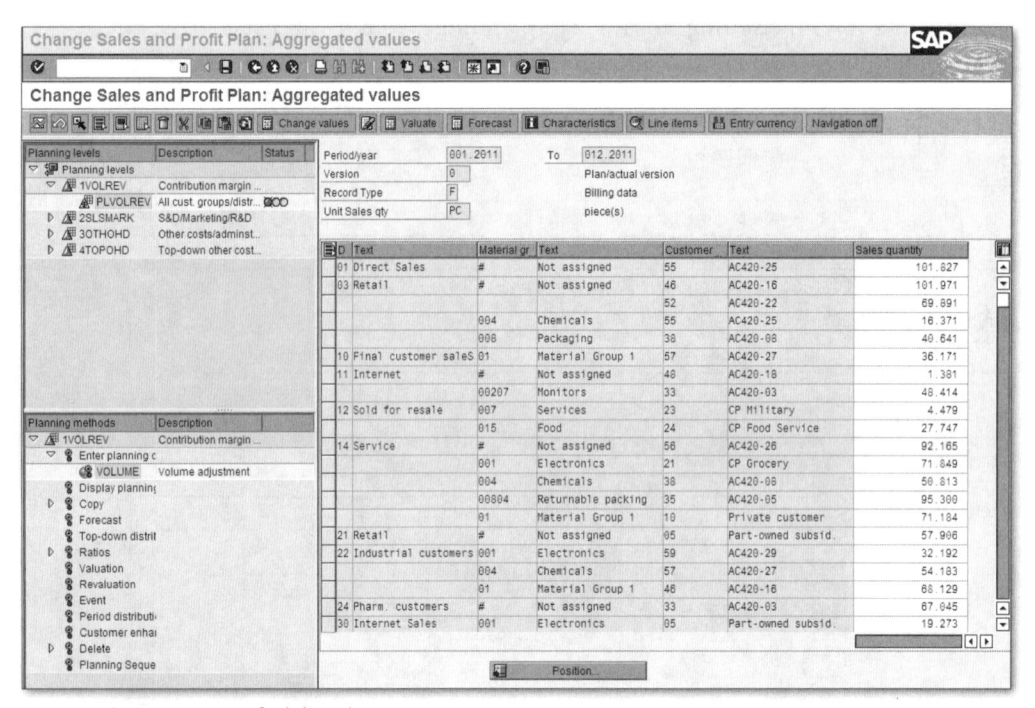

Figure 10.4 Profitability Planning

10.1.2 Structure of Planning Applications in SAP NetWeaver BW

Now let's look how planning applications built on SAP NetWeaver BW are structured.

- **The database layer**
  In SAP ERP the planning data is stored in exactly the same tables as the data from the operational processes. You can identify it for reporting by the value type (1 for planning) and business transaction (such as RKP1 for primary cost planning). The fixed structure of this database layer means that planning in SAP ERP can never be completely flexible, since it won't otherwise be possible to store data in the relevant tables. The same applies to any of the partner products that offer an update to SAP ERP. Ultimately the BAPIs for the data transfer are subject to the same restrictions as the SAP ERP transactions.

  In SAP NetWeaver BW the database layer is multidimensional, storing the data in logical cubes rather than in relational tables. This is exactly the same as the database layer used for reporting that we discussed in Chapter 8. This layer stores not only the planning data, but also any reference data that has been extracted from SAP ERP or other systems. The two types of cube look very similar, the difference being that the reporting InfoProviders are designed to display data extracted from SAP ERP or other systems, while the planning InfoProviders are designed to receive the data entered in the planning layouts (SAP SEM-BPS and SAP NetWeaver BW-BPS) or queries (SAP NetWeaver BW-IP).

  From a controlling perspective, this gives you a degree of freedom. If you want to plan wage costs by cost element group, rather than by the 10 accounts coming over from Payroll Accounting, you can do that. Only if you want to retract data to SAP ERP do you have to make sure that the two data structures are in synch. If you want to plan by quarter rather than by period, you can set up your InfoProviders to include the quarter as a time dimension, alongside periods and fiscal years. Again, if you want to retract to SAP ERP, you'll have to build a planning function to split the figures for the quarter to the relevant periods. You can even plan by week if your business requires it, but this dimension must stay in SAP NetWeaver BW, since the CO tables do not include the week.

- **The OLAP layer**
  In SAP ERP the planning processor underlies all transactions used for cost center, order, project, and profitability planning. The exception is product costing, which stores cost estimates as a list of costing items. The planning processor provides generic planning functions, such as distribution that spreads values entered for a fiscal year to the periods using a distribution key as we saw in Chapter 5 (see Figure 5.12).

  In SAP NetWeaver BW an OLAP engine supports these generic functions. You can build much more complex planning functions within this OLAP layer and link them to form planning sequences to automate various planning steps (such as copying the figures from last year and then applying a 3% markup).

From a controlling perspective, this allows you to perform much more sophisticated planning functions than the "copy and adjust" functions available in SAP ERP. However, such functions come at a price. They require a level of expertise to build and have to be modeled and tested properly, but if you want to perform sophisticated calculations during planning, such functions are essential.

- **The presentation layer**
  The presentation layer is what you see during planning. In SAP ERP you select planning transactions, such as Transaction KP06, and then planning layouts, such as 1-101 or 1-102, in which to enter your data.

  In SAP NetWeaver BW-IP you enter your data either in Web queries or in SAP BEx queries. Technically, these are like the queries we saw in Chapter 8 for reporting except that they're input-enabled, meaning you can enter and display data. This is the logical extension of the situation we saw in SAP ERP, where the planning layouts use the same definition layer as Report Painter for reporting. However, you cannot define a query by simply selecting an InfoProvider as we did in Chapter 8. Instead, you have to define an *aggregation level* for your InfoProvider that tells the system which characteristics you intend to capture data for. In SAP ERP we did this simply by either entering data in the activity type or leaving it blank during cost center planning.

  In SAP SEM-BPS and SAP NetWeaver BW-BPS, you enter your data in planning layouts that use either SAP GUI or business server pages (BSPs) (an early Web technology) and report on it using SAP BEx queries. In this case, you need to define a *planning level* to tell the system which characteristics you intend to plan on.

Probably the most fundamental difference is that the new planning tools are designed to *stand alone*. They may share master data with SAP ERP, in the sense that you can extract cost center hierarchies, cost element hierarchies, and so on and use these as a basis for planning, but you are not bound by the same constraints, since the SAP ERP data and the SAP NetWeaver BW planning data are stored in separate databases.

10.1.3 Multidimensional Database Layer in SAP NetWeaver BW

To illustrate the difference between the tables used to store data in SAP ERP and in SAP NetWeaver BW, let's have a look at the InfoProviders for Corporate Investment Management.

New Options for Planning | **10.1**

To display the relevant InfoProviders, log on to SAP NetWeaver BW, select SAP BUSINESS INFORMATION WAREHOUSE • ADMINISTRATION • DATA WAREHOUSING WORKBENCH ADMINISTRATION and then MODELING • INFOPROVIDER (this menu path is exactly the same as for reporting). From the list of InfoProviders select FINANCIAL MANAGEMENT AND CONTROLLING • INVESTMENT MANAGEMENT • CORPORATE INVESTMENT MANAGEMENT. Figure 10.5 shows the InfoArea for Corporate Investment Management with a MultiProvider (a cube that combines data from several InfoProviders) for Corporate Investment Management that brings together a reporting InfoCube containing operative data (0IMFA_C03) and a planning InfoProvider that stores the data entered in the planning applications (0SEM_C03). Notice that InfoProvider 0SEM_C03 has a special icon that denotes that you can write data to it, rather than merely reading data.

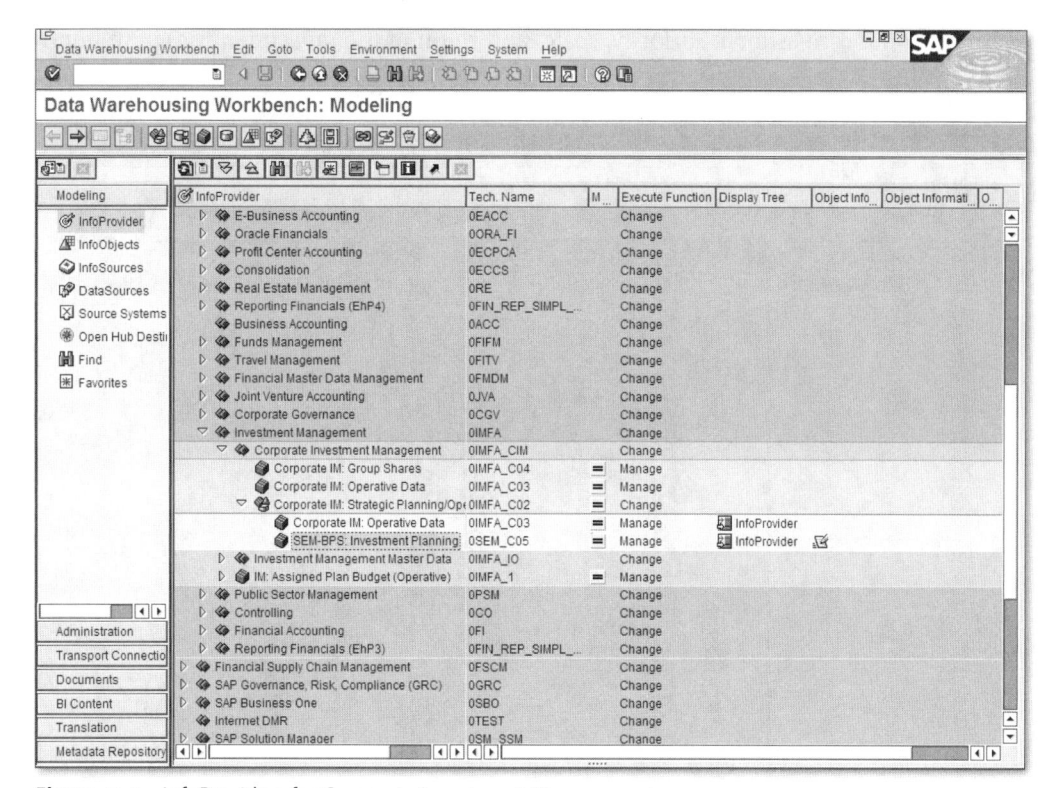

Figure 10.5 InfoProviders for Corporate Investment Management

You may wonder why you need the reporting InfoProvider (0IMFA_C03) at all. The purpose of this InfoProvider is to provide reference data for planning. This might allow you to do a simple copy from the previous year and then add a certain percentage (typical planning functions) or merely to view the previous situation as a reference for planning.

To display the details of this InfoProvider, double-click on InfoProvider 0SEM_C05. Figure 10.6 shows the dimensions of the delivered planning InfoProvider. You'll recognize the items in the INVESTMENT DIMENSION as the fields we saw in the investment program in Chapter 4. In the KEY FIGURES DIMENSION, you'll recognize elements from Chapter 5, including the planning item and version.

What's important in SAP NetWeaver BW is that you can either stick closely to the structures in the investment program in SAP ERP or you can add new attributes for planning and reporting that only exist in SAP NetWeaver BW. This allows you to define new attributes for classifying the investment that go beyond the attributes reason for investment, priority, scale, and so on in the investment program item.

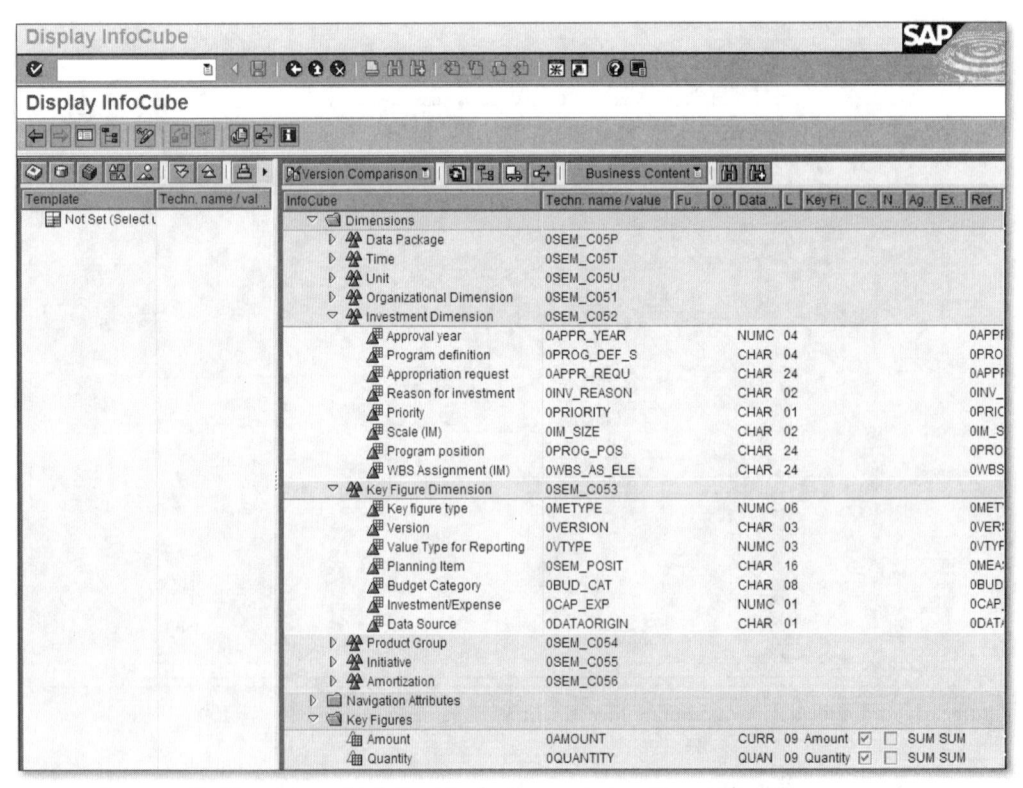

Figure 10.6 Dimensions of InfoProvider for Corporate Investment Planning

You perform the next step in the planning modeler. To access the planning modeler, select Transaction RSPLAN or SAP BUSINESS INFORMATION WAREHOUSE • BUSINESS PLANNING AND SIMULATION • MODELING BI INTEGRATED PLANNING. You can then choose whether to work with a wizard (where a roadmap guides you through the steps) or without (where the steps are provided on tabs). To use the tab option shown in Figure 10.7, select START MODELER in the initial screen.

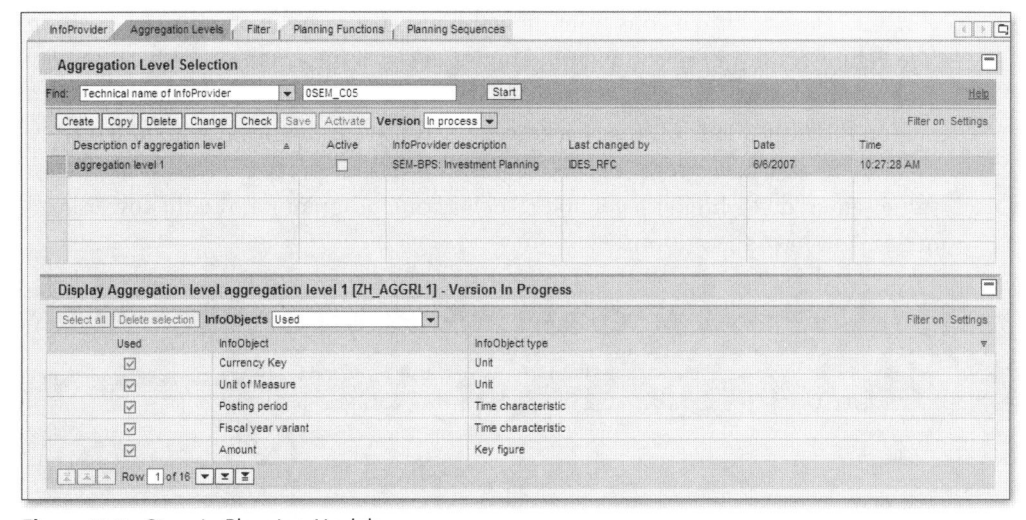

Figure 10.7 Steps in Planning Modeler

Perform the following steps in the PLANNING MODELER:

1. Select the INFOPROVIDER to be used to store the data in SAP NetWeaver BW.

2. Create an aggregation level in SAP NetWeaver BW-IP to determine the characteristics for which you want to capture planning data.

3. Create a filter. This provides the selection characteristics, such as version and time frame that you'll use in your query.

4. Create planning functions. These will allow you to copy data, revaluate data, delete data, and so on.

5. Create planning sequences. You can use these to link planning functions, so you might link a copy function and a revaluate function, allowing you to copy last year's plan and then add a factor entered by the user.

10 | Planning in SAP NetWeaver BW or SAP SEM

To enter data, in SAP SEM-BPS or SAP NetWeaver BW-BPS you need to define a *planning layout* to enter the relevant data about your planned investments. In SAP NetWeaver BW-IP you need to create a *query* to enter the planning data. To create a query, you need to call up the Business Explorer Query Designer from your desktop, connect to the relevant BW system, and select QUERY • NEW. Use the INFOAREAS folder to select the aggregate level for Corporate Investment Planning (see Figure 10.7) and then define the columns and rows of your query by dragging the relevant dimensions from the left-hand area into the appropriate position (see Figure 10.8). In the context of planning it's also important to determine how different nodes will be handled by choosing the correct settings in the PLANNING tab (on the right). This means checking the settings for distribution (familiar from Chapter 5) and disaggregation. Disaggregation is the process of breaking down values entered at a higher level node, such as one program item to the lower level nodes. You have the options:

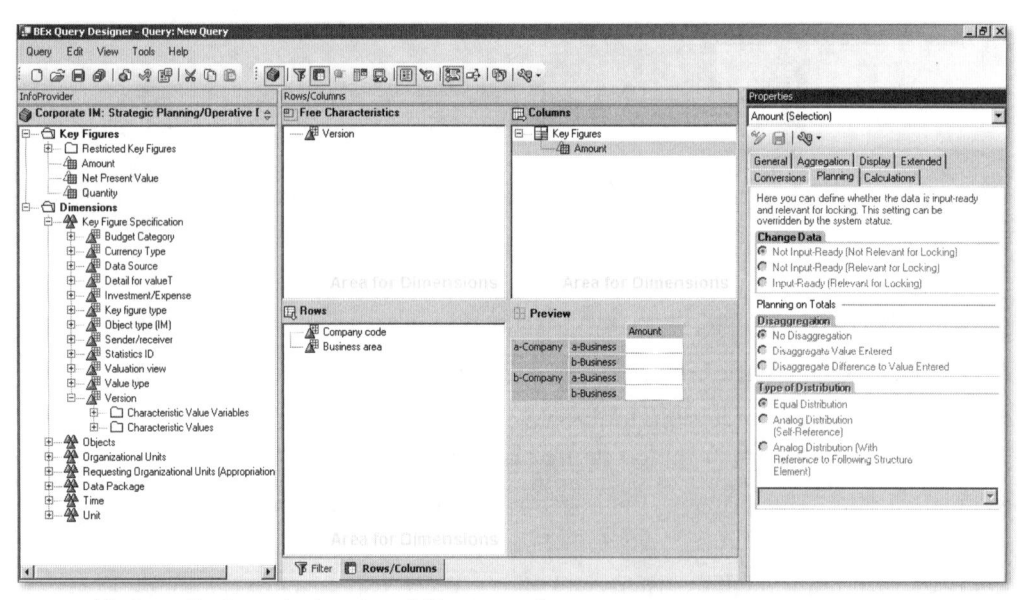

Figure 10.8 Query for Investment Management

▶ No Disaggregation (data entered at the higher level node is not broken down to the lower level nodes)

468

- Disaggregate Value Entered (break down the data entered at the higher level nodes to the lower level nodes)
- Disaggregate Difference to Value Entered (if data has been entered for the lower level nodes, aggregate these and then break down the difference with respect to the aggregated value to the lower level nodes)

10.1.4 Data Entry and Planning Functions

Data entry for planning can use one query, like the one shown above, that writes back to one INFOPROVIDER. However, the real power of the solution emerges when you start to use multiple queries (or planning layouts) in combination with planning functions. We'll now look at an example of a very simple product cost estimate.

Figure 10.9 shows a planning layout in SAP NetWeaver BW-BPS with a simple product cost estimate that was built for demo purposes. To execute such a query, follow the menu path SAP BUSINESS INFORMATION WAREHOUSE • BUSINESS PLANNING AND SIMULATION • WEB INTERFACE BUILDER • EXECUTE and enter the interface Z800UPSUSPRDCST (only available in IDES demo systems). If you compare the entries in this planning layout with the data we looked at in Chapter 5, you'll see that the structure has been simplified and changed to make it easier to plan at a high level.

- The value fields in SAP ERP have been mapped to account numbers, and no distinction has been made between fixed and various costs.
- All costing items in the planning layout have been assigned to cost centers. You may remember that the operations in SAP ERP are assigned to cost centers via their work center and that overhead costs include a cost center, but material items do not. Here the assignment of the BOM item to the operation in the routing has been used to determine the relevant cost center during extraction to SAP NetWeaver BW.

This is a typical example of the transformations that take place when data is extracted to SAP NetWeaver BW to make it easier for planners who are not familiar with the data structures in SAP ERP to work with the data.

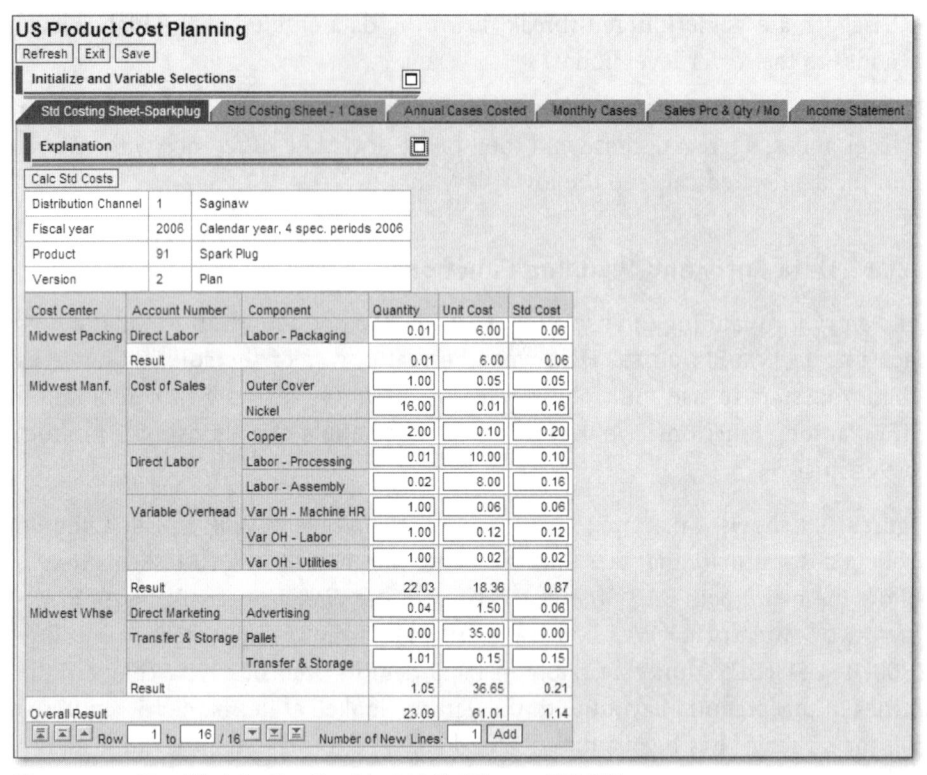

Figure 10.9 Simplified Costing Sheet in SAP NetWeaver BW-BPS

The next step is to transform the costs for one spark plug to a case of spark plugs in the second tab. If you navigate to the ANNUAL CASES COSTED tab shown in Figure 10.10, you'll see how a quantity can be applied to this basic data to provide the total costs for the year. The calculation is performed using a *planning function* that you start by clicking on the CALC OF CASES ANNUALLY button. This takes the number of cases to be sold in the year and scales up the unit costs to determine the product costs associated with this quantity.

The power of such a planning tool is in the *simulation* functions. In this example, you can enter various assumptions concerning the sales quantity and product price by choosing the SALES PRICE AND QUANTITY/MONTH tab and then using the planning functions (on the buttons shown in Figure 10.11) to have the system calculate the annual sales and a product income statement based on these entries.

New Options for Planning | 10.1

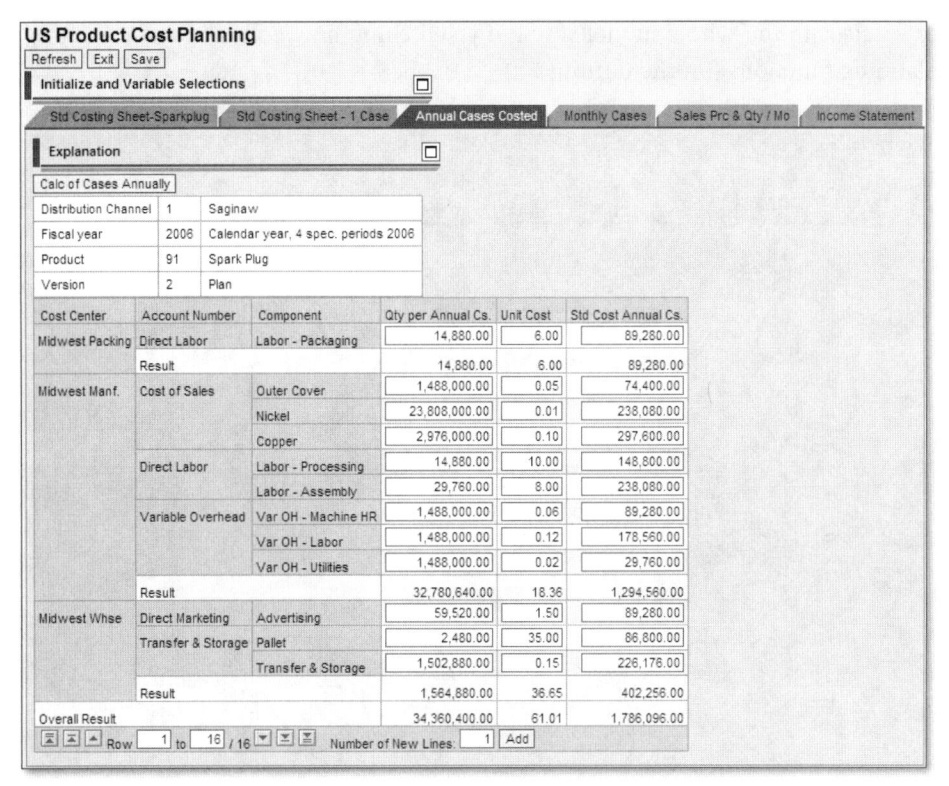

Figure 10.10 Simplified Cost Estimate in SAP NetWeaver BW-BPS

Figure 10.11 Product Price and Sales Quantity per Month in SAP NetWeaver BW-BPS

Figure 10.12 shows the result of such a simulation. The valuation function in CO-PA that we discussed in Chapter 5, Section 5.1.4 also pulls together sales quantities and product costs, but it does not allow you to change the prices of the products or recalculate the whole model simply by switching between tabs and executing planning functions (on the buttons).

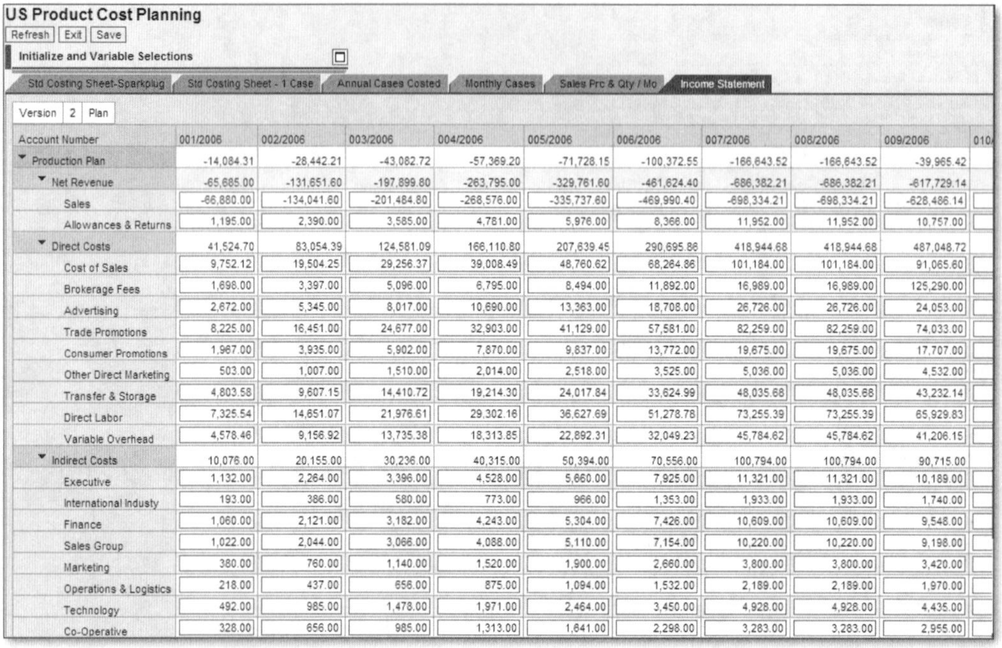

Account Number	001/2006	002/2006	003/2006	004/2006	005/2006	006/2006	007/2006	008/2006	009/2006
Production Plan	-14,084.31	-28,442.21	-43,082.72	-57,369.20	-71,728.15	-100,372.55	-166,643.52	-166,643.52	-39,965.42
Net Revenue	-65,685.00	-131,651.60	-197,899.80	-263,795.00	-329,761.60	-461,624.40	-686,382.21	-686,382.21	-617,729.14
Sales	-66,880.00	-134,041.60	-201,484.80	-268,576.00	-335,737.60	-469,990.40	-698,334.21	-698,334.21	-628,486.14
Allowances & Returns	1,195.00	2,390.00	3,585.00	4,781.00	5,976.00	8,366.00	11,952.00	11,952.00	10,757.00
Direct Costs	41,524.70	83,054.39	124,581.09	166,110.80	207,639.45	290,695.86	418,944.68	418,944.68	487,048.72
Cost of Sales	9,752.12	19,504.25	29,256.37	39,008.49	48,760.62	68,264.86	101,184.00	101,184.00	91,065.60
Brokerage Fees	1,698.00	3,397.00	5,096.00	6,795.00	8,494.00	11,892.00	16,989.00	16,989.00	125,290.00
Advertising	2,672.00	5,345.00	8,017.00	10,690.00	13,363.00	18,708.00	26,726.00	26,726.00	24,053.00
Trade Promotions	8,225.00	16,451.00	24,677.00	32,903.00	41,129.00	57,581.00	82,259.00	82,259.00	74,033.00
Consumer Promotions	1,967.00	3,935.00	5,902.00	7,870.00	9,837.00	13,772.00	19,675.00	19,675.00	17,707.00
Other Direct Marketing	503.00	1,007.00	1,510.00	2,014.00	2,518.00	3,525.00	5,036.00	5,036.00	4,532.00
Transfer & Storage	4,803.58	9,607.15	14,410.72	19,214.30	24,017.84	33,624.99	48,035.68	48,035.68	43,232.14
Direct Labor	7,325.54	14,651.07	21,976.61	29,302.16	36,627.69	51,278.78	73,255.39	73,255.39	65,929.83
Variable Overhead	4,578.46	9,156.92	13,735.38	18,313.85	22,892.31	32,049.23	45,784.62	45,784.62	41,206.15
Indirect Costs	10,076.00	20,155.00	30,236.00	40,315.00	50,394.00	70,556.00	100,794.00	100,794.00	90,715.00
Executive	1,132.00	2,264.00	3,396.00	4,528.00	5,660.00	7,925.00	11,321.00	11,321.00	10,189.00
International Industy	193.00	386.00	580.00	773.00	966.00	1,353.00	1,933.00	1,933.00	1,740.00
Finance	1,060.00	2,121.00	3,182.00	4,243.00	5,304.00	7,426.00	10,609.00	10,609.00	9,548.00
Sales Group	1,022.00	2,044.00	3,066.00	4,088.00	5,110.00	7,154.00	10,220.00	10,220.00	9,198.00
Marketing	380.00	760.00	1,140.00	1,520.00	1,900.00	2,660.00	3,800.00	3,800.00	3,420.00
Operations & Logistics	218.00	437.00	656.00	875.00	1,094.00	1,532.00	2,189.00	2,189.00	1,970.00
Technology	492.00	985.00	1,478.00	1,971.00	2,464.00	3,450.00	4,928.00	4,928.00	4,435.00
Co-Operative	328.00	656.00	985.00	1,313.00	1,641.00	2,298.00	3,283.00	3,283.00	2,955.00

Figure 10.12 Simulation of Product Income Statement in SAP NetWeaver BW-BPS

Having given a brief introduction to planning in SAP NetWeaver BW, we'll now look at new developments in SAP ERP that combine the planning queries and planning functions in SAP NetWeaver BW with the database layer in SAP ERP to provide a planning environment that can bring together the best of both solutions.

10.2 Options in SAP ERP from SAP Enhancement Package 6 for SAP ERP 6.0

SAP enhancement package 6 for SAP ERP 6.0 will include new planning applications for project planning that will offer an alternative to Transactions CJ40 and CJR2, which we looked at in Chapter 5. These planning applications are designed to be easier for occasional users such as project managers to use.

- The idea is that you'll use the SAP ERP tables as the database layer, so your project plan will be available for active availability control, as we saw in Chapter 6, or as a basis for results analysis as we saw in Chapter 7.

- However, by activating the SAP NetWeaver BW content on the SAP ERP server you'll be able to use the reporting functions to automatically aggregate data for each node of the project structure and planning functions to distribute values from year to period and so on. To make it easier to work with these queries, they're delivered as content bundles that your administrator can activate in SAP ERP by selecting Transaction BSANLY_BI_ACTIVATION or following the menu path CROSS APPLICATION COMPONENTS • PROCESSES AND TOOLS FOR ENTERPRISE APPLICATIONS • ANALYTICS • BI CONTENT ACTIVATION WORKBENCH and then selecting the content bundle /ERP/FCOM_PLANNING in the IMG.

- Probably the most significant difference is the user interface itself. You might want to refer back to Chapter 5, Sections 5.2.2 and 5.2.3 to remind yourself what the original transactions look like.

10.2.1 Role Project Planner and Cost Estimator

Where we previously used the planner profile to determine which planning applications were active, the new applications were delivered as roles (see Appendix A at *www.sap-press.com*) that must be assigned to the user using Transaction SU01. Figure 10.13 shows the role structure for the project planner and cost estimator. The applications for overall planning and cost element planning are built using the combination of SAP NetWeaver BW-IP and SAP ERP.

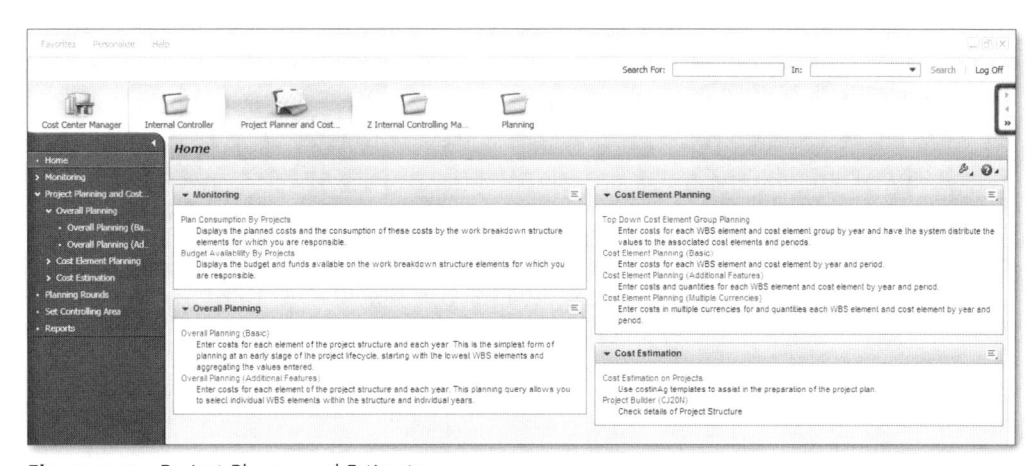

Figure 10.13 Project Planner and Estimator

10.2.2 Overall Planning

To execute overall planning, click on the link OVERALL PLANNING (BASIC) in Figure 10.13. Figure 10.14 shows one of the new applications for Overall Planning. This includes a selection area that allows you to select the projects and version to be planned, a list area that shows the costs per WBS element, and two charts showing the total project costs and the project costs by year. One of the main differences (other than the look and feel) with respect to Transaction CJ40 is that you can plan several projects in one sitting by entering multiple projects in the selection screen, whereas the existing transaction forces you to enter data for each project definition separately. In this example, to keep things simple, we'll just enter data for one project.

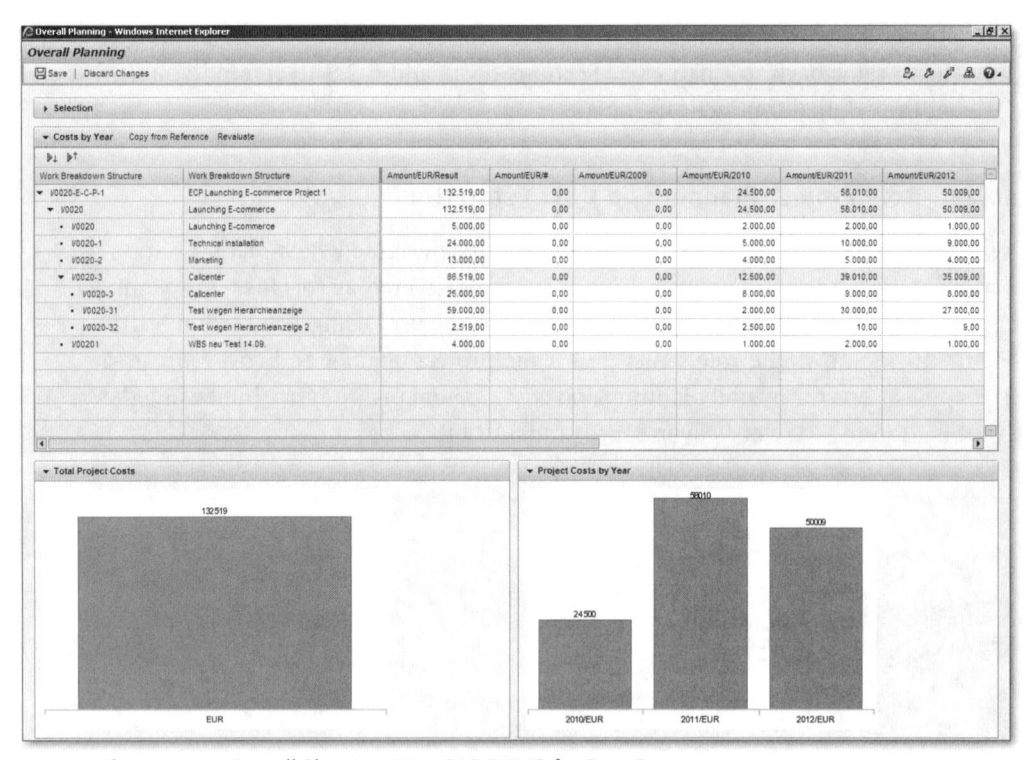

Figure 10.14 Overall Planning Using SAP BW-IP for Data Entry

Returning to our basic architecture discussions, we find the following structure:

- **Presentation layer**
  The planning applications are embedded in Web Dynpro applications that can be configured using Floorplan Manager (a small icon in the top-right hand corner allows you to define which application should appear where). The planning applications use input-enabled queries in which the project expenses can be entered. SAP delivers standard queries (basic and advanced in Figure 10.13), but you can replace them with your own queries if you need to show different fields. So instead of having your project managers enter data for three years, you might put in queries that offer columns for more or less years.

- **OLAP layer**
  The OLAP layer uses a local SAP NetWeaver BW-IP system to perform all standard planning functions. In this example a COPY FROM REFERENCE function has been included that copies data from alternative versions, since many organizations use different versions to document planning progress at different stages of approval. A revaluation function allows you to apply a percentage markup or markdown to the values in the query.

- **Data base layer**
  The database layer is in SAP ERP, so the master data you're planning against are the work breakdown structure elements (see Chapter 4) in SAP ERP, and the planned expenses are stored in the SAP ERP tables rather than a separate reporting InfoProvider. Such a solution is not as flexible as a dedicated reporting solution, but it has the advantage that the data entered is immediately available for budgeting. This also means that the application can perform checks against the master data, determining which elements are flagged as planning elements, which have a status that allows planning, which are locked, and so on and issuing messages if the WBS element is not available for planning or a version is locked.

Another aspect that characterizes these applications is the use of Floorplan Manager. If you don't like the two charts at the bottom of the application and want to focus on the figures only, you can click on the PERSONALIZE icon (top right) and remove the charts altogether or reposition them on the screen by using the personalization options shown in Figure 10.15.

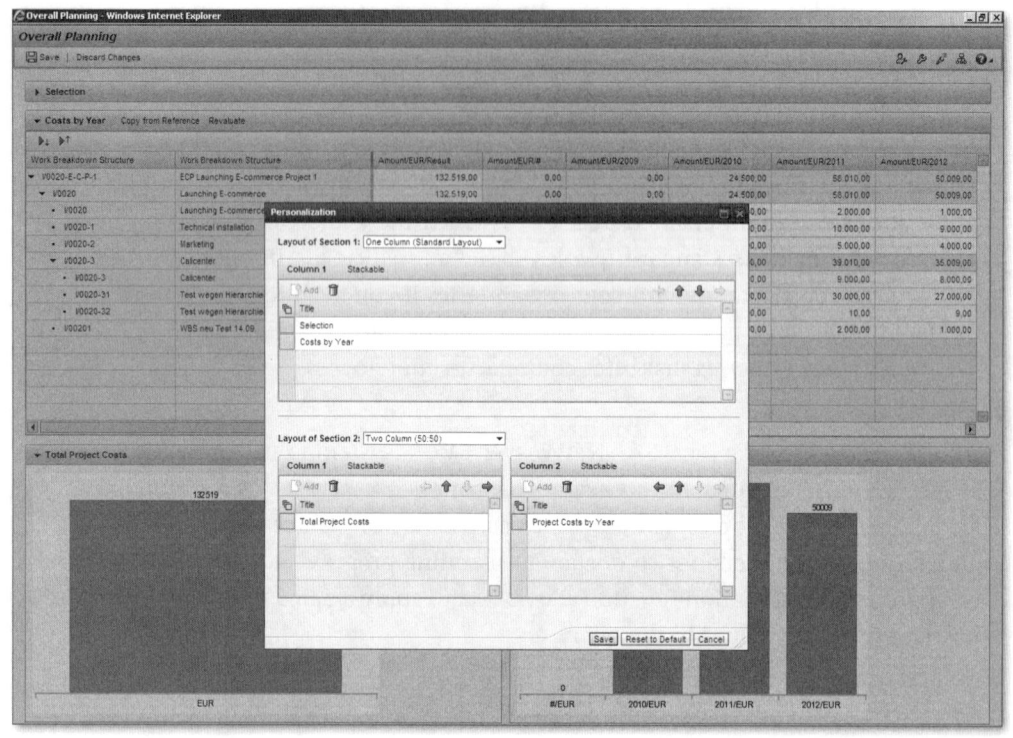

Figure 10.15 Personalization for Overall Planning

10.2.3 Cost Element Planning

Figure 10.16 shows where the new cost element planning parts company with Transaction CJR2. As we said in Section 10.1.2 planning transactions in SAP ERP are limited by the data structures used to store the actual data. While the cost center/cost element combination can be irritating for cost center planning, for project planning it can make data entry almost impossible since the number of cost elements that can be potential inputs for a WBS element can be even greater. If you choose form-based planning (see Chapter 5), you can easily have hundreds of cost elements in each layout. You can enter data by cost element as before, but there's also a new query that allows you to enter data for a cost element group and have the system distribute the costs to the underlying cost elements. To use this planning application, select TOP DOWN COST ELEMENT GROUP PLANNING in Figure 10.13.

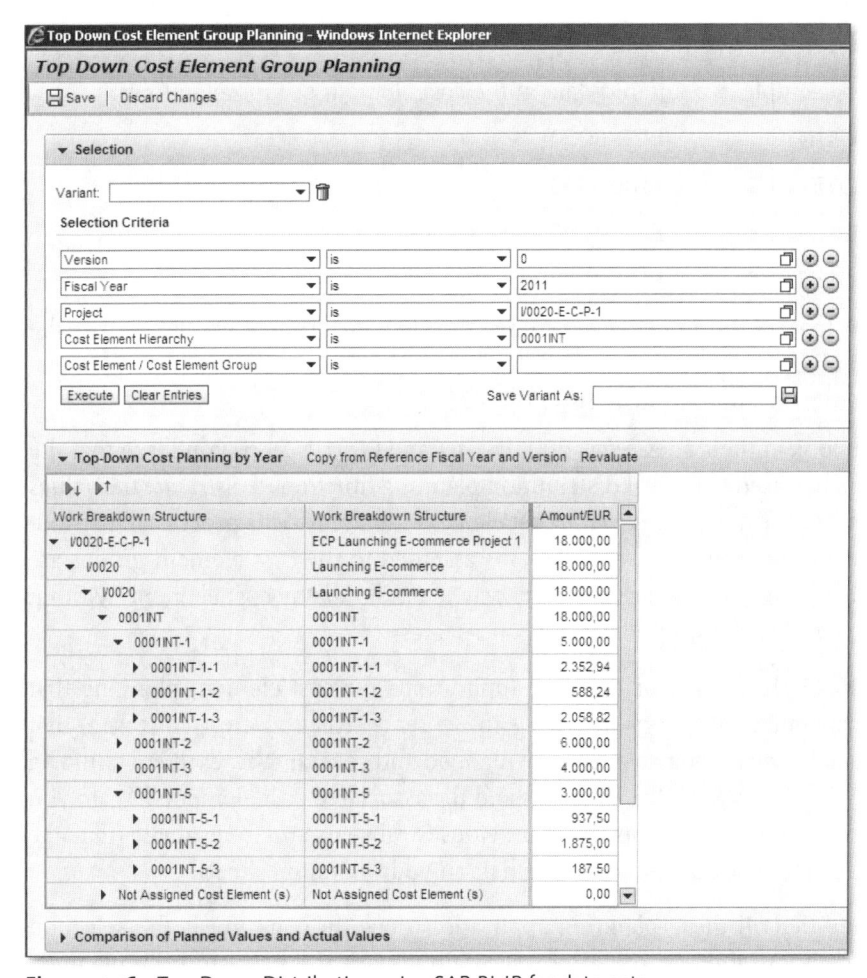

Figure 10.16 Top-Down Distribution using SAP BI-IP for data entry

1. Enter the version, fiscal year, project, and top node of the cost element hierarchy in the selection panel and click on EXECUTE.

2. You'll see a hierarchy comprising the work breakdown structure elements assigned to your project.

3. To display the cost element group, click on one of the WBS elements.

4. Usually the root or top node in the cost element hierarchy is too high to be useful, since it includes all cost elements, so scroll down to the level of detail that makes sense for your needs.

5. In our example, we entered data in the cost element groups as follows:

    - 0001INT-I-1   EUR 5000
    - 0001INT-I-2   EUR 6000
    - 0001INT-I-3   EUR 4000
    - 0001INT-I-5   EUR 3000

6. If you look at the nodes *above* these cost element groups, you'll see that the system has *added* the values for cost element group 0001INT and the WBS element to give a total of EUR 18000.

7. If you look at the nodes *below* 0001INT-I-1 and 0001INT-I-5, you'll see that the system has used the equal distribution planning function to *distribute* the values entered to the next nodes in the cost element hierarchy. This process of distribution continues until the cost elements assigned to the cost element groups are reached, providing a quick and easy way to enter data by cost element, without being faced with hundreds of data entry lines.

Figure 10.17 shows one of the new applications for cost element planning that allows data entry by cost element. Again we see a selection area (collapsed) that allows you to select the projects to be planned and several tabs, each containing a list area that shows the WBS elements and the associated cost elements. Again you see planning functions to copy from previous fiscal years and to revaluate (to make percentage increases/decreases to the data in your planning sheet).

One thing that all these planning applications have in common is the selection screen to choose the appropriate project, along with the version to be planned. Another is a need for status information to document whether the plan has been approved and so on. So we'll now look at Express Planning as a way of providing a framework for several planning applications and managing comments and status information for each planning step.

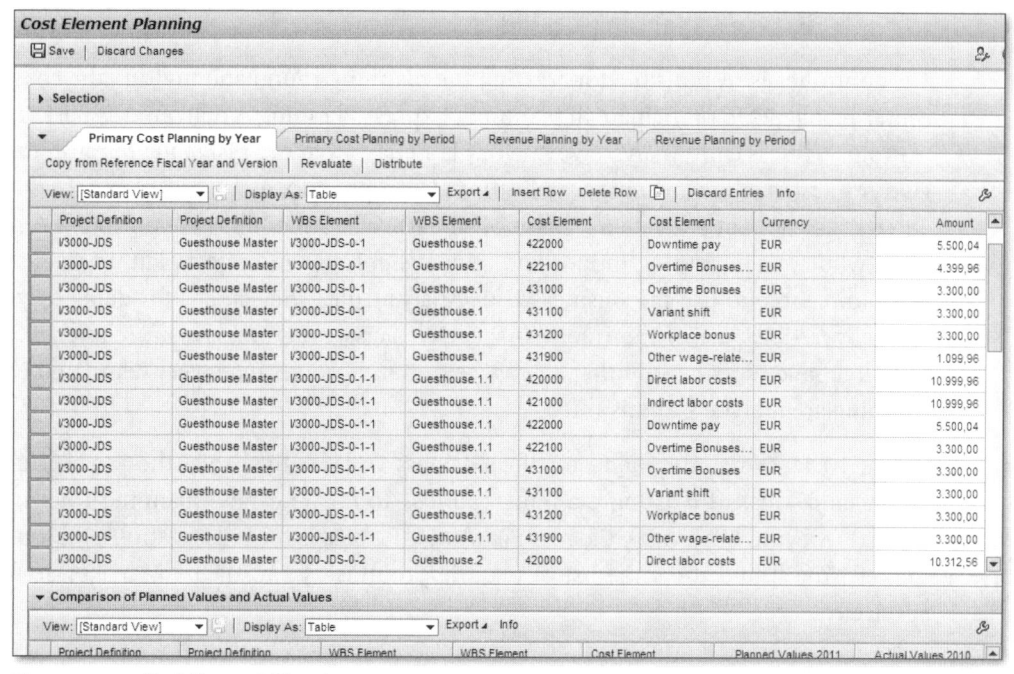

Figure 10.17 Cost Element Planning

10.3 Express Planning as a Framework for the Planning Process

When we looked at the planning transactions in Chapter 5, we talked about the collaboration between the controller as owner of the planning process and sales managers, cost center managers, project managers, and so on who were required to submit planning data for their unit. Express Planning acts as the framework around the collaborative part of planning, allowing the controller to create a planning round, for example, to handle the annual operational plan, invite cost center managers to participate, define who should review and approve the data entered by the managers, and monitor which managers have submitted their data and which plans are still outstanding. Express Planning was introduced in SAP ERP 6.0 and will be enhanced in SAP enhancement package 6 to include the new planning applications that we looked at in the previous section.

10.3.1 Creating a Planning Round

The controller is responsible for creating the planning round and inviting the cost center managers to participate in planning. Express Planning is delivered as part of the role Business Unit Analyst, which your IT department can assign to your user to give you access to such planning applications (see Appendix A at *www.sap-press.com*). Since enhancement package 6 it's also been part of the role Internal Controller. All users who create planning rounds and review, approve, and reject planning steps need to be able to use the Business Unit Analyst role. The screens for data entry are delivered as part of the role Manager Self Service (as we saw in Chapter 3), so you'll have to make sure that all cost center and project managers who will be planning are assigned to this role.

Figure 10.18 shows the menu for the Business Unit Analyst role, the PLANNING folder, and a list of existing planning rounds. To create a new planning round, select PLANNING ROUNDS • CREATE PLANNING ROUND in the navigation area on the left. You'll find the same list of planning rounds as part of the Manager Self Service role.

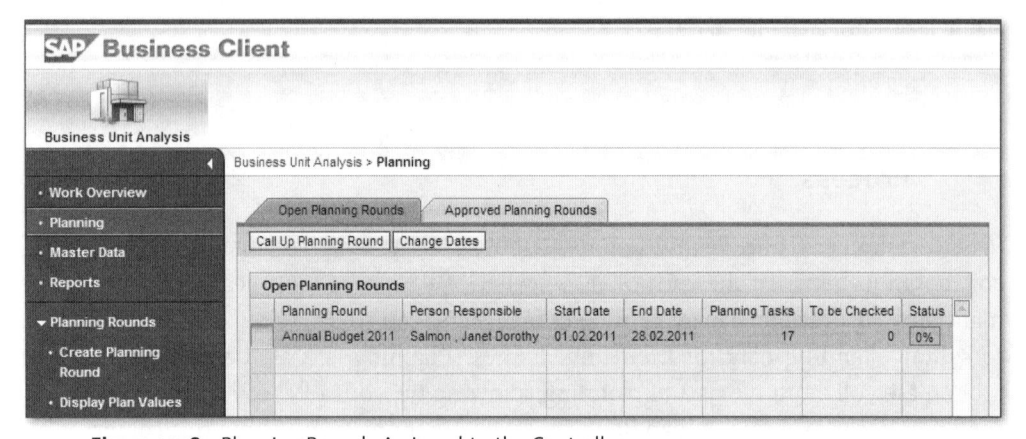

Figure 10.18 Planning Rounds Assigned to the Controller

A roadmap now guides you through the process of creating a planning round. Before you start, you'll need to create a *planning scenario* and a *planning instance*.

- The planning scenario determines what steps and substeps are included in the planning process. Each step can include one or more planning services. Express Planning acts as a framework around the individual planning steps, keeping track of the objects to be planned (the cost centers each manager is responsible for), the status for each step and substep, and any comments entered by the managers.
- The planning instance contains the technical data associated with each planning round. The two things that will probably change with every planning round are the fiscal year for which you want your cost center managers to enter data and the version under which you need to store this data (operational plan, forecast, and so on). You need to create a new planning instance for each planning round to ensure that you have a separate storage area for each set of status data, comments, and so on.

In your planning scenario, you can use the following planning services to *enter* data in SAP ERP.

- Primary cost planning for cost centers (as an alternative to Transaction KP06, without activity types)
- Primary cost planning for internal orders (as an alternative to Transaction KPF6)
- Statistical key figure planning (as an alternative to Transaction KP46)
- Activity type plan primary costs (as an alternative to Transaction KP06, with activity types)
- Activity type plan quantities (as an alternative to Transaction KP26)
- Activity type plan prices (as an alternative to Transaction KP26)

In your planning scenario, you can include the following planning services to *display* data in SAP ERP.

- Cost center assignment (displays the cost center(s) for which the manager is responsible)
- Cost review (displays the costs assigned to the cost center in the previous year)

- Internal order review (displays the internal orders for which the manager is responsible)
- Equipment review (displays the assets and equipment for which the cost center manager is responsible)

In addition, several generic services are available for planning that allow the manager to:

- Enter planning data in an SAP NetWeaver BW-BPS planning layout
- Enter planning data in an SAP NetWeaver BW-IP planning layout
- Enter planning data in another SAP ERP transaction
- Upload documents from Microsoft Office applications

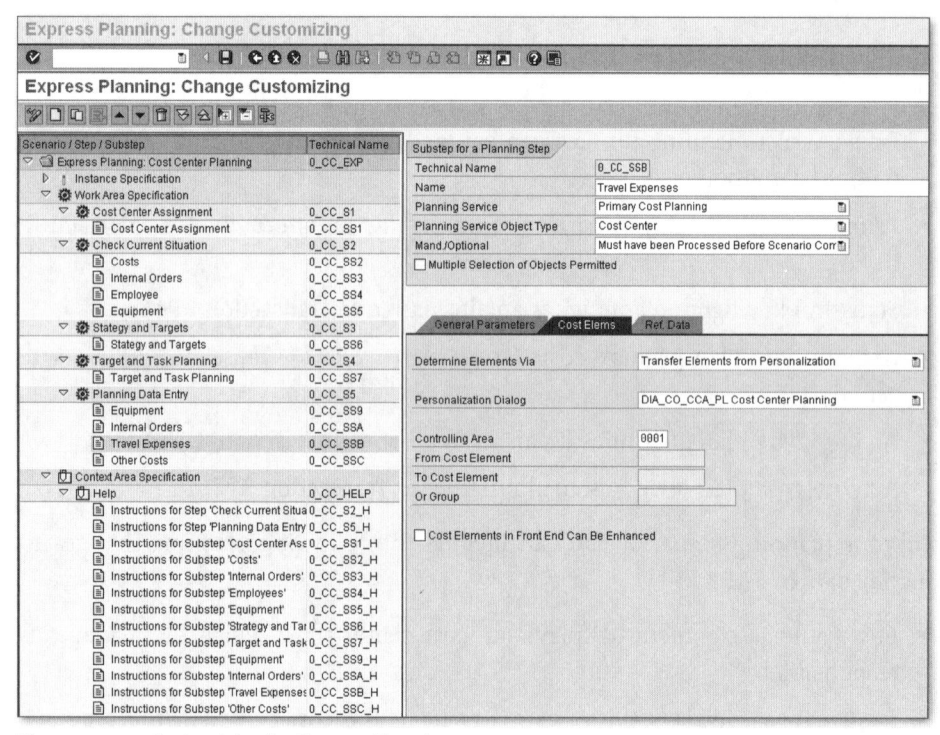

Figure 10.19 Customizing for Express Planning

The best way to get a feel for the possibilities of Express Planning is to use Transaction EXP_CUST and take a look at the delivered planning scenario and then create a simple planning scenario of your own. Figure 10.19 shows the steps in the planning scenario as folders: COST CENTER ASSIGNMENT, CHECK CURRENT SITUATION, STRATEGY AND TARGETS, TARGET AND TASK PLANNING and PLANNING DATA ENTRY. These settings are delivered as standard, so you'll find them in any SAP ERP 6.0 system. For testing, copy this planning scenario into your own name space and then remove those planning services that you don't need or add new services as required.

> **Planning Services in Web Dynpro ABAP and Web Dynpro Java**
>
> The earliest version of Express Planning (SAP ERP 6.0) was built using Web Dynpro Java. In SAP ERP 6.0, support package 8, the planning services were rewritten in Web Dynpro ABAP, with the exception of workforce requirements, which is only available in Web Dynpro Java. If your organization isn't using Web Dynpro Java, simply remove the workforce requirements step from the tree when you copy it.

In Figure 10.19 we've selected the TRAVEL EXPENSES step, which allows cost center managers to enter primary costs for any cost element contained in personalization dialog DIA_CO_CCA_PL. The personalization dialog is one of the central constructs of Express Planning. Instead of having the managers manually select the cost centers they are responsible for and the cost elements they need to plan as in Transaction KP06, the personalization dialogs act as a central repository of the entities for which a manager is responsible. To maintain the personalization settings, select Transaction FPB_MAINTAIN_PERS_M and enter the dialog DIA_CO_CCA_PL and the name of the relevant user.

> **IMG Settings for Manager Self-Service**
>
> Your administrator can find full details of how to set up personalization by following the menu path INTEGRATION WITH OTHER MYSAP.COM COMPONENTS • BUSINESS PACKAGES/FUNCTIONAL PACKAGES • MANAGER SELF SERVICE (mySAP ERP) • PERSONALIZATION • PERSONALIZATION OVERVIEW in the IMG.

Figure 10.20 shows the entities for which one of the managers in the demo system can enter plan data. He's responsible for planning all cost centers in group H3810 and all cost elements entered in the dialog shown. Your administrator can prefill these settings with the cost centers that your user authorizations allow you to see using settings available in Customizing.

10 | Planning in SAP NetWeaver BW or SAP SEM

Notice that the bottom folder in Figure 10.19 includes instructions to guide managers through each step of the planning process. Once you're up and running, the steps to be included in planning should be fairly stable and you'll have to make only minor changes to your planning scenario to include, for example, additional supporting documentation about the process or instructions for filling out certain steps.

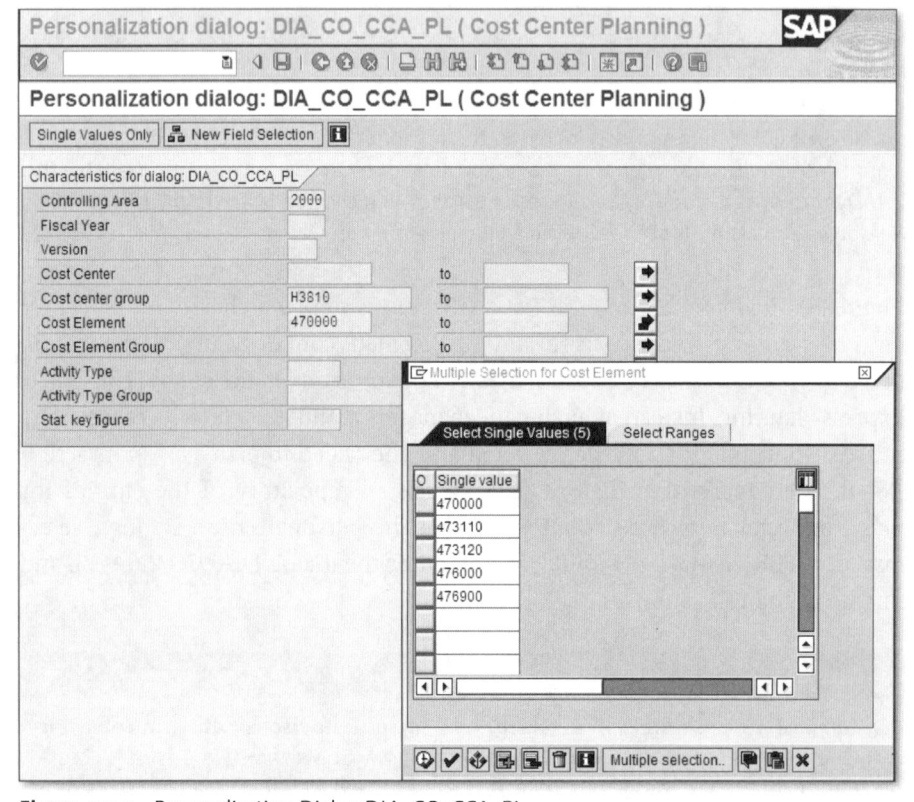

Figure 10.20 Personalization Dialog DIA_CO_CCA_PL

Let's now go ahead and create a planning round by selecting CREATE PLANNING ROUND in the navigation panel in Figure 10.18. Figure 10.21 shows the roadmap that guides you through the creation of the planning round. Here you enter the link to the planning scenario and planning instance and set deadlines for planning so that the correct steps and substeps will be generated for which the managers will be required to plan.

484

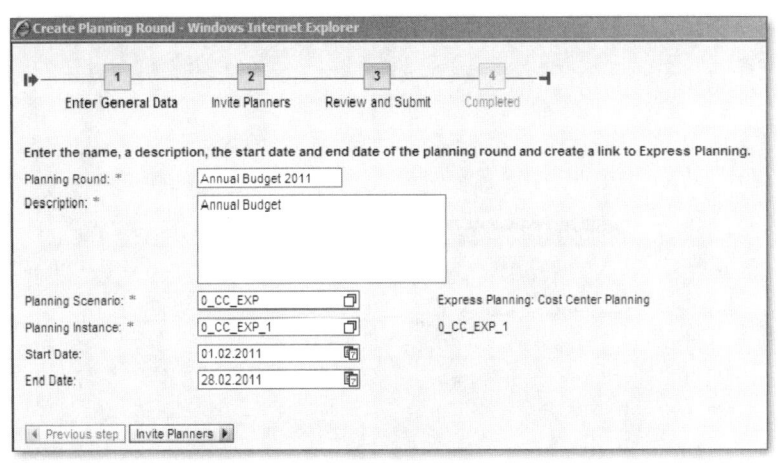

Figure 10.21 Link Planning Round with Planning Scenario and Instance

The next step is to invite the managers who need to plan. There are several ways to do this.

- If you refer back to Chapter 3, you'll remember that each cost center now includes the user name of the cost center manager. As the planning round is created, the system can use the user names of the managers of each cost center to prepare the invitation list. If you've maintained the user names of all your cost center managers in the cost centers, all you have to do is update the personalization settings in personalization dialog DIA_BUA_SNI* for your own user to include all cost centers that you want to plan against. This will allow you to generate the invitation list automatically.

- You can also manually choose the cost center managers to be invited (see Figure 10.22). If you use this option, you should ensure that the settings in Figure 10.20 have been maintained properly for all managers or you'll send them an empty planning sheet in which they cannot enter any data, because their responsibility is not defined in the system.

- Once you're up and running, you can simply copy the names of the managers who participated in last year's planning round and adjust as required (see Figure 10.22). Remember again, that if you add managers to the list you will need to make sure that the personalization settings have been maintained properly so that these managers will see their own cost centers in the planning application.

485

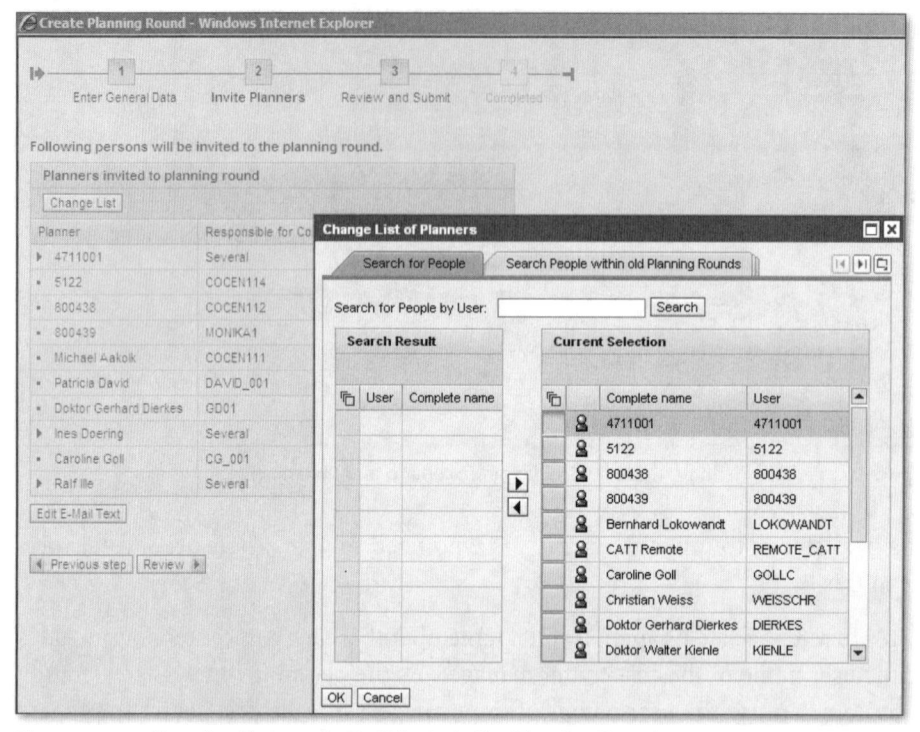

Figure 10.22 Choosing Planners to Participate in the Planning Round

You should also click on the EDIT E-MAIL TEXT button in Figure 10.22. This will ensure that an email is sent to all the cost center managers in the list, using the email address entered in their user master records (maintained using Transaction SU01). Each manager receives a generated link to the Web application containing Express Planning in this email. Alternatively, they can access their planning round using the list of planning rounds shown in Figure 10.18.

Before the mail is sent, it makes sense to review the planning round and specify who is responsible for reviewing and approving each step in the planning process. To do this, call up the planning round (see Figure 10.18). If you're using the Business Analyst role, this will take you to Figure 10.23, where you can display the steps either by user, by object (cost center, in our example), or by object hierarchy (cost center hierarchy) and enter both the user(s) who will approve the plan and the user(s) who will review the plan. These users also need to be assigned the business unit analyst role to access the planning round and perform their tasks (see Appendix A at *www.sap-press.com*).

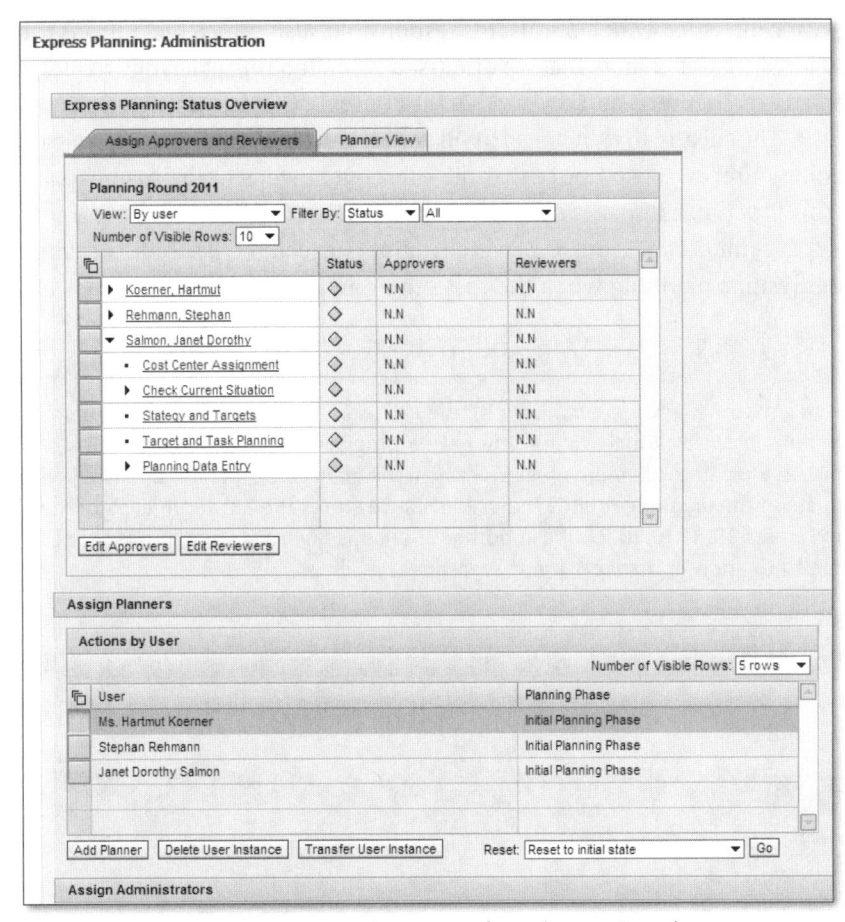

Figure 10.23 Entering Reviewers and Approvers for a Planning Round

This completes the steps to prepare the initial planning round for distribution.

10.3.2 How Cost Center Managers Submit Their Data

Let's now look at what happens if a manager clicks on the link in the email or chooses the application from the list of open planning rounds in Manager Self-Service. He'll see a roadmap containing the steps defined in the planning scenario. The first step (see Figure 10.24) is to check that the cost center assignment is correct. The planning process has a dual purpose for the controller. First, you're preparing the operational plan for the following year, but you're also implicitly checking that the underlying master data is correct, or you'll be building on false assumptions. Under the three cost centers for which our user is responsible, also notice the buttons for requesting a cost center change that we discussed when looking at change requests for master data in Chapter 3 and revisited in the context of master data governance in Chapter 9. The idea is that managers will report out-dated master data as part of the planning process. Also notice that the subsequent steps in the roadmap are inactive. This is because it makes no sense for the manager to continue planning if one of his cost centers is missing or needs changing. Instead, he'll submit a change request and resume planning when the cost center assignment is correct.

> **User Instances in Express Planning**
>
> Each planning sheet assigned to a manager is called a *user instance*. Don't worry too much about the term *instance* as such, unless you have a programming background. Think of the instance as a separate planning sheet for each of the managers that have been invited to participate in the planning round. The user instance stores the entries in each of the screens in Figures 10.24 to 10.27. It's important if one manager's planning sheet has to be transferred to another manager for any reason.

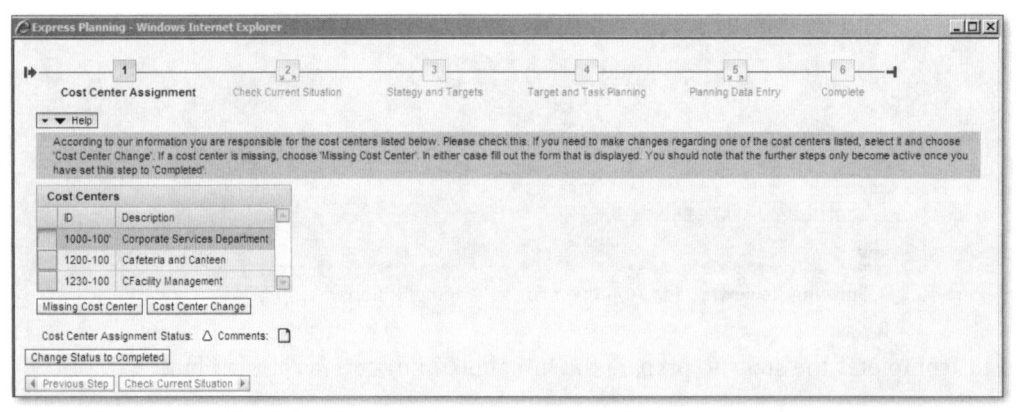

Figure 10.24 Check Cost Center Assignment in Express Planning

Moving on, the next steps are active in Figure 10.25 because we've confirmed the cost center assignment. In a similar vein, we can now check the cost center expenses in the previous year, the assigned internal orders, and the employees and equipment for which the manager is responsible. We've included the strategy and targets step to share more strategic goals with the cost center manager as part of the planning process. From a pure controlling point of view steps 3 and 4 are irrelevant, but from an organizational point of view, the planning process can be a good time to share strategy and get commitment from managers on how they plan to execute on the strategy.

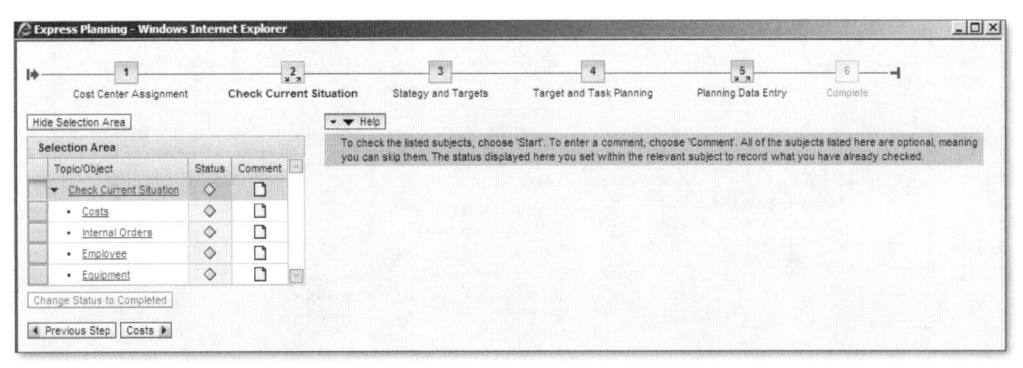

Figure 10.25 Check Current Cost Center Expenses

Let's skip now to step 4, planning data entry, and look at the data the manager can enter. Step 4 includes a series of substeps (see Figure 10.18): (workforce requirements), equipment, internal orders, travel expenses, and other costs. The top cost center (1000-100) is passed to the planning service as a parameter. This is the equivalent of entering the cost center in the selection screen of Transaction KP06. We can switch the time buckets by changing the planning period to be either quarterly or monthly by switching the drop-down list box PLANNING PERIOD from Planning on an Annual Basis to Planning on a Quarterly or Monthly Basis (see Figure 10.26). If you do this, the planning table will become very wide and you'll probably want to hide the cost centers on the left by selecting HIDE SELECTION AREA. As you enter and save data in this screen, the expenses will be written to the same tables as are used to store the planning transactions in CO.

Also notice that a status is set for each cost center and that you can enter comments for both the cost center and lines in the plan, so that managers can explain the reasons for their high travel expenses. These are not stored with the CO planning data, but in separate tables that relate specifically to Express Planning (the user instances we discussed earlier). Reviewers and approvers see these comments and the status information when they review the plan as part of the planning round.

Figure 10.27 shows the same framework (cost centers, status, comments) but a different planning service, namely, primary cost planning for an internal order. You may remember that in Chapter 3 we talked about internal orders that provide additional detail to a cost center and included the RESPONSIBLE COST CENTER field in their master data. These two orders have been selected as belonging to cost center 1000-100 and are planned in this context.

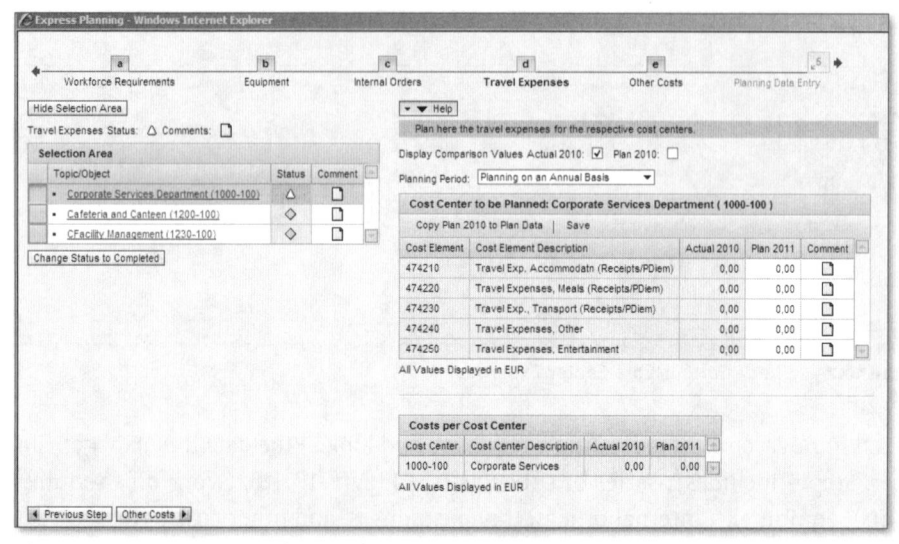

Figure 10.26 Primary Cost Planning for Travel Expenses on a Cost Center

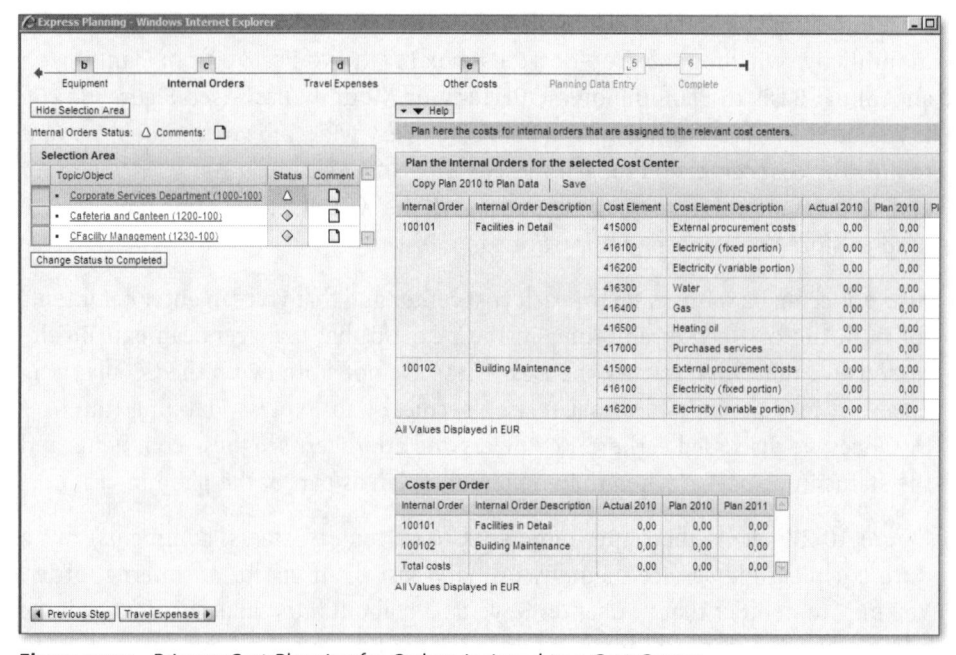

Figure 10.27 Primary Cost Planning for Orders Assigned to a Cost Center

Whatever steps are configured in Express Planning, the final step is always the status overview, where the manager can check his own progress. Notice that some steps have been flagged as mandatory and some as optional. The manager can also see who is responsible for approving each step. Figure 10.28 shows our current progress through Express Planning. Only when all the mandatory steps are complete, will the SUBMIT button become active.

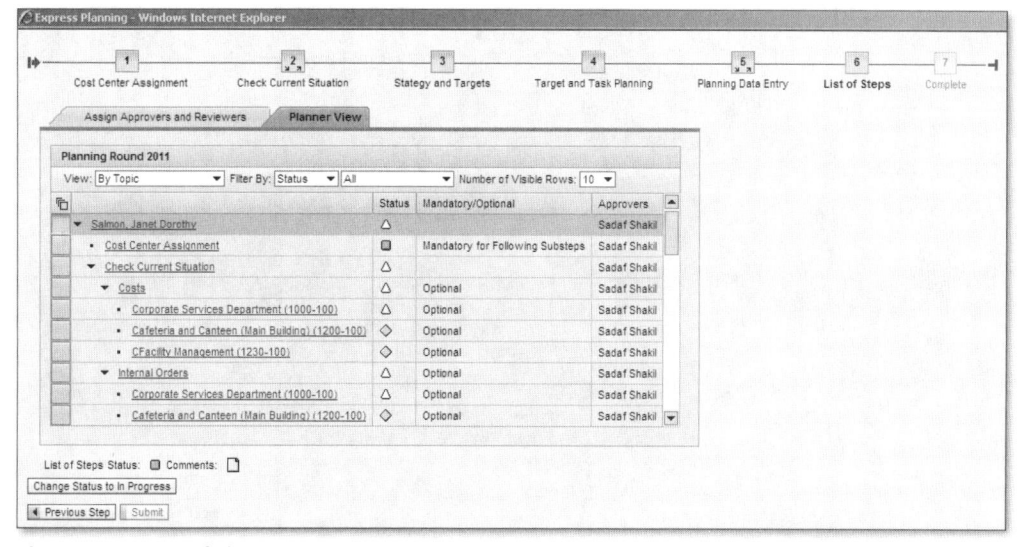

Figure 10.28 List of Planning Steps Prior to Submission

10.3.3 Monitoring, Reviewing, and Approving the Planning Process

As the cost center managers work through the steps in Express Planning, the controller can monitor progress. Figure 10.29 shows the users working in Express Planning and the steps they've completed. As a controller, you can click on any of the links and display the data the planners have entered, but you can only approve and reject it or add your comments when the cost center managers have submitted the data to controlling at the end of the process. Technically, submitting the planning data releases the user instance for each cost center for comment by the reviewers and approvers. Also notice in Figure 10.29 that our user is the administrator for the planning round. This is typically the job of the controller who creates the planning round initially and monitors progress.

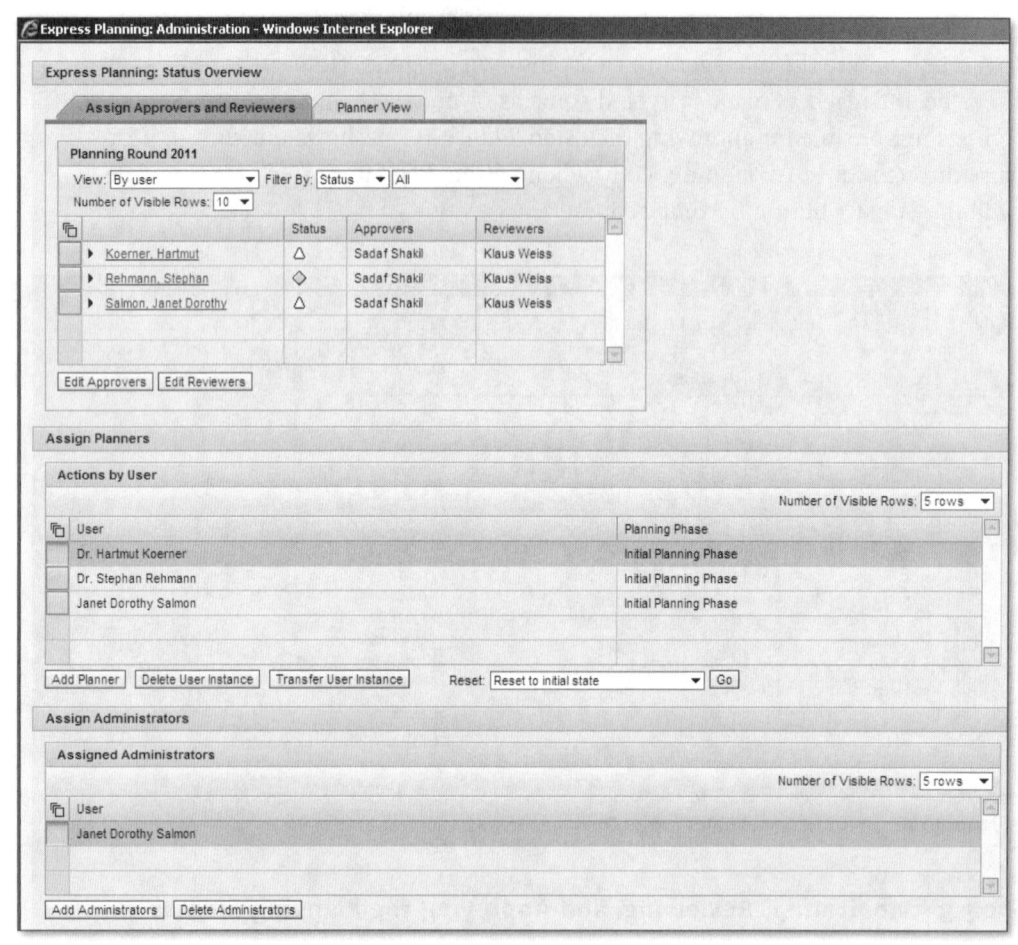

Figure 10.29 Express Planning Status Overview

The approval process starts with the planner submitting the initial plan. On the Approval tab the approver sees those parts of a planning round he is responsible for and that are currently in the approval phase. This is important if more than one approver is responsible for checking and approving a planning round. If the approver rejects the cost center manager's plan, the user instance or planning sheet is sent back to the planner for revision and disappears from the monitor shown in Figure 10.29. Likewise, once the plan is completely approved, it disappears from the monitor.

The approver can either use the buttons on the status overview to approve or reject selected parts of the planning round or use the hyperlinks of the status overview to navigate directly into the planning and process approval there.

In the status overview the approver can select several lines (even across different planners) and can perform mass approval or rejection.

When the approver navigates to the individual planning of a planner, it's for doing detailed approval work (e.g., looking at the individual planning results and using the comment functionality to explain reasons for rejection).

After finishing the approval work, the approver sends back the planning to the planner for revision (in case of rejections) or finalizes the planning of the planner (in case of complete approval).

The planners automatically receive email notifications.

- In the revision phase the planner is not allowed to make any changes in areas that already have been *approved*.
- If the planner selects a *rejected* part of the plan, he can make adjustments and then change status to COMPLETED again.

After the planner revises all rejected parts of the plan and marks them as completed, the SUBMIT button is active again, and the planner may submit the plan for approval again.

Afterward, another approval phase is performed. This process may iterate until the plan has been completely approved.

10.3.4 Embedding Overall and Cost Element Planning in Express Planning

In enhancement package 6 several new services are included in Express Planning. Figure 10.30 shows the newer version of Transaction EXP_CUST with the configuration for calling the planning application as a Floorplan Manager application and for passing the parameters project, version, and fiscal year variant to the application. If you compare this with the screen shown in Figure 10.19, you'll see that the new version is significantly more dynamic in terms of the applications that can be embedded and the parameters that can be passed.

10 | Planning in SAP NetWeaver BW or SAP SEM

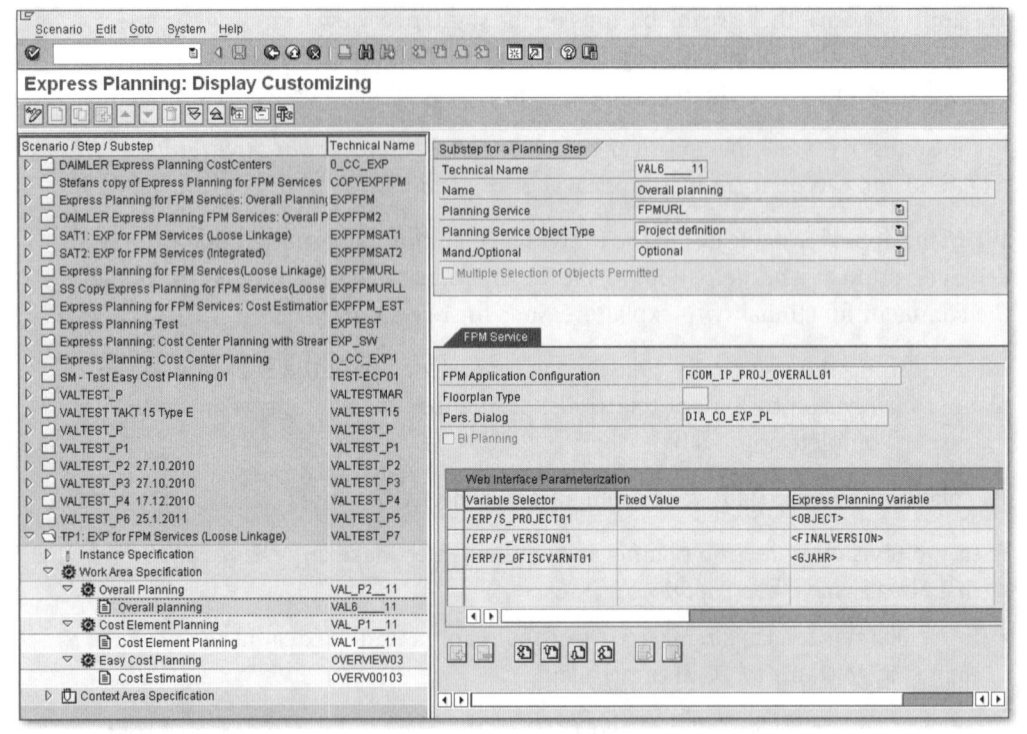

Figure 10.30 Floorplan Manager Service in Express Planning

Figure 10.31 shows the result of executing this application. Here you see the same planning application for overall planning as in Figure 10.14. This time the projects for which the manager is responsible don't have to be entered in the selection screen, but are transferred as parameters from the Express Planning instance using the variables we saw in Figure 10.30. By clicking on the SHOW SELECTION AREA button you can enter a status or a comment for each project to be planned.

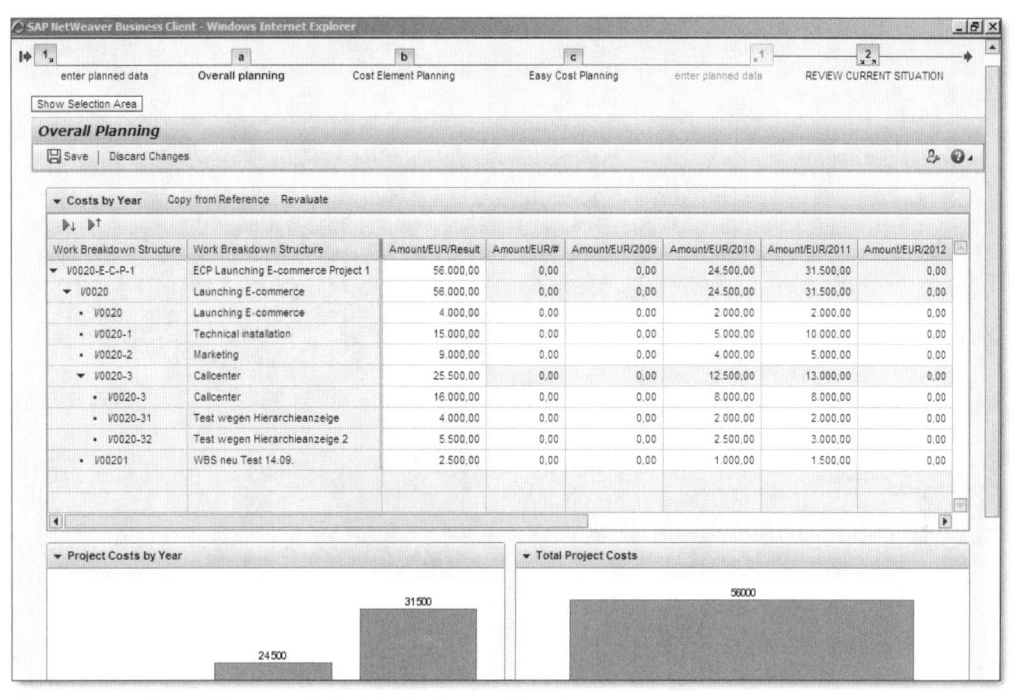

Figure 10.31 Overall Planning Embedded in Express Planning

10.4 Summary

In this chapter we revisited the planning transactions from a slightly more technical point of view and compared the planning transactions in SAP ERP with the newer planning applications available in SAP SEM-BPS or SAP NetWeaver BW-BPS and in SAP BW-IP. We then introduced a hybrid form of planning using SAP NetWeaver BW-IP in SAP ERP and discussed Express Planning as a tool that allows controllers to initiate and monitor the collaboration with the cost center managers needed for proper cost center planning.

The chapter looks at new ways of performing allocations to provide a full cost to serve model both in SAP ERP and in SAP BusinessObjects Profitability and Cost Management and looks at how these allocations can coexist with existing CO functions.

11 Allocations Using SAP Cost and Profitability Management

We've talked about allocations in various forms throughout this book. Just as a reminder, we need to perform an allocation whenever we want to move primary costs such as payroll, materials, depreciation, and so on from the original cost center or order under which they were posted in the general ledger to the final profitability segment whose costs we want to analyze. We looked at this value flow in detail when we discussed the use of *assessment cycles* to move costs from cost centers to profitability segments in Chapter 7. In addition, allocations are used to move costs between *supporting* and *operational* cost centers as we discussed when setting up master data in Chapter 3, planning in Chapter 5, or performing allocations in Chapter 7. We also looked at direct activity allocations in Chapter 6, when we discussed what happens when we confirm a production order or record time to a work breakdown structure element.

You may remember that when we introduced the value flows used in the Controlling component of SAP ERP Financials (CO) in Chapter 1, Figure 1.2 showed not only the cost centers, internal orders, sales orders, production orders, projects, and profitability segments that we've looked at until now, but also an additional account assignment object, the *business process*. SAP introduced the business process as part of its Activity-Based Costing solution in Release 4.0 of SAP ERP to extend its existing cost allocation capabilities. It makes sense to use a business process to capture costs for activities that cannot easily be described in an employee time sheet or the routings, recipes, maintenance plans, networks, and so on that we find in Logistics.

When you consider the elements that make up product costs, a routing describes all the steps to make the product but does not necessarily cover the costs associated with the procurement, quality management, maintenance, transport, shipping, and so on associated with delivering that product. When we looked at make-to-order production in Chapter 6, for example, we saw that we could capture the costs of the raw materials needed to manufacture the configured material and associated manufacturing steps but did not capture the costs placed on the organization for handling complex configuration rather than a standard product. When we looked at this sales order in CO-PA, we ignored the costs of late changes to the order by the customer and the costs of chasing late payments and handling disputes if the customer was slow to pay. This is the domain of Activity-Based Costing, where you can create business processes to cover tasks such as configuring a sales order or chasing late payments and then set up a *template* to establish rules for when the costs for this extra task are to be charged.

More recently SAP has acquired SAP BusinessObjects Profitability and Cost Management (SAP BusinessObjects PCM), a tool designed from the start for building activity-based costing models. In this chapter we'll look at template allocation in SAP ERP and then at how to build cost models in SAP BusinessObjects PCM that can take the data you already have in SAP ERP as their starting point. We'll explain in what context each tool makes sense and how they differ.

- Activity-Based Costing (CO-OM-ABC) is tightly integrated within the CO component, providing an extra "layer" between the cost center and the cost objects in Cost Object Controlling or the profitability segments in CO-PA and accessing information available in SAP ERP to determine when the costs for performing particular activities should be charged.

- SAP BusinessObjects Profitability and Cost Management is a dedicated allocation tool designed to take resource costs out of SAP ERP (or any other source system) and allocate them to activities and cost objects using rules that you establish in SAP BusinessObjects PCM independently of whatever assessment cycles and direct activity allocations you may have built in SAP ERP.

One of the guiding principles of this book has been to leverage whatever data is available within SAP ERP to support cost accounting, whether it's the information in the bills of material and routings that tell us what needs to be done in manufacturing or the square footage of floor space that tells us the relative size of the different cost centers for cost allocation. This same understanding will help us as we consider the practicality of the different allocation options. Consider these three cases.

- If we already have BOMs and routings in place and our main goal is to include the costs of a quality check performed once for each production order in our costing model, then we can use Activity-Based Costing (CO-OM-ABC) to extend the existing product costing process to include the costs of such a quality check. All we have to do is create a business process for the quality check and a template that will determine under what circumstances the costs of that quality check are to be charged to our production orders.

- If we're only using Cost Center Accounting and basic allocations to move costs between cost centers, as might be the case for a bank or other financial service organization, then we often have almost no driver information for more complex cost allocations in SAP ERP, since most of the information about the loans handled is in separate industry-specific systems. If this is the case, you might find it more practical to create a costing model in SAP BusinessObjects PCM to determine the costs of opening accounts, handling various insurance policies, and so on.

- If we're capturing information on collections and disputes in SAP Financial Supply Chain Management and marketing activities in SAP Customer Relationship Management, then bringing this information into Profitability Analysis (CO-PA) is going to involve setting up extra value fields and data loads from external systems. Again, you might find it more practical to create a costing model for this purpose in SAP BusinessObjects PCM that's not subject to the constraints in CO-PA.

> **Data Structures in CO-PA**
>
> For many years the rule of thumb for an operating concern was that you should have no more than 50 characteristics as dimensions and no more than 120 value fields. This limit can be extended using SAP Note 1029391. The option of 200 value fields is standard in enhancement package 4.

Before we go into detail about the various costing models, it's worth clearing up a few terminology issues up front. SAP BusinessObjects PCM works with the terms *resources*, *activities*, and *cost objects*, but these terms are used differently in SAP ERP. You can map your SAP ERP model against this, as follows.

- The *cost objects* in SAP BusinessObjects PCM are equivalent to the market segments in CO-PA (product, customer, channel, region, and so on), rather than the more short-term production orders, process orders, and so on. Generally the steps you perform in the Cost Object Controlling menus will be completely unaffected by any use of SAP BusinessObjects PCM, since you aren't going to change how you assign material and labor to your products, update inventory, or charge time to a WBS element. If you do want to include the costs of a quality check in your product costs, then it's generally more practical to add an extra step in the form of a *template allocation* to the process you have in place in SAP ERP.

- The *resources* are generally your cost centers, though they can be individual items in the general ledger or a different grouping of the cost centers. Normally this isn't a one-to-one mapping exercise. It often makes sense to pull out the costs of certain service departments or supporting cost centers rather than your whole cost center hierarchy and allocate these costs using SAP BusinessObjects PCM. This is perhaps a key difference between CO and SAP BusinessObjects PCM. The assumption in CO is that *all* costs will ultimately be allocated to CO-PA. In SAP BusinessObjects PCM you decide how much of your organization the model will embrace. It can be a complete costing solution (and often is in the financial services or healthcare sectors), or it can be a partial model to answer a single business question (such as the cost impact of your receivables process on customer profitability).

- The *activities* might not exist in SAP ERP at all if you haven't been capturing marketing activities or collection activities in SAP ERP. If they do exist, it will be as a business process defined in the ACTIVITY-BASED COSTING menu or sometimes a cost center/activity type combination. Generally, activity types associated with time sheets, routings, recipes, maintenance plans, and so on do not belong in SAP BusinessObjects PCM.

11.1 New Tools for Performing Allocations in SAP ERP

We'll start by looking at template allocation, to show you how you can extend your CO implementation to include the costs of activities or business processes in your normal product costing approach.

11.1.1　Template Allocations in SAP ERP

Let's first look at how to represent the activity in SAP ERP. The most common way to do this is to create a business process for each activity. The business process has master data that combines the following elements.

- The assignment to a company code, business area, profit center, and so on works exactly the same as for the cost center we looked at in Chapter 3, Section 3.1. Since you're going to be performing allocations that potentially cross company codes or profit centers, bear in mind that the general ledger will also be affected (see Chapter 3, Section 3.1.3). The business process also has a responsible manager, which is important in the context of process management and the whole notion of process ownership.

- The assignment to a secondary cost element and the parameters for price calculation are exactly the same as for an activity type (see Chapter 3, Section 3.5). The fact that you can calculate a price for a business process using the same mechanisms as for an activity price is often seen as an advantage over the percentage-based overheads we looked at in Chapter 7, Section 7.2, where it's almost impossible to set the overhead percentage to completely clear the cost center at period close.

To create a business process, follow the menu path ACCOUNTING • CONTROLLING • ACTIVITY-BASED COSTING • BUSINESS PROCESS • INDIVIDUAL PROCESSING • CREATE and enter the name of the business process or use Transaction CP01. Figure 11.1 shows the basic data for business process 300900 (work scheduling). Notice the assignment to a company code, business area, and profit center, as we saw for the cost center, and also to a hierarchy area. You can group business processes into hierarchies for reporting and to make it easy to select them as the senders or receivers of an allocation, using the same functions we used to group cost centers in Chapter 3.

If we return to the pump example that has accompanied us throughout this book (see Figure 11.2), we now notice that the cost estimate contains two items of item category X in the itemization. These cover activities not described in the routing (these have category E). The costs for one unit of each activity have been applied to every subassembly in our bill of material. In our example, this means that the costs of work scheduling (business process 300900) and sales order processing (business process 400900) have been included in the product costs, but this same approach could also be used for a quality check that has to be performed in every manufacturing order regardless of lot size, and so on.

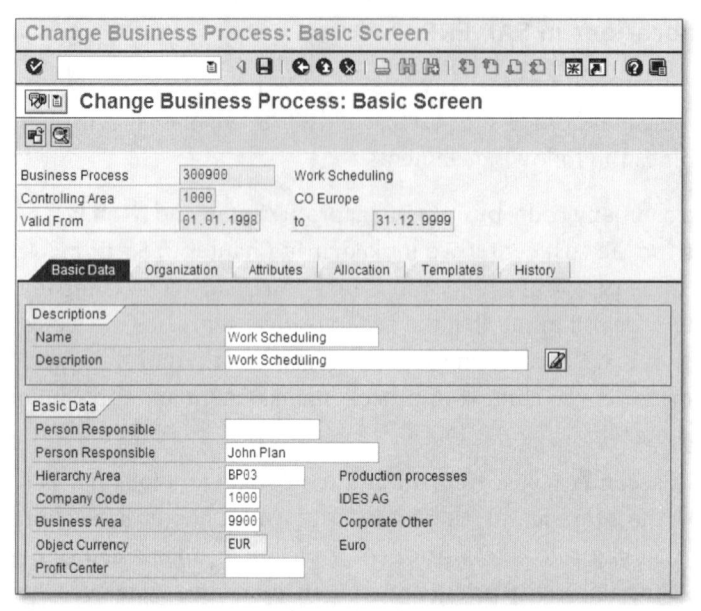

11 | Allocations Using SAP Cost and Profitability Management

Figure 11.1 Business Process for Work Scheduling – Basic Data

The business process costs are assigned to a cost element and from there to the cost components. This link is the same as those we discussed when we looked at Product Cost Planning in general in Chapter 2, meaning that you can distinguish between business processes that are part of the cost of goods manufactured (work scheduling) and those that are part of the cost of goods sold (sales order processing). In Figure 11.2 we're looking at the cost of goods manufactured view, so the value in item 9 is zero, since this value will only show up in the cost of goods sold view (you can switch between the two views using the COSTS tab).

You create the link between the cost estimate and the business process by setting up a template in Customizing. If you're not sure which template has been used in your cost estimate, select the VALUATION tab (see Figure 11.2). In our example we used template CO-PC-10-1. The logic used to select the template is the same as the logic for overhead calculation that we looked at in Chapter 7, Section 7.2, with the template being selected based on the costing sheet (here COGS) and the overhead key in the material master during planning (here SAP10) and in the production order at period close. This link is created during configuration. Figure 11.3 shows the template, CO-PC-10-1, that was used to apply the activity costs to our cost estimate. The easiest way to display this is to double-click on the template field in Figure 11.2. The template shown in Figure 11.3 comprises two calculation lines. The sales order processing line assigns a unit of one for our business process 400900. The order processing line refers to a subtemplate that in this example includes our other business process, 300900, and a unit of one. In this example, you don't need to stack the template, but could have included both lines as business processes, though this gives you a feel for the potential of the template.

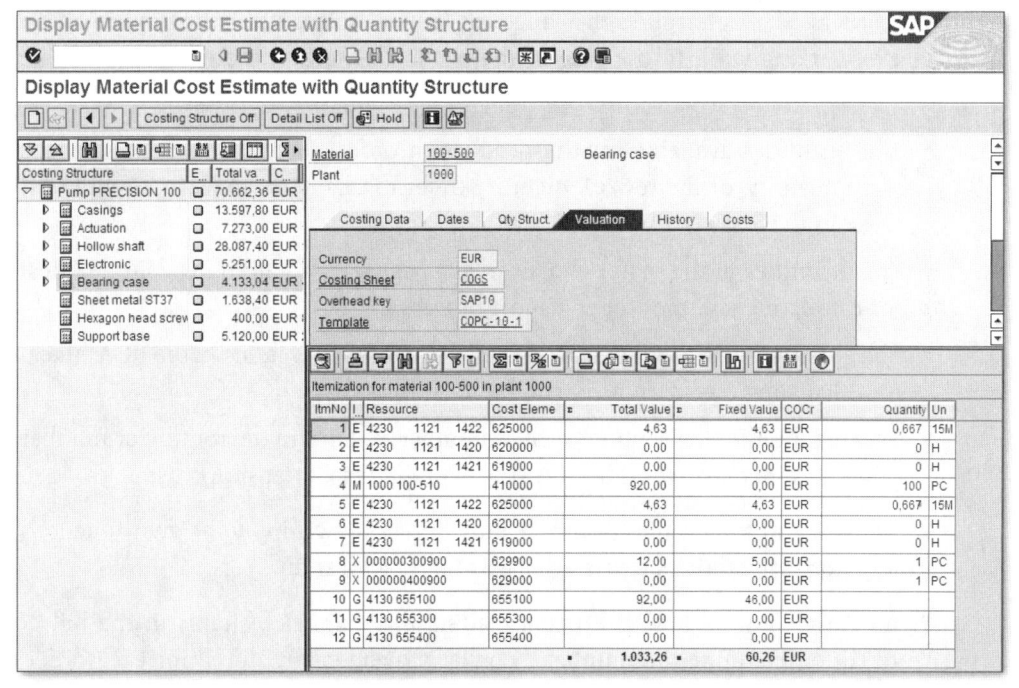

Figure 11.2 Cost Estimate – Business Processes

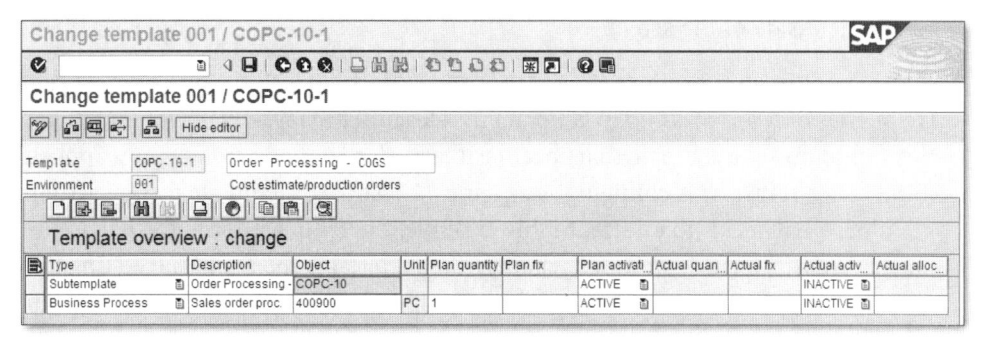

Figure 11.3 Template – Work Scheduling and Order Processing Costs

Having a unit of one is clearly the easiest way to work but won't get you beyond the simplest examples. If instead of entering a 1 in the PLAN QUANTITY field you double-click on the field, the system will offer you a series of standard functions for calculating quantities in the context that your template is being used in. This context is stored as an environment in SAP ERP. Notice in Figure 11.3 that we're in environment 001, which is used for both Product Cost Planning and production orders. This determines the functions that are relevant for the type of object you're working with. In the case of the production order, the quantities can be calculated using:

- The quantities available for the production order, such as order lot size, the scrap quantity, or the rework quantity (refer to Chapter 6 to learn how to post these in the first place)
- The quantities in the material master, such as weight, length, or volume (ideal for calculating volumes for transport processes)
- The quantities in the bill of material, such as number of items in the BOM (ideal for calculating the costs of procurement processes)
- The quantities in the routing, such as number of items in the routing or number of work center changes (ideal for calculating internal transport costs)

You can extend these options almost indefinitely by writing your own functions to select other quantities to use as a basis for an allocation.

Figure 11.4 shows a template that's reading the number of items in the bill of material to determine the number of pallet movements required for each order. Notice that this time the PLAN QUANTITY column includes a function name instead of a 1. You'll also see some of the other options you can use to calculate quantities on the right side of the screen.

Another option to consider is the PLAN ACTIVATION column. If the business process is not sales order processing in general but sales order *configuration*, you might use this option to set up a logic that specifies that order configuration is only applied if the material master is configurable. Figure 11.5 shows a template for the assignment of activity costs to CO-PA. In this example, the template reads the flag in the material master that determines whether the material is *configurable* (see Chapter 4, Section 4.3.4) to decide whether customer-specific configuration is necessary or not. The activity costs for order configuration will only be charged if the material is configurable.

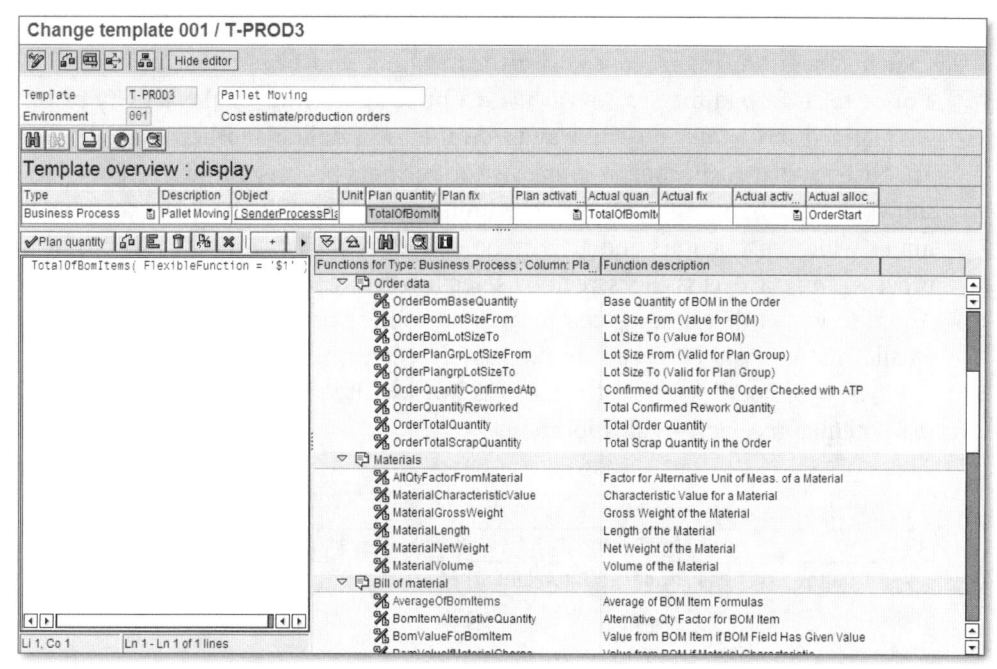

New Tools for Performing Allocations in SAP ERP | **11.1**

Figure 11.4 Template—Quantity Calculation Functions

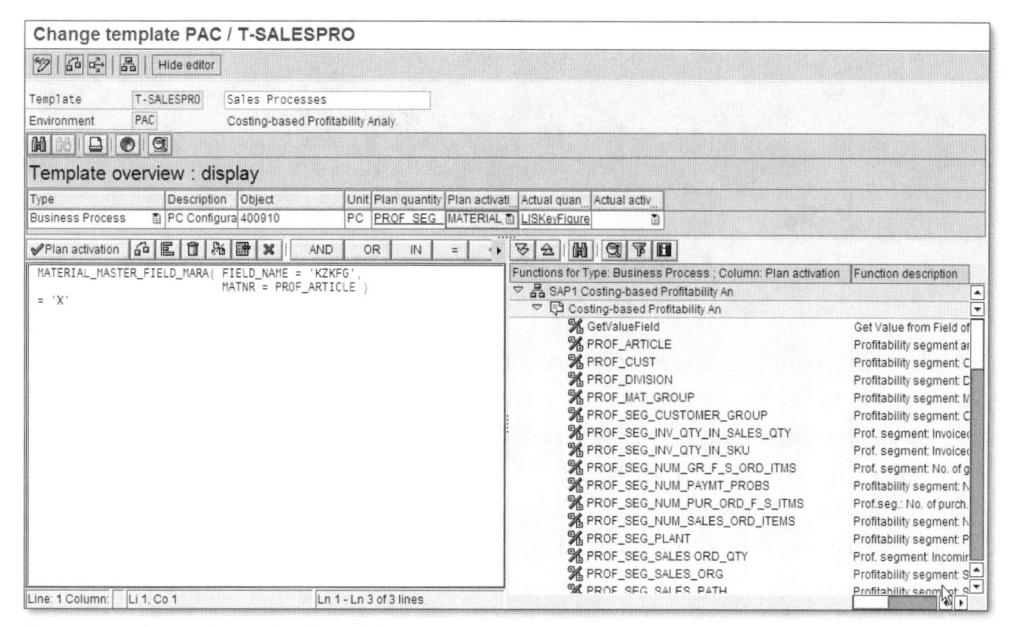

Figure 11.5 Template—Activation of Process

Whatever method of quantity calculation you choose, you won't be able to include your business process in your cost estimates until you have either manually set a price for it or had the system calculate a price as we saw for the activity prices we planned in Chapter 5. One way to do this is to define another template that establishes what cost center resources your business process will use. Figure 11.6 shows the link between our work scheduling process and the template that determines which cost centers and activity types are providing work for this business process. You can access this screen by selecting the TEMPLATES tab in Figure 11.1. Another way of determining the costs of a business process is to make it part of an allocation. If you refer back to the list of receivers for an allocation in Chapter 7, Figure 7.5, you'll see that the business process (BUSINESS PROC. field) is one of the potential receivers of an allocation.

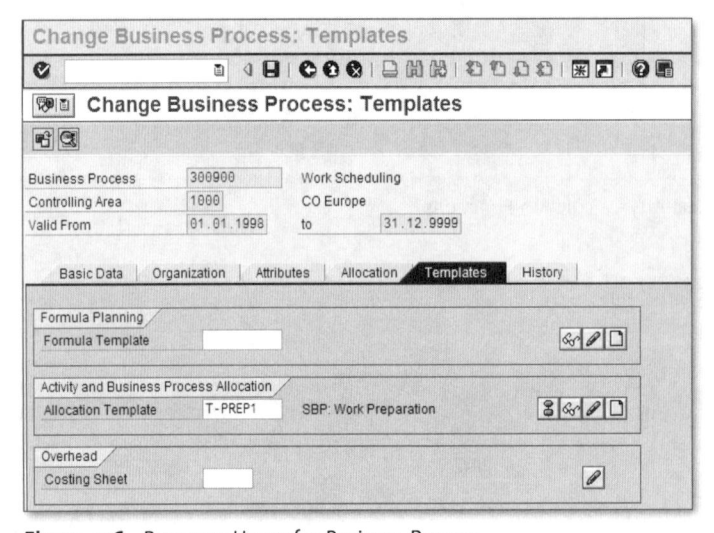

Figure 11.6 Resource Usage for Business Process

Since this template can refer to other templates, the best way to view the whole chain is to select the first icon (DISPLAY ALLOCATION STRUCTURE) to the right of the ALLOCATION TEMPLATE field and click through the different levels. Figure 11.7 shows the allocation structure used to determine the costs for our work scheduling process. You'll see that it uses a fixed number of CPU minutes for the MRP run (an internal activity) and a unit of work from the Order Scheduling process. The order scheduling process in turn uses CPU minutes for order planning and wage hours (also internal activities). When you build up templates this way, the thing to remember is that you always start with the *receiver* and specify the *senders* from which it is receiving costs.

- You set up a template in CO-PA to define when order configuration is needed for a sales order.
- You set up a template for a production order or cost estimate to define when work scheduling or quality control is needed for the product.
- You set up a template for the business process to determine the amount of internal activity required to perform the work scheduling process.

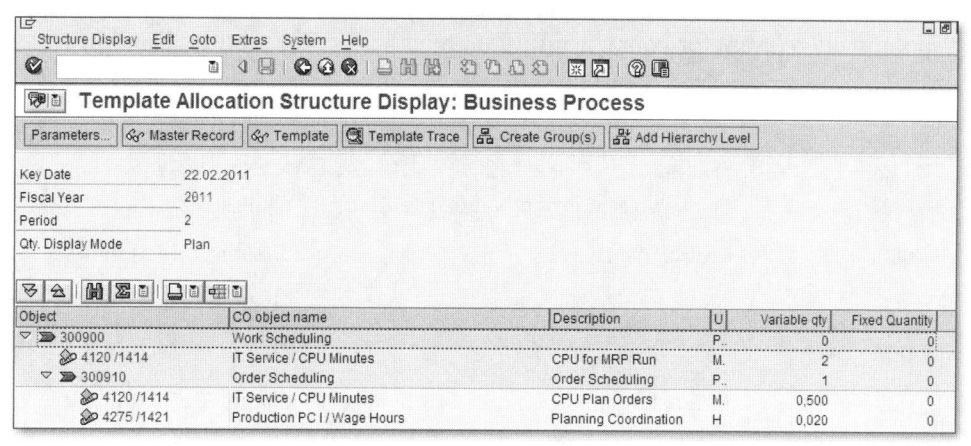

Figure 11.7 Allocation Structure for Template Allocation

In our example, the template allocation took place during product costing (in either the costing run or Transaction CK11N). To assign *actual costs*, you'll find the functions to run template allocations in all the menus we used to demonstrate allocations as part of the period close in Chapter 7. To calculate the planned costs of performing work scheduling, refer back to the menus we used for planning in Chapter 5. For example, Figure 5.2 shows the menu path for starting Template Allocation to CO-PA.

11 Allocations Using SAP Cost and Profitability Management

In Figure 11.3 and the figures that followed each template was created with reference to an *environment*. There are many environments for which you can create a template to apply process costs. The functions available within the environment will vary, so environment PAC for CO-PA allows you to reference any value field in the operating concern as a driver for template allocation, whereas environments 001 for production orders and 009 for process orders allow you to reference quantities referring to a production campaign (see Chapter 2, Section 2.4).

To create a template, go to any of the template allocation transactions (for instance, ACCOUNTING • CONTROLLING • COST CENTER ACCOUNTING • PERIOD-END CLOSING • SINGLE FUNCTIONS • ALLOCATIONS • TEMPLATE ALLOCATION) and then select EXTRAS • TEMPLATE • CREATE or go directly to Transaction CPT1. Then give your template a name and select the relevant environment. To decide which environments are potentially relevant for your organization, refer back to the sections listed in Table 11.1.

Environment	Object	Reference
PAC	Costing-based profitability analysis	Chapter 2, Section 2.6
SLI	Cost centers	Chapter 3, Section 3.1
SLD	Cost center/activity type	Chapter 3, Section 3.4
006	Cost object hierarchy	Chapter 3, Section 3.8
007	Internal orders	Chapter 3, Section 3.2
010	Product cost collector	Chapter 3, Section 3.7
004	Network	Chapter 4, Section 4.7
005	WBS element	Chapter 4, Section 4.7
SOP	Transfer sales and operations planning	Chapter 5, Section 5.1.1
CPD	Activity-dependent cost center planning	Chapter 5, Section 5.1.2
CPI	Activity-independent cost center planning	Chapter 5, Section 5.1.2
001	Cost estimate/production orders	Chapter 5, Section 5.1.3

Table 11.1 Template Environments for Master Data

Environment	Object	Reference
001	Cost estimate/production orders	Chapter 6, Section 6.1
008	Sales order	Chapter 6, Section 6.3
009	Process order	Chapter 6, Section 6.3

Table 11.1 Template Environments for Master Data (Cont.)

Then proceed as follows.

1. Depending on whether you're allocating the costs of a business process or the combination cost center/activity type, choose either business process or cost center/activity type in the TYPE column. You can also build stacked templates as we saw in Figure 11.3 by entering the name of another template.

2. Enter the relevant business process or the combination cost center/activity type. The system will select the description from the relevant master data, as well as the unit of measure (usually pieces).

3. Enter the planned quantity either as an integer (one unit of work scheduling) or by choosing a quantity function. You can access the quantity functions by double-clicking on the QUANTITY column. They'll vary depending on the environment you're working in.

4. If your costs will only apply under certain circumstances, choose an activation function by double-clicking on the PLAN ACTIVATION column.

For the business process and the cost center, you can now include your template in the relevant master data (select the TEMPLATES tab for the business process or cost center). For the other objects the selection is in Customizing, so you have to discuss with your configuration team how to ensure that the correct template is selected during product costing or in the period close.

> **Template Maintenance in a Productive System**
>
> Normally template maintenance is a Customizing activity and cannot be changed in a productive system. If you do want to maintain templates in a productive system, ask your IT department to use Transaction SOBJ to adjust the settings for object CPT2 (the template change transaction) to permit template maintenance as current settings. This will allow the same kind of maintenance as we saw for the allocation cycles in Chapter 7, Section 7.1.

While template allocations can be a useful tool for performing allocations in SAP ERP, you may find that most of the driver quantities you want to use for allocations are actually outside of SAP ERP. In this case, it's worth looking at whether SAP BusinessObjects Profitability and Cost Management (PCM) can help you.

11.2 New Tools for Performing Allocations in SAP BusinessObjects PCM

The template allocation we just looked at makes perfect sense when the information we need for the allocations is already available in the material master, BOM, routing, or wherever. For CO-PA we can set up templates that can read any value field in the operating concern. The discussions start when the *quantities* you need as a basis for your allocation aren't readily available in SAP ERP.

The question of where the majority of the drivers reside that you want to use as a basis for your allocations can determine whether to perform allocations in SAP ERP, SAP BusinessObjects PCM, or both.

- In SAP ERP we've already looked at how to enter key figures such as square footage to use as a basis for an allocation or how to configure a template to pick up quantities available in Logistics. You can use any value field in your operating concern as the basis for an allocation. The issues start when you find yourself adding value fields for both drivers and the result of each allocation in CO-PA. If you have a complex model with a lot of drivers, you can easily find yourself running out of fields.

- SAP BusinessObjects PCM has its own data bridge to pull data out of an external system, or you can use SAP BusinessObjects Financial Information Management to extract the relevant data from SAP NetWeaver BW, SAP ERP, SAP CRM, or any data warehouse. SAP BusinessObjects PCM also includes a Web-based data collection tool to collect information from managers in the form of a survey.

Once you have collected the relevant data, the next stage is to think about your *model*. Before you start drawing out any details, think about the type of model you're interested in.

- If you're looking at *modeling* to understand the drivers for a single area of your business, your corporate costing system, where all allocations can impact the general ledger, may not be the best place for experiments. In these circumstances, it's good to ask yourself how stable your model is. Even in SAP ERP, cost center structures change over time, but ask yourself whether the business process or activity you're describing describes your core business or is something you're experimenting with. If you want to keep changing that model because of the lessons you've learned from your calculations, building in your corporate costing system where every change involves gaining the consensus of all involved parties may not actually be what you want.

- If you want to run different *simulations* based on your model, costing several plan versions as we saw in Chapter 5 may not give you sufficient flexibility to model the impact of different scenarios. One thing that makes simulations cumbersome in SAP ERP is that so many different applications are involved, as we saw when we followed the annual operating plan from start to finish. In these circumstances, it's good to ask yourself what the purpose of your simulation is. We saw how budget data is used in SAP ERP to limit spending on a project (see Chapter 6) and how planned data is used as a basis for variance calculation (see Chapter 7), but as we discussed in Chapter 10 some plans are just plans—a modeled set of assumptions.

- Further discussions typically start around the dimensions you use in your model. As we discussed in Chapter 2, setting up your operating concern for CO-PA is very much about deciding how to map the low-level detail, such as customers and products, and how these roll up via customer groups, material groups, product hierarchies, regions, and so on to provide a consistent profitability model for the whole organization. You may find, however, that for some parts of the organization, you need more detail—going right down to the SKU level—and for others less. Another question is the product view versus the customer view. As we saw in Chapter 5, the product is very central to the planning process in SAP ERP. The customer dimension exists, but if you don't set up templates in CO-PA to handle questions about how much it costs to serve a particular customer, all other customer-related costs are merely overhead and are applied using assessment cycles.

11.2.1 Mapping the Costing Model in SAP BusinessObjects PCM with SAP ERP

You can build models in SAP BusinessObjects PCM that have almost nothing to do with CO, but that isn't the focus of this book. We want to understand how to use the two models in *combination*. If you've installed SAP BusinessObjects PCM, you can log on by selecting MODEL BUILDER on your desktop. Once you've filled in your log-in credentials, select the relevant model, as shown in Figure 11.8.

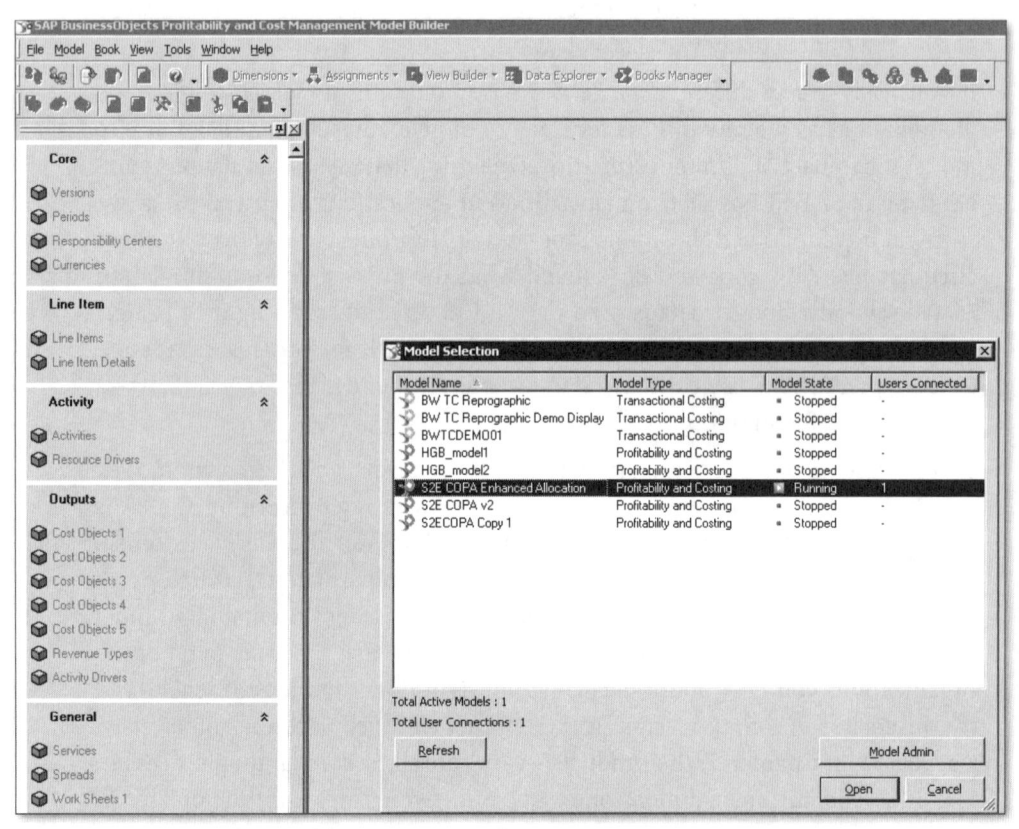

Figure 11.8 Select Model in SAP BusinessObjects PCM

Notice that our demo system includes two main sample models.

- One model is used to demonstrate overhead allocation in a bank. In such an example, there may be a link to a business process in SAP ERP, but it's more likely that the main purpose of CO is simply to capture the initial staff costs (from payroll), building costs (from asset accounting), and office costs (from the General Ledger) and bring them into Cost Center Accounting. All subsequent steps to assign these costs to the activities performed by the bank and understand their impact on customer profitability can take place in SAP BusinessObjects PCM.

- The other model is used to demonstrate an alternative form of overhead allocation, where the relevant profitability segments in CO-PA are modeled as cost objects in SAP BusinessObjects PCM and activity costs assigned to these cost objects. Here both the cost centers and the cost objects will be extracted to SAP BusinessObjects PCM, but activities will be described in SAP BusinessObjects PCM.

11.2.2 Dimensions of the Costing Model

Most models start with a series of *line items*. Don't be misled by the SAP term *line item* that we say in Chapter 2, which meant any document written to record the posting to a cost center, internal order, and so on. The line items in SAP BusinessObjects PCM are not line items in the sense that they correspond to a document in Table COEP that you would view using Transaction KSB1 or KOB1. They are as likely to be totals records if you're extracting data from CO, since you're unlikely to need all the detail available in a CO line item. In SAP BusinessObjects PCM the term *line item* simply means the list of expense records that you're taking as the starting point for your model. Figure 11.9 shows the line items in SAP BusinessObjects Profitability and Cost Management. You'll find this view by following the menu path MODEL • DIMENSIONS • LINE ITEM • LINE ITEMS or selecting LINE ITEMS on the left.

In this example we've loaded STAFF COSTS, BUILDING COSTS, OFFICE COSTS, and IT COSTS into the model as nodes, and these contain the detailed elements SALARIES, PENSIONS, TAX, and so on. There may be a one-to-one relationship between these nodes and the cost element groups in SAP ERP (see Chapter 3), or you may find yourself performing a mapping exercise to restructure your cost elements and cost element groups as you establish the data transfer mechanisms.

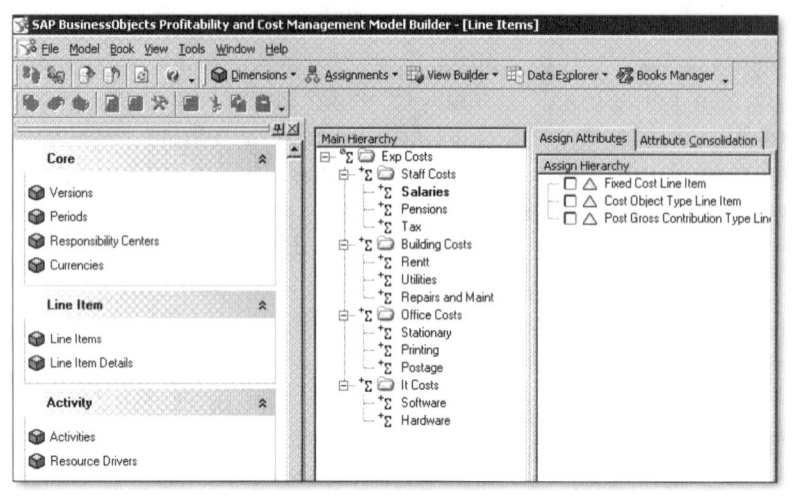

11 | Allocations Using SAP Cost and Profitability Management

Figure 11.9 Line Items in SAP BusinessObjects PCM

Just as in SAP ERP, the cost element information is always linked with the question of *where* the expense occurred, so SAP BusinessObjects PCM includes information about the responsible center, as shown in Figure 11.10. You can access this view by following the menu path MODEL • DIMENSIONS • CORE • RESPONSIBILITY CENTERS or selecting RESPONSIBILITY CENTERS on the left.

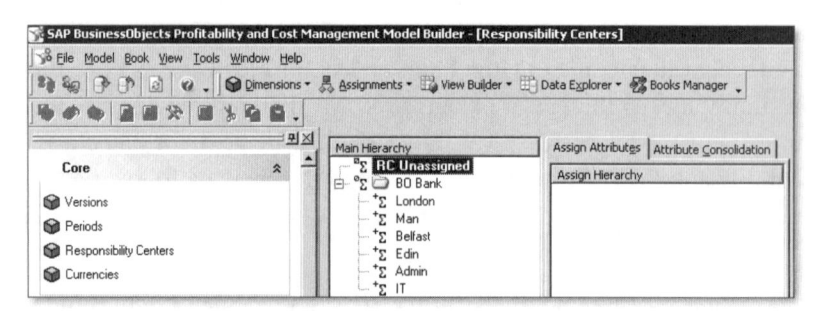

Figure 11.10 Responsibility Centers in SAP BusinessObjects PCM

In this example, the responsibility centers are a series of bank locations. These usually link with the cost centers in SAP ERP, though occasionally you'll find a group of General Ledger accounts or even a profit center represented here, depending on how you configure the data bridge.

You can perform a simple allocation from a marketing cost center to the cost objects, but you're more likely to add *activities* to your model. These might be business processes you've set up in CO, but they're more likely to be activities with no equivalent in CO—setting up a bank account, checking a customer's credit history, and so on. Figure 11.11 shows the sample activities performed by our bank. You can access this view by following the menu path MODEL • DIMENSIONS • ACTIVITY • ACTIVITIES or selecting ACTIVITIES on the left.

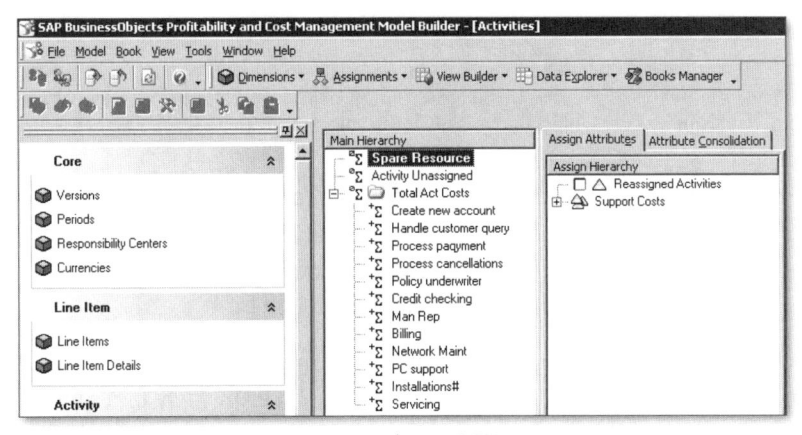

Figure 11.11 Activities in SAP BusinessObjects PCM

In this example you can see activities such as CREATE NEW ACCOUNT, HANDLE CUSTOMER QUERY, PROCESS PAYMENT, and so on. It's possible to perform an allocation that ends with the activities, simply helping to understand the relative costs of each activity performed by the bank.

More often, however, the ultimate aim is to assign these expenses to *cost objects*. As we said earlier, these aren't the production orders and product cost collectors you'll find in SAP ERP, but the characteristics you'll normally model in CO-PA. Figure 11.12 shows how the sold-to party (or customer) is loaded into SAP BusinessObjects PCM as a cost object. To display this dimension, follow the menu path MODEL • DIMENSIONS • OUTPUT • SOLD-TO PARTY or select SOLD-TO PARTY on the left.

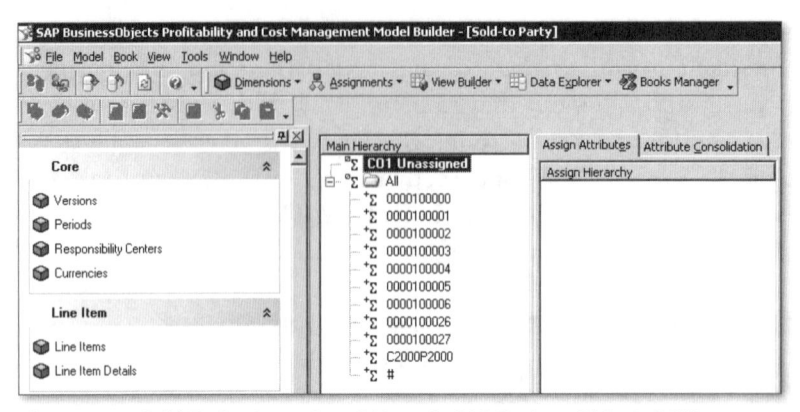

11 | Allocations Using SAP Cost and Profitability Management

Figure 11.12 Sold-To Parties as Cost Objects in SAP BusinessObjects PCM

Compare the sold-to party with the use of the material as a cost object shown in Figure 11.13. To display this dimension, follow the menu path MODEL • DIMENSIONS • OUTPUT • MATERIAL or select MATERIAL on the left. We could continue this process and also look at channels in the same way.

Controllers with almost 50 characteristics in their existing operating concerns are often concerned by the fact that SAP BusinessObjects PCM has only five cost objects and how characteristics in CO-PA can map to cost objects in SAP BusinessObjects PCM. Two things are worth bearing in mind here.

- Organizational dimensions in CO-PA, such as versions, valuation views, and so on, don't count as cost objects. Entities such as versions and currencies are modeled as separate dimensions in SAP BusinessObjects PCM, so you can ignore these in your characteristic count.

- Dependent dimensions, such as customer groups for customers or product groups for products, are considered as attributes of the main cost object, so you would model a dimension Customer with an attribute Customer Group in SAP BusinessObjects PCM. Again, this will reduce the number of potential cost objects. If you have SAP NetWeaver BW in place, look at the dimensions you used to model your operating concern there or refer to Chapter 8, Figure 8.12 for an example. Your aim is to identify the *separate* dimensions that are relevant for profitability reporting and model them as cost objects.

New Tools for Performing Allocations in SAP BusinessObjects PCM | **11.2**

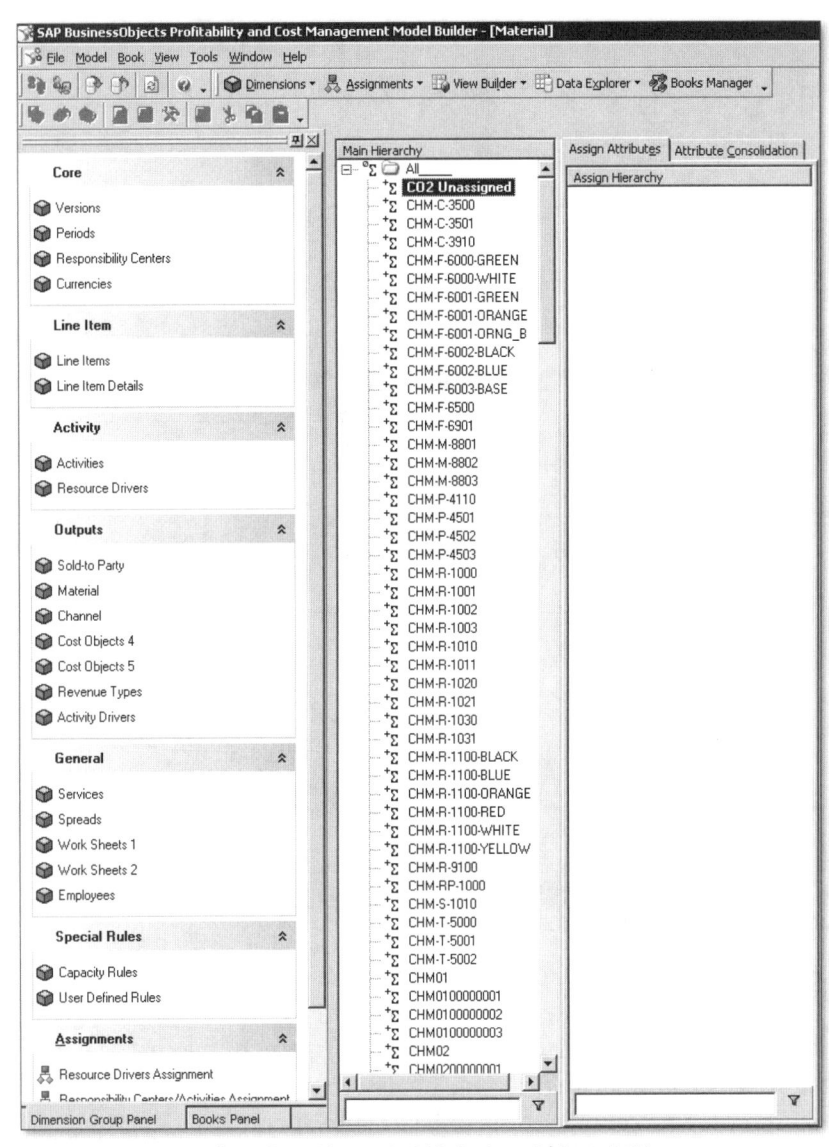

Figure 11.13 Materials as Cost Objects in SAP BusinessObjects PCM

In Figure 11.12 and 11.13, we renamed the delivered dimensions Cost Object 1, Cost Object 2, and Cost Object 3 to suit our purposes. You can do the same by selecting MODEL • RENAME DIMENSIONS as shown in Figure 11.14. Here you'll also see that Versions, Periods and Currencies are separate dimensions rather than one of the many characteristics included in the operating concern in CO-PA.

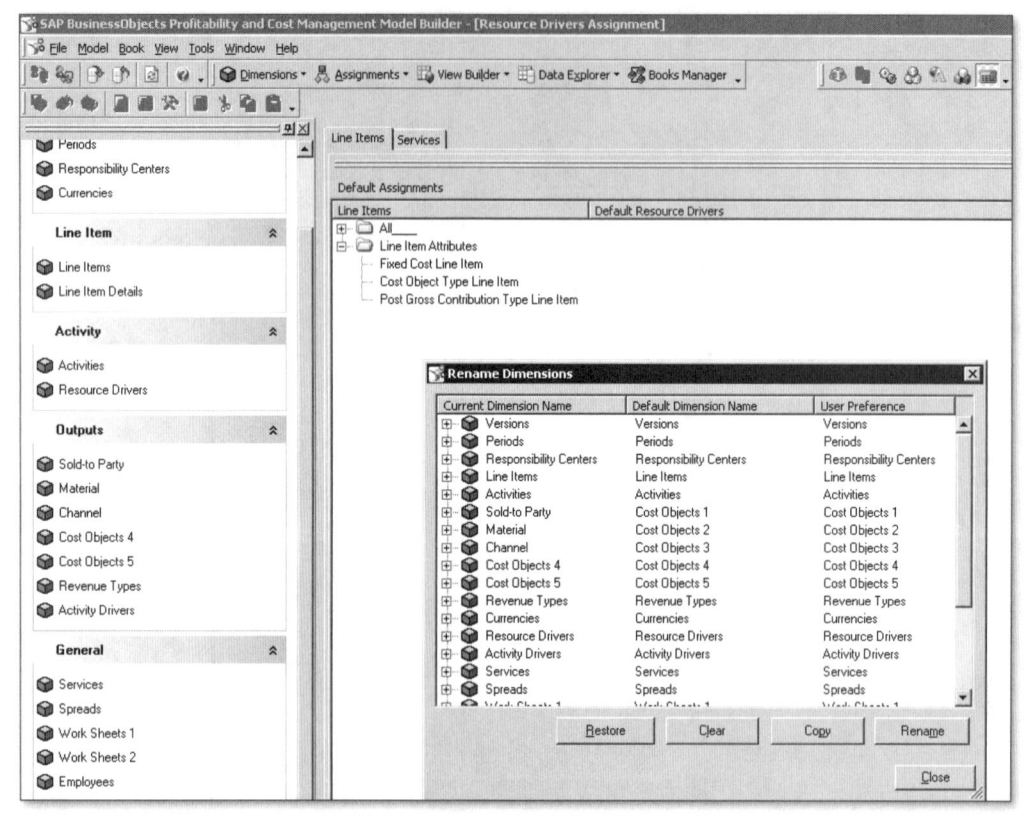

Figure 11.14 Dimensions Table in SAP BusinessObjects PCM

11.2.3 Assignments in the Costing Model

Now that we have the three levels (resources, activities, and cost objects) in place, the next stage is to link these three levels. In SAP ERP we did this by assigning statistical key figures, such as square footage of office space, to the cost center or planning the activity types, such as machine hours, for the production cost center. Figure 11.15 shows the resource drivers to be used to allocate each type of cost. You can access this view by following the menu path MODEL • ASSIGNMENTS • RESOURCE DRIVERS ASSIGNMENT or selecting RESOURCE DRIVERS ASSIGNMENT in the bottom left.

New Tools for Performing Allocations in SAP BusinessObjects PCM | 11.2

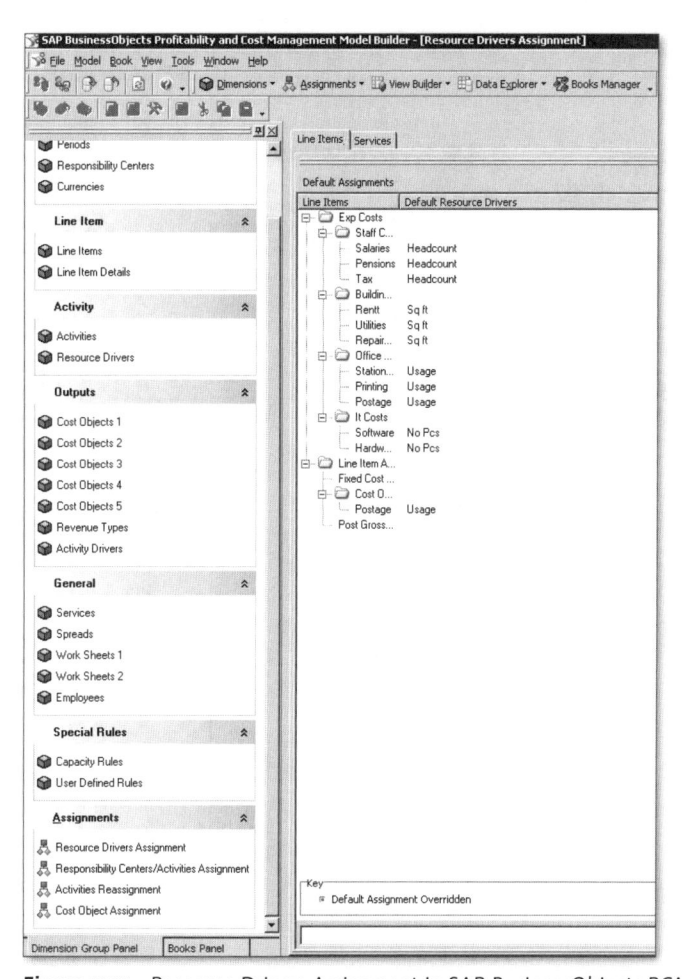

Figure 11.15 Resource Drivers Assignment in SAP BusinessObjects PCM

In this example we see headcount being used to allocate salary costs, square footage being used to allocate building costs, usage being used to allocate office costs, and pieces being used to allocate IT costs. This is essentially the same as working with statistical key figures in SAP ERP.

We then need to map the responsibility centers to the activities they're performing. Figure 11.16 shows a sample assignment from the branches of the bank to the activities performed by those branches. You can access this view by following the

11 | Allocations Using SAP Cost and Profitability Management

menu path MODEL • ASSIGNMENTS • RESPONSIBILITY CENTERS/ACTIVITIES ASSIGNMENT or selecting RESPONSIBILITY CENTERS/ACTIVITIES ASSIGNMENT in the bottom left.

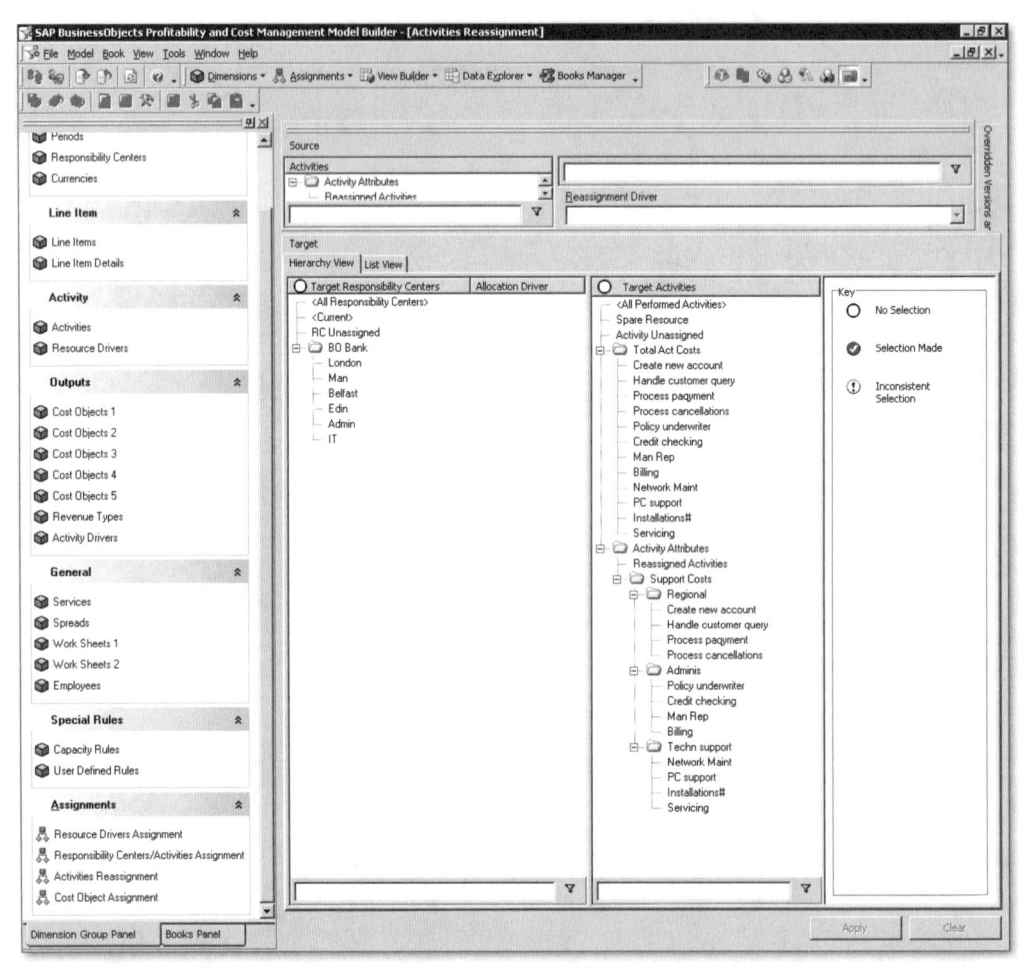

Figure 11.16 Responsibility Center Assignment in SAP BusinessObjects PCM

Finally the activities have to be assigned to cost objects, as shown in Figure 11.17. You can access this view by following the menu path MODEL • ASSIGNMENTS • COST OBJECT ASSIGNMENT or selecting COST OBJECT ASSIGNMENT in the bottom left. This assignment will behave much like the assessment cycles we looked at in Chapter 7, Section 7.1.4, with all costs being assigned to each activity and then charged to all cost objects. You can be much more sophisticated in SAP BusinessObjects PCM and use the rules editor to build a template that provides options closer to those we discussed earlier when talking about building up templates in SAP ERP.

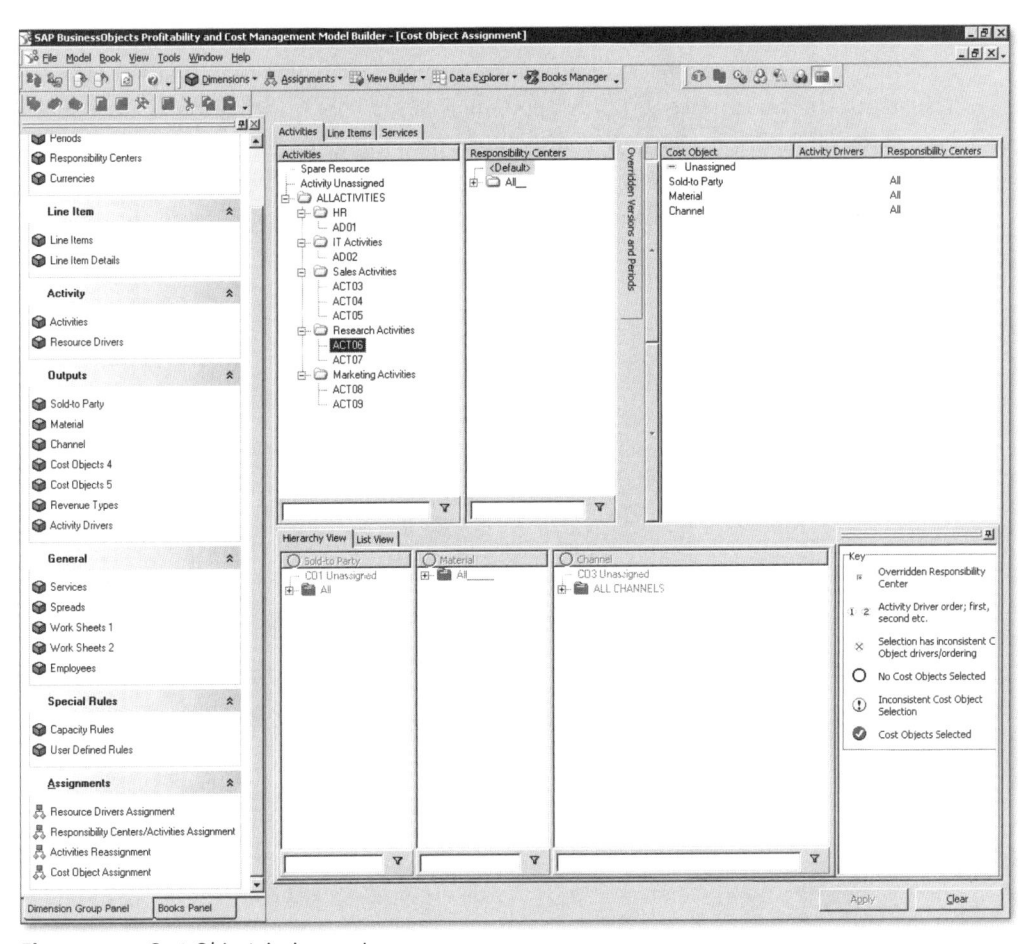

Figure 11.17 Cost Object Assignment

11.2.4 Loading Data to the Model

Once we've built our dimensions and established the links between them, we've effectively built the master data for our costing model. The next step is to load data to the model and run the allocations. To understand what's required in this step, take a look at Figure 11.18, which provides an overview of the SAP Business-Objects PCM architecture. In the bottom of the figure you'll see the various options for bringing data out of SAP ERP or a data warehouse. For the data we've been looking at, the first decision to make is whether you're going to load data from the CO tables in SAP ERP or via an SAP NetWeaver BW query. As we mentioned earlier, SAP BusinessObjects PCM has its own data bridge to pull data out of these systems, or you can use SAP BusinessObjects Financial Information Management to extract the relevant data. Once the data is loaded, the data calculated can then be extracted to the reporting tool of your choice for analysis. This can mean extracting the results back to SAP NetWeaver BW, but there are several other options, as Figure 11.18 illustrates.

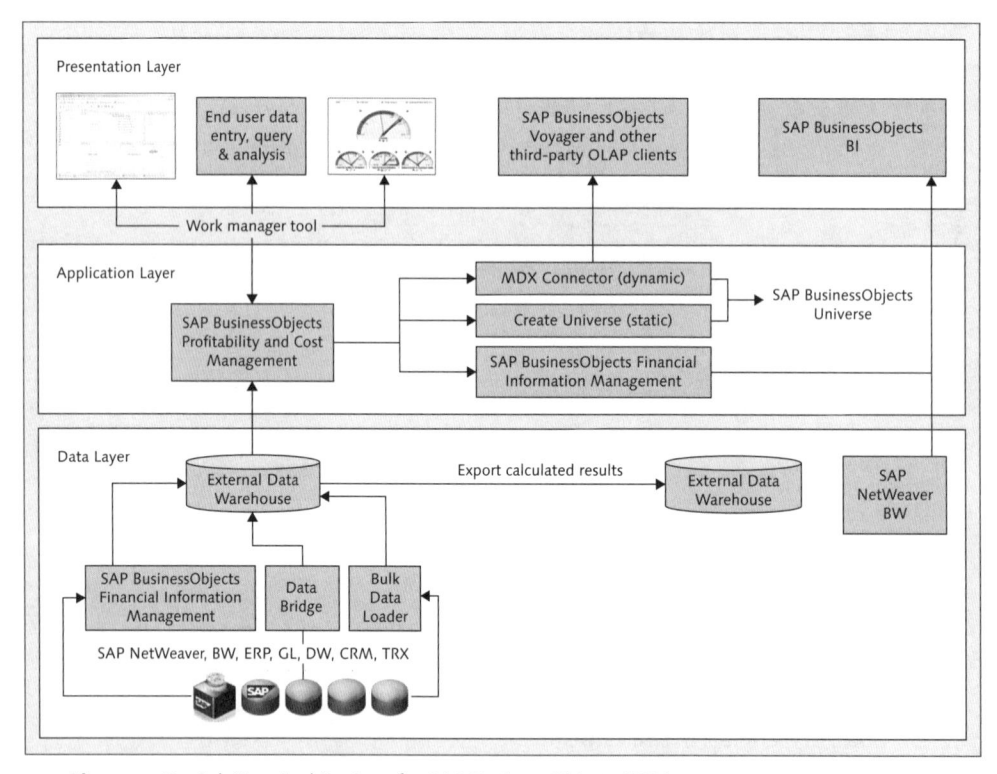

Figure 11.18 Solution Architecture for SAP BusinessObjects PCM

To explain exactly how this load process works is beyond the scope of this book, since there are many options. The important thing at this stage is to understand how the CO component can integrate with SAP BusinessObjects PCM and whether there are benefits for your organization in investigating the solution further. Now that we've looked at how to build models in SAP BusinessObjects PCM, we'll finish by looking at the kind of insights into customer profitability that such calculations can provide.

11.3 Customer Value Analysis Using SAP BusinessObjects PCM

The reason we've looked at how to build a costing model in SAP BusinessObjects PCM is to understand how to extend our understanding of customer profitability in CO-PA with additional information calculated in SAP BusinessObjects PCM. This brings us into the realm of customer value analysis. We'll therefore have a look at some sample dashboards that were built using data determined using SAP BusinessObjects PCM.

When we log on to a dashboard application like the one shown in Figure 11.19, we see the customer situation at the company level. The key performance indicators (KPIs) in the top left of the screen refer to the whole company and indicate that revenue and gross margin are on target and growing, but the net margin is below target. The other areas of the dashboard explain this situation in more detail, so in the bubble chart in the top right of the screen, we see that net margin varies significantly by customer segment, with print shops being a particular concern. We can investigate this situation further in the chart on the bottom left and the heat map on the bottom right of the screen.

Faced with this type of problem, the controller analyzes the customer segment in more detail, by selecting the CUSTOMER SEGMENT tab. In Figure 11.20 we see more details on the situation for the commercial segment. The whale curve on the right ranks customers by cumulative profitability, showing the customers on the left that create profit and those on the extreme right that are unprofitable. The dashboard in the bottom right allows you to view the two extremes of that whale curve and select either the top 10 or the bottom 10 customers in the segment. In this kind of analysis, you'll be looking at the discounts enjoyed by your less profitable customers and their cost to serve. Often a high cost to serve is the result of a disproportionally high use of activities such as technical support or expensive delivery processes.

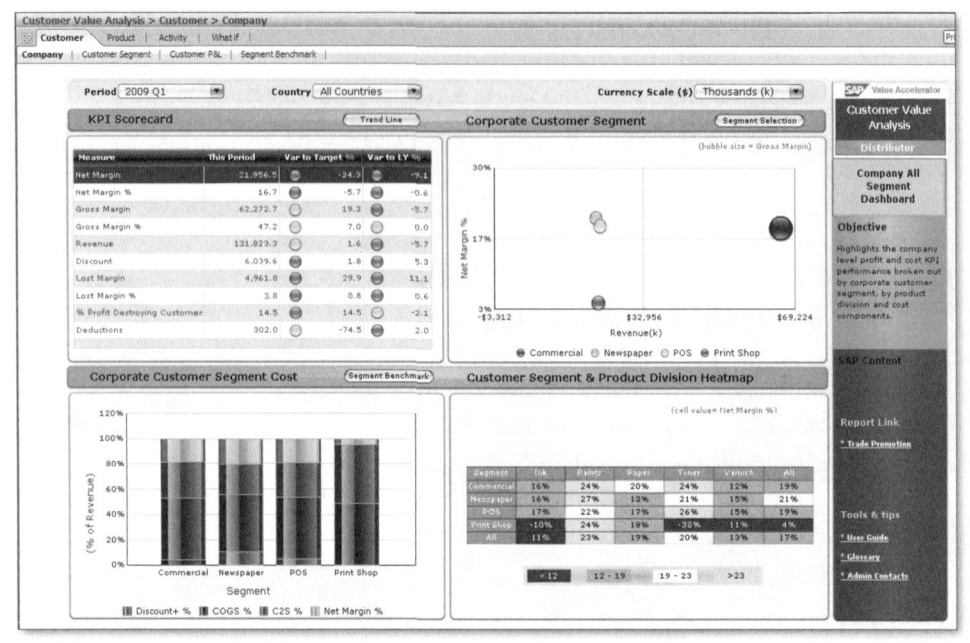

11 | Allocations Using SAP Cost and Profitability Management

Figure 11.19 Sample Scorecard for Customer Profitability for Company

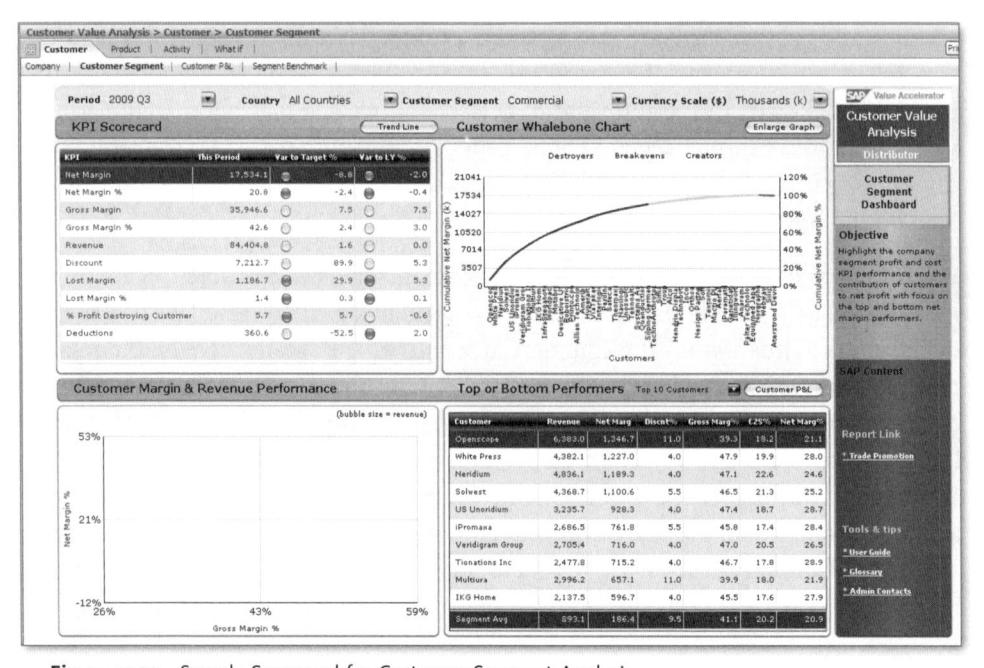

Figure 11.20 Sample Scorecard for Customer Segment Analysis

Finally to display a tabular illustration of the same results, select the CUSTOMER P&L tab, as shown in Figure 11.21. The focus here is on exactly those problematic activities—the costs incurred for activities such as distribution, order processing, marketing campaigns, and so on.

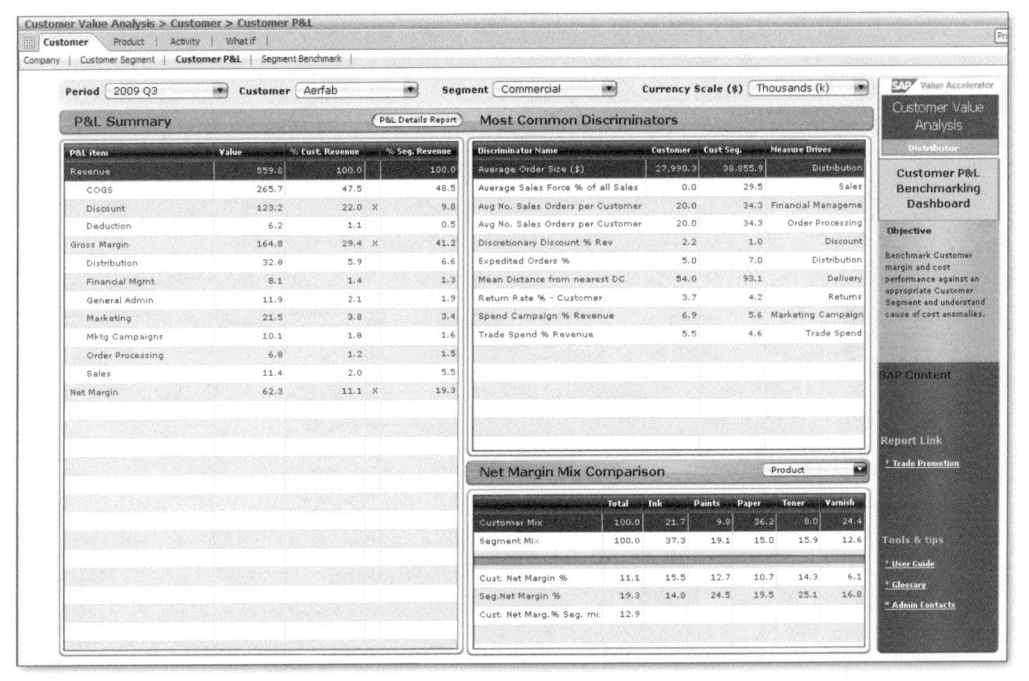

Figure 11.21 Sample Customer Profit and Loss Statement

This example is simply an illustration of the kind of analysis an activity-based model can enable, but it should help you decide whether you want to embark on such a journey or not.

11.4 Summary

In this chapter we looked at how to use template allocation to include the costs of certain business processes in our product costs and profitability analysis and how to use SAP BusinessObjects PCM to build an alternative costing model that extends what you already have in SAP ERP to include other activities and cost drivers. We then looked at the type of insights into customer profitability that such allocations can enable. While such profitability calculations can be performed at any time, the availability of the relevant data means that they are typically part of the period close process. In the next chapter we'll therefore look at how to organize and automate your close process to free up more time for cost analysis and simulation, allowing you to act on the insights the costing model has provided.

This chapter picks up where Chapter 7 left off and looks at how to organize, schedule, and monitor the steps of the period close. It shows you how to handle the huge volumes of data in a real period close and perform a close across multiple systems.

12 Period Close Using SAP Financial Closing Cockpit

When we looked at the details of the period close in Chapter 7, we focused on what was happening in the individual close steps, rather than on how to optimize the close as a whole. The most obvious difference between a real-life close and what we described in Chapter 7 was that in Section 7.2 we looked at individual production orders and product cost collectors and ignored the options for *collective processing*. Only when you're testing will you calculate work in process or variances for an individual production order and then settle the order. In the real world, you'll use collective processing for all the steps in Section 7.2 to make sure that all relevant orders were selected and that all the steps were completed successfully. In this chapter we'll focus on the close as a whole and how to perform the tasks to make the best use of system resources because of the volumes of data to be processed.

If you skip through the various sections of Chapter 7, you'll get a sense of the flow of a close. We discussed the importance of not running the allocation cycles until you're sure that all the data from payroll, billing, and asset accounting is available. This represents a *dependency* between closing steps. There are many examples of dependencies in Chapter 7, where one closing step builds on the result of a previous step.

- You can only run periodic revaluation in CO-PA when you've completed the revaluation of consumption step in the Material Ledger to calculate the actual costs for the finished materials whose sales were captured in CO-PA.
- You can only settle your production orders when you've finished calculating work in process, scrap, and variances for each of the orders.

The individual menus give a sense of this flow simply by the sequence in which they present the tasks, but you'll inevitably find yourself hopping between menus. Internal orders are a good example of where the menu is of only limited help.

- Internal orders that belong to their parent cost centers must first be settled to the cost centers before you can allocate the cost center expenses and calculate activity prices.
- Once you've calculated the actual activity prices, you have to assign the new activity prices to a different set of orders (perhaps for research and development or investment) before settling these orders.

As you draw up your list of steps for the close, it's a good idea to look at the groupings you'll use for selection. You might want to refer back to Chapter 3, where we looked at how to define order groups and selection variants to make sure that your objects are grouped in suitable blocks for processing. Refer back to the settings shown in Figure 3.11 to remind yourself which selection parameters are available for use in closing.

12.1 New Options for Accelerating the Period Close

Fortunately the first solutions to help you manage the closing process have been available since Release 4.6C. The menu screenshots throughout Chapter 7 show the Schedule Manager as the first step of the period-end closing menus for Cost Center Accounting, Internal Orders, Cost Object Controlling, and so on. The Schedule Manager is a generic tool that allows you to list your closing tasks, assign task owners, prepare a schedule for the tasks, and then execute each task in the correct sequence. We also saw the Schedule Manager in the planning menus in Chapter 5. You can use the mechanisms we describe for the period closing tasks to execute the plan allocations and plan settlements in exactly the same way.

The release of SAP ERP 5.0 coincided with demands from the Securities and Exchange Commission (SEC) for faster reporting. SAP's response was the Closing Cockpit. This uses much of the same coding as had been used in the Schedule Manager but allows you to visualize the individual controlling areas and company codes participating in the close, flag closing tasks by *closing type* (month-end close, year-end close, and so on), and define *dependencies* between tasks. To access the Closing Cockpit, select Transaction CLOCOC or ACCOUNTING • FINANCIAL ACCOUNTING • GENERAL LEDGER • PERIODIC PROCESSING • CLOSING • CLOSING COCKPIT (MANAGE

TEMPLATES AND TASK LISTS). Don't be misled by the fact that the Closing Cockpit is offered in the GENERAL LEDGER menu. The idea is that it should cover tasks that cross the whole of SAP ERP Financials, including the Controlling component (CO). Since the initial release of the Closing Cockpit coincided with the introduction of the SAP General Ledger, some people assume that they cannot use the Closing Cockpit in combination with the classic General Ledger, but this is not true. When you build up your templates, you simply have to make sure that you include the correct transactions for whichever general ledger you are using.

> **Moving from Schedule Manager to Closing Cockpit**
>
> If you've already started using the Schedule Manager but are now on SAP ERP 5.0 or later, you can import your lists from one environment to the other by selecting TEMPLATE/TASK LIST • IMPORT TEMPLATE FROM SCHEDULE MANAGER. This also means you can start building task lists in Schedule Manager now and move them to the Closing Cockpit without problems when you upgrade.

The SAP Financial Closing Cockpit was released with SAP enhancement package 3 for SAP ERP 6.0 and was further enhanced in enhancement packages 4 and 5. In this release the name of the product was changed from Closing Cockpit to SAP Financial Closing cockpit, though menus and system documentation still refer to the Closing Cockpit. You can activate the enhancements using the business functions FIN_ACC_LOCAL_CLOSE in enhancement package 3, FIN_REP_SIMPL_2 in enhancement package 4 and FIN_ACC_LOCAL_CLOSE_2 in enhancement package 5. Before we discuss the details of these product iterations, let's look at what these solutions have in common, namely, the orchestration and automation the close tasks.

The first step in accelerating your period close is to draw up a list of the period closing steps that you already perform. Let's use the tasks we discussed in Chapter 7 as a starting point (the numbers refer to the chapter sections).

Close Transactions in Controlling
7.1.3: Assessment cycles (KSU5)
7.1.3: Distribution cycles (KSV5)
7.1.3: Reposting cycles (KSW5)
7.1.3: Indirect activity cycles (KSC5)

> **Close Transactions in Controlling**
>
> 7.1.4: Assessment cycles to CO-PA (KEU5)
>
> 7.1.5: Activity price calculation (KSII)
>
> 7.2.1: Revaluation at actual prices (CON2)
>
> 7.2.1: Overhead calculation (KGI2 or CO43)
>
> 7.2.2: WIP calculation (KKAS, KKAX, or KKAO)
>
> 7.2.3: Variance calculation (KKS6, KKS2, or KKS1)
>
> 7.2.4: Settlement (KK87, KO88, or CO88)
>
> 7.3.2: Periodic costing run (CKMLCP)
>
> 7.3.3: Alternative valuation run (CKMLCPAVR)
>
> 7.4.1: Periodic revaluation (KE27)
>
> 7.4.2: Top-down distribution (KE28)

> **Other Tasks in the Close**
>
> When you think of closing tasks, you tend to think of tasks that have to be executed to create the necessary postings before you close the books. Remember that we discussed scheduling Report Writer reports in the background and preparing extracts in Chapter 8, Section 8.1. Don't forget to add these tasks to your list if you have not removed all your reporting to SAP NetWeaver BW.

In a new implementation people typically keep a list like this with notes about task dependencies in a spreadsheet and check them off when they complete each task, making notes about any issues they encounter.

12.1.1 Orchestrating Your Closing Tasks

Figure 12.1 shows the same list of transactions as a list in the SAP FINANCIAL CLOSING COCKPIT, with folders that correspond to the sections to make it easier for you to refer back to Chapter 7 for details of what happens in each step. To create a new template, select Transaction CLOCOC or ACCOUNTING • FINANCIAL ACCOUNTING • GENERAL LEDGER • PERIODIC PROCESSING • CLOSING • CLOSING COCKPIT (MANAGE TEMPLATES AND TASK LISTS), switch to CHANGE mode, and select TEMPLATE/TASK LIST • CREATE TEMPLATE. For this example, choose the organizational hierarchy

CONTROLLING AREA. Since all close tasks in CO are performed either with reference to the controlling area or with reference to the plant(s), we've left out the other organizational units. This makes the entries in the Closing Cockpit look the same as in the Schedule Manager. We'll come back to how to add other organizational units in Section 12.1.8.

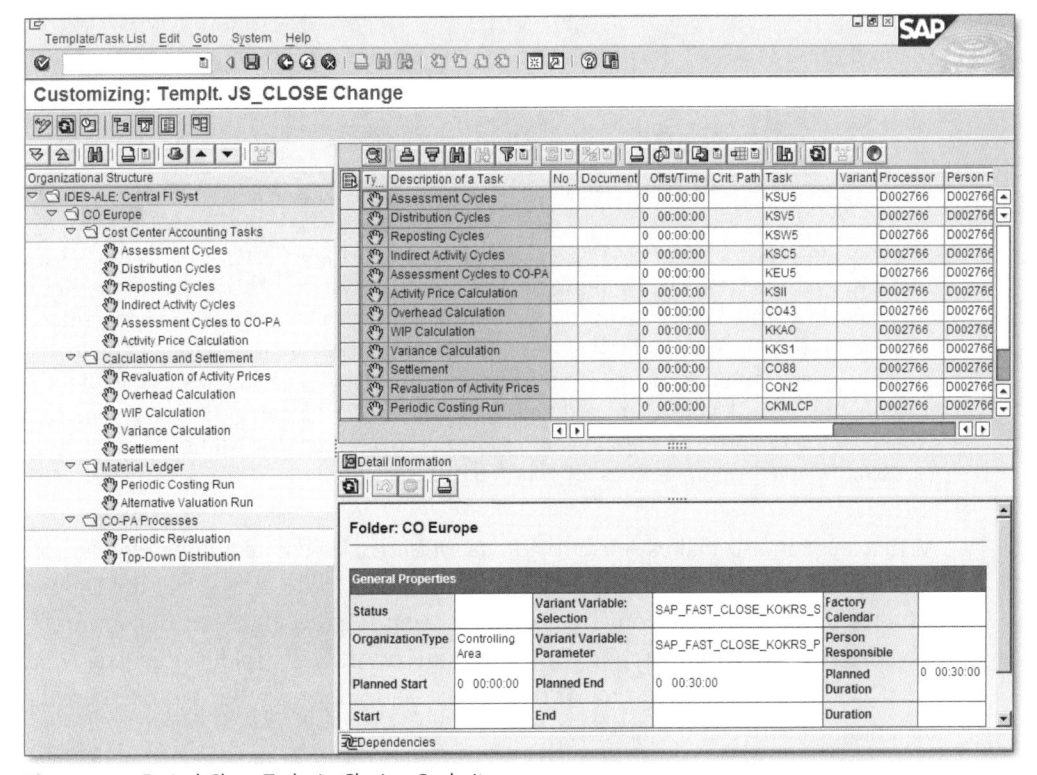

Figure 12.1 Period Close Tasks in Closing Cockpit

To add transactions to the list, right-click on the tree on the left, select ADD TASK, and create a task for each of the transactions in the list. You can structure this list by adding folders for each section by right-clicking and selecting CREATE FOLDER. You can cut and paste folders to move tasks around in the list until you're happy with the sequence.

Once you have the list in place, consider adding any other information that you've collected over the last few months. In the list on the right of the screen, you'll see two columns: NOTES and DOCUMENTS.

- To add a note as a reminder, right-click on the task and select CREATE NOTE. This is a good way of including quick tips and simple instructions in your template.
- To add a Microsoft document to explain a closing step in more detail, right-click on the task and select CREATE OFFICE DOCUMENT. You can then upload your chosen document from the server. This is a good way of providing more sophisticated job aids to guide users and explain possible pitfalls with screenshots.

Keeping these kinds of documents up to date can be a great way of ensuring that what you're learning is available to everyone who participates in the close and help other people take over your tasks if you're unavailable at any time.

> **Where to Maintain Templates**
>
> As you can see from Figure 12.1, the template settings are Customizing settings by default, which means you can transport them between systems. This is fine if you want to maintain a central template in your Customizing client and then transport it into your productive system. Many controllers feel that this will make them overly reliant on their IT department for quick changes to the template. If you want to take ownership of the closing process, ask your IT department to implement SAP Note 1179482 so you can maintain the template settings in your productive system. Implementing this note will switch off the transport settings for your templates.

At this stage it also makes sense to add *dependencies*. To create a dependency, you need to link the successor task with its predecessor. To do this, select the DEPENDENCIES block at the bottom right of the screen (Figure 12.2). In our example, the periodic revaluation step in the PROFITABILITY ANALYSIS folder uses data from the periodic costing run in the MATERIAL LEDGER folder (in other words, there's a dependency between the tasks).

1. Click on the PERIODIC REVALUATION step (the successor) to move it into the DEPENDENCIES part of the screen (lower right).
2. Mark the predecessor (PERIODIC COSTING RUN) on the left-hand part of the screen.
3. Go back to the DEPENDENCIES block, right-click on the follow-up task (periodic valuation), and select CREATE DEPENDENCY. The system will then show this dependency as a task hierarchy (see Figure 12.2).
4. Continue like this, working from the back of the close to the front until you've identified all dependent tasks.

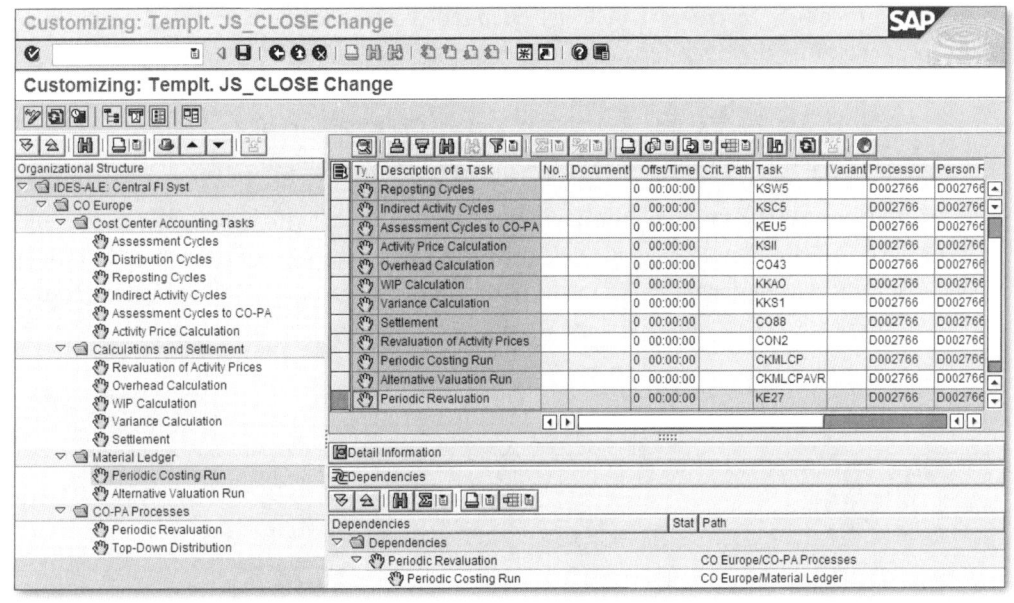

Figure 12.2 Maintaining Dependencies in the Closing Cockpit

Maintaining Dependencies

It makes sense to think about dependencies immediately since they're important to your understanding of the close as a whole. However, until SAP enhancement package 5 for SAP ERP 6.0 the system only checked dependencies between jobs (programs with variants) prior to scheduling. Defining dependencies between other types of tasks merely serves as a reminder. In the latest release, the system checks all dependencies and issues a message if the predecessor does not have the correct status when the next task is started.

12.1.2 Executing Your Close Tasks

It's not yet possible to execute the transactions shown above. To do this, we must first create a *task list* from our template by selecting TEMPLATE/TASK LIST • CREATE PERIODIC TASK LIST. Then enter the key date, the period, and the fiscal year for that close in the task list header (see Figure 12.3). This will result in the creation of a task list with reference to your template for the next period close. When you're ready to start the closing activities, switch the status from Not Released to Released.

The procedure to create a task list changed in enhancement package 5 to allow organizations to separate the task of maintaining templates (generally the job of a select group of power users) from the task of creating a task list (usually more widely used). There's now a new transaction, CLOCOT for the creation of task lists. This transaction calls up the same pop-up as we see in Figure 12.3.

SCHEDULE MANAGER does not have templates with separate task lists. To schedule a task in Schedule Manager, click on the task and move it into the appropriate slot on the calendar view. You can then monitor its progress by navigating to the Monitor.

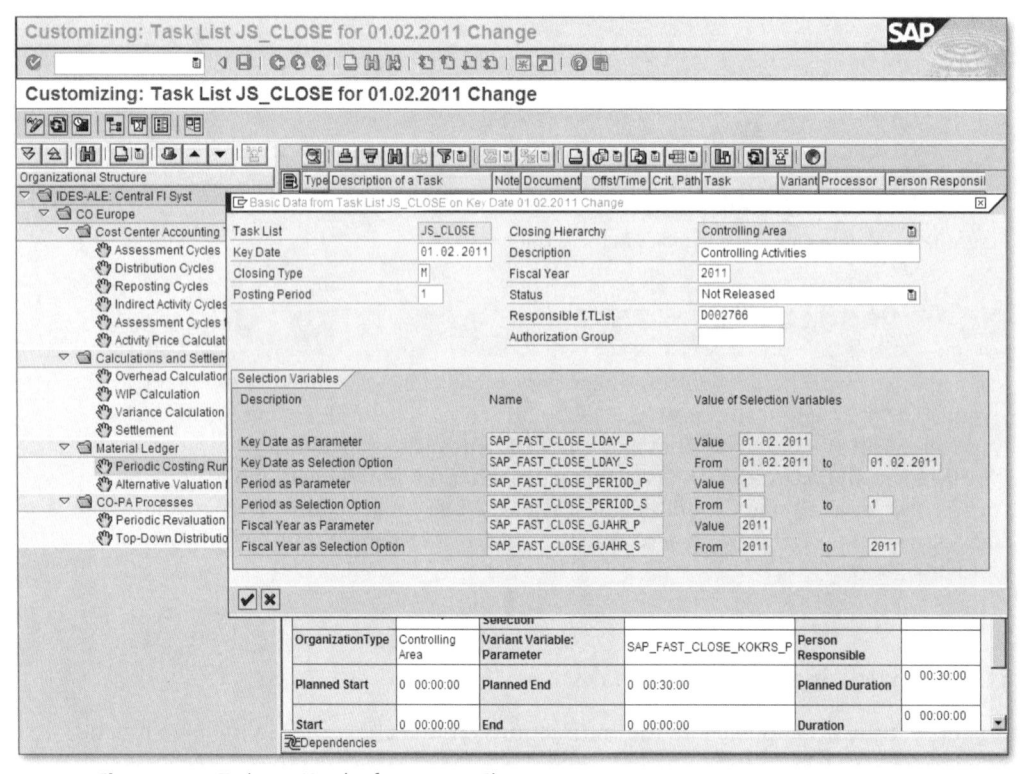

Figure 12.3 Task List Header for January Close

Once we've released the task list, we can perform any of the tasks by right-clicking on the task in the right-hand part of the screen (Figure 12.4) and selecting EXECUTE TRANSACTION. The documentation we added to the template is available to support us in performing the steps. We can also add additional documentation about events encountered during the close by selecting CREATE OFFICE DOCUMENT. If you look at the ASSESSMENT CYCLES task in Figure 12.4, you'll see that an office document has been uploaded for this task. You can update status information for each task by switching the STATUS field from NO STATUS to ENDED when you've successfully run the transaction. In so doing, you've effectively moved your spreadsheet and associated checklist online.

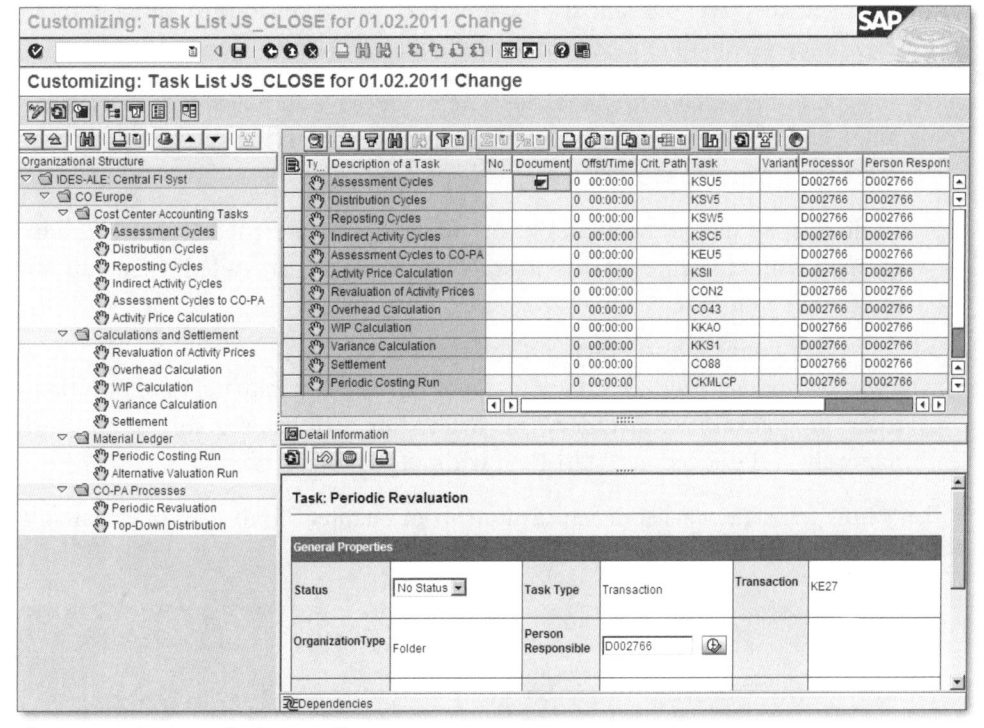

Figure 12.4 Task List for January Close

When a couple of successful closes start to make you feel comfortable with your template, you're ready to make the move from running these transactions online to automating them. When working with the closing steps, you may have noticed that there's always an option of background processing that allows you to schedule the job to run at some time in the future, ideally when system load is low. You can continue to call up each step and schedule each one in turn, but there's a more elegant way to do this, which is to enter the offset for each task (in other words, how many days before or after the key date of the close it should start) and the start time for each task. The system can then use this schedule to start the assessment cycles task at 8 am on Day 1, the distribution cycles task at 9 am on Day 1, and so on through the close.

12.1.3 Automating Closing Transactions

To allow the close steps to start at the scheduled time, you need to go back to your template (Figure 12.1) and enter a start time for each of the steps in turn (hopefully you've been keeping notes about how long each one takes to run). Initially these times will merely serve as a reminder of when each action is due.

To automate the execution of the close step, you have to make sure that all the parameters that you've entered manually until now are in the system when your close step is scheduled to run.

- To do this, exchange the names of the transactions (designed to run with you present) with the names of the *executable programs* that are called when you run the transaction.
- To replace your manual entry of the fiscal period, fiscal year, controlling area, and so on, enter a *program variant* that will store these parameters and pass them to the program as it's scheduled. This will ensure that the program can run automatically at the scheduled start time without you being present.

Let's now translate our list of transactions from Chapter 7 into a list of executable programs.

Close Programs in Controlling
7.1.3: Assessment cycles (RKGALKSU5)
7.1.3: Distribution cycles (RKGALKSV5)
7.1.3: Reposting cycles (RKGALKSW5)
7.1.3: Indirect activity cycles (RKGALKSC5)
7.1.4: Assessment cycles to CO-PA (RKGALKEU5)
7.1.5: Activity price calculation (RKSPI_KSII)
7.2.1: Revaluation at actual prices (RKAZCON2)
7.2.1: Overhead calculation (RKAZCO43)
7.2.2: WIP calculation (SAPKKA07WL)

New Options for Accelerating the Period Close | **12.1**

Close Programs in Controlling

7.2.3: Variance calculation (RKKKSWL0)

7.2.4: Settlement (RK07COWLCO88)

7.3.2: Periodic costing run – separate programs for each step:

7.3.3: Alternative valuation run (AVR) – separate programs for each step:

7.4.1: Periodic revaluation (RKEBPBATCHGIPB)

7.4.2: Top-down distribution (RKEBPBATCHGITD)

To switch the first task in your list from transaction to program, return to the template (Transaction CLOCOC) switch to CHANGE mode, right-click on the task, and select EDIT TASK, as shown in Figure 12.5. Since the assessment cycle is usually one of the first tasks of the close, we've scheduled it to run at 8:00 am on the first day of the close. When we schedule the tasks, the offset of one day will be used to set the task start time as 8.00 am on the key date (entered in Figure 12.3) plus one day.

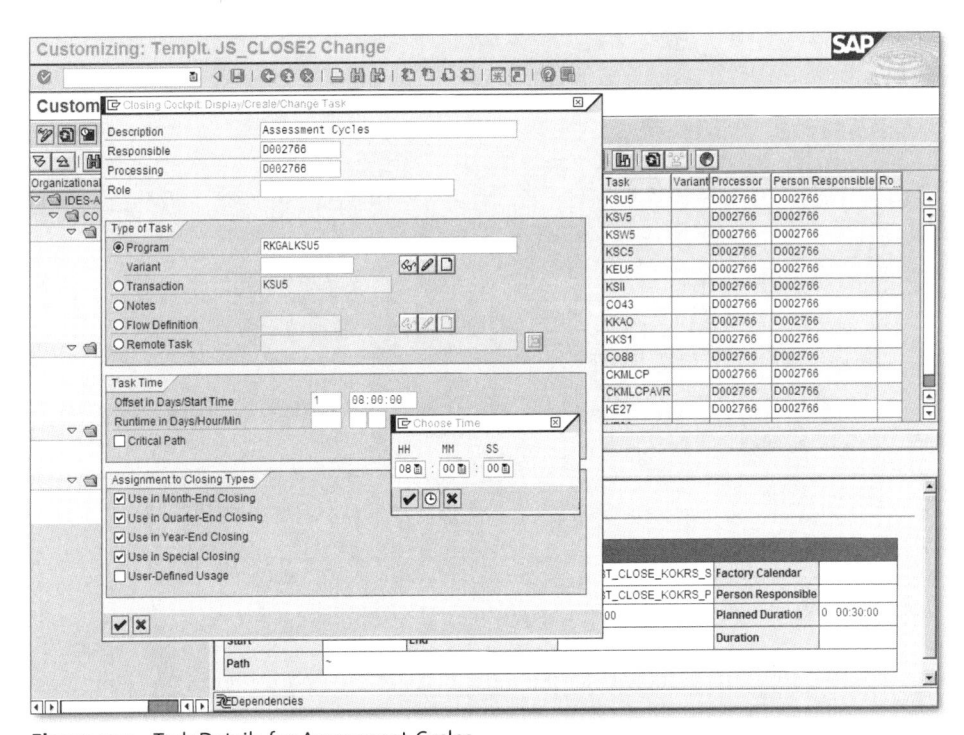

Figure 12.5 Task Details for Assessment Cycles

537

You can cross-check your list and add any programs you might be missing by selecting Transaction CLOCOC and GOTO • REGISTER PROGRAM FOR CLOSING COCKPIT. If you're working with the Schedule Manager, select Transaction SCMA (SCHEDULE MANAGER) and ENVIRONMENT • CLOSING SCMAPROGRAMS instead.

> **Including your own ABAP Reports in the Template**
>
> If your organization has written its own ABAP reports for some tasks in the close, you can manually add these tasks to the list. To make sure that such programs will be able to send status information back to the Closing Cockpit or Schedule Manager to confirm that they've been properly completed, have your IT department implement the code described in SAP Note 325118 for each of these reports.

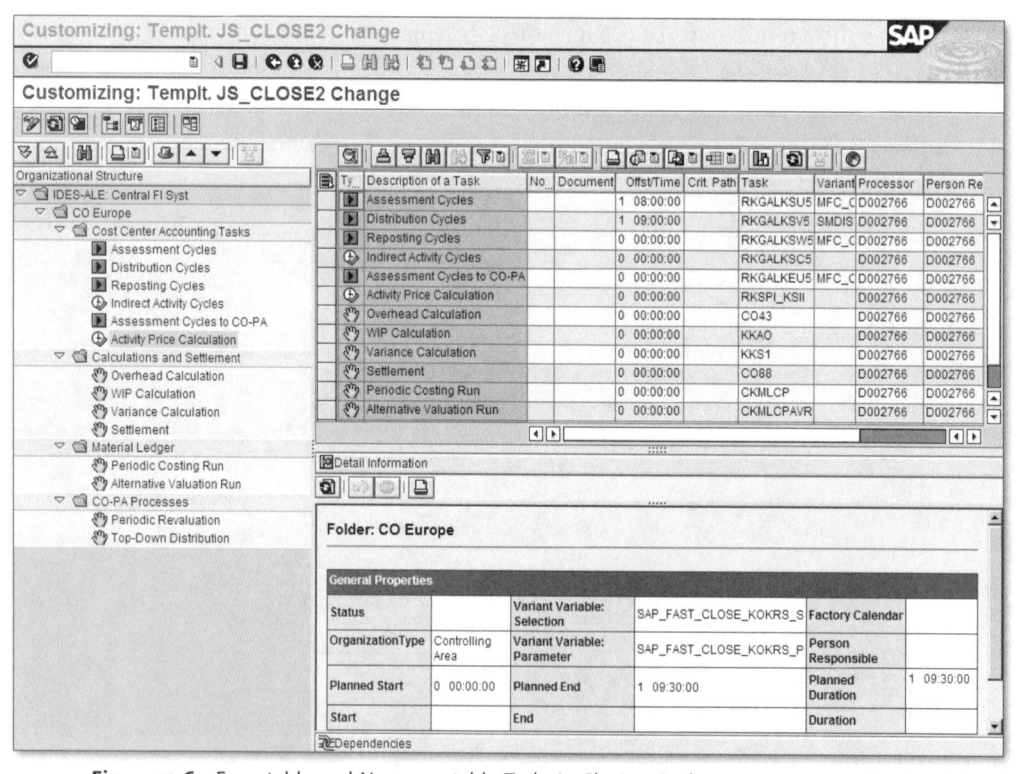

Figure 12.6 Executable and Nonexecutable Tasks in Closing Cockpit

Figure 12.6 shows the result of changing the tasks in the first folder of our template. We've replaced the transaction codes with the programs for executing the close in all six tasks. However, we've only maintained variants for four of the tasks. The system shows that these four tasks are executable (in other words, they have all the parameters they need to start immediately), whereas the other two tasks need the user to enter the parameters to be able to start. To completely automate the close, we need to create program variants for all the tasks, so let's have a look at how to maintain these program variants.

> **Responsibility for Program Variants**
>
> In some organizations, the IT department is responsible for maintaining program variants, while in others the controlling department is allowed to create variants. Let's assume that you'll work with the IT department to complete the next section.

12.1.4 Creating Program Variants for Your Close Tasks

To maintain variants, for each of the above programs, select Transaction SE38 or TOOLS • ABAP WORKBENCH • DEVELOPMENT • ABAP EDITOR. Enter the name of the relevant program (see list above) and select GOTO • VARIANTS, as shown in Figure 12.7.

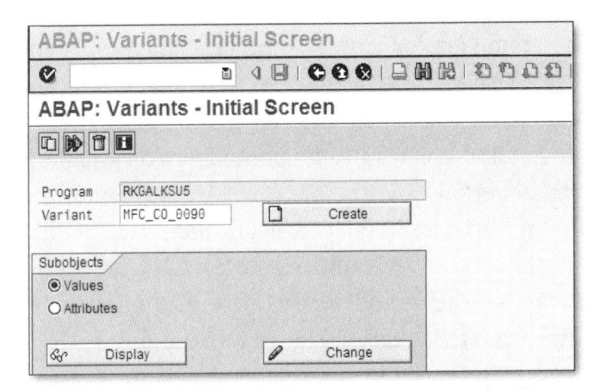

Figure 12.7 Program Variant for Assessment Cycles (Program RKGALKSU5)

To create a new variant for the program, click on CREATE. If a variant already exists (you'll see it in the F4 help on the VARIANT field), select VALUES and click on the CHANGE button. Figure 12.8 shows the selection parameters needed to execute an assessment cycle. Most of the parameters can be set once and will not change from close to close. Be sure to enter the cycle or cycles that you want to execute by clicking on the ENTER CYCLES button, or nothing will happen when you schedule the closing task.

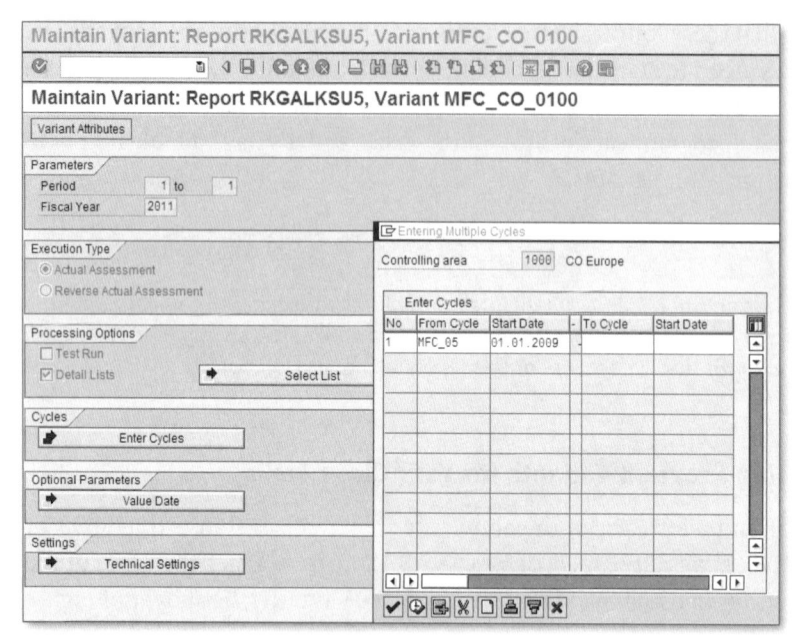

Figure 12.8 Variant for an Assessment Cycle

Once you've entered all the fixed parameters for your closing task, the next step is to ensure that the period and fiscal year don't have to be set manually, but can be passed from the task list header when you schedule each closing task. If you refer back to Figure 12.3, you'll see that the task list header contains two variables, SAP_FAST_CLOSE_PERIOD_P for the fiscal period and SAP_FAST_CLOSE_GJAHR_P for the fiscal year. To link the variants with the variables in the task list header, click on the ATTRIBUTES button in Figure 12.7 or the VARIANT ATTRIBUTES button in Figure 12.8. This will allow you to have the system set the period and fiscal year automatically based on the settings in the task list header (January 2011, in our example).

To have the system set the fiscal year and fiscal period during the close, enter "T" in the SELECTION VARIABLE column (see Figure 12.9) and then make the following links using the F4 help.

If you're using the Closing Cockpit, enter these parameters.

- FROM_P – SAP_FAST_CLOSE_PERIOD_P
- TO_P – SAP_FAST_CLOSE_PERIOD_P
- GJAHR – SAP_FAST_CLOSE_GJAHR_P (this is German for fiscal year)

If you're using Schedule Manager, the procedure is similar, but the TVARV variables are not set in the task list header, so it's a good idea to define your own variables just for controlling. Use the following parameters as a reference, but *copy* them under your own naming convention.

- FROM_P – SAP_SCMA_PERIOD
- TO_P – SAP_SCMA_PERIOD
- GJAHR – SAP_FISC_YEAR

To find out more, read the information in SAP Note 502482.

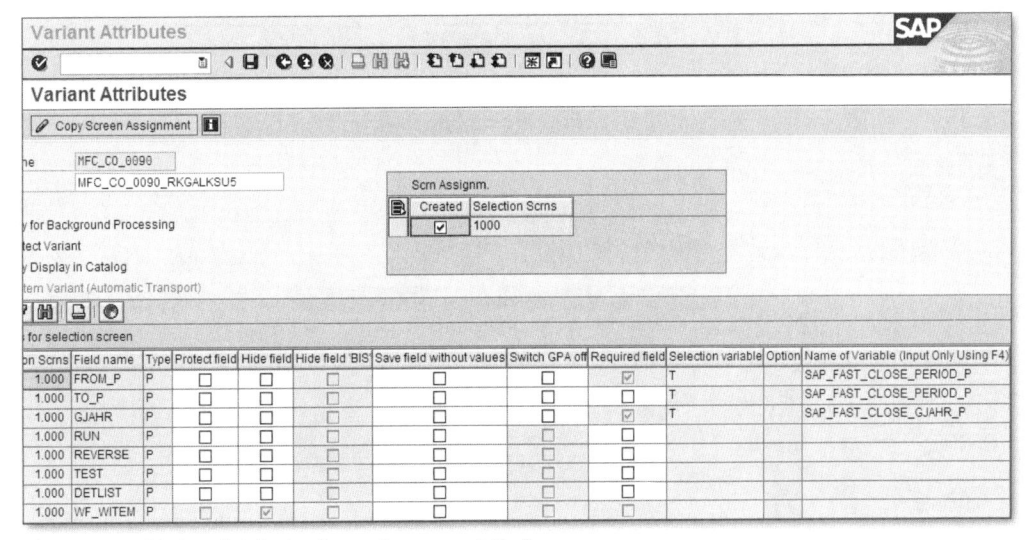

Figure 12.9 Variant Attributes for an Assessment Cycle

12.1.5 Scheduling Tasks

Once you've entered programs and variants for all relevant tasks, you can choose whether you execute each program separately from the SAP Financial Closing Cockpit or establish your closing calendar using the start times in Figure 12.5 and then schedule the whole period close automatically.

- To start the tasks from the task list (see Figure 12.3), select one or more tasks and then select SCHEDULE SELECTED TASKS.
- Since there may be dependencies between some of the tasks, select CHECK START CONDITION for the task before you schedule, if you're in doubt.

As the job completes, it will update status information (completed, completed with errors, and so on) and any logs created to the task list for analysis by the task owner. Figure 12.10 shows the result of completing an assessment cycle. The STATUS of the task is ENDED, the START and END times have been recorded (notice that we were two days and two hours behind schedule) and the SELECTION CRITERIA updated. We'll now look at the information in the LINKS section to display the information the system creates automatically while executing the close task. You might want to refer back to Chapter 7, Section 7.1.3 to compare the results of running the transaction manually with scheduling it to run in the background.

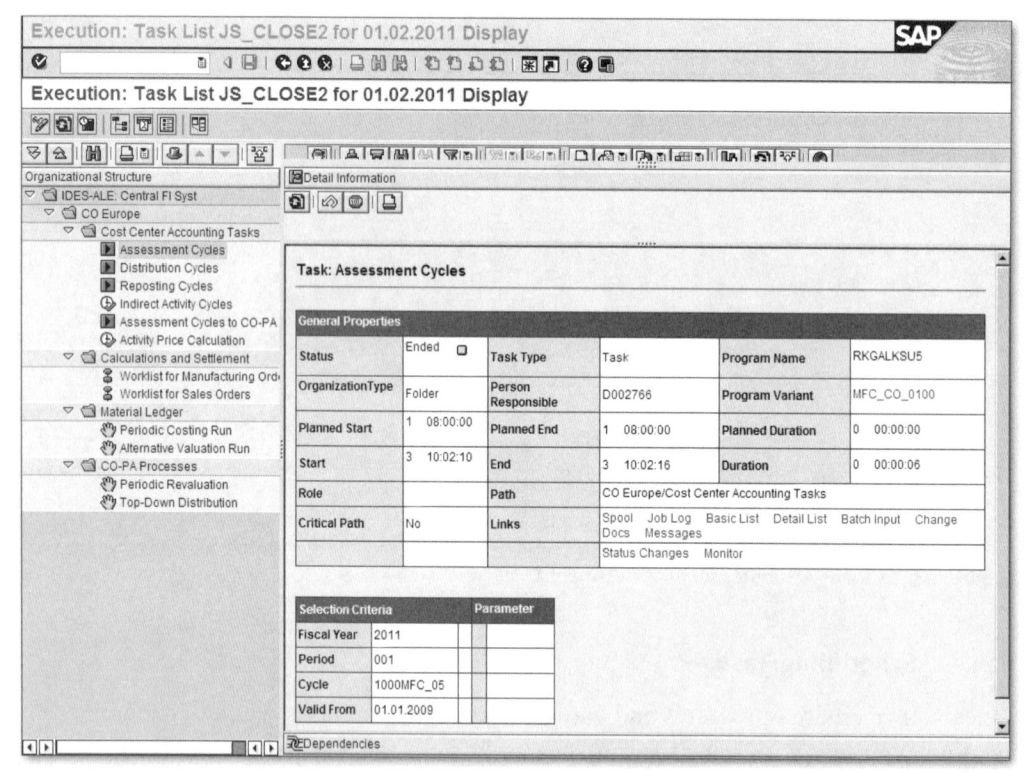

Figure 12.10 Status and Selection Criteria for Completed Close Task

First, let's look at the job log by selecting JOB LOG in the LINKS section of the task details.

New Options for Accelerating the Period Close | **12.1**

Figure 12.11 shows the entries in the job log for the assessment cycle. These are largely technical. The main thing to notice is that although the program name is what we entered for the task (see Figure 12.5), the variant name has been switched to a technical name beginning with T$. This is because we used selection variables of type T for the time variables (see Figure 12.9). The generated program variant replaces the place holders in the variant with the period and the fiscal year from the task list header and with the relevant organizational units (controlling area, company code or plant) from the folders in the template.

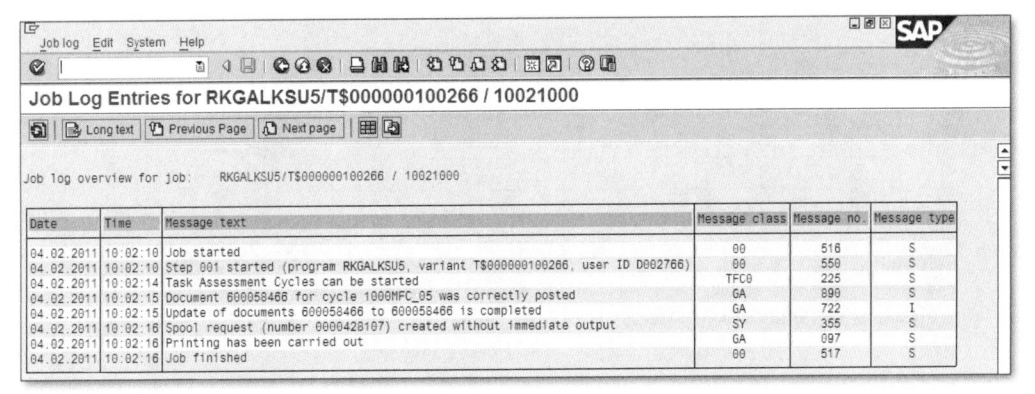

Figure 12.11 Job Log Entries for Assessment Cycle

Caution: Job Logs

The job log is potentially dangerous because error messages from the application will appear as information messages, implying that things went smoothly when you should really be stopping the close and fixing the issues before you move onto the next step.

The spool list will give you a better impression of what happened when the job was processed. To display the spool list, select SPOOL LIST in the LINKS section of the task details. You might want to compare the next two figures with Figures 7.7, 7.8 and 7.9 in Chapter 7.

Figure 12.12 shows the result of executing a single cycle MFC_05 (usually several cycles are scheduled at once). This cycle included one segment (MFC_05_01) with one sender cost center and three receiver cost centers. Scrolling down, Figure 12.13 shows the clearing posting to the sender cost center and the allocation to the receiver cost centers based on the fixed percentages 20, 50, and 30.

543

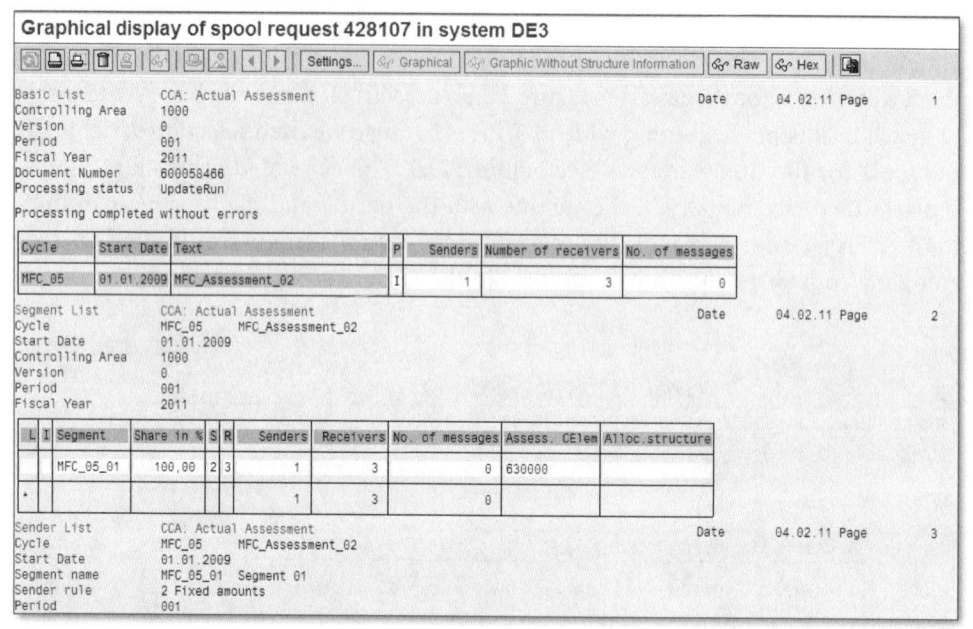

Figure 12.12 Spool List for Assessment Cycle (Pages 1-2)

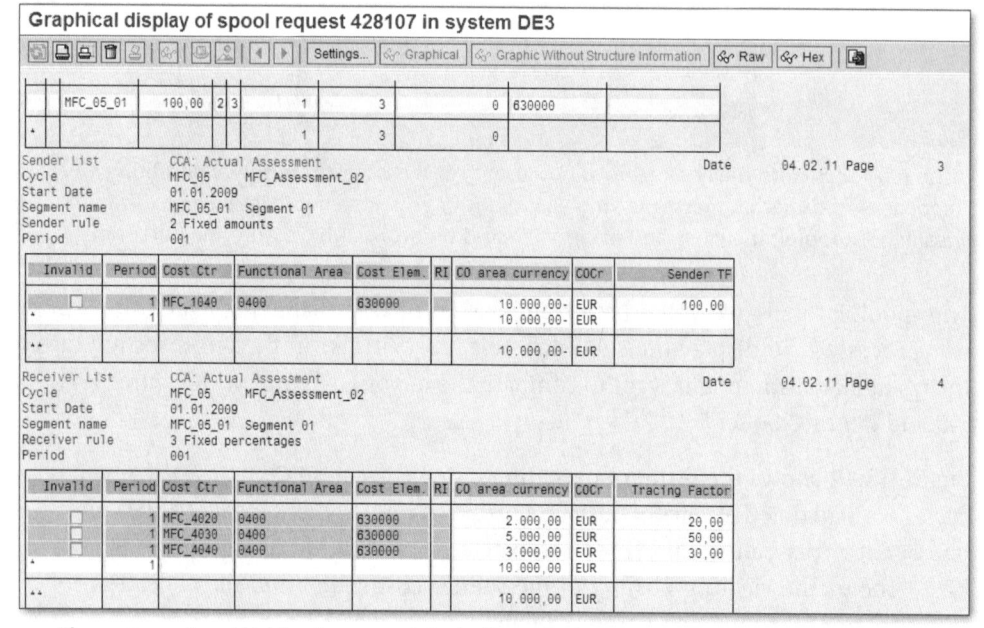

Figure 12.13 Spool List for Assessment Cycle (Pages 3-4)

From SAP enhancement package 5 for SAP ERP 6.0, you can also access the Closing Cockpit Monitor in the LINKS section (see Figure 12.14). Make sure that you check this view for every step. At first glance it looks like it's just repeating information we saw in the previous figures, with the addition of the business transaction (RKIU in this example), but it's here that you'll see whether errors really happened that should be corrected before you start the next step.

> **Schedule Manager Monitor**
>
> You might have wondered why you had to go through all the effort of including the code described in SAP Note 325118 in all your own programs. The reason is that this code updates the Schedule Manager Monitor. It's this monitor that will tell you if errors happened from an application perspective. Any external scheduler (there are several on the market) can only read the job log and the spool list. The real truth of what happened during posting is set by the application and passed to the Monitor using the code described in SAP Note 325118.

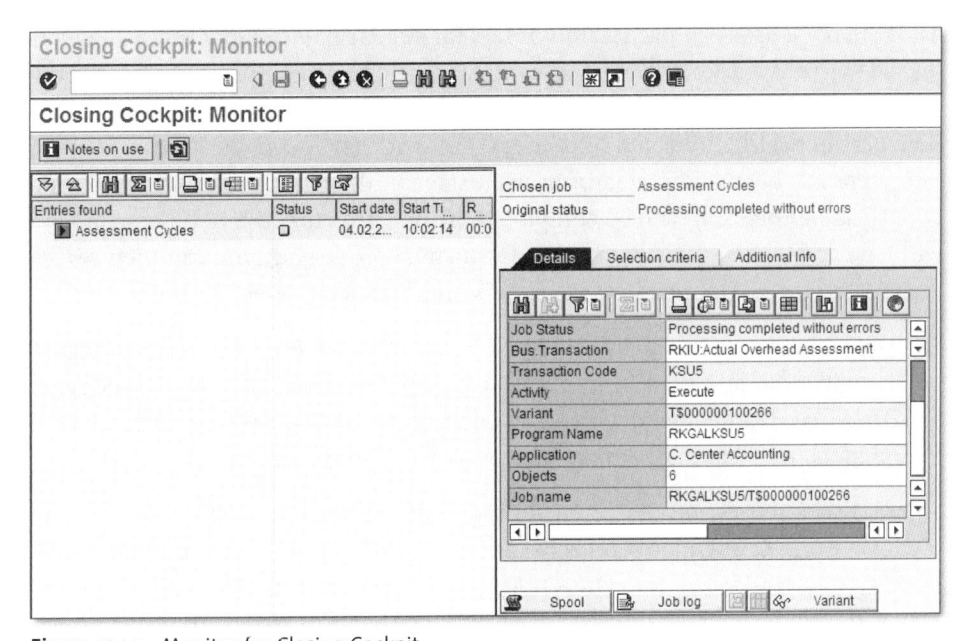

Figure 12.14 Monitor for Closing Cockpit

12.1.6 Using Workflows In the Close

Going back to Figure 12.6, you could carry on and define program variants for each of the closing steps in the calculation and settlement steps. There is, however, a key difference between running an allocation cycle and settling a group of orders. In an allocation cycle, the system works with a group of senders and receivers, typically a large number of cost centers, passing the costs from the senders to the receivers and sometimes back to the senders again, iterating through this cycle until the task is complete. Only when the whole cycle is complete will the cost centers be released and the next task can be performed.

When handling orders, each order is essentially a separate object for which overhead can be calculated, then work in process, then variances, and so on. You'll be able to complete all the tasks for one production order, even though the next might have errors. The only exception to this rule would be the rework orders that we discussed in Chapter 6 that must settle to their parent production order before it can be settled. Out of this basic idea, the concept of a work list was born. A work list is simply a list of all production orders (or similar objects) that the system has selected as relevant for the close, plus the tasks that must be performed for these production orders. In our example the tasks are overhead calculation, WIP calculation, variance calculation, and settlement. The work list documents that each of the four steps has been completed or at what stage in the chain errors occurred. In a typical case, processing will be completed the first time for 95% of orders, and 5% will have to be parked in an error list for manual processing. You can then restart the task for the 5% that had errors, significantly reducing selection time.

To display the workflows delivered by SAP, return to the EDIT TASK screen (Figure 12.5), switch the task type from TRANSACTION or PROGRAM to FLOW DEFINITION, and press [F4]. The delivered workflows begin with 0 or 1 (there are some delivered by the industries that may or may not be active in your system).

Figure 12.15 shows the delivered flow definitions for Cost Center Accounting (CO-OM-CCA), Cost Object Controlling (CO-PC-OBJ), Product Cost planning (CO-PC-PCP), internal orders (CO-OM-OPA), and project systems (PS). For workflows that also include a work list, the WORK LIST checkbox is selected. To display more details of the workflow, select one of the entries.

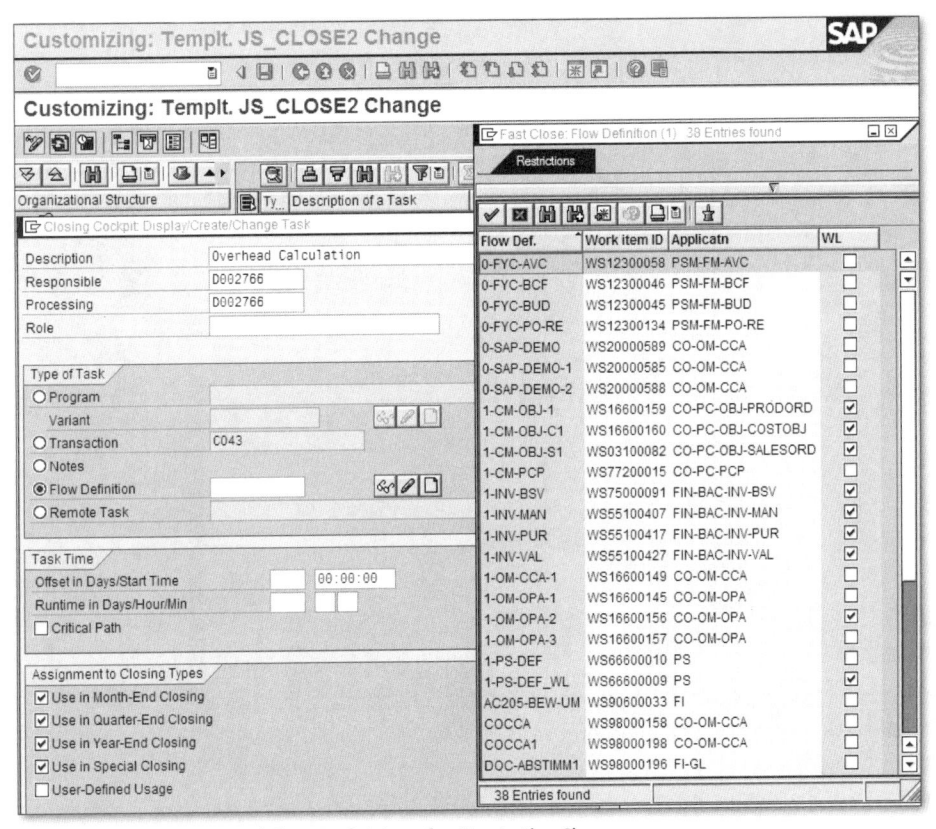

New Options for Accelerating the Period Close | **12.1**

Figure 12.15 Sample Workflow Definitions for Use in the Close

Figure 12.16 shows details of workflow 1-CM-OBJ-1. You could copy this workflow and make minor adjustments, to replace all the steps in the CALCULATIONS AND SETTLEMENT folder. In the first close step, the system selects all production orders that are relevant for processing. This may sound obvious, but without this step, each step would reselect the same group of production orders before processing them. Selecting the orders once and then passing the results to the next step saves time in the close, because only production orders that have successfully completed each step will be passed on to the next step.

547

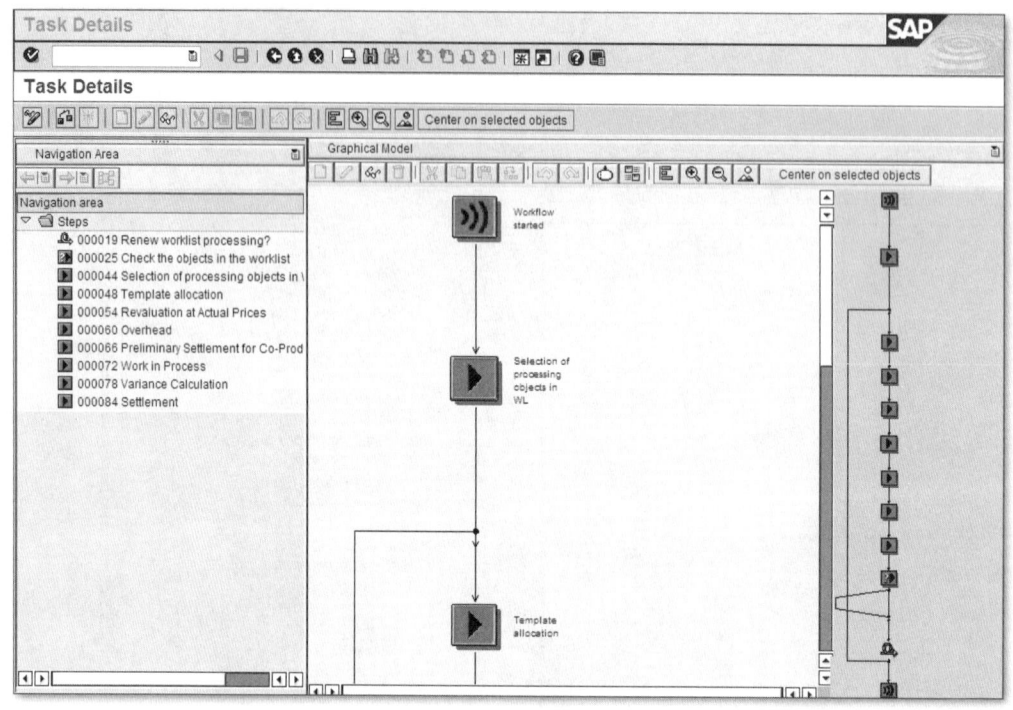

Figure 12.16 Work List for Production Orders

Figure 12.17 shows the key step in this workflow, where the relevant production orders are selected using the program variant entered and stored as a work list. To make sure that you can use the workflow in each step, click on the tasks shown in Figure 12.16. Once you're in the detail screen, check the program variant (see Section 12.1.4). You should also decide who should be informed about errors (usually it's the user who scheduled the workflow, but you can use the full workflow functions if you want to be more sophisticated in your choice of processor) and how authority checks will be handled. Continue in this way, checking the parameters for all the relevant steps in the workflow.

We discussed template allocation in Chapter 11. Whether we need the template allocation step will depend on whether we're running Activity-Based Costing in SAP ERP. Similarly, whether we need the preliminary settlement of co-products and rework step will depend on whether we have co-products or orders with rework (see Chapter 6). Assuming we choose *not* to use either step, we'd have to copy this workflow and remove these steps before we include the workflow in the template. To copy a delivered workflow, go to Transaction SCMA and select EXTRAS • FLOW DEFINITION • ADMINISTRATION OF FLOW DEFINITION and copy your chosen workflow under a new name. Now mark the node you want to remove and select CUT BLOCK.

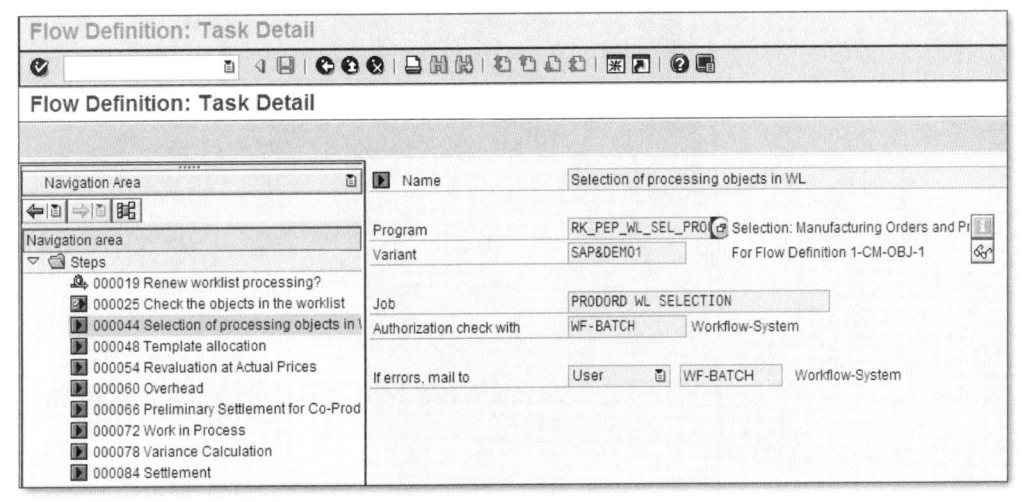

Figure 12.17 Selection of Objects for Processing

> **Responsibility for Workflows**
>
> In some organizations, the IT department is responsible for maintaining workflows, while in others the controlling department is allowed to create its own workflow definitions. The Closing Cockpit and Schedule Manager use a subset of all workflow functions. The workflows shown can be maintained directly from the Schedule Manager transaction. To find out more about using workflow in the context of the Schedule Manager, refer to SAP Note 332149.

As you can see from Figure 12.16, one workflow can cover many programs. If we use workflows, we can drastically reduce the number of tasks in the list, as shown in Figure 12.18. We've removed the individual closing transactions from the CALCULATIONS AND SETTLEMENT folder and replaced them with two workflows, for production orders and sales orders. When you schedule the workflows, the main difference you'll see compared to the programs and variants is the result of the Monitor shown in Figure 12.19.

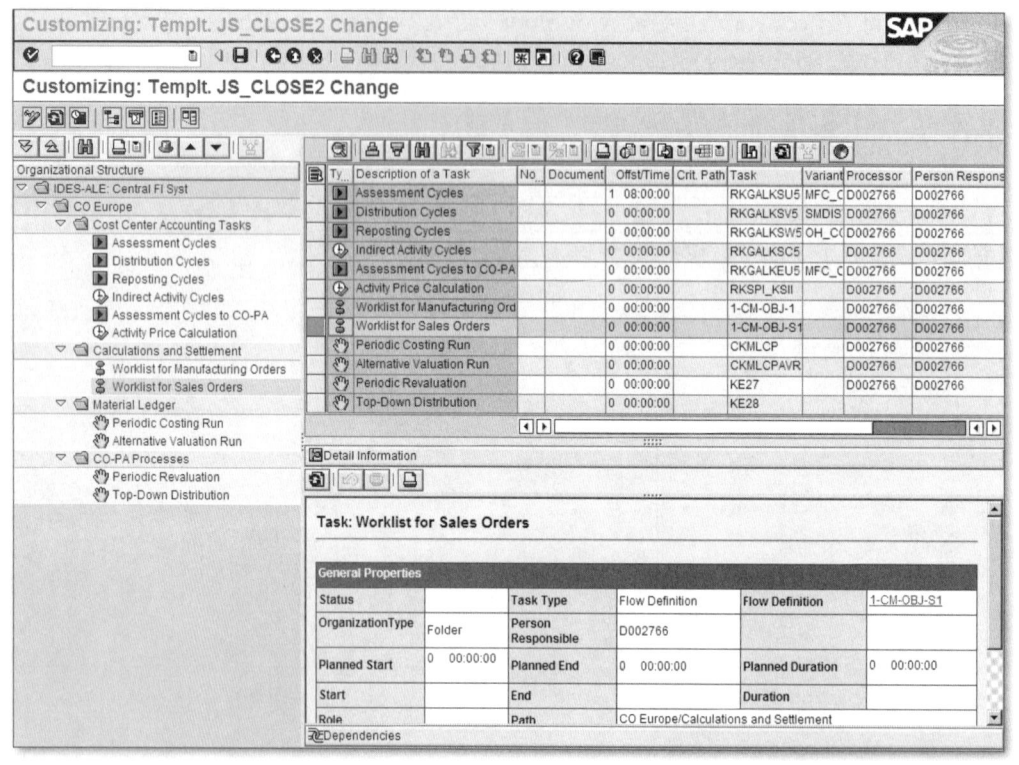

Figure 12.18 Closing Cockpit with Workflows

Figure 12.19 shows the results of scheduling a workflow. This looks similar to the single task we saw in Figure 12.14, but we can see all the tasks in the workflow. Here you see the critical difference compared to the entry in the job log. Technically the job has completed, but from an application perspective it was not completely successful, since the status is PROCESSING COMPLETED, BUT HAS ERRORS. Run 1 has encountered errors you can display by clicking on the step with the error status. The system displays the four production orders that encountered errors. Normally the controller would then check the details of the error (probably the wrong results analysis key has been entered in the production order), correct the affected orders using the information in the list, and then repeat the step for those objects that encountered errors. Only when the application status is green, would he move on to the next step.

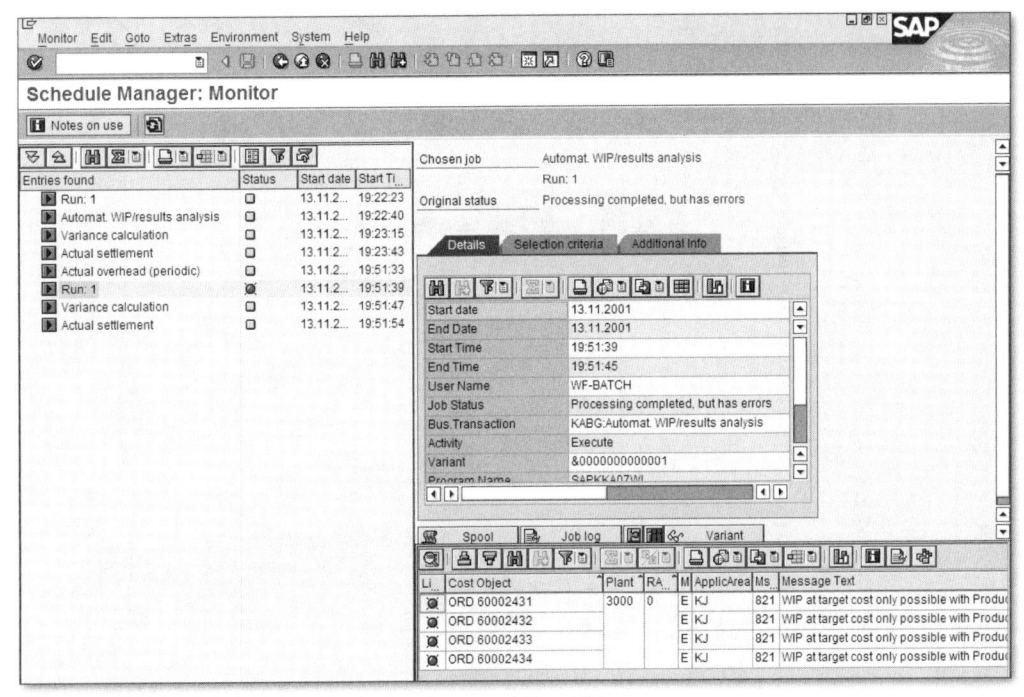

Figure 12.19 Monitor Showing Work Flow Steps and Error List

12.1.7 Handling Costing Runs in Your Close

If you now go back and look at the screenshots of the periodic costing run (Figure 7.40) and alternative valuation run (Figure 7.44) in Chapter 7, Section 7.3, you'll notice that under the flow steps for each costing run, there's a SCHEDULE MANAGER button. Each flow step has its own program and variant (you're actually maintaining the program variant when you maintain the details in the PARAMETERS column). As you execute the costing step, the system schedules the job and updates the Schedule Manager Monitor. If you click on the SCHEDULE MANAGER button in the periodic costing run or the alternative valuation run, you'll see exactly the same screen as if you clicked on the MONITOR link in the Closing Cockpit (see Figures 12.14 and 12.19). Figure 12.20 shows the Monitor for the periodic costing run. Errors have occurred during the post closing step. To display the errors, click on the line. This time errors have been caused by the requirement to update the commitments.

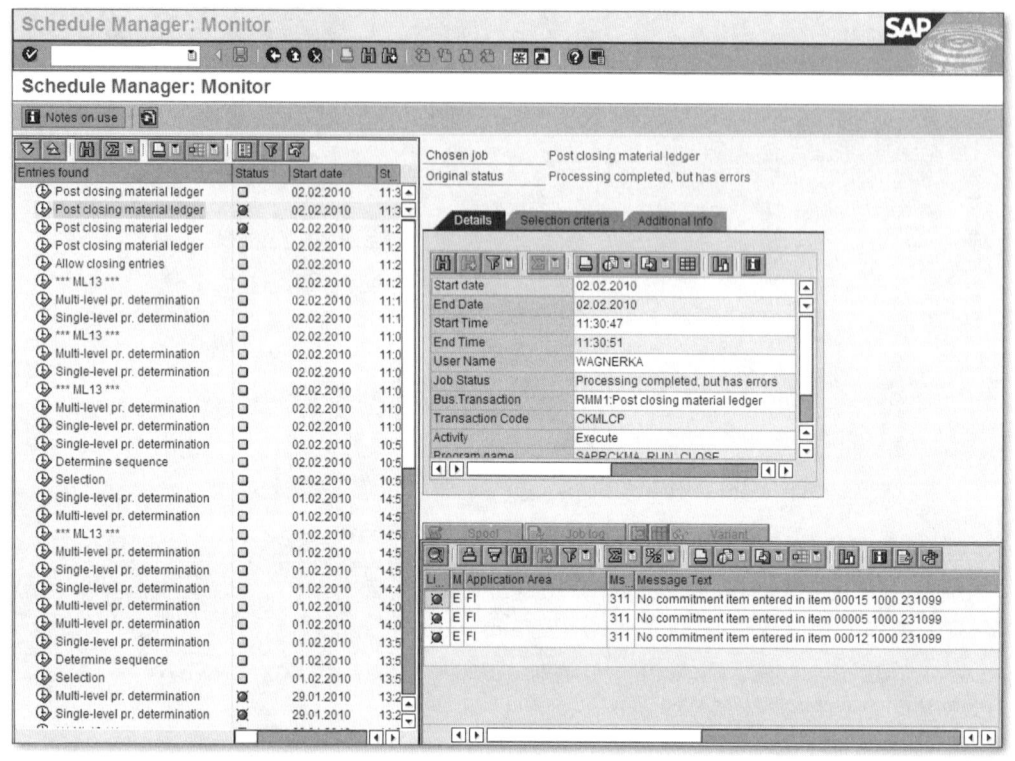

Figure 12.20 Monitor for Periodic Costing Run

Even though the approach for costing runs is slightly different from the previous steps, it makes sense to include the costing runs in the template as transactions. You can then call the costing run manually before executing the jobs and set a final complete status when you've completed each step in the costing run. This will prevent the periodic revaluation step in CO-PA from running before the closing run is flagged as complete.

12.1.8 Handling Organizational Units in the Closing Cockpit

So far, with the exception of the dependency definition, everything we've looked at for the Closing Cockpit could also have been done in the Schedule Manager. Probably the most obvious difference between the two is the inclusion of a closing hierarchy in the Closing Cockpit that organizes the closing steps according to the organizational unit responsible for performing the step.

New Options for Accelerating the Period Close | **12.1**

When you create a new template in the Closing Cockpit, the system asks you to select a closing hierarchy, as shown in Figure 12.21. Most organizations use the CONTROLLING AREA/COMPANY CODE option. If you choose this option, the template will automatically include a folder for every active controlling area and a folder for every active company code in your system. If you use Product Costing, your plants may perform their closing activities independently. If this is the case, choose the closing hierarchy CONTROLLING AREA/PLANT (see Figure 12.21), and the template will automatically include a folder for every active controlling area and a folder for every active plant.

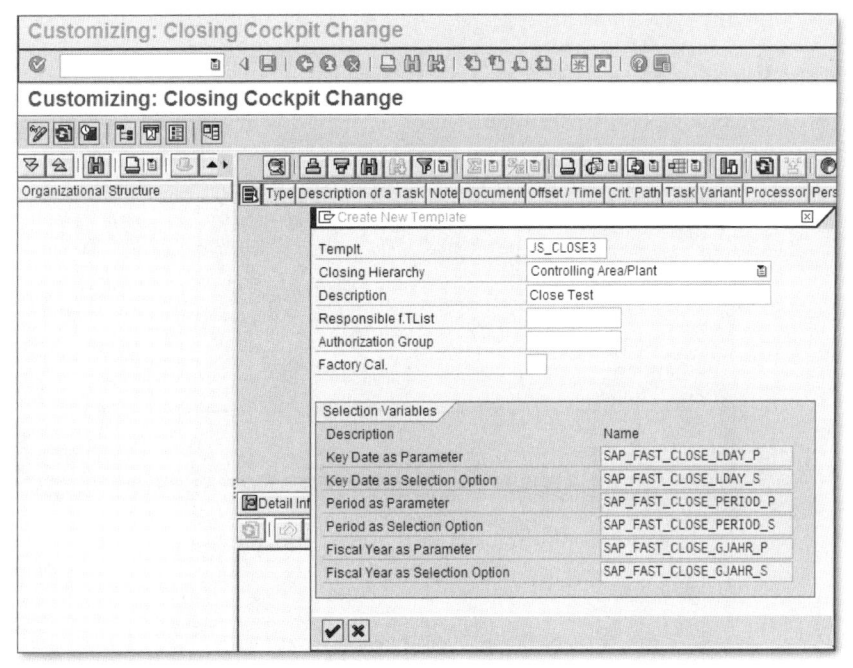

Figure 12.21 Organizational Hierarchy

Figure 12.22 shows all the controlling areas in our demo system and all the plants assigned to the North American controlling area. Selecting the NEW YORK folder reveals that this folder is of organization type Plant (see lower right of screen). As we saw with the time variables in Section 12.1.4, the organizational unit represented by the folder is passed to the jobs when they're scheduled.

553

- Folders that represent the organizational unit Controlling Area can pass the variable `SAP_FAST_CLOSE_KOKRS_P` during scheduling.
- Folders that represent the organizational unit Company Code can pass the variable `SAP_FAST_CLOSE_BUKRS_P` during scheduling.
- Folders that represent the organizational unit Plant can pass the variable `SAP_FAST_CLOSE_WERKS_P` during scheduling.

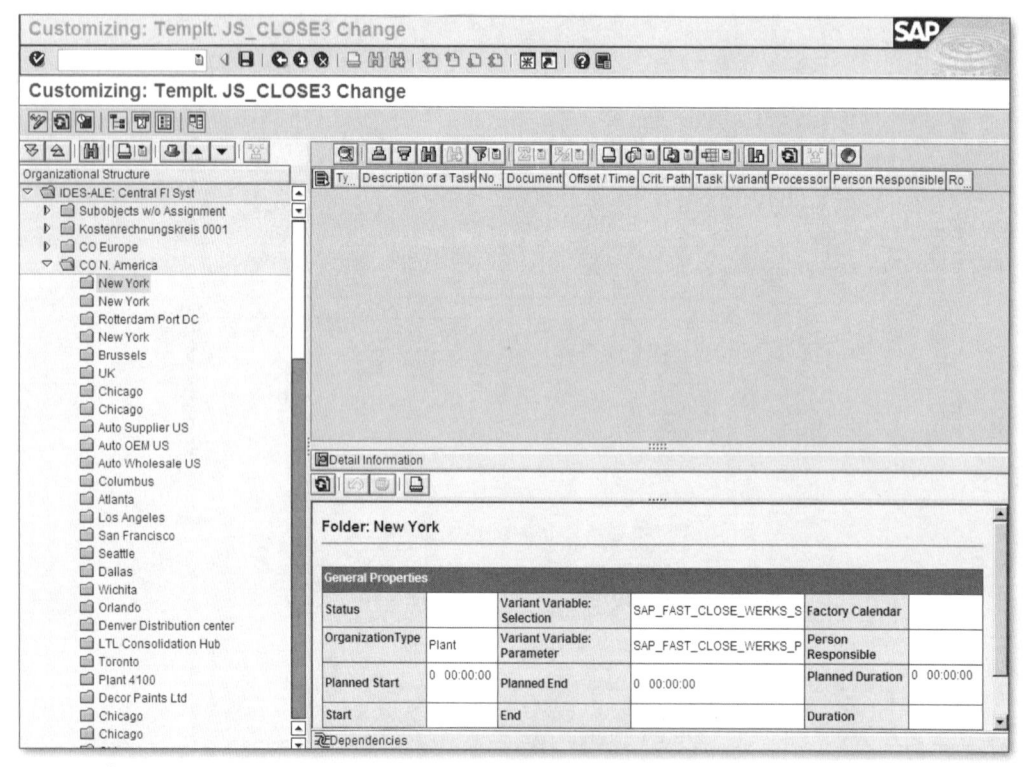

Figure 12.22 Controlling Areas and Plants in Closing Cockpit

If you're not sure which parameters the folder will pass, right-click on the folder and select CHANGE VALUES. Figure 12.23 shows controlling area 2000 assigned to the folder CO NORTH AMERICA. The controlling area is needed to schedule all jobs in CO, so it makes sense to define the closing tasks under the controlling area, by creating additional folders and subfolders under the CO NORTH AMERICA folder.

To add folders, position the cursor on the folder CO NORTH AMERICA, right-click, and select CREATE FOLDER or CREATE SUB FOLDER.

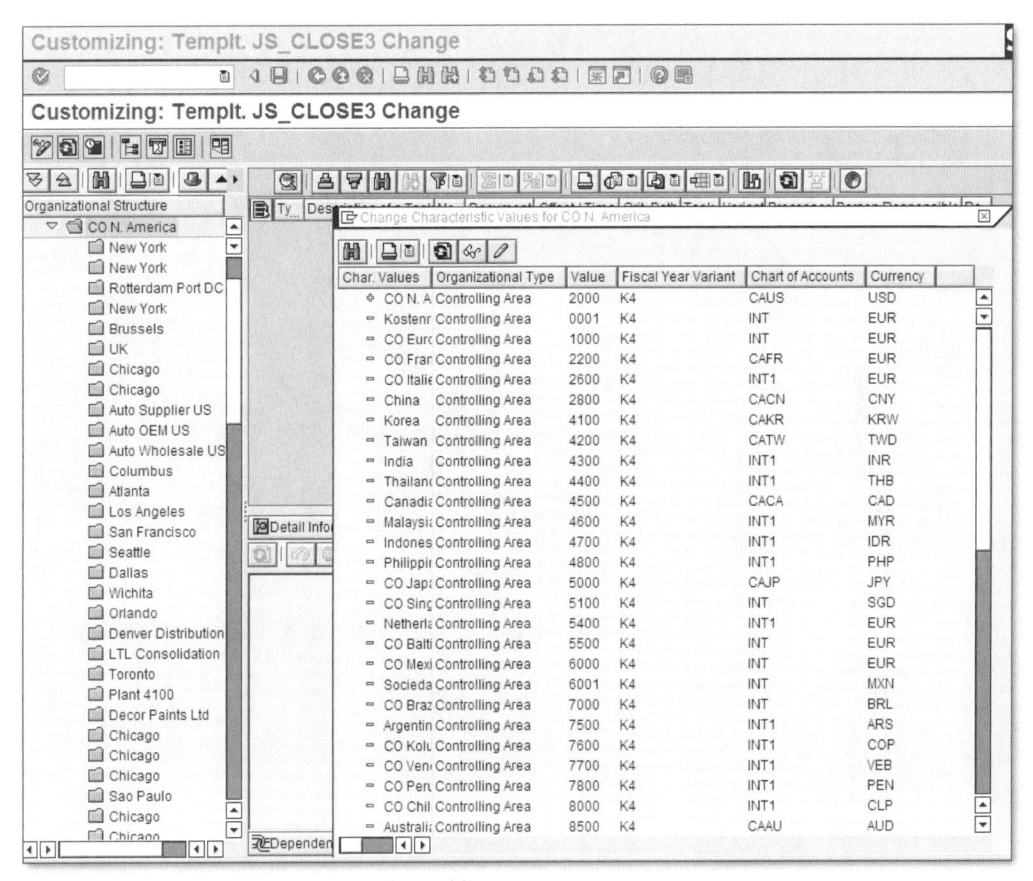

Figure 12.23 Controlling Area Assigned to Folder

If your plants are in different geographical locations, it can also make sense to include the relevant factory calendar. This means that when you schedule a task with respect to the key date of the close (such as on key date plus one day), the system will first check whether that day is a working day for the plant. If the proposed day is not a working day, it will schedule the task on the next available working day. Where tasks are scheduled for key date minus one day, as might be the case for a billing run or payroll run prior to the close, the system will schedule the task on the first working day before the proposed day. The folder also includes a field for the person responsible. You should consider entering the plant controller or similar person here (see Figure 12.24).

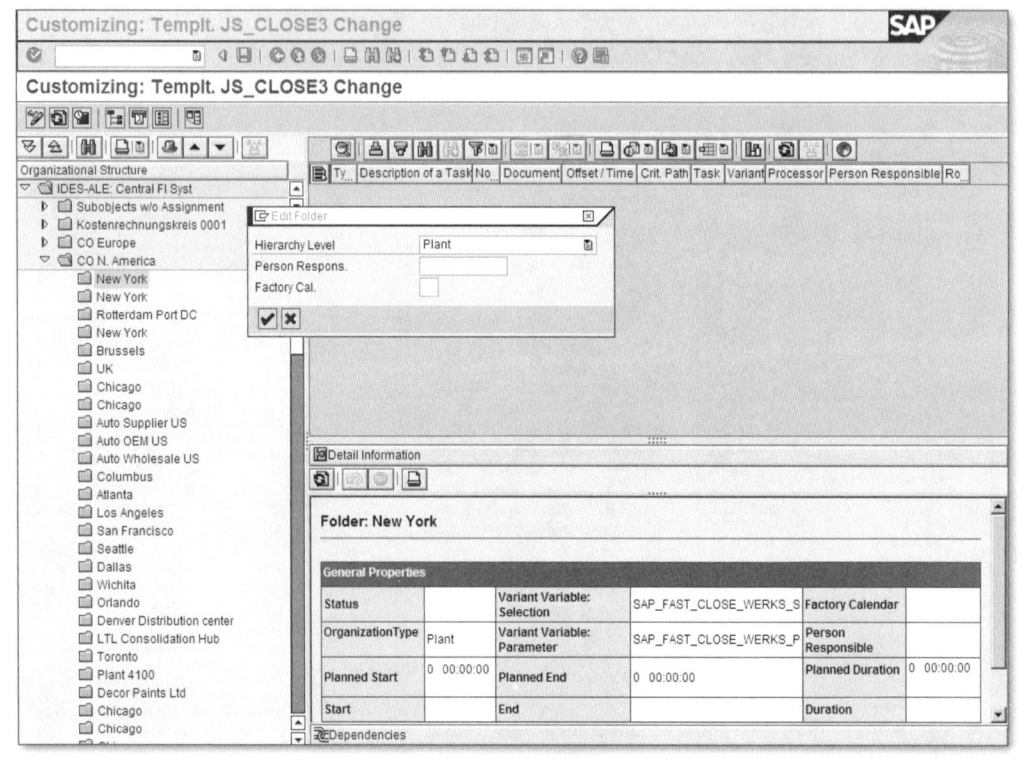

Figure 12.24 Assigning a Factory Calendar to a Plant Folder

If you find the hierarchy tree confusing and prefer the list view only, you can remove the tree by pressing [F9] (Show/Hide Hierarchy Tree) as shown in Figure 12.25.

Notice the names of the processor, person responsible, and a role in the list. If you're not going to perform all tasks yourself, you should maintain the proper user names here. As of SAP enhancement package 3 for SAP ERP 6.0 there's a new authorization object, F_CLOCO, that your administrator can use to determine who can set statuses, change tasks, and so on in the Closing Cockpit. Since enhancement package 5 you can also set authorizations by template. This is useful if different teams are responsible for individual templates.

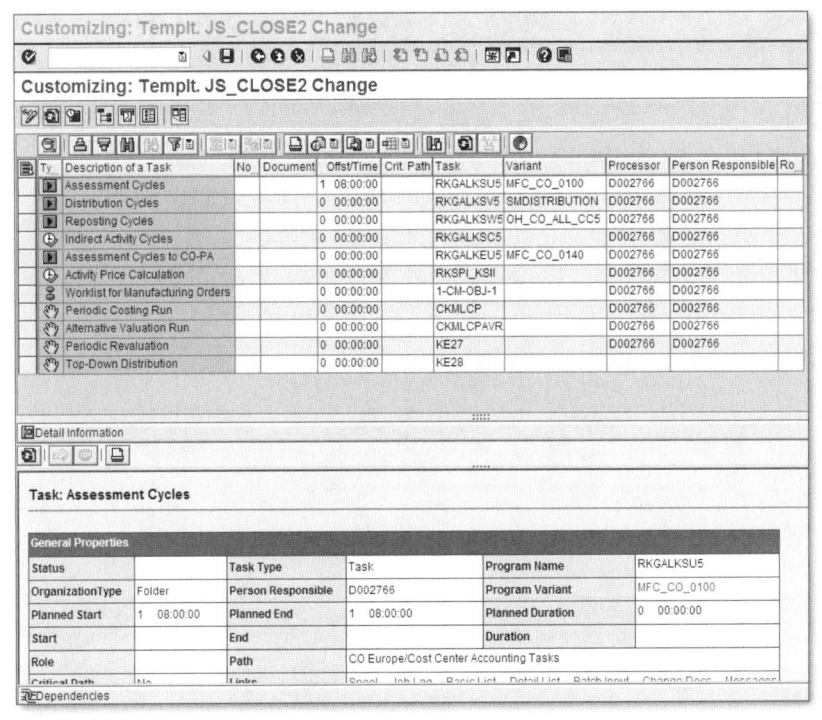

Figure 12.25 Closing Cockpit Without Organizational Hierarchy

12.1.9 Closing Cockpit and SAP Financial Closing Cockpit

SAP Financial Closing Cockpit covers all the enhancements of the closing cockpit from SAP enhancement package 3 for SAP ERP 6.0 onward. From a visual point of view, the main difference is that there's an alternative user interface to replace Transaction CLOCO that is delivered using the role SAP_FAGL_CLOCO_WD_15 or the business package Closing Cockpit (see Appendix A at *www.sap-press.com*). Figure 12.26 shows a list containing all the task lists in which the user is included (our two examples). In this example, we've selected all task lists that contain tasks assigned to our user ID.

To access details of the close tasks, select a line (JS_CLOSE2 in our example). Figure 12.27 shows the close tasks and task details. If several users are responsible for executing steps in the close, you can toggle between the two using ALL TASKS and MY TASKS in the DISPLAY field. You can change the start and end time until the task has been scheduled, which is why some of the cells are white (open for entry) and some are blue (locked).

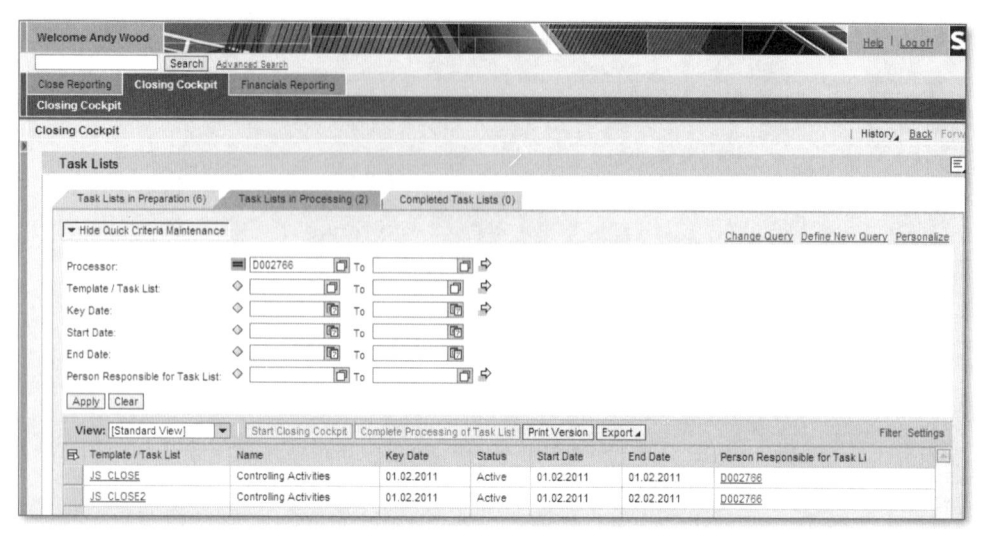

Figure 12.26 Finding Task Lists in Which a User Is Active

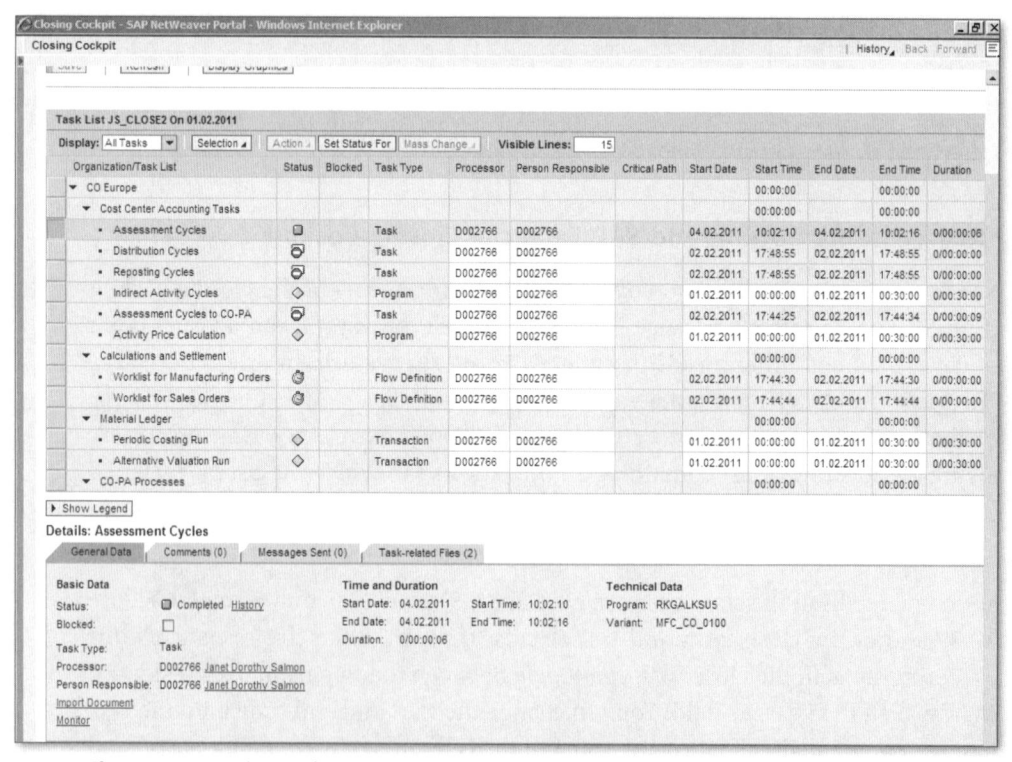

Figure 12.27 Task Details

On completion, all logs the system creates are attached to the TASK-RELATED FILES tab. Figure 12.28 shows the links to the spool list and job log created when our assessment cycle was scheduled. To view the MONITOR, choose the GENERAL DATA tab,

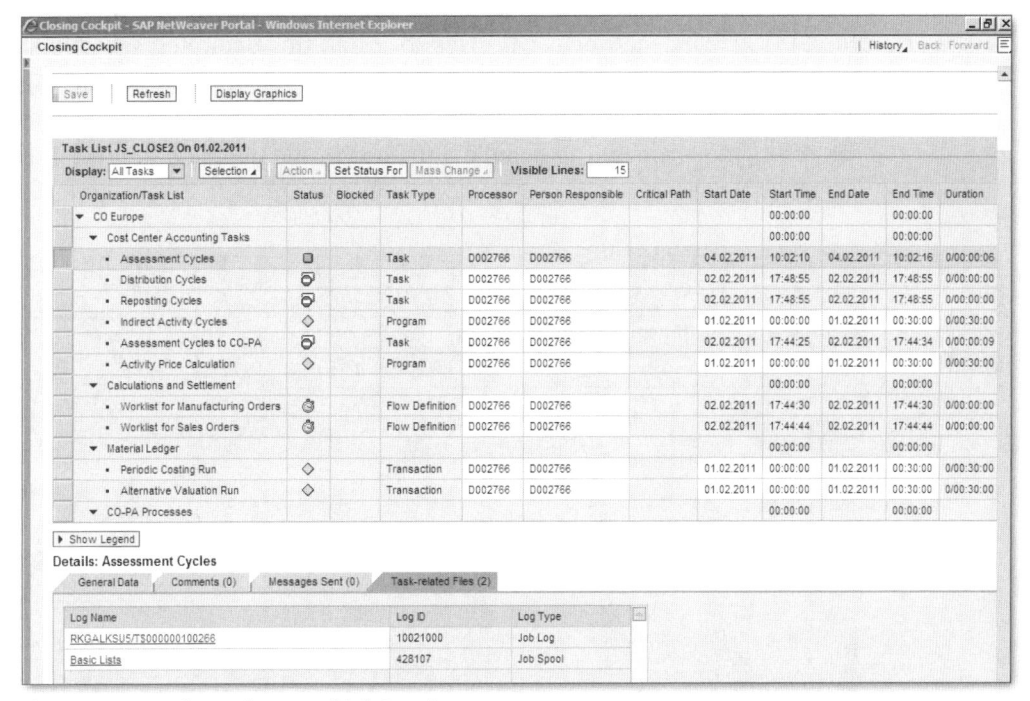

Figure 12.28 Link to Job Log and Job Spool

If all your closing tasks take place on the same SAP ERP system, you can skip the next section. However, in large installations, it's common to have multiple installations of SAP ERP, and dependencies can exist between the closing tasks in each instance. We'll now look at how to manage the close in such an environment.

12.2 Closing Tasks in Multiple Systems

Probably the most pressing reason to consider using the newer enhancement packages is the question of whether your close crosses multiple systems. In larger organizations, it's common to have the production running on a different SAP ERP system than finance. This raises many questions concerning how best to orchestrate the close and handle cross-system dependencies.

In SAP enhancement package 3 for SAP ERP 6.0, there's a new task type, remote task, which allows you to schedule tasks on different ERP systems. The technology to perform this scheduling is provided by SAP Central Processing by Redwood (or SAP CPS). Your IT department will have to install this dedicated scheduling software on SAP NetWeaver and set up a queue for each system on which closing tasks will run and jobs for each type of job that you'll want to schedule. People in the controlling department can complete the rest of the template in much the same way as we saw earlier.

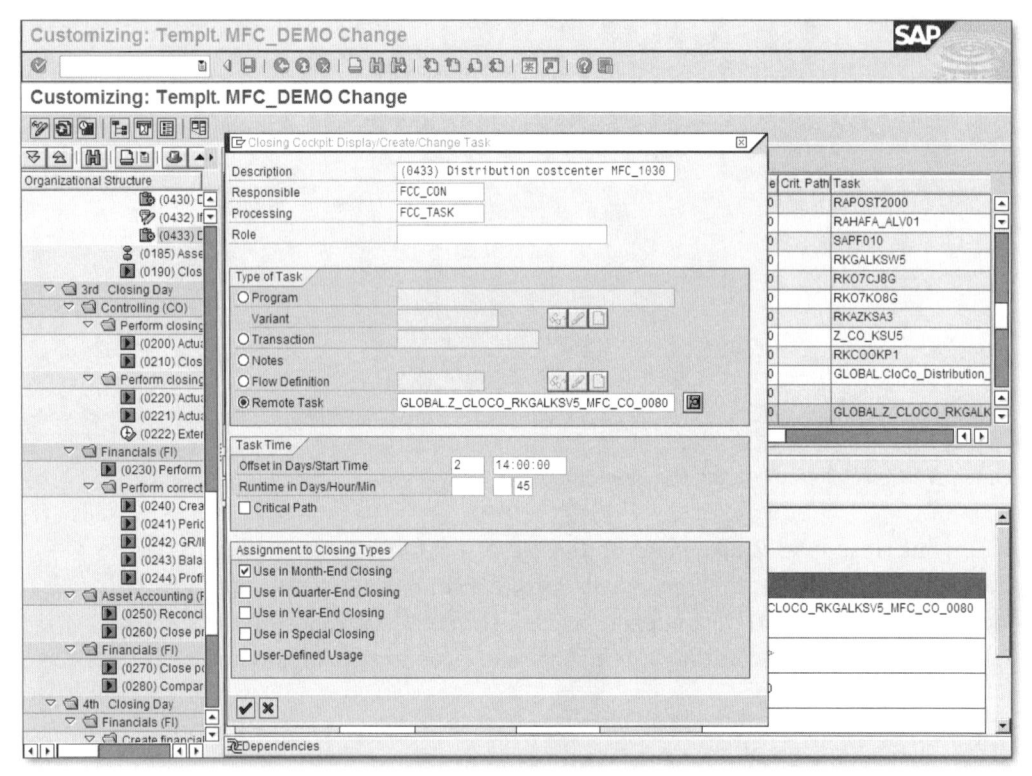

Figure 12.29 Remote Task in SAP Financial Closing Cockpit

Figure 12.29 shows the DISPLAY/CREATE/CHANGE TASK screen again, this time with a remote task. In this scenario, the SAP ERP system on which the template has been created will call the remote system to schedule the distribution cycle. The SAP ERP system on which the *template* is defined must be on SAP enhancement package 3 for SAP ERP 6.0 or higher, because this release level is needed for delivery of the interfaces to call SAP Central Process Scheduling by Redwood. The other SAP ERP system on which the *remote task* is performed can be on a lower release, since the call that initiates the task is performed using a remote function call (RFC). To display details of the job parameters, click on the DETAIL VIEW icon to the right of the text field. Note that you will only be able to access this icon if your user also exists in SAP CPS.

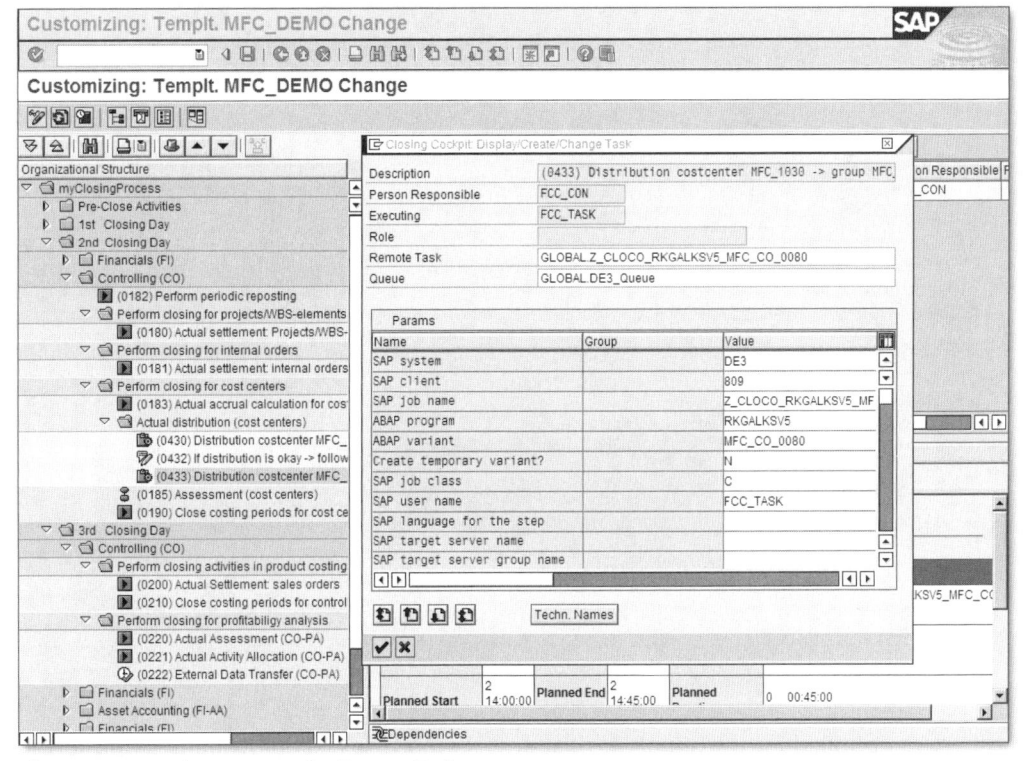

Figure 12.30 Task Parameters for Remote Task

Figure 12.30 shows the parameters for the remote job. In this example, we're scheduling a distribution cycle (see Chapter 7) on a different client of the demo system (the DE3 queue). The IT department generally creates the job definition (the shell) in SAP Central Process Scheduling by Redwood and sometimes also the program variants (as we discussed earlier). However, once the template is complete, both departments will have their own view of the closing task. The IT department will work with SAP Central Process Scheduling by Redwood to ensure the system performance and all technical issues relating to load balancing as the heavy lifting of the close begins, but the controlling department will see the task as usual and can display all related logs from the Closing Cockpit. Figure 12.31 shows a remote task that's currently being executed from the SAP Financial Closing Cockpit in an additional tab, REMOTE TASK DATA.

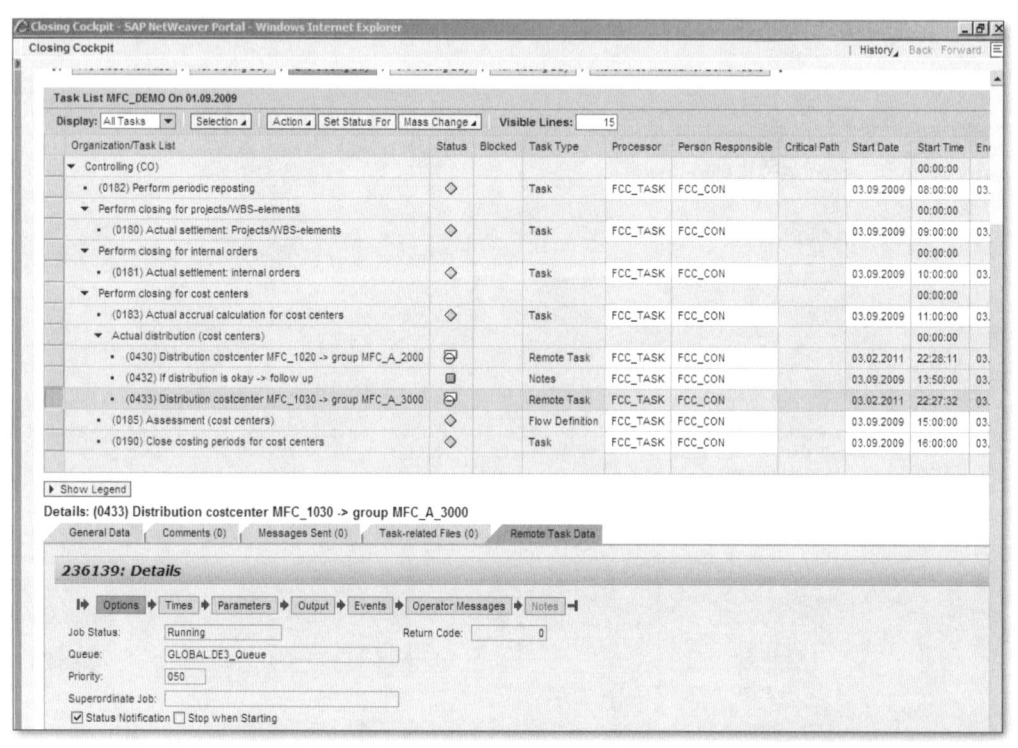

Figure 12.31 Remote Task Parameters

On completion, the remote task attaches its job logs, spool list, and so on to the TASK-RELATED FILES tab (see Figure 12.32), just as we saw for a locally executed task. Once SAP Central Processing by Redwood has been set up, a central controlling department can schedule and monitor tasks on multiple systems without having to log on to the individual systems.

Storing Log Files

Generally the IT department is responsible for storing spool lists and job logs. This can mean that the spool lists are deleted fairly quickly and the links in the Closing Cockpit won't take you back to old spool lists. If you use SAP Central Process Scheduling by Redwood, the lists and log files are stored there, and the SAP Financial Closing Cockpit links to them. So it makes sense to talk with your IT department to make sure that logs for jobs initiated from the SAP Financial Closing Cockpit are stored for longer to enable a proper audit.

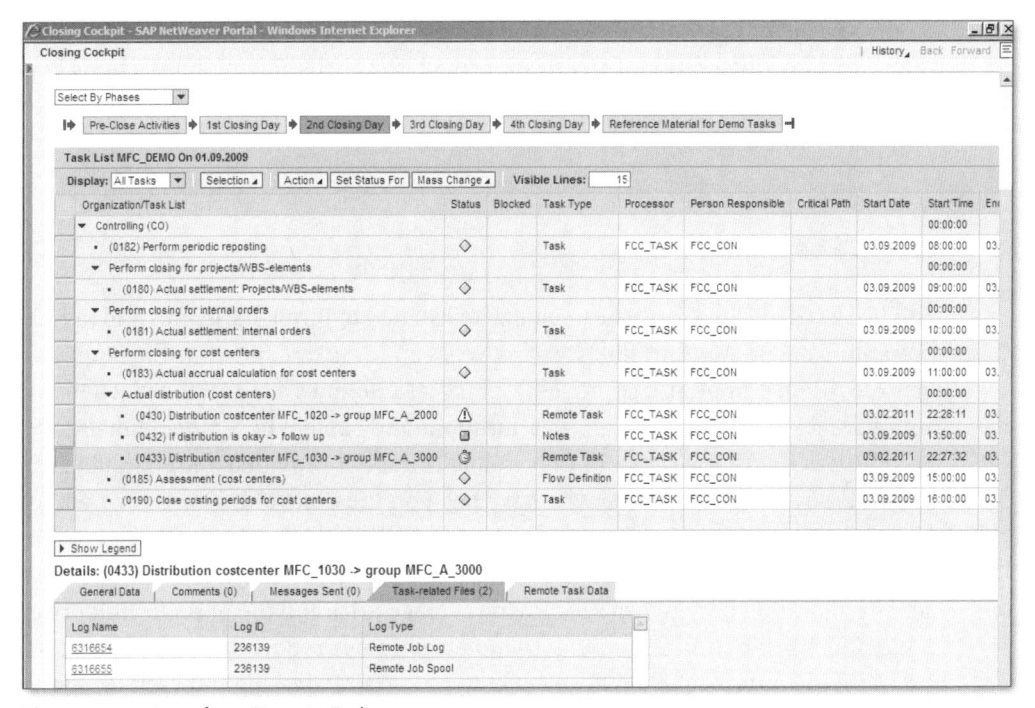

Figure 12.32 Logs from Remote Task

Once you've automated the execution of the allocation cycles and settlements that we looked at in Chapter 7 and automated the creation of extracts as we discussed in Chapter 8, the next stage is to look at what checks you're doing on the data to ensure consistency. This can be as simple as checking that the balance on each cost center is zero after all the allocation cycles have run or that the balance on the orders is zero after all the settlements have run. Having the log files in SAP Central Process Scheduling by Redwood allows you to build scripts that automate the checks on these log files. If the balance on a particular cost center is not zero, you can set up exceptions that send an email to notify you if the cost center still has a balance even though all assessment cycles have run.

12.3 Summary

The Closing Cockpit and Schedule Manager are tools that systematically support the application of your own best practices for the period close, documenting what has to be done, by whom, and when. You can add to your skeleton plan both technically, by including workflows and so on, and in a business sense, by including supporting documentation. You can start small, simply listing the transactions you use in the close, or go global with one master schedule for a multisystem close, depending on the nature of your requirements.

12.4 Post-Script

This book is dedicated to all the people who listened to Birgit Starmanns and myself presenting our "T-Account slides" in Las Vegas and Amsterdam while the book was being written. I hope it has proved a practical reference for the times when we aren't available personally to answer questions and explain how "the others" do it. For those of you starting out in Controlling, I hope it provided a useful guide for your journey ahead. For those who have been on the Controlling road for a while, I hope that it provided some new ideas and insight. If the book got you out of just one hole, whether it's explaining the difference between an indirect and a direct activity allocation or between the moving average price and the periodic unit price, it has done its job. If it helped you to modernize your reporting approach or take a day out of your close schedule, even better. I've already caught myself using the manuscript to find the ten essential SAP Note numbers when I'm not online.

The Author

Janet Salmon is currently Chief Product Owner for Management Accounting at SAP AG and has accompanied many developments to the Controlling components of SAP ERP Financials as both a product and a solution manager. In this role, she works with the controllers from many international organizations to understand new software requirements and explain how to use the existing software.

She joined SAP AG as a translator in 1992 having gained a degree in Modern and Medieval Languages from Downing College, Cambridge and a post-graduate qualification in Interpreting and Translating from the University of Bath.

She became a technical writer for the Product Costing area in 1993 and a product manager in 1996. In 1998 she received an award from the Society of Technical Communication for *Functions in Detail: Product Cost Controlling*, which the judges described as "refreshingly free of fluff." She is an advisor and regular contributor to SAP Financials Expert (*http://www.financialsexpertonline.com*) and regularly presents at Financials conferences.

Index

A

Access method
  in queries, 413
Account
  link to cost element, 25
Account assignment
  for material issue, 272
  in purchase order, 260
  purchase for project, 308
Account assignment elements
  for project, 181
Account-based CO-PA
  introduction, 82
Accounting document
  for goods receipt from purchasing, 262
  for incoming invoice, 266
Accounting principle
  in alternative valuation run, 380
Accounting view
  of material master, 147
Active availability control
  for project, 308
  introduction, 47
Active budgeting, 47
Activities
  as basis for price calculation, 122
  dimension in SAP BusinessObjects PCM, 515
  in SAP BusinessObjects PCM, 500
Activity allocation
  to project, 312
Activity-based Costing
  introduction, 28, 498
Activity-dependent planning, 218
Activity-independent cost
  planning, 216
  target costs for, 348
Activity/output prices
  planning, 213

Activity price
  analysis of, 351
Activity price calculation, 228, 350
  approaches, 121
  settings in activity type, 121
Activity quantity
  as basis for planning, 205
Activity type
  activity unit, 119
  in Material Ledger, 375
  in work center/resource, 174
  introduction, 117
  use in allocations, 326
Activity type groups, 122
  in planning, 213, 216
Activity type plan
  as service in Express Planning, 481
Actual costs, 32
  business requirements, 77
  for production orders, 276
  material master, 196
Actual postings, 20, 257
Adobe Interactive Form
  change request, 140, 434
Allocation
  cross-company, 189
  cycles overview, 331
  introduction, 326
  real-time integration of CO and Financial Accounting, 332
  using SAP BusinessObjects PCM, 497
Allocation template
  in business process, 506
Alternative cost center hierarchies, 100
Alternative valuation run
  costing steps, 378
  introduction, 372
  link to Schedule Manager, 551
Annual budget, 203
Annual operating plan, 203
Apportionment structure

Index

for co-products, 162
  in process order, 296
Appropriation requests, 185
Approval
  for change requests, 449
  workflow, 48
Approval year
  for investment program, 183
  in investment planning, 253
Arm's length trading, 320
Assessment cost elements, 334
  use of, 337
Assessment cycles, 332
  cyclical relationships, 338
  introduction, 98, 330
Asset Accounting
  link with Cost Center Accounting, 94
  period close tasks, 328
Auditing
  CO-PA reporting, 403
Auxiliary cost component split, 238

B

Backflushing
  distribution of usage variances, 289
  for production orders, 272
Background processing
  for period close activities, 535
Balance sheet valuation
  price fields, 151
  tax and commercial prices, 195
Basic view
  of material master, 146
Batches, 155
Billing
  prior to period close, 328
Billing document
  for sales order, 287
Billing elements
  for project, 181
Bill of material
  cyclical structures, 164
  in production order, 268
  introduction, 158

long-term planning, 210
  material usage, 66
  recursive, 164
  usage, 158
Bottom-up planning, 248
Budget change
  change request, 431
Budget change request, 254
Budget changes, 48
Budgeting, 19
  for projects, 251
  introduction, 43
  value flow, 46
Budget planning
  for investment programs, 247
Budget request
  change request, 431
Budget transfer request, 254, 431
Business area
  in cost center, 96
Business function
  CO_ALLOCATIONS, 313
  FIN_ACC_LOCAL_CLOSE, 529
  FIN_CO_COGM, 196, 329, 350, 381
  FIN_GL_REORG_1, 94
  FIN_MDM_ACC, 437
  FIN_MDM_ORG, 437
  FIN_MDM_SOA_CU, 443
  FIN_MDM_SOA_ORG, 443
  FIN_REP_SIMPL_1, 61
  FIN_SSC_ISS_1, 453
  LOG_EAM_OLC, 173
  LOG_MM_SIT, 321
  LOG_PP_PROD_ORDER_SPLIT, 298
Business process
  in allocations, 506
  introduction, 497
  master data, 501
Business Transaction
  RKIU, 336
  RKP1, 463
Business unit analyst, 480
By-products
  in BOM, 161

C

Capacity
  as basis for price calculation, 122
  in cost center planning, 213
  of cost center, 175
  of work center, 175
Capital investment projects
  planning of, 246
Change documents
  for master data, 134
Change request
  action box, 434
  approval of, 449
  configuration, 430
  for budget, 254
  for cost center, 488
  form settings, 434
  master data governance, 443
  notification type, 433
  reviewing related requests, 448
  scenarios, 430
  shared service framework, 452
Characteristics
  for profitability analysis, 282
Chart of accounts, 187
  data model for SAP MDGF, 437
  link with primary cost elements, 186
  master data governance, 429, 436
Closing Cockpit
  in period close, 528
  scheduling extracts for reporting, 391
Closing hierarchy
  in Closing Cockpit, 553
Collective processing
  during period close, 527
Commitments
  for project, 310
Company code
  in cost center, 95
Completed contract
  valuation, 370
Conditions
  for purchasing, 259
Configurable BOM, 165
  classification, 165

Configurable material
  manufacture of, 303
Configurable materials, 165
Confirmation
  for production orders, 275
Control key
  for operation, 170
Controlling, 18
Controlling document
  for production order, 274
Co-products, 153
  in BOM, 161
  in process orders, 295
  settlement rules, 162
Corporate Investment Management
  planning activities, 464
Cost and activity inputs
  planning, 215, 461
Cost center
  approval processes, 34
  as account assignment, 34
  change request, 430
  difference from order, 90
  groups, 101
  hierarchies, 97
  introduction, 29
  link to work center, 173
  master data, 90
  master data governance, 437
  operational, 91
  output measure, 30
  outputs, 37
  purchasing costs, 34
  responsibility for, 29
  responsible managers, 92
  supporting, 91
  typical expenses, 36
  validity period, 136
Cost Center Accounting
  actual postings, 313
  creating cost centers, 90
  introduction, 26
  line items, 52
  period close activities, 327
  planning, 211
Cost center change request, 488

Cost center group
    in Express Planning, 483
Cost center line item, 277
    layouts for reporting, 55
    simplified reporting, 59
Cost center planning, 211
Cost centers
    finding cost centers in allocation cycles, 332
Cost components
    for activity prices, 229
    introduction, 66
Cost component split
    in Product Cost Planning, 238
    manual change to, 376
Costed multilevel BOM
    report, 67
Cost element, 25
    examples, 25
    primary, 25
    secondary, 25
Cost Element Accounting
    introduction, 25
    master data, 124
Cost element category
    for primary cost element, 188
Cost element group, 127
    in planning, 216
Cost element master data
    reports, 128
Cost element planning
    for projects, 248
    new version in enhancement package 6, 476
Cost elements, 123
    for goods issues and receipts, 274
    for recording WIP, 359
    in activity types, 119
    in primary cost component split, 229
    in product costing, 66
    in Profitability Analysis, 82
    link to cost components, 239
    link to SAP BusinessObjects PCM, 513
    master data governance, 437
Costing-based CO-PA
    introduction, 82
Costing lot size, 151, 236

impact of scrap, 154
in material master, 152
Costing run
    in Material Ledger, 371
    introduction, 230
Costing sheet
    in production order, 354
Costing variant
    in Product Cost Planning, 233
Costing version
    in Product Cost Planning, 233
Costing view
    of material master, 151
Cost object controlling
    master data, 131
    MRP class, 154
    period close activities, 351
    production orders, 270
Cost object hierarchy, 132
    introduction, 75
    options at period close, 133
Cost objects
    dimension in SAP BusinessObjects PCM, 516
    in SAP BusinessObjects PCM, 500
Cost of goods manufactured, 66
Cost planning
    introduction, 201
Country chart of accounts, 187
Cross-company allocations, 189
Cross-company costing, 196
Cross-company postings, 319
    allocations, 95
Crystal Reports
    in SAP List Viewer, 421
    link to query, 418
Cumulation
    in Material Ledger, 378
Currencies
    for reporting, 59
Customer account
    assignment in Customer master, 157
Customer invoice, 287
Customer master, 156
    reconciliation account, 285

Customer value analysis
  using SAP BusinessObjects PCM, 523
Cycle run groups
  for allocations, 338

D

Dashboard reports, 422
Data modeling
  master data governance, 437
Data provisioning
  in SAP NetWeaver BW, 412
DataSources, 21
  for controlling, 396
Data warehousing
  introduction, 395
Dependencies
  in period close, 532
Depreciation, 328
  cost center assignment, 36
Derivation
  in profitability analysis, 282
Determine delta postings
  in alternative valuation run, 379
Direct access
  using SAP NetWeaver BW, 398
Direct activity allocation, 117
  category of activity type, 120
  correction of, 317
Distribution cycles, 338
  introduction, 330
Distribution key
  in planning, 218
Distribution of activities, 293
Distribution rules
  settlement rules, 109
Division
  in material master, 148
Drill-down reporting
  in Cost Object Controlling, 393
  in Profitability Analysis, 392
  unassigned data, 415
Driver-based planning, 43
Drivers
  for cost centers, 30
  for products, 30

E

Edition
  how to create, 440
  list of, 441
  master data governance, 438
Enterprise Extension
  EA_FIN, 290, 373, 376
Entity types
  use in MDGF, 437
Environment
  use in templates, 508
Equipment
  link with Cost Center Accounting, 94
Equivalence numbers
  for co-products, 164, 296
Error handling
  in period close, 550
Exceptions and conditions
  in SAP NetWeaver BW, 415
Executable programs
  for period close transactions, 536
Expenses
  to be capitalized, 38
Express Planning, 21
  change requests, 138
  for cost center planning, 215
  introduction, 479
  order planning, 226
  user responsible for cost center, 92
Extracts, 388

F

Factory calendar
  in Closing Cockpit, 555
FIFO (first-in, first-out), 151
Finished product, 158
Fixed assets
  depreciation, 328

Fixed costs, 29
Fixed cost variances
  on cost centers, 350
Floorplan Manager
  for planning applications, 475
Flow definition
  for period close activities, 546
Formatted reports
  using Crystal Reports, 420
Form-based planning, 216
Formula key
  in work center/resource, 173
Free planning, 216
Functional area
  in cost center, 96
Future standard price
  in material master, 242
  marking/releasing, 242

G

General Ledger
  link to Cost Center Accounting, 95
  link with internal orders, 108
Goods movements
  real-time valuation, 40
Goods receipt
  for purchasing, 260
Grenzplankostenrechnung (GPK), 28
Group chart of accounts, 187
Group costing
  use of costing versions, 234
Group valuation
  for intercompany trade, 323
  in material master, 196

H

Hierarchy area
  for cost centers, 97
High-Performance Analytic Appliance
  (HANA), 21, 424

I

Incoming invoice
  from vendor, 265
Indirect activity allocation, 118
  category of activity type, 120
  for energy, 120
  in planning, 224
Indirect activity allocation cycles, 341
  introduction, 330
InfoArea
  in SAP NetWeaver BW, 396
InfoObjects
  in SAP NetWeaver BW, 405
InfoPackages
  for data extraction, 395
InfoProviders, 21
  for corporate Investment Management, 464
  for planning, 463
  in SAP NetWeaver BW, 396
Information system
  Cost Center Accounting, 53
  internal orders, 63
  product cost by order, 73
  product cost by period, 75
  product cost by sales order, 76
  product cost planning, 67
  Profitability Analysis, 83
InfoSet queries, 416
Input price variances
  for production orders, 362
  on cost centers, 349
Input quantity variances
  for production orders, 362
  on cost centers, 350
Intercompany trading, 321
Intermediate → see Semifinished product
Internal order line items, 62
  delivered layouts, 64
Internal orders
  change request, 430
  introduction, 26
  master data, 105
  planning, 225
  reporting options, 63
  settlement rules, 108
  statistical, 110

status management, 136
Internal service request, 21
  for master data changes, 137
International Financial Reporting Standards (IFRS), 16
Inventory
  introduction, 37
Inventory counts
  handling of variances, 289
  recording of, 290
Inventory valuation, 40
  scrap, 41
  work in process, 41
Investment Management
  introduction, 32
  orders, 32
  planning, 247
  projects, 32
Investment planning, 246
Investment program, 33
  introduction, 183
  planning, 249
Investment programs
  introduction, 246
Item category
  in BOM, 159
Itemization
  Delivered layouts, 69
  reporting options, 69

J

Job log
  for period close activities, 542
  in Web application for Closing Cockpit, 559
Joint production, 153
  product cost by order, 295

K

Kilger, Wolfgang, 15

L

Layouts
  how to change, 56
Lean accounting, 33
  introduction, 27
  value streams, 94
Legal valuation
  in material master, 196
  intercompany goods movement, 321
LIFO (last-in, first-out), 151
Line items
  cost center, 54
  order line item, 64
  in SAP BusinessObjects PCM, 513
List report, 54
Long-term planning, 209
Lot size
  for costing, 236
  for production order, 268

M

Main cost component split, 238
Make-to-order production, 303
Manager Self-Service
  internal orders for cost centers, 108
  user responsible for cost center, 92
Manufacturing order → see Production order
Marking
  of cost estimates, 242
Master Data, 18
  controls, 47
  Governance, 21
Master data reporting
  cost centers, 103
Master recipe, 168
Material account
  use of valuation class, 147
Material group
  for sales order item, 282
  in material master, 146
Material Ledger, 374
  activation of, 149

Index

cross-company trading, 196
in material master, 148
introduction, 77
performance, 261, 375
period close activities, 371
Material master, 144
master data governance, 437
selection list for costing, 235
views, 145
Material origin
use of checkbox, 151
Material types
in material master, 145
Material usage
for production orders, 272
Mixed costing
introduction, 175
Mixed price variances
for production orders, 363
Mixing ratios
for product costing, 178
use of, 239
Model builder
in SAP BusinessObjects PCM, 512
Moving average price, 148
in combination with Material Ledger, 150
MRP variances
source of, 268
Multidimensional reporting
in Cost Center Accounting, 403
in SAP NetWeaver BW, 401
Multilevel price determination, 373

N

Navigation attributes
in SAP NetWeaver BW, 404
Networks
for projects, 39
introduction, 181

O

Offset
timing of period close, 535

OLAP engine
use in planning, 463
Operating concern
dimensions used for planning, 207
in SAP NetWeaver BW, 399
introduction, 80
link with cost objects in SAP BusinessObjects PCM, 516
Operating rate
for cost center, 349
Operational chart of accounts, 187
Operational cost centers, 91
Operation-level costing, 172
Operations
BOM items for WIP calculation, 360
Operation values, 170
Order confirmation
introduction, 35
Order groups, 111
Order items
for co-products, 296
Order line items
simplified reporting, 65
Order lot size, 268
Order master data
reporting options, 112
Order networks
use of, 160
Orders
typical expenses, 38
Order settlement
introduction, 39
Order split, 299
Order to cash, 281
Organization types
in Closing Cockpit, 553
Original budget
for projects, 251
Origin group
material master, 151
Outbound delivery
for sales order, 285
Output
of planning, 205
Output measure
for cost centers, 30
for planning, 30

574

for products, 30
for work center, 174
Output parameters
 for extracts, 391
Output price variances
 for production orders, 363
 on cost centers, 350
Output side variances
 on cost centers, 350
Outsourced manufacturing
 with CO production orders, 299
Overall plan
 investment planning, 247
Overall planning
 in Express Planning, 494
 new version in enhancement package 6, 474
Overhead calculation
 for production orders, 355
Overhead group
 in material master, 152
Overhead key
 in production order, 354

P

Parameters
 for closing activities, 540
Partner cost component split, 66
Partners
 in an allocation, 58
Passive budgeting, 47
Payroll costs
 cost center assignment, 36
Percentage of completion, 42
 valuation, 370
Period close, 20
 automation of, 536
 introduction, 40
 process controls, 48
 use of SAP Financial Closing Cockpit, 527
Periodic costing run
 costing steps, 372
 introduction, 372
 link to Schedule Manager, 551
 underlying data, 261
Periodic unit price

goods receipts for purchases, 261
 in costing run, 372
 in Material Ledger, 150
Personalization dialog
 in Express Planning, 483
Person responsible
 for cost center, 92
Physical InfoProviders
 in SAP NetWeaver BW, 414
Physical inventory
 handling of variances, 289
Physical inventory differences
 distribution of, 292
PI document, 290
P&L accounts
 link to CO, 187
Plan integration
 for internal orders, 225
Planned scrap
 in BOM, 161
 settings in material master, 154
Planner profile in planning applications, 459
Planning
 driver-based, 43
 introduction, 43
 process controls, 48
 steps involved, 43
 supply and demand, 45
Planning area
 for planning applications, 460
Planning elements
 for project, 181
Planning functions
 in SAP BW-BPS, 470
Planning instance
 in Express Planning, 481
Planning layouts
 for cost center planning, 215
 for secondary cost centers, 221
 in SAP SEM-BPS, 468
Planning options, 16
Planning package
 in profitability analysis, 207
Planning round
 creation of, 480
 introduction, 479
Planning scenario

575

for sales and operations plan, 209
  in Express Planning, 481
Plan quantities
  inclusion in template, 504
Plan reconciliation, 213
Plan to manufacture, 267
Plan version, 203
  how to look, 245
Plaut, Hans-Georg, 28
Post closing
  in material ledger, 374
Preliminary cost estimate
  for production order, 270
Price conditions
  for intercompany sales, 196
  for purchasing, 259
  in purchasing info record, 195
Price control
  in material master, 148
Primary cost component split, 66
  for product costs, 238
  in planning, 229
  use of, 175
Primary cost distribution, 338
Primary cost elements, 25, 124, 186
  in distribution cycles, 339
Primary cost planning
  as service in Express Planning, 481
Primary cost postings
  reporting options, 57
Prior year rates, 313
Process controls
  period close, 48
  planning, 48
  Price Calculation in Material Ledger, 375
Process costs
  in product costing, 501
Procurement alternative, 175
  product cost collector, 300
Procure-to-pay
  introduction, 258
Product cost by order, 295
  introduction, 72
  period close activities, 352
Product cost by period, 300
  introduction, 74

Product cost by sales order
  introduction, 76
  period close activities, 369
Product cost collector, 130
  introduction, 74
  product cost by period, 300
  variance calculation, 365
Product Cost Controlling
  introduction, 27
Product costing, 15
  reporting options, 65
Product Cost Planning, 230
  Procurement Alternatives, 239
Product costs
  Simplified Reporting, 71
Product costs by period
  product cost collectors, 130
  period close activities, 360
Product costs by sales order, 302
Product hierarchy
  for sales order item, 282
  in material master, 146
Production alternatives, 130
Production campaigns
  reporting options, 73
Production order, 268
  introduction, 299
  reporting options, 72
  settlement, 279
Production plan, 209
Production quantity
  as basis for planning, 205
Production variances
  calculation of, 362
  sources of, 276
Production version
  in material master, 152
  product cost collector, 131, 300
  reporting options, 74
Product roll-up
  via BOM, 159
Profitability Analysis
  allocations to, 343
  Billing Document, 287
  BW content, 399
  direct posting from FI, 263

    drill-down reports, 84
    introduction, 80
    planning, 205, 245
    Period close activities, 384
    reporting options, 83
    sales order entry, 281, 282, 306
    settlement to, 368
Profitability planning, 245, 462
Profit center
    cost center, 96
    in material master, 152
    in purchase order, 260
Program variant
    generation of, 543
Program variants
    in workflows, 548
    use of in period close, 539
Project
    account assignment, 148
    change request, 430
    controlling, 307
    definition, 179
    introduction, 39, 179
    line items, 311
    size, 182
    stock
Proportional costs, 29
Purchase order
    purchase to stock, 258
Purchase price variances
    in procure-to-pay process, 259
Purchasing info record, 193
    in purchase order, 258
    use of conditions in costing, 195

Q

Quantity structure
    in Material Ledger, 79
    link to BOM, 159
Queries
    for Profitability Analysis, 410
    for SAP BusinessObjects tools, 418
    in SAP NetWeaver BW, 397

R

Rate routing, 168
Raw material, 160
Receiver cost centers
    in planning, 221
Receiver rule
    allocations to Profitability Analysis, 344
    assessment cycle, 334
Receivers
    allocations, 99
    in an allocation, 58
Reconciliation ledger, 95
Record types
    in Profitability Analysis, 80
Recursive BOMs, 164
Reference order
    use of, 105
Release
    of cost estimates, 242
    production order, 271
Remote tasks
    for period close activities, 562
Replicated data
    in SAP NetWeaver BW, 398
Reporting, 18
    introduction, 51
Report Writer
    use of extracts, 388
Reposting cycles, 340
    introduction, 330
Reposting line items, 314
Reposting values, 318
Requirements type
    in sales order, 304
Resource drivers
    in SAP BusinessObjects PCM, 518
Resources
    in process industry, 173
    in SAP BusinessObjects PCM, 500
    supply and demand, 31
Resource-usage variances
    for production orders, 363
    on cost centers, 350
Responsibility accounting, 27

Responsible centers
   in SAP BusinessObjects PCM, 514
Responsible cost center
   internal order, 108
Responsible managers
   in Express Planning, 487
Results analysis
   introduction, 42
   revenue-based, 42
Results analysis cost elements, 359
Results analysis key
   in production order, 354
Results analysis version
   use of, 358
Revaluate at actual prices, 351
Revaluation
   in Profitability Analysis, 384
   of consumption, 373
Revision phase
   in Express Planning, 493
Rework
   confirmation of, 275
   for production order, 298
Routing, 168
   in production order, 270
   long-term planning, 210
   manufacturing steps, 66
   work in process calculation, 360

S

Sales and operations plan, 205
   transfer from CO-PA, 209
Sales order, 281
Sales order controlling
   period close activities, 369
Sales order costing
   reporting options, 76
Sales order stock, 303
   account assignment, 147
   introduction, 76
   unvaluated, 370
   valuated, 370
Sales planning, 206
Sales quantity

   as basis for planning, 205
SAP BusinessObjects, 20
SAP BusinessObjects Explorer
   for profitability reporting, 424
SAP BusinessObjects Profitability and Cost
   Management
   introduction, 498
   options for loading data, 510
SAP Catch Weight Management
   equivalence numbers for co-products, 164
   multiple units of measure, 146
SAP Central Processing by Redwood, 560
SAP Cost and Profitability Management, 21
SAP ERP General Ledger
   Cost Center Accounting, 95
SAP Financial Closing Cockpit, 22
   introduction, 529
   Web application, 557
SAP List Viewer, 54
   Crystal Reports, 421
   layouts, 55
   tree report, 69
SAP Master Data Governance for Financials,
   429
   introduction, 436
SAP NetWeaver BW, 20, 396
SAP SEM, 21
SAP Shared Service Framework, 429
Sarbanes-Oxley Act, 47
   master data compliance, 137
Scheduled activity, 213
   in long-term planning, 210
   transfer from SOP/LTP, 214
Schedule Manager
   for planning, 206
   in period close, 528
   scheduling extracts for reporting, 391
Schedule Manager Monitor
   use of, 545
Scheduling
   for period close activities, 541
Scrap
   calculation of, 366
   confirmation of, 275
   introduction, 41
Secondary cost element, 25, 124

use, 125
Secondary postings
  reporting options, 58
Segments
  within allocation cycles, 332
Selection list
  for costing run, 234
Selection variants
  internal orders, 106
Semifinished product, 160
Sender cost centers
  in planning, 221
Sender rule
  for assessment cycle, 333
  for indirect activity allocation cycles, 341
Senders
  allocations, 99
  in an allocation, 58
Sending emails in Express Planning, 486
Settlement, 367
Settlement rule
  automatic generation, 110
  for production order, 306
  internal orders, 108
Shared service center
  introduction, 452
Simplified reporting
  order master data, 112
  cost center line item, 59
  Cost Centers, 103
  order line items, 65
  product costs, 71
Simulation
  using SAP BW-BPS, 471
Single-level price determination, 373
  in Material Ledger, 150
Source structure
  in joint production, 162
Special procurement key
  in material master, 153
Splitting
  of production orders, 298
Splitting cost center costs, 219
Split valuation
  for batches, 156
Spoilage, 41

in BOM, 161
Spool list
  for period close activities, 543
  in Web application for Closing Cockpit, 559
Stakeholder, 19
Standard cost center hierarchies, 97
Standard cost estimate
  in material master, 148
Standard costs, 30
  for raw materials, 192
  use of costing run, 231
  variances, 31
Standard price, 148
  marking/releasing, 242
Standard routing, 168
Standard-setting
  in planning, 201
Standard values
  in operation, 170
Star schema
  for multidimensional reporting, 401
Statistical internal orders, 110
Statistical key figure
  as service in Express Planning, 481
  groups, 117
  introduction, 114
  use in assessment cycles, 334
Status
  for an internal order, 136
  in Express Planning, 489
Status management
  for internal orders, 136
  for orders and product cost collectors, 136
Stock
  urestricted use, 260
Stock in transit, 320
  valuation of, 375
Stock revaluation
  release of standard costs, 240
Stock transfer order, 320
Structure explosion
  in Product Cost Planning, 236
Summarization levels
  in Cost Object Controlling, 393
  in Profitability Analysis, 392
Supplier

Index

master data governance, 437
Supporting cost center
    indirect activity allocation cycles, 341
    use of, 338
Supporting cost centers, 91
    cost center planning, 220

T

Target costs
    for product cost collector, 300
    for production orders, 361
    on cost centers, 347
Target Cost Version, 361
Task list
    for period close, 533
Template
    definition, 508
    display in product costing, 502
Template allocation
    as part of period close, 507
    instead of overhead calculation, 356
Templates
    for period close, 532
Time buckets
    in planning applications, 489
Time dependency
    in BOM, 159
Time-dependent data
    Asset Accounting, 94
Time-dependent fields
    for cost centers, 135
Time recording
    by order, 35, 39
    by project, 35
    to project, 310
Time sheet
    data entry, 310
Top-down distribution
    in Profitability Analysis, 385
Top-down planning
    for investments, 248
Totals record
    Cost Center Accounting, 61
Transaction, 16
    C203, 169

CA03, 168
CA23, 168
CAT2, 310
CAT5, 311
CJ13, 311
CJ20N, 180
CJ30, 252
CJ40, 248, 474
CJR2, 249, 460, 476
CK40N, 231
CK91N, 176
CK94, 178
CKM3N, 78
CKMATCON, 234
CKMATDUV, 292
CKMCCD, 376
CKMDUVACT, 294
CKMDUVREC, 293
CKMLCP, 372
CKMLCPAVR, 378
CKMLQS, 276
CLOCOC, 530
CLOCOT, 534
CO01, 268
CO8B, 298
CO15, 272
CON2, 351
COR1, 295
CP01, 501
CPT1, 508
CR03, 173
CRC3, 173
CS03, 159
EXP_CUST, 482
FSSO, 187
IM32, 251
IM34, 183, 249
IM52, 252
KA01, 124
KA06, 124
KA23, 128
KALC, 95
KB11N, 318
KB21N, 312
KB61, 314
KB65, 317
KE24, 282

KE27, 385
KE28, 385
KEPM, 205, 245, 462
KEU2, 344
KEU5, 347
KGI2, 356
KK01, 115
KK87, 367
KKAS, 360
KKAX, 358
KKBC_ORD, 359
KKF6N, 131
KKPHIE, 133
KKS2, 362
KKS6, 365
KL01, 118
KL13, 123
KLH1, 122
KLH2, 127
KO04, 105
KOB1, 64
KOH1, 111
KP04, 459
KP06, 215, 459
KP26, 213, 459
KPF6, 226, 459
KPSI, 214
KS01, 90
KSB1, 53
KSBL, 222
KSBT, 351
KSC2, 341
KSC5, 342
KSH1, 101
KSII, 350, 380
KSPI, 227
KSPP, 214
KSS4, 219
KSU2, 98, 332
KSU5, 336
KSV2, 339
KSV5, 339
ME13, 193
ME21N, 259
MI01, 290
MI04, 290
MI07, 291
MIGO, 260
MIRO, 265
MM03, 146
MS01, 210
OKEON, 98
RKIL, 342
RKIV, 340
RKU3, 317
RSA3, 396
XD01, 157
XK01, 197
Transaction-based price determination
  in Material Ledger, 150
Transfer control
  in Product Cost Planning, 234
Transient InfoProviders
  for reporting, 416
Travel expenses
  cost center assignment, 36

U

Unit of measure
  for material master, 146
  in material master, 146
User exit
  COOMKS01, 93
User responsible
  for cost center, 92

V

Valuated Quantity Structure report, 276
Valuation
  during planning, 207
Valuation class
  for materials, 147
Valuation function
  in Profitability Analysis, 384
Value fields
  for profitability analysis, 283
  in Profitability Analysis, 82
Value flows
  in Controlling, 28
Value streams

cost center assignment, 94
Variable costs, 29
Variables
  for organizational units, 554
Variance analysis
  introduction, 325
Variance calculation
  for cost centers, 347
  for product cost collectors, 366
Variance key
  in material master, 152
  in production order, 354
Variances
  settlement of, 279
Variation
  in Report Writer reports, 390
Vendor master, 197
Version
  for sales and operations plan, 209
  plan version, 203
  purpose of, 204
  use in period close, 329
Views
  in BW queries, 414
Virtual InfoProviders
  in SAP NetWeaver BW, 413

W

WBS element, 180
  change request, 430
Web queries
  for planning, 464

Weighted average price
  in Material Ledger, 150
  using Material Ledger, 148
Where-used lists
  for cost centers, 103
Work breakdown structure, 20, 39
  elements, 179, 180
Work center, 173
  in production order, 270
  link with Cost Center Accounting, 95
Workflow
  approvals, 48
  for period close activities, 546
Working time
  recording of, 310
Work in process
  account determination, 190
  calculation of, 357
  for product cost collectors, 360
  introduction, 41
Work lists
  for period close activities, 546
Work orders
  reporting options, 72

X

xCelsius dashboard, 422

Z

Zero-based planning, 206

www.sap-press.com

Discover best practices for the design and configuration of SAP ERP Financials

Understand the configuration process by using a real-world, project-implementation approach

Completely revised to include real-world examples and extended coverage on account assignments, the new SAP General Ledger, and much more

Naeem Arif, Sheikh Tauseef

SAP ERP Financials: Configuration and Design

Master the issues involved in designing and configuring an SAP ERP Financials implementation using this overview guide. This is an invaluable reference that covers what you need for the configuration and design process, the enterprise structure, reporting, data migration, Accounts Payable and Receivables, Financials integration with other modules, and all other critical areas of SAP ERP Financials. This new edition is updated for SAP ERP 6.0, Enhancement Package 4.

664 pp., 2. edition 2011, 79,95 Euro / US$ 79.95
ISBN 978-1-59229-393-3

>> www.sap-press.com

SAP PRESS

booksonline

Your SAP Library is just a click away

1. Search
2. Buy
3. Read

Try now!

www.sap-press.com

- ✓ Easy and intuitive navigation
- ✓ Bookmarking
- ✓ Searching within the full text of all our books
- ✓ 24/7 access
- ✓ Printing capability

Galileo Press

Interested in reading more?

Please visit our Web site for all
new book releases from SAP PRESS.

www.sap-press.com

SAP PRESS